GW00703112

The Strategists

ALSO BY PHILLIPS PAYSON O'BRIEN

The Second Most Powerful Man in the World

The Strategists

Churchill, Stalin, Roosevelt,
Mussolini, and Hitler—
How War Made Them
and How They Made War

PHILLIPS PAYSON O'BRIEN

DUTTON

DUTTON

An imprint of Penguin Random House LLC
penguinrandomhouse.com

Simultaneously published in the United Kingdom by Viking,
an imprint of Penguin Random House UK.

Copyright © 2024 by Phillips O'Brien

Penguin Random House supports copyright. Copyright fuels creativity, encourages diverse
voices, promotes free speech, and creates a vibrant culture. Thank you for buying an authorized
edition of this book and for complying with copyright laws by not reproducing, scanning, or
distributing any part of it in any form without permission. You are supporting writers
and allowing Penguin Random House to continue to publish books for every reader.

DUTTON and the D colophon are registered trademarks of
Penguin Random House LLC.

Insert #1, page 1, photo 2; Insert #2, page 2; Insert #2, page 3, bottom photo; Insert #3, page 3; and Insert #3,
page 8: Courtesy of the Franklin D. Roosevelt Presidential Library & Museum, Hyde Park, New York.
Insert #1, page 3; Insert #2, page 4, top photo; Insert #2, page 5, bottom photo; Insert #2, page 7, top photo;
Insert #3, page 2, top photo; Insert #3, page 7, bottom photo: Alamy Photo Stock
Insert #3, page 6, bottom photo: Bundesarchiv, Bild 146-1970-097-76/ o.Ang.

LIBRARY OF CONGRESS CATALOGING-IN-PUBLICATION DATA
has been applied for.

ISBN 9781524746483 (hardcover)
ISBN 9781524746506 (ebook)

Printed in the United States of America
1st Printing

While the author has made every effort to provide accurate telephone numbers,
internet addresses, and other contact information at the time of publication,
neither the publisher nor the author assumes any responsibility for errors
or for changes that occur after publication. Further, the publisher does not have
any control over and does not assume any responsibility
for author or third-party websites or their content.

For Payson
May you know as little as possible about war

Contents

Acknowledgements

The writing of this book spanned a period of some of the most important milestones in my life. It started with the birth of our son, Payson, to Mathilde and me. As someone who has come to fatherhood later in life, Payson's arrival was both wondrous and, at first, more than a little daunting. What soon became clear, however, was that instead of being a challenge, he provided the most amazing support in helping to create this book. He allowed me to focus the mind, provided the most wonderful perspective on what matters in life, and was—through his laughs, his natural warmth, and his constant growth into a really remarkable little person—a form of emotional buoyancy that I never would have expected. Mathilde, without whom I could not have written my previous book, and I are so lucky to have him. Indeed, the making of our little family is the most wonderful thing ever to have happened in my life, and though writing such words hardly does it justice, it is to Payson and Mathilde that I need to pay the greatest thanks.

This book also corresponds with the passing of my father, William O'Brien. As I look back on my life, his love of books, ideas and learning rubbed off on me and has constantly influenced my career progression and choices. It is sad to think that he won't read this book and gain some pleasure in it. And that he will not be able to order countless copies from the local bookstore, which he liked to do with the sole purpose of telling the cashiers that the book was written by his son. I hope to pass on to Payson the same love of ideas that he helped instil in me.

And, as always, I would not have been able to get through this period without the support of my mother Nancy, my sisters Elizabeth and Sarah, my brother William, my brothers-in-law Jamie and Sam, my aunt and godmother Anne, and my nephews Andrew, Sam and Ben. Though I get to see them all far less than I would like, they are always there on video or the phone for a chat. When I get back to New England, they provide the wonderful solidity of home.

I also am blessed with a group of the best possible friends, who provide the good humour, the strength and the kindness that make a far greater difference than they can understand. Roddy and Anne and Will and Kate, the four of you and the weekends we spend together have been some of the high points of every year in which this book was written (pandemic permitting). This was also the period that saw Mathilde, Payson and I move from Glasgow to Fife, and doing so made me realize the great importance of our Glasgow friends. Matt, Stuart, May and Ed (and Oren and Jesse), Peter and Jacqui, John and Alison—thanks to you all, and it's very hard not to see you as much as I used to. Scattered further afield, I have so many friends—some very old, and others who I just met during the last few years—to whom I would like to pay thanks. Whenever I get to see or even just speak with Gary and Joan, Guy and Ina, Lori and Steve, Randall and Alison and Alexander and Michael, Eliot and Judith, Cian, and Marilyn—I gain so much.

I would also like to pay a special tribute to three of my dearest, oldest friends, all of whom passed during the writing of this book, in a way that still seems inexplicable and beyond cruel. Carolyn and Catherine Frazer were friends from before memory (I have pictures of us all in the bathtub for proof), and Brian Nicholson was someone who was extremely kind to me in my early teens at a time when he could not understand how much it meant. While I never saw the three of them as much as I would have liked as we aged and went in our different directions, I need to say how much they are missed. Life is short.

Having moved to Fife, and now spending more time with colleagues (and friends) at St. Andrews, it's clear how important my new home has become. Stephen, Brad, Gurch, Fiona, Tony—thank you for being so supportive with the move and establishing a new home. The strategic studies group has been a key part of my intellectual development, and has provided the kind of environment that has made this book possible. Hew, Kristen, Marc, Guy and the rest of the team at ISWS—thank you. I would like to list all of my colleagues in the School of International Affairs for their kindnesses—though the list would be too long. I would also like to acknowledge the role of the University of St. Andrews in making this book possible. In supplying me with research leave, and providing a supportive research culture, the university allowed this book to be better and produced more quickly than I would have imagined.

For this book I must pay particular thanks to three young academics all starting in their careers: Dr. Sofya Anisimova, Dr. Jacopo Pili and Dr. Tim Kucharzewski. The three of them provided the linguistic and research skills needed to make the sections on Stalin, Mussolini and Hitler coherent and well sourced. They helped scour for sources, provided constant feedback and correction on the manuscript, and helped provide the assurance that the picture I painted of these three most dreadful of men was sensible. Please do watch out for them as their careers grow and blossom.

Finally, I would like to pay thanks to two editors at Penguin Random House. Brent Howard was the person who first brought me on board to write the biography of William Leahy and then agreed to the contract for *The Strategists*. He has taught me a great deal about writing and concision, and the feedback he provided for this manuscript was always invaluable and made the final product that much better. Recently I've started working with Daniel Crewe, who has not only helped see this book to completion, but has also agreed to work on my next book, *War and Power*. I'm not sure what this says about his judgement—but I, at least, remain grateful.

Introduction

Strategy, War and Personality

On October 29, 1941, as Adolf Hitler picked at his ostentatiously simple vegetarian dinner and sipped his favourite fizzy mineral water, his mind raced. He could taste victory, the greatest triumph in military history. German troops had just captured almost three-quarters of a million Soviet soldiers around the city of Kyiv, the last of a series of smashing defeats inflicted on Joseph Stalin's Red Army since the launch of Operation Barbarossa, the invasion of the Soviet Union, on June 22. From his spartan, bug-ridden headquarters in East Prussia, codenamed Wolfsschanze (Wolf's Lair), Hitler saw the unfolding campaign as confirmation of his own genius. Only his daring and strategic vision, he believed, could have brought his nation to this precipice of victory. Soon Germany would have a massive new empire in which to settle genetically healthy Germans, while wiping out anyone or anything that stood in Hitler's way.

With ideas cascading in his head, Hitler had taken to giving long monologues to hand-picked military officers and political cronies, who sat obediently at his dinner table. On this night, Hitler's guests included Günther von Kluge, a Prussian-born field marshal whose military service had commenced in 1901. Von Kluge was commander of the 4th German Army, one of the most powerful forces attacking the Soviet Union. As Hitler well knew, even as the German Army as a whole was winning battles, some senior commanders were worried that these victories were drawing their troops ever further into the unconquerable vastness of Russia, threatening to buckle the entire German logistical system.

Major problems were appearing for the Germans on both rail and road. Since the days of Tsarist Russia, railway lines in the Soviet Union had been built with a wider gauge than those of the rest of Europe. Knowing this, the Germans had hoped to capture Soviet railcars to keep supplies moving forward as quickly as possible.

Soviet forces, however, withdrew almost all their locomotives as the Germans advanced, and destroyed as much railway infrastructure as they could. Thus, the Germans were left with the laborious and time-consuming task of rebuilding the Soviet railway system to run their own trains and keep up their advance. It slowed their pace considerably.

The Germans were also running short of trucks. On paper, the German Army was one of the most advanced in the world. The troops that invaded Russia were carried in 600,000 motorized vehicles. But it was a motley force, drawn from across a conquered continent, and needed a wide array of tyres and spare parts, to say nothing of fuel, to keep going. There were far too few German-made military-grade trucks—the backbone needed to supply large, armoured break-throughs and maintain a constant tempo of operations.

As the German Army struggled with both rail and road control, supplying troops scattered across a thousand-mile front was becoming a logistical nightmare. With trains stymied and trucks scarce, the Germans were forced to take long operational pauses to allow the supply situation to be rectified. Hitler, however, did not seem concerned. Mobility, he insisted, was overrated. "It's the infantryman who, when all's said, sets the tempo of operations with his legs," he informed his audience that night. He instructed them to focus on providing more and more firepower to the army to allow the German soldier to blast through any enemy, and stop worrying about moving too quickly. After all, "in the choice between mobility and power, the decision . . . is given too easily in favour of mobility."[1]

Adolf Hitler's confidence was rooted in a conviction that he understood modern war. After all, he was no stranger to the battlefield. As a corporal in a Bavarian regiment, Hitler had spent almost all of World War I on the Western Front. Serving mostly as a dispatch runner, he was wounded during the Battle of the Somme in 1916, and in 1918 was temporarily blinded by a British mustard gas attack. Such experiences had physically and psychologically scarred millions of soldiers, but Hitler looked upon the war as the most wonderful and meaningful experience of his life. Prior to the conflict, he had been a drifter with no prospects. The German Army and the war gave him purpose, and he devoted himself to both, revelling in his new-found sense of direction.

World War I also stamped him indelibly with strategic ideas he would bring to World War II. One of them was that firepower and armoured protection were more important than speed and mobility. As a soldier he had marvelled at the largest German howitzers and mortars and became convinced that heavy steel was the way to victory. When, in 1918, he first came across tanks, adopted by German forces in response to the British Mark I, Hitler quickly found a preference for the biggest and strongest over the fastest with the longer range—hardly a surprise for a foot soldier in a trench war. As he told his audience in 1941, in the trenches he had learned that "only the heaviest and most thickly armoured tank had any value."[2] As a dictator, he took this prejudice and forced it on the modern German Army. The next year, during another evening monologue, Hitler boasted how he had overruled those who insisted that "light and fast" vehicles had value and "after a hard struggle, I imposed my will and ordered the manufacture of heavy tanks."[3]

Hitler's fetish for the heaviest and most powerful, and his disinterest in mobility and logistics, had a major impact on how World War II developed. The German armies, which he created and threw into battle, were woefully short of light vehicles and trucks, while large and inefficient investments were made in building ever heavier and more powerful tanks. Indeed, German industry developed some of the most awesome and complex tanks in the world, including the Panther, the Tiger, and the behemoth Tiger II, known to Allied troops as the King Tiger, whose heavy armour and massive long-range gun gave it a fearsome presence in combat. Yet the sheer size and technological complexity of these lumbering fortresses meant that Germany could only manufacture a small number of them when compared to the more robust and speedier Allied tanks. The stress Hitler placed on German industry to produce heavy tanks meant fewer resources to build trucks and other support vehicles; as a result, German troops were chronically short. The Wehrmacht often relied on horse-drawn vehicles to keep itself supplied and moving. The German Army may have had a great punch concentrated in a few armoured units, but there was a surprisingly weak body of foot soldiers, supplied by horse.

As Hitler was pontificating in late October 1941, he was about to receive a lesson in the consequences of this lack of mobility. A month later, the German Army would fail before the gates of Moscow, its advance halted by supply problems, exacerbated by a Russian winter and a Red Army counterattack. Hitler, however, refused to learn from this lesson, and instead doubled down on his own perceived brilliance and understanding of war. Because of his fixation on power over speed—and his refusal to adapt—within a year the German Army would be on the defensive in every theatre of war. Two and a half years after that, Hitler would shoot himself while completely immobile, entombed in a concrete fortress hidden deep below the streets of Berlin.

The central role that Hitler played in determining German strategy throughout the war, with his particular prejudices, irrationalities and fundamental errors, does not fit easily into how we see grand-strategy-making, or foreign policymaking in general, in a modern state. There is a widespread discussion in militaries, governments and universities that likes to see strategy as emerging from a linked process of "ends-ways-means." In this Clausewitzian world, strategic choice is seen as the pursuit of a clear political end through the employment of the means available to a state (such as its military force) in certain well-thought-out methods (the ways). It seems logical in theory, but as Hitler—and indeed all the dominant grand strategists of World War II—demonstrated, it's typically a mirage.

In many cases that is because strategy, grand or otherwise, has been turned into something more complex than it actually is. A strategy is simply an implemented decision which starts a dynamic process. For the purposes of this book, the strategic decision is the choice by the leader, with or without the opinions of advisers, of the strategic plan that the state should follow. The implementation is the translation of that plan into action. This second step can be messy and disruptive at times, particularly in peace during moments of weak leadership. In the cases of Adolf Hitler, Joseph Stalin, Benito Mussolini, Winston Churchill and Franklin D. Roosevelt in World War II, the bureaucratic checks that we like to think of as limiting leadership were often ineffective. The five were strong, ego-driven leaders, and often they were able to see their strategic plans put into action. In many cases they either crushed any possible bureaucratic challenges to their power, as did Hitler and Stalin, or they outmanoeuvred other power centres (government offices, political rivals, their militaries) that could have thwarted the implementation of a strategy that they wanted, as in the case of Roosevelt.

Once the strategic decision has been implemented, the process is far from over. The enemy always has a say and all strategies remain dynamic and subject to rapid changes or even destruction. A sign of a successful strategist and strategy is one that can cope with this process of challenge and change. This was in many ways the greatest test of the Five. If all of them usually got their way in getting their strategic choices adopted as policy, in many cases those choices had to be changed when confronted by an enemy response. Stalin's greatest advantage over Hitler was that, while both were bloodthirsty dictators with an innate desire to control as much as possible, he learned to respond practically when the reality of the war did not correspond to his expectations. Hitler, if anything, became worse at adjusting his strategies to reality when confronted with failure.

The difference between grand strategy and strategy, using World War II as a model, can be simply defined. To be considered an issue of grand strategy, two basic tests need to be passed. First, to be a "grand" strategic question the implemented decision must be put into action by an authority that has nothing above it, such as a commander-in-chief or a dictator, to which it must defer. Only a Hitler, Stalin, Mussolini, Churchill or Roosevelt—for the purposes of this book, they will be called the Five—could make a grand-strategic choice. The second test is that it needs to be for actions above the conduct of operations on the battlefield. In other words, grand strategy is about the creation and allocation of armed forces. The creation step is often terribly understudied, but in many ways the most important, as it determines later choices. The militaries of the great powers were the result of years-long choices, balancing the industrial and technological capabilities of their nations with the personal priorities of their leadership. One could not just wish up thousands of aircraft, tanks, trucks or naval vessels in a short period; nations had to have workable models in the production stage. In World War II all of these kinds of production choices were dominated by the Five, and reflected their own perceptions. The Allies were able to dominate the air-sea war, for instance, because Churchill from the start of the Battle of Britain prioritized aircraft and naval production, and Roosevelt in 1941 made air-sea weapons his clear priority.

The other part of grand-strategy decision-making in World War II was where to send the finished equipment. Except for Stalin—who had a relatively straightforward allocation situation (everything to the Eastern Front, to fight the Germans in a great land war)—the leaders had to balance different theatres and different types of war. Perhaps the greatest clash between Roosevelt and Churchill was over Churchill's desire to make the Mediterranean the primary area of Allied effort and Roosevelt's desire for a cross-Channel invasion.

Once you go below this level, you have left grand strategy and are in the area of strategy or even tactics. Some of the grand strategists— particularly Hitler, but also at times Mussolini and Stalin—blurred the lines between the two, almost always badly. One of the great tests of grand-strategic leadership is learning what not to do as well as what to do.

If it's not difficult to define grand strategy in World War II, what is murkier is to clearly make a connection between the choices and a definite set of intended ends. The five grand strategists were all riven with prejudices, preferences, irrationalities and mental tics that made their strategic choices highly individualistic, even unstable. When it came to the basic ends of the war, it is not easy to say exactly what they wanted, or whether their ends were remotely achievable. More-over, the connection between these unstable ends and the ways/ means available to them was often tenuous at best. They could create misshapen means, not actually understand the means they helped create, or have little idea how these means would behave when used in different ways. Grand strategy in World War II was made in a chaotic, dynamic situation, not a rational and planned one.

This analysis also directly attacks the idea that states in war are following something comprehensible such as a national interest or the greater good—even when the structures of government are there to make it look like this is the case. The bureaucracies of each World War II government produced pages and pages of strategy documents, with numbered points, well-reasoned arguments, and in some cases definitive maps of eventual goals that the strategies were meant to obtain. They were almost all meaningless and in some cases were either entirely disregarded or quickly overruled by the Five in action.

The best example of this is easily the most famous strategic idea produced by the United States in World War II: the policy of Germany First, or Europe First. This grand-strategic concept, developed in the years before the Japanese attack on Pearl Harbor, was the consensus view of many in the US military, State Department and the White House. The foundation of Germany First was that the United States, upon entry into the war, should throw the majority of its armed forces against Hitler and leave Japan to be dealt with later. Strategically, the view made some sense. Germany was the larger economic power, with more resources, and was in control of most of the European continent. Germany First was based on the idea that once Germany was defeated, Japan would have no strategic future, but that the defeat of Japan would play little role in driving Hitler out of the war.

Yet at no time did Franklin Roosevelt ensure that the United States followed a Germany First plan, and as such the United States fought a very different war than its strategic planners said that it should. For political and personal reasons, Roosevelt, who paid lip service to Germany First, was happy to allow the US to divide its forces approximately equally between the Pacific and Europe.[4] Roosevelt was content to adjust his strategy to the dynamic situation being presented by his enemies, an important sign of why he succeeded. The US would send as much equipment to fight Japan throughout the war as was dispatched to fight Germany.* This is

---

* In 1942 the United States dispatched considerably more war material (particularly aircraft and naval vessels) to fight Japan than it did to fight Germany. Starting in 1943, the US war effort diverged, with the Army and Army Air Force sending

why implementation matters. A great strategic plan can be announced, but if grand strategists take no steps to make sure it is followed, it cannot be called national strategy. As a rule of thumb, it could even be said that, during World War II, the more detailed a plan, especially if it was written down by a team of practitioners a few layers below the real centres of strategy-making—Hitler, Stalin, Mussolini, Churchill and Roosevelt—the more unimportant it was.

The Five might have believed that what they were doing was in the best interests of their people—but they were mostly doing what they wanted to do, and used the idea of national interest to justify their decisions, not to make them. This is even the case with Roosevelt, normally seen as the most benign of the Five. He had a very personal policy, in which his individual participation in many ways transcended what was best for the United States. That individual focus can best be seen when in 1944, as he was perceptibly weakening and coming close to death, he chose a new vice president with whom he rarely spoke and in whom he never confided. It was one of the most irresponsible decisions in grand-strategic history.

To demonstrate the personal, as well as the chaotic, nature of the actions of the Five, this book is divided into two sections. The first half covers the creation of their strategic mindsets, and their individual perspectives, by showing how they experienced and reacted to war long before they became the leaders of their respective nations. Beginning with Winston Churchill's first encounter with war as a young soldier in British India, and stretching through World War I then to the end of the Russian Civil War, the war experiences of the Five, along with their emotional and intellectual reactions, will be outlined.

The second part of the book will look at World War II as a series of clashes of these mindsets. The end result will not be an overall model about grand-strategy-making, beyond this focus on the

---

approximately 70 per cent of its material to fight Germany, while the US Navy sent more than 90 per cent of its material to fight Japan. Overall, the US war effort between 1942 and 1945 would have been spread approximately equally between the European and Pacific theatres.

process of those at the top of the strategic pyramid. In that sense it will bring the study of grand strategy away from the bureaucracies and the well-thought-out, written-down plans and towards the dynamic state of flawed individuals making personal choices.

As this book is being completed, the greatest example of this reality of personal grand-strategy-making is playing out before us. Vladimir Putin's invasion of Ukraine, an attempt to create a greater, more powerful Russia, shows once again that grand strategy can be hijacked by deeply flawed individuals over bureaucracies or structures. In no rational world could the Russian invasion of Ukraine be seen as something well thought out or in the Russian national interest. It was poorly conceived, based on a hopeless misreading of Ukrainian intentions and capabilities. The Russian Army was also constructed in such a way that it was far less than the sum of its parts. While Putin might have had an ends-ways-means plan in his own mind, we can say now that he had poorly constructed means, which he employed in wholly unrealistic ways in a vain attempt to achieve completely unrealistic ends. Yet just before the invasion he was considered perhaps the most savvy and intelligent leader of a major power in the world.

Putin's grand-strategic performance has in many ways combined the worst strategic traits of Adolf Hitler and Benito Mussolini. In a rational world, with a sober evaluation of the Russian Army, one would have imagined a state's decision-making bureaucracy would have tried to halt his invasion of Ukraine—as one would have imagined the Italian state might have restrained Mussolini from invading Greece, or German influences might have kept Hitler from attacking the Soviet Union with Britain still fighting. Yet the Five were usually not restrained, and for better or worse they did what they wanted.

1. Winston Churchill: The Making of an Imperial Strategist

In September 1897, twenty-two-year-old Winston Churchill first set eyes on the Himalayas. He was entranced, and a little horrified. Raised in the tidy countryside of southern England, he found the topography of north-west India all out of proportion. High slopes were intersected by deep valleys, fertile and green, watered by fish-filled rivers and dotted with prosperous villages swarmed by late-summer butterflies. On the slopes above, the change was stark. The vegetation became stumpy and sparse, eventually thinning out entirely. Constant wash had eroded the soil, exposing black "primeval" rock.[1] Near the tops of the mountains the ground was completely barren, crowned by masses of jagged rock. It was a difference that would soon be a matter of life and death.

For the first time in his young life, Winston Churchill was going to war. He was joining a campaign of pacification, waged to force the local population to accept British rule. This was the border area of India, Britain's imperial jewel in the crown, and Afghanistan. These valleys were the homeland of numerous Pathan peoples.* For years the British had mostly let the Pathans alone, but now, under their "Forward Policy," they had recently moved military forces as far north as possible. It was typical imperialist politics; the British wanted to secure the territory before the Russians, who were pushing southwards from central Asia, got too close.

To impose British authority, a series of military outposts were constructed throughout Pathan country. One of these small fortresses controlled the traffic through the Malakand valley, a key route into Afghanistan. On July 26, 1897, local Pathans launched a surprise

---

* Today the Pathans are known in the English-speaking world as Pashtun, which might mean something to those interested in the continuation of futile wars.

attack against the Malakand camp, lighting a fuse that spread quickly to other valleys. More and more Pathans joined the attempt to drive the occupiers away, and by early August more than 150 British officers and soldiers had been killed or wounded in the fighting.[2]

When Churchill first heard about the attacks, he was on leave in England. A cavalry lieutenant with the 4th Queen's Own Hussars, then stationed in the south of India, he was desperate to see action and craved notoriety. He quickly pulled every string available in his socially rich shadow box and was taken on board by Sir Bindon Blood, the commander of the expedition sent to break the Pathans. The journey from England to the front was over 10,000 miles by train, boat and then train again, and even though Churchill set off immediately, it took well over a month. He was in such a rush that he left without all the necessary equipment and had to buy important items from the possessions of fellow officers who had just been killed in the fighting.

Churchill's first brush with combat took place on September 16, when he was attached to a force of about a thousand soldiers whose job it was to "chastise" the inhabitants of the Mamund valley. This valley was a cul-de-sac—approximately ten miles wide, pan-shaped and framed by rocky ridges. The Pathans of the Mamund, a particularly warlike bunch in British eyes, were to pay the price for joining the fray after the Malakand attacks. British troops were ordered to lay waste to the valley, executing any tribespeople who stood up to them. For Churchill it was "lion-taming," needed to teach the Pathans about the inherent "superiority" of the British race.[3]

The British troops that entered the valley—the majority of whom were Indians themselves, from regiments including the 35th Sikhs, 38th Dogras and 11th Bengal Lancers—believed that one day would be more than enough to inflict this devastation. Many expected that the Pathans, faced with an organized army, would simply run away; and during the first few hours of the day they would have felt rather smug. Starting just before sunrise, the troops advanced methodically along the valley floor. The Pathan fighters, who could see their enemy approach, kept their distance, occasionally waving swords that flashed in the early morning light. They waited until the troops got close, and then slowly, almost insolently, retreated up the valley slopes. To try to force a fight, the British shot at them as they retreated, but the Pathans would not take the bait. They continued upwards, disappearing into the grey-black moonscape. By mid-morning, with hardly a casualty suffered and no enemy in sight, the British commanders decided to move into the hills. Churchill was attached to a unit of fewer than a hundred men aiming for the village of Shahi-Tangi, which stood at the end of a spur road high up along a ridge, at the end of the valley.

As they approached their objective, everything changed. Human shapes started dropping from much higher up, and five British soldiers were shot in an instant.[4] The Pathans could move more quickly up and down the ridges than the British troops, and had decided to make a stand. Churchill, exhilarated that he could finally shoot another human being, grabbed a rifle from one of the Sikh soldiers under his command and started to pump round after round into the advancing enemy. Unconcerned with his own safety, he viewed the actions of others pitilessly. Perhaps that was all he could do, because the fighting in the Mamund quickly revealed the brutality of war.

British soldiers executed prisoners who came into their hands and blamed the Pathans for butchering their comrades.[5] Churchill claimed to have seen British bodies, including one of his friends, savagely hacked to pieces. He considered the shooting of Pathan prisoners an understandable response.[6] But if the Pathans seemed barbaric to the British, the feeling was more than mutual. For the first time in large-scale combat, British soldiers were armed with soft-nosed dum-dum bullets.* During the nineteenth century, as firearms had become more advanced, with stronger metals, industrially made fittings and more powerful mixtures of gunpowder, they were able to fire rounds with a far greater muzzle velocity. This could make them ineffective. By the 1890s, modern rifles fired hardened metal bullets with such

---

* They were so nicknamed after the British armoury in India, the Dum-Dum Arsenal, at which they were first developed. It took many years to declare them illegal because the British government waged a lone battle against international opinion, only relenting in 1907.

force that if they did not hit a bone or vital organ, they could pass smoothly through a human being, making only small, non-lethal entry and exit wounds. The dum-dums corrected this "problem" by using a soft lead tip that would split and tumble in different directions when it hit flesh, gouging out swathes of the innards. Churchill told his grandmother that previously dum-dums had been used only on wild game such as tigers, but they had now decided to use them on the Pathans. They caused the most gruesome injuries, with "shattering effects . . . which are simply appalling." Nevertheless, in articles and books he wrote after the event, Churchill went to great lengths to defend their use. He described the dum-dums as having the "wonderful" impact of a "beautiful machine."[7] The purpose of a bullet was to kill, he pointed out, in which case the dum-dums did their job admirably. Dum-dum-type bullets were declared inhumane and illegal by the Hague Convention in 1899, but the British government refused to accept the decision. They would do so, belatedly, in 1907.[8]

Having access to dum-dums allowed Churchill and the others to stem the first Pathan attack. Armed with a mishmash of firearms—some smuggled, some stolen, some taken from British dead—the Pathans could not produce the sustained firepower of their enemy. Yet, no matter how many Pathans were shot, more and more dropped down from above and it became clear that the British position was in danger of being overrun. Spread out in small detachments throughout the far end of the valley, their entire force was engaged, with no reinforcements available for hard-pressed units such as Churchill's. The decision was made, however humiliating, to retreat.

The way back down the hill was perilous. Struggling to take the wounded and dead with them, the British had to crawl back slowly, with small groups holding off the Pathans while others carried the bodies. If the Pathans shot a carrier, the whole unit had to stop under fire and arrange another group to carry the newly wounded man. Eventually the number of dead and wounded proved too much, and one officer and twelve men were left behind on the hillside to "be cut to pieces."[9] It was not until noon that Churchill's force was back at the beginning of the spur road and in touch with other British forces. Despite being exhausted and now broiling in the midday sun, the officers determined to return and destroy the village and recover the body of the white officer. A much larger force, six companies, was mustered and ordered up the road. Faced with such force, the Pathans gave way. The British reached Shahi-Tingi by mid-afternoon and wiped the village from the map.

Retreat was once again ordered, and by the following morning, exhausted British forces were outside the valley. The cost was sobering. Of the thousand men who had marched into the Mamund, nine British officers, four Indian officers and 136 soldiers had been killed or wounded. Churchill claimed this was the highest casualty rate that the British had suffered for many years. Instead of admitting that the operation was a fiasco, however, he tried to argue that it was a success. After all, Shahi-Tingi had been destroyed and more than 200 Pathan fighters killed.[10] It was a feeble effort on his part.

Blood, understanding that the Mamund Pathans now had to be broken beyond redemption, sent an entire brigade into the valley on September 29. He told his men to "lay it waste with fire and sword in vengeance."[11] They did their job. All day the Mamund echoed with the booms of exploding buildings—so regular they sounded like an artillery barrage. In the end the soldiers levelled fourteen villages and forty different forts, and filled all the wells, broke all the reservoirs, cut down all the trees, and burned all the food and crops they could find. The Pathans, unable to resist such might, sat high up on the hillsides watching their lives below being obliterated.* Churchill supported the use of such terror tactics, telling his mother that the great slaughter of the Pathans had cowed them into submission.[12]

These battles in the Mamund valley were but one small part of a larger and more expensive conflict that went on for months. In private Churchill voiced some doubts about the Forward Policy, which had pushed the British into a position where they had to spend so much treasure defending this distant frontier. This has led some to

---

* Churchill, as an older man, would write about these operations with a hint of irony, saying that "honour had been satisfied." In his public writings at the time, however, he was a strong supporter of the policy of destroying villages. He made an explicit argument for it in his 1898 book *The Story of the Malakand Field Force.*

argue that Churchill was opposed to the whole plan. That is wrong.[13] Winston Churchill in 1897 believed in only two things with conviction: his own destiny, and that of the British Empire. While he might have been sceptical of some of the finer details of imperial policy, he never wavered in his determination that the British Empire should be as powerful as it could be, and that he was the right person to lead it.

Such self-confidence was no accident. Churchill was raised to be a servant of the empire and, in return, to view the empire as a servant of his greatness. He was born in the only non-royal house in England to be deemed a palace—Blenheim, the Oxfordshire seat of his grandfather, the 7th Duke of Marlborough. The creation of the architect Sir John Vanbrugh, Blenheim was gifted to the 1st Duke of Marlborough by the English government for that most important of acts, beating the French in battle. Three-sided, with soaring heavy towers and grand baroque architecture not offset with the slightest hint of whimsy, its immensity can only really be appreciated at a distance. Up close, its vastness overwhelms. Churchill's father, Randolph, was the third son of the duke. An ambitious, up-and-coming politician in the Conservative Party, from relatively early in his career Randolph was seen as a possible prime minister. Churchill's mother, Jennie, was American, though she much preferred life in refined and sophisticated Europe. Vivacious and alluring, she was the daughter of an alternately successful and bankrupt New York financier, Leonard Jerome. Randolph and Jennie met during a summer holiday in 1873 when he was twenty-four and she nineteen. They were engaged after three days, married after eight months, and Winston was born a little more than seven months after that, on November 30, 1874.

Randolph and Jennie were extremely well suited, both being emotionally stunted. Preferring their pleasures—including horse racing and love affairs—over all else, they spent as little time as possible with their new son. Winston was deposited with nannies, then tutors, and finally at boarding schools (most famously Harrow, which he entered and loathed in 1888). The young boy was desperate for parental affection and wrote them letters begging for visits or even just signs of attention. He was usually disappointed. At one point his mother cut off contact when she became irritated with his pleading, admonishing him that his tone "does not please me." His father was known to schedule meetings practically next door to where Winston was living, without ever informing his son.*

Churchill was not born into a meritocracy, or else he would have achieved little. As a young man he demonstrated at best modest talents and was prone to laziness. Uninspired by his upbringing, he hated school and studied erratically, receiving marks near the bottom of his class. The only thing that excited him was war. The first surviving letter he wrote to his mother was to thank her for sending him toy soldiers, flags and castles.[14] As soon as he entered Harrow, he joined the school's Rifle Corps, revelling in the smoke and confusion of the mock battles they fought. He learned to shoot and fence, believing that they would be useful if he joined the army.

During vacations, Churchill spent days playing soldier with his younger brother, Jack, and their friends. He was known to drill the young boys in proper military technique—building little fortresses on the estate grounds and then planning attacks. He threw himself into these games with a recklessness that he would later show on real battlefields. Once, when playing a game where he was on the run, trying to elude capture by his brother and a cousin, Churchill found himself trapped in the middle of a rickety old bridge with a pursuer at each end.[15] Mortified at the prospect of surrender, he decided to leap twenty-nine feet to the ground below, hoping that the slender branches of the fir trees beneath him would break his fall. He ruptured a kidney and was unconscious for three days. It would take harder lessons than this before his childish idea of war matured.

Considering his fascination with war, it is not surprising that Churchill decided to join the army, yet even doing this proved to be

---

* In defence of Randolph and Jennie it is sometimes argued that aristocratic parents of the late Victorian era were societally conditioned to be distant from their children. This is a caricature used as a convenient excuse, however. They were not living up to some ideal; they simply did not want to spend time with their son and were much more interested in their own lives. Other elite Victorians could be and were loving and attentive parents, even if they sent their children to boarding school.

a challenge. To be accepted he had to pass the admission test for the Royal Military College at Sandhurst. Even with the help of tutors, he failed at his first two attempts (his mother took advantage of this to argue that because he needed to study, she couldn't see him at Christmas). Only in June 1893, on his third try, did he make the grade, just scraping by. With marks too low to gain admission into the infantry, his only option was to join the cavalry.* If he expected praise from his father, he was quickly disabused of this notion. Randolph, irritated that he had to bear the extra cost of supporting his son in the cavalry, sent Winston a stinging rebuke. He complained that, despite being given every advantage, Winston continued his pattern of "slovenly" work.[16]

Once Churchill joined the cavalry, however, something inside him clicked. Preparing for war sparked an inner drive. He graduated from Sandhurst twentieth in his class of 130, having spent so much time in the saddle that his whole body ached.[17] With the Hussars he finally found a happy home. He loved the nightly formal meals, the mess tables heavy with ornate regimental silver, the officers in dress uniform and the menus written in French (which, he admitted, was the only French thing about the food). He enjoyed drinking with his fellow officers—the beginning of a lifetime love affair with alcohol.

He was also willing to take on more responsibility. When Churchill was at Sandhurst his father's health had deteriorated. Randolph's speeches in Parliament became erratic, gruesome spectacles, as his mind wandered uncontrollably. For decades it was thought by many (including Churchill himself) that Randolph was suffering from the advanced stages of syphilis, though this now seems unlikely. More likely he was suffering from an undiagnosed neurological condition such as a brain tumour. Regardless, his decline was humiliating. Lord Rosebery, the prime minister, famously said of Randolph that there "was no curtain, no retirement, he died by inches in public." Eventually his condition became so acute that it was considered necessary to hide him away on a world tour. In India in late 1894 Randolph

---

* The cavalry had a lower admission threshold because of the extra expense needed to join the service. The purchase and upkeep of the right horses were not cheap.

became so ill that he was shipped back to England, where he died in January 1895.

Randolph's death was a liberation for Winston. Now head of the family, he no longer had to endure constant paternal insults, and Jennie, with her husband gone, was transformed. She moved from being a distant, uncaring figure to Winston's greatest patron, and made furthering his career one of her overriding occupations. Churchill, slightly dumbfounded by the change, noted that henceforth he and Jennie worked as a team, though he was also careful to say more like brother and sister than mother and son.

One of Jennie's strongest skills was helping Winston secure the appointments he so desperately craved. And this is important in understanding the true wealth of Churchill's background. He was not capital-rich; Randolph's debts had been almost as large as his assets, and mother and son had only a modest living. What the Churchills possessed in spades was social capital. The family was one of the most famous and powerful in Britain, and Jennie spent much of her time cultivating connections throughout British politics and society (it was rumoured that among her many lovers was the future King Edward VII). When Winston wanted to bend the rules in his favour, which was most of the time, he could go right to the top.

This social capital was needed, for Churchill had a real worry: that he would fail to see combat. When he entered the army there was a generation of officers above him who had not seen real action.[18] But the British Empire had been relatively quiescent since the early 1880s, with occasional outbursts of violence but no large-scale conflict. That would not do for Winston Churchill. His career in the army was not being undertaken for its own sake. It was part of his plan— indeed he believed it his destiny—to become a man of fame and political power.[19] He was more than aware that the best way for him to gain notoriety was through the publicization of some dashing military exploits.[20]

Therefore, he had to attract attention, even as an observer. In 1895 he heard that the Spanish were about to send 80,000 troops to their colony of Cuba, led by their most famous commander, Marshal Arsenio Martínez Campos. This force was being sent to crush an uprising by the Cuban people, and Churchill wanted to witness the fight. Arranging this was relatively easy, as the long-serving British ambassador to Madrid, Sir Henry Drummond Wolff, was one of Randolph Churchill's oldest friends. The ambassador provided excellent introductions to everyone who mattered in the Spanish Army, and promised Churchill that Martínez Campos would personally welcome him in Cuba. Displaying for the first time the instinct for publicity and money-making that would typify his career, Churchill also contacted the *Daily Graphic*, the first daily illustrated paper published in the UK, which had previously published articles written by his father. He quickly received a contract to publish any stories from Cuba he might supply, at five guineas a piece.[21]

In the summer of 1895 Churchill set off to observe the "thrilling and immense" experience of war.[22] When he arrived off Havana, he later recalled, he felt like Long John Silver gazing upon Treasure Island.[23] He even got his hands on some excellent Cuban cigars, which helped kick-start another of his life's passions.

Once in Cuba, Churchill's connections proved invaluable and he received anything he needed. After an escorted trip on a specially protected train, he was welcomed warmly by Martínez Campos and advised where he could see action immediately. Churchill hurried over to the disease-ridden town of Sancti Spiritus, a place he judged as in "a dreadful state with about four separate pestilences raging."[24] He spent the night in a tavern waiting for a Spanish force of 3,000. The Spaniards were due to attack rebel forces hidden deep in the Cuban jungle and Churchill intended to march with them.

His first day witnessing operations was a shock. It began with an early, brisk march just as the sun was rising. The Spanish made surprisingly quick progress through the jungle and Churchill was impressed by how they used their machetes to slice through the dense growth with ease.[25] At nine in the morning the column halted, and a large breakfast was prepared, including a thick stew and, most delightfully, rum cocktails. Then, instead of the march recommencing, hammocks were slung between trees in the canopy for all the officers. Soon the entire force was asleep and did not move for the next four hours. Only in the afternoon were the troops roused from their siesta and the advance continued. Churchill, much to his surprise, found this schedule remarkably efficient. He calculated that the men covered as much ground as they would have had they been forced to walk all day, and with the siesta they arrived at their destination more refreshed. Being a committed racialist, Churchill attributed these Spanish successes to their being "closer to nature" than the more analytical and technically advanced Anglo-Saxons.

Churchill also became restless. This pleasant rhythm of march-siesta-march continued for the next few days, with hardly an enemy seen or a shot fired. Finally, just when it looked like the campaign would achieve nothing, the Spanish came across some rebels. On Churchill's twenty-first birthday he gleefully experienced being under fire when a rebel bullet passed within a foot of his head and killed a horse standing beside him. For the next three days there was sporadic rifle fire between the rebels and the Spanish, though the enemy was desperately difficult to see, mostly visible only through the occasional puff of gun smoke.

Eventually, it seemed that a real battle would take place. The Spanish came upon a rebel camp and deployed their entire force to attack, the infantry and artillery aiming straight at the rebel line, with the cavalry sent to move around the flanks. Heavy fire soon erupted from all sides. To Churchill, the rebels' Remington rifles released a "deep" moan, while the Spanish line, firing more efficient Mausers, emitted a "shrill rattle."[26] Yet for all the noise and smoke, the combat was unsatisfying. Though they were able to take the position—indeed, they were able to force the rebels from any area in which they were discovered—the Spanish were never able to kill or capture many of the enemy. The rebels were too skilled at retreating, carting away their wounded and dead. It was like fighting a phantom.

If this type of combat taught Churchill little concrete about war (except for its innate confusion), it revealed how important empire was becoming as the keystone of his strategic ideology. Churchill had gone to Cuba sympathizing with the rebels, thinking they were fighting against injustice. When he realized this was an anti-imperialist war, he flip-flopped. During one of the days of quiet jungle marching, he fell into conversation with a Spanish officer, who stunned him by describing the mission of the Spanish Empire in Cuba in the exact same way Churchill himself portrayed the British Empire's presence in India. At first Churchill thought it showed real arrogance on the part of the Spaniard that he could dare compare Spain's imperial possessions to Britain's.[27] Yet being forced to view the Spanish as fellow imperialists was transformative, and Churchill became strongly sympathetic to their cause. When his tour ended, his hosts awarded him the Red Cross, a military decoration that was normally only awarded to Spanish officers.

Despite wanting the Spanish to win, Churchill worried they were immersed in an "interminable" conflict that might overwhelm their limited economic resources. If Spain were to be forced out, the last thing he wanted was an independent Cuba. The idea of non-white people ruling themselves was something he would not or could not believe possible. An independent Cuba, he argued, would be taken over by its "negro element" and descend into chaos.[28] In his final article for the *Daily Graphic*, the twenty-one-year-old confidently told his audience that all the "impartial people" who lived in Cuba saw independence as a pipe dream and that a rebel victory would lead to a "bankrupt Government, torn by race animosities and recurring revolutions."[29] It would be better for all, he believed, if the United States stepped in as the new imperialists. His real fear was that the United States, which was criticizing Spanish rule with increasing vigour, might force Spain out of Cuba but not re-imperialize the island. In his eyes this would be "monstrous."[30]

The future of Britain's empire as a strategic pivot would strengthen with Churchill's further exposure to war. His next major assignment was one of the most important in his life—the 1896 deployment of the 4th Queen's Own Hussars to India. When Churchill arrived in India, the British Empire seemed serenely entrenched. British rule had been in operation for more than a century and had developed its own institutions and traditions. There was a large Indian Army (with British officers), a British-dominated bureaucracy and entrenched British business interests that controlled India's economy, all reporting to a British viceroy who lived in massive, ornate palaces while affecting an air of haughty supremacy. This entire bureaucracy operated under the nominal authority of seventy-seven-year-old Queen Victoria, the crowned Empress of India (she never set foot on Indian soil), though the real oversight was exercised by the government in London, which maintained a separate India Office with a secretary of state who sat in cabinet.

This layered structure of control was needed because the British understood, if they did not admit, that their authority was maintained by the constant threat of violence. Since their arrival in India in the seventeenth century under the auspices of the East India Company, there had been a series of violent attempts to overthrow British rule. After a major Indian uprising in 1857, the British decided to institute direct rule with the creation of the "Raj," but that was not able to stop the violence. As Churchill's time there would demonstrate, conflict could erupt at a moment's notice.

Naturally, Churchill wanted to believe that most Indians were delighted to be ruled by the British. When he reached the Hussars' camp near Bangalore, he discovered that he could hire three servants at tiny wages and all his needs would be met. "If you like to be waited on and relieved of home worries, India . . . was perfection," he later recalled. "All you had to do was hand over all your uniform and clothes to the dressing boy, your ponies to the syce, and your money to the butler, and you need never trouble any more . . . [Your servants] would devote their lives to their task. For a humble wage, justice, and a few kind words, there was nothing they would not do."[31]

Freed from mundane tasks, Churchill indulged two growing interests. He became one of the British Army's most enthusiastic and skilful polo players. The game's aristocratic nature appealed to him, and it stimulated his intensely competitive streak. Polo practice took up much of every day, primarily in the late afternoon when it was not too hot for the horses. But of more interest to the budding strategist was what Churchill did before this, when the heat of the day was at its most intense and the officers stayed in the shade. He started to read, trying to make up for his slovenly work at school. He began by devouring Edward Gibbon's six-volume, eighteenth-century classic, *The History of the Decline and Fall of the Roman Empire*. It was not by chance. Behind the imperial bravado, Churchill was worried about the future of his empire. When he read Gibbon, with its stories of the fall of Rome through religious weakness, internal corruption and the threat of ruthless barbarians, his mind raced.

Not long after he read Gibbon, Churchill made his first political speech. It was given while on leave in England, to the Primrose League of Bath on July 26, 1897 (the day Churchill first heard of the attack on the Malakand camp).★ In this political setting, Churchill ridiculed those who said that the empire was weakening "as Babylon, Carthage and Rome had declined," and called for the British people to stiffen their resolve and fight to maintain the empire against the doom-mongers. "Do not believe these croakers . . . but give the lie to their dismal croaking by showing by our actions that the vigour and vitality of our race is unimpaired and that our determination is to uphold the Empire that we have inherited from our fathers as Englishmen."[32] After all, the British Empire was the greatest force for good in the world, bringing "peace, civilization and good government to the utmost ends of the earth."[33]

Over the coming years he would argue for different schemes— some to toughen up the British people to fulfil their mission, some to reward them so that they would love the system more, but all with the aim of reinforcing imperial strength. This need could occasionally drive Churchill to take more progressive positions, as he made clear in the third political speech he ever gave—to the Conservative Party membership in Southsea in 1898. There he argued that social reform was needed to make the British people better servants of empire: "To keep our Empire we must have a free people, an educated and well fed people. That is why we are in favour of social reform."[34]

He even devised his own version of a perfected British society, which would function as a vehicle to maintain the empire. He paid particular attention to the education and training of young men. In

---

★ Randolph Churchill had been one of the founders of the Primrose League in 1883. It was established to provide an organization to disseminate and discuss Conservative Party policies.

Churchill's vision of Plato's Republic, manliness was to be prized over education. "When they are sixteen or seventeen they [young men] begin to learn a craft and do healthy manual labour, with plenty of poetry, songs, dancing, drill and gymnastics in their spare time," he said. "They can thus let off their steam on something useful. It is only when they are really thirsty for knowledge, longing to hear about things, that I would let them go to the university. It would be a favour, a coveted privilege, only to be given to those who had either proved their worth in factory or field or whose qualities and zeal were pre-eminent."[35]

In private he was just as determined. In December 1897, right after participating in the brutal pacification of the Pathans, Churchill wrote to his mother and his brother. He urged Jack to travel and see as much as he could "of this great Empire of ours—to the maintenance of which I will devote my life."[36] To his mother he pledged, "I shall devote my life to the preservation of this great Empire and to trying to maintain the progress of the English people."[37]

It is important to note that Churchill referred specifically to the English people—and not the English-speaking peoples. A romantic notion has been peddled that Churchill was naturally pro-American—or, as it has been termed, had a lifetime "true love" for the United States.[38] This is bad poetry. Even though Churchill's mother was American, he always approached strategic affairs from a British-centric perspective. During his first two visits to the United States he was struck by how alien American culture was to his own. While he liked many things about the US—its newness, its aggression, its swagger—he loathed just as many, including its populism, its lack of respect for tradition, and what he considered its "odious" foreign policy that only served to "disgust polite people."* He certainly wanted friendship between the United States and Great Britain, but now and throughout his career he was worried that America could not be trusted to serve the needs of the British Empire. As he told his

---

* Always the aristocrat, Churchill particularly hated American paper money, which he considered unspeakably common. He preferred heavy, precious-metal coins.

mother, "One of the principles of my politics will always be to promote the good understanding between the English speaking
communities. At the same time alliances nowadays are useless . . . As
long as the interests of two nations coincide & as far as they coincide—
they are and will be allies. But when they diverge, they will cease to
be allies."[39] When his mother proposed starting a new journal entitled
The Anglo-Saxon, which would emphasize the close connection
between Britain, the British Empire and the United States, Churchill
tried to persuade her to rename it *The Imperial*.[40]* His allegiances
were not to be diluted.

After Cuba, this focus on empire continued to fire his desire to get
into war. It was why he was so desperate to see action in the Malakand campaign and, once that was over, to take part in a similar
pacification campaign in the Tirah valley.[41]† It was also why he was
furious when his first news reports failed to garner him publicity. To
defray his personal expenses during the Malakand campaign (as
Churchill's regiment was not assigned to the fighting, he had to pay
his own upkeep), he had agreed to write reports for the *Daily Telegraph*. To his surprise, his articles were published as the work of an
anonymous officer. When he found out, he fumed to his mother, "I
will not conceal my disappointment at their not being signed. I had
written them with the design . . . of bringing my personality in front
of the electorate. I had hoped that some political advantage might
have accrued."[42]

Frustrated, he decided to push his efforts on the British public
even more spectacularly by writing a book. Filled with an energy
that surprised himself, he completed the manuscript in a few months
and sent it off to publishers in early 1898. The book itself, titled *The
Story of the Malakand Field Force*, revealed that Churchill had a way
with words, both in painting pictures and making arguments. He
presented the war vividly, with sounds and smells, and peppered the

---

* Jennie was indeed able to help produce a few issues of what was eventually titled
The Anglo-Saxon Review, between 1899 and 1901, but the journal was not a success.
† Unfortunately for Churchill, he arrived at the Tirah after the fighting had died
down, so he could not make a greater name for himself there.

narrative with different opinions (all arguing the same thing: that Britain was absolutely right to be doing what it was doing).

The book gained Churchill surprising notoriety. One of its greatest fans was the long-serving prime minister and foreign secretary, Lord Salisbury. A scion of another of England's most famous families, the Cecils, Salisbury had been a fixture in British politics for half a century. As a young associate of Randolph Churchill, he had originally been an opponent of attempts to democratize the British system. He later relented so he could play a role in his area of greatest interest: foreign and imperial policy. Salisbury was prime minister for all but three years between 1886 and 1902, serving as foreign secretary for most of that time as well. Courtly, distant and cynical, he physically embodied the British aristocracy holding modern life at bay, and Churchill loved him for it. In foreign policy, Salisbury worked to maintain the empire in the face of the relatively faster growth of its international rivals—the Germans, Russians and, dare it be said, Americans. It was Salisbury, very much ironically, who spoke of Britons wanting to follow a policy of "splendid isolation"— while himself knowing that such a position was impossible.

After reading *The Story of the Malakand Field Force*, Salisbury sent Churchill a letter "out of the blue" asking for a chat. So, in the summer of 1898, the young lieutenant was ushered into the vast, ornate foreign secretary's office in Whitehall and given half an hour with the most powerful person in the world. Salisbury praised the book richly and told Churchill, "If there is anything at any time that I can do which would be of assistance to you, pray do not fail to let me know."[43]

The timing could not have been better, for Churchill wanted a big favour. For months, a new war had been brewing, this time in East Africa. The war in question was a British campaign, waged to recover from perhaps their most famous defeat of the imperial age, the 1885 destruction of Major General Charles George Gordon and his force during the fall of Khartoum. Gordon, a Christian religious zealot, had tried to hold the largest city in Sudan against an Islamic uprising led by another zealot known as the Mahdi, who was in charge of a force the British called the Dervishes. For most of 1884, the British population had watched transfixed while Gordon and his soldiers were besieged in Khartoum (Gordon refused to follow orders and retreat). In January 1885, with a relief force heading down the Nile and only a few days away, Khartoum fell and Gordon was killed—quickly entering the pantheon of imperial heroes.

By 1898, the British were ready to wreak their revenge. The Mahdi had died, but his regime lived on, with Khartoum the capital—a constant reminder of their earlier defeat. A large force was collected in Egypt and put under the command of the dramatically moustachioed Sir Herbert Kitchener, referred to as the sirdar (leader) to maintain the fiction that he was doing the bidding of the Egyptian government.* Churchill was desperate to take part in the campaign but had run into a Kitchener-shaped road block. The sirdar, like many senior officers in the British Army, had grown to despise Churchill as a shameless self-promoter who was using the army for personal advantage. Kitchener thus coldly rebuffed every attempt by Churchill to gain a posting to the theatre. With no one else left to ask, Churchill went to the prime minister for help. Even though Kitchener remained hostile, a special, bureaucratic exception was found just for Churchill. Certain units taking part in the invasion—including the 21st Lancers, a new and unsung cavalry regiment—were formally under the control of the War Office in London, and not Kitchener. Taking advantage of this loophole, Churchill was assigned to the Lancers at the very last minute and hurried off to war.

And what a war it was. The battle with which the campaign culminated was fought in front of the city of Khartoum (however, much to Kitchener's chagrin, the battle was officially designated Omdurman, not Khartoum, by the War Office) and marked the end of one particular era of imperial warfare. Methodical and humourless, the sirdar had no intention of doing anything but wiping out the Sudanese forces and regime. He had a modern railroad constructed

---

* Not formally part of the British Empire, Egypt was a client state of the United Kingdom and its government was completely under the control of British officials—most famously Lord Cromer, who for more than twenty years ruled in Cairo as a new pharaoh.

across the Sahara desert so that troops and supplies, including Maxim guns (early machine guns) and artillery pieces, could flow unhindered down the hundreds of miles from the Egyptian border to Khartoum.[44] He even sent modern gunboats, in pieces, down the railway, and had them assembled on the upper Nile. Kitchener's army was thus bristling with firepower as it approached its objective. Though his army of 25,000 men (17,000 of whom were Egyptian or Sudanese) was still considerably smaller than the Dervish army of approximately 60,000, he was never going to lose. The Dervishes had only 20,000 rifles, a motley collection at best, and most of their men were armed with swords and spears. Churchill went into battle with a light heart.

He would also have one of the most spectacular views of the coming clash.[45] By September 1, 1898, Kitchener had camped his army along a bend in the Nile in a defensible crescent shape, just north of Khartoum. Two large ranges of hills provided protection for both of his flanks, and funnelled all approaching troops onto a flat, sandy plain directly in front of his line. To provide more cover for his troops, he had them fortify their position with a zariba, lines of tightly packed, thorn-covered vines. Kitchener had created a killing field, and on the morning of September 2 the Dervishes marched directly into it.

The 21st Lancers were at first kept within the zariba, but early in the morning Churchill was given a special assignment to scout Jebel Surgham, the rocky ridge which protected the left flank of Kitchener's camp. Taking seven soldiers with him, he trotted as quietly as possible up the uneven terrain, unsure whether the Dervishes had already fortified the hill. In the half-light of early morning, Churchill ordered his men to separate themselves by one hundred yards, so that if they did stumble into the enemy, those at the rear could get away and warn Kitchener.

When they finally reached the top of Jebel Surgham, the first strong rays of morning sun were peeking over the horizon, revealing that the ridge was unprotected and also uncovering almost the entire Dervish army on the move. At first the Dervish formations looked like miles of long, dusty smudges in the distance. As they came closer, however, they became frighteningly distinct. Churchill could see the Dervishes in their white robes, waving colourful banners in the morning air and raising their weapons in exultation. Soon their indistinct low rumble of a war cry became piercing and loud, as the Dervish lines generated the courage needed to march to almost-certain death. For Churchill, it was "an hour to live."[46]

The first part of the battle went exactly to Kitchener's script.[47] The Dervishes went straight for his well-defended lines. At more than 2,000 yards, British artillery opened fire into the attacking troops, cutting down masses of closely packed men. Those Dervishes lucky enough to survive the artillery were then mowed down by machine-gun and concentrated rifle fire, starting at about 1,000 yards. Still, they pressed forward until their forward line was cut down almost entirely, allowing only small groups of disorganized, disheartened men to retreat. Any Dervishes unlucky enough to be captured by the British Army were often summarily executed.[48]★ Hardly a British soldier had been touched. Churchill, on his ridge, was so high up he could feel the air-pressure rushes from the British artillery shells as they dropped onto the Dervishes. Later, when he saw their white-clad, dead bodies piled in heaps before the British lines, he likened them to "snowdrifts" on the desert floor.

Once the first Dervish attack was broken, Kitchener decided to move his troops forward to engage the rest of the Dervish army closer to Khartoum. This promised to be a trickier task, as his army would have to leave the safety of the camp. As part of this movement, the 21st Lancers were ordered out of the zariba to scout out the territory between the camp and Khartoum. Moving around Jebel Surgham to the left, they were isolated on the edge of Kitchener's army. As they came around the hill, they were the first British troops who could see the great mud-built city in the distance, with its large minarets and cityscape dominated by the grand tomb of the Mahdi himself. Coming across what looked like a small group of Dervishes,

---

★ Once again Churchill was more than aware that soldiers under British command were responsible for war crimes such as the killing of helpless prisoners. In the case of Omdurman, he tried to blame most of the killings on non-white troops.

the commander of the Lancers ordered a charge, and Churchill took control of a squad of twenty-five men for what he thought would be one of the great moments in his life.[49]

The desert, however, had played a deadly trick. As the 21st Lancers pounded down on the enemy, at full gallop with swords drawn, they had no idea of what they were doing. Instead of there being a few hundred enemy on a flat plain, the Lancers were charging directly into a large depression they could not see, full of 2,000 crouching Dervishes. The unseen enemy forces, in ranks ten to twelve deep, leapt to their feet as the cavalry crashed in on them, slashing with swords and firing weapons. The Lancers wheeled around frantically, all with one thought—to stay on their horses. If dragged out of the saddle, a rider would be consumed by a furious mass of enemy, like a whale eviscerated by sharks. There might be a few pathetic cries, then the man was gone.

Churchill, in the midst of the mayhem, grabbed his pistol—a Mauser semi-automatic that he had fortuitously purchased when back in London—and started shooting all around him. He kept his horse moving, and once again gave thanks for the dum-dums that could stop an enemy dead in his tracks, a necessary advantage as the fighting was so intimate. One Dervish he shot was so close that when Churchill pressed the trigger, the barrel of his Mauser was touching its target. He was convinced that he had shot at least five men in a few seconds.[50]

Yet he also experienced something new. For the first time during a battle, maybe for the first time in his life, Winston Churchill was truly afraid. The charge of the 21st Lancers, the last real charge in British cavalry history, was stupid and unnecessary and he very well might have died.[51] Many others did. In less than five minutes, the regiment suffered 70 killed and wounded out of the 300 officers and men.[52] Compared to the extraordinarily light casualties in the rest of Kitchener's army, it was an appalling toll.* Churchill, however, was

---

* Kitchener's entire army suffered fewer than 500 casualties at Omdurman, fewer than 50 of which were killed. So, in a few minutes, the Lancers suffered almost half of all the soldiers in the army killed during the battle.

still unwilling to learn from his fear. Like much of the British public, he focused on the heroism of the Lancers, not the pointlessness of the attack. The charge was considered so brave that three men received the Victoria Cross, the nation's highest award for valour. Even that was not enough for Churchill. He wished that more of his men had died. He complained to his mother that if only the 21st Lancers had suffered fifty or sixty additional casualties, it "would have made the performance historic—and have made us all proud of our race and blood."[53]

Still, Churchill did his best to capitalize on those soldiers who did die, by entering politics. When he finally returned to England in 1899 (after a redeployment back to the 4th Hussars in India so that he could compete in a polo tournament), he left the army and tried to enter Parliament. He was selected as one of the Conservative Party candidates for Oldham, a marginal two-seat constituency full of industrial workers and not a naturally Conservative borough. The party had won both seats in its national landslide of 1895, but it was feared that the opposition Liberal Party might win them back. Churchill, a young, energetic candidate with one of the most famous names in the country and a budding reputation as a war hero, was considered the perfect candidate to try to hold on for the Conservatives.

The election itself was an eye-opener. By-elections were short and intense. Churchill's campaign went from late June 1899 to early July, a blur of speeches and discussions of local issues. He ran as an orthodox Conservative. He was strongly opposed to women's suffrage, though he did call for improvements to the conditions of the working poor (the only sensible thing he could do in a working-class district).[54] What excited him most, however, was the issue of the empire.[55] He ended his opening address with an enthusiastic call for the British Empire to be strengthened, even enlarged—saying he would support a government that took as its mission to "consolidate the Empire, to strengthen the bonds of union between its widely scattered posts, to preserve its frontiers from aggression and to encourage a healthy principle of growth."[56] The voters had different priorities. Indeed, the question of the power of the Church of England proved far more contentious (and motivating) than the empire.

In the end Churchill lost, but ran a creditable campaign. It made him realize that as a domestic politician he needed to broaden his appeal. He would put this lesson into practice when he next ran for office.

Before Churchill could try, though, one final war—the most important in his early career—exploded into action: the Boer War. The Boers were Dutch settlers who had moved to South Africa in the seventeenth and eighteenth centuries (*boer* is the Dutch word for "farmer"). Like the American Puritans, they were religious fanatics looking to create a holier world by conquering a territory and subjugating the people who already lived there. For decades, no one in Europe had paid them much attention, but in the late nineteenth century, gold and silver were discovered in South Africa, and everything was transformed. The British, who had colonized most of the region, started casting envious eyes on Boer territory and arguing that they were the region's imperial overlords. In 1895, a group of pro-British adventurers, led by Sir Leander Starr Jameson (a business associate of the famous diamond miner Cecil Rhodes), launched a raid into Boer territory, trying to bring the area under the British umbrella. The Jameson Raid, as it came to be known, was a disaster. After a few days the Boers surrounded and arrested the raiders. They then utilized their new-found wealth to equip their forces with modern weapons, and the tensions between Great Britain and the Boer republics ratcheted up.*

Churchill was as determined as anyone to add the gold, silver and diamonds of South Africa to the British Empire. He supported the Jameson Raid when he first heard about it in 1897, and in perhaps the most hyper-aggressive article he ever produced, called for a pre-emptive war to crush the Boers. "Sooner or later," he wrote, "in a righteous cause or a picked quarrel, with the approval of Europe, or in the teeth of Germany, for the sake of our Empire, for the sake of our honour, for the sake of the race, we must fight the Boers."[57]†

---

* By the late nineteenth century the Boers had established two large republics in South Africa: the Orange Free State and the Transvaal.

† Kaiser Wilhelm II of Germany, after hearing of the Boer capture of Jameson, wrote to the Boers congratulating them on their success. For British imperialists such as Churchill this was an insult that needed to be avenged.

He would get his war, but it would be very different from the one he expected. In October 1899, negotiations between the British government and the Boers over the control of the region broke down and war was declared. Churchill was overjoyed. He was instantly hired by the *Morning Post* to head to South Africa for the huge salary of £250 per month plus all expenses (which probably made him the most highly paid war correspondent in the world). He considered the Boers a "miserably small people" and was confident that the might of the British Empire would crush them quickly in another jolly victory.[58] Churchill told his mother that he believed the British Army would be ready to strike by Christmas Day and that all the major Boer cities should be safely conquered within two months—making it possible that he would be home in time to see the Derby.[59]

Once in South Africa, it became clear that this war was something else entirely. The Boers were at home on horseback and could move over the South African plains with a rapidity and decisiveness that the British found disconcerting. The Boers were also determined to fight by their rules, not those of nineteenth-century imperial warfare. British forces soon found themselves on the defensive, and the early battles were almost all won by the Boers. What British forces remained near Boer territory were often besieged, most famously in the town of Ladysmith. The situation grew worse in December 1899, during what was known as Black Week. The Boers inflicted defeats on three separate British armies, leading the British government to understand that they would have to mobilize almost the entire empire to put down this force of angry Dutch farmers.[60]

Churchill's personal experience of the early war was just as disastrous. Almost immediately after arriving, he went deep into the war zone and joined some units in Natal being organized for the relief of Ladysmith. It was a chaotic time, the British having little idea where the elusive Boers were deployed. Befuddled, they had to send patrols into the countryside daily to see if the enemy was anywhere around.

Normally these patrols were done by cavalry, but not long after Churchill arrived in November the commanding officer of the region had the bright idea of sending out some of his best infantry in an armoured train. Churchill, "eager for trouble," happily jumped aboard. This probably seemed wise. Made up of open-top train carriages to which thick steel plates with gun holes had been fastened, armoured trains bristled with weapons, looking like impregnable, mobile fortresses. They were not.

As the train trundled on into unknown territory, everything seemed under control. For fourteen miles it travelled without an enemy being seen or a shot being fired. Then, looking back, Churchill and the rest could see Boer troops that had quietly come up behind them. The Boers started peppering the cars with rifle fire, and even brought into play one of their artillery pieces. Their fire caused a great racket, but the train was completely unaffected. It was thought better to head back to camp, and the locomotive, which was kept in the middle of the train for safety, was set in reverse and quickly picked up speed.

It was a ruse. The Boers wanted the train to speed up. As it came around a bend, the heavy carriages ran smack into an obstruction that they had laid across the tracks. Churchill and the soldiers went flying in different directions, and the cars at the front of the train derailed and were left lying scrambled across the tracks.

Churchill instantly gave up the fiction that he was a war reporter and almost tried to take command. While many of the soldiers refused to leave the protection of those cars still on the tracks, he strode up and down the line under constant fire, trying to find a way to escape capture. They had one chance. The centrally placed locomotive car had not been dislodged, so some of the train could still move—if a way could be found to clear the tracks. It was decided to use the engine, decoupled, as a great battering ram to force a way open to safety. For an agonizing while the plan seemed to work. The obstructing cars were gradually pushed outwards. When it seemed that one more shove might finish the work, the locomotive was sent at full force into the last blockage. It smashed its way through, but when Churchill looked back things were worse. In knocking the last block out of the way, the locomotive had caused a cascade, forcing some of the derailed cars back over the rail line behind it. The locomotive was now stranded from the troops in their armoured cars. When Churchill started running back to what was left of the train, all hell broke loose and Boer soldiers descended, taking him prisoner. He only just had time to throw away his beloved Mauser before they apprehended him.*

Brought to Pretoria a prisoner of war, he and other British officers were kept in a schoolhouse, under relatively light guard. Churchill hated being a prisoner, finding it even worse than Harrow, and maybe for the first time in his life he started to show the signs of clinical depression that would emerge regularly later. He became desperate for escape, to keep his sanity as much as anything else.

On December 12, 1899, he took advantage of a gap in the patrolling of the school perimeter to leap over a wall, but certainly not to freedom. He was still marooned hundreds of miles from British forces, with little in the way of provisions, no weapons, and no knowledge of the terrain. First, he had to get out of town, a trick he achieved by simply walking. Thinking no one would pay attention to an individual going about his business in a large town, Churchill strode right through the Boer capital until he reached the outskirts of Pretoria, where he was able to find a place to hide out.

From there he had the foresight to use the train lines. He would hop on trains at night, when no one could see, and ride in the direction that he thought meant freedom. Eventually, luck intervened. Near the end of his tether, with food running out (for a while he had survived eating just a few slabs of chocolate), Churchill entered a small mining camp at the end of a spur railroad. There he was discovered not by the Boers, but by a friendly English mining official whom the Boers had allowed to stay behind. Now with an ally, Churchill had a chance. For days he was hidden away, deep in an abandoned mine shaft, eating roast chicken and trying not to be bothered by the masses of rats always underfoot. Eventually a plan was hatched to bury Churchill in a trainload of wool and send him not through British lines but to the Portuguese colonies to the

---

* Churchill was in the process of throwing away his trusty dum-dums when he was captured. For a moment he was worried he might be executed for having such ammunition, but the Boer who captured him did not recognize what they were, so let him throw them away.

east. Cocooned in downy comfort, Churchill rode without event to the town of Lourenço Marques, where he presented himself to the British consulate. News of his escape made it out to Britain just as the war seemed at its darkest, and it helped make him a national hero.

Churchill would even decide to return to combat. Finding that his celebrity had made him an outcast in the army, he signed up to fight with a locally raised, pro-British unit, the South African Light Horse. This allowed him to take part in the large invasions of conquest that the British Army undertook in 1900. Sending almost a quarter of a million troops from around the empire, the British overwhelmed the Boers, eventually seizing their major cities. At this point Churchill left for home, to reap the political benefits of his new-found notoriety.*

He was a changed man—in a few respects. He had learned the value of moderating some of his earlier harsh rhetoric and strategic notions about the need to crush imperial resistance. Having been a Boer prisoner and been surprised by the generosity and kindness with which he had been treated, he decided that a punitive peace would be counterproductive—at least against whites. He publicly supported giving the Boers a great deal of self-government, even committing the British government to providing medical care to the Boer wounded. In a public letter he chided those who wanted to punish the Boers. "Beware of driving men to desperation. Even a cornered rat is dangerous. We desire a speedy peace and the last thing we want is that this war should enter a guerrilla phase. Those who demand 'an eye for an eye and a tooth for a tooth' should ask themselves whether such barren spoils are worth five years of bloody partisan warfare and the consequent impoverishment of South Africa."[61] Of course, Churchill's gentle peace came at a steep cost. The Boer republics would be wiped from the map, and the Boer knee had to be bent to accept the supremacy of the British Empire: "the

---

* The war, however, would continue for a number of years, as the Boers resorted to guerrilla warfare and the British imposed almost total control on Boer society, most famously using concentration camps to confine Boer women and children. These camps cost the lives of tens of thousands of their inhabitants.

Republics and the Dutch flag must go. I would rather fight another year and leave a Republic the size of a sixpence in South Africa."[62]

Churchill needed to have the empire as his focus because, as he admitted about himself, he had few strong convictions. As he told his mother, "I do not care so much for the principles I advocate as for the impression which my words produce & the reputation they give me. This sounds v[er]y terrible. But you must remember we do not live in the days of Great Causes."[63] He had come to view human beings as base, self-interested animals, and admitted that he was one—just a spectacular one. As he said after the Boer War, "We are all worms, but I do believe that I am a glow-worm."[64] For the rest of his career, he would change his political positions on almost every issue, putting on and discarding ideological stances like fashionable clothes—but the empire remained his lodestar.

By the time of Churchill's return to Britain, the wars he had fought over the previous five years had started him along the path to developing the strategic mindset with which he would fight future wars. He was coming to understand the relationship between cost and benefit, though he instinctively favoured the most daring, bloody or famous of actions. What had already been fixed, however, was that preserving and strengthening the British Empire was and would remain his great strategic goal. His ideas were encapsulated in one of his favourite songs, which he had loved belting out at night with his fellow officers, a few drinks in his belly and a warm glow in his heart:

> Great White Mother, far across the sea,
> Ruler of the Empire may she ever be.
> Long may she reign, glorious and free,
> In the Great White Motherland.[65]

2. Joseph Stalin: The Making of an Ideological Strategist

When World War I erupted in August 1914, the man who would be the worst and best grand strategist of the next world war was isolated in one of the most remote spots on Earth. Joseph Jughashvili, better known as Stalin—Bolshevik revolutionary and gangster—was a prisoner of Tsarist Russia, exiled in the tiny Siberian fishing village of Kureika. Located above the Arctic Circle on the Yenisei River, Kureika was inaccessible by road and lay hundreds of miles of rolling tundra and dense forest from the closest railway. Its flat landscape, punctured by a few low-rises, was uninspiring, lacking the pastoral beauty one would hope for in such a wild location. "In summer the river and in winter the snow, that's all nature offers here," Stalin lamented.[1] It was so remote that in late 1916, when the Russian Army was desperate enough for soldiers that they even called up politically unreliable criminals, it took Stalin a six-week sleigh ride to reach the draft board.*

Isolated and irrelevant, Stalin spent much of the first two years of the war brooding. He alienated his fellow Bolshevik exile and rising star in the party Iakov Sverdlov with his selfishness and slovenly habits. He seduced the youngest girl he could find and stole a dead man's books. He even claimed to be better than the locals at fishing. If an area of river was not producing fish, Stalin would move to a new one in the hope that it would produce more. He later claimed that the locals were amazed at this technique and considered him a great angler—though this seems to be another example of Stalin trying to convince himself and others that he was superior. His need to be dominant in even the wilds of Siberia could not

---

* Stalin failed the physical examination for entrance into the army, due to his left arm being permanently weakened because of a childhood injury.

obscure the fact that his life had been a series of failures to that point. Given that he was thirty-five years old in 1914, middle-aged for the time, the idea that he was soon to be the dictator of the largest country in the world would have seemed impossible—as it would at any moment of his early life.

Stalin was born in 1878, thousands of miles away from Kureika, in Gori, Georgia. Situated in the heart of the Caucasus Mountains, Georgia had hot summers, spicy food and produced wagonloads of fruit. It was also located at the intersection of competing greater powers. For centuries, Russians had pressed down from the north, Turks from the south and Persians from the east, leaving Georgians waging a constant struggle to maintain their identity. For most of the nineteenth century, Georgia had been a province of the Russian Empire, though Georgian nationalism had remained strong. Both of Stalin's parents (and the young Stalin himself) considered themselves Georgians first and foremost.

Stalin's illiterate parents were also poor in a way that would have been shocking to Winston Churchill.[2] His father, Besarion Jughashvili (better known as Beso), was a hard-drinking shoemaker who believed that Joseph should follow in his footsteps—and this meant that his son should not be educated. Stalin's mother, Ekaterine, was made of sterner stuff. Known by the nickname Keke, she was determined that the young Stalin make something of himself. In her mind, that meant becoming a priest in the Orthodox Church.

This disagreement was an indication of the terrible couple Keke and Beso made. Stalin told his own daughter that Beso beat Keke and in turn Keke beat him. At one time Stalin, who hated his father, reportedly threw at knife at Beso.[3] As Beso turned more and more to the bottle, he and Keke became estranged. Eventually Beso moved to the Georgian capital, Tbilisi, to ply his trade, and dragged the young Joseph along with him. Stalin escaped as soon as he could and returned to Gori. To forestall it happening again, Keke, who had struck up a connection with a local priest and a well-to-do family while working as a cleaner (and possibly a prostitute), became determined to see her son educated by the Georgian Orthodox Church. She triumphed in 1893 when Stalin, who had revealed himself to be a precocious student, voracious reader and skilled writer of Georgian-language poetry, passed the entrance exam for the Tbilisi Seminary.

It was a pyrrhic victory. The years that Stalin spent in the seminary made an indelible, entirely non-spiritual, mark. Though the teenage boy enjoyed the church singing (Stalin had a lovely singing voice), he quickly embraced atheism. The monotonous daily prayers and monastic living conditions did nothing to rekindle faith in a benevolent God. It did, however, educate him about the power of suspicion and control. Stalin later recalled that the seminary authorities monitored the trainee priests through a system built on "spying, penetrating into the soul, humiliation."[4] All of these would be key stratagems employed by the Stalinist state. The seminary also drummed into him a catechismal mindset. He emerged with a penchant for ordering his points methodically, often with numbers, as if building a structure with his thoughts.

This way of thinking was important because, while Stalin was not spiritual, he was about to adopt the great secular religion of his age—Marxism. At the seminary, the young Stalin spent much of his time reading radical literature, including Karl Marx's *Das Kapital*. He was immediately enthralled by Marx's avenging historicism. Marx laid out a historical progression that he claimed was bound to happen. In the future there would be a revolution brought about by the cruel, oppressive, capitalist regimes that governed the globe. Their greed would drive them to extremes in a desire to extract profit from an increasingly destitute proletariat. The oppressed industrial working classes would rise up, a new world would be born, superstition would wither, and the fruits of economic production would be rationally spread.

The young Stalin was drawn to this violent view of history. He did not love the poor but saw himself as a force to avenge the wrongs from which they suffered. The first pseudonym he adopted emerged straight from this resentment. He started calling himself Koba, the name of an avenging hero in a popular Georgian novel. This character was a dispenser of the roughest justice, including murder. His favourite targets were wealthy Georgians, accused of selling out their poor countryfolk to Russian forces. Renamed and reborn as a radical,

Stalin/Koba left the seminary in 1899 determined to destroy the capitalist system.*

The Georgia into which he emerged had much to avenge. It contained both a large peasant class and a growing proletariat, both of whom were some of the poorest in Europe. As the Russian Empire industrialized, Georgia saw new railways and factories built, upending its artisan-farmer economy. Beso's small shoe business, for one, was undercut by the appearance of cheaper, factory-made shoes. Stalin's father was forced to give up his craft and go to work in a factory, after which he drank himself to death in 1909.

Stalin spent much of his first years after the seminary trying to organize those who were similarly angry, suffering and resentful. He drifted from place to place, holding a series of odd jobs, the longest of which was as a meteorologist at the Tbilisi observatory. No matter where he went, trouble quickly followed, and he soon came to the attention of one of the most effective police forces of its time, the Okhrana.

Russia's autocrat, Tsar Nicholas II, was a simpleton, spectacularly unsuited to running the country's vast empire, yet through the Okhrana his Tsarist state had established a formidable bureaucracy of control. Anyone deemed a threat quickly came to their attention, and they infiltrated most radical groups, including many with which Stalin associated. By 1901, Stalin had been forced to go underground and first used murder as a weapon, allegedly killing a supposed Okhrana informant. In 1902, he was arrested for the first time, bolstering his career as a revolutionary. Incarcerated, Stalin came across a population of violent, angry men whom he could organize. He became a version of a prison mafia boss, showing once again his need to dominate his fellow man. The Russian state then sentenced Stalin to his first exile in Siberia, but he escaped almost immediately and made his way back to Georgia.

While Stalin was embarking on his career as a revolutionary

---

* Keke never fully recovered from this blow. Practically the last thing she said to her son as she was dying—and he was the world leader of communism—was "What a shame that you did not become a priest."

gangster, a major split occurred amongst Russian communists. Marxists often disagreed on one fundamental question: how should
revolution be achieved? A strict reading of Marx seemed to make it
clear that a nation needed a large population of industrial workers
before it could progress to the stage of revolution. If so, imperial
Russia in 1900 would have been the last major power to qualify.
Compared to Britain or Germany, it was an industrial laggard, overwhelmingly populated by illiterate, religious peasants—a class that,
according to Marx, would make very poor revolutionaries.

   Many Russian Marxists therefore argued that they needed to work
with other leftist groups to try to usher in economic and societal
change before the country was ready for revolution. Opposed to
them were radicals who despised such caution. They argued for
immediate action, even if it was led by a small core of professional
revolutionaries (many educated and from wealthy backgrounds).
This disagreement led to a 1903 split within the most important
Russian Marxist political group of the time, the Russian Social
Democratic Labour Party. The leader of the hard-line forces, who
were in the minority at the time, was Vladimir Ilyich Ulyanov, better
known as Lenin. He was determined to lead the Russian communist
movement no matter what, and called his faction the Bolsheviks
(meaning "the majority") as opposed to the moderate Mensheviks
("the minority"). For not the last time in their rise to power, the Lenin-
ists were happier with the lie.

   When Stalin learned of the split, he jumped into Lenin's camp, and
from that point onwards vied to be valued by the older man. In 1906,
Stalin wrote his first ideological pamphlet, *Anarchism or Socialism?*,
and it was clear that he supported revolution without delay.[5] In this
short work, Stalin communicated both his complete adoption of a
Marxist world view and his belief that there should be no accommo-
dation with parties not committed to revolution. He started by
attacking those who argued that Marxism was just a theory, saying it
was far more than that: "It is an integral world outlook, a philosophical system." Later Stalin used one of his favourite tricks, answering a
self-posed rhetorical question. Asking whether communists should
or should not work within the existing system, he opted for the

uncompromising position. "The proletariat cannot achieve socialism by making peace with the bourgeoisie—it must unfailingly take the path of struggle, and this struggle must be a class struggle, a struggle of the entire proletariat against the entire bourgeoisie. Either the bourgeoisie and its capitalism, or the proletariat and its socialism!"

Stalin's identity as a Leninist defined his early career. Before the Russian Revolution, the two met only a handful of times, mostly when Stalin went to Bolshevik conferences—the first time in Finland in 1905. While few, these meetings whetted Stalin's appetite. To bring himself closer to Lenin, he began shedding his Georgian skin and adopting a Russian identity. Until late 1907 he was still writing his pamphlets and articles in Georgian, and then he switched to Russian.[6] In what seems like an echo of his hero Lenin, in 1912 he adopted the name Stalin, which means "Man of Steel" in Russian. More and more, Stalin spoke about being Russian and would eventually become a Russian patriot with an intensity that would surprise family members. Lenin was aware that the younger man was both eager to please and would do whatever was needed on his behalf. In 1912 he supported making Stalin a member of the party's Central Committee. When a Menshevik complained about Stalin's unorthodox methods, Lenin replied, "This is exactly the kind of person I need!"[7]

Lenin was a shrewd judge of character. Stalin would not shirk from taking extreme action to achieve any goal Lenin desired. He robbed banks and killed enemies. His most famous exploit was the Tbilisi bank heist of 1907, which netted approximately 100,000 roubles.[8] His methods, while extreme, were not that unusual in the chaos of the Russian Empire. The Tsarist state was riding a tiger as Russia modernized, trying to maintain its absolutist structure in the face of a transforming economy and society. Peasants were increasingly restive with their impoverished lot, while the new working classes in the major cities started to flex their political muscles, and a growing middle class wanted to have its contributions and capital recognized.

At times, the tiger could turn on its master. There was a failed revolution against Tsarist rule in 1905. Defeat by the Japanese in the Russo-Japanese War exacerbated this growing uneasiness and resulted in mass protests and eventually a mutiny amongst the armed forces. Cornered, the tsar agreed to reforms, including the creation of the Duma—an elected assembly with consultative more than actual powers. The concession bought the regime time, though Nicholas II was too obtuse to grasp that his system needed more thorough reformation. He disbanded the Duma as soon as he could and returned to absolutist rule.

Stalin's role in the events of 1905 was not consequential, though this was a result of geography. The most important protests occurred in and around the Russian capital of St. Petersburg, while at the time Stalin was operating as a revolutionary bandit in some of the least accessible parts of Georgia.[9] He had some dashing exploits, leading packhorses laden with weapons and stolen cash over mountain passes, but he was on the fringes. And the failure of the 1905 uprising ushered in the most frustrating period of Stalin's life. In 1907, his wife Kato died from typhus, leaving Stalin with a young son whom he promptly abandoned. Between 1908 and 1913 he was regularly hauled off by the Okhrana and placed in one remote location after another, fathering another child in at least one more place, and then escaping and making his way to St. Petersburg or some other city before starting more trouble. In 1913, to keep him well and truly out of the way, Russian authorities sent him to Kureika, where he would remain until war ignited Europe a year later.

World War I would be his salvation. The strains of the conflict brutally exposed the deficiencies of the Tsarist state and the relative backwardness of the Russian economy and army. The tsar used the war as an excuse to leave the capital—now renamed Petrograd to make it sound less German—and act as a warlord. He was not successful. Russia's greatest problem was that no matter how many soldiers were drafted into its army and no matter how bravely those soldiers fought, they were unable to cope with the more modern, better-trained and better-equipped German forces. When in 1915 the Germans switched some of their army from the Western Front to the east, the Russians found themselves in relentless retreat. Once they were pushed back deep into Russia itself, their casualties reached levels hardly seen before in any war (more than two million Russians would be killed in World War I, the highest number of any combatant nation). Faith in Nicholas began to crack.

In the end it was food, or the lack thereof, that destroyed the Tsarist state. In February 1917, as Petrograd began to emerge from the worst of its winter freeze, the working population lost faith that the state would deliver them the necessary food to sustain life. The comparison between their lot and Russia's fabulously wealthy elite became even more acute. Protests spiralled out of control, and for once the Tsarist system was unable to crush the dissent. Nicholas attempted to calm things by ordering food rationing, but that made things worse as people panicked, thinking it was a sign that supplies would soon run out. By the end of February 1917, elements of the army started siding with the protesters and their councils (called soviets), which were calling for drastic change. Faced with the nightmare that they would lose control over their troops, a delegation of Russian generals and politicians confronted the tsar. He was told that if he did not abdicate, the army might disintegrate. Stunned, Nicholas abdicated in his own and his son's names, in favour of his brother. However, power soon was handed to a provisional government dominated by moderate-left figures including the socialist lawyer and rumoured cocaine fiend Alexander Kerensky. The Russian Revolution had begun.*

In the midst of this chaos, Petrograd transformed into one of the freest, most anarchic cities in the world. Newspapers of every ideological position bloomed overnight, and just as quickly folded. Orators of different stripes whipped crowds into a fervour against the provisional government. Popular entertainments were raucous and rude, and violence could erupt out of nowhere. The Russian Army was in almost as much chaos as the city, with different commanders duelling with each other for authority. Mass desertion was a fact of life, and even many of the soldiers in Petrograd—ostensibly there to keep order and protect the provisional government—were

---

* The phrase Russian Revolution will be used to describe the upheaval in all of 1917, while the specific revolutions in February and October will be described using their months as names.

showing a dangerous fondness for subversive ideologies such as communism. Looming over all the chaos was the very un-anarchic German Army, only 200 miles away and so far able to puncture any line the Russians had tried to put in its path.

It was the perfect opportunity for Joseph Stalin. He hurried to Petrograd from Siberia as soon as possible—arriving in March 1917, just weeks after the tsar abdicated. At once he threw himself into politics, and by the end of the Russian Revolution and the Civil War that followed he had learned—and failed to learn—a great deal. For a while it was common to portray Stalin as a minor figure in 1917, a vision that emerged mostly from the caricature created by his great nemesis, Leon Trotsky. A rival for Lenin's favour, Trotsky claimed that Stalin "did not exist, in a political sense" in 1917 and that the Georgian remained uninvolved in the great events that led up to the second revolution later that year.[10] It was a comforting fiction that Trotsky created to make himself feel better after Stalin had him exiled from the USSR—and perhaps it did so, until Stalin had one of his agents drive an ice pick into his rival's head in 1940.

The Russian Revolution and Civil War would transform Stalin into one of the most powerful political figures in the world. By the end he had secured for himself a more senior military command than any of the other great World War II strategists. He controlled armies while Churchill commanded brigades and Hitler carried messages. He headed major departments of state while Franklin Roosevelt was an assistant secretary, and he had a political standing in his country that could only be rivalled by Mussolini after his seizure of power in Italy.

Stalin's education as a strategist during these years was both profoundly ideological and practical—establishing the template that would determine his actions going into, during and leaving World War II. At times these impulses could go to war against each other, and lead him down a self-destructive route. When they worked together, however, he could crush opponents both domestic and international. Stalin's strategic outlook was also very different from Trotsky's. Trotsky, who had spent most of the previous ten years as a minor revolutionary celebrity in the great capitals, cafés and salons of

Europe, was a mesmerizing speaker and intellectual thinker who came to Petrograd in 1917 and took the city by storm, performing in what he called the "Modern Circus."[11] Nightly, Trotsky would dazzle packed crowds with his soaring oratory, denouncing the provisional government and calling for ever more radical action. Stalin, in comparison, avoided such public shows. Still speaking a heavily accented Russian, with a surprisingly soft voice that did not project well in a noisy hall, he expressed himself more robustly in print. Working with his good friend Lev Kamenev, whom Stalin later would have tortured and executed, he quickly seized the editorship of the leading Bolshevik newspaper *Pravda*.

Before Stalin arrived in Petrograd, *Pravda* had been run by the stone-faced Bolshevik Viacheslav Molotov. Stalin simply brushed Molotov aside, taking control of the paper and stealing Molotov's girlfriend at the same time. Instead of being resentful, Molotov, a good Bolshevik in need of a guiding force, accepted his demotion and humiliation without protest and even transformed into one of Stalin's more devoted acolytes. It ended up being a wise career move, and Molotov became a trusted servant with whom Stalin could plan his rise to the top. It would culminate with Molotov becoming Stalin's foreign minister and diplomat of choice during World War II, showing that Stalin prized loyalty more than anything.

Having seized *Pravda* and turned it into their personal mouthpiece, Stalin and Kamenev initially were a little uncertain about what line to take. Instead of calling for immediate revolution, they at first supported cooperation between all socialist groups, including the hated Mensheviks and the provisional government.[12] The idea that all of Russia could be seized by a small Marxist sect was probably too much to imagine for a Georgian bandit who had spent the previous years in isolated village communities. In his first *Pravda* editorials that March, Stalin spoke simply of the need to "put pressure" on the government to start peace negotiations with the Germans.[13]

His moderation would not last long. In April 1917, Lenin arrived in Petrograd, smuggled in by the Germans in a sealed train boxcar. Too impatient to wait for united socialist action and disdainful of the provisional government, he seized control of the Bolsheviks and called for the immediate overthrow of the Russian state. Stalin quickly fell into line.

Stalin's work in the early days after the February Revolution was clearly noted and had made him popular amongst the grassroots of the party. Not long after Lenin arrived, party members voted to select a new Central Committee and Stalin came in a surprising third, trailing only Lenin and Grigory Zinoviev (another close associate Stalin would later have killed).[14] Crucially, he received the strong backing of Lenin himself, who told the party members, "We have known Com[rade] Koba for very many years . . . He handles any responsible job well."[15]

Stalin used his power in the party over the next few months to make himself one of Bolshevism's most effective propagandists, and to inch ever closer to Lenin. Whereas Trotsky was developing such a following that he was seen as a possible rival to Lenin for power, Stalin made himself into an agent of Lenin's demands. As a sign of Stalin's status, he was given the title of "special assistant to Lenin for special assignments."[16] Certainly Lenin showed that he trusted Stalin with his life. Though the provisional government had no Okhrana, it did try to assert its power, and in July 1917 it ordered that Lenin be arrested. Stalin played a major role in keeping the Bolshevik leader safe, and Lenin was first hidden in Stalin's own bedroom in the house of the pro-Bolshevik Alliluev family (Stalin would soon marry Nadia Allilueva). When it was decided that Lenin needed to be spirited out of Petrograd for his own safety, it was Stalin who shaved the older man's distinctive moustache and sharp chin beard. Suitably disguised, Lenin fled to Helsinki where he stayed for months, using Stalin as one of his most reliable conduits. With Lenin out of the capital, Stalin played a more prominent role in Bolshevik politics, addressing the party's sixth congress, which was held in secret that July–August.[17] And while Trotsky was definitely a more important player in the events leading up to the second great Russian revolution, in October 1917 (or November in the new Gregorian calendar, which the USSR would adopt), Stalin was clearly exercising power in Bolshevik circles.

What the Bolsheviks did between March and October 1917 was

one of the most impressive feats of historical organization and action ever witnessed. When the tsar abdicated, the Bolsheviks were a fringe of a fringe—a small radical sect within a much larger socialist movement made up of Mensheviks, social democrats, anarchists and others. Under Lenin's direction, the Bolsheviks became determined to act like the majority and take over as much of the left as they could, while constantly stoking tensions amongst the workers, disaffected soldiers and discontents in Petrograd.

This is where Stalin did his important work. He published almost daily articles in *Pravda* and other Bolshevik journals, which became increasingly radical in their calls for action. If Stalin lacked the ability to write the kinds of intellectual treatises on Marxism that other Bolsheviks often used to burnish their credentials, he had an ordered, direct and simple way of expressing himself that could be very effective. By October he was directing his fire not only on the capitalists and the provisional government, but also on Mensheviks and other socialists who held back from launching a true revolution—and even Bolsheviks such as Kamenev and Zinoviev who were hesitant to back Lenin's call for immediate action.[18] On October 24 he all but called for another revolution, making it clear that he was more than aware about what was going to happen.[19] "It was the soldiers and workers who overthrew the tsar in February. But having vanquished the tsar, they had no desire to take power themselves. Led by bad shepherds, the Socialist-Revolutionaries and Mensheviks, the workers and soldiers voluntarily turned over the power to representatives of the landlords and capitalists . . . If you all act solidly and staunchly no one will dare to resist the will of the people. The stronger and the more organized and powerful your action, the more peacefully will the old government make way for the new. And then the whole country will boldly and firmly march forward to the conquest of peace for the peoples, land for the peasants, and bread and work for the starving."[20] The October Revolution exploded into life one day later.

When sailors from the main Tsarist naval base of Kronstadt came out in support of the Bolsheviks, events took on an irresistible momentum. They joined with workers and disaffected soldiers who had joined the Bolsheviks, some of whom had been named Red Guards. They would give Lenin the most effective fighting force in Petrograd, a huge advantage going forward. Railway workers also rallied to their cause, shutting down transportation for Kerensky's supporters, who started melting away. Kerensky himself gave up hope and abandoned the city—some said disguised in a woman's dress. On the night of October 25–26, they occupied the great Winter Palace while facing almost no opposition. They were the masters now—but the real question was for how long.

Stalin's role during these two days was far from prominent, and it is hard to find any real evidence of what he did (though this did not stop Soviet-era films from creating an entire mythology about his supposed central role in the revolution). His lack of a definite achievement was another reason that Trotsky, who was in the middle of the action—and next to Lenin the person most responsible for leading the revolution—would later charge that Stalin was insignificant in events. As always, Trotsky missed the real point. Stalin had been extremely important in the build-up of Bolshevik power in Petrograd, he had earned Lenin's confidence, and he had acquired a reputation amongst the party for his effectiveness. So what if he hadn't led forces on the day? His position in the party was secure, as shown by the fact that as the Bolsheviks moved to consolidate their power, he was one of the highest-ranking members of the new authority.

Stalin was one of only seven members elected to the new Bolshevik Central Committee that was installed almost immediately after the October Revolution. Moreover, he was widely considered the fifth-highest-ranking member of the party's leadership, trailing only Lenin, Trotsky, Zinoviev and Kamenev. Now having to set up a proto-government in the midst of chaos, Lenin entrusted Stalin with a portfolio that covered the nationalities question—his supposed speciality. So, while Stalin was certainly not the equal of Trotsky, who was made the head of the new Bolshevik Foreign Office and would soon create and lead the Red Army, he was amongst a handful of the most important Bolshevik leaders in the new state. Moreover, he had something Trotsky still lacked: the complete confidence of Lenin. Stalin was one of only two people in Petrograd given permission to enter Lenin's private apartment at party head-quarters.[21] Though Trotsky still outranked Stalin in the governmental hierarchy of the Bolshevik state (as chaotic as it was), Stalin could rightly point to signs of Lenin's favour such as this to support the belief that the two were close to equal rivals.

Of course, for any of these positions to matter, Stalin and the Bolsheviks had to survive in power. In late 1917 and early 1918, that seemed far from certain. The Bolsheviks controlled Petrograd, Moscow and most of the larger cities in European Russia, but they were faced with a host of enemies both internally and externally. First and foremost, the Bolsheviks needed an army to keep control, and once the Imperial Army was dissolved in March 1918, Trotsky started recruiting the tsar's former soldiers for the Bolshevik cause. A surprisingly large percentage of the tsar's officers, including some of the most committed fighters, believed that their loyalty was to Russia regardless of who controlled the state, and rebadged themselves into the Red Army. This included the most successful Russian general of World War I, General Aleksei Brusilov.

A significant percentage of the peasant soldiers in the Russian Army likewise accepted their new government. One of the first things the Bolsheviks did after seizing power was to decree that the peasants could now own the land that they worked, appropriating millions of acres from the aristocracy and middle classes. It was a brilliant move, creating an economic interest amongst the peasantry to support the continuation of Bolshevik rule.

Still, having access to an army meant little if the Bolsheviks could not stop the Germans. It was here that Lenin made one of his most important grand-strategic choices, which caused great divisions in the Bolshevik leadership, providing Stalin with an important example of the need to make short-term concessions for long-term gain. Lenin was convinced that it was the domestic enemy that needed to be conquered first, and as such it would be best to try to negotiate an armistice with the hated Germans (as onerous as that might be). Almost immediately after the October Revolution, Lenin reached out to the Germans to try to end Russia's participation in the war.

Trying to reach a deal with a highly developed capitalist country such as Germany was bound to be controversial for the Bolsheviks. Germany, also led by a monarch (and cousin of the tsar), stood for everything the Bolsheviks supposedly hated. Germany also had active socialist and communist movements that the Bolsheviks were hoping would start its own revolution—which according to Marx would have been far more likely than a revolution in backwards Russia. Furthermore, as a condition to agree to peace, the Germans were demanding control over large areas that had previously been part of imperial Russia. Lenin did not blink. Better to cut a deal with the devil, so that Bolshevism could survive, than risk everything against a stronger power. Many of his supporters, including Trotsky, thought the move unnecessarily cowardly, and believed that if the Bolsheviks stood firm, revolution would break out in Germany and capitalism would begin to be swept away. Stalin, still finding his feet, hedged his bets.

The original negotiations revealed just how impractical Trotsky could be. As the man in charge of foreign affairs, it fell to him to lead the Bolshevik negotiating team. He arrived at the talks at Brest-Litovsk in January 1918 and lectured his increasingly exasperated German counterparts about the evils of capitalism, imperialism and militarism, often grandstanding for the foreign press. He declared that Russia would be leaving the war in short order, but in the same breath said he would not agree a treaty with Germany that handed over large parts of formerly Russian territory. He was gambling that the Germans were too focused on their coming great struggle in the west to expend much force against Russia.

He lost. The truth was that the Germans didn't need a large army to push forward against the chaotic rabble that made up much of the Russian forces. Almost immediately after Trotsky returned to meet with Lenin and the Central Committee, the Germans attacked with what forces they could muster, and Russian Army resistance crumbled. It was the closest that Bolshevik rule ever came to collapsing in its early days. Stalin, torn between his ideological self which opposed any deal with the Germans and his practical self which understood the immediate need, initially tried to have it both ways. Meanwhile Lenin looked at the unfolding disaster and called for the immediate resumption of the peace talks and a signing of a deal—or, he claimed, the revolution would be over "in three weeks." Stalin at first supported the resumption of the talks, but argued that no deal should be automatically approved.[22] Lenin overruled him, and the party fell in line.

When the Bolshevik negotiators returned to the talks, the full extent of Trotsky's failure became clear. The Germans, holding an even stronger hand, offered even worse terms. With no alternative, the Bolsheviks caved, agreeing to the famous Treaty of Brest-Litovsk, one of the greatest losses of territory in diplomatic history.[23] This treaty, signed in March 1918, handed Germany control of all of Poland, the Baltic states and Ukraine, as well as parts of Belarus. At a stroke, Russia lost much of its natural resources and agricultural production. Yet it was a necessary humiliation, and allowed the Bolsheviks to triumph in the end. They would let the western Allies carry the responsibility of defeating the German Army, while they looked after more immediate concerns.

When Corporal Adolf Hitler, sitting snugly in his dispatch runner's dugout, heard about the Treaty of Brest-Litovsk, he saw it as confirmation of the superiority of the German Army and an important marker on the road to an eventual German victory. The opposite was true. By turning Germany fully against the capitalist powers of the west, Lenin had given the Bolsheviks time. What they did with that time was to take over all of Russia, from Vladivostok to Minsk, triumphing in one of the greatest wars of atrocity ever fought.

The Bolsheviks' enemy in the Russian Civil War was an extraordinary medley of forces collectively referred to as the Whites. Many were former members of the Imperial Army, devoted to the old regime, who were trying to turn back the clock. Others were less concerned with reinstating the tsar than enriching themselves and creating personal empires. Some Whites had no interest in restoring imperial Russia at all, and were fighting for their national or ethnic identities. Hailing from all parts of the enormous polyglot Russian Empire, these included Ukrainians, Cossacks and, to Stalin's mortification, Georgians (to name just a few). There were even groups of fighters from far outside the old Russia, including a force of Czech prisoners of war who had been serving in the Austro-Hungarian Army when captured years earlier. Together, the Whites could have been a large and powerful force—but their disparate concerns weakened them fatally in comparison to the extraordinarily united Bolsheviks.

For Stalin, the Treaty of Brest-Litovsk led directly to his first major independent command—taking charge of the control and shipping of food in and around the city of Tsaritsyn, which would later be named Stalingrad and is today known as Volgograd.★ As in all wars, there was a struggle to control and transport resources in the Russian Civil War, and no resource was as important to the Bolsheviks as the grain needed to make the rich, dark bread that was ubiquitous in European Russia. As Bolshevik strength lay in the larger cities, and with access to grain produced in Ukraine cut off, they were desperate to get food from the fertile regions straddling the Volga and Don rivers. That was what made Tsaritsyn so important.

The city, named after the golden sands of the Tsaritsa River, which flowed into the Volga at that place, had been founded in the late sixteenth century, but for its first 300 years it remained a small backwater. During the nineteenth century, Tsaritsyn's strategic location on the Volga made it a crossroads for modern communications. Railways appeared in the 1860s, and Tsaritsyn found itself on one of the main lines from Moscow to the Caspian Sea and on to central Asia. The city boomed with the growth of heavy industry, and transformed into a bustling centre of trade, with a modernist grid of streets containing shops, entertainments and housing. If the Bolsheviks were going to get food from the south-east to the cities, much of it was going to be shipped through Tsaritsyn, and Stalin was sent there to make sure it happened.

In the early days of the Russian Revolution, Stalin had grasped the importance of controlling Russia's trains to protect food shipments.

★ There are some people in Volgograd today who wish to restore the name Stalingrad, believing that it would give the city a much higher global profile. If they succeed, it could be argued that Stalin's rehabilitation has taken a major step forward.

In August 1917, in one of his *Pravda* editorials, he had pinpointed the issue of Russia's "underdeveloped" rail network, which was failing to supply the cities and the army at the same time.[24] At this point in his career he had been careful not to propose anything too violent. Instead he called for food supply problems to be solved by cooperative peasant and industrial worker committees. When presented with the reality of the food/rail situation in Tsaritsyn, however, Stalin acted in a very different manner. He went to war against any and all enemies to get the grain he needed. He was given the bland title of General Director of Food Affairs in South Russia, but he has more accurately been described as Tsaritsyn's "bandit in chief."

When Stalin arrived to take up his command on June 6, 1918, he sent Lenin a telegram revealing both his egocentricity and a desire to impress his patron. The situation in Tsaritsyn, he reported, was rife with "chaos and profiteering," and the rail network was "completely dislocated" due to the different incompetent Red Army agencies competing for power.[25] Yet Stalin boasted that he would quickly put things right. He had already appointed a number of new commissars and had started collecting a massive quantity of grain. He promised to dispatch one million poods of grain to Moscow in a few days.* Things would not turn out to be so easy. Though it is not entirely clear how much grain Stalin was able to send north, he soon started making excuses to Lenin as to why his promises never fully materialized. And as he explained his failures, Stalin gave glimpses into his grand-strategic outlook.

Stalin was acting as much as a military commander as a political one. He even started wearing quasi-military dress. Favouring collarless tunics with no decorations and high black leather boots, he could also be found wearing army-style caps at jaunty angles. It was a militarized outfit he would wear frequently until his death.†

---

* Pood was the common Russian measure of grain at the time, and one pood weighed 16.4 kilograms.

† Though as Stalin grew in power and international prestige, his uniform became slightly more elaborate. During World War II he favoured more traditional outfits, with striped trousers and decorated collars and shoulder boards.

Stalin did not just dress like a soldier; he created a military-style headquarters. His base was a specially kitted-out railway car, where he surrounded himself with trusted aides—including his new teenage bride, Nadia Allilueva, who had come to act as his secretary, and Nadia's brother. Stalin arrived in Tsaritsyn with 400 fresh troops to help fight, but he kept 50 of these around him for his personal protection.[26] Soon, this force was considered too few, and the number of soldiers assigned as his bodyguards was doubled to 100—and nicknamed the Stalinist Guard.[27]

Protected as well as he could be, Stalin immediately instituted a reign of terror. So much of his later actions when in power—the terror, the mass arrests, the beatings and murders and above all the use of secret police—were first tested by him at Tsaritsyn. The secret police, called the Cheka, were greatly expanded in the city by Stalin on his arrival. A ubiquitous part of Bolshevik rule throughout Russia, their brutality was hardly confined by Stalin's command. Yet the force Stalin used in Tsaritsyn was particularly large and particularly unpleasant. It was said that the Tsaritsyn Cheka had a fondness for torturing and dismembering their prisoners with handsaws.[28] Certainly killing people seemed a trivial matter in Stalin's Tsaritsyn, and suspicion alone was enough to merit the loss of life. Not long after Stalin's arrival, the main market was raided by the Cheka and some people were executed on the spot, on the grounds that they might have been speculators.[29]

It was the start of a series of mass arrests. Almost daily, Stalin's forces claimed to discover some new conspiracy in what had outwardly been a reliable and loyal sector of society.[30] Some of these may have been real, but many were not—though this difference never mattered much to Stalin. The Cheka arrested so many people that prisons soon were overflowing, and prisoners had to be confined on large barges moored on the Volga—where, kept in cramped quarters, they suffered from exposure and starvation. Bloody beatings were common and many would die from "a bullet in the neck" before Stalin was through.[31] He even gave orders that, were the city to fall, the barges should be blown up and sunk to kill all the prisoners. He was gaining a "taste" for this type of rule.[32]

Stalin himself ordered the summary execution of an engineer named N. P. Alexeev, who was suspected of being an agent of the Whites sent to Tsaritsyn to spread subversion.[33] Even though there was no hard evidence of Alexeev's guilt, Stalin believed the chance of his being guilty was enough to justify not only his execution without trial, but that of his staff and the two sons who were with him.[34] The template that Stalin would use during the Great Terror in the 1930s was being set—political loyalty, particularly when demonstrated by someone of an uneducated or poorer background, was what mattered. Expertise, even when desperately needed, and especially when exhibited by those from a wealthier or more educated background, created suspicion. At Tsaritsyn, for instance, nothing was more important than the efficient functioning of the rail lines and rail stock. Yet when Stalin grew suspicious of some railroad specialists because they hailed from the wrong class, he did not hesitate to call for their arrest and summary execution.[35] Far better that a few innocent people were killed than anyone guilty escape justice.

Stalin's brutality in ruling Tsaritsyn eventually made even Lenin a little squeamish. A proponent of mass killing as a tool of power, Lenin heard so many reports of Stalin's excesses that he complained that Stalin had gone overboard and was shooting people "incorrectly."[36] Of course, being Lenin, he could not go too far in criticizing Bolshevik crimes, saying just after the killings, "that's why we are humans."[37] Yet Stalin's particular form of terror was somewhat different when compared to other mass murderers such as Trotsky or Lenin. His wrath was directed as much towards the internal enemy as the external—a fundamental tenet of his ideologically based outlook. He needed to explain why things did not and would not work out exactly as he would have liked, or as Marxism said they should—and his explanation was almost always the nefarious deeds of internal saboteurs and subversives.

Stalin suspected enemies everywhere. The most dangerous were not the Whites, but closet traitors in the Red Army who, in Stalin's mind, had been put in power by none other than Trotsky. By the summer of 1918 Trotsky, as war minister, had become the biggest supporter of using formerly Tsarist officers in the Red Army. He had come to the conclusion early in the Civil War that the only way for the Red Army to triumph was with competent, experienced leadership. And so he started assigning major commands to such defectors. In doing so, he made one of his most important contributions to the Bolsheviks' eventual triumph in the Civil War, though at the same time he unwittingly handed Stalin another tool with which to later bash him over the head.

Much of the Red Army in the area was under the command of a former Tsarist general, Andrei Snesarev. Tall, with "impeccable military bearing" and prone to wearing immaculate pre-war uniforms complete with medals won in the Tsar's service, Snesarev could have walked out of a classic Russian novel straight into a formal ball in the palaces of St. Petersburg.[38] Cautious and sensible, Snesarev had been building up a large force at Tsaritsyn before launching any operations. Stalin, however, was determined to destroy him.

Stalin's telegrams to Lenin show a man desperate to gain control over Red Army military forces, whom he was blaming for his personal failures. Enraged over military bungling that had nearly allowed the Whites to sever a vital railway line, Stalin told Lenin he was going to seize all the command authority he needed. "For the good of the world," he cabled Lenin, "I need military powers . . . I shall myself, without any formalities, dismiss army commanders and commissars who are ruining the work. The interests of the work dictate this and, of course, not having a paper from Trotsky is not going to deter me."[39]

Stalin didn't just dismiss. Having claimed military authority, he ordered Snesarev and members of his staff arrested and confined on the infamous Volga barges. Luckily for Snesarev, he was freed when Trotsky personally intervened, though many of his officers died. A few weeks later, Stalin had Snesarev's replacement, Colonel Anatolii Nossovitch—along with more officers—arrested. Trotsky again had to intervene to save him, but Stalin got his way.*

---

* Nossovitch eventually escaped from Bolshevik authorities and defected to the Whites. Though, before he was arrested, he seems to have been working for the Red Army.

Stalin had revealed one of his formative strategic traits—he would go to great, even self-destructive lengths to purge anyone he viewed as a threat to himself or Bolshevism (which, in his mind, were basically identical). And he prized loyalty over ability. It was at Tsaritsyn that Stalin first came to work closely with Klim Voroshilov.[40] Possessing a Platonic form of mediocrity, Voroshilov's defining characteristics were a cheerful nature, shallow mind, humble background and a dog-like devotion to Stalin. (He was also one of the Red Army officers in the region not favoured by Trotsky.) As such, he was quickly taken on by Stalin as a favourite. As Stalin kept sidelining and arresting officers like Snesarev and Nossovitch, he kept building up Voroshilov, assigning more and more resources to him and allowing him to plan military operations. By the end of August 1918, Stalin felt confident enough in Voroshilov's loyalty that when he heard of the famous assassination attempt on Lenin,* he had the official condolence telegram signed by both Voroshilov and himself.[41]

Thankfully for Stalin, he was eventually to leave Tsaritsyn before Voroshilov's and his own military incompetence and lust for power led to total defeat.[42] While he might have surrounded himself with people he trusted, he still had a long way to go to understand how to win wars.

---

* This was easily the most serious of many assassination attempts against Lenin. Fanny Kaplan, a Marxist from a dissident group opposed to Bolshevik policies, fired two bullets in Lenin at close range on 30 August. Though he recovered, this attempt was used to justify the Bolsheviks bringing in their first open policy of Red Terror.

3. Franklin Roosevelt: The Young Maritime Strategist

In 1887, a five-year-old Franklin Delano Roosevelt wrote his first letter.[1] It was to his mother, Sara, who was laid up in bed with a bad cold. To cheer her up, Roosevelt had sketched two pictures of what he loved more than anything else in the world: ships at sea. These were not warships, with large guns trained at some unseen enemy, as might have been drawn by a young Winston Churchill. They were boyish visions of graceful sailing ships. One sketch was of three vessels with different mast and sail configurations, showing that the young boy had already paid close attention to the mechanics of sailing. The other, done in finer detail, was of a yacht that would have had pride of place for a wealthy family like the Roosevelts. The yacht was a handsome, two-masted vessel, sporting a row of large portholes along the side and the newest, cutting-edge advance that any self-respecting millionaire would have coveted: a steam-powered engine. The picture also revealed a great deal about the little boy.

Throughout his life, Roosevelt spent as much time as he could on the water, thinking about the seas or reading about the oceans. Along with stamp-collecting, naval history was his greatest recreational passion. He accumulated a private library of thousands of volumes on maritime history, collected naval memorabilia, and even periodically started writing his own books on naval history (although, unlike his cousin Theodore, he would never be able to complete and publish one). He was a skilful sailor and fisherman who delighted in piloting both sailing vessels and steamships. He could judge winds and tides, and surprised even professional naval officers with his ability to handle larger vessels.

Luckily for him, Franklin Roosevelt had been born into a Gilded Age family which gave him the ability to indulge his expensive tastes. He appeared in 1882, the one and only child of Sara Ann Delano

Roosevelt and James Roosevelt. Sara was attractive, feisty and twenty-seven years old when her son was born, while James was reserved, hypochondriacal and fifty-three—and yet for all their differences, both of Franklin's parents were bound by a profound conventionality. Perhaps that was because society had favoured them both. Each came from an established, wealthy, north-eastern family; the Delanos had been Massachusetts-based opium traders and the Roosevelts one of the oldest Dutch families in New York, who at one point farmed what is now Midtown Manhattan. Franklin's parents lived and acted as members of America's aristocracy, and raised him to sit atop American society.

The small family shuttled between three residences. There was the obligatory Manhattan townhouse, and a "cottage" (really, a rambling mansion) on Campobello Island in Nova Scotia that was used during the summer months when more southerly climates were considered unhealthy. Their most important home was a country estate named Springwood, on a hillside that rose up along the east bank of the Hudson River in Hyde Park, New York—the place in which young Franklin was born and which he would always consider his true home.

The Roosevelts' life of privilege included regular trips across the Atlantic. James, in a never-ending quest to treat his various ailments, became a devotee of different spas scattered around western Europe. A favourite pastime of those with a great deal of money and free time, these mineral baths promised better health to those who would drink their fizzy, smelly waters, take strolls in well-maintained pleasure gardens and eat prescribed foods—all overseen by teams of serious doctors. By the time Franklin was fourteen, he had followed his father to such spas eight times. These trips provided Franklin with some of his earliest ideas on Europe and Europeans.

James particularly favoured a spa in Bad Nauheim, Germany. There Franklin learned to speak German tolerably well and was exposed to German culture, but the Roosevelts remained firmly disapproving of the locals. James taught Franklin to look on the Germans as "swine"—an emotion the young man was never able to shake.[2] German society felt alien to him, and German manners not to his tastes. The British and French guests at the spa were much more to his liking.

The journeys themselves also shaped Franklin's view of the world. Crossing the Atlantic in the 1880s was not for the faint-hearted. The era of grand ocean liners had yet to start, and though the Roosevelts travelled in style, they went on relatively small vessels which bobbed up and down in the relentless North Atlantic seas. Franklin handled himself like a seasoned sailor in even the roughest waters. He was rarely seasick (a fact about which he would boast for the rest of his life), and studied intently as the different ships manoeuvred in the unpredictable waters. When given the chance himself, Roosevelt became an avid sailor. In his early teens James gifted him a twenty-one-foot skiff, which Franklin piloted skilfully around the remote coves of Campobello.

Franklin's parents were more than happy to indulge their only child. After he was born, Sara chose abstinence as the most effective form of birth control and devoted herself to raising her son. She smothered Franklin, both infantilizing him and inflating the boy's ego. She dressed him in the stylized outfits of the time, first as a young girl with flowing, curly hair and then as a Scottish Highlander with a kilt and sporran, always making him the centre of attention. Sara had Franklin educated at home by tutors until the demands of society forced her to release him to the world. It was not until he was fourteen years old that she accepted that he needed to leave home to complete his education. He was sent to boarding school at Groton, a relatively new establishment a little over thirty miles to the north-west of Boston. She was devastated. He was delighted.

Sending Franklin to Groton said a great deal about what the Roosevelts wanted their son to become. Founded by the Reverend Endicott Peabody, an Episcopalian athlete and do-gooder, Groton was designed to produce physically strong, morally sound boys who would help guide America to its global destiny. Set in a bucolic but austere part of Massachusetts, Groton was as much a philosophical idea as a school. Every boy played every sport; there was daily bathing in cold water, strict honour codes and little privacy. Teamwork, God and rule-following were all stressed, and those who were different were ostracized; a Groton man had certain standards to live up to. When Roosevelt was sailing across the Atlantic during World War I and heard tales of the supposedly underhand tactics employed by German submarines, he exclaimed in his diary, "At Groton we were taught that the worst thing to do was to play 'dirty ball.'"[3]

Roosevelt fit snugly into this conformist environment. He was a diligent student and sportsman, doing his best to succeed in all activities, usually ending up near the middle of the pack. He was a consistent B student (back in the day before grade inflation, when a B was a respectable mark), a determined but not particularly skilled baseball and football player and a moderately successful debater. Eventually, most of the other boys liked him.

At Groton, Roosevelt began his intellectual love affair with the ideas of the great naval and geopolitical theorist Admiral Alfred Thayer Mahan. A US Navy officer who was better at writing than sailing, Mahan had burst onto the world scene in 1890 with the publication of *The Influence of Sea Power Upon History, 1660–1783*.[4] In this, and other books and articles which he proceeded to produce prodigiously, Mahan argued that naval power was the foundation of global power, using illustrations collected from classical history up until the present era. Mahan was convinced that the Royal Navy's dominance was the reason for the present greatness of Britain and the British Empire. He urged his fellow Americans to build up their navy if they too wished to play a great role on the world stage and protect their blossoming industrial economy.

Roosevelt first mentioned Mahan during a Groton debate on whether the United States should annex the Hawaiian Islands. Taking the non-imperialist line, the sixteen-year-old argued that seizing Hawaii was morally and strategically counterproductive, referring to Mahan to bolster his points. Mahan had commented that holding Hawaii would require a massive investment by the United States in building a large naval base—and, Roosevelt argued, no right-thinking person would want to spend so much so far from American soil.[5]

This argument makes Roosevelt stand out from the other men who would lead their countries in World War II. The adolescent (and in some cases adult) Churchill, Hitler and Mussolini saw war as a romantic, exciting event, with waving flags and dashing uniforms. The battlefield was to them an important test of manhood, a theatre of bravery and commitment, a way to separate the worthy from the weak. When the young Roosevelt looked at the world and war (and the older Roosevelt for that matter), he was less emotional and rarely romantic. The outcome of war was to be decided by money, equipment and strategy, and the control of the seas.

A few months after the debate, when Roosevelt was faced with the reality of war, this more detached side again emerged. In 1898, relations between the United States and Spain had reached a crisis point. The issue that divided the two was Spanish rule in Cuba, which was becoming increasingly brutal and incompetent, and had caused a backlash amongst nationalistic Americans who believed that the United States was the overseer of the Americas—and had a duty to step in and save the Cubans. Where Winston Churchill would view the Spanish–American War as an exciting chance to see combat for the first time, Franklin Roosevelt took the position that bloodshed was unnecessary. With war clouds gathering, he wrote to his parents, "I feel that every moment of delay is in the interests of peace, and that the President is doing all he can to prevent war."[6] A few weeks later, when war seemed "inevitable," Roosevelt analysed the expected outcome functionally: "We are awaiting Spain's reply to our ultimatum. She will of course refuse to leave Cuba and on Saturday our army is to cross over and invade Cuba. I think by the time this reaches you, that Cuba will have been rid of Spaniards and Spain will be soon ready to give in."[7]

When war did break out, Roosevelt, not personalizing his emotions, claimed that "everyone" was "wildly excited." There have been tales told (unsubstantiated) that he and his classmates were planning on running away from school and enlisting. If so, any such notion was fleeting. He came down with scarlet fever just after war was declared, and spent the next few months in bed. He rarely mentioned the Spanish–American War again.

One of the reasons for Roosevelt's reluctance to discuss the conflict was undoubtedly because it resulted in the establishment of a large American empire. Using the strength of the growing American navy, the United States not only forced the Spanish out of Cuba; they seized much of Spain's overseas territories, most famously Puerto Rico and the Philippines. In the latter they launched a brutal war of pacification to hold on to the islands when faced with a Filipino independence movement.★ Roosevelt was never at ease emotionally or rationally with America having an empire. It struck him as unnatural for the United States to control territories that would never become states. While he was a "paternalist" and believed that the US—as an enlightened, advanced, white, Christian power—should help mentor non-white peoples, he was never an imperialist.

He was also distinctly not a supporter of the British Empire. Not long after the Spanish–American War ended, the Boer War broke out—and Roosevelt came out with a strong declaration in favour of the Boers. On November 10, 1899, while Churchill was sailing down to South Africa, Roosevelt wrote to his parents, "Hurrah for the Boers! I entirely sympathise with them."[8] Sara was obviously shocked at her son's anti–British Empire views, and scolded him in reply. A contrite Franklin tried to communicate his ideas in his next letter—adding a less than convincing explanation to mollify his mother: "I cannot help feeling convinced that the Boers have the side of right and that for the past ten years they have been *forced* into this war. I am sure you will feel this if you only read up the Boer case. *However*, undoubtedly, now that the war is actually on, it will be best from the humanitarian standpoint for the British to win speedily and civilization will be hurried on, but I feel that the same result would have been surely obtained without war."[9]

In calming his mother's wrath, Roosevelt revealed one of the skills that would stand him in great stead as he grew as both a political and a strategic leader—his charm. From an early age he showed the ability to ingratiate himself with almost anyone, to make that person feel that they had a close connection—was respected, even loved. Where

---

★ In another Groton debate Roosevelt argued strongly for Filipino independence from US rule. While we cannot be sure whether he took these positions because they were assigned or because he believed in them, it is interesting to note that he only recorded debates in which he took a non-imperialist stance.

Hitler and Churchill often used lectures to make their case, relying on the power of their rhetoric to overwhelm their targets, Roosevelt used a smile, a laugh and pleasant conversation. He would establish an air of faux intimacy to make the other person think that he agreed with them, that they were working together for a common cause. But Roosevelt's charm was not just a tool; it was a mask. He used it to keep people from understanding what he was really thinking. He was by nature a sceptic about human nature and generally saw individuals in utilitarian terms. He was also ruthless and ambitious, determined to use others in his climb to the top.

For the young Roosevelt had a secret: he hankered after political glory. Most Gilded Age gentlemen eschewed the dirty world of politics, preferring to focus on business, philanthropy or the pursuit of pleasure. The Roosevelts were different. Part of Sara imbuing her son with ideas of greatness was because she believed he could be a political leader (she kept practically everything Franklin ever gave her, convinced of his eventual historical importance). James was also politically active, though he himself would never run for office. He was a financial supporter of the campaign of President Grover Cleveland, who even visited the family at Hyde Park. This highlighted something else unusual about this branch of the Roosevelt family: they were Democrats through and through, and Franklin would make the Democratic Party a part of his identity.

In 1900, Roosevelt left boarding school for university. At one point he had thought about attending the US Naval Academy at Annapolis, but his parents were never going to let that happen.[10] Instead, he moved thirty miles down the trainline from Groton to Harvard. There, Roosevelt continued his pattern of middle-of-the-road production in sports and academics, while also honing his political skills. Most usefully, he became the editor of the student newspaper, the *Harvard Crimson*, which he used to make himself one of the truly "big" men on campus. Deploying his charm—an acquaintance at Harvard referred to it as Roosevelt's "frictionless command"— he guided the *Crimson*, gaining an appreciation for a snappy phrase and a powerful headline.[11] He also took part in his first political rally, though it was for a Republican (the one and only time he would campaign for a non-Democrat). In this case he could be forgiven, for the Republican was his cousin, the Republican vice-presidential nominee, Theodore Roosevelt.

After Harvard, Franklin was determined to carve out a political career as a Democrat, though for a few years he played at being a New York lawyer. He attended Columbia Law School and opened a practice with a Harvard classmate, but was never invested. In 1910 he ran for and was elected to the New York State Senate from a district taking in Hyde Park and the surrounding counties. He had positioned himself as an anti-machine Democrat, running against the power of Tammany Hall, New York City's famed Democratic organization. His victory was a stepping stone to greater things. He quickly used his entrée into Democratic Party politics and his charm to secure one of the decisive moves of his career.

It happened because of a chance meeting at the 1912 Democratic National Convention in Baltimore. The Democrats had chosen the left-wing populist William Jennings Bryan as their presidential candidate for three of the last four elections—and had lost every one. A fundamentalist evangelical, and almost socialist/pacifist, Bryan fired up the Democratic base like no politician had befoɪe. But his more radical ideas and Billy Sunday personality terrified much of Middle America.

By 1912, many Democrats, such as Roosevelt, had had enough of losing and were pushing the more centrist governor of New Jersey, Woodrow Wilson. Roosevelt, a delegate from New York, went to Baltimore early to help organize Wilson's forces, and there he met Josephus Daniels. Daniels, formerly a committed Bryanite and a life-long white supremacist, had likewise switched to backing Wilson in 1912. Daniels had used his position as a major newspaper editor to become a power in the Democratic Party in the South, and it was a real coup for Wilson when Daniels switched sides. It was widely assumed that, in return for backing Wilson, Daniels would be offered a cabinet position if the Democrats won. Roosevelt, on meeting a powerful man who could further his career, smiled his best Cheshire cat smile and dropped his charm bomb.

The results were more dramatic than he could have imagined.

Daniels was smitten—and would be for the rest of his life. The chapter in his memoirs where he describes meeting Roosevelt is entitled "Love at First Sight—F.D.R. and J.D.," and Daniels wrote dreamily about being "strongly drawn" to the younger man.[12] He was so bowled over that when Wilson won and Daniels was offered a cabinet job, he demanded that Roosevelt be named his assistant. Rather surprisingly for a man who had shown little interest in international affairs, none in strategic policy, and probably had never been on a warship, Daniels elected to be secretary of the navy.* Though Wilson was less impressed by the young Roosevelt, Daniels would not be denied, and in April 1913 Roosevelt was named the new assistant secretary of the navy (ASN). It was a great coup for Roosevelt, making him one of the few civilians with real influence over America's war-fighting in the World War I era.

Daniels had been duped; the "Love at First Sight" was unrequited. When Roosevelt first cast eyes on Daniels, with his pleated shirts, string tie and homespun Southern manners, he considered him the "funniest looking hill-billy" he had ever seen.[13] While Roosevelt could be fond of Daniels, often in a patronizing way, he was sceptical of the North Carolinian's grasp of naval policy and his outlook on the world. Roosevelt had no intention of being a loyal deputy, and from the moment he took office he worked around, or even flat out undermined, the secretary of the navy.

Not naturally aggressive, Daniels hated thinking about the possibility of war and instead wanted to focus on social reform in the fleet. He talked about turning the navy into a great university for the enlisted men, to better them intellectually and morally. In the end, his most famous reform, which still bedevils American sailors to this day, was to ban the consumption of alcoholic beverages on US warships. Roosevelt, who was quite fond of a cocktail or two, had little interest in such policies. He wanted to take control of naval policy for himself, and it was almost always in one direction: to make the US Navy more powerful and more prepared to fight.

---

* He was offered the choice of a number of cabinet posts, but certain senior ones such as secretary of state and of the treasury were already allocated to others.

The Roosevelt who first strode into the Department of the Navy was just thirty-one years old, almost six feet tall, thin but broad-shouldered and strong. He could move with energy and purpose, radiating good health (when not off with illness).★ His exuberance as assistant secretary of the navy made a huge impression on those who met him. William Leahy—who first encountered Roosevelt in the department in 1913, became his friend and would serve as his chief of staff during World War II—was in his own reserved way as wowed as Daniels. Decades later he described the Roosevelt he first met as a "handsome, companionable, athletic, young man of unusual energy and decision."[14]

A man on the rise, Roosevelt invariably had a smile on his face—from the moment he sat down at the breakfast table with his large and growing family, until he had his final cigarette of the night. In 1905, he had married a niece of Theodore Roosevelt named Eleanor, and by the time they moved to Washington, DC they had four children and would soon produce two more. Franklin was eager to blend into the Washington social scene, and soon became a fixture at the private members' clubs, dinner parties and golf courses that dominated life for the elite of the nation's capital. The shy and introspective Eleanor found this a chore, and unlike her vivacious husband often found excuses to leave parties early. For months at a time, sometimes all summer and well into the autumn, she would retreat to the healthy climes of Campobello with the children. Franklin would act sad when she was away, but he almost always found excuses to stay in Washington longer than he had first promised.

In Roosevelt's first month in office, the United States became embroiled with Mexico in a dangerous military confrontation. In April 1913, Mexican authorities detained some American sailors who were ashore picking up supplies in Veracruz, and though they were quickly released, the US commander on the spot, Henry Mayo, decided to humiliate the Mexicans by demanding a twenty-one-gun

---

★ For all his strength and activity, Roosevelt did have a remarkable susceptibility to illnesses. He caught serious bugs on a regular basis, and at one time suffered from appendicitis. He was regularly out of work for weeks and sometimes months.

salute be fired in respect of American forces. The Mexicans were irate, and popular protests spread against American heavy-handedness. Things quickly spiralled out of control, and Wilson authorized the dispatch of American forces to seize Veracruz.

By late April, US sailors were ashore and exchanging fire with Mexican soldiers and civilians. Daniels was aghast and wanted to take steps to dial down the confrontation, while Roosevelt was keener on preparing the navy to fight.[15] He blurted out to the press that the United States was at "war and we're ready," admitting in public for the first time that his ultimate goal was to create an American fleet "second to none."[16] During his time as ASN, Roosevelt was the most openly warlike that he would ever be in his life.

Roosevelt was more than happy to try to subvert his own administration to get his way on naval policy. One of the first letters he wrote in the job was to his cousin Theodore, asking the former president to use his popularity to argue against dividing the American fleet between the east and west coasts. "We shall be in an unpardonable position if we permit ourselves to be caught with our fleet separated," he wrote.[17] He was worried about two things. One, that a divided fleet would be a tempting a target for a surprise Japanese attack. Relations between America and Japan—two growing, expansionist powers—had become increasingly hostile. The two had started amassing empires in the Pacific, and as the European powers turned to face each other, they became the dominant forces in the region. The Japanese were also incensed at the racist treatment meted out to their emigrants to the United States, who were being singled out for discrimination. While Roosevelt did not think war was imminent, he was worried that if the Japanese did decide to fight, they would attack without warning. And just in case they did, he argued that the fleet be concentrated and ready for war at all times.

The second worry that lurked in Roosevelt's mind, and drove him to enlist Theodore to make his case, was that the American people were not invested enough in strategic policy. While he was desperate for a stronger navy, he understood that it was a relatively low priority for the American people, who regardless of how often they were warned, flattered or cajoled still thought mostly about domestic issues. Roosevelt would later complain of the American people having an "inability to visualize our position in the world."[18]

Plotting with his cousin, the former president, was an act of disloyalty on Franklin's part against the sitting president, whom he served. Theodore Roosevelt and Woodrow Wilson were the two political titans of their time, and they loathed each other. Theodore had run for the presidency against Wilson in 1912 (and it was rumoured that he would run again in 1916), and during the campaign it became clear that they looked at the world very differently. Theodore believed in strong military forces and competitive nation states, and saw war as a great test of virility. Wilson claimed to hate war (though did not mind bossing around weaker Latin American countries), spoke religiously of the value of international cooperation and saw himself as a morally superior being. Wilson considered Theodore a warlike cowboy, and Theodore saw Wilson as a fussy moralist. Theodore said later that, instead of "speaking softly and carrying a big stick," Wilson "spoke bombastically and carried a dish rag."[19] Yet Franklin showed no hesitation in using his cousin to put pressure on Wilson.

Roosevelt's focus on keeping the fleet concentrated was another sign of how he had been influenced by Alfred Thayer Mahan, who held that a concentrated fleet was stronger than one divided.* Indeed, during his time as ASN, Roosevelt regularly espoused both the tactical and the strategic ideas that Mahan had popularized. Mahan's tactical thinking was a creation of the moment and place he inhabited. He was writing during the era of the enormous steel-belted battleships, which reached a peak of design and destructiveness in the dreadnought revolution. By 1914, some dreadnoughts were sporting massive fifteen-inch naval guns that fired shells as heavy as automobiles for a distance of more than five miles. They were heavily

---

* One of Mahan's cardinal rules was that fleets should always be concentrated to keep them from being destroyed piecemeal. He believed that a great modern war at sea would be decided in one or a small number of pitched battles, during which large battlefleets would engage—leaving control of the sea in the hands of the fleet that emerged triumphant.

armoured with massive steel belts along their sides, some more than a foot thick.★ Mahan's assumption was that these floating fortresses would engage in a decisive sea battle, the victor in which would become arbiter of the world's waterways. Preparing for this battle was why Roosevelt was so committed to keeping the American fleet concentrated. He understood that, because of the large distance between the east and west coasts of the US, there were powerful domestic pressures to split the fleet—which would leave the country with two small, non-mutually-supporting forces vulnerable to easy destruction.

Eventually Roosevelt's worry about concentration became so intense that he felt the need to enlist Mahan himself. The opening of the new Panama Canal, Roosevelt reasoned, would only add to political pressures to split the fleet between east and west, and in June 1914, just before the war clouds started gathering in Europe, he wrote to Mahan asking him to agitate on the navy's behalf.

> When the canal is finally opened next Winter there will undoubtedly be a great deal of pressure brought to bear—political and sectional— to have the Fleet divided, and to have one half kept on the Pacific and one half on the Atlantic. I am just back from a trip to the Pacific Coast and was struck by the total lack of any correct conception of fleet operations. The people can be educated, but only if we all get together ahead of time and try to show the average "man on the Street" the military necessity of keeping <u>The Fleet</u> intact. Your voice will carry more conviction than that of anybody else.[20]

This opening started up a flurry of correspondence between Mahan and Roosevelt. The admiral was intrigued and wanted to

---

★ There were two types of dreadnought capital ship, the battleship and the battle-cruiser. Both were heavily armed with the largest guns possible, but battleships were built with far more armoured protection than battlecruisers (which sacrificed armour for greater speed). As World War I would show, the battlecruiser was far more vulnerable than the battleship, yet going into the war the different nations compared their naval strength by counting both classes.

know more about the younger man. Soon Roosevelt started angling for a meeting, telling Mahan that he could only divulge more information face to face (probably to let him know about Daniels's prevarications). When war erupted in August, Mahan sent Roosevelt a series of letters pressing him to get the fleet ready to fight the Japanese. Showing how much their thinking had synchronized, Mahan argued that Japan was a greater threat than any European country and might take advantage of the war to attack the United States.[21] The admiral could not have been more committed.* On his final trip to Washington, not long before he died on December 1, 1914, Mahan made an uninvited trip to the Navy Department in the hope of speaking with Roosevelt—to find, much to his regret, that the ASN was out of the office.

If Mahan's tactical ideas on fleet concentration helped the two men bond, his larger strategic ideas on the importance of naval power made an even longer-lasting impression. These boiled down to the control of global communications—and by this Mahan, and Roosevelt, meant the movement of all goods and supplies (both civilian and military) over the surface of the ocean. Naval power, or so Mahan argued and Roosevelt agreed, bestowed the ability to control communications, and this led to much greater strength in peace and war, a stronger economy, more influence abroad and, if needs be, the ability to attack an enemy passively or actively. The specific Mahanian phrase that Roosevelt returned to again and again in these years was "control of the sea." What Roosevelt meant by this was "the ability to keep the oceans open for one's warships and merchant ships and for any military expeditions desired."[22] He believed that controlling the seas would lead to victories, no matter what happened in any specific battle on land.

Roosevelt had started making these arguments years before he wrote to Mahan, and continued making them for years after, usually in short-form pieces. He was an undisciplined writer who would periodically keep a diary, for a few days devotedly making entries

---

* He eventually produced a 5,000-word article which was published in the *North American Review*.

before the commitment bored him and the effort petered out. Where Churchill, Hitler, Mussolini and Stalin all wrote or dictated books about themselves and their ideas, Roosevelt was never able to muster the enthusiasm or commitment to write a large piece.* He could write short pieces, however—newspaper or journal articles that he produced in a clear if unexciting prose.

In these short pieces, naval power and history were regular themes, and Roosevelt liked to present communications control, not land battles, as the determining factor in wars. One of his favourite historic examples of this was the fate of General Louis-Joseph de Montcalm, who had led French forces during the Seven Years War (1756–63). Roosevelt considered Montcalm a military genius who for the first years of the war had outfought British forces, most famously in the battles of Fort Oswego and Ticonderoga, when his small force of fewer than 4,000 held off a British army almost four times as large. Yet for all his victories, Montcalm ended up cut off from the French state, and eventually died in 1759 leading his troops on the Plains of Abraham outside of the city of Quebec. The fundamentals of warfighting mattered much more than the results of battles.[23]

Another historical subject that fascinated Roosevelt was the American Revolution. He was convinced that naval power had played a decisive, if mostly hidden, role in the American victory.[24] Knowing that it would be "impossible to fight" the might of the Royal Navy, the motley assortment of American vessels—usually small, some nimble and captained by a mixture of pirates and fishermen—concentrated on attacking British trade and launching hit-and-run raids on the British coast. They stole British commerce and sank British merchant ships, and in doing so drove up insurance premiums in London and brought the war home to the British people.

Roosevelt took this lesson and applied it in reverse to the America of his time. In an article he wrote about the importance of naval power for the United States he felt the need to warn the American

---

* Roosevelt occasionally toyed with writing a book. When he was young he had started accumulating material for a biographical study of naval officers of the American Revolution. A few pages of these notes still survive in his papers.

people about the devastating impact of communications attacks. If the US lost the ability to ship goods and military force on the oceans, Roosevelt argued, it would implode the American economy.[25]

This warning was written near the outbreak of World War I. In early August 1914, the news came to Washington that the great powers of Europe had decided that diplomacy was finished and shooting should begin. With war looming, Roosevelt rushed to the Navy Department, excited and full of energy, expecting to find the building buzzing. What he found was a sleepy government office going about its business as if nothing out of the normal was happening. Roosevelt let rip in a letter to Eleanor, who was on Campobello Island with the children (whom he called his "chicks"), writing that "to my astonishment on reaching the Dept. nobody seemed the least bit excited about the European crisis." He blamed the secretary of the navy: "Mr. Daniels feeling chiefly very sad that his faith in human nature and civilization and similar idealistic nonsense was receiving such a rude shock."[26] Disgusted at this hemming and hawing, Roosevelt decided that it was up to him to get the navy ready for war. "I started in alone to get things ready and prepare plans for what *ought* to be done by the Navy end of things." Even days later, Daniels still seemed paralysed by indecision and Roosevelt remarked that his boss was "bewildered by it all, very sweet but very sad."[27]

Roosevelt's doubts about Daniels blended with his misgivings towards Wilson. The president, in his first major address after the outbreak of war, asked Americans to be neutral in "thought and deed." Roosevelt, anything but neutral, saw the war as a fight between good and bad—between the western Allies, with whom he felt an instant attachment, and the haughty, militarist Germans who needed to be taught a lesson. He wanted a clear result, confiding to his wife that rather than a "long drawn-out struggle I hope England will join in with France and Russia and force peace *at Berlin!*" Later he joked with Eleanor, "I just *know* I shall do some awful unneutral thing before I get through."[28]

He was true to his word. For the next year and a half, the young assistant secretary acted as a subversive agent within the administration, clandestinely (or sometimes openly) pushing the US Navy and

the nation down the line of preparedness. The Preparedness Movement, as it came to be known, was a pro-Allied grouping of American
politicians, opinion-makers and industrialists who believed the United
States needed to ramp up its preparations to fight in Europe. It overwhelmingly consisted of Republicans and its most famous advocate
was Theodore Roosevelt, but many others began banging the drum for
more military spending and greater assertiveness by the United States.

Wilson saw the Preparedness Movement as an enemy, as did most
of his cabinet. Roosevelt, on the other hand, while never publicly
endorsing the movement, immediately started using similar rhetoric
and taking similar positions. He was worried that the Republicans
would monopolize the defence issue and wanted the Democrats to
show that they were willing to do what it took to make America
strong. By 1915 he was drafting articles arguing for a stronger, better-
prepared fleet that could assure communications control for America.
One of his most bellicose was a plea for a powerful fleet dominated
by battleships, a reflection of Alfred Thayer Mahan's influence upon
Roosevelt's understanding of war.

Yet the war at sea had developed in a surprising way by 1915, one
that Roosevelt—and Mahan—had not foreseen. Refusing to fight a
Mahanian decisive battle with the British, the Germans held back their
battleships and instead launched a war against British trade using a relatively new weapon: the submarine. It was a strategy that revealed itself
to be potentially effective. The German submarines sent to the ocean
floor numerous British merchant ships hauling food and supplies, causing real concern in London. At the same time, German submarine
warfare brought the first signs of possible war with the United States.

Before the war, the sinking of unarmed merchant ships by submarines had been considered illegal, but the Germans argued that the
British were stopping all trade into Europe (which was also considered
illegal) and at the same time arming merchant ships secretly, which
made it impossible for them to tell which ships were unarmed. The
Germans turned to "unrestricted" submarine warfare around Britain in
early 1915, declaring that they might attack any ship without warning
in an area approximately 100 miles around the British Isles. The problem they quickly found was that Americans were often on these ships.

Woodrow Wilson decided that he would use the threat of US force to keep the Germans in line. As 1915 went on and more Americans were lost at sea—most famously on the British passenger ship *Lusitania*, which was sunk off the coast of Ireland in May—Wilson demanded the Germans back down, and they did. But in making unrestricted submarine warfare an issue of such confrontation, Wilson had set a tripwire that would soon trigger an escalation.

As the submarine war around Britain ramped up, some American voices started arguing for fewer American battleships and more submarines. Roosevelt was horrified at this attack on Mahanian orthodoxy. He wanted more battleships, not fewer, and he tried to set his fellow citizens straight. As always starting from the premise that control of movement on the oceans was crucial, Roosevelt claimed that this would go to the fleet "which can go up and down the length of and breadth of the sea at will."[29] Submarines had some purpose, but they were still far too slow, vulnerable and limited to fulfil this role, and it would be many years before this change occurred—if it even did. In the meantime, the battleship remained dominant, and Roosevelt assured the American people these vessels had "most decidedly not been given up by the men who are experts on naval warfare."[30]

Roosevelt would play a crucial role in making sure that the United States had as many battleships as possible. In the summer of 1915, he told Daniels that, instead of planning naval building on a year-by-year basis, which left the US Navy unable to plan rationally for the future, and having to adjust to the whims of Congress, he wanted the navy to ask for an unprecedented, multi-year building programme.[31] The result was the grandest naval building programme in American history to that time: the Naval Act of 1916. The origins of the Act are some-what obscure, as it seemed to emerge practically out of nowhere in President Wilson's address to Congress in December 1915 (four months after Roosevelt had started pushing for a large, multi-year pro-gramme).[32] Certainly Wilson was desperate to burnish his preparedness credentials in a presidential election year, but it ran strikingly counter to most of his rhetoric since August 1914. Daniels, likewise, was hardly an enthusiastic supporter of a massive new programme. Franklin Roosevelt, however, was, and once Wilson spoke, he did a great deal of the public lobbying for the programme. He promptly wrote an article which once again repeated his alarmist proposition that without a larger fleet the United States was threatened with economic collapse. "If we were attacked tomorrow by a nation with a stronger navy than ours not one bale of cotton, not one pound of tobacco . . . could leave our shores. We could survive a year or so of that, but not much longer, and the enemy could keep up an indefinite blockade at comparatively little cost even if it did not seek eventually to land."[33]

Behind this defensive smokescreen lurked Roosevelt's hope that the United States might end up with the most powerful navy in the world, though he was careful not to say that openly. When he testified to the House Naval Affairs Committee in March 1916, Roosevelt discussed how the United States should build the second most powerful fleet in the world, saying that America should aim to replace Germany in this slot by building eleven of the largest warships afloat. "We have been slipping behind Germany for ten years . . . to put our fleet on an equal basis with the German fleet we should need eight battle cruisers and three dreadnoughts."[34]

Roosevelt was playing fast and loose with the truth with such a claim, as he well knew. If the US Navy built eleven new capital ships (battleships and battlecruisers), it would not just numerically match the Germans (and probably surpass them), it would qualitatively blow the Germans, and even the British, out of the water. With World War I raging, the European powers had stopped construction on capital ships. They were considered too expensive and time-consuming to produce at a time when immediate help was most important. This European neglect meant that if the United States did undertake a massive new programme of capital ships, they would be building unchallenged. Moreover, they would be building ships that could be designed in the light of wartime experiences—with better protection, more powerful guns and faster speeds.

Amazingly, Congress went along with these plans. In August 1916, both Houses passed the bill, which authorized the construction in the coming years of the sixteen largest capital ships in the world: ten super-dreadnoughts and six battlecruisers. If completed, it would give the United States a "Navy second to none," with firepower that could crush any other fleet at sea. Roosevelt was ecstatic at the prospect of an American fleet mightier than the British. He drafted a list of eventual American battleships and compared it to the Royal Navy's. The US Navy clearly came out on top in the most modern, powerful vessels, and Roosevelt wrote expectantly, "I hope for as good as this."[35]

He certainly struck as aggressive a public tone as any member of the Wilson administration. 1916 was a presidential election year, and one that looked to be balanced on a knife's edge. The Democrats had renominated Wilson as their candidate, while the Republicans had chosen the somewhat dull if respectable governor of New York, Charles Evans Hughes. With such a close race looming, Roosevelt hit the campaign trail, mostly in New York. His speeches were patriotic calls for more military spending and national service—the creation of a military force that could go to war. As he told a crowd in Malden-on-Hudson in October, the United States Navy was "only about one-half or one-third as large as it should be . . . Every citizen must take his part. That means we must have universal military service."[36] His rhetoric was more bellicose than most Democrats', including the president and Daniels, whose campaigning stressed the theme of the administration keeping Americans out of the great war in Europe.

As Wilson made his bid for a second term, Roosevelt's friendship with William Leahy, the man who would become his chief of staff and chairman of the Joint Chiefs of Staff during World War II, moved from the professional to the personal. Leahy had taken over as the captain of the secretary of the navy's dispatch boat, USS *Dolphin*. But as Daniels was more of a landlubber, the *Dolphin* was often available for Roosevelt to use—and he took advantage of the perk with gusto. In 1916 he used the ship to shepherd his large family to and from Campobello, and came to trust Leahy, even inviting the officer to spend some days with him at Hyde Park. As the presidential campaign was ending, Roosevelt went out of his way to write Leahy a note telling him that he would need to cruise with him again soon. "I have been leading a hectic life since I saw you, jumping to Washington for a day and then off again to the campaign, but our trip on the *Dolphin* has been a great help and by January 1 I shall certainly need to go off again with you all."[37]

As Roosevelt trusted very few people, this relationship mattered. Because he learned to like and work with Leahy before he became a major figure, it made their relationship different than any other Roosevelt would have with a military/strategic policymaker during the war. Moreover, the two shared a Mahanian view of the world when it came to the importance of sea communications, and would become a self-reinforcing team at the top of US strategy-making from 1942 to 1945. His relationship with Leahy also provided Roosevelt with an extra layer of assurance that was not open to most of the other World War II grand strategists.

In February 1917, the Germans, in an attempt to sever the North Atlantic trade routes with their U-boats, restarted unrestricted submarine warfare. President Wilson, newly re-elected, had reached his limit with German aggression, and decided that American force needed to be thrown into the war to make sure the result was in the American (and, in his mind, global) interest. Roosevelt was delighted. In March, he arrived back in Washington expecting to find the administration running at peak efficiency, preparing to fight the greatest war in human history. He railed against Daniels's "procrastination" and complained about his boss to Wilson's famous confidant Edward House.[38] He could not believe that Daniels was acting so nonchalantly, and was livid that the US Navy was not studying British methods in preparation for entering the war. He also blamed the sitting Chief of Naval Operations, Admiral William Benson, a Georgia Roman Catholic, who was probably the most anti-British man in the American Navy.

But Roosevelt would not have to wait much longer. In April, Congress acceded to the president's request to declare war. The US Navy would finally get the fight Roosevelt wanted.

4. Benito Mussolini: The Birth of a Nationalist Strategist

Private Benito Amilcare Andrea Mussolini of the 11th Bersaglieri Regiment was giddy. It was September 16, 1915, and he was about to cross the Isonzo River as a soldier in an invading Italian Army. The Isonzo, which ran through the Austro-Hungarian Empire's province of Küstenland, began high amongst vertical rises in the Dalmatian Mountains before descending into a rocky valley and broken countryside, and finally emptying into the Adriatic Sea. When earlier that year Italy had joined World War I on the side of the Allies against the Germans and Austrians, one of its first moves was to seize the Isonzo. The river ran almost halfway between the Austrian border and the coveted city of Trieste.★ The river's glacier-fed waters were an electric light blue, and a dazzled Mussolini thought them "wonderfully" unlike any other he had ever seen. He bent down and drank, exclaiming, "This is a sacred river."[1]

Or at least that is what he wanted people to think he believed.† Reaching the Isonzo as part of an invading Italian Army represented both the culmination of a remarkable career change for the thirty-two-year-old and an opportunity for personal glorification. He had only embraced the cause of violent, expansionist Italian nationalism eleven months before, and in doing so had turned himself into a minor celebrity, unlocking the reasons for much of his future success. Making Italy great, and himself even greater, would be his

---

★ Trieste had a majority population of Italian nationals, with a significant German minority, though the population around the city was a majority of other nationalities from the Austro-Hungarian Empire, including Slovenians.

† Much of Mussolini's diary, in which this story was recounted, was being serialized in the nationalist newspaper *Il Popolo d'Italia*, so anything that he wrote in it needs to be understood in that light.

foundational strategic mindset—even if he had as of yet no clear idea how to achieve it.

Mussolini's embrace of nationalism and violent expansion was surprising, considering that most of his early life had been spent in radical, left-wing circles, raging against militarism and capitalism. Until World War I, Mussolini seemed more determined to become an Italian Lenin than an Italian Hitler. He was born in a hamlet just outside the nondescript Emilia-Romagna hill town of Predappio.[2] A place on the fault line between old and new, Predappio was sandwiched between the Apennine Mountains, which rose steadily to the west and south, and the enormous, fertile Po valley, which stretched eastwards towards the Adriatic Sea and northward towards Italy's new, growing industrial heartland. An agricultural settlement in which life had changed little for centuries, Predappio was nevertheless close enough to modernized Italy that radical ideas circulated.* This mattered hugely in Mussolini's life, as his father Alessandro, a skilled, lazy blacksmith, became a significant figure in Romagna radical politics.

In his memoirs, Mussolini boasted that his family had been major characters in Renaissance Bologna. If true, the Mussolinis had been downwardly mobile ever since. Mussolini's father was good-looking, and he drank, chased women, brawled, and spent what little money he could get his hands on without hesitation. As a young man, he had taught himself left-wing politics by reading Marx and Bakunin, and soon started agitating amongst the poor. His precise ideology was fluid—at times he favoured anarchism, at others violent socialism—but he always wanted to overthrow the established order. He eventually came to the attention of the police and, after radical literature was found during a raid, was sentenced to six months in prison. He emerged as a figure of some repute in socialist circles.[3]

---

* Though Predappio has existed as a settlement for millennia in one of the most historically significant regions of Italy, it barely figures as a tourist destination. Its major draw today is as the birthplace of Mussolini, and it attracts both morbid tourists and modern fascists on pilgrimage so successfully that it has a working infrastructure to provide for their needs.

Once released from jail, Alessandro fell in love with Rosa Maltoni, a local schoolteacher. Like the Mussolinis, the Maltonis came from a petit bourgeois background and had fared almost as poorly over the years. They had dealt with their decline by clinging tightly to traditionalism and orthodoxy. They were devout Roman Catholics, and in the nineteenth century became patriotic Italian nationalists. Rosa's parents were repelled by the idea of marrying their daughter to a deranged radical and made Alessandro promise to give up politics before letting them wed. Alessandro made the pledge and the Maltonis were foolish enough to believe him.

Alessandro and Rosa, like all the parents of the World War II grand strategists, were a terrible match, though Mussolini in his memoirs painted them as fascist caricatures. Alessandro was described as a valiant fighter for the people and Rosa the prototypical dutiful, family-obsessed Italian mother. In fact, their relationship was tempestuous and they duelled over control of their young son. Alessandro dominated at first. In July 1883, when Mussolini was born, Alessandro broke with Italian tradition and named him after Benito Juárez—the radical, reforming Mexican politician.* He did his best to make the boy politically aware, bringing Benito to rallies and immersing him in a life of clandestine meetings and class resentment. Mussolini was in awe of his larger-than-life father.

Rosa, though, was planting deeper seeds. Her motivations were partly caused by resentment at the precarious lifestyle Alessandro's politics had forced on the family.[4] Because Alessandro spent all the money he could acquire, including Rosa's wages as a schoolteacher and her inheritance from her father, the Mussolini family existed on the edge of poverty. Rosa was forced to work long hours at her schoolhouse (where the family lived in two rooms) and do odd jobs to keep her family fed. Even so, the Mussolinis ate worse than peasants, usually getting by with pottage for lunch and stewed radishes or

---

* In much of Italy it was the custom to name the first son after one of the grandfathers. Alessandro not doing this was a statement that he was not bound by custom. Alessandro also made sure that his subsequent two children, Benito's siblings, were also named after radical figures.

chicory gathered from the local fields for dinner.[5] They were only able to afford meat on Sundays, when a pound of mutton had to be shared amongst the five of them. Unimpressed with the wages of radicalism, Rosa tried to turn Benito into a devout Roman Catholic and Italian patriot.

She failed utterly in the first task. When Rosa dragged the young boy to mass, Mussolini reacted in the normal way he did when angered—with violence. Instead of going into the church, he climbed a nearby tree and threw stones at the more devout children heading off to pray. Acknowledging a god meant accepting a force higher than himself, and this was something he was always loath to do. Later in life he would occasionally pretend to be a Catholic for political purposes, and when dictator he famously signed a concordat with the Catholic Church—but he did it all from the vantage of a sceptic.

Rosa worked hard to make her son a committed Italian nationalist, and she eventually succeeded to a greater degree than she ever understood. She regularly made him sing patriotic songs from the Risorgimento era (Italian Unification)—a powerful political statement in the newly formed Italy. As the Risorgimento had only been completed in 1871, the new state's unity was still far from universally accepted. There were strong regional identities throughout Italy, stretching from Sicilians in the far south to Lombards and Venetians in the north, to say nothing of those from Romagna in the middle, from where the Mussolinis and Maltonis hailed. All of them competed with Italian-ness for the people's loyalty. But Rosa was determined that her son believe in Italy first and foremost, above regionalism and above Alessandro's stress on class. And there were signs that even while the young Mussolini espoused radical socialism, Italian nationalism was lurking in the back of his mind. As a student he would periodically proclaim his devotion to the Italian Empire, and even mused at times about volunteering for the Italian Army.

If the boy was being torn by his parent's differing agendas, Mussolini also revealed that he had a personality very much his own. He was a nasty piece of work: disruptive, querulous, a terrible student and an even worse friend. Above all he was determined to dominate his fellow human beings. He was so difficult that Rosa, who believed that her son showed signs of greatness, eventually convinced Alessandro to educate him at a boarding school, in the nearby town of Faenza. Things did not go well. Mussolini was haughty and affected poses of disdain towards other students. Matters were made worse by the fact that the Salesian brothers divided the students into three tables for meals, based on the level of money their parents could pay. Mussolini thus had to sit with the poorest students, and away from most of his classmates.[6] Unsurprisingly, he made only one friend—a boy with a particularly hard head, over which Mussolini would amuse himself by breaking tiles.[7]

Like Stalin, Mussolini detested the close control and monotonous schedule of prayers that the priests imposed on their students, and in return he was detested by the Salesian fathers for his insolence. Mussolini quickly revealed a hair-trigger temper that saw him whip out the knife he always carried and attack people who angered him. In his second year at Faenza he got into a fight and stabbed another pupil. He was quickly expelled for refusing to "bend to Salesian discipline."[8] Rosa was not to be dissuaded, however. She enrolled Mussolini in another school, named after the famous Italian nationalist poet Giosuè Carducci and run by the poet's brother. History repeated itself. Mussolini soon drew his knife and plunged it into the buttocks of another student, whom he accused of spilling ink on one of his essay papers. He was swiftly expelled as a boarder, though at least allowed to continue taking classes as an external student.

As well as revealing his predilection for unexpected stabs in the back, Mussolini as a student exhibited other distinct personality traits that would typify his war leadership. He could be a quick learner but tried to get by without much study. He would eventually achieve good marks in history, Italian literature and singing, though he often needed to needed to resit examinations to progress. One reason for his uneven progress was his egocentrism; nothing anyone else said seemed to compare to the brilliance of his own thoughts. "I do not believe in the supposed influence of books," he would later write. "I do not believe in the influence which comes from perusing the books about the lives and characters of men . . . I have never, with closed eyes, accepted the thoughts of others." One of the few things

Mussolini really seemed to enjoy was music. Always wanting to be the centre of attention, he played a large, loud trumpet in the school orchestra.

Mussolini was not popular with his classmates, though personal relationships mattered little to him in comparison to personal glory. He would boast later that "during my life, I believe, neither my school friends, my war friends, nor my political friends ever had the slightest influence upon me . . . I am sure that whenever I took an extreme decision I have obeyed only the firm commandment of will and conscience that came from within."[9]

Mussolini's obsession with satisfying his own desires was revealed in its most grotesque form when he started pursuing the opposite sex—or, to put it more accurately, raping them. To Mussolini, women were objects to be conquered and discarded. He started frequenting brothels at a young age, and there were rumours that he contracted a venereal disease. When he could not purchase a woman, he was known to attack her. As a young man he forced himself on a neighbourhood girl he described as "discreet and generous." He grabbed her, threw her violently into a corner behind a door, and raped her. Afterwards, the traumatized young girl accused Mussolini of dishonouring her. Years later he joked about the assault, writing "what honour was she talking about?"[10] This rape was not an exception.

When Mussolini finished school, he chose a profession poorly suited to his talents—teaching. A sign that, for all his talk of being a man of the people, his petit bourgeois background meant that he also craved respectability, he applied for positions in local schools. He was offered a post as a substitute teacher in the Reggio Emilia village of Gualtieri, during which he could be seen walking angrily around town wearing a large black hat and a black tie, scaring the locals. Any chances he had for a permanent position were doused when he started a violent affair with a local married woman, Giulia Fontanesi.[11] Being Mussolini, he tried to break Giulia's autonomy, stabbing her at one point when he was particularly angry. When the infidelity was discovered, Giulia was thrown out of her marital home and Mussolini fled, promising Giulia he would call for her once he was settled in a new location—a promise he had no intention of keeping.

Mussolini then made a decision that would shape his international outlook. He left Italy, and for much of the next eight years would live in foreign lands. His exposure to the outside world in some ways sharpened his Italian identity. He was outraged at what he saw as the second-class treatment meted out to Italians outside of his country, but at the same time he was a strong believer that Italians who emigrated ended up improving themselves. This seemed particularly the case if an Italian emigrated to the United States. Up through World War I, Mussolini seemed almost in awe of Italian Americans, especially ones who later returned to their homelands. They seemed to him more modern, more determined, more reliable. He even flirted with emigrating to America himself, and supposedly had plans to move to New York City in 1903 to write for the socialist paper *Il Proletario*. Only Rosa falling ill kept him from the move—alas for Italy.

As it was, Mussolini's moves outside of Italy were only to neighbouring countries—Switzerland first, and then Austria-Hungary. Both trips played a role in helping create the personality he would later manifest as a war leader. In 1902 he moved to Zurich and immediately embarked on a career as a revolutionary firebrand and propagandist. He threw himself into socialist politics in Switzerland, which was popular amongst the sizeable Italian population there. He moved amongst different radical groups and revealed the ability to write passionate, inflammatory articles in the socialist papers.[12] He also became a skilled orator, and veered ever more towards radical policies in his attempts to delight his hardcore followers.

While he explored various socialist or radical ideologies, he settled on none, taking different elements from anarchism, communism, anti-clericalism, syndicalism, and sometimes espousing anti-militarism while at other times seeing himself as an "apostle of violence."[13] In many ways, this "flexibility" pointed out a reason for his later political success. He seemed as interested in collecting followers as hewing to one ideological line.

He was so successful that he came to the attention of the Swiss police in 1903 after giving a particularly fiery speech in the very unfiery town of Bern, and was expelled from the country. At first, he was determined to go back (and avoid being drafted into the Italian Army), and a few months later he slipped back into Switzerland to continue his political work. Showing how quickly he could change his colours, however, in December 1904 he returned to Italy and did his military service, joining the Bersaglieri, who were based in Verona.

Mussolini's first military experience revealed that the radical organizer still had profoundly conventional impulses that would have shocked his radical followers. As a soldier, Mussolini followed orders compliantly, later recalling that "the sense of willing subordination suited my temperament."[14] He was obedient, eager to please his officers and spoke to others about the importance of doing service to the fatherland.

He also liked being a soldier, especially in an important regiment. The Bersaglieri was (and still is) one the most well-known Italian military units. Originally a Sardinian formation, they were adopted by the Italian state as sharpshooters and shock troops and turned into one of the new country's elite units. Befitting their special status, Bersaglieri wore large, dark capercaillie feathers in their floppy soft hats. Originally these might have been used to camouflage Bersaglieri sharpshooters hiding in vegetation, but by Mussolini's time they were ornamental and very distinctive. Bersaglieri were never supposed to walk from place to place but instead to move using a fast-paced trot. Mussolini loved the special status and naturally considered himself a great success, later writing that "in every regard I was an excellent soldier."[15] He even claimed that if his mother had not died in 1905, he might have stayed in the army for longer and become an officer.

Instead, Mussolini returned to radical politics almost immediately after leaving the army in 1906. He tried his hand at teaching in Italy one more time before in 1909 moving to Trento, the Italian-populated part of the Austro-Hungarian Empire to the north-east of Lake Garda. In Trento he once again enthusiastically threw himself into the world of radical newspapers, writing pieces criticizing his fellow Italians for being too nationalist. He got roaring drunk in public and caused trouble wherever he found himself. Eventually the Austrians had had enough, and in 1909 he was expelled for "irredentism," which only made him more of a radical celebrity.*

When Mussolini returned to Italy, this time for good, his life seemed as divided as always. On the one hand, he started behaving more soberly. He gave up drinking and watching sport, and was even later elected as a municipal councillor in Milan. He started contemplating marriage, though exactly when and to whom was a mystery for years. Mussolini also supposedly fell in love with the daughter of his father's new lover. Mussolini claimed Alessandro had been heartbroken when Rosa died, although if so he had an odd way of showing it. Almost immediately after his wife's death, Alessandro moved in with a new paramour, Anna Guidi. Mussolini was soon drawn to Anna's youngest daughter, Rachele, and as normal was willing to use violence to get his way. Alessandro and Anna were reluctant to bless the courtship between their children, so Mussolini grabbed a gun and threatened to shoot Rachele if the parents did not give their approval.[16] It's here that the story gets rather confusing. Mussolini, and some of his biographers, would claim that the two were married not long after. In his autobiography Mussolini described how he and Rachele were living humbly as husband and wife in 1914 when World War I started.

The claim of a marriage at this time was a lie. He might have forced himself on Rachele in 1909 and threatened to kill her if he could not possess her, but in typical Mussolini fashion he seems to have abandoned her afterwards. In 1914 he married a woman named Ida Dalser, a beauty salon owner in Milan, who sold her business to help support her new husband.[17] The two of them soon had a son, whom they named Benito Jr. Being who he was, Mussolini quickly abandoned Dasler once he had benefited from her largesse—and the two were divorced.[18] When Mussolini was dictator, one of the first things he did was have any records of the marriage destroyed. He had Dalser beaten and incarcerated in an asylum, where she died in 1937. Benito

---

* Italian irredentism was mostly an informal movement calling for the unification of all Italian speakers in one Italian Republic. It was thus considered threatening to Austria-Hungary, with its significant Italian-speaking population.

Jr. was ostracized and given strict orders not to refer to himself as a Mussolini. In 1942, Mussolini's first-born son died, possibly due to injections given him to induce a coma. Mussolini never showed the slightest remorse. Indeed, he had ended up marrying Rachele Guidi in 1915, not long after his first marriage ended.

Mussolini also gained a measure of prominence in Italy between 1909 and 1914. His most public role at that time was as the lead editor of the official Italian Socialist Party newspaper *Avanti!* Under his control, the paper doubled its circulation and, ironically, became a leading defender of the right to freedom of speech and expression. Mussolini used *Avanti!* to dominate the more radical wing of the party. Continuing a tactic he had used in his Switzerland days, he almost always staked out extreme positions, regularly arguing for revolution and the overthrow of the present political system. He spoke approvingly of socialists using "barbarous violence" to achieve their political aims, and even praised political murder.

While Mussolini was turning himself into an advocate of domestic insurrection, in foreign policy terms he was a strident non-interventionist, almost pacifist at times. In 1911, a war between Italy and the Ottomans began for the control of Libya, and Mussolini savagely criticized Italian participation, even organizing demonstrations against the conflict. In September, while he was trying to whip an anti-war crowd into a frenzy, loud bangs went off in the background. The crowd immediately fled, leading Mussolini to call his fellow Italians a "people of cowards."[19]

Mussolini was arrested for his anti-war agitation in October, on the grounds of being a rabble-rouser and saboteur. Not wanting to suffer too much for his convictions, he pivoted and claimed that he was really driven by patriotic ideals and wanted a "rich and free" Italy. His obsequiousness worked and he was only imprisoned for five months. When released, he once again espoused extreme rhetoric and attacked the war. In 1913, rather ironically considering his later hyper-militarist positions, he claimed that the war was a bad thing as it led to "a sort of hardening of moral sensibility and . . . a devaluing of human life."[20]

Mussolini's constant shifting revealed that ideology was for him a tool to achieve an end—his greatness. He could argue for extreme positions with intensity and outward commitment, but then abandon these heartfelt stances easily if he thought a new stance would benefit him more. He did this most spectacularly—and successfully in terms of his career—at the start of World War I.

When the great powers of Europe embraced war in August 1914, Italy stood apart. Though Italy had been since 1882 a member of the Triple Alliance, along with Germany and Austria-Hungary, this pact was defensive and only to be triggered by an attack against one of the signatories. The Italians claimed, with justice, that as the Germans and Austrians had launched military operations first with their invasions of Belgium and Serbia, Italy was under no obligation to go to war. For a brief while, then, the Italian people were given a precious gift, staying neutral in what would be at that time the bloodiest war in human history. Sadly for them, people such as Mussolini decided that neutrality just wouldn't do.

The change in Mussolini's position on Italy and the war was breathtaking. Following the outbreak of fighting, Mussolini, still claiming to be a socialist, had strenuously argued against the war in *Avanti!* He wrote on August 16: "Socialists must be indifferent to the arguments for war, based these days on irredentism, on the notion that democracy needs to be saved, on the borders to be corrected, of the more or less stable 'balances' to be maintained and so on."[21] Indeed, in September he claimed that the war was a competition between two similar evils: the imperialism of colonialist Britain and the imperialism of industrialist Germany.[22]

But it soon became clear to him that while neutrality might save Italian lives, it would not benefit him, nor his vision of what he wanted Italy to be. In October, barely two months into the conflict he had so vociferously denounced, he publicly changed his stance in an editorial "thunderbolt."[23] He now derided absolute neutrality, arguing that all good socialists had to be free to go to war if need be. He shifted from opposing Italy joining the war to arguing for intervention. Still portraying himself as a socialist/Marxist and a supporter of the poor, Mussolini argued that war would usher in important social, political and economic changes that would benefit the working classes. He also tried to couch his arguments in ideals, saying it was vital that France, a beacon of Latin liberty, had to be saved from militarist, oppressive Germany and Italian-hating Austria. The second of these was almost certainly the most important, for he also spoke of joining the war as an opportunity for Italy to solve the "problem of Trento and Trieste."[24]

The switch was made even more pronounced when Mussolini gave up the editorship of *Avanti!* to start a new nationalist and pro-war newspaper, *Il Popolo d'Italia*. Favouring populist calls for robust military action against Germany and Austria-Hungary, *Il Popolo* quickly gained in popularity and seemed to have real influence over Italian popular opinion.[25] Having his own newspaper (funded by right-wing, pro-war industrialists) allowed Mussolini to develop a completely new image.[26] He no longer had to worry about Socialist Party members and their infuriating ideological anti-nationalist pretences, and could instead embrace Italian greatness and argue for seizing ever-larger amounts of Austrian territory. Now it was not only Trento and Trieste that needed to be conquered; Italy taking most of the Adriatic coast had become a "must."[27] To do this, Italy needed to be reborn spiritually, and this happy day could only be achieved through the shedding of blood.

This obsession with a blood sacrifice revealed just how much Mussolini saw war in emotional, not rational, terms—as a contest between two "wills." In the pages of *Il Popolo*, he regularly fetishized the bayonet, and enthused boyishly at the notion of one and a half million Italian bayonets driving the Austrians and Germans back.[28] On the other hand, he wrote almost nothing about machine guns and artillery—the industrial, unglamorous modern weaponry that was already making a mockery of the virtue of sacrifice on the battlefields of Europe.

Having such an effective propagandist as Mussolini was important to pro-war forces, as the Italian people seemed happy to remain neutral and there was only a somewhat motley group publicly agitating to fight. As well as Mussolini in the pro-war camp there were hardcore nationalists such as the poet Gabriele D'Annunzio, some socialists who believed that war would lead to revolution and some capitalists who believed that war represented an economic opportunity—but they were in no way a majority of the Italian people. Thus, having some vocal and very visible supporters for war remained important for those at the top of Italy's political leadership—who increasingly saw the war as a once-in-a-lifetime opportunity.

Prime Minister Antonio Salandra and Foreign Minister Sidney Sonnino started an auction with both the Allies and the Central Powers to see which would offer the best deal to get Italy to enter the war. It was an unequal competition. The Germans pressured the Austrians to offer the Italians some of their sovereign territory (hinting that the Austrians could take it back after the war), but the Allies, led by the British, could always dangle more in front of the greedy politicians. They promised Italy even larger swathes of Austrian territory, as well as the possibility of parts of the German overseas empire. It was too tempting for Italy's leaders, and in early 1915 Salandra and Sonnino signed (in secret) the Treaty of London, in which Italy was promised all of the province of Trento up to the Brenner Pass, as well as Trieste and a large hinterland around the city including much of the Isonzo valley and large parts of the Dalmatian coast. They presented the Italian king, the short and indecisive Vittorio Emanuele III, with a fait accompli. He backed the deal and then the rest of the Italian system fell into line, and almost like pressing a switch the nation transitioned from peace to war. On May 23, 1915, Italy officially joined the Allies. It was one of the most sordid events of the twentieth century—and Mussolini could not have been happier.

Like a number of pro-war Italians, he believed that Italy possessed spiritual advantages that would allow its soldiers to defeat the Austrians. In *Il Popolo* he promised his readers that the war would be a short and glorious campaign, maybe lasting no more than a few weeks.[29] The Italians would be fighting a just war to liberate their dispossessed fellow nationals in Trento and Trieste, and this would instil Italian forces with the will and elan to drive them forward against Austria's ethnically divided, linguistically polyglot, conscript soldiers.* In an editorial written immediately after the Italian

---

* When the war started in 1914, the Austro-Hungarian Army had to issue its mobilization orders in eleven different languages, to make sure that all the different nationalities understood what was happening.

declaration of war, he proclaimed that "Italy must conquer the Dal-matian archipelagos and the littoral. Austria must be expelled from the Adriatic sea."[30]

Mussolini was also aware that the Italians would have a significant numerical advantage in the coming battles. A nation of 36 million people, Italy would be able to throw almost its entire army against divided and scattered Austrian forces. To their east, the Austrians had deployed the largest part of their army against the Russians. Even then things had gone badly, and the Russians had seized large parts of Galicia, which the Austrians were desperate to seize back. To the south, the Austrians had 200,000 soldiers committed to the invasion of Serbia—a task they had failed to complete in 1914 and would have to press on with in 1915. Nor could the Austrians expect to receive additional support from the Germans in any war with Italy. The Germans had the majority of their army deployed on the Western Front, facing the combined might of France and Great Britain. Beyond this, they still had to keep significant forces in the east fight-ing the Russians, and had even deployed an army to help the Austrians conquer Serbia. The Italians, not wanting to provoke the Germans in any way, even refused to declare war on Germany until August 1916, unwilling to give the greatest land power in the world any reason to send aid to their Austrian allies.*

Italian intelligence believed that the Austrians could deploy only 250,000 soldiers to cover their entire border with Italy,[31] a figure that was almost exactly accurate. The Italian Army, in comparison, under the leadership of Marshal Luigi Cadorna, commenced hostilities with around 400,000 soldiers, with plans to add hundreds of thou-sands through the calling-up of different classes of conscripts. Cadorna could thus quicky outnumber the Austrians wherever he

---

* Italy and Germany took part in a strange shadow war between May 1915 and August 1916. Small numbers of German troops did show up on the Italian front, but they generally avoided overt action. German submarines in the Mediterra-nean also regularly sank Italian vessels, but usually flew an Austrian flag when they did so.

wanted. Both he and Mussolini believed that a glorious war of conquest beckoned.

It would not be so easy. If the Italians had a numerical advantage, everything else, especially the terrain, favoured the Austrians. The areas the Italians were hoping to seize stretched from some of the most mountainous, remote parts of Europe to rocky, marshy plateaus where movement was ponderous and the attackers would be exposed as soon as they pressed forward. In a nutshell, almost everywhere the Italian Army was sent they would be confronted by dug-in Austrian soldiers shooting down at them from above. Italian soldiers—brave, mostly untrained, many illiterate and poorly equipped—were marching to the slaughterhouse.

Indeed, the terrain determined much of the opening stages of the war. In June, the Italian Army made its initial moves towards Trento and Trieste, advancing a few miles into Austrian territory at both locations. It was a chaotic, spasmodic and slow advance. The Austrians originally expected to retreat further into the interior, but the slow pace of the Italians allowed them to dig in much closer to the border.[32] Trento was little more than fifteen miles from the border with Italy, but the Italian Army never reached it.

To the south and east, things were if anything worse. The road to Trieste began well enough: relatively flat until the turquoise Isonzo was reached. Across the river, however, the Italian soldiers entered the Carso plateau—a large swathe of boggy upland, marked by sinkholes and bleached white rocky outcrops.[33] Entrenching there was practically impossible, and there were few roads for efficient movement. The Italians were exposed, forced to attack in the open against Austrian forces on the higher ground. One Austrian general described their advantage like firing "from a ten-storey building" down on the exposed Italians.[34] They were soon decimated by Austrian machine guns and artillery, and on the cratered moonscape of the Carso they found it difficult to cover, let alone bury, their dead. The Italian Army never reached Trieste, stopped in its tracks about halfway between the city and the Italian border.

Mussolini missed these opening campaigns. It's not clear whether he tried to volunteer at the start, but regardless he did not enter the army until called up to serve. This meant that he remained a civilian until September 1915, missing the first bloody advances. Only then did he enter the army, assigned to his old Bersaglieri, where he once again donned the capercaillie feather.

The Mussolini who went to war in late 1915 was halfway between the angry, small-town rapist and the world-famous dictator that he would become. He was solidly built, showing a slight pudge in the middle (something he would fret about when he was in power). He still had a fringe of thinning black hair, as he hadn't yet plucked up the courage to shave it all off, and he sported a narrow moustache that made him look ever so slightly like a dandy. He was physically vigorous, strong and liked to strut—physical affectations that he would push to the extreme while giving speeches from the balcony overlooking Piazza Venezia. His military career over the coming two years would ensure he was exposed to the realities of World War I soldiery more than any of the other war leaders, aside from Adolf Hitler—though the lessons he took from it were different in important respects.

The most detailed information we have of Mussolini's war experience comes from his diary, much of which was written for public effect and published in the newspaper. Still, there are many flashes of honesty, and it needs to be treated seriously as a historical source—if one can overlook the later fascist bombast that surrounds it.[35] Yet it reveals that the war as Mussolini experienced it was very different from the one he had confidently told his readers would be a glorious campaign of victory.

The early recollections are all predictable, positive homages to the unifying impact of war on the Italian soldier. He wrote that he had "noticed—with pleasure, with joy—that there is a most cordial camaraderie among soldiers and officers. The life of constant risk draws men together."[36] Mussolini argued that the war broke down the existing regional loyalties of the Italian soldier, creating a national—indeed a racial—awareness. The one-time Marxist/anarchist exclaimed that in the army "no one says, 'I am going back to my hometown.' They all say, 'I am going back to Italy.' Perhaps for the first time Italy has come to take her place, in the consciousness of her sons, as a living reality."

And of course, all that camaraderie and national unity were fused to make the Italian soldier, particularly in his own unit, eager to attack the enemy. The Bersaglieri, according to Mussolini, never spoke of being in "combat" or even in "action," but only of taking part in an "advance." With such an "aggressive spirit which animates the Italian soldiers," victory was assured. When gravely injured during these terrible advances, the Italian soldier was portrayed by Mussolini as stoic and unemotional: "The superb silence of these humble sons of Italy, when their flesh is torn and tortured by the ruthless steel, is a proof of the magnificent sturdiness of our race."[37]

In Mussolini's eyes, the only thing that could rival the greatness of the warlike spirit of the Italian soldier was Mussolini himself. Though only an enlisted soldier, he regularly claimed to be hailed as a great leader by those around him. One enlisted Bersaglieri supposedly came up to Mussolini in September 1915 and begged him: "Signor Mussolini, since we have seen that you have so much *spirit* (courage) and have led us in the march under shell fire we want you to be our commander."[38] Famous officers also supposedly sought him out for comradely embraces, thanking him for his pro-war agitation, while others lamented that he was not part of their units. Mussolini claimed none of this went to his head. He refused all entreaties to become an officer himself, also turning down the opportunity for a safe job in the rear lines, as he just wanted to serve as a simple soldier upholding the "magnificent sturdiness of our race." It reeked of hogwash, and after a time, in his darker moments, Mussolini admitted as much.

For all of his paeans to the purifying impact of war on the Italian race and claims that war revealed his personal greatness, Mussolini did let slip that the reality of the war, and his role within it, was not so rosy. Italy, at that time only partially industrialized and considerably poorer per capita than France, Germany or Austria, had difficulty equipping its soldiers. Mussolini was forced to compliment the sturdiness of Austrian shoes, and admitted that enemy corpses were quickly stripped of their footwear by Italians, who were wearing an inferior product. He also had to admit that when the Italian soldiers in his unit were first given steel helmets, they came from France, as there were no Italian versions to be had. The general lack of steel helmets at the start of the war left Italian soldiers at great risk of terrible head injuries from the small splinters of hot metal that pinged around the battlefield like insects.

Yet the soldiers themselves presented the greatest dilemma. Though Mussolini liked to portray the average Italian as committed to the war and determined to make the ultimate sacrifice in the cause of a greater Italy, the reality was different. The Italian Army was made up of a mass of conscripts—most of them illiterate, and many bewildered by being taken so far from their small farms and villages, the only world that they had ever known. Considering the transformation, the Italian soldier did his duty magnificently and accepted hardships that would have appalled his British or French counterpart on the Western Front. Mussolini tried to make a virtue of this deprivation, contrasting the supposed depth and sturdiness of "English trenches . . . furnished with all the comforts—they even have heating apparatus" to the Italian trenches, which had to be scraped out of the rocky soil and were "mere holes dug between rocks, shelters which are exposed to all kinds of weather."[39] He portrayed the soldiers as uninterested in money or pleasure of any kind, able to subsist on bland rations, the highlight of which was the daily coffee allowance. It was an admission that this was not the glorious war he had promised.

And as a soldier himself, Mussolini had a great deal of time to observe his fellows, though partly that was due to extraordinary good luck which kept him on the fringes or completely removed from the great bloodletting that was going on all around him. After the Italian Army was halted not long after crossing the Isonzo, its main preoccupation was to try to break the Austrian lines and reach Trieste. To do this, it would have to break the Austrian lines on the Carso while neutralizing the Austrian forces in the mountains to the north—who held vantage points that helped them dominate movement. Eleven times between June 1915 and August 1917, Marshal Cadorna built up and then launched Italian forces against the Austrian lines in the area. He tried different tactics—massed artillery barrages, surprise attacks, mountain operations and even straightforward frontal assaults. There were so many battles that historians have been left simply numbering them from one to eleven—and distinguishing between them is difficult because of the repetitiveness of their horror. No matter what they tried, the Italian soldiers were left assaulting soldiers who were in prepared positions, almost always having the high ground, and usually with superior military technology. The results were slaughter upon slaughter for the Italians—and advances that were easier to measure in yards than in miles.

Mussolini witnessed two of these slaughters not long after reaching the front, though during each he was far enough away from the action that he missed the greatest danger—being either at the rear, on the edges or even isolated higher up in more mountainous blockhouses. He could hear, see, even smell what was happening, but was rarely fired upon. These two battles were some of Cadorna's early offensives to try to break out towards Trieste—the third and fourth battles of the Isonzo.

These battles were part of the Italian Army's destructive learning curve when it came to modern war. Cadorna was just starting to see the first waves of mass reinforcement of recruits, and he had decided that a battle of movement would be almost impossible with the technology they possessed and the terrain. Therefore he tried to achieve the "big breakthrough" by simply blasting his way through the Austrian lines.[40] Italy was scoured for all spare artillery pieces, some of which came from naval bases far to the south, and all the guns that could be found were rushed to the front. In the end, Cadorna deployed more than 1,300 artillery pieces on a thirty-mile front, the largest mass concentration of firepower that the Italian Army had ever used. His plan was to shatter the Austrian lines with a mass bombardment, allowing Italian forces to take the town of Gorizia (barely over a mile from the start point) and open up a new road to Trieste.[41] On October 18, the attack began.

Mussolini was likely located just to the north and at the rear of the action.* When the Italian guns opened fire, he exulted at the

---

* In his diary, Mussolini was often maddeningly vague on where he was posted, perhaps for reason of military discipline but also perhaps because he often seemed to miss out on major battles.

"distant and prolonged bombardment . . . The mighty concert of our artillery begins." After two days of listening to this bombardment, which he assured himself would crack Austrian morale, Mussolini excitedly claimed that action was imminent. And yet he never seemed to get into it. He claimed his unit was set to "protect the advance" of other units, which seemed to mean that they were to stay at the rear and watch hordes of wounded Italians returning from the front line. He had time to muse about soldiers' drinking, the sound of artillery, the willingness of the Italian soldier to attack—mostly ephemera. He clearly was not on the front line, and after a few days he asked himself: "Has the 'action' ended? I don't know anything about it."[42]

In reality, if not in Mussolini's diary, Cadorna's plan had caused a bloodbath for his own troops. Of the great mass of artillery he had foraged from across Italy, the large majority were small-calibre guns that made little impact on the fortified Austrian defences. When the Italian soldiers advanced with their customary bravery, Austrian machine guns—mostly undamaged and firing from higher ground— cut them down with ease. The front line barely moved, and after losing 67,000 men in a few days, Cadorna called off the assault.[43] He was not to be deterred, however. Instead of rethinking, he spent the next few weeks building up for a repeat assault. He would change his tactics not at all, the only difference being that when the Fourth Battle of the Isonzo started on November 10, the weather was considerably worse. Now there was blood and snow.

The 11th Bersaglieri was destined to play a prominent role in this attack. Yet Mussolini, with extraordinarily good fortune, was away from the front line—sent to Vernazza for the training required for his recent promotion to corporal (the same rank that Hitler would obtain in the war). There he spent a few days he described as "dull enough" before being ordered to rejoin his unit. The 11th Bersaglieri had gone into action and needed every man it could get. Mussolini did not reach the front until November 16, and admitted that even then he was the only person who had come back when ordered. By that point, it seems, the real fighting for the Bersaglieri was almost over. Mussolini stepped away from his diary, not writing in it again until February

1916. There is no mention of combat during the Fourth Battle of the Isonzo, with the last entry ending "This morning the sun shines."[44]

He thus came through two of the bloodiest battles the Italian Army would fight without seeing any real action. Many of his comrades were not so lucky. When Cadorna finally called off the Fourth Battle of the Isonzo, another 50,000 Italians were officially recorded as casualties. It was an undercount. More recent estimates place the combined Italian losses in the third and fourth battles at closer to 170,000 soldiers.[45] Yet for all this blood, the front line had only moved incrementally.

Mussolini's fortuitous experience of war made some impression on him—but not nearly enough. He was forced to admit in October 1915 that the war was much harder than he had anticipated (or had led his readers to believe): "Our war, like all other wars, is one of position, a fight for place. A dreary war . . . All the picturesque attributes of the old-fashioned war have disappeared."[46] And yet he could not shake his basic belief that it was willpower that would triumph in the end. The more the memories of these battles retreated in his mind, the more his old sureties of the importance of will—or the "unquantifiable" over quantifiable material—reasserted themselves.[47] As he would write some months later: "He wins who wills to win. He wins who has the greatest store of mental energy, of will power. A million cannon will not bring victory if the soldiers have not the courage to attack."[48]

He had been given a brilliant opportunity to learn—he just didn't like the lesson, so rejected it. As always with Mussolini, what he wanted to be was more important than what he was, which would be of cold comfort to the hundreds of thousands of Italian soldiers in World War II who would face the millions of British, Soviet and American cannons with the same bravery as their World War I predecessors—and die just as easily.

5. Adolf Hitler: Art and War

Adolf Hitler was just good enough as an artist to get by, and because of that the history of the world was different. It was August 1914, and he was twenty-five years old, living in Munich, and painting pictures. They were pale, uninspiring works, often copied from tourist postcards of major city landmarks. But the rigidly drawn sketches of grand baroque buildings appealed to a certain class of the petit bourgeois who patronized the city's cafés and beer halls, and Hitler was able to make a basic living hawking his work. Having the ability to live off his art was what allowed him to be in Munich in the first place, and it was from Munich that Hitler would begin a path towards the destruction of Europe.

Hitler was born and raised in Austria-Hungary, and had lived in that empire until he moved to Munich in early 1913. Austria-Hungary was one of the most ethnically diverse nations in Europe, if not the world, with a population including Germans, Hungarians, Czechs, Italians, Slovenians, Serbians, Croatians, Romanians, Albanians, Poles, Slovaks and Jews, amongst others. The Hitlers were an ethnically German family living within this multicultural space, and this fact came to dominate Adolf's outlook. To him, the influence of these different cultures and races, particularly that of the Jews, fatally weakened the Germanness of what he was convinced should be Austria's dominant ethnic group.

Before Munich, Hitler had spent six years living in the Austrian capital, Vienna, ranting at the lack of strong racial identity that he saw in this cosmopolitan, intellectually vibrant and relatively tolerant place—or as he called the graceful Austrian capital, "incest incarnate."[1] Yet he refused to leave, and needed to find a way to support himself until he turned twenty-four and received an inheritance from his father's estate. He flirted with real poverty, yet even in the most difficult times Hitler was able to survive on the small amounts he made from his art, and he never had to take up a wage-paying job or start training in a profession. By holding on in his state of unemployment, when he did get his hands on the family money he was free to do what he had dreamed of doing for years—move to the more racially pure and muscular Germany. This was how he found himself in Munich when World War I started, and why he was able to enlist in the German Army and not that of Austria-Hungary. This was a decisive factor in shaping the war experiences and subsequent strategic outlook of the maniac who would one day start World War II.

Like Benito Mussolini and Joseph Stalin, Adolf Hitler's family hailed from far outside the ruling elite. Unlike the other two dictators, however, he came from a family that was relatively prosperous, even upwardly mobile. His father, the formidable Alois Schicklgruber, was the son of a peasant woman and a father whose identity to this day is not easy to confirm. Alois was a determined social climber, obsessed with beekeeping, and had originally trained as a shoemaker. Aiming to get ahead, he changed his name to Hitler to associate himself with the family of the more prosperous man with whom his mother had taken up after his birth.* He eventually joined the Austro-Hungarian civil service as a customs officer—a not inconsiderable achievement for someone who had only an elementary level of education. As a sign of his devotion to his employer, Alois grew heavy side whiskers modelled on the long-time Austrian emperor, Franz Joseph.

As a career customs officer, Alois was able to provide a comfortable living for his three wives and numerous children, eventually even employing a cook and maid. The catch with this comfort was that his family had to live with Alois, who has been described as "pompous, status-proud, strict, humourless, frugal, pedantically punctual, and devoted to duty."[2] Hitler was terrified of this paragon of Austrian officialdom, who treated his son with a mix of formality

---

* Alois changing his name from Schicklgruber to Hitler was one of the few things for which his son Adolf would later praise him. "Heil Shicklgruber" does not exactly roll off the tongue.

and condescension. Once, when the young Hitler asked his father to think through a problem, Alois replied, "I have no need to think, I'm an official."[3] When Hitler was later dictator of a genocide-committing, continent-spanning Nazi empire, he would tell his generals of how scared he had been of his father and how one of his clearest memories was the constant stings that Alois's bees inflicted upon him.[4]

Hitler's mother, Klara, was an entirely different creature. The third of Alois's wives, she was twenty-three years younger than her husband, kind, shy, and submissive. She and Alois had six children, but only two—Adolf, who was born in 1889, and his younger sister Paula—survived to adulthood. She loved her only son without reservation and, in return, might have been the only person Adolf genuinely cared for. He was known to carry her portrait until the moment that he shot himself in a bunker in Berlin.

Hitler's devotion to Klara was dependent on the fact that she devoted herself to indulging him. Her obsequiousness helped shape his vision of the ideal woman—dull, not particularly intelligent, uninterested in politics and focused on her family. In early 1942, Hitler would speak about how his mother was the perfect paragon of German womanhood. "Intelligence, in a woman, is not an essential thing," he said. "My mother, for example, would have cut a poor figure in the society of our cultivated women. She lived strictly for her husband and children. They were her entire universe. But she gave a son to Germany."[5]

When both of his parents were alive, Hitler was a passable student and seemed almost normal. He liked playing Cowboys and Indians, and though an egomaniac, he interacted well with schoolmates. In 1903, Alois dropped dead while drinking his daily glass of morning wine, and Hitler was left to indulge his true nature.* Alois had wanted his son to become a civil servant like himself, but Adolf had no desire to work for any other person or institution. His state of self-absorption was exacerbated by the widowed Klara, who was now devoted full-time to providing everything her son desired. She

---

* Hitler believed that Alois's heavy smoking was the actual cause of his death, and used his father as an example to try to get others to give up tobacco.

made sure all household chores were done to the boy's standards, provided him with food and clean clothing, gave him money, and allowed him to indulge his passions. The results were monstrous.

As a boy and a young man, Hitler revealed many of the traits he would later bring to his dictatorship and war leadership. He was lazy but demanded to be the centre of attention. He always saw things in intense black and white—one side pure and good (the side he supported) and the other degenerate and dishonest. He also found it impossible to take into consideration the feelings of other people, making friendship difficult except with the most submissive of personalities. Indeed, the one close friend he made in the years after Alois's death was the lacklustre August Kubizek.

Hitler met Kubizek in 1905 after he and Klara moved to the city of Linz. At the age of sixteen, Hitler loved to get dressed up as a dandy in immaculate suits, complete with a thin black cane which he would twirl energetically when angry, and attend the opera. Kubizek, a fellow opera devotee who shared Hitler's passion for the works of Richard Wagner, was captivated by the forceful young Adolf. Kubizek had the ability to listen devotedly and unquestioningly to Hitler's endless rants on opera or whatever else came into his mind. They were a perfect match, and Hitler considered this time one of the best of his life, and Linz became his favourite city.*

At this time, Hitler had not the slightest interest in a military or political career. Instead, he intended to "devote his whole life to art," and expected to make his mark on the world as a painter.[6] To help launch himself, Hitler was determined to attend the Academy of Fine Arts in Vienna. In 1907, not long after Klara had been diagnosed with breast cancer, Hitler left to take the entrance examination, which he assumed would be a formality. Sadly for humanity, he was not nearly good enough to be admitted, and was turned down because of an inability to draw human faces.[7] He could draw static shapes and straight lines well enough, but living, flexible forms were

---

* When he became dictator, Hitler showed his "affection" for Linz by drawing up plans to make the city into a great metropolis, with large galleries to be stuffed with artworks plundered from Europe.

always too difficult for him to master. This blow was magnified when he returned to Linz and had to nurse Klara through her painful last few months of life. When she died in December 1907, he was devastated and fled back to Vienna, pretending to the world that he had been accepted to the academy.[8]

In fact, he lived for six years as a parasite, surviving on an orphan's pension he received from the Austrian government, some generous financial gifts from relatives, and the money he was paid for his insipid pictures. Vienna was a fascinating study in contrasts: a grand European capital, at the forefront of modern art and psychology, the metropolis was home to some two million people, many living in the most terrible poverty amongst some of the worst slums in Europe.[9] Hitler ended up on a general trajectory towards the latter in these years, and it would have seemed to the outside world that he was more likely to end up a homeless vagrant than an infamous dictator. We have a good description of Hitler's life in these years, because Kubizek, who was embarking on a career in music, eventually came to Vienna to live with him.

When Kubizek arrived, Hitler was still living the lie that he had been accepted into the Academy of Fine Arts. The two ended up sharing a bug-infested room which smelled strongly of paraffin. It was large enough for two beds, Kubizek's piano, and a span of floor where Hitler could pace for three steps back and forth while unleashing his inevitable tirades. At first Hitler seemed to be his old self. He kept up appearances and dressed in immaculate clothes, even sleeping with his trousers folded neatly under his pillow to keep their creases sharp. Yet clearly not all was well. Hitler seemed aimless and needed to watch his expenses. He devoted almost all of his spare money to going to the opera, usually Wagner, and always in the cheap, standing-room-only seats. Even then he had to ration his visits to those he considered the most important "spectacles."[10] To free up money for the opera, he ate sparingly, often subsisting on milk and bread, and he frequented different canteens across the city that served food at subsidized prices. One of these canteens was at the music academy where Kubizek was a student, and it served a nut cake that the sweet-toothed Hitler could not resist. He liked it so much that he was even willing to sit next to the many Jewish students of the academy who also used the canteen, which must have irritated the future architect of the Holocaust.[11]

After a while, Kubizek realized something was up. Hitler was forced to admit that he had not been accepted into the academy, even after a second attempt, and had no clear path to becoming an artist. He compensated for this failure by devising one grandiose plan after another. Moving on from a career in painting, he next decided he would become a world-famous architect and came up with a plan to tear down much of Vienna's appalling workers' slums and rehouse the proletariat in cleaner, brighter modern housing. At another time he decided to become a great composer like Wagner, and started writing an opera based on the historic German myth about Wieland the Smith, which involved the rape and killing of children.[12] In typical Hitler fashion he would become obsessed with different projects for a few weeks, working with manic intensity until the early hours of the morning and then, when the work became too difficult or the truth started dawning that they would go nowhere, he would lapse back into indolence.

With his life a series of such failures, Hitler became bitter, particularly towards the Austro-Hungarian Empire and its cosmopolitan capital. Much of this resentment revealed his fundamentally contradictory view of ethnic Germans, which would influence almost everything he did strategically in World War II. With masses of time on his hands, Hitler started attending sittings of the polyglot Austrian parliament, even once dragging along a bewildered Kubizek to witness the proceedings. Hitler did not go to understand legislation or learn about politics, but instead to spark an intense rage at what he observed. Kubizek watched mystified as Hitler, staring down on the legislators with their various cultures and agendas, became increasingly enraged and "jumped to his feet, his hands clenched, his face burning with excitement."[13]

Hitler's rage was against what he believed to be the constant insult to the Germanness of Austria-Hungary. In Hitler's mind, the empire's German population was responsible for all that was "good and honourable," but was being shunted aside in favour of multiculturalism.

The enemies of Germanness in his paranoid world were varied and nefarious, being linguistic, religious, artistic and racial. There were Czechs who spoke in a non-Germanic tongue that Hitler talked about abolishing, Roman Catholics whose religion made Germans soft and which Hitler wanted to excise from German life, Slavs who were completely alien in outlook and needed to be forced into subservient positions. Then there were the Jews, who represented a threat in every one of these areas.

It was in Vienna that Hitler's antisemitism first manifested—which made him not atypical in the city. As the city's Jewish communities produced some of the greatest successes in Europe, from the founder of psychoanalysis Sigmund Freud to the modernist author Arthur Schnitzler, they also became a focus of resentment and suspicion. Different Austrian political movements, which clearly influenced Hitler, made antisemitism part of their creed, arguing that Jews diluted the purity of the Germanic race and perverted society by making it too material and modern. Hitler, who believed that the Jews controlled all the press in Vienna, started seeing Jews as a particular threat to his idea of a dominant German people.[14] When he first saw Orthodox Jews in Vienna, with their distinct hairstyles and clothes, he wondered, "Is this a German?"[15] Making Vienna purely German would become one of his great ambitions as dictator. In 1943 he would boast about having cleared the Jews out of Vienna, and stated that his next step would be to drive out the Czechs.[16]

Hitler's belief that non-Germans were poisoning Vienna was more than an example of national paranoia; it was personal. It helped him explain what to him seemed the inexplicable—why he had failed to be accepted into the Academy of Fine Arts and at everything else he tried. When Hitler was turned down the second time, he had gone to the academy's rector to demand a reason.[17] The older man, who seems to have wanted to let the angry young Hitler down easily, explained that Adolf's skills, which always tended to the linear, were not well suited to painting but could be better suited to architecture. On the one hand this began Hitler's obsession with becoming an architect, but it did not fully answer his doubts.

His personal rejection certainly helped sour him on Vienna and

Austria as a whole, and led him to see the invisible hand of enemies thwarting him personally. In *Mein Kampf*, he would string together his personal misery at this time with the paranoia he felt about the enemies of all Germans. "My eyes were opened to two menaces of which I had previously scarcely known the names, and whose terrible importance for the existence of the German people I certainly did not understand: Marxism and Jewry. To me Vienna, the city which, to so many, is the epitome of innocent pleasure, a festive playground for merrymakers, represents, I am sorry to say, merely the living memory of the saddest period of my life."[18] A first mythical stab in the back had occurred.

Hitler's obsessions with the challenge posed by Jews and non-Germanic groups also revealed the dirty little secret of his extreme nationalism. Though he was convinced that the Germans were the greatest people in the world, he was also worried at how easily they could be corrupted. The Austrian Germans were the most extreme example of this. Where they should have exercised dominance, to Hitler they had been too willing to accommodate other groups to try to make the empire work, and in doing so had put themselves beyond redemption. He asked himself about the Austrian Germans: "Are these people human, worthy to belong to a great nation?"[19] The answer was clear—no—and no renaissance of them within the Austro-Hungarian Empire would ever be possible.

So Hitler would move to Germany itself, though he needed to find a way to reach the age of twenty-four before he could do so. In the intervening years he had to survive by whatever means possible. This involved a steady deterioration in his living standards. He fell out with Kubizek (perhaps ashamed at his constant failures in life while his friend was carving out a mediocre career in music). He moved lodgings to even less salubrious surroundings. For a while Hitler was even homeless, and became acquainted with the deepest squalor in the city. Later in life he would speak of the enormous Vienna "gutter rats, such as aren't found anywhere else."[20] Money became so short that he would later claim he went "long months without ever having the smallest hot meal."[21] Eventually, though a heavy smoker, he threw his "cigarettes into the Danube" so that he could buy a little butter for his bread.[22] It was the moment when he became a committed opponent of smoking, and he would hector his tobacco-mad generals about the evils of smoking throughout World War II. Eventually he took up residence in one of Vienna's working men's hostels, where he played the educated intellectual in front of mystified labourers. When things were at their bleakest he was able to get by on selling his art—and he disregarded suggestions, such as that from his legal guardian after Klara's death, that he should take up a real job and become a baker.[23]

His political outlook in Vienna was a mixed bag. While clearly an extreme nationalist, he was also flirting with drastic social reform to try to improve the lives of the poor. His plans to rehouse Vienna's workers were part of a larger ideology that called for the forced redistribution of wealth and power from the rich to the poor. Where he broke from left-wing socialists, however, was in his underlying reason for social reform. Hitler wanted change to make the Germanic working classes more patriotic and national-minded. The more time he spent with workers, the more shocked he was by just how weak their patriotism was.

When it came to military service and war, Hitler was unengaged, even hostile. Kubizek spoke of Hitler being a pacifist in Vienna— though that seems to be mistaking a specific hatred for a general principle. Hitler was an anti-militarist, if being a militarist meant serving in and fighting for Austria-Hungary. One of the reasons he changed residences so often (usually not leaving a forwarding address) and why he is so difficult to track in these years is that he was a skilful draft dodger, on the run from doing his Austrian compulsory military service. When Kubizek mentioned at one point that he was heading back to Linz to do his military service, Hitler was furious. He declared that "on no account was I to serve in the Austro-Hungarian Army. This moribund Habsburg Empire did not deserve a single soldier."[24]

Once he had his hands on Alois's money, Hitler could finally move to Germany itself. He did this almost immediately after his birthday, aiming for Munich. The capital of Bavaria, Munich was Roman Catholic like Austria but considerably less cosmopolitan. Hitler arrived in May 1913 "full of enthusiasm," determined to build a career as an architect.[25] On the surface his life in Munich resembled that of his more prosperous times in Vienna. He rented a room from the family of Joseph Popp, a tailor, started painting again, sold his works, and spent his free time either reading or hanging out in cafés and beer halls, where he would pontificate with fellow cranks and conspiracy theorists. According to his landlady, he was formal, had not a single visitor the entire time, and was difficult to get to know.[26]

In January 1914, Austrian authorities tracked him down in Munich and ordered him back across the border for military service. Hitler panicked, wrote a grovelling letter to Austrian authorities, and obediently returned to his homeland. Fortunately for him, doctors took one look at this pale, frantic artist and judged him to be medically unfit for service. He returned to Munich greatly relieved.

Then the war came.

Adolf Hitler's World War I experiences show the complexity in trying to understand the man and his ideas. There are thousands of books written on his life, and still major disagreements exist on some of the basic details and interpretations. Hitler often said contradictory things, told exaggerations or complete fabrications, leaving biographers the opportunity of cherry-picking different comments to assemble different composite pictures. Even the photograph that for decades defined our vision of Hitler in August 1914 has been challenged. When Hitler was leading the Nazi Party and on the verge of political power, his court photographer Heinrich Hoffmann discovered an astonishing picture of the young Hitler in Munich on August 2, 1914. In it, Hitler can be seen clearly, one small figure in a mass tumult on the Odeonsplatz. The crowd had come to cheer the war and Hitler looks ecstatic, mouth slightly open in wonder, eyes riveted, looking forward. But there are serious questions about the photograph's legitimacy, with some arguing that Hoffmann, trying to embellish the Hitler myth, found a way of skilfully inserting him into the picture.[27]

With Hitler, it is best not to dwell on one single source or comment. In the case of Hitler's reaction to the outbreak of war, we don't need a picture to know that he was ecstatic—because his actions speak as loudly as any words. He volunteered immediately to serve in a Bavarian regiment and in a very short time transitioned from mediocre painter and café philosopher to soldier. In fact he volunteered so quickly that for a few weeks Bavarian authorities were unsure what to do with him.* Hitler registered his willingness to fight on August 3, 1914, but was at first sent home as Munich was full of eager young men and authorities were unable to process them all. Only on August 16 was he accepted into the army, and assigned to the Bavarian 16th Reserve Regiment.† With "pure idealism" in his heart, Adolf Hitler was ready to march off to war.[28]

Hitler's war service was different from—and makes him stand apart from—the other strategic leaders of World War II. Churchill, Roosevelt and Stalin all had positions of political authority sometime between 1914 and 1919. Mussolini, meanwhile, possessed a certain celebrity. Hitler, however, was an insignificant soldier in an insignificant regiment. The 16th Reserve Regiment—which came to be known as the List Regiment after its first commander, Colonel Julius von List, who was killed early in the war—was one of the less distinguished units that fought for Germany.[29] It was made up of a mixture of volunteers and conscripted men, and few if any of its soldiers had military experience and had to be trained up from scratch.[30] It was not considered terribly combat-effective, achieved few battlefield distinctions and was often sent to hold less important parts of the front. For Hitler the war would not be glamorous, and he would not be in the papers. It would, though, expose him to the reality of combat. Of all the war leaders, his service on the front was the most extensive, and he faced the prospect of death far more often than the rest—perhaps combined. He would also see the war from

---

* Because of the federal composition of the German Reich before World War I, Bavaria, which still had its own king and governmental structure, was responsible for raising its own military formations in 1914. However, these units were under the command of the German Army as a whole when the Reich went to war.

† Legally, as an Austrian citizen, Hitler should have returned to Austria to serve in the army, yet in the chaos of the start of war, no one in Bavaria was bothered with legal niceties, so Hitler got away with the move.

the ground up—as a cog in a larger machine who had no real understanding of the full picture but had to intuit things by observation.
The experience would change some of Hitler's perceptions and
heighten other pre-existing ones, and in doing so it would be formative for him as a war leader—setting his view of Germans, Jews,
grand strategy, weapons, tactics and soldiers.

In October 1914, after a period of basic training, the List Regiment
was sent to the Western Front. The trip alone seemed to Hitler a vindication of his nationalist ideology. For the first time he visited the
beating heart of the German economy and in some ways culture—the
Rhineland. "I saw the Rhine for the first time in 1914," he wrote later,
"when I was on my way to the Western Front. The feelings which the
sight of this historic stream inspired in me remain for ever graven on
my heart. The kindness and spontaneity of the Rhinelanders also
made a profound impression on me; everywhere they received us and
feted us in a most touching manner."[31] As always with Hitler, this
monochrome vision was partly fantasy. Hitler was determined that
Germany be presented as united in overwhelming enthusiasm for the
new war, and never mentioned any signs of reluctance—of which
Germany had many.

On October 23, the List Regiment crossed the border into Belgium, and for the first time in his life Hitler was in a non-Germanic
country. He remained in his excited pre-combat mood, thinking victory was all but assured. Having no idea of modern war, Hitler even
wrote to Frau Popp that he was hoping he would "get to England
soon."[32] The idea of Germany launching a successful amphibious
assault on Britain, in the teeth of the maritime dominance of the
Royal Navy, would have required a science-fiction novel to justify.
Still, Hitler was dreaming of it.

The next few weeks would reveal that the real war was rather
different. When Hitler reached the Western Front in October 1914,
it was a moment of transition in World War I and warfare in general. The German, French and British armies were starting to
construct the famous trench lines that would come to define their
war. The first few months of combat in the west had been fluid.
When the Germans invaded Belgium and France in August, they

moved rapidly, often advancing ten to fifteen miles a day. They seized Brussels by August 20, and for a while seemed on the verge of sweeping through Belgium and coming down from the north into France to seize Paris. Yet the faster and further they moved, the more German forces became spread out over a large area. Ominously wide gaps appeared between their marching armies. On September 9, with the Germans only twenty miles from Paris, the French Army counterattacked. In what is now known as the First Battle of the Marne, the French exploited the gaps between the German forces, rocking the invaders back on their heels and causing panic.[33] Soon the Germans were in headlong retreat and the chief of the Prussian and German General Staff, Helmuth von Moltke, seemed close to a nervous breakdown. Yet after the Germans were pushed back thirty miles, the French attack lost momentum and the front started to stabilize.

Then something unexpected occurred. Instead of continuing to move forward or back, the two armies dug down. The Germans and the French and British began marking out a line which would run through northern France before nipping back into Belgium and reaching the English Channel. Throughout the rest of September until early November, their forces met in continual engagement, known collectively as the Race to the Sea, to determine where the line would be. Both sides built ever more extensive systems of trenches and fortifications to protect themselves, stretching from the border of Switzerland to the coast, and in so doing gave a crucial advantage to whatever side was lucky or smart enough to find itself on the defensive during the coming years of war.

In January 1915, Hitler, who witnessed these early trench lines being constructed, revelled in their strength, though even he found them unspeakably dirty. "Because of the eternal rain . . . the meadows and fields look like bottomless swamps," he wrote, "while the roads are covered ankle-deep in mud. Through these swamps run the trenches of our infantry—a maze of dug-outs, trenches with loopholes, entrenchments, barbed wire entanglements, pitfalls, landmines, in short an almost impregnable position. The French and English have been on the offensive since the beginning of

November. But they have always been repulsed with tremendous losses."[34]

Hitler was right. Changes in military technology over the previous decades meant that the defender in World War I was in a much stronger position than the attacker. Machine guns and artillery fire magnified the fighting power of well-protected defenders located in prepared trenchworks. They could lay down such a destructive field of fire that attackers, even in significantly larger numbers, were at a critical disadvantage. For the next three and a half years, the attacker, usually the British and French, tried various tactics and technologies to break these trench lines on the Western Front, including mass artillery fire, tanks, and various poison gases. The results were invariably the same. Their attacks might start promisingly and take a few trench lines, but eventually they would collapse before a full breakthrough could be accomplished. In the meantime, the attackers would have been killed or maimed in very large numbers and the line barely moved from that laid down in September–November 1914.

Hitler's first experiences of combat involved one of the many small engagements that occurred while the Germans and the Allies were trying to stake out where this line of trenches would be. Unlike most of Hitler's World War I story, a detailed record exists, in letters to his Munich acquaintances, of how he first experienced—or at least wanted to portray—combat.

These letters, sent to a few of his Munich acquaintances, reveal a certain tension about the war. Hitler did not portray conflict lightly. He was willing to describe some of the horrors he encountered—though he also seemed to revel in horror at times, particularly if it was imposed by German action. In Belgium, Hitler looked upon towns such as Louvain—"a heap of ash and rubble," he wrote—or the Belgian city of Liège, where "the blast of German shells" had shattered the glass windows, leaving only the iron frames still standing. The reality of German military muscle reassured him. A grotesquerie he dwelt upon in detail was the "half-decomposed" corpse of a horse he had to stare at one night as it lay only four paces in front of his position. The next day, he discovered a large shell crater that had been created by the constant German and "English" artillery fire, and "after much effort" he and his comrades dragged the rotting carcass into it.★

Eventually the List Regiment went into action near the small Belgian town of Messines, not far from one of the most famous battle sites of the war—the once-grand medieval city of Ypres. There they were part of the opening stages of what would be known as the First Battle of Ypres. It was a typically chaotic early operation involving an inexperienced unit. Hitler could make no sense of the battle area, and was able "to see next to nothing in the foggy witches' cauldron spread out" in front of him. But he would soon be exposed to the destructive reality of modern firepower. When given the order to attack, the List Regiment rushed forward, immediately taking casualties. Thankfully for the Bavarians, the British at this point in the war still had limited supplies of machine guns, but the few on hand started extracting a bloody toll. Trying to keep themselves from being exposed, Hitler and the other List soldiers were forced into a disjointed series of leaps "across meadows and turnip fields . . . wire entanglements and hedges." Eventually the Bavarians, accompanied by a unit of Württembergers, attacked over the bodies of "dead and wounded Englishmen." British resistance was fierce and the Germans were forced into "many bloody hand-to-hand skirmishes" before the first line of British trenches was taken. Some British soldiers surrendered with their hands in the air; those that did not, Hitler claimed, "were mowed down."[35]

German casualties were heavy. When Hitler and his fellow soldiers discovered that one of their favourite officers, a "madcap major," was "lying on the ground with his chest torn wide open, and a heap of bodies all around him," they thirsted for revenge. They badgered the dead major's adjutant to allow them to make a fresh attack. The fight then reached a climax. Four times the List Regiment tried to break through the British lines and four times they were thrown back by defensive firepower. At one point a bullet tore through the left

★ Much of Hitler's World War I military experience occurred across from British lines on the Western Front. However, for him the enemy was invariably the "English," a habit that expressed an outlook he would keep throughout his life.

sleeve of Hitler's uniform. He claimed that only a "miracle" had saved him.

In the end, it was the introduction of heavy artillery that Hitler was convinced made the difference. The Germans brought up some of the largest field guns they had, 21cm howitzers.* These wide, stubby guns fired shells weighing 250 pounds. Hitler exulted at their destructive power, claiming that they produced enormous craters, "each large enough for a hay-cart to turn around in without difficulty."[36] The British, who had not yet constructed a full trench line, seemed to him unable resist the weight of explosives that descended on their lines and were forced to pull back, leaving the field to the Germans.† A small part of the Western Front had now been defined.

Hitler's descriptions should be taken with a large grain of salt. The German attack with such raw soldiers was not nearly as straightforward, and his description of the badgering of an officer to allow the soldiers to expose themselves again in a revenge attack seems more than a little mock-heroic. In reality, the German performance was mixed, and a large number of their casualties seem to have been caused by friendly fire. What is true, however, is that the attack happened, Hitler experienced it, and it helped to develop his view of war.

The List Regiment suffered extreme casualties. Hitler claimed that in a four-day period the regiment had shrunk from 3,000 men to 600, a calculation that seems only slightly exaggerated. The regiment's official rolls say that only 725 of the original 3,000 men were ready for combat when the dust settled, and it had suffered an even higher casualty rate amongst its officers, with only four of the original thirty or so officers fit for duty.[37] It would be a long while until the List Regiment was considered strong enough to undertake significant operations. They were put in a relatively quiet part of the line until their strength could be rebuilt with fresh recruits.

---

* These were often called mortars by the German troops and Hitler refers to them as such, but they were howitzers firing high-arcing, low-velocity shells.

† Another view is that the British were forced to withdraw because they ran out of ammunition. Hitler, however, was determined to tell acquaintances back in Germany that it was the German heavy artillery that made the difference.

Hitler's descriptions also reveal how he liked to mix reality with exaggeration. In *Mein Kampf*, he made a great deal about the transformative impact of his early war experiences; how the "romance of battle had been replaced by horror" while "exuberant joy was stifled by mortal fear."[38] Many soldiers with similar experiences were gripped by a revulsion towards war, and a cynicism towards power and authority. Hitler, however, reacted to war by taking his pre-existing nationalist chauvinism and turning his paranoia up a notch. He now claimed that the war was one to cleanse Germany of foreign sickness. If he was "lucky enough to return to the fatherland" he wanted to find it "a purer place, less riddled with foreign influences, so that the daily sacrifices of hundreds of thousands of us and the torrent of blood that keeps flowing here day to day against an international world of enemies, will not only help smash Germany's foes outside but our inner internationalism, too, will collapse."[39]

Hitler was an enthusiastic participant in this war of smashing. His initial performance under fire showed that he had no doubts, and for the rest of the war he was known to do his duty diligently. Not long after the First Battle of Ypres, it is said that Hitler risked his own life to save that of the List Regiment's commander. In November, when Lieutenant Colonel Philipp Engelhardt walked into an open, exposed position, leaving him an easy target for enemy sharpshooters, Hitler and another soldier rushed to protect him. They blanketed their commander's body until they could usher him back to cover.[40] During the battle itself, Hitler was commended for risking his life by running back to headquarters to tell them that his unit was being fired on by other German units.[41] He was eventually awarded the Iron Cross, Second Class, for his actions, the highest award that could be bestowed on someone of his rank. When he received his medal, he called it the "happiest day of my life."[42] As a sign of his standing, Hitler was promoted to corporal and at the same time named a regimental dispatch runner. War and the German Army, for the first time in Hitler's life, had brought him real success.

These developments, particularly becoming a dispatch runner, also determined how Hitler would see, hear and smell the war until 1918.[43] A dispatch runner in the era before efficient combat radios and telephones was the link between the commanders and the units in the front line. They were soldiers considered particularly reliable, who could be trusted not to shirk their duty. There were eight runners assigned to the List Regiment's headquarters, responsible for taking orders to the battalions and bringing back reports. In *Mein Kampf*, Hitler never admitted to serving as a dispatch runner, making it seem like he spent most of the war in the front-line trenches. Later, when the truth came out, the role of dispatch runner was held up by Nazis as particularly heroic, a sign of his willingness to expose himself to enemy fire for the sake of the regiment.

The truth was more prosaic. Being a dispatch runner was a much superior posting to being in the front line—in ways that had great appeal to Hitler. Headquarters were kept far out of machine-gun range and direct sight of the enemy. The List Regiment headquarters, for example, was usually about ten kilometres (more than six miles) from the front line. Even then, he would not normally be asked to take messages to forward front-line positions, but to battalion headquarters, which were also kept a way back to provide protection.

When not carrying messages, the runners could relax in relatively peaceful, at times sunny, surroundings that were the envy of soldiers at the front. Hitler was known to spend his free time reading or even painting, drinking tea or brooding. Being around headquarters, food was also easier to scrounge and often of better quality. As a soldier Hitler had a voracious appetite and became adept at squirrelling away extra food. He discovered a way to remove sweet biscuits from the bottoms of boxes, making it look like the containers had been undisturbed. Later in the war, when food was running short, Hitler, who had not yet embraced vegetarianism, became skilled at scrounging dogs and cats to eat. He was known to prefer cat.[44]

Being at headquarters was also considerably more hygienic. Soldiers at the front had to live in the mire, keeping their heads below the tops of the trenches, wet from the constant rain and covered in the mud of their subterranean world. They could even be swallowed up by the muck. In May 1915, during the Battle of Aubers Ridge, the British exploded a mine under the soldiers of the List Regiment's front line.[45] Scores of Hitler's comrades were buried alive. Soldiers at the front also lived amongst the constant sights and smells of death. Particularly after battles, no man's land between the trenches could be covered in decomposing bodies, and their distinctive smell of sweet putrescence would pervade the front line. When the hyper-fastidious Hitler told his Munich acquaintance Ernst Hepp he had been made a runner, he made great play about it being more danger-ous but admitted that it was "slightly less dirty work."[46]

Indeed, Hitler clung tight to his position as a dispatch runner throughout the war. Offered the opportunity of promotion, he always refused. A promotion would have in all likelihood returned him to the front line, and he had no desire to part from the relative comfort and his fellow soldiers that he lived with at headquarters. As time went on, this group became a surrogate family to Hitler, and he was more attached to them than to any other people he encountered during his life, apart from Klara. In return, his colleagues, even though they saw Hitler as a strange fish, trusted him.

He was certainly different to most soldiers. Compared to his com-rades, Hitler was intense, sullen and outrageously prudish—and because of this was the target of constant teasing by his new family. His comrades would, for instance, deliberately make defeatist com-ments about the course of the war, just to provoke him into one of his inevitable angry rants about the enemies of Germany. Even more cutting, they regularly teased him about women—which would cause deep embarrassment. Hitler was a lifelong misogynist who found intelligent women threatening. Even when dictator, he pre-ferred the company of younger girls who did not find him a bore and never challenged him personally and intellectually. He was terribly shy when it came to sex, and during his time in Vienna had gone out of his way to avoid women at all costs. There is a good chance that by the time the war started he was still a virgin, which made him a target of the others at headquarters. They teased him about not visiting the brothels that inevitably followed the army. Hitler would get flus-tered, once responding to such a provocation by falling back on nationalism. He accused his tormentors of having "no German sense of honour left at all," which was met with hoots of laughter from his more cynical comrades.[47]

The greatest friend Hitler made as a dispatch runner was a dog named Foxl. Hitler viewed human beings as biological imperatives, controlled mostly by their racial characteristics. Dogs, on the other hand, were worthy of affection, as long as they could be controlled, and Foxl became the uber-Hitlerian pet. Hitler stumbled across him in January 1915, when he saw Foxl hunting for rats in the trenches. The dog "fought against me, and tried to bite me," but Hitler wrestled him into submission. He took pains to keep the dog nearby at all times, sleeping beside Foxl, taking control of his feeding, training him in tricks and even tying the dog up in a trench so he couldn't escape when Hitler had to deliver his dispatches. This smothering did the trick, and after a while Foxl became the devoted, submissive companion Hitler had always craved. He would even growl if anyone he didn't recognize approached Hitler. "It was crazy how fond I was of the beast," Hitler recalled. Later in the war Foxl disappeared. Hitler believed he was stolen by a shifty railway worker who tried at one point to buy the dog from him. Years later he still raged at the loss, saying that the "swine who stole my dog doesn't realize what he did to me."[48]

If being a dispatch runner had its perks—from food to relative safety, and even the ability to keep pets—it could still be dangerous work. When runners had particularly important information to deliver, often two were sent with identical messages in case one of them was killed. Hitler claimed he was made a regimental dispatch runner because three of the eight men in the position had been killed during the first day of fighting around Ypres.[49] As a runner Hitler was seriously wounded twice during the war—once by shrapnel and once by gas. And a number of other times, even allowing for his penchant for dramatic licence, he came very close to death.

One of the greatest dangers that he regularly faced in World War I helped cement an assumption that would govern his thinking in World War II: the decisive power of modern, heavy artillery. Far more than the machine gun, Hitler feared artillery fire. When German armies were marching through Russia in October 1941, and victory seemed in his grasp, during one of his evening meditations Hitler thought back on the dangers he had faced when delivering messages in the last war. "How often I myself have had to face a powerful artillery barrage, in order to carry a simple post-card!"[50] He raged against the commanders who had forced him and other runners out into the open against modern guns, claiming that "throughout the 1914–1918 war, some twenty thousand men were uselessly sacrificed by employing them as runners on missions that could have been equally well accomplished by night, with less danger."

Hitler's fears about artillery did not end when his messages were delivered—for it represented the greatest threat to his safety when relaxing back at headquarters too. Even though regimental headquarters were deliberately placed out of sight of the enemy, if found they could be targeted. Since the Napoleonic Wars a century earlier, artillery had developed as much as, if not more than, any form of weaponry. When Napoleonic armies met, artillery had been a line-of-sight weapon made of crude iron that could fire a projectile less than a kilometre and with little accuracy. In the intervening century, leaps in metallurgy—particularly the development of high-strength, higher-purity steels—combined with industrial-specification precision manufacture meant that guns, like the 21cm howitzer which so impressed Hitler near Ypres in 1914, had exponentially longer ranges. They could fire identical factory-range shells so high in the air that they could reach far beyond human visibility—more than ten times as far as the cannonballs at the Battle of Waterloo.

This made long-range bombardment a particularly stressful event. Soldiers, usually unable to see the weapons firing at them, often had to rely on their ears to know if they were under attack. British, French and German shells all made distinctive sounds as their different shapes passed through the air. Soldiers had to guess from these sounds if they were soon to be hit, leading to panic-stricken dashes into cover. In 1942, thinking back to his World War I experiences, Hitler argued that it was a good thing that German projectiles were noisier than their Russian equivalents. German weapons made "such a hellish din that nobody can endure it . . . It has a psychological effect in addition to the material effect. There's no point in hiding the discharge of the shot from the enemy, for in any case there's no means of protecting oneself against it."[51] He was right in one sense. It often made no difference whether a soldier heard a shell coming or not. By the end of the war, it was estimated that 60 per cent of all casualties suffered on the battlefields had been caused by artillery.[52]

And these casualties could come from behind-the-lines personnel, such as Hitler at headquarters. This was because of improvements in distance spotting. In 1914 much of this was done by balloon spotters, but as the war went on and aircraft technology developed, spotting by plane became increasingly important.[53] With such improvements in spotting, targeting previously difficult-to-see headquarters became a high priority. Once located, headquarters could instantly find themselves transformed into the object of high-intensity bombardments, with the first salvos only revealing themselves as their shells were arcing downwards, emitting their distinctive cries.

Even though headquarters were sturdily built and solidly reinforced—increasingly so as the war went on—shells weighing hundreds of pounds, descending from a mile in the air, could smash through almost any protection, killing or wounding the inhabitants. This was a worry that regularly played on Hitler's mind. Once, he was actually spared by an accurate Allied artillery attack, which wiped out a command bunker so quickly that he was unable to get inside and take cover. In 1916, his luck would not be so good. In October, around the town of Fromelles, he was in a dispatch runners' dugout when accurate British artillery found them. A shell made an almost direct hit, and Hitler's thigh was torn by shrapnel, leading to a long convalescence in Germany.

It was one example of how World War I combat was setting certain ideas in his mind that he would never shake. The largest, most powerful, most spectacular weapons—particularly those built by German ingenuity—were the best. Having the ability to blast away at soldiers such as himself was the key to victory. More lessons, of course, remained to be learned.

6. Winston Churchill:
Learning Strategic Restraint

Winston Churchill returned home from South Africa in 1900 determined to re-enter the world of politics. He again stood as one of the candidates for Oldham and was elected to the House of Commons in October, becoming a Member of Parliament at just twenty-five. At first a Conservative like his father and grandfather, Churchill soon drifted from the party of his birth, repelled as the Conservatives abandoned their free-trade policy to support higher tariffs. This, Churchill feared, would lead to substantially higher food prices for his working-class constituents. Moreover, he remained worried about any possible alienation of the British worker from the empire, and this made him more interested in social reform. He began to identify with the opposition Liberal Party, and in 1906, just after the Liberals won a huge majority in Parliament, Churchill "ratted" (in his own words) on the Conservatives and joined the party in power.

As a Liberal, Churchill came very much under the sway of the most mesmerizing politician of the age, David Lloyd George—who had come to politics from as different a background from Churchill as one could have imagined in late nineteenth-century Britain. Born into an obscure family in rural Wales, Lloyd George worked himself up from practically nothing, using his cunning, cynicism and wits. He was also a spellbinding public speaker. After becoming a lawyer, he entered politics, camping himself squarely on the left wing of the Liberal Party. He made a name as one of Britain's most outspoken critics of the Boer War, and jingoes such as Churchill thought of him as a traitor, labelling him a "pro-Boer."

By the time the Boer War ended, Lloyd George was a rising star. When the Liberals took power, he entered the cabinet first as the president of the Board of Trade, and in 1908 was named Chancellor of the Exchequer, the second-most-important office in the British state. In charge of national finances, Lloyd George took the audacious step of calling for old-age pensions for the working class, to be funded by higher taxes on rich landowners—the first stirrings of a redistributive welfare state in British history. This move precipitated a political crisis, as the unelected House of Lords, dominated by Conservative aristocrats, played into Lloyd George's hands by noisily defending its hereditary rights—allowing the chancellor to cast himself as the protector of democracy and the people.

By his side in the fight against the Lords stood the grandson of the Duke of Marlborough, Winston Churchill. Indeed, after 1908, when Churchill himself entered the cabinet as Lloyd George's successor at the Board of Trade, he seemed almost a clone of the radical Welshman. In every major dispute Churchill sided with Lloyd George, making similar arguments in support of the latter's position, and often acting as the shield-maiden to Lloyd George's radicalism. Most incongruously, Churchill joined the Chancellor of the Exchequer in the battle against more naval spending when the Anglo-German naval arms race started in earnest in 1909.

It was a fateful time in the origins of the coming global war. Before 1908, the German Navy was not seen as a particularly great threat to the Royal Navy—that was the position usually held by the combined French and Russian fleets. In 1908, however, British intelligence sources warned the government that the Germans, with their advanced industrial economy, had started building as many dreadnought battleships (considered the most important vessels afloat and the key to winning any great naval war) as they possibly could, as a direct challenge to Britain.* Had this been the case, the Germans would have soon presented an existential threat to the British Empire. Densely populated due to the nineteenth-century boom in urbanization and

---

* Dreadnoughts were big-gun battleships, an innovation the British introduced in 1906. They had a much heavier weight of fire than earlier battleships and could engage at greater ranges. It was decided by most of the major navies that dreadnoughts made all earlier battleships obsolete, and soon after they came into service naval strength was calculated by comparing numbers of dreadnoughts possessed by each country.

industrialization, Britain could not produce enough food to feed itself. It needed to control the world's seas in order to import huge amounts of foodstuffs from North and South America.[1] A German Navy capable of cutting British trade would be able to starve the United Kingdom into helplessness in short order. This was why the Anglo-German naval race became so intense.

In 1909, the Royal Navy, with strong support in the cabinet, argued that Britain should start a mammoth and expensive construction programme of eight dreadnoughts to meet the supposed German threat. A public cry of "We want eight, and we won't wait!" went up amongst the fleet's supporters. Lloyd George, who needed government money to fund his old-age pensions, found himself on the defensive. He decided to try to contain this extra naval spending, arguing that there was no need to build so many warships, and he received Churchill's undiluted support. In fact, it was Churchill who supplied most of the written arguments in cabinet for those arguing for a smaller naval programme and a smaller naval budget.[2]

In the end, Lloyd George and Churchill were overwhelmed by the larger pro-navy majority in the cabinet, but their alliance was cemented. However, soon they would find themselves on opposite sides of the naval debate when in 1911 Churchill was named First Lord of the Admiralty—the civilian head of the Royal Navy, representing the fleet to the cabinet, and much of the time to the people. Considering how central the Royal Navy and sea power were to the might of the British Empire, it was one of the most important, and well-publicized, positions in the country.

Churchill was an ideal selection. Only thirty-seven years old, with thinning, red-tinged hair, a short, squat body, and a countenance described by the prime minister's wife as "ugly," he had enough dynamism to counteract his appearance. In a cabinet filled with Liberal grandees and chaired by Prime Minister H. H. Asquith—a sophisticated lawyer with a preternaturally calm air and a tendency towards detachment—Churchill was an *enfant terrible*. Even though he was a civilian, he often ostentatiously appeared in military dress, complete with a sword, rows of medals and, when possible, a large, cocked naval headdress. He spent many days touring naval facilities, speaking to the press, making trips on the First Lord's yacht, and turning himself into the public face of British naval power.

Churchill's showiness should not hide the reality that he was also effective. Almost immediately after he became First Lord, the naval race with the Germans reached a crescendo. When it looked like the two countries might embark on a new round of dreadnought construction, the German government caved in and decided not to push up their pace. It was a comprehensive victory for the British government and the Royal Navy, and meant that when war broke out their dreadnought fleet would be much larger than the Germans'.

Having forced the Germans to give way seemed to heighten Churchill's interest and excitement at running the Royal Navy. Between 1911 and 1914 he immersed himself in the understanding of naval technology and strategy, visited practically every naval facility in the United Kingdom, lived much of the time on the First Lord's yacht and let his mind rehearse constant war plans with Germany.

When the war started in 1914, Churchill was thus poised to be one of the driving forces in the Liberal government and had at his disposal all the necessary tools to make himself a historic First Lord of the Admiralty. And yet his impulsive, still boyish view of war and strategy continued to hold him back. For all his knowledge of the economic and technological nature of modern sea power, Churchill retained a love of risk and danger that clashed repeatedly against a more sober understanding of strategy. The British went into World War I with such naval dominance that they had no need to seek out the German fleet and risk battle. They could, and did, quickly shut down Germany's worldwide trade, confining the great land power to the European continent and limiting the German war machine and population to only the resources that could be acquired on its doorstep. At the same time, the British—and through them their allies the French and Russians—were given access to the supplies of the entire world, which soon began flowing into their ports, factories and stomachs.

The Germans could sometimes make headlines with daring raids in distant seas—such as those carried out by Admiral Graf Spee's East Asia Squadron, which operated in the far Pacific and around the coast of South America during the first few months of war. Yet these were flea-bites on the course of the war. After Spee managed a few minor victories, the Royal Navy obliterated his entire force in the Battle of Coronel on November 1, 1914. After that, the British Grand Fleet, based in the wonderfully large and strategically located Orkney Island harbour at Scapa Flow, was left to watch and wait, hoping that the Germans would be rash enough to send out their main High Seas Fleet for battle. In the meantime, the balance of world production would start to turn decisively in the Allies' favour.

In the end the Germans would, unexpectedly, turn to a new form of weapon, the submarine, to attack British trade. But in 1914 Churchill was not worried about this, dismissing any notion of an unrestricted submarine offensive as extremely unlikely, arguing that the Germans would not attempt anything so "uncivilized."

Such quiet dominance sat uneasily with Churchill. From the moment shooting started, he bombarded Asquith with plans and notions, even pushing the idea that the British should schedule operations in accordance with the predictions of astrologer R. G. Hickling, who Churchill believed was uncannily correct in hitting auspicious dates.[3] Churchill was also desperate to get as close to the fighting as possible. One of his first forays was to Belgium, where, if he had had his way, he might have ended his life fighting a heroic if doomed fortress battle.

The speed with which the Germans first moved through Belgium and northern France had come as the rudest of shocks to the entire Asquith government. By early September 1914, a forbidding gloom took hold of London when it seemed that the Germans might capture Paris. Even after the front stabilized with the French victory at the Battle of the Marne, things looked ominous as the Germans moved to seize as much of Belgium as possible while a trench line was dug from the Alps to the sea.

On October 2, the Belgian government informed the British that they were going to abandon Antwerp, one of the largest ports in Europe and one of the few remaining Belgian cities in Allied hands. When the news came, Churchill was alone with only the foreign secretary, Sir Edward Grey, and the new secretary of state for war—his old nemesis from the Sudan, Sir Herbert Kitchener. Churchill decided immediately to head to Belgium and see the situation for himself. Leaving at midnight, the "intrepid" Churchill, according to Asquith, set out to "infuse" into Belgian backbones "the necessary quantity of starch."[4] Commandeering government trains, warships and even cars, he was at the front by noon the following day.

What a sight he was. Always aware of the power of military fashion, the civilian First Lord of the Admiralty had decked himself out in a dashing blue military uniform with gold buttons and all the trimmings. It was actually the uniform of a London trade organization, but the Belgians would have had no idea.[5] Confronted by what seemed to him a demoralized Belgian government and depressed king, Churchill, relying on the dynamism of his personality, temporarily lifted their spirits. He promised to send British reinforcements to hold Antwerp, telegraphing London to immediately dispatch two Royal Navy Marine brigades with five days of rations and two million rounds of ammunition.[6] Within hours, he was demanding another two million rounds. By October 4, Churchill had decided that he alone would be able to save the day. He telegraphed Asquith saying that he would resign his office as First Lord if he was given a military command at the appropriate rank and made supreme commander of all forces fighting to save Antwerp.* Churchill, according to Asquith, had "tasted blood" and felt like a "tiger to raven for more."[7]†

The reaction in London showed Churchill's peculiar reputation in action. When his melodramatic telegram was read out in cabinet, there was sniggering around the table and it was met with a "Homeric laugh."[8] Yet when Churchill returned home on October 7, his daring and energy proved infectious. In a private meeting, he lectured Asquith on his need to eventually be given a major military command, exclaiming that "a political career was nothing . . . in comparison

---

* As two major generals would have been put under his command, Churchill would have to have been given the rank of at least lieutenant general to meet his requirements—two steps below field marshal.
† Here Churchill used the word "raven" in the archaic sense of needing to devour voraciously.

with military glory."[9] Asquith told his mistress that Churchill was "certainly one of the people in the world one would choose to go tiger-hunting with."[10] Asquith's wife, the eternally forbearing Margot Asquith, was also complimentary of Churchill's daring—with one caveat. She wondered what it was that made Churchill such a compelling figure when he had such a disorganized, indeed "noisy," mind. She decided it was his "courage and colour—his amazing mixture of industry and enterprise." And yet, something inside her realized that this quality also posed a huge problem, and she added, "*He takes huge risks.*"[11] She had summarized Churchill's strengths and weaknesses perfectly. In 1914–15, he argued that the war would be won by the side that took a series of great risks and emerged victorious. As he said: "Victory is only wrested by running risks."[12] The question for him was picking the right ones.

Though he was thwarted in his desire for the Antwerp supreme command (thankfully, as it turned out, as the Belgians evacuated the city and the Germans marched in almost immediately after he left), Churchill was determined to find some other bold enterprise to support. His need for action was so strong that it even overrode his sober understanding of the present state of military technology. The rational side of Churchill's nature told him that the offensive was becoming increasingly dangerous. Ever since his experiences in the Boer War, Churchill had remarked on the killing power of modern weapons. Once the trench lines had been constructed through France and Belgium, he became wary of large-scale offensives on the Western Front.[13]

Yet this wariness did not stop him from devising risky operations in other theatres. In October 1914, in a fit of frustration brought about by inactivity, he concocted a wild plan to use old British battleships to fight their way into Germany by steaming down the Elbe river system.[14] By the end of the year, he was pressing Asquith to undertake what would probably have been one of the most disastrous seaborne invasions in history. Desperate to come up with a way to use the Royal Navy against the Germans, Churchill wanted to force a way into the Baltic Sea. He pushed for a D-Day-type attack on the northernmost German province, Schleswig-Holstein, and the insertion of British troops into Denmark (which he assumed would simply decide to throw in with the British government at that time). In late December he sent Asquith a detailed proposal for an attack that he wanted launched by March.[15] The British were to send their navy directly into the Heligoland Bight, just off the German coast and only a few miles from the German Navy's main base at Wilhelmshaven. There the British were supposed to seize an island, construct a supporting base and quickly lay down a large minefield to keep the Germans in harbour. When that was ready, another invasion, this time of the north German mainland, would ensue. Ultimately, the neutral Danes were supposed to acquiesce, and thus the Royal Navy would be given access to the Baltic. Thankfully, Churchill received little support from his colleagues and his plan went nowhere. But soon he found another dangerous operation to back, one that would almost end his political career—the attempt to force the Dardanelles, better known as the Gallipoli campaign.

The Dardanelles is a narrow waterway separating Europe from Asia; the Gallipoli peninsula comprises the northern bank, the Troad peninsula the southern, and the strait connects the Mediterranean and Aegean to the Black Sea by way of the Sea of Marmara. On the northern shore of the Marmara lay the Ottoman capital of Constantinople, guarding another tight waterway leading directly into the Black Sea. Passage through the Dardanelles was the first stage in the journey to reach Russian ports by ship, but the channel was completely within the Turkish Ottoman Empire, a belligerent against the Allied powers. Any attack was sure to be met by fierce resistance.

Some have insisted that Churchill was a late convert to the Dardanelles attack because he only endorsed the specific plan in January 1915. This gives the wrong impression. Churchill started planning for an attack on Turkey in August 1914, months before the Ottomans even joined the war.[16] Such an offensive was fundamentally rooted in his strategic vision, which, regardless of his more left-wing domestic stances over the previous fourteen years, remained fixed on the strengthening and even the extending of the British Empire. An attack on Turkey would allow the British to seize more parts of the Ottoman Empire, while also strengthening their hold over

Egypt and its vital waterways to India and the Pacific empire. In November 1914, Churchill made this connection explicit when he argued in the War Cabinet that "the ideal method of defending Egypt was by an attack on the Gallipoli Peninsula. This, if successful, would give us control of the Dardanelles, and we could dictate terms at Constantinople."[17]

When it became clear to Churchill in January 1915 that he would get no support for his proposed attack into northern Germany, he redirected his energy on the Dardanelles. The specific plan he supported had been brought to him by the most remarkable British naval officer of the generation, Admiral Sir John (Jackie) Fisher. Just as energetic as and even more combustible than Churchill, Fisher had been First Sea Lord—the professional head of the Royal Navy—from 1904 to 1910, and had started the dreadnought revolution which laid the groundwork for British naval dominance in 1914. Fisher was also a force of nature who would bombard politicians and friends with notes full of exclamation points, underlines, and letters so large that a few lines would fill the whole page. He had so attached himself to the notion of British naval supremacy that, when World War I started, Churchill had Fisher brought out of retirement and made First Sea Lord again—a move that was greeted with acclamation.

It was a bad idea. Fisher and Churchill were naturally competitive and started butting up against each other immediately. After a few weeks back in office, Fisher complained that Churchill had so imposed his will on the Admiralty that he had cowed all the naval staff, making them incapable of taking initiative.* Fisher, however, was not to be cowed. He proposed to Churchill a naval bombardment on Turkish forts protecting the Dardanelles. Like Churchill, he was worried that Russia, cut off from its two great western Allies, needed support, and he believed that opening the Dardanelles would be both strategically and psychologically heartening to the Russians. Fisher was interested in a low-risk, naval-only operation that would use ships not needed

---

* Fisher had a point. While Churchill was more than happy to have senior generals at the War Cabinet, he often tried to block senior admirals from attending. He wanted to make sure that his voice was the only one heard from the Admiralty.

by the Grand Fleet in Scapa Flow. He wanted to do nothing that would give the Germans any advantage if they did sortie out to the North Sea in search of battle.

Churchill swiftly took Fisher's plan and made it his own. He called for the use of bigger, more powerful warships, and was willing to significantly weaken the Grand Fleet's superiority over the Germans to make the attack happen. Indeed, he was willing to reduce the Royal Navy's number of dreadnoughts in North Sea waters to only parity with the Germans in order to attack the Dardanelles—making the argument that British warships were individually more effective than their German equivalents.★

His support pushed the attack ahead with extraordinary speed. Within weeks a large British naval force in the Eastern Mediterranean started battering the Turkish forts which protected the opening to the Dardanelles—at first destroying their walls and guns from such a distance that the Turks could not respond. The plan was to force an opening into the Dardanelles, to be followed up by a landing of troops on the Gallipoli beaches on the European side of the waterway. Eventually, it was assumed, British forces would victoriously march into Constantinople, having opened a naval route to Russia and transformed the balance of power in the Near and Middle East. Unfortunately, it was a plan that had almost no chance of success.[18]

Launched on February 17, the campaign went well for the British during the first few weeks. Word came out that the Turks were running out of ammunition and Churchill was ablaze, calling for more forces to be thrown into the battle. Envisaging the historic triumphs about to happen, he lectured the War Cabinet that "the prize we ought to seek from this action [is] nothing less than the occupation by the Allies of Turkey in Europe. All must pass into our hands, and

---

★ This was not the case, as the Battle of Jutland would attest. If British battleships generally had a heavier weight of fire than their German equivalents, the latter were better built and more survivable. Had there been a great sea battle between equally matched German and British fleets, the Germans might very well have won, and the course of history been very different.

we ought to accept nothing less."[19] To Margot Asquith, Churchill's bluster became "insufferable," and she added that it was "all *vanity*—he is devoured by vanity."[20]

He would get his comeuppance. On March 18, as a large British and French force attempted to fight their way up the entrance of the Dardanelles, three British capital ships (two early battlecruisers and an older battleship) were struck by mines in rapid succession. These losses, the most damaging the Royal Navy had suffered since the Battle of Trafalgar, led the commander on the spot, Admiral John de Robeck, to ask for ground troops to land on the Gallipoli beaches ahead of schedule to help reduce Turkish resistance. Churchill supported the escalation, optimistic that British soldiers would be enough to bring the Turks to heel.

There was an assumption on the part of Churchill (and many other British leaders at the time, both civilian and military) that, in the end, the Turks would be unable to stand up to British forces. Decades of killing non-Europeans had convinced them of their innate superiority, and when faced with real resistance they seemed unable to rationally calculate the odds of defeat. On April 25, a large British Empire force, almost half of which comprised Australian and New Zealand troops, started landing on the Gallipoli beaches. Churchill had at first estimated that 50,000 British ground troops should be enough.[21] As it was, approximately 70,000–80,000 landed—and quickly went nowhere.

The Turkish Army proved far more effective than Churchill had expected. Near to their bases of supply, they were able to move forces to the landing areas quickly and entrench themselves on the higher ground overlooking the beaches. The result was a British catastrophe. The British, Australians and New Zealanders were soon staring upwards at a numerically larger, well-equipped and determined enemy. After battering themselves fruitlessly against the Turkish lines, the invaders were left huddling in soft, sandy trenches searching for whatever cover they could find. The Turks, up on the ridges, could drop artillery shells right on the exposed troops.

Churchill received a first-hand account from his brother, Jack, who had been one of the first soldiers ashore and quickly learned that the Turks were an enemy who would not be brushed aside. In early May, he wrote to Churchill describing the unfolding disaster: "Here we are, a comparatively small force clinging on to the end of the Gallipoli Peninsula, and having the prospect of fighting the whole Turkish Empire!"[22] Yet, having committed himself, Winston Churchill could not retreat. He called for the massive reinforcement of failure, claiming that landing thousands more men would turn the tide. It was a desperate move, but one that he was becoming powerless to see enacted. The growing debacle was eating away at his political position.

The first casualty was his already combustible relationship with Fisher. The First Sea Lord, who had envisaged a far more limited operation in the Dardanelles, wanted to pull back from the ongoing disaster and do nothing that might jeopardize British superiority over the Germans. He chafed at Churchill's domineering behaviour, and in acts of extreme disloyalty made his feelings known to both the government and the opposition Conservatives (who considered Churchill a traitor for switching parties in 1904). By the middle of May 1915, Fisher had had enough and resigned in a huff as First Sea Lord. Before he could be stopped, he had jumped on the first available train to Scotland.

Fisher's resignation, coming on top of the Gallipoli failures, destroyed Churchill's political position. With a false rumour about a shortage of shells being provided to the British Army adding more pressure, the entire Asquith government was soon at risk, and Churchill would be their first sacrifice. To bring the Conservatives into a coalition government, Churchill was demoted as First Lord and made Chancellor of the Duchy of Lancaster, a title which allowed him to sit in on the cabinet, but crucially not the War Cabinet, the small group of senior ministers who made most of the important strategic decisions. Indeed, as chancellor, Churchill had no governmental responsibilities or department to run; it was a position usually bestowed on elder statesmen on the downslope of their careers. One could not have chosen a worse office for Churchill—at the table of power but with no cutlery—and it caused him to sink into a depression. Deciding his only choice was to don a soldier's uniform once again, he asked Asquith to make him a major general and give him command of an entire corps. Asquith demurred at this extraordinary request, but did promise to help him secure a decent command. With no other option, Churchill resigned from the government and headed back to war.

On November 18, 1915, Churchill slipped across the English Channel to rejoin his old regiment, now called the Queen's Own Oxfordshire Hussars. Invited to dine by the commander of the British Expeditionary Force, Sir John French, an old acquaintance from the Boer War, he was quickly offered the command of a brigade (about 5,000 men). This would have come with a promotion to brigadier—not a major general, but still a dramatic promotion from the rank of major, which he had been when he left the army.[23] Before taking command, however, Churchill believed he needed some exposure to the realities of trench warfare and was posted as an observer to the Grenadier Guards, one of the British Army's most well-trained and looked-after units.

What Churchill discovered was a type of warfare transformed from the pageantry of the imperial age. One of the first operations he saw being prepared was a prisoner snatch by a squad of ten Guards. This small group was being sent out under the cover of darkness, to sneak up on one of the German advanced posts, capture some enemy soldiers and smuggle them back to British lines for interrogation. In case the British captured more Germans than expected, the men were given clubs to beat the surplus prisoners to death quietly.[24]

As he surveyed this new battlefield, the different sides of Churchill's "noisy" mind latched on to very different things. The journalist in him was intrigued by the sights, sounds and smells. The Guards were stationed near the town of Neuve Chapelle, in a topography that had been completely reshaped by the war. Once prosperous farmland with tidy villages and bustling churches, it was now desolate and muddy, the fields abandoned, the buildings shattered, the trees skeletal—a hellish landscape criss-crossed with lines upon lines of deep, dank trenches. During the day, soldiers were careful to keep their heads down, while at night the moon could shine brightly, silhouetting large bats fluttering overhead. The British trench lines, garbage-strewn and chaotic, were a gruesome spectacle. The previous occupiers had buried dead bodies in the embankments, and now decaying human feet or bits of clothing could be seen breaking through the earth.

The strategist in him was alarmed. What Churchill was finally observing up close was something that he had feared from the start of the war—though the reality was far worse. The trenches dug by both sides were so well constructed, stretching back in line after line, that they made any offensive operations an impossibility. Even the heaviest artillery barrages made little difference to their integrity. Sure, artillery might smash one line, allowing for an initial British advance, but there would be others manned by determined Germans armed with machine guns, trench bombs and artillery. The more he saw it in action, the more he was convinced of the efficiency and deadliness of the German Army. Everything from its artillery bombardments to its trench lines seemed well planned and well executed. Breaking them would require a tremendous toll of casualties, and for the moment at least this looked practically impossible.

The politician in him was terrified at the loss of life this bloodshed meant for the British working man. Even during this quiet period at the front, there was a steady drip of losses—a soldier killed by a crack German sniper here, a squad gruesomely injured by a direct shell hit on a dugout there. Already, a generation of experienced soldiers had been decimated, their ranks replaced by raw recruits who had recently been civilians of the most non-martial type. Churchill could see this new generation now being prepared for the slaughter, and understood that if something was not done, the very integrity of the United Kingdom and the entire British Empire was at stake.

Those first impressions of modern war would only strengthen as Churchill spent another six months at the front. His tour occurred at a fortuitous time, between the bloody Battle of Loos (the first time the British used poison gas), which ended in October 1915, and the cataclysm of the Battle of the Somme, which started in July 1916. Had he been present for either of these events he would have undoubtedly acted with his characteristic aggression and risked being killed or badly wounded. Yet even this relatively quiet time was enough to convince him that the British needed to drastically rethink their strategy.

After only two weeks at the front, Churchill wrote a memorandum trying to organize his thoughts, which he titled "Variants of the Offensive." Faced with the reality of trench warfare, Churchill's opposition to any offensives on the Western Front under the present conditions had become adamantine. He now envisioned the defeat of Germany as something that could only be achieved through attrition—not daring and great risk. The sacrifice of a British life should only be made if it would at least result in the loss of a German one. "Any operation on the Western Front is justified if we take at least a life for a life."[25] He was willing to make this sacrifice because the Allies had more men and a much larger worldwide economic base that they could exploit, meaning that in a true war of attrition the Germans stood no chance.

Yet he also knew that as the Germans were occupying practically all of Belgium and much of northern France, it would be incumbent on the Allies to attack—and that put their soldiers at a far greater risk of being killed or seriously wounded than the Germans. Faced with this conundrum, Churchill looked for a technological/industrial solution. He meditated on different technologies that would allow the attacker mobility to go forward and not be mowed down in waves, including increased body armour, hand-held shields, and new trench mortars. He was particularly interested in developing tanks (or, as he called them in the paper, caterpillars).

Churchill had been one of the earliest British backers of tanks. In late 1914, when the secretary to the Committee for Imperial Defence, Maurice Hankey, brought to Churchill's attention a plan to build armour-plated tracked vehicles, the then First Lord was supportive. As the War Office, which ran the army, was uninterested in the new technology, he made tanks an Admiralty project, forming the Landship Committee in 1915, to provide the first real support for their development.[26] His exposure to the trenches brought home to him how important this new technology truly was, and "Variants of the Offensive" was fundamentally a document pressing for the construction of different types of tanks.* He imagined massed formations of armoured fighting vehicles breaking through the German lines, then fanning out on either side to open the breach, allowing troops to push forward and exploit these openings.

Before he could argue for his new strategic ideas in the halls of power, however, Churchill still needed to serve a reasonable tour at the front—though he made sure that his life in the trenches was as comfortable as possible. Immediately after heading into action, he sent his wife Clementine a list of the special clothes and equipment that he would require. He was particularly desperate for sturdy, waterproof footwear—and only boots from the fashionable Fortnum & Mason department store in Piccadilly would do. He also asked for a wide range of goodies, including sardines, chocolates, cheeses (particularly Stilton) and potted meats, and instructed Clementine to send him three bottles of brandy (one of them had to be peach brandy) every ten days.

If he was not going to deny himself some of the finer things in life, Churchill was determined to get stuck in, even when things did not work out exactly as planned. After his tour with the Guards, Churchill was only offered the command of a battalion of fewer than a thousand men, and not the brigade of almost 5,000 that he felt he had been promised. Though he fumed at what he considered a great insult (he blamed Asquith for abandoning him, thinking that the prime minister was afraid of bad publicity), Churchill took the smaller command, determined to make it a success.

His battalion was in the 6th Royal Scots Fusiliers, whose soldiers came from a very different world than that of the Guards or the Hussars. During the Battle of Loos, the battalion had suffered grievous losses in experienced officers and NCOs, and Churchill described the replacement officers as "small middle class Scotsmen— v[er]y brave & willing & intelligent; but of course quite new to

---

* In the document Churchill also stated he believed that other technologies, such as special trench artillery, held out the prospect of more safety for troops taking the offensive, but they received less coverage than his sections on tanks and tracked vehicles.

soldiering."[27] He went in determined to bend the officer corps to his will. When he was first introduced to them, at lunch, he made it clear that things would be run his way, and his way alone. "Gentlemen, I am now your commanding officer. Those who support me I will look after. Those who go against me I will break."[28]

The enlisted men were even more alien to him. Throughout his life, Churchill looked at the average British working man as an exotic creature in need of either appeasement or the smack of firm government. Much of the battalion came from Glasgow's lower middle class; Churchill described them as "grocers, fitters, miners—all Trade Unionists probably." He drilled them in the fundamentals of trench warfare—machine-gun fire, grenade throwing, and digging and maintaining the embankments. To try to understand the culture of the Scottish soldiers, whom he considered to be of a different "race," he asked Clementine to send him a volume of the poetry of Robert Burns. He felt he could comfort the men if he occasionally quoted Burns to them, though had enough self-awareness to worry that any attempt to put on the Scots accent would make him sound ridiculous.[29]

By late January 1916 the battalion was ready to return to the front line, and Churchill led them forward with confidence. The Churchill who brought the Royal Scots Fusiliers into the line near the small town of Ploegsteert (inevitably called Plugstreet by the men) had evolved from the young man who regretted more of his men not being killed charging the Dervishes in Sudan. He now looked after his soldiers with an almost motherly devotion, and inspected their positions assiduously. At night he could be found in the most forward and exposed part of the line, making sure his men were supplied and fed, or preparing them for small operations such as prisoner snatches. During the day he did his best to keep casualties down and liked to make sure that his men were in "safe places along the front line—always the safest."[30] He was a notably lenient commander with those troops he trusted. He avoided imposing harsh penalties for soldiers who disobeyed regulations if he believed the offender was not a shirker. He was so lenient, in fact, that he was eventually reprimanded by headquarters for being too soft.

His lenience was an understandable reaction to the randomness of death in this war. There was no romance on the Western Front. Churchill himself almost became a casualty of German artillery a few times—once being saved by simple good luck. One day he was ordered out for lunch with his commanding general. He tramped across the desolate fields to meet the car that was supposed to take him to his meal, but none ever appeared. After hours of waiting, he stomped back to the lines, cursing his misfortune, only to discover that his headquarters had been demolished by a direct hit just moments after he had left. At another time he was torn when one of his officers was so pleased to have been wounded by German artillery—meaning he would be sent home—that in front of Churchill he kissed a fragment of the shell that had struck him. If Churchill did not endorse such behaviour, he went out of his way to protect himself as much as possible and avoided the ostentatious risks that typified his conduct in India, Sudan and South Africa. Early on during his time at the front, Churchill paid a visit to French forces in a neighbouring sector, and he was gifted a French Adrian helmet. Churchill loved its extra-protective powers—and its distinctiveness, as he liked being photographed in it. As he told Clementine, "I have been given a true steel helmet by the French wh[ich] I am going to wear, as it looks so nice & will perhaps protect my valuable cranium."[31] He also constantly monitored the strength of the sandbag barricades that surrounded his lodgings, and his favourite headquarters was a farmhouse inside which large tree trunks had been placed to support the walls and ceilings.

Churchill now understood that modern weapons had made a mockery of bravery. Machines would determine the outcome of this war, and exposing oneself was more likely to lead to injury or death than anything else. He took his battalion into line with only 700 men (a battalion should have been a thousand), but he didn't mind because they were oversupplied with machine guns. He was convinced that these more than made up for the missing men, and would have taken a terrible toll on the Germans were they stupid enough to attack this part of the line—which they never did.

Soon he was railing against attacks of almost any kind, claiming that this "war is one of mechanics & brains & mere sacrifice of brave & devoted infantry is no substitute & never will be."[32] By April 1916, he had decided that any attacks that year by the British and French armies should be stopped. "I have formed definite opinions about the war. First, we must now make up our minds that there is no chance of our winning in 1916. That is the beginning of wisdom—we must make our plans for a combined attack in the summer of 1917." By that time, he hoped, the "piling up munitions and arming the limitless manhood of Russia" would make a decisive difference. In the meantime: "Let the Germans attack if they will."[33]

Having formed such clear plans in his head, Churchill felt increasingly frustrated by his lack of power to see them implemented. One of the great lies that he liked to tell himself and others while in the trenches was that the focus of war had provided him with a clarity that he had been missing during his political career. When he first went into the line with the Guards, he wrote to Clementine that he had "found happiness & contentment such as I have not known for many months."[34] In truth, the longer he stayed at the front, the more depressed he became at his fall from power. His depressions became so regular that he tried to explain them away, telling his wife that they were at least "real things," not the "terrible and reasonless depressions" that had afflicted him back when he was in office.[35] He raged at what he saw as the betrayals of his former colleagues and scrapped around anywhere he could for political gossip. He felt ignored when hardly anyone in power wrote to him or visited, and complained of the attacks by "spiteful newspapers or gossiping people," though he was careful to hide how much he hurt, claiming "I do not ever show anything but a smiling face to the military world."[36]

He was thus always calculating when he should return to Parliament (he had not resigned his seat when he rejoined the army). He was eventually driven to do so by the appointment of an official Dardanelles inquiry committee, which he felt might besmirch his name. In early May 1916 he determined to "attend to my Parliamentary and public duties," and his battalion was broken up and distributed to other units.[37] If he had retained many boyish traits when the war started, the man that returned to London was more sober, cautious and methodical in his strategic outlook. He now had a holistic war strategy that stretched from the production of weapons to the deployment of forces in the field, all underlined by a coherent geopolitical vision.

The problem he had was that, while still an MP, he had no power. He was thus left fuming when, not long after he returned to politics, the British Army did the exact thing that Churchill had desperately warned against and launched the Somme offensive. The expectation going into the attack was that massed British artillery would smash the Germans, allowing for the kind of breakthrough that the war had not seen in the west since August 1914. Nothing was held back. The Fourth Army, the unit leading the offensive, had about twice as many artillery pieces per mile of front as the British had displaced during the Battle of Loos less than a year before. This concentrated firepower was supposed to smash German barbed wire and pulverize their forward trench lines while killing or at least disorienting the German soldiers on whom their shells were to rain down relentlessly.

It was all a strategic delusion. The German wire was not broken, and their trench lines were left mostly intact. German soldiers, expecting an assault, were safely kept as deep underground as possible. On July 1, the brave soldiers of the Fourth Army left the British trenches and, following orders, moved in slow, orderly formation towards the German lines, expecting to find only destruction and dead enemies. They were massacred. German defenders laid down such a withering defensive fire that many of the British attackers died within sight of their own lines. By the end of the day, almost 20,000 Britons had been killed and more than 37,000 had been wounded, the greatest one-day slaughter in the history of the British Army.

Yet there would be no respite. Once again reinforcing failure, but on an even more massive scale, the Somme attacks were kept up all summer, in the vain hope that the German line would eventually crack under the sustained pressure. By the time the offensive was finally called off in November, the greatest British penetration of the German line was only five miles, while in many places they had moved forward less than a mile. To gain such a small amount of territory, 420,000 British soldiers had been killed or wounded.

Churchill, who had foreseen it all, was alternately irate and despondent. By August he had prepared a memorandum beseeching the cabinet to call off the attacks, which he had passed on via his close friend F. E. Smith (later Lord Birkenhead). "Do you think we should succeed in an offensive," Churchill wrote, "if the Germans cannot do it at Verdun with all their skill and science? Our army is not the same as theirs; and of course their staff is quite intact & taught by successful experiment."[38] Yet he might very well have remained a man with little influence whose political career was all but over, had Lloyd George not stepped in and provided Churchill with the most understudied, but perhaps most important, step in his strategic career.

Lloyd George had remained surprisingly devoted to Churchill during the period of the latter's political absence. Realizing that Churchill instinctively adopted the position of a supplicant towards him and knowing that Churchill had only a small base of political support and would be dependent upon him, Lloyd George wanted Churchill back in the cabinet as soon as possible. He also approached military developments with a mindset similar to Churchill's. He was growing aghast at the carnage on the Western Front and believed that the British Army was being pig-headed in its desire to keep attacking the Germans. Like Churchill, he wanted to halt all offensive actions until a new way to attack had been found.

Finally, Lloyd George had a strong grasp of Churchill's strengths and weaknesses and felt he could control him. To Lloyd George, Churchill was "one of the most remarkable and puzzling enigmas of his time" whose "fertile mind," "undoubted courage" and "thorough study of the art of war" made him extremely valuable. On the other hand, Churchill was beset by "erratic impulses" and "judgement" and needed "exceptionally strong brakes" to keep him under control.[39] Lloyd George was happy to be those brakes. He feared the damage Churchill could do from the backbenches if kept out of power. As he said about Churchill in a less diplomatic way years later: "He would make a drum out of the skin of his own mother in order to sound his own praises."[40]

Lloyd George was coming into his own as Britain's great World War I leader. For much of the war he had been growing disenchanted with what he saw as Asquith's restrained leadership. To keep Lloyd George happy, Asquith had stared delegating more and more authority to him. In the summer of 1916, after Kitchener was killed, sunk by a German submarine while on his way to talk to the Russians, Asquith made Lloyd George his secretary of state for war. Even this was not enough, however, and the failure of the Somme offensives, and Lloyd George's overall frustration with the British Army, made the Welshman move for the top job itself. In December 1916, he cut a deal with the Conservatives, who abandoned their coalition with Asquith and sided with him. The Liberal Party split in two, with some staying with Asquith but a large bloc siding with the new coalition. Lloyd George was now prime minister—and one of the first things he wanted to do was get Churchill back into the cabinet.

The only problem Lloyd George faced was getting the Conservatives to agree. For the first few months of 1917 they remained resolutely opposed to Churchill's rehabilitation, and whenever the prime minister pushed the issue it threatened to destroy the government. Only by the summer was he able to wear out the opposition—on the condition that Churchill not be included in the War Cabinet. Faced with this conundrum, Lloyd George asked Churchill to be the new minister of munitions. It was an ideal role at the ideal time.

Placed in charge of Britain's production of war materiel, the more mature, forty-two-year-old Churchill could try to impose his vision of war through machinery, not manpower. It was also a time when the government was increasingly willing to listen to his advice. When Churchill was named munitions minister in July 1917, the British Army was starting another one of its muddy, bloody slugfests: the Battle of Passchendaele. Like the Battle of the Somme, this engagement produced no big breakthroughs and resulted in months of attacks and hundreds of thousands of casualties. For Churchill, it was madness. He decried the waste of effort on the Western Front and believed it would have been far better for Britain to protect its valuable manpower resources and provide support in order for its allies to do more of the fighting. In this case, he wanted to call off the Passchendaele offensives to send aid to the Italians, whose front was threatening to collapse under the pressure of German and Austrian attacks. When the attacks were finally over, he rejoiced: "Thank God our offensives are at an end. Let them make the pockets, let them trapse across the crater fields, let them rejoice in the occasional capture of placeless names & sterile ridges."[41]

By the time he wrote this, in late 1917, he was preparing to argue for his strategic ideas in the cabinet, and prepared some memoranda about Britain's war production plans for 1918 and 1919. Churchill, who usually wrote with clarity and forceful expression, was particularly pointed in these papers. First and foremost, he started from the perspective that there should be no offensives in 1918. He ridiculed any idea of throwing British forces against German trenches until the following year. "Ever since the autumn of 1914 we have heard the same accounts of the exhaustion of the enemy's man-power, of the decline of his *morale*, and of how near we stand, if we only make the effort, to the supreme and final result. Every year we have in consequence made exertions on the greatest possible scale, and every year the close of the campaign has seen the enemy's front, however dinted, yet unbroken."[42]

Attacks in 1918 should therefore be halted and the troops kept in excellent defensive order in case the Germans attacked. All British efforts on the Western Front should be turned to 1919, when Churchill believed that two major developments, one geopolitical and the other industrial, would finally allow for the possible destruction of the German Army.

The war in late 1917 had undergone a dramatic transformation. The Russians, Britain's ally since the outbreak of war, were on their knees, their country torn apart by revolution and starvation. The Russian Army had mostly dissolved, and the country was in chaos, with a growing Communist/Bolshevik Party (one of whose leaders was Joseph Stalin) in control of the major cities of St. Petersburg and Moscow. The Communists were determined to get Russia out of the war, which would free up a million German soldiers, who were presently on the Eastern Front, to go west.*

---

* They would do so in March 1918, when they concluded the Treaty of Brest-Litovsk with the Germans, fully withdrawing what became known as the USSR from World War I.

Counterbalancing this was the entry of the United States into the war on the side of Britain and France. In April 1917, America, in reaction to the decision of the German government to restart unrestricted submarine warfare in the Atlantic, had declared war on Germany. The entry of America's massive industrial power, with its large number of military-age males available for service, more than made up for the loss of Russia—if American force could be brought to bear. From Churchill's perspective, however, it was taking far too long for the US to mobilize and send its force to Europe, and the German submarine menace still needed to be surmounted. He thus calculated that a large American army would not be able to fight until 1919 and he was more than happy to wait for that to happen. The British had done enough dying; if the Americans could handle much of the load in fighting the Germans, so much the better.

The second development Churchill expected would allow for the destruction of the German Army was increased British production. While the British were waiting for American power to arrive, Churchill was determined to use his position as munitions minister to provide all the materiel of war needed to offer British troops protection and support. His up-close look at modern war had led him to an important calculation: firepower was all well and good, but in a static environment it would always drastically favour the defender. More important than anything was the establishment of what he called "moving power."[43] Mobility would have to come from technology, and it was incumbent on him to provide the right equipment to make it happen. He pushed ahead with plans for the tank, and now added to it a powerful corps of aircraft.

Churchill had long been intrigued by the military uses of airplanes, and as the war went on he seemed convinced that they were transforming into a battlefield-winning weapon. He wanted not only to outbuild the Germans in numbers (which the British were already doing) but to equip British aircraft with the kinds of weapons that would allow for effective attacks on ground forces. He wanted an independent air staff appointed, rigorous work on improving bombing accuracy and a British air force that could seize air supremacy anywhere it wanted. Churchill was convinced that, once this

Two aristocrats: Winston Churchill and Franklin Roosevelt as boys.

Adolf Hitler showing arrogance
in a school photo.

Joseph Stalin while at the seminary:
he supposedly sang like an angel.

Churchill as a young Hussar in 1895, two years before he saw combat in the Malakand Valley.

A young Mussolini in one of his more respectable phases.

A young, confident Roosevelt not long after becoming the Assistant Secretary of the Navy.

Two mugshots: Mussolini and Stalin were both arrested for their radical activities before World War I.

Бакинское Губернское Жандармское Управлеіе.

Mussolini as a Bersaglieri during World War I. He had a long posting in the
mountains, which was safe and he found enjoyable.

Hitler and some of his fellow soldiers during World War I. The German Army gave him a community he had never had before—as well as a dog.

Churchill serving on the Western Front in early 1916. His exposure to war in the trenches hel[...] give him a healthy respect for the German Army and a desire to keep British casualties dow[...]

happened, the war could be taken to the Germans—in a new, modern way, with airborne forces, the strategic bombing of factories and transport systems and attacks on the German Army's supply systems.

Once the "real mastery" of the air was obtained, he wrote, "all sorts of enterprises which are now not possible would become easy. All kinds of aeroplanes which it is now not possible to use on the fighting fronts could come into play. Considerable parties of soldiers could be conveyed by air to the neighbourhood of bridges and other important points . . . The destruction of particular important factories could also be achieved . . . All his [the enemy's] camps, depots &c., could be made the object of constant, organized machine-gun attack from low-flying squadrons."[44]

Churchill proposed using an equipment-centric, technologically advanced and industrially produced armed forces to fight the enemy through the control of movement, all while keeping British casualties to a minimum. He was so convinced that this was the way forward that even while the war was going on, he believed that internal dissent should be crushed by similar methods. When Ireland exploded into rebellion in 1916 and 1917 after the Easter Rising and the crackdown instituted afterwards by the British government, Churchill was a hawk. He wanted to crush any move towards Irish independence and thought about using the most cutting-edge military equipment to keep Ireland in line. In late 1917, when he was trying to economize on military deployments on the Western Front, he suggested sending more armoured cars, machine-gun cyclists, aircraft and even tanks to fight the Irish Republicans.[45]

As it was, Germany would be easier to defeat than Ireland. 1918 developed far more dramatically than anyone expected, and the war ended before Churchill's new strategy could be brought to bear. The first part of the year had seemed like a disaster for the Allies. With Russia out of the war, the Germans transferred hundreds of thousands of men to the west and in March launched their spring offensives. For the first time in almost four years, they achieved a clear breakthrough, shattering some French and British lines. They had found a way tactically to get through the trench lines, using small groups of storm troopers to seize positions without the heavy artillery barrages which alerted their enemies. At one point the Germans penetrated twenty-five more miles into French territory, and for a moment Paris once again seemed about to fall. Churchill fell into a despair. Stunned that the Germans had broken British and French trench lines, his already healthy respect for the German Army became outsized. He called for the conscription of all men below the age of fifty and even envisaged fighting on without France. And yet, the German tactical masterstroke turned out to be a strategic disaster.

The German Army could not keep up the pace, and in pushing forward suffered staggering casualties—almost 700,000 men had been killed and wounded by the time the last attacks were called off in July. The Germans could provide no great protection for their men on the attack, and the weapons of the defensive soon reasserted themselves in their deadly fashion. The losses were so great that the German Army was fatally weakened, and in a matter of months transformed from an organization in good spirits to one its leaders felt they could not trust. The Germans asked for an armistice in November 1918 and the war on the Western Front was over. The abrupt end of the conflict meant that Churchill's ideas of how war should be fought were never trialled. That would have to wait until World War II.

7. Joseph Stalin and the Strategy of Practicality

Joseph Stalin was no romantic. Unlike Churchill, Hitler and Mussolini, he never saw war as a boyish adventure, moral test of courage or great redemptive crusade. When he surveyed the Red Army fighting around Tsaritsyn in the summer of 1918, he did not see a group of valiant, politically aware communists willing to make the ultimate sacrifice in their battle against the Russian Whites to bring about a Marxist utopia. Except for a cadre of Bolsheviks, he saw most soldiers as unreliable—even treacherous—cutthroats. The most devious, in his eyes, were the Cossacks who claimed they were fighting for the Bolsheviks. Stalin believed that they had joined the Reds only for access to weapons and intelligence, and would refuse to fight White Cossacks when the moment came. He even doubted the average Russian soldier—or "competent muzhik," as he called him. This soldier, Stalin told Lenin, had previously been fighting for Soviet power but had turned against the Bolsheviks because of the policy of the forced requisitioning of grain. Stalin's solution to this problem was, as always, brutality imposed from above—or, as he termed it, the use of his "iron discipline."[1]

A sceptical vision of human nature might have been one of Stalin's advantages as a strategist—if he could have kept his suspicions and ideology from taking him down too dark a path, thereby sabotaging all the benefits his cynicism provided. During his time at Tsaritsyn and until the end of the Russian Civil War, he was a long way from maintaining the right balance. Stalin's fundamental problem was that he was not competent enough to fulfil the purposes of his command. Often he made bad decisions and needed a way to justify to Lenin and others why he was not responsible for the disasters that followed in his wake. He needed an explanation for the lack of the large food deliveries he was always promising—an excuse that would both satisfy the monstrous needs of his own ego and mollify Lenin.

To be fair to Stalin, at Tsaritsyn he was confronted with a challenge far more difficult than those faced by any of the World War II grand strategists during their World War I careers. Peasant farmers in the area had become disillusioned with the Bolsheviks, who were forcibly requisitioning grain for price far below the market. Disincentivized, they hid as much of their output as possible. What's more, the Civil War had led to the destruction of so much equipment that there was not enough machinery to process the grain and hay that the Bolsheviks did get their hands on.[2] These problems cascaded down. The inability to get hay, for instance, severely handicapped the shipment of livestock. Animals needing to be sent north had to be provided with food for the journey, but Stalin said finding the hay to do this would be "impossible."[3]

When Stalin was able to get his hands on food, he found it difficult to ship. The issue which overhung everything and would determine the fate of his mission (and would later determine the course of much of World War II on the Eastern Front) was the control and efficient functioning of railways. Stalin needed to make sure that the lines running to the south of Tsaritsyn, particularly to the northern Caucasus, could get food to him so that he could then dispatch it north. Then he had to make sure that the lines to the north, from Tsaritsyn to Moscow, were free of White forces.

Stalin's paranoia had already made this a more difficult task. He had arrested and executed many railroad specialists because he did not trust their backgrounds. Soon his military endeavours would make things worse. Stalin's first test as a military leader had come when White forces began cutting the railway lines running both south and north of Tsaritsyn.* General Andrei Snesarev had prudently been building up forces before deciding where the greatest threat lay. Stalin, demanding action, accused Snesarev of keeping Red Army forces "bound hand and foot." Making a quick visit to the front south of Tsaritsyn, Stalin decided that he understood the

---

* An episode first mentioned in Chapter 2.

situation better than the general and insisted on an attack. He asked Moscow for eight armoured trains, turned 12,000 of Snesarev's troops over to the hopeless Klim Voroshilov and authorized an offensive.

The exact reasons for the failure of the attack are difficult to know, as honest sources are scarce and Stalin, desperate to avoid responsibility, tried to shift the blame to Snesarev and his supposedly untrustworthy staff. The likely explanation is simple: the Red Army in the region was not yet able to sustain major operations, especially under the incompetent leadership of Voroshilov. Regardless, when the attack did fail, it led to a permanent cut in the rail lines running south, physically severing Stalin from one of his largest sources of food. He admitted to Lenin that there were 700 wagonloads of grain ready to go in the North Caucasus, to the south, but there was no way to get them north to Tsaritsyn. He had even lost access to the river-borne communications between Tsaritsyn and the Caucasus, so could not use the Volga as an alternative. The importance of controlling logistics was beginning to sink in.[4]

Beyond this offensive and perhaps scared off by it, Stalin and Voroshilov changed tactics and started favouring guerrilla operations.[5] This change put Tsaritsyn itself at risk. Guerrilla tactics might have worked if the Bolsheviks wanted to cut railway lines as insurgents, but they were now the government and needed to keep the lines operating. Before long, the railway lines running north from Tsaritsyn were also periodically cut, leaving Stalin relying at times only on the Volga river to send grain in that direction.[6] Stalin's incompetence was starting to lose the benefits that Snesarev's more traditional tactics had gained.

For a moment, Stalin was left trying to bluster his way out of a disaster that he was making worse. After two months in charge, far from protecting his command, Tsaritsyn was closer to falling to the Whites than when Stalin arrived.[7] On August 31, he sent Lenin a fantastical, slightly cloying telegram begging for significant naval support from the practically non-existent Bolshevik navy, but also boasting that things would soon be put militarily right.

Dear Comrade Lenin,

The fight is on for the South and the Caspian. In order to keep all this area (and we *can* keep it!) we need several light destroyers and a couple of submarines . . . I implore you, break down all obstacles and so facilitate the immediate delivery of what we request. Baku, Turkestan and the North Caucasus will be ours (unquestionably!), if our demands are immediately met.

Things at the front are going well. I have no doubt that they will go even better (the Cossacks are becoming completely demoralized).

Warmest greetings, my dear and beloved Ilyich.[8]

Little was true in Stalin's short message, but thankfully for him he would never get called out on it. Almost immediately after sending this telegram, Stalin received news about the assassination attempt on Lenin that left the Bolshevik leader with two bullets lodged in his body. Stalin was shocked, but the act gave him an excuse to employ greater brutality. He had already crushed most of the opposition he had faced in Tsaritsyn, but now he telegrammed the party (which at the time was being run by Stalin's estranged roommate from Kureika, Iakov Sverdlov) saying he would institute "systematic mass terror" in response. Attempting to create a false impression of success, on September 1 he sent a telegram to Moscow fallaciously describing how the Whites had been sent reeling in panicked retreat.[9] It's hard to find any example of what he was talking about.

Lenin's shooting also made a showdown between Stalin and Leon Trotsky unavoidable. Many of the officers Stalin had arrested, and whose power he had usurped, had been put in place by Trotsky. Lenin, seeming to want to support Stalin in his difficult task and believing what he was being told by Stalin's fantastical telegrams, had refused to intervene. But with Lenin temporarily out of commission, Trotsky, working with Sverdlov, decided to take Stalin to task. In early September, they recalled him to Moscow to discuss the situation around Tsaritsyn.

At first, without Lenin's decisive intervention, a fudge was attempted. Stalin was forced to share military authority with two officers backed by Trotsky, who remained in charge of the Red Army, under the renamed Military Command of the Southern Front.[10] It would never work—Stalin was emotionally incapable of sharing power except with acolytes. Even while in Moscow, he was trying to micromanage Voroshilov back at the front, urging him to attack and demanding success.[11] When Stalin returned to Tsaritsyn, he immediately tried to subvert the agreement with Trotsky. On October 3, he and Voroshilov sent Lenin a telegram making a personal attack on the war minister, full of Stalinist tropes about the threats posed by so-called experts. "It is necessary to discuss with the Central Committee of the party the question of the behaviour of Trotsky," read the message, "who mistreats the most prominent members of the party to please the traitors from military specialists to the detriment of the interests of the front and the revolution. To raise the question of the inadmissibility of Trotsky issuing individual orders . . . To reconsider the question of military specialists from the camp of non-party counter-revolutionaries."[12]

Trotsky had finally had enough. The day after this telegram arrived, he fired back on Stalin and Voroshilov. He claimed that even though Stalin's command regularly outnumbered the Whites by up to three to one, Tsaritsyn remained constantly in peril.[13] Trotsky took particular (and truthful) aim at Voroshilov when he claimed that Stalin's client general might be competent to command a regiment but never an army of 50,000 men. He "categorically" demanded that Lenin remove Stalin from Tsaritsyn.[14] Finally, forced to choose, Lenin recalled Stalin, who had to return to Moscow.

If Stalin had been capable of understanding what Trotsky had done, he might have thanked his great rival. By pushing Stalin out, Trotsky cleansed a possible disaster from Stalin's record while allowing him to start creating an entirely new myth of military success. Indeed, Stalin could now go back to Moscow, claiming he had done a brilliant job at Tsaritsyn but in actuality leaving it to the military specialists that Trotsky brought in to try to clean up the mess he'd left behind. He certainly wasted no time trying to establish the perceived reality of his military glory. In late October 1918 he gave a speech to the Moscow soviet and a detailed interview to the Communist Party newspaper *Pravda*, and in both described how his command had been the great focus of White attacks. "It is on Tsaritsyn that the enemy is concentrating his heaviest fire," he claimed.[15]

According to Stalin, the Whites had combined three large armies, a huge force of "forty regiments" and a "number of generals," in order to seize Tsaritsyn by mid-October.[16] The valiant Red Army forces (which Stalin, of course, had organized and prepared before returning to Moscow) had sent the Whites and their generals to "seek safety in flight—so that one of them [a general] even lost his boots." It was the first major instance of Stalin's lifelong habit of spinning his own narrative boasting of his military foresight and greatness—and while he lived, it was probably the most successful rewriting of history in history.

In 1929, Voroshilov, whom Stalin still had loyally by his side, wrote an article called "Stalin and the Red Army." It was full of the expected praise of Stalin's genius, but Voroshilov, always a little obtuse, included one half-truth when he wrote that, though mistakes at Tsaritsyn had been made, Stalin "made fewer mistakes than others." Stalin, reviewing a draft of the article, wrote in the margin: "Klim! There were no mistakes. This paragraph should be thrown away."[17] It was.

In 1942, during one of the most difficult periods for the Soviet Union in World War II, a film about the campaign, titled *The Defence of Tsaritsyn*, would be released, portraying Stalin and Voroshilov working hand in glove to save the city from massed attacks by the Whites, who were abetted by devious forces in the Red Army. The myth had become history in a way that revealed a great deal about how Stalin could view strategy (until punched in the face by reality). You can work very hard to create the reality you want, and with enough power you can often succeed.

In fact, there were certainly White efforts to advance in the Tsaritsyn area, but they were often disjointed and involved forces that failed to cooperate. Their most serious effort, which happened after Stalin left, was a siege by Cossack forces that was only lifted in late 1918. The Cossacks were so brutal with the local population and plundered so widely that they helped push many of the peasants, who had been disillusioned by the Bolshevik policies of forced requisition, back to supporting the Red Army. At this point, Stalin's own shortcomings as a commander and strategist were far more responsible for the failure of his time at Tsaritsyn than the Whites.[18]

If Stalin was drawing on more fiction than fact in describing the overall course of the military campaign around Tsaritsyn, he relayed his view of war and strategy. In doing so, he gave glimpses of both the ideological and practical strategist in action. As always, the ideological/paranoid view of strategy was dominant, and the practical added as an important afterword once the former had been aired.

Stalin's ideological analysis of what made for the best Red Army started as it always did with ideological commitment. "The successes of our army are due in the first place to its political consciousness and discipline," he wrote. To have any chance of success, the army had to have soldiers who were fighting with the right political ideals—and this would always trump expertise or education.

After paying homage to the importance of ideological commitment, Stalin mentioned that logistics and supply were also prerequisites to any successful military operations. "The strength of the army is not due to its personal qualities alone," he wrote. "An army cannot exist for long without a strong rear. For the front to be firm, it is necessary that the army should regularly receive replenishments, munitions and food from the rear. A great role in this respect has been played by the appearance in the rear of expert and competent administrators, chiefly consisting of advanced workers, who conscientiously and indefatigably attend to the duties of mobilization and supply."[19]

Tsaritsyn had whetted Stalin's appetite for military glory and his need to be seen as an equal of Trotsky. When he returned to Moscow, he did everything possible to re-ingratiate himself with Lenin, and quickly succeeded. What stands out during the post-Tsaritsyn period was how forgiving Lenin was towards Stalin, how he continued to invest great confidence and authority in his protégé, and how he continued to push significant military commands on him. It revealed, as much as anything, that Lenin was actually more of a Stalinist than a Trotskyite when it came to war. He did begrudgingly accept former Tsarist officers and trained experts into the Red forces, but like Stalin he was always doubtful of their loyalty and suspicious if their operations turned out poorly. Just how forgiving Lenin was to Stalin can be seen in the major military commands the former gave the latter in 1919.

Before he undertook these, however, the Russian Civil War was transformed by German capitulation to the western Allies. Lenin's gamble in agreeing to the demeaning Treaty of Brest-Litovsk had finally paid off handsomely. Even after transferring a large part of their Eastern Army to the Western Front in 1918 and launching their most successful attacks there since 1914, the Germans lacked the resources to fight the British, French and Americans combined. By November 1918, a German Army in retreat and a German population with little faith in victory had had enough. Bowing to the inevitable, Germany's government asked for an armistice—a formality short of throwing themselves at the Allies' feet and begging for mercy.

For the Bolsheviks, this would be decisive. The Germans had forced them out of Ukraine and large parts of European Russia. Now, with the collapse of the German Army, the last thing many people in these lands wanted was to be forcibly integrated into a Bolshevik empire. Germany's collapse was also disheartening to the Whites, who had been backed by the Germans. With Germany out of the equation, the competing White interests were faced with a much greater challenge in taking on a centralized, brutal and ever more experienced Red Army. The Civil War still had to be fought to its conclusion, and the Reds would suffer setbacks, but the chances of a White victory were severely lessened by the German defeat.

Stalin's immediate military experience after Tsaritsyn and the German capitulation revealed how much he and Lenin had in common and how much he was still valued by the Bolshevik leader. His next assignment was when he was sent by Lenin to investigate one of the Whites' last great successes: the seizure of Perm in the Urals by the White forces of Admiral Aleksandr Kolchak.[20]

The story of Admiral Kolchak is one of those that make the Russian Civil War stand out for its bizarreness. A mousy Tsarist naval officer who spent the end of the war outside of Russia, Kolchak had first tried to work with the British before returning to his homeland.

There, this "historical misfit" first watched from the sidelines, fleetless and thousands of miles from the sea, as the Civil War unfolded.[21] In late 1918, he was put forward by disparate groups of rightists as the leader of the counter-revolution, and he accepted. He declared himself the heir to Alexander Kerensky's provisional government, and started collecting forces under his command. Soon, Kolchak was arresting socialists, trying to turn the clock back by undoing the Bolsheviks' economic changes and marching his motley force west. For a while, he became the greatest threat the Bolsheviks faced, and was anointed by the Allies as the leading figure for all White forces.

Kolchak's armies—a strange combination of Tsarist units, Cossacks and even freed Czech prisoners of war—were concentrated to the east of Moscow in the vast area of the Urals. Kolchak set up his capital in the city of Yekaterinburg, and his first offensives were, from the Bolshevik perspective, worryingly effective. When his troops seized the town of Perm, an important logistics hub, and a large surrounding area, it set off a panic in Moscow.[22] As a sign that Stalin's performance in Tsaritsyn had not materially damaged him in Lenin's eyes, he was dispatched to go to the area and determine why the disaster had unfolded. He travelled east with the overall head of the Bolshevik Cheka, the Polish-born Felix Dzerzhinsky—another person growing in power within the party. Stalin's military thinking revealed that he remained the same ideological paranoid that he had been at Tsaritsyn, with the dash of practicality still intact.

His analysis for Lenin, which was passed on in a detailed joint report signed off by Stalin and Dzerzhinsky at the end of January 1919, predictably placed the greatest responsibility for Perm on the lack of party discipline and devotion in the Red Army.[23] As always, the difference was between the wealthier, experienced soldiers who could not be trusted, and the poorer ones who (mostly) could. Stalin and Dzerzhinsky recommended that the army henceforth divide its soldiers into propertied men, whom Stalin called "unreliable," and the poor, propertyless who were "alone suitable for Red Army service."[24] The overall picture he painted was of an officer corps—put in place by Trotsky, of course—that was either incompetent, disorganized or suspect in loyalty. To put the Red Army on the right political footing, Stalin wanted to have the party step up its efforts in overseeing army operations and spreading the right propaganda amongst the soldiers.

If the discipline and organizational shortcomings brought on by political unreliability were mostly responsible for the Red Army's defeat, Stalin dwelt at significant length on the logistical shortcomings of the Red Army in the region. The lack of supervision of the railways, according to Stalin, left them liable to "skilfully organized sabotage of railway personnel."[25] His strategic outlook was hardening.

As was his influence in the party and with Lenin. During the official party conference held that March, Stalin's command at Tsaritsyn came in for criticism. Not only did Stalin fire back strongly, and let Voroshilov take the blame for most of his failings, but he received robust support from the party's leader. Lenin, who had stated in 1918 that he thought Stalin's widespread killings in Tsaritsyn had been too extreme, now claimed that he had come to believe that they were "not a mistake."[26] It was a sign of how similarly they viewed the world, and a sign of how happy Lenin was to see Stalin improve his own standing in the party. At the conference, Trotsky turned out to be the most controversial figure, gaining a great deal of support but also more criticism than any other member of the Politburo, the small council that was coming to dominate Bolshevik politics through its role guiding the Central Committee of the Communist Party. When it came time to select the next Politburo, Stalin, along with Lenin and Trotsky, was one of only five voting members.

Fresh from this honour, Stalin was sent into the field to fight various political fires, dispatched to a range of areas where Lenin wanted more information or believed the situation was serious. This was during what might best be seen as the crescendo of the Russian Civil War. The party conference of 1919 ushered in the last periods in which the Reds would come under sustained attack. With World War I over, and the Versailles Treaty agreed, the great powers were growing increasingly less committed to being deeply involved in the huge, amorphous mass that Russia seemed to them. The British, for instance, were withdrawing troops from one part of Russia, and though they were still willing to aid the Whites, they were not going to do it effectively once they had left.

As the Reds still held the heart of European Russia and the cities of Moscow and Petrograd, it was incumbent on the Whites to launch attacks to try to dislodge them from their central redoubt. At this point, the lack of unity shown by the different White forces revealed itself as particularly disastrous. They launched numerous attacks from the south-west towards Petrograd, from the south out of the Don valley and east from the Urals towards Moscow, but there was little coordination or even a shared political identity between the forces. This gave the Bolsheviks the crucial advantage of being able to react to each one in turn.

The most important of Stalin's military experiences during this crescendo was spent in and around Petrograd in the late spring and early summer of 1919. Petrograd was a vulnerable and yet tricky city for the Whites to attack. With the Germans in chaos and Poland and the Baltic states trying to establish control over their new countries, much of the area of far western Russia was up for grabs. The Tsarist General Nikolai Iudenich, who had fled to Finland early in the Civil War, moved to build up a White Army in this free-for-all and attack Petrograd.[27] Yet Iudenich was operating in an area that contained different groups, such as Estonians and Poles, who had their own agendas, and this hampered his attempts to build up large forces. Stalin was sent to Petrograd to check on defences in and around the last Tsarist capital and to try to organize as many resources as possible for the Red war effort.

Stalin's reports to Lenin showed, if anything, that he remained even more hyper-suspicious of plots and betrayals, particularly from members of the Red Army. One of his first reports from Petrograd to Lenin claimed that deceit was to be found everywhere and that the two men had to work together to root it out. "The whole situation of the White Guard offensive against Petrograd makes us assume that there is an organized betrayal in our rear, and perhaps on the front itself," he wrote. "Only this can explain the attack with relatively insignificant forces, the rapid advance, as well as the repeated explosions of bridges on the highways leading to Petrograd. It seems that the enemy has full confidence in the absence of any organized military force for resistance and, in addition, counts on help from the rear . . . Please pay increased attention to these circumstances and take urgent measures to uncover conspiracies."[28]

Playing up the idea of a vast conspiracy of traitors in their midst also helped Stalin appeal to Lenin. He might not have been terribly competent, but he would take extreme measures to protect the Leninist line against all possible enemies—even those who were not enemies yet. Lenin approved of Stalin's willingness to use the most brutal means against possible enemies, even when he was aware Stalin was making things up. Such was the case with Stalin's description of the seizing of a coastal fortress from insurgents.

Krasnaia Gorka was a Tsarist fortress which lay about thirty miles from Petrograd, on the south bank of the entrance to the great city's inner harbour. It was under the command of a former Tsarist officer who had joined the Reds. However, in early June 1919 the officer and many of his men mutinied.[29] Communist troops were taken prisoner and the rebels eventually declared for the Whites.

One could have scripted Stalin's reaction: expose plots, crack down brutally and proclaim his own brilliance. He told Lenin the mutineers were part of a vast, hidden conspiracy, and so rooted out suspected bourgeois cells in Petrograd.[30] He even had all suspect foreign embassies and consulates searched, claiming he was looking for stockpiles of guns and ammunition that had been hidden for the Whites.* Having satisfied his need to find ideological enemies, Stalin then exhibited his military ego and incompetence in his plan to retake the fort. Possessing no real naval expertise, he nevertheless tried to bully local Red Army commanders into attacking from the sea. It was a gratuitous and needlessly complex plan, as Krasnaia Gorka was accessible by land and more vulnerable to assault from that way regardless. It seems that Stalin's instructions were not followed, and the fort was assaulted by Red Army forces from land, leading to the mutineers fleeing to link up with Iudenich's forces further to the west.

---

* Supposedly, one gun was found in the Romanian embassy.

Stalin, however, not only pretended that his plan had been followed, but claimed to Lenin that it was the major reason the fort was retaken and yet another sign of his ability to understand matters better than the military professionals. The telegram that Stalin sent to Lenin on June 16, and the notations Lenin wrote while reading it, reveal a lot about both men. The telegram opened with Stalin saying that the fort had been retaken, and Lenin added in the margin a very Stalin-like exhortation to "purge" the personnel still there. The next part of the telegram was basically an ode that Stalin wrote to his own genius: "Naval experts assert that the capture of Krasnaia Gorka from the sea runs counter to naval science. I can only deplore such so-called science. The swift capture of Gorka was due to the grossest interference in the operations by me and civilians generally, even to the point of countermanding orders on land and sea and imposing our own. I consider it my duty to declare that I shall continue to act in this way in future, despite all my reverence for science." Lenin was more than aware that Stalin's boasts were nonsense, and wrote in the margin that the fort had obviously been captured "from the land."[31]

If Lenin knew Stalin's description of the attack was fanciful, Stalin, once again, would make sure that the historical record was rewritten to fit his purposes. In 1951, the Soviets would produce a lavish colour film titled *The Unforgettable Year 1919*, with a particularly rousing score by the great composer Dmitri Shostakovich. It laid out a fabulous fictional/heroic vision of these events, with Iudenich's forces marching on Petrograd and the Red Army riddled with Tsarist traitors. Only the arrival of Stalin on the scene saves the day, culminating with his brilliant leadership in retaking Krasnaia Gorka from the Whites (complete with a dashing seaborne assault). The film ends with a great spectacle when Lenin bestows the grateful thanks of the Soviet people on Stalin as well as the Order of the Red Banner, the highest military decoration in the new Soviet state.

The Unforgettable Year 1919 quickly became one of Stalin's favourite films. Nikita Khrushchev, a future post-Stalin premier, claimed he "loved" seeing it; and Stalin would force his entourage to sit through endless screenings late at night as he relived military triumphs that never happened—except in his head.[32] The Civil War in that sense had created in Stalin the idea that he was a military genius, and he was desperate to have that idea validated. He did indeed end up receiving the Order of the Red Banner, though it was given for political reasons, not martial achievements.

In November 1919, on the second anniversary of the October Revolution, Trotsky was seen as the greatest military hero of the struggle, widely celebrated in the way Stalin craved, and it was decided that he would receive the Order of the Red Banner. Lev Kamenev proposed that Stalin also receive the award. A confused Bolshevik asked why, and was told, "Can't you understand? This is Lenin's idea. Stalin can't live unless he has what someone else has."[33]

Lenin understood Stalin well, and had decided that his political reliability mattered more than his military ability—or lack thereof. He also liked that Stalin provided a counterweight to Trotsky, whose actual military success seemed to make him the second-most important person in the Soviet state and, in some western eyes, a rival to Lenin himself. Certainly, at this point, Stalin was not considered someone who could challenge for the leadership, and this made him doubly useful to Lenin. So much so that when a new war broke out not long after the Russian Civil War ended, Stalin would be given one of the most senior military positions in the party.

By the end of 1919, the Whites had been routed, and their largest army, headed by Aleksandr Kolchak, was in the midst of headlong retreat into Siberia, where it would soon dissolve. In early 1920, some of Kolchak's remaining forces handed him over to Bolshevik allies, who had him executed and his body dumped in a frozen river. It was a moment that effectively marked the end of the Civil War—though there were a few White forces left in the field. Yet the Bolshevik victory did not instantly lead to a period of peace. Though the fate of most of the old Russian Empire had been decided, the parts to the far west were still up for grabs, and the new USSR would soon find itself at war with another new state.

Other than the foundation of the USSR, the single most important development in eastern Europe after the Russian Civil War was the re-creation of a large and potentially powerful Poland. One of the great states of Europe in the sixteenth to eighteenth centuries, Poland had been crushed and partitioned by its neighbours Russia, Prussia and Austria. By 1800 it had ceased to exist, though Polish identity, sharpened by an intense Roman Catholicism, remained strong. With the collapse of Germany in 1918, the western powers called for the re-establishment of an independent Poland, and provided it, on the map at least, with enough territory to make it one of the larger states in Europe. It stretched on its eastern side from close to Minsk, deep into the Russia of 1914, to only sixty or so miles from Berlin in the west.[34] Drawing lines on a map, however, did not guarantee Poland's existence. The Poles would have to fight for that—and, as it turned out, the greatest threat to them in the short term would be the Bolsheviks.

When it was clear that the Civil War was going to end with a Bolshevik victory, a debate ensued about what to do with the western border of Russia—a particularly charged question for Marxists, who argued that they were fighting for worldwide revolution. One of the greatest difficulties in making this decision was that the proletariat of Europe, far from behaving as Marx had prophesied and rising up in revolution, refused to play their expected part. While there were some worker uprisings in Germany, they were never able to consolidate power, and as 1919 went on it became more and more apparent that the Bolshevik revolution might not be part of a global transformation. In such a world, the existence of a large and powerful Poland on the Soviet Union's border was a real worry.

Indeed, the re-created Poland instantly revealed itself to be unabashedly assertive. Led by the long-time underground Polish fighter Józef Piłsudski, a new Polish Army made up of veterans of the German, Russian and Austro-Hungarian armies quickly entered the field. Piłsudski, who had been a socialist before 1914, quickly had himself promoted to marshal, renounced socialism in favour of nationalism and started to push out the borders of the Polish state wherever possible—most controversially into Ukraine, which was struggling to gain its own independence after a long period of Russian imperial rule, and which had been particularly devastated by the Russian Civil War. The Polish leader aimed his forces at Kyiv, the long-time Ukrainian capital and at one point the capital of Russia itself.

Lenin decided to act. He looked at Poland not as a new state born of freedom but as a dangerous example of imperialist capitalism reaching its tentacles deep into what rightfully should be the Soviet Union. He also convinced himself that the Red Army, hardened and made more ideologically aware by two years of civil war, was more than up to the task of crushing Polish forces. After he and Piłsudski exchanged disingenuous peace proposals in the first half of 1920, Lenin opted for full-blown war.[35] He claimed that this would be a true war of liberation for the Poles, and that once they understood that the Red Army was bringing freedom, the war would be won quickly and decisively.

Stalin would end up playing a major role in the eventual outcome of the war, and it would be seen as another one of his military blunders. Yet it also showed that the practical Stalin remained alive, as long as his ideological/paranoid side could be kept in check. Stalin seemed to see the war with Poland as a classic war between states, rather than an ideological knife fight like the Civil War. He was concerned that, regardless of Marxist homages to the unity of the proletariat, the Polish people also viewed this war from a nationalist perspective and would refuse to see the Soviets as liberators, and instead fight against them as invaders. Moreover, Stalin saw Poland as a stalking horse for the western powers, and was convinced that the Poles would receive a great deal of support. As he said in an interview for *Pravda* in May 1920: "It is beyond all doubt that the campaign of the Polish gentry against workers' and peasants' Russia is in actual fact a campaign of the Entente."[36]

Stalin seemed able to view wars with outside powers more rationally than internal struggles, likely because he was unworried about hidden Polish deviants subverting the Red Army from inside. In his mind, neither a Polish victory nor a Soviet march on Warsaw seemed likely, making him one of the least hawkish among the Bolshevik leadership (along with, mortifyingly enough for him, Trotsky). As late as July 1920, Stalin was advising that Lenin be cautious in attacking Poland, and instead devote forces to one of the last remaining White armies in the field, controlled by Piotr Wrangel. On July 11, he gave another interview to *Pravda*, ostensibly on the war with Poland, but he ended with a stirring cry that "so long as Wrangel is intact, so long as he is in a position to threaten our rear, our fronts will be unsteady and insecure, and our successes on the anti-Polish Front cannot be lasting. Only with the liquidation of Wrangel shall we be able to consider our victory over the Polish gentry secure. Therefore, the new slogan which the Party must now inscribe on its banners is: 'Remember Wrangel!' 'Death to Wrangel!'"[37]

Two days later, Stalin made a complete reversal, coming out in favour of a full-on offensive against Poland, though the reason seems as much rooted in his own ego as in any strategic lessons that warfare had afforded him. It had become apparent that the optimists had been correct, and that Warsaw would fall relatively quickly. Stalin became desperate not to be left on the sidelines as success beckoned. On July 13, he wrote to Lenin from the front, almost seeming to take a share of credit for the Soviet triumph: "The Polish armies are completely falling apart, the Poles have lost contact, control; Polish orders, instead of getting to the addressees, often fall into our hands; in a word, the Poles are going through a collapse, from which they will not recover soon."[38]

Left unstated was that Stalin had militarily misjudged the conflict, at least at the outset of the war. While Stalin was being cautious, the commander of the largest Red Army front, Mikhail Tukhachevsky, had been acting decisively and aggressively. A rising star in the Red Army, Tukhachevsky had been a Guards officer in the Tsarist army before becoming a German prisoner of war. Once freed, he joined the Red Army and played a prominent role in its victories at the end of the Civil War. He would later go on to be one of the most important military thinkers in Russian history (at least until Stalin had him shot on trumped-up charges during the army purges of the late 1930s). Dashing and a bully, Tukhachevsky had attacked Polish forces furiously and advanced rapidly. Soon he was approaching Warsaw and was on the verge of destroying the new Polish state.

Seeing how quickly Tukhachevsky was advancing spurred Stalin into action, and he joined the war with gusto—though it would be his war for his objectives. Stalin's choices once again revealed that while victory was important, the right kind of victory was more important, and the right kind of victory involved personal glory for himself. Once he decided to press forward with an offensive, Stalin did not cooperate with Tukhachevsky in attacking Warsaw, as he was supposed to do—which would have been smart by any measure of military science. Instead, he decided to use his front for a success that could be completely his own: the capture of the city of Lviv.[39]

In August 1920, Stalin obfuscated, delayed and simply disobeyed orders that called for him to have the south-west front support Tukhachevsky's assault on Warsaw.[40] Between August 5 and 13, Stalin received a number of direct orders from Moscow to send forces to take Warsaw, and Trotsky, believing it would happen, boasted that the Polish capital would be captured by August 16.[41] Stalin's responses to orders he did not want to follow showed that he did not always need to suck up to Lenin like before. On August 13, he replied to Lenin that he would not comply with orders to send calvary troops commanded by Semion Budennyi to assist Tukhachevsky in taking Warsaw, as they had already been deployed towards Lviv. "Your last directive . . . unnecessarily overthrows the existing grouping of forces in the area of these armies, which have already begun the offensive," he wrote. "This directive should have been given either three days ago, when the 1st Cavalry was in reserve, or later, after the 1st Cavalry took the Lviv region; at the present time it only confuses the matter and inevitably causes an unnecessary harmful interruption in the business for the sake of the new grouping. In view of this, I refuse to sign the corresponding decision of the South-Western front [command] as a follow-up to your directive."[42]

Stalin's insubordination was part of the transformation of the war from one that looked like an imminent victory to a rather humiliating draw. In an engagement which lasted almost two weeks, known as the Battle of Warsaw, Polish forces counterattacked against Tukhachevsky.[43] The Soviet armies, strung out by their advance, were so widely separated that communications were cut off. Up to 100,000 Red Army troops were taken prisoner in the chaos, while others retreated pell-mell into Russia. The rout was the start of a remarkable recovery by the Polish Army, and it forced Lenin into another humiliating agreement, the Treaty of Riga, signed in March 1921.

Poland ended up with a greater geographic area than that which they had been assigned by the Versailles Treaty, though Lenin did secure Ukraine as part of the USSR.

Stalin received much of the blame—though the way he handled it revealed a great deal about how three years of war had created his strategic mindset and what the future would hold.[44] The Stalin who returned from the war against Poland in defeat was defiant and cocksure. At a special Ninth All-Russia Conference of the Communist Party, held in late September specifically to discuss the war in Poland, there was a great confrontation. The conference started with an apologetic, slightly embarrassed speech by Lenin in which he tried to explain the stunning turnaround in the fighting.[45] He accused Stalin of neglecting to do what was necessary to take Warsaw, and of being biased towards the needs of his own front at Lviv. Trotsky was even more aggressive, charging Stalin with peddling wildly optimistic stories of Polish collapse, and deceiving the Central Committee as a way of disobeying their orders.[46]

Stalin in response stood up to both and threw their arguments back in their faces. Numbering his points like the catechistic young trainee priest he had been, he snidely attacked the heads of both the Red Army and the Communist Party, declaring their criticisms to be delusions:

1) Comrade Trotsky's statement that I have depicted the situation at our fronts in a rosy light does not correspond with reality. I was, it seems, the only member of the Central Committee who ridiculed the slogan of a "march to Warsaw" and openly warned comrades in the press against being carried away by successes and against underestimating the Polish forces. You could just read my articles in *Pravda*.

2) Comrade Trotsky's statement that my calculations about the capture of Lvov were not justified contradicts the facts. In mid-August, our troops approached Lvov at a distance of 8 versts [1 versta was 1,066 metres], and they probably would have taken it, but they did not take it because the high command deliberately refused to take Lvov, and at the moment when our troops were 8 versts from Lvov, the command transferred Budennyi from the Lvov region to the

western front to rescue the latter. What do Stalin's calculations have
to do with it?

3) Comrade Lenin's statement that I am biased towards the western
front, that the strategy did not let the TsK [Central Committee of the
Communist Party] down—does not correspond to reality. Nobody
has denied that the TsK had a telegram from the military command
[of the western front] about the capture of Warsaw on 16 August. The
point is not that Warsaw was not taken on 16 August—this is a small
matter—but the fact is that the western front, as it turns out, was
about to face a catastrophe due to the fatigue of the soldiers, due to
the lack of order in the rear, and the command did not know, did not
notice . . . If the military command had warned the TsK of the actual
state of the front, the TsK would undoubtedly have suspended an
offensive, as it is doing now. The fact that Warsaw was not taken on
16 August is, I repeat, a small matter, but the fact that it was followed
by an unprecedented catastrophe, which cost us 100,000 prisoners and
200 guns, is already a big oversight of the command that cannot be
ignored. That is why I have demanded the appointment of a commission in the TsK, which would clarify the causes of the catastrophe and
would prevent a new defeat. Com. Lenin, apparently, spares the military command, but I think that it is necessary to spare the business,
not the command.[47]

From his point of view, Stalin was being honest about war and
strategy. The practical Stalin appears a number of times—such as when
he states (truthfully) that he had been one of the only senior Bolsheviks warning against attacking Poland at the start, and in his response
to Lenin where he says that the real problem was the lack of proper
supply chains in the rear of Tukhachevsky's army, which led to a collapse of the front. Overhanging it all, however, is Stalin's profoundly
suspicious ideological/paranoid view of war. Responding to Trotsky, he simply ignored the fact that aid was late to help Tukhachevsky
because Stalin had kept the focus on Lviv. Yet his response to Lenin
displayed his true, untrusting self. The real problem that Stalin
wanted to highlight was, as always, senior army commanders. They
had botched things, he charged, and an investigation was needed to

find those responsible. But even Lenin was too squeamish to do what Stalin believed had to be done—which Stalin probably understood.

It was the statement of a future dictator who was done listening to others. Stalin was ready to take power, and woe betide those who had stood or would stand in his way—Lenin included. He was also lucky enough at this point that the basic lies that underpinned his explanations never led to any repercussions, and in some ways even helped his rise to the top. That would only materially change when he had to come up with a strategy in order to contend with Adolf Hitler—and he could no longer simply make the narrative fit his wish.

8. Franklin Roosevelt and the Domestic Politics of Strategy

The ships were operating in total blackout, taking advantage of the brief hours of darkness available on a midsummer night in the middle of the North Atlantic. It was July 1918 and the convoy, composed of fast troopships, was bringing 20,000 freshly trained American soldiers to fight on the battlefields of northern France. Amongst the fleet were giant, converted German liners which had been seized by the United States government and were now being used to squeeze the life out of the country that made them. To confuse any German submarines lurking nearby, the troopships had been camouflaged with futuristic designs painted in clashing shades of greys and blacks, their odd shapes and shades making it difficult for any attacker to judge speed and direction. The bulk of the large troopships made their silhouettes stand out as "great black lightless masses" and allowed them to cruise "steady as churches" through the unpredictable North Atlantic waters. Around them scurried much smaller destroyers, "built for speed,"[1] darting around like birds of prey, hoping, searching for German U-boats.

Sleeping on board one of these destroyers, USS *Dyer*, was Assistant Secretary of the Navy Franklin Delano Roosevelt.[2]★ Or, it might be better said, trying to sleep. As the destroyer whipped from side to side in the swell, he had wedged himself between his bunk's light mattress and the wall to which the bed was fixed. It was the only way to keep himself from being thrown to the deck. From the moment he had embarked from the Brooklyn Navy Yard on this "adventure," Roosevelt's greatest hope had been to see a German U-boat on the high seas—and his excitement made him jumpy. He

★ The USS *Dyer* was a Wickes-class destroyer that had just been built and was making its maiden voyage to Europe.

found himself jolting awake at the slightest noise.[3] That night a warning whistle went off, and Roosevelt, with "lightning rapidity," leapt from his bed and barrelled his way to the *Dyer*'s bridge, hoping for some action. Only when he arrived in front of the destroyer's captain did Roosevelt realize he was still in his pyjamas and had forgotten to put on his slippers. It was a false alarm; they were just crossing paths with another convoy. Roosevelt laughed, loving "every minute."[4]

The journey was the realization of a lifelong dream. Roosevelt could have chosen to travel in comfort, either on a liner or in a larger warship like a cruiser or a battleship. Yet he had deliberately elected to make the crossing in the smallest ship on offer. Thin, manoeuvrable destroyers were the backbone of the fleet. They ran patrols, scouted for enemy vessels, and protected the prima donna battleships from torpedo attacks. A destroyer's size made travelling on them a test of seamanship, which is exactly what Roosevelt wanted. The *Dyer* bobbed up and down violently in the Atlantic, causing many in the crew to vomit and leaving the vessel, as Roosevelt noted, smelling like "a street in Haiti." None of this bothered the assistant naval secretary. He was "entirely without fear," and the rougher the experience, the more Roosevelt "seemed to like it." Once again, he could boast that no matter how topsy-turvy the seas, he was never seasick.[5]

Another reason Roosevelt wanted to experience life on a destroyer was because he understood how these ships had transformed the war at sea. In the first six months of 1917, German submarines had taken a frightful toll on Allied shipping. Freed to attack whenever they wanted, they sank so many merchant ships that it looked like the British might starve if something drastic were not done. That something turned out to be the convoy system, which was started in late May. Instead of sending merchant ships out on the high seas individually, hoping that the ocean's vastness would provide protection, they were now herded together and guarded by escort vessels—and the destroyer had shown itself to be the most effective of these. Armed with new weapons such as depth charges, destroyers scared off or sank large numbers of German submarines. Immediately the number of merchant ships lost plummeted, while German submarine losses reached record highs. By September 1917, the Germans were losing more submarines than they were building. They were about to lose the war at sea, which meant that they would eventually lose the war as a whole.

From the moment the United States had entered the war, winning this struggle against German U-boats became its most important naval objective. For Roosevelt, controlling sea communications in the Atlantic became an obsession, though he could not simply impose his ideas on the US government. His job was more concerned with the nuts and bolts of the fleet than grand strategy. In June, he toured the naval districts of the north-east, in Boston, Newport, Rhode Island and New York City.[6] In a report he sent to Josephus Daniels, his boss, Roosevelt slammed the commanders of the latter two districts, accusing them of incompetence. He asked the secretary of the navy to replace them, but Daniels refused to act. In September, Roosevelt returned to the districts and once again wrote a report saying that the two commanders had to be removed.[7] Worried Daniels would still do nothing, Roosevelt requested that his letter be officially acknowledged, making his objections a matter of public record.

If much of his time was spent on naval administration and ship-building, Roosevelt also continued his role as a public lobbyist for a larger and more powerful navy. He was always keenly aware of the political issues involved in strategic questions—though it took him years to hit the right tone. In 1914, he had made an abortive bid for nomination as the Democratic candidate for New York's US Senate seat. Roosevelt attempted to leverage his naval experience and strategic outlook to bolster his candidacy, lecturing a Dutchess County crowd about how the United States was much weaker navally than most people assumed.[8] With the nation at that point determined to stay out of a European war, such appeals had little resonance and Roosevelt was easily defeated. Back in the Navy Department, he was determined that he would be smarter the next time.

When America finally entered the war, Roosevelt drew on his campaign experience to write a series of articles explaining why the growth of the US Navy was good for the nation. In June 1917, he published a piece in the *Ladies' Home Journal* titled "What the Navy

Can Do for Your Boy."[9] Refusing to start with all the material advantages or educational opportunities a new naval recruit would gain, Roosevelt instead appealed to parents by laying out the fundamentals of a Mahanian strategy, but in the folksy tone that would become his trademark:

> We all know more or less that our Navy is the first line of defense and we are coming to realize that the definition of the word "defense" does not mean the prevention of hostile armed forces from landing on our seaboard, but that in its broader sense and in the light of modern conditions the word "defense" means also the keeping open of our highways of commerce across the seas . . . If merchant ships are tied up in New York Harbor it is not New York City alone that suffers, but that the effect of this tie-up spreads quickly back to the interior parts of the nation, tying up transportation, filling up grain elevators to capacity, upsetting enormous markets for manufactures and produce, and causing general confusion throughout the land.[10]

While Roosevelt was touting the importance of naval power, a squadron of American dreadnought battleships embarked to join the Royal Navy's main battlefleet in Scapa Flow. Since the British had effectively kept the German surface fleet bottled up in port since 1914, the biggest American warships had little prospect of seeing combat. Instead, it was the smaller ships—the destroyers which so delighted Roosevelt—that would fight the German submarines.[11] Indeed, some 70 per cent of America's modern destroyers were sent to Europe during the war. A United States base, under British command, was established in Cork in Ireland (called Queenstown at the time), and it soon became a hive of activity as the Americans learned the most up-to-date British methods to convoy merchant ships and attack German U-boats. Roosevelt had little influence over these forces, as they were under the command of the supreme American naval commander in Europe, Admiral William Sims. Sims, who spent most of his time in London, had excellent relations with the British and showed himself to be a forceful theatre head, leaving Roosevelt champing at the bit back in Washington.

If Roosevelt had almost no say over American ships at sea, he did make one significant foray into naval strategy. Roosevelt considered the German submarine to be the greatest threat to the Allies. The question, of course, was how to destroy, or at least stop, those submarines before they sank more merchant ships. Finding a submarine in the open ocean was an almost impossible task in an era without effective sonar and air patrol.* They were simply too small—and, with the ability to submerge, almost impossible to locate before they revealed themselves.

Faced with this conundrum, Roosevelt adopted the idea of a defensive minefield on a heroic scale. Minefields had proved effective in narrow seas where they could control the passage of vessels. Ottoman mines had helped stymie the Royal Navy when it tried to force its way up the Dardanelles, and German mines had deterred the British from pursuing the German Navy when it fled back to its home bases after the Battle of Jutland in 1916.

Roosevelt pushed the idea to the extreme, arguing for the construction of a minefield straddling the entire North Sea, from the coast of Scotland to Norway, a distance of 240 miles. Completing such an enormous barrier would take approximately 100,000 of the most modern "antenna" detonator mines laid in fields 15–35 miles wide and at various depths.[12]† Roosevelt, however, was convinced that the cost was worth it. The North Sea barrier would use machines, which the United States could manufacture in unprecedented number, to wage an industrial war against Germany, thus saving American lives while seizing control of communications in the

---

* This did not stop people from trying. During both World War I and World War II a great deal of effort was put into the deployment of submarine hunter-killer forces, which were sent out to find German U-boats before they could attack convoys. They were mostly a failure.

† They were referred to as antenna mines because they were connected to a 100-foot cable. All a target needed to do was brush the cable for the mine to explode, leading to a much greater area covered by each mine. Submarines were considered so delicate that the water pressure change from an explosion within that range would be enough to do serious damage.

Atlantic Ocean. All that was missing, in Roosevelt's mind, was the ambition and drive to make the barrier a reality.

It is difficult to understate Roosevelt's passion for the North Sea Mine Barrage, as it came to be known. He referred to it as his "pet hobby," and was convinced that it was his lobbying that made the Navy Department eventually support the plan.[13] He had started pushing the idea long before the US joined the war.[14] Once America was fighting, he pressed ahead with even more force. In May 1917, Roosevelt personally approached both Daniels and Woodrow Wilson on the issue.[15] At first, he found little support. The secretary of the navy and the president had little enthusiasm for such a grand defensive undertaking. Indeed, the administration as a whole, including the president, was pushing for far more risky, offensive operations in order to attack German submarines. Wilson seemed keen that Americans "do something audacious in the line of offense," such as venturing out to the German submarine bases themselves—or as he liked to call them, their "Hornet's Nest."[16] For Wilson, this need was personal as much as anything else; he wanted the Americans to be seen to play the decisive role in defeating the Germans, so as to strengthen his own negotiating position during the post-war peace talks. But he had no idea what attacking German bases entailed, and was pushing a reckless policy.[17] German bases were extremely well protected with large minefields, and the key facilities were miles upriver from the sea. Any such attacks would require American vessels to put themselves in great danger and could involve the landing of ground troops in Germany itself—a bit like Churchill's plans of 1914 to threaten the north German coast.

The British, who understood how dangerous attacks on German bases would be, at first fended off both Roosevelt's plans for a great North Sea Mine Barrage and Wilson's for offensive actions on the German submarine bases. However, with the Americans putting pressure on the British to do something, in the summer of 1917 they relented on the North Sea barrier, with the proviso that the United States pay for and provide almost all the mines needed for the herculean effort.

Having got the British on board, Roosevelt had to return to his own administration. In October, he reached a new high point in his assertiveness, writing a memorandum to Daniels demanding action on the North Sea barrier, and then sending a copy of that memorandum to Wilson, in a rather naked power grab, asking for someone—probably himself—to be given responsibility for the plan. "It is my duty to tell you that if the plan is put into execution with the same speed and method as employed in the past other priceless months will be wasted," he wrote. "Some one person in whom you have confidence should be given the order and the necessary authority to execute the plan without delay." Just in case Wilson needed to brush up on his Mahan, Roosevelt ended the letter with a lesson on sea power: "I dislike exaggeration, but it is really true that the elimination of all submarines from the waters between the United States and Europe must of necessity be a vital factor in winning the war."[18]

The letter was not only an indication of Roosevelt's growing confidence; it was a plea for a change in his position. Touring American naval bases and writing articles to soothe nervous parents was all well and good, but these jobs were a long way from being the responsibilities of a real war leader as Roosevelt envisioned them. He considered leaving the Navy Department and fighting at the front—and he even had a specific unit in mind, because he had created it.

As Roosevelt had spent more time on the technical side of naval construction, he had become drawn to the idea of mounting on rail carriages the massive fourteen-inch naval guns normally placed on American dreadnoughts.[19] These would be the American response to Germany's famous super-large artillery pieces—the Big Bertha and the Paris Gun. They would be constructed using American industrial might, shipped across the Atlantic, and assembled in France, where they would batter strategic German targets with unprecedented explosive power. When completed, these pieces could fire a shell weighing 1,400 pounds for a range of twenty-four miles.[20] By December 1917, plans were drawn up to build the huge rail carriages needed to support the weight of the naval guns, and in January 1918 construction started on the final product. It was the largest Allied artillery piece of the war, and it was hoped that they would be ready for action by the summer.

Roosevelt had been "responsible for the acceptance of this extraordinary proposal."[21] As with the North Sea Mine Barrage, he became territorial about their progress. This would be the unit he would fight with—if he chose to do so. Serving with these guns would allow him to become a member of the navy while also speeding up the time required to get him into action (training to command a vessel would have taken many years). The only decision was if he would take the plunge.

One thing that kept Roosevelt from enlisting was that he was hopeful that he would be sent on a special mission to Europe. He had been keen both to see the state of the conflict and to engage in some high-level international diplomacy long before the US entered the war, and first proposed that he be sent to Europe on an inspection trip in 1914. When the US finally joined the fighting, his pleading became incessant. He told Daniels: "One of us ought to go and see the war in progress with his own eyes, else he is a chess player moving his pieces in the dark."[22] Yet the naval secretary seemed reluctant to spare Roosevelt from the department. Daniels would not say no, but would find reasons for delay.

For a while in early 1918 it looked like any Roosevelt mission might never get off the ground. The war from the point of view of the Allies took a depressing turn when the Germans launched their famous spring offensives in March. Using one million troops transferred from the Eastern Front now that Soviet Russia had signed a peace treaty with Berlin, the Germans attacked using stormtrooper tactics. When news reached Washington that they had punched a wide hole in French and British lines and had once again started to march on Paris, there was a moment of despair as it was feared that France might be driven out of the war. On March 28, after Roosevelt had discussed the military situation with General Leonard Wood, he described himself to his mother as being "somewhat blue," adding: "Not much likelihood of my going over, though they ought to send me."[23]

And then, miraculously, the German attacks petered out and the Western Front stabilized again. It was finally agreed that a Roosevelt mission could move forward. Few realized at the time that he was heading into a war that was almost over. He believed he was about to glimpse in person a struggle that held the prospect of years more blood and toil.

On July 8, 1918, Franklin Roosevelt boarded the *Dyer*, bound for Europe.[24] At thirty-six, he was a far cry from the wheelchair-bound president later generations would remember. With a level of energy one aide compared to that of his cousin Theodore—a compliment that Franklin would have adored—Roosevelt spent his days walking the *Dyer*'s deck, watching a warship in action. He spent hours on the bridge, observing everything and everyone. He tracked how the convoy zigzagged, always making sure never to revert back to their true course for more than fifteen miles—which was considered far longer than a German U-boat could visually observe.[25] This civilian aboard a ship filled with professional sailors dazzled those around him with his encyclopaedic knowledge of the fleet, with one observer saying that the ASN "knew more about the many activities of our navy than anyone else."[26]

Much of the *Dyer*'s time was spent on drill. The ship just built, her green crew still had much to learn. They practised on the weapons they most expected to use against German submarines, dropping depth charges and firing their new guns. The depth charges made a far greater impact than Roosevelt had expected. Drums packed with 300 pounds of high explosive, they were jettisoned off the stern and set to detonate at a certain depth. The first time the *Dyer* dropped a depth charge it exploded after the destroyer had moved only a few hundred yards away. At that distance, it was so powerful that the ship shuddered violently, as if it had run into a fixed rock in the middle of the ocean. Roosevelt admitted ruefully that it would take "a lot more" than a few days of drill "to get a crew efficient." And that was a minor hiccup, compared to another moment when a crew in charge of one of the *Dyer*'s five-inch guns fired backwards, narrowly missing the bridge where Roosevelt stood watching. His reaction was to laugh.[27]

In London, Roosevelt was immediately introduced to the First Lord of the Admiralty, Sir Eric Geddes. A successful businessman with a reputation as an organizational genius, Geddes did his best to ingratiate himself with the younger man. For days he personally shepherded his guest, even travelling all the way to Ireland to keep Roosevelt company. But Geddes had an ulterior motive. The Briton was thinking about the post-war world, and like many in the Royal Navy had been discomfited by the American 1916 naval programme with its pledge to build massive new US capital ships. The problem that Geddes had was that, while he was determined to keep naval supremacy in Britain's hands, he could afford to do nothing to antagonize the US government.

Faced with this dilemma, Geddes charmed the charmer. When he and Roosevelt chatted about shipbuilding priorities, the First Lord talked amiably about how unnecessary new capital ships were in the war against Germany. What they really needed from the Americans was more and more anti-submarine vessels. Britain had stopped all its capital ship construction for the duration of the war and the United States should do so as well. Roosevelt bought the story—hook, line and sinker. He immediately reported back to Daniels of an excellent idea "to discuss the possibility of dovetailing the British programme for new construction in with our programme, in order that between us we may not build too many of one type of vessel."[28]

Later in the trip, Roosevelt met David Lloyd George, and the prime minister, much like Geddes, wooed the young ASN. Roosevelt was drawn to Lloyd George's "tremendous vitality," and the two men, domestic politicians to their core, discussed labour relations over lunch. Roosevelt revealed how hawkish he could be at this time, criticizing the British for not adopting conscription at the outbreak of war, which, the American said, deprived the government of a powerful weapon to keep the trade unions in line.

The high point of his time in London was Roosevelt's private audience with King George V. On the morning of July 30, he was driven to Buckingham Palace, where he was hurried through vast corridors lined with fine naval paintings and ushered into a waiting room. There he spied a number of exquisite Chinese lacquer ornaments. Still not entirely comfortable with the global, imperialist aspirations of the British state, Roosevelt hoped the ornaments had not been seized during the looting following the Boxer Rebellion. Finally, he was escorted before the king. The American did his best not to be overawed, and dealt with George as a fellow elite. The two hit it off instantly. The king, a naval officer, praised Roosevelt for making his Atlantic crossing in a destroyer. Most of their time was spent discussing the beastly Germans. The king's jaw "snapped" as he spat out details of supposed German atrocities, and he confided to Roosevelt that, even though he had many German relatives, "I can tell you frankly that in all my life I have never seen a German gentleman." Roosevelt later boasted that even though the interview was supposed to have lasted fifteen minutes, the two "got going so well" it was closer to forty-five before he was ushered out.[29]

Roosevelt seemed to get along with everyone—with the exception of Winston Churchill. The two met only briefly, during a dinner party, and the older Briton rubbed the young American up entirely the wrong way. It's not clear what happened between them, but years later Roosevelt was still angry about it and told Joseph Kennedy, whom Roosevelt would make the US ambassador to Britain from 1938 to 1940, that Churchill had "acted like a stinker."[30] Churchill claimed to have no recollection of the event, which might have been the issue in the first place. Roosevelt's specific charge was that Churchill had been "rude" to him.[31] This could mean that Churchill had ignored Roosevelt, finding him unworthy of his attention, which Franklin would have taken as a real insult—and never forgotten.

Churchill's judgement aside, the great attention Roosevelt was paid in London seemed to go to his head. As British policymaker after British policymaker did their best to win over the young man, they pitched different initiatives. One suggested that Roosevelt help install a British naval commander in the Mediterranean, who could take control of Italian forces and compel them into action. Roosevelt was taken by the idea, flattered at the idea of dabbling in international politics. During his visit to Rome, he argued the British case directly to the Italian prime minister, Vittorio Emanuele Orlando.[32] Yet the Italians had no intention of turning their forces over to the British, nor were the French supportive of a dominant British command in the area—and neither was it official American policy. Rebuffed, Roosevelt quickly dropped the idea.

If Roosevelt spent much of his time with high political leaders, he spent just as much visiting American naval units, so that he could assure Daniels and Wilson that their boys were well looked after. The first major facility he toured, starting three days after his arrival, was the base in Cork that housed a large detachment of US destroyers on anti-submarine operations. Roosevelt inspected the facilities for the enlisted men: their hospitals, theatres and clubs. He was also introduced to one of the best-kept British secrets of the war: the Q-ships. These were what looked like innocent merchant ships that had actually been equipped with powerful, concealed naval guns and were staffed by select Royal Navy officers and enlisted men. The job of a Q-ship was to cruise the North Atlantic looking like a juicy target for any German submarine that might stumble across it. The hope was that a U-boat, thinking this was an unescorted civilian ship, would surface to destroy the Q-ship with its deck gun (saving a torpedo and giving the crew a chance to abandon ship). When the unlucky submarine surfaced, the Q-ship was to manoeuvre closer and, when the range was right, quickly run up the Royal Navy ensign, reveal its heavy weaponry and blow the submarine to smithereens before it could react. It was dangerous, ungentlemanly work—and, by the international law standards of the time, probably illegal. That didn't bother Roosevelt. He was gripped listening to the "hair-raising" stories of a Q-ship captain who had sunk "4–5" submarines.[33]

Roosevelt was even more interested in his North Sea Mine Barrage. His return trip to the UK in August involved an extensive tour of the naval facilities in Scotland. He visited the British Grand Fleet, the world's dominant battleship force, then based in the Firth of Forth around Edinburgh, but was most excited when he left Edinburgh for the Highlands and could see his mine barrage being laid. What he discovered was an operation in full swing. The British had started laying down the first mines in March;[34] the Americans had followed suit in June.[35] By the time Roosevelt arrived, the area was bustling, with mines being unpacked, assembled, loaded onto vessels and then carted out to their locations. After seeing the mine operation in action, he proposed that a similar barrier be constructed in the Mediterranean, to bottle up the Austrian Navy in the Adriatic.

Confident in his abilities to analyse and guide the naval war,

Roosevelt arrived in France to observe the ground war. He was fascinated by the sights and sounds of the battlefield, and the stories of the brutality and heroism that supposedly occurred in the terrain in front of him. In his journal, the Germans were invariably the "Boche" or the "Hun," responsible for committing the most horrible atrocities. They destroyed churches, pointlessly shelled buildings, "deliberately and maliciously" ransacked and stole whatever they wanted. Through their horrors the Germans had created a generation of French citizens who would, Roosevelt judged, never forgive their invaders. It was an impression that Roosevelt, too, would carry with him for the rest of his life.

In Paris, he had a private meeting with France's prime minister, Georges Clemenceau. Short and sprightly, Clemenceau had been fighting the Germans since the 1870s. Calculating that Roosevelt was a man worth impressing, the French leader tried to shock him with stories of German depredations. He wanted to disabuse the fresh-faced American of the idea that the war might end soon—"that the Germans have stopped fighting or that they are not fighting well."[36]

Germany needed to be broken, and to bring home just how much effort this would take, Clemenceau told Roosevelt of a tableau he had witnessed during one of his many visits to the front. He had come across two dead bodies, one German and one French, partially buried in a shell hole. The men had been killed by artillery while locked in combat, weapons gone, trying to bite each other to death.

Roosevelt set off to see such sights for himself. Discarding an itinerary filled with abandoned battlefields and cushy hotels, he asked local French commanders to be allowed as far forward as possible. For four days, from August 4 to 7, he moved in and out of combat areas, felt blasts as shells fell nearby, crawled into dugouts and fortresses, catalogued the destruction in his head and saw grave after grave marking where a man had recently fallen, be he French, German or even American.

He started his tour with the US Marines near Belleau Wood, where he was entertained by the commander of the 4th Marine Brigade (part of the 2nd Infantry Division), Major General John LeJeune.

Roosevelt listened to stories of Belleau Wood, the "largest American battle since Lee surrendered at Appomattox" and believed the whispers that the army had made this one Marine brigade do twice as much fighting as any two army divisions combined. Indeed, like a good navy man, he was convinced that the army would do anything to piggyback on the Marine Corps' glory. When he heard it was being suggested that Belleau Wood, which the French renamed Bois de la Brigade de la Marine to commemorate the bravery of the Corps, should be renamed Bois des Americains, he had his objection put on the record.

After a few days with the Marines, Roosevelt joined the French Army at the site of their most famous battle of the war, Verdun. Like Winston Churchill two years earlier, Roosevelt donned the distinctive French military helmet and carried a gas mask as he made his way forward. He would need it. As a sign of how in some areas the intricate, layered trench systems of either side made attacking almost impossible, Verdun in the summer of 1918 was still in the front line, as it had been when the battle commenced two years earlier.

Roosevelt was driven down the famous Voie Sacrée, the narrow road that the French had used to reinforce their beleaguered troops during the battle, and brought up to the Citadel, the large—now heavily battered—fortress which sat on a ridge overlooking the town. Looking down on Verdun, he was shocked. Roosevelt tried to find one roof still intact—and failed. There were "great gaps" where large buildings had once stood and detached "jagged walls" everywhere. Touring the battlefields outside of town, Roosevelt was at first confused at the empty expanse unfolding in front of him. It was only after a moment that he realized the entire area had been so saturated by shot and explosion that all trees, shrubs and structures had simply been blown away, leaving a blank canvas of dirt. He wrote in his diary, "You see no complete shell holes, for one runs into another, and trench systems and forts and roads have been swallowed up in a brown chaos."[37]

Roosevelt's tour of the battlefield allowed him to show real courage. One of the most important sights was Fort Douaumont, the largest fortress in the Verdun line, which had been captured by the

Germans in 1916 before falling again into French hands. As the fort was still very much a target of German fire, Roosevelt and his group could only file into the fort single-file, leaving forty paces between each of them, in an attempt to not attract attention.[38] Even then they were spied by the Germans, who started lobbing shells in Roosevelt's direction. Each time they heard a shell whine, a French officer would lift his hand and the ASN would leap into an abandoned shell hole. (One can only imagine the repercussions if the Germans' artillery fire had been accurate; the Americans' most stalwart leader of World War II would have been snuffed out before he could even begin.) Inside the fort, more than 800 officers and men were crammed together, filling every cranny, and the whole building shook with the explosion of German shells. Roosevelt smiled, but probably hated every minute.

After a day visiting the sights of Verdun, Roosevelt was driven back up to the Citadel for a "delightful dinner" with French officers and, he hoped, a restful sleep after all his exertions. As he lay in bed, eighty feet below the Citadel's floor in a cramped tunnel, he realized how alien the land war was to his sensibilities. It smelled wrong. In the caves and fortresses of Verdun he had felt cramped, damp and dirty, and exclaimed in his diary that he would "hate to have to live in this spot."[39] There was something grubby and unhygienic about being in a large infantry formation that made Roosevelt's skin crawl. He could not rest in the Citadel either, where the air had to be circulated by pumps, "feeling that it is the same air being breathed over and over again."[40] Other odours constantly bombarded him, most obviously the rotting and dead animals strewn everywhere. To Roosevelt's "sensitive naval" nose, "the smell of dead horses is not only evident, but very horrid."[41] He had watched the army officers and been amazed that they were not bothered in the least by the stench.

Indeed, when this navy man looked at the land war, he viewed it through the lens of Alfred Thayer Mahan. Roosevelt was not particularly engaged on the question of land-power tactics, but he seemed most critical about issues of communications and logistics. Though he was extremely respectful of French efforts, he chided his hosts for not rebuilding the rail lines and bridges over the Marne, which the Germans had destroyed as they retreated from the failures of spring.

If Roosevelt was unfamiliar with the nuances of land warfare, he was fascinated with what was happening in the air. The growth of military aviation had become one of the great talking points of World War I, with people either praising aircraft as revolutionary vehicles that threatened to upturn all established notions of how nations would fight or believing they were expensive, dangerous distractions that accomplished little. When the United States had joined the war, millions of new dollars were appropriated for aviation.[42] Roosevelt wanted to see just how effective the new weapons were going to be.

When Roosevelt first left Paris on his way to the front, he had visited a French airfield. He was amazed to see fighter planes lined up, out in the open, and asked whether French authorities were worried about Germans bombing them. The Germans, he was told, preferred bombing at night, in which case they were safe because the Germans could never find them.

That night, Roosevelt had hoped to see an American bombing raid leave from an air base near Saint-Inglevert.[43] After two hours of fruitless waiting, he was informed that the ground mist made any raid impossible. Frustrated, he went to bed, only to be woken up a little later by the sound of bombs dropping on the nearby port of Calais. "Evidently the Boche did not think the ground mist too heavy," he recorded in his diary. Still, he saw the limits of air power. Even though the Germans had bombed Calais for months, the port—crucial for bringing in troops and supplies—still busily "teem[ed] with movement," the harbour had "never been out of commission" and the railways to the front had "been continuously used."[44]

If Roosevelt was underwhelmed by the effectiveness of aerial bombing, he was aware that technological advances were changing warfare almost moment by moment. Over a short period, the bombs being dropped by aircraft had grown from fifty-pounders—capable of light damage, like blown-out windows or scorched walls, and only from a direct hit—to the 1,200-pound giants being used by the German night bombers that could flatten buildings. Roosevelt personally inspected a street where one of the largest bombs had fallen. It had destroyed "six houses on each side" and killed many of their inhabitants. As Roosevelt was beginning to understand, the weapons of the future were going to be ever more powerful and effective.

Of course, Roosevelt was convinced that the institution that would reach that future first was the US Navy. One reason he went to Italy was to see the navy's new night bombers, which were soon to be flown over the Alps for deployment on the Western Front. They were capable of carrying the new super-heavy 1,750-pound bombs, which were intended to wreck German works and batteries in Belgium.

Roosevelt's faith in the US Navy also drove him to take one of his final stops on his tour—and maybe the most revealing—when in mid-August he visited ports in Bordeaux and Brittany. Key transit hubs for the transportation of American troops and war equipment to France, they hummed with activity. The US Army had taken over the main harbour of Bordeaux, and for two miles along the shore all one could see were "ships, traveling cranes, railroad tracks, freight cars, and storehouses," with all the heavy work being done by crews of African-American troops.[45] Yet Roosevelt was more interested in what was happening up the coast, in Saint-Nazaire. There, his beloved fourteen-inch naval guns were being assembled on railway carriages, with each enormous gun supported by a train of thirteen cars. There was the "huge gun car," three construction cars needed to maintain the gun, two ammunition cars in which to store the massive shells, a workshop car, a fuel car, a kitchen car, and four cars to house the crew and headquarters.[46] Each train was so heavy that the French worried that they might collapse some of the older bridges that they would have to cross to reach the front.

This was hardly Roosevelt's concern, however. Watching Americans prepare these immense, cutting-edge guns for combat, he felt an irresistible tug to join them. That was certainly what Cousin Ted would have done—indeed, had tried to do, until halted by President Wilson. As Franklin Roosevelt made his final preparations to leave France and head back to America, he seems to have decided that this was his moment to join the fight. On August 20, as he sat awaiting departure, he wrote to Eleanor that "the more I think of it the more I feel that being only 36 my place is not at a Washington desk, even a Navy desk. I know you will understand . . ."

He would not get the chance. On September 11, as he sailed from Brest on the liner USS *Leviathan* (originally built as the SS *Vaterland* for a German company) for the trip back to the United States, Roosevelt was a very ill man. He had caught a case of the Spanish flu, quickly compounded by pneumonia. One of the deadliest outbreaks in modern history, influenza ravaged much of the globe during the last year of the war, leaving millions dead.★ Though Roosevelt survived, he arrived home so weak he had to be brought off the boat by stretcher. He would not be back at work at the Navy Department until October 15.

By then the German Army was in headlong retreat, and the idea of Roosevelt signing up to fight had become pointless. Part of him would regret his inability to serve for the rest of his life. And if his illness changed his public life, it also transformed his private existence. With Roosevelt so unwell when he arrived back in the United States, Eleanor was left to unpack his belongings. Sorting through his clothing and souvenirs, she made a discovery that revealed her life to be a lie. Franklin had been involved for years in a passionate love affair with her own correspondence secretary, Lucy Mercer. Eleanor had been betrayed by two of the people closest to her in the world.

Franklin's life was at a crossroads. He probably loved Lucy, but divorce would have been a major political handicap. Still, part of him wanted to run away with the younger, beautiful Mercer. In the end, it was his mother, Sara, who drove him down the path of conventionality. The price Eleanor made him pay was the professionalization of their marriage. From then on, they rarely shared a bed, and never shared each other. Their private lives increasingly diverged and their cooperation was mostly on the political issues about which they both

★ This pandemic, often called the Great Influenza epidemic, stretched from 1918 until 1920. It started in the US before spreading worldwide, and took an unusually high toll on young adults. Estimating a global toll is extremely difficult, but it has been claimed that up to 50 million people died.

cared. In many ways, they made a better political couple than a personal one—as the future would demonstrate.

The crisis in his marriage pushed Roosevelt to hanker for another trip—to get back to Europe as soon as possible. Three days after the Germans surrendered, he started pressing Daniels to send him back, ostensibly to oversee the demobilization of American naval forces, which were dotted around western Europe from the Scottish Highlands to the south of Italy.[47] Once again Daniels demurred at first and kept Roosevelt by his side, but by early 1919 the younger man's pleading became incessant and Daniels relented. Soon Roosevelt was again at sea—though to make sure he behaved himself, Eleanor went with him this time.

He might have been sailing back to Europe with his personal life in chaos, but Roosevelt was more confident than ever of his strategic ideas. He remained convinced that his choices during the war were the right ones, even the controversial North Sea Mine Barrage. Yet history has not been kind to the mine barrage on a cost-benefit basis.[48] More than 70,000 mines were laid before the Germans surrendered. Even then, the barrier suffered from technical problems, such as the antenna mines being prone to fratricidal explosions. The biggest issue, however, was that the barrier was never completed. The Allies had refused to lay any mines in Norwegian territorial waters, for instance, which left a clear path for German submarines to skirt the field.* In the end, relatively few German submarines were actually destroyed by the barrier—perhaps four to six—and that has led some to criticize it as ineffective. It's an interesting judgement, and partly impossible to justify as the barrier was only in operation for two months and was "barely hitting its stride" when Germany surrendered.[49] Roosevelt, however, remained devoted to the idea of the mine barrage, and if its impact in World War I was minimal, it revealed two important aspects of his approach to strategic questions that would manifest in World War II. The first was that winning the communications war was always the foundation on which any war

---

* After the British and Americans started laying mines, the Norwegians said that they would mine their own waters.

would be won, and the United States would have to pour resources into that as a first priority. The second was that, when faced with a strategic problem, if possible use machines, even on the grandest scale, rather than sacrificing soldiers' lives to do the dirty work. Machines don't vote. The parents, siblings and loved ones of dead soldiers do.

For with the war over, Franklin Roosevelt was once again looking ahead to grander things. The war had raised his public profile. Attractive, with a strong speaking voice and, unlike Daniels, a passionate interest in naval issues, it was Roosevelt who was increasingly the public face of the fleet. In summer 1919 he was the lead subject of a *New York Times* editorial which praised his stance in favour of increasing naval officer pay.[50] This was staid compared to much of his publicity. Whenever possible, Roosevelt tried to attach himself to the cutting edge of the navy's technology, and in 1919 that meant taking part in air shows—to display aviation's possibilities to an interested American citizenry.

In April, he had made a public flight in the navy's newest flying boat, the Curtiss NC-2, built with an eye towards crossing the Atlantic. Speaking to reporters afterwards, Roosevelt reminded them: "The last time I was up was in active patrol off France."[51] A few weeks earlier, he had taken part in an air show in New York's Madison Square Garden. Speaking from the cockpit of the navy's newest and largest bomber, a Handley Page, he had made a passionate plea for the United States to become the world's leading air power. He even took the Mahanian concept of control of the seas and adapted it to this new technology. "Control of the air," Roosevelt claimed, "[is] absolutely necessary in this country for commercial purposes, for travel, and for defense in future possible wars."[52]

He was warming more and more to the possibilities of air power, and as assistant secretary he did the US Navy one final service when he played an important political role in making sure that it kept control of its own air arm. The birth of aviation had unleased a bureaucratic debate over how these new machines should be controlled. Britain, the leading air power, took a decisive and controversial step in establishing a distinct Royal Air Force in 1918, giving the new service the control of all flying vehicles for the army and navy.★ There were advocates for this in the United States, most robustly from the man who would become America's most famous air enthusiast, Brigadier General William "Billy" Mitchell. In 1919, Roosevelt wrote an article for the magazine *US Air Service*, which was republished in its entirety in the *New York Times*, arguing for the continuation of an independent American naval air arm. It would be "unthinkable" to deprive the fleet of its own air force. "Not until we do away with armies and navies altogether," he wrote, "or until the development of aircraft relegates land forces and the Navy to the scrap heap will the time arrive for a United Air Service."[53]

All this publicity helped Roosevelt as a rising star in the Democratic Party, but even he would have been surprised to see just how dramatically he was about to leap up. At the end of the war, many had assumed that Woodrow Wilson would run for a third term in 1920. However, while out campaigning for the Versailles Treaty in 1919, the president suffered a terrible stroke. He would never fully recover. Though Wilson still coveted the Democratic nomination, he was far too weak to run again, and the party eventually turned to the safe, somewhat boring governor of Ohio, James Cox.

In an attempt to add some stardust and energy to their campaign, the Democrats chose Franklin Roosevelt to be their vice-presidential candidate. Roosevelt showed himself to be a tireless campaigner, criss-crossing the country on behalf of the party. At one point, he visited twenty states in eighteen days, giving multiple speeches each day from the back platform of a train car. From the moment Roosevelt accepted the nomination until the day of voting, he hammered home the message of internationalism, American power and the importance of the League of Nations. He could at times

---

★ This ended up being a very controversial step. While it helped the British maintain a first-rate strategic and tactical air force in the interwar years and through World War II, it has been argued that it was a serious handicap to the development of British naval air power, one of the reasons British aircraft carriers flew such terrible planes until well into World War II, when they received American ones designed specifically for the navy.

personalize issues by going on about the North Sea Mine Barrage, a stronger merchant marine or the importance of US naval power, but mostly he struck a Wilsonian internationalist line.[54] His final campaign statement was a call for a US worldwide commitment: "Lastly, the whole conduct of the campaign in regard to the single paramount issue of the League of Nations is in line with the foregoing: On one side a clear-cut programme for the future for the carrying out of the highest purpose of our participation in the war, for the progressive accomplishment of a new purpose—on the other side a backward going policy which would result in a return to the international relationships of 1914."[55]

If Roosevelt was an inspired choice for the vice-presidential nominee, he also proved how irrelevant the vice presidency was in campaigning. The American people listened to the Democrats drone on about the importance of the League of Nations and the need for the United States to be internationally engaged—and switched off. Bored with lectures about their international responsibilities, they opted overwhelmingly for the Republicans, who promised a return to "normalcy." It wasn't so much that they rejected the League of Nations, it's just that they didn't care.

When the electoral votes were tallied, the Republican ticket of Warren Harding and Calvin Coolidge won 404, while Cox and Roosevelt received only 127.★ Roosevelt handled the results with outward calm, but he learned an important lesson that would shape his outlook on the next world war: the American people could never be motivated to support pre-emptive international engagement, and talking about using American force around the world was a vote-loser. In the wake of the election loss, he pivoted from being perhaps the most bellicose member of the Wilson administration's foreign and strategic policymaking team to becoming an apostle of peace. By March 1921, he was claiming to the public that he had always been opposed to the US being the greatest naval power in the world.[56] He had decided that a strong navy and anything that smacked of possible

★ The Republicans also received more than 60 per cent of the popular vote, making this the greatest landslide since before the Civil War.

war was to be avoided. As he sadly told a friend from his Navy Department days, the American people had little interest in naval power.[57]

This caution was the final piece in the puzzle in creating the strategist that would lead the United States in World War II. Naval power, particularly the control of communications, would determine the outcome of any war.* To allow this to happen, the United States should limit land battles whenever possible, prioritizing sea and air weaponry technology and production. However, politically one had to assume that the American people would be reluctant, even hostile, to going down the internationalist route, so any strategy had to be crafted to keep them on board. In many ways, it was a "say one thing but do the other" policy—and time would show that Franklin Roosevelt was a master of it.

---

* By the time of World War II, Roosevelt broadened his understanding of communications control to take in air-sea power, which he saw as a combined area of modern war to be won by constructing the largest possible navy and air force.

9. Benito Mussolini and Bluffing as Strategy

Benito Mussolini sat high up amongst ridges and peaks, staring across empty expanses at snow-covered mountains, starry skies and the occasional Austrian soldier. "From on high there is a marvellous view of the mountains," he wrote in his diary. "On the left of the Cadore the sharp peaks of the Dolomites are outlined against the sky. The soul is expanded and uplifted by such a sight. The mountains, like the sea, make one *feel* the immensity of space."[1] At times, the scenes were so awe-inspiring that, arrogant as he was, he felt he could not do them justice: "A soft purple line marks the coming of the sun. If I were a poet . . . !"[2]

Mussolini's string of good fortune had continued. It was the spring of 1916, and his new posting was one of the best in the Italian Army. For four months, from February through to the end of May, the Dolomites would be his home. Though he stressed in his diary the dangers he supposedly faced, Mussolini clearly enjoyed himself—but it would not be entirely true to say he had it easy. Italian soldiers who served in the mountains had to fight in a treacherous landscape and endure extreme weather. Once the front moved thirty miles north of the Adriatic, almost until it reached the Trento area, it followed high mountain ranges—some of the tallest in Europe—which could only be crossed by narrow foot passes. This made the movement of large bodies of troops impossible.[3] Reduced to small units, soldiers in the Dolomites made life-threatening treks, often strapped to lines of supply-laden donkeys, along narrow mountain trails, with the constant possibility of plunging to death with one misstep.* They had to worry about being buried alive by avalanches or

---

* Mussolini was particularly complimentary of the role of donkeys in keeping the Italian Army provisioned in the war. For many Italian soldiers these animals were the most reliable means of supply they had.

blizzards that could descend without warning. Their lives could also be monotonous. Often tasked with holding isolated blockhouses or mountain entrenchments, they could go long stretches with few breaks; and if the Austrian sharpshooters were operating nearby, they would have to keep under cover all day—unable to contemplate the immensity of space.

What Mussolini did not have to worry about, however, was being ordered to charge headlong into Austrian machine-gun fire, and that alone made his a prized position. Emilio Lussu, a soldier in a Sardinian unit who spent the same period fighting on the Carso plateau, envied soldiers such as Mussolini who were in the Dolomites, later reflecting: "We had always talked of the war in the mountains as if it were some privileged rest."[4]

Mussolini's experiences reinforce Lussu's suspicions. Moving from blockhouse to blockhouse, from ridge to mountaintop, occasionally going to the rear to rest, he rarely saw, let alone engaged, the enemy. He marched many miles a day up mountain trails, becoming physically stronger, and he revelled in his sense of well-being. One May morning, after a "deep, sweet and refreshing sleep," he seemed to glow with good health. "Bright sunlight this morning," he gushed in his diary. "We have laid down fir boughs in the tents and have put trees against the sides so that we are concealed from above. Simple life—I think of Rousseau and his 'return to nature.'"[5]

With time on his hands, Mussolini thought a great deal about Italy and the war, and this presented him with what would be one of his constant conundrums. He wanted the Italian soldier to be (and liked to portray him as) an aggressive nationalist, eager to attack any enemies without hesitation. He certainly did his best to find evidence of such, recording conversations that reinforced his prejudices about the strength of Italian nationalism. In the mountains, he encountered one officer, a Sicilian from Catania, who told him exactly what he wanted to hear. The Sicilians were the "very best soldiers possible," the Catanese crowed to Mussolini, and then added: "My little Sicilians have given every proof of their courage and loyalty. All they want is a bayonet to attack and then . . ."[6]

Yet Mussolini also understood that many Italian soldiers were hardly nationalist zealots. In April 1916, he did a mental exercise and divided up a typical company of 250 men based on their support for the war. Out of 250 soldiers he guessed that only 20 per cent strongly backed the war. These included 10 per cent who had returned to Italy from abroad—many from the United States—whom Mussolini considered "splendid soldiers from every point of view." Then there were another 20 per cent, mostly younger men, whom were mostly trustworthy, as they had volunteered. The other 60 per cent of the company, a significant majority, did not support the war. He guessed that 100 men, 40 per cent of the total, accepted their duty with resignation and "would have liked to have remained at home." The remaining 20 per cent were at best silently hostile, including "the unscrupulous, the riffraff"—those who only stayed in line for fear of military discipline. For one of Italy's leading interventionists, it was hardly an optimistic summary.[7]

But Mussolini was not pessimistic enough, as he would soon discover. One of the difficulties of judging his war record is that he spent long stretches away from the front, either on leave or writing articles to try to keep up Italian hopes for ultimate victory. These long gaps are usually just left blank in his war diary. He says almost nothing about them in his autobiography, and his biographers have been unable to uncover specifics about his whereabouts.[8] That was the case for most of 1916, when his final diary entry during his mountain phase was for May 16, and his next on November 30. During the intervening six months it is difficult to say exactly what he was doing.

It certainly seems plausible that he was being protected from dangerous action by the military, or at least accorded special leave to keep him away from the front during particularly dangerous times. For Mussolini's absences from the front coincided with some of the worst battles between the Italians and the Austrians. Just before his diary stopped in May, the Austrians caught the Italians by surprise by launching an offensive in Trentino. They punched a hole in the middle of the Italian line, and for a while they threatened to get down onto the Venetian plain with their spearheads, only twenty miles from Vicenza. Marshal Cadorna rushed in reinforcements to plug the gap, and then a Russian attack on the Eastern Front caused the Austrians to withdraw half their troops. When the fighting stopped, another 80,000 Italian soldiers had been killed, wounded, captured or declared missing.

At the other end of the line, on the Carso, Cadorna went on the offensive again in his Don Quixote-like quest to capture Trieste. Starting in August 1916, he launched a series of attacks against the Austrian lines: the Sixth, Seventh, Eighth and Ninth Battles of the Isonzo. The first of these was one of his few significant successes in the war. Italian soldiers, now strongly supported by well-prepared artillery fire, attacked with elan towards Gorizia and Monte San Michele.[9] In the mess that was the Carso, they often ended up fighting hand-to-hand with the Austrian troops, but in the end they secured both objectives. Yet the Austrians simply retreated to the next line of high rocky ridges, and the Italian drive petered out. That did not stop Cadorna from launching three subsequent offensives, each trying to further extend the Gorizia bridgehead. He had a few local advances, but no major breakthroughs. By the end of the Ninth Battle, in early November, Italian elan had turned into exhaustion, if not outright depression.[10] Combined, these four battles on the Carso had cost Italy around 150,000 more casualties. Trieste remained obstinately in Austrian hands.

As soon as Italian offensive operations ceased, Mussolini appeared at the front, as if by magic. This time, however, there would be no glorious mountain vistas. He was forced to confront the horror of the war—or at least the detritus—that he had helped unleash. "It has been a cruel war on the terrible Carso," he wrote in his diary. Yet despite the staggering amount of bloodshed and lives lost, he at first tried to spin the carnage he witnessed as a necessary step on the road to rebirth. "The muddy and gory trenches are swallowing up our men, but the Europe of tomorrow will see that from this tragic soil there will spring the purple flowers of a greater liberty."[11]

The average Italian soldier, however, had no wish to become fertilizer for Mussolini's freedom. He could see all around him too many real examples of such sacrifice. So many men had died on the Carso, and movement over it could be so dangerous that many bodies remained unburied—with others only partially covered, in shallow, hastily dug pits. Mussolini saw one of these makeshift cemeteries hit by an artillery shell which blew corpses into the sky, leaving the area littered with body parts. He could come up with nothing poetic, simply recording: "Macabre!"[12]

Such sights were not unusual. While there were no large-scale attacks during Mussolini's months on the plateau, there were regular patrols, artillery and sniper fire, freezing mud and constant premonitions of death. Mussolini was horrified to see the corpse of a fellow Bersaglieri soldier left unburied, within clear sight of his living comrades. "Why does no one bury him?" he asked his diary, and then tried to explain away his fellow soldiers' nonchalance. "In order to allow his family to keep the illusion that he is 'missing'? Perhaps."[13]

What Mussolini didn't want to admit was that his fellow soldiers could not give a damn. They had no desire to expose themselves to danger for the mundane sight of a corpse—even that of a friend. The morale of the Italian Army, regardless of all of Mussolini's homages, was plummeting. Both at home and on the battlefield the soldiers were beset by tragedy. On the home front, the winter of 1916–17 was a time of great deprivation, and the Italian mortality rate leapt due to disease and inadequate food supplies.[14] Many of the soldiers—peasants who had worked their entire lives on farms—were desperate to get home to help. Of course, the main reason many wanted to get away was that they had endured one of the most trying battle experiences of the war. A year and a half of constant fighting, most of which saw the Italian Army struggling to advance over useless terrain and suffering significantly higher casualties than their Austrian enemies, had taken its toll in both lives and minds.

Much of the time within the narrative of World War I, the Italian experience is overlooked in favour of the great battles of the Western and even Eastern Fronts. Yet by Western Front standards, the Italian soldier made an equal, and in some ways greater, sacrifice to that of his British and French comrades. By the end of the war, five million Italians had served in the armed forces, and 650,000 of them had died (or would soon perish because of war-received wounds).[15] Cadorna, in launching an offensive every three months between May 1915 and August 1917, asked more of his troops than the British and

French did of their own.[16] The Italian death rate, approximately equal to the UK's, occurred in a timespan only three-quarters as long.

Italian soldiers also lived in worse conditions and fought on more treacherous ground, which led to an even more stressful environment. For instance, artillery shells fired on the Italian Front were more likely to land on rocks, which would send deadly shards into the air, multiplying the killing effect. Compared to the soft, rock-free farm fields of northern France, artillery fire on the Italian Front was 70 per cent more deadly.[17]

Across the Italian Army, desertions rose almost exponentially, and incidents of self-mutilation became a serious problem.[18] In 1917, one squad of Sicilian soldiers deliberately infected their own eyes with gonorrhoeal mucus. Four of them were permanently blinded, but that didn't stop the army handing them all harsh prison sentences of up to fifteen years.[19]

Mussolini's cycle of pleasant, relatively danger-free postings followed by long periods away from the front was an extraordinary exception to the normal life of an Italian soldier. Italian units, even elite ones such as the Bersaglieri, could be kept stationed in dangerous, forward postings for extended periods. Too worried by how the soldiers might behave if allowed too far behind the lines, Cadorna and other senior officers often kept their units at the front out of a misbegotten fear that they could make serious trouble or even desert if not under the strictest military discipline.

In 1916, Cadorna received a report that the 5th Bersaglieri, which had not been rotated out of the line regularly, was experiencing a morale crisis. Its soldiers were suffering from mental and physical "exhaustion" and desertions were increasing.[20] Cadorna replied that the Bersaglieri would have to suck it up. Faced with such a reality, it is not surprising that many Italian soldiers were fed up with the war— and this was politically and personally dangerous for Mussolini as one of the country's most prominent interventionist agitators.

Rumblings of anger had been directed towards interventionists from the start of the war. A fellow interventionist and friend of Mussolini's, Filippo Corridoni, had been killed in late 1915, shot in the head fighting the Austrians. Not long after, Mussolini came upon an

Italian soldier who accosted him, saying, "I have good news for you: they killed Corridoni. It serves him right, I am glad of that. All these interventionists should die."[21] By late 1916 such sentiments were spreading.

On the Carso, Mussolini had to search out fellow interventionists for emotional support. On New Year's Eve 1917, he was showing signs of depression and needed to do something to keep up his spirits.[22] He banded together with a group of interventionist comrades and they talked boldly about preparing for an offensive in the spring, while also admitting that they would need "several weeks of quiet" in an Italian town far behind the lines before any attack was launched. Mussolini and his group had a pathetic need to vindicate their pro-war stance, and he declared that only after the war would their value be recognized: "These humble sons of the people who have felt the righteousness of our war, deserve to be highly 'honoured' when victory comes."[23]

At the time there was little honour for them. Mussolini's war record, combined with his pro-war agitation, was leading to personal attacks on his integrity. Stories circulated that he had been granted leave from the front line far more than the average soldier (which only seems to have been the truth). He became so worried by the rumours that he started searching out people to defend his war record, going so far as to try to mobilize the Church on his behalf. On the day after Christmas 1916, Mussolini's unit had been visited by their chaplain, Father Michele. Mussolini "spoke to him of the polemics which arose on account of my winter leave and asked him to testify for me." The priest promised to come to his defence.

This need for vindication revealed the depth of the emotional crisis Mussolini was suffering. The constant presence of death combined with torrential winter rains had taken their toll. He complained that he lacked the motivation to do basic tasks, neglecting to improve fortifications to protect against enemy gunfire. As his mental condition deteriorated, the agnostic even engaged with the idea of Catholic devotion. On New Year's Eve, Father Michele returned to Mussolini's unit and handed out devotional prayer sheets, which were politically constructed to give Italian soldiers comfort that their sacrifice had value and that victory would be theirs in the end. Mussolini read the prayers closely, and recorded them verbatim in his diary: "We indeed want victory; a two-fold victory: one over our political enemies, for the glory of our country, and the other over ourselves for our own purification and uplifting."[24] Though clearly moved by the words, his mood failed to improve. On January 21, 1917, he admitted, "I have been low in morale," and for January 27 and 28 he wrote simply: "Snow, cold, infinite boredom. Orders, counter-orders, disorder."[25] By February, his need to calm his nerves became so acute that he took up smoking.[26]

Had Mussolini been left at the front for much longer, he might have lapsed into an inescapable depression. As it was, he was spared. On February 23, he was part of a team manning a trench gun when a projectile exploded in the barrel, peppering the soldiers with shrapnel. Mussolini was brought to the hospital incoherent, muttering, "I have seen tragedy." He would never again see the front as a soldier.

His recovery was typical of World War I. He had his ups and downs, running high fevers when infections hit and suffering from delirium. Eventually, most of the shrapnel was removed from his body. The only atypical development, and one that rather reinforced the notion that he was given special treatment throughout the war, was that the king himself paid a hospital visit to the wounded corporal and praised his devotion to duty.

Once recovered enough to work, Mussolini's career as a soldier was over and he returned full-time to the job of pro-war agitator. Having been wounded in action, he now felt even more liberated to press his case for Italian greatness in general—and his own greatness in particular.[27] He took back the reins as editor of *Il Popolo d'Italia*, which had suffered during his absence. The replacement editors lacked Mussolini's aggression and the paper had gone into significant debt—having to be bailed out by friendly nationalist industrialists.[28] Mussolini energized the paper and made it his mission to keep up Italian spirits and assure the nation that victory would be theirs. He put the government on notice that it would have to make major social changes to "give the fighters the certainty that the country they are going back to when the war is over will be a different one."[29]

No longer at the front, where he had to worry about soldiers angry at interventionists, he started pushing a cultish notion of an aristocracy of politically aware veterans. This *trincerocrazia* (rule by those who had served in the trenches) would form the core of a "new and better elite" which he claimed should rule Italy after the war.[30] Of course, he was too modest to point out that a prominent newspaper editor who had served in the army would be ideally suited to lead this new trench-ocracy. Mussolini was coming closer and closer to arguing for an overthrow of the Italian state.[31] The journey to a personal dictatorship was shortening.

The articles he published after his return give an indication of how his time at the front had shaped his outlook on war—and how much he had wilfully decided not to learn. In June 1917, he gave his readers a detailed overview of the war from a grand-strategic perspective. By this time two major developments had reshaped the conflict: the entry of the United States as a supporter of the Allies, and the almost concurrent withdrawal of Russia after the Bolshevik revolution. To Mussolini, partly because of his great respect for American power, this made victory for the Allies inevitable. He told his readers that while the war would not end in 1917, it had entered its "decisive and conclusive phase."[32]

Beyond this judgement, however, much of the article showed how much he still saw this "sacred" war as a contest of will, with material factors secondary. He argued that US entry was important because of the political awareness of American soldiers, more than the fact that the largest productive power in the world had joined the fray. In Mussolini's world, half a million Americans "well aware of why they fight" were worth more than five million politically unaware Russian troops.

Indeed, Mussolini made much of the importance of will over equipment—or as he put it, "material superiority is not enough to win the war." He said the Germans had made a terrible mistake going on the defensive on the Western Front in 1917, as this was actually "more expensive" than going on the offensive. How anyone who had witnessed how machine guns and modern artillery could devastate attacking infantrymen could still think the defensive was more expensive boggles the mind. However, instilling the right values remained to Mussolini the key to preparing soldiers to advance. He believed that the failure of the Italians to secure their offensive goals was not down to the fact that they had constantly ordered attacks on well-prepared defensive lines, but because the Italian Army had failed to politically educate and motivate its soldiers. In the balance between morale and equipment, willpower always triumphed over steel. Mussolini was "certain that thousands of cannons and machine guns are not enough for victory, if the spirit of the soldiers is lacking."

Mussolini's relative lack of interest in the importance of production and technology to the winning of war stands out because he had plenty of time to see both in action. Aircraft had played an increasingly prominent role on the Italian Front as the war went on, a presence he did not fail to notice. He even wrote from his hospital bed in March 1917 about hearing the "usual whirring of aeroplanes."[33] Yet he gave little thought as to how they would or could change warfare.*

The irony for Mussolini was that his focus on the will of the Italian soldier was about to undergo its greatest test—though the results would differ from his expectations. Throughout the summer of 1917, Mussolini assured his readers that the morale of the army was in excellent shape and that soon the march on Trieste would recommence. The Germans had other ideas. Though Germany and Italy had declared war on each other in 1916, the Germans had sent very little support to the Austrians on the Italian Front. That changed in late 1917. That year the Germans had sensibly disregarded Mussolini's advice and adopted a defensive strategy on the Western Front. They bunkered down in well-prepared positions and allowed the British and French to launch their catastrophically bloody attacks known as the Battle of Passchendaele and the Nivelle offensive (the latter of

---

* Mussolini's relationship to aircraft explains a lot about his strategic thinking. He used airplanes as a way of improving his personal image. He became a very early pilot and used this to help establish a personal narrative for daring and bravery. What he never did, however, was try to understand the importance of air power in war.

which almost broke the morale of the French Army). Cadorna, however, acting just as Mussolini would have liked, built up for two more major attacks, the Tenth and Eleventh Battles of the Isonzo. At this point, details are unnecessary. The Italian Army did its best to advance into the teeth of Austrian defensive firepower, but even with significant numerical advantages they hardly advanced at all. A few hills were seized during the Eleventh Battle, but at a prohibitive cost. These offensives were the two bloodiest Cadorna would ever oversee, inflicting a combined 300,000 casualties and leaving the Italian Army catatonic when they ended in September. This was precisely the moment when the Germans decided to make a major effort.

Able to reduce their casualty losses in the west in 1917, the Germans had started thinking about an offensive against Italy. With the Bolsheviks in charge of Petrograd and conducting peace negotiations with Berlin, the German Army and its Austrian ally could both free up significant numbers of troops for the attack. They formed a new joint German-Austrian force, the 14th Army, made up of fifteen divisions. The German troops selected for the operation were those with great experience fighting in mountainous terrain—including the "illustrious" Bavarian Alpenkorps, which included a young Erwin Rommel. Adding the troops concentrated to the north and south of the 14th Army, the Austrians and Germans now had numerical superiority in the area of attack and they would be moving forward from the hills towards better terrain, not directly into the high ground as the Italians had been doing for more than two years.

Cadorna, however, even though he was receiving accurate reports of a German build-up, was too obtuse to realize his army was under threat. Until only a few days before the attack he didn't take the prospects of an enemy offensive seriously.[34] When he did accept that an attack might be coming, he seemed to welcome a German-Austrian offensive, telling his daughter that his troops were "on the eve of great events."[35] He was convinced that his troops would blunt the coming attack, which would make his own next great offensive that much easier. Plus, the weather was dreadful, which would lead to chaos for the attackers, only increasing their losses.

As was typical for Cadorna, things did not work out as expected.

When the Germans and Austrians launched their attack on October 24, in what is known as the Battle of Caporetto, the Italian Front collapsed. The Germans used the terrible weather and their skills in the mountains to manoeuvre close to the Italian lines before attacking. Instead of signalling their intentions with a long, heavy artillery bombardment, they used a short, sharp barrage followed by a swift infiltration of Italian lines by small groups of skilled soldiers who aimed for weak points.[36] Ridges and mountaintop fortifications that were thought to be almost impregnable were swiftly captured.

Chaotic Italian leadership made things much worse. Cadorna gave orders for a retreat, then countermanded them and ordered the soldiers to fight to the death, before finally ordering a retreat again. Other senior officers abandoned the battlefield entirely and could not be located for days. Outnumbered, exhausted after years of bloody attacks, poorly and incompetently led, the Italian Army on the Carso had had enough. Soldiers started abandoning the front lines and all heavy equipment they could not carry, and headed back to the rear.

It quickly turned into a rout.[37] The Germans moved so swiftly that they threatened to get behind the Italian 2nd Army, Cadorna's most reliable formation. Not wanting to be trapped on the wrong side of the Isonzo, most of the 2nd Army's soldiers, without orders, chose to try to get across the river. They crowded the roads leading to the major bridges, one of which was the site of Mussolini's sacred drink as a conqueror crossing eastwards two years earlier. They created a disorganized mass of humanity with the thousands of civilians who were also trying to get away. Along the front, upwards of a million people were fleeing for their lives. The only benefit of this was the relatively small number of Italians who were killed—though the number captured or who deserted was gargantuan.* The area was also strewn with discarded equipment.

The collapse was so swift and total that even the Germans and Austrians were surprised.[38] Having expected the assault to clear the Carso and push the Italians back to the 1915 borders, they found the

---

* By some estimates, 280,000 Italian soldiers were taken prisoner and 350,000 deserted. In comparison, only 30,000 were wounded and 10,000 killed.

door to Italy itself unlocked. It was here that the terrain now moved to help the attackers. Once they left the mountains and hills and headed west, the Germans and Austrians reached the broad and mostly flat Venetian plain. They could move quickly, and advanced at a rate that had not been seen before on the Italian Front and had only been matched on the Western Front in 1914, before the First Battle of the Marne.

Mussolini's reaction to Caporetto was extraordinary. Having assured his readers that the Italian Army was motivated and combat-ready, he first tried to pretend that all was well. On October 28, the day before the Germans seized Udine, where Cadorna had his long-time headquarters, Mussolini told his readers this was all part of a cunning plan cooked up by the Italian high command: "Our Command was not surprised . . . among all the possibilities of the Austro-German manoeuvre, what happened has been taken in account by our Chief of Staff, as well it must have. Even before the offensive . . . our Command must have studied and taken all the measures for the counter-manoeuvre."[39]

Two days later, when it became clear that Cadorna had no cunning plan, Mussolini started blaming the Russians for pulling out of the war.[40] Meanwhile, the Germans and Austrians continued with their swift advance. By November 12, just over two weeks after they had attacked, their forces had penetrated more than 100 miles into Italy and were only twenty miles from Venice itself. To the west of Venice lay Italy's industrial and economic heartland; Italy's entire position in the war was hanging in the balance. The British and French started wondering if the benefits of having an Italian ally were worth the cost.

Then, stunningly and unexpectedly, the Italian soldier stood his ground. When news of the disaster of Caporetto reached the nation, the war was recast for many from one of useless attacks and meaning-less deaths into one of the defence of home and hearth from brutal Germanic invaders.[41] The number of desertions dropped steeply and fresh recruits started turning up for their draft enlistments in higher numbers than they had before Caporetto.

That being said, the Italian recovery was functional as well as emotional. By the time the first phase of the German-Austrian offensive was petering out, the front line was at one of the few excellent defensive positions for the Italians on the Venetian plain—the broad, fast-flowing (in winter) Piave River. Once the Italian soldiers were safely on the west bank of the Piave, its bridges were blown, and for the first time since fleeing over the Carso the Italian Army regained the territorial advantage. Moreover, major material and organizational changes soon helped make things even better. Cadorna was finally removed, in one of the few valiant steps taken by King Vittorio Emanuele. His successor, General Armando Diaz, a Neapolitan, was cut from very different cloth: prudent and with no desire to sacrifice his men unnecessarily.[42] Sceptical and rational where Cadorna was highly religious and cocky, Diaz prioritized building a solid defensive line and put off any ideas of an offensive. After holding the Germans and Austrians during their last attempts to cross the Piave in late December and early January, he concentrated on making his army holistically better. That meant delaying any offensive. Even when the British and French put pressure on him to attack in early 1918, he refused to budge.

Diaz also took advantage of the fact that Italian war production had risen significantly since 1915.* Stocks of machine guns and shells were now particularly high.[43] He even saw to it that the soldiers' pay was raised and the harsh punishments of the Cadorna era moderated. Regular leave, for instance, was made policy, and the Italian soldier was treated like a man—not some untrustworthy, misbehaving child.

Finally, the Allies decided to provide Italy with some significant support. One of the most impressive aspects of Diaz's performance is that he was able to get a great deal of front-line equipment and infantry support from the Allies while resisting their entreaties to go on the offensive. Not long after the scale of the disaster at Caporetto

---

* Getting precise figures on Italian armaments production during World War I is not easy, as detailed, consolidated records were not kept. What seems to have happened was that war production rose significantly from the outset of war through the first half of 1917. At that point something close to full production was reached and then the building of war materiel flattened before declining in 1918.

became clear, the British and French promised to send six divisions each to Italy to help stem the tide. In this case they were (almost) true to their word.* Between October 30 and December 8, 1917, more than 1,400 trains carried 261,000 soldiers, 1,000 artillery pieces and 24,000 vehicles to help stabilize the front at the Piave.[44]

When the Austrians and Germans returned to the offensive in June 1918, they were faced by an entirely different enemy—motivated, better equipped and with significant French and British support. When they tried to force their way across the Piave, they were met with fierce, well-constructed defences and mowed down with machine guns as if they were Italians on the Carso. After a few days of useless slaughter trying to break the Italian line, the Germans and Austrians called off the offensive. Their casualties were massive and now their armies were breaking.

Ever prudent, Diaz took his time to launch a counterattack. He didn't believe things were ready until October 23. By that time, Austrian and German armies were melting away throughout Europe, and the Italian attack, which came to be known as the Battle of Vittorio Veneto, quickly shattered what remained of their lines. The Austrian retreat that ensued was just as chaotic and destructive as the one the Italians had experienced exactly one year earlier at Caporetto. The war in Italy, and all of Europe, was ending.

While Diaz was rebuilding the army, Mussolini was spending much of his time thinking about how to destroy the Italian state and replace it with something new—something more Mussolini-like. One of the first things he talked about was using state power to crush all opponents of the war and direct the efforts of the people. When the enormity of the disaster at Caporetto first became undeniable, he had called for a form of total war including the closing of almost all forms of recreation such as concert halls, racetracks and even coffee shops.[45] This was just a precursor. Soon he was demanding that all Italian media be ruthlessly purged and centralized under one authority. As he told the readers of *Il Popolo d'Italia* on February 2, 1918, "I am

---

* In the end the Allies only sent eleven divisions as one of the British units was kept on the Western Front because of the Battle of Cambrai.

strongly convinced that it is necessary to put all newspapers down, killing them, organize their massacre." These newspapers depressed the public spirit while focusing on bad news and defeats, he thought. Far better to have only one national newspaper that could provide the news he thought was best. It would not have been difficult to imagine which editor Mussolini would want to run the one national newspaper.

Controlling the media was but one step on the road to a nationalist dictatorship. A few days after he called for the "killing" of all other newspapers, Mussolini mused in a speech to pro-war supporters that the great mistake the interventionists had made was in not over-throwing the Italian government at the start of the war. Leaving power in the hands of the "old establishment" had weakened national resolve and the willingness to take the radical action needed to make the war a success.[46] In this vision, dictatorship during the war was a good thing. Being particularly pro-American at this time in his life, Mussolini praised Woodrow Wilson extravagantly for taking war-time powers that were equivalent to those of a "dictator." Taking such powers, Mussolini argued, "will mean, in a few words, that Wilson will have a dictatorship. When a stateman owns unlimited powers, he is a 'dictator,' even if he does not give himself such a title."[47]

If Mussolini was marching down the road to personal rule, he was also losing any inhibitions in terms of manipulating patriotism for his own ends. Now Italy must be made even more powerful, dominating both sides of the Adriatic. "The Italian people have changed during these three years of war," he declared. "Italy must become a great power, expanding on the sea, to the east. The Adriatic Sea must become a sea which is militarily Italian and only Italian."[48] As part of his extreme nationalist stance, he started spinning patriotic delusions. Thus the Battle of Vittorio Veneto moved from being but a contrib-uting part in the overall collapse of Germany and Austria-Hungary to the "greatest victory in world history."[49] Mussolini was trying to bluff the Italian population into believing that Italy was a great power entitled to a more prestigious standing in the world.

But bluff could only carry one so far, as Italy discovered at the Paris Peace Conference in 1919–20. The Italian delegation—led by

Premier Vittorio Orlando, who came to power after the catastrophe of Caporetto, and spurred on by nationalists such as Mussolini—went into the conference wanting more than that promised to Italy by the sordid Treaty of London in 1915. In particular, they demanded the Austro-Hungarian city of Fiume (now known as Rijeka, in Croatia) and talked about further Italian advances down the Adriatic coast. Though Italian paramilitaries, led by Gabriele D'Annunzio, seized Fiume on behalf of Italy in 1919, the Italian delegation at Paris ran into a brick wall and the relative power balance between Italy and its more influential partners was made very clear. The British and the French no longer saw Italy as being important to their victory, and Woodrow Wilson refused to say that the United States, which had only joined the war in 1917, was bound by the Treaty of London in the first place.

The Italian delegation was stymied and walked out of the negotiations in a huff. Yet when it was clear that the Allies wouldn't budge, they had no choice but to return to Paris and accept dictation on what they would receive. Italian victory in the war was quickly turned into another national humiliation—at least according to Mussolini. His Italy, a "powerful and prolific" nation with an "exuberant" population, received only a few scraps from the table (such as Trieste, which was now seen as something insignificant), while the rest of the Allies carried off the greater prizes.[50]

This resentment served Mussolini well. If the Allies had unfairly thwarted Italy at Paris, Mussolini would be the man to make Italy great again. He created his own political movement in the midst of this supposed humiliation—the National Fascist Party. Styled as a patriotic movement dominated by politically minded former soldiers, as Mussolini had started prophesying in 1917, the Fascists were to be his vehicle to make himself dictator. At first, loosely organized groups called Fasci were assembled in March 1919, in the midst of Orlando's humiliation. In November 1921 the Fascist Party itself was founded with Mussolini as its leader, and in 1922 he seized power over all of Italy. It was the culmination of his wartime learning.

Mussolini viewed the Italian state, not insensibly, as too weak and chaotic to save itself. He thus threatened a march on Rome more as an act of bluster than any widespread violent action. Indeed, he was prepared to call the whole thing off if the government reacted with force. Luckily for him they didn't, and the indecisive King was only too happy to invite Mussolini to take power to end the chaos. Il Duce was made.

World War I had taught Mussolini how to seize and manipulate power, and the value of acting like a great power even if you were not one. The only trouble with this strategic outlook would come if someone called Mussolini's bluff.

10. Adolf Hitler: Victory and Defeat

Wandering the streets of Berlin in October 1917, Adolf Hitler found the German home front transformed. When he was last in the capital, a year before, it had been full of desperately hungry residents quickly losing faith in final victory. Now the city was pulsing with energy. Berlin was "magnificent, a real metropolis." A busy hive of activity, the "traffic" Hitler saw on the streets passing by was "tremendous." Hitler spent his time as a tourist "getting to know the museums better" and seemed content with everything he encountered. As he wrote in a very self-satisfied postcard to another soldier at the front, "I am short of nothing." [1]

Hitler was in Berlin because things at the front seemed so quiet. For what would be the only time in the war, he had voluntarily asked for leave, a request that the regiment was more than happy to grant. When he returned to France from his pleasant holiday, Hitler found a situation which only magnified his sense of well-being. The List Regiment was serving in one of the quietest sections of the Western Front, guarding the Oise–Aisne Canal in Picardy, not far from the heart of the champagne-producing regions of France. From late 1917 through early 1918, Hitler could go back and forth along the flat lands and low hills of the region, with little to fear from what seemed to him to be unnaturally subdued French artillery. He became triumphant, believing that Allied forces across from him were "visibly depressed." [2] And why not? They had spent two years battering away against the German Army, hardly gaining any territory, and would soon be pummelled by the greatest German offensive of the war.

Almost everywhere that Hitler looked on the Western Front was evidence that the German Army was growing in strength and preparing to attack. Lines of fresh soldiers were materializing, unloading from a constant procession of trains appearing from the east. These were veterans of Germany's victory over Russia. In the end almost a million men were moved to the Western Front in preparation for the great offensive. These reinforcements were accompanied by more and heavier equipment which, knowing what we do of Hitler, would have caused him even greater excitement. Along with the thick, 42cm howitzers—nicknamed Big Berthas because of their girth and punch—there were long-range Paris Guns, looking like suspension bridges tilted upwards, and heavy A7V tanks that clanked along like moveable, lumbering fortresses. These behemoths were supported by new, technologically advanced aircraft flying overhead, including the formidable Fokker D.VII, more manoeuvrable than its British and French counterparts. This force, Hitler was convinced, would crush the French and British forces facing them, leading Germany to a final victory. Looking back on this time when dictating *Mein Kampf*, even after the war had been lost, he still couldn't restrain his excitement. "Even enemy propaganda was having a hard time of it; it was no longer so easy to prove the hopelessness of German victory."[3]

Another reason Hitler's faith in the German Army was at an apex in late 1917 and early 1918 was that up until that time he had avoided most of the catastrophic battles that define our understanding of the Western Front. His deployments were normally along quiet sections, or occasionally on the fringes of great battles. This had insulated him from seeing the worst that the war could offer. In 1915 the List Regiment had spent much of its time stationed near the town of Fromelles in far northern France. They did take part in the battles of Neuve Chapelle in March and Aubers Ridge in May, but these were small compared to what would come later on the Western Front, including the two great battles of 1916, Verdun and the Somme.

Verdun was first great battle of the trenches, and it arose from the plan of General Erich von Falkenhayn, chief of the German General Staff after Moltke, to attack the symbolically important French city. Whether or not Falkenhayn's actual plan was to use Verdun to draw the French Army into combat and "bleed France white," he certainly succeeded in killing unprecedented numbers of soldiers.[4] The Germans started their operation in February 1916 and the French reacted as expected by throwing huge numbers of troops into the area to hold the town. Fighting went on for the rest of the year, making it the longest battle of the war and one of the bloodiest, but Verdun remained defiantly French. In the end both sides bled white. The German Army incurred almost 150,000 dead out of almost 340,000 total casualties. French casualties were even higher. For many of the soldiers who took part in the bloodbath it was a scarring, debilitating struggle that left them shell-shocked and demoralized. Even though the Germans had to transfer in more and more troops from other parts of the front to take part in Verdun, the List Regiment missed the whole campaign.

They did take part in the Battle of the Somme, initially on the fringes. The Somme was the first great offensive of the massively enlarged and industrially equipped British Army, and started on July 1. The British attempted to use their artillery to pound the German defenders into submission, allowing the following waves of infantry to break through their trench lines. It did not work out as planned. The first day of the Somme was the bloodiest single day in British military history, when almost 20,000 British soldiers were killed and 40,000 injured.[5] This slaughter was only the start of what would be a five-month campaign that would leave each side suffering about half a million casualties. Hitler avoided almost all of it. In July, the List Regiment served on the western edge of the battle area, holding its line well and suffering small numbers of casualties.[6] In October, however, it was deployed to the thick of the action. Hitler and his comrades were put on a train and shipped to a new German line on Warlencourt Ridge, right in the middle of the fighting line.[7] Hitler was in high spirits as he approached the great battle. In 1942 he reminisced about how he and his comrades had "laughed and made jokes all night" as they headed to the Somme battlefield.[8]

In Hitler's case the results of the battle would be short and inglorious. The List Regiment entered the line on October 2 and just three days later he was hit, suffering what Americans in World War II would refer to as a "million-dollar wound." As he was taking cover in the dispatch runners' dugout, a British shell fell outside. Shrapnel blasted through the dugout's opening, grazing Hitler and two other soldiers. Hitler's wound, in the thigh, was relatively light, but he was pulled off the line and sent to a military hospital near Berlin. Once there, due to the vagaries of military bureaucracy as much as any-thing, he would wait approximately six months before returning to the Western Front.

Hitler was shocked by what he discovered in Germany.* Instead of a people united in support for the war, he came face to face with widespread dissatisfaction, even defeatism, in both the army and the general public. In hospital he listened, seething, while soldiers boasted about avoiding combat. One, Hitler claimed, said he "pulled his hand through a barbed-wire entanglement" so that he would have to be admitted to hospital, and once inside found endless ways to extend his convalescence.[9] When Hitler was able to walk, he was allowed to visit Berlin and then returned to Munich—and visiting both only added to his anxiety. Though he tried to calm himself by visiting museums and galleries, he grew increasingly angry. Hitler had returned to Germany right in the midst of the greatest food shortages of the war, the famous Turnip Winter of 1916–17. With transatlantic trade cut off by the Royal Navy, and no access to imported food from Russia or France, Germany was left to try to feed its very large, densely packed population using only its own resources. Things were made worse when the 1916 harvest was one of the worst on record, and strict rationing had to be introduced.[10] Caloric intake, which had averaged 3,000 calories a day in Germany before the war, was cut by a third.[11] Soup kitchens were ordered to be constructed in all German cities in an attempt to ward off mass starvation. When Hitler toured Berlin, he found hunger and discontent everywhere.

Things were worse when he reached Munich. Instead of finding German unity, Hitler again became furious when he heard Bavarians blaming Prussians for their misery and hunger, even going so far as to advocate for the restoration of Bavarian independence. In Munich, Hitler claimed, successfully shirking duty had become a badge of honour for soldiers back from the front.[12] The city, which had been his favourite before 1914, would never recover fully in his eyes.

---

* Hitler wrote no letters that have survived from this time, so the only details we have are his recollections in *Mein Kampf*. In this case, as he is so critical of Germans, it's probably true that he was accurately recalling what he felt at the time.

Who was to blame for this crisis? In answering this question, Hitler let his paranoid inner world range free. Though his doubts about the true resilience of the German people remained, he did not want to admit that Germans might honestly doubt that this miserable war, which had already killed hundreds of thousands and brought misery and famine to their doorstep, was a mistake. No, the real culprit had to be the Jews. In his fact-free world, the Jews had used the war to embed their domination throughout the production process and to stoke animosity between Bavaria and Prussia, all the while skilfully avoiding military service themselves.[13]

Reading his delusions, it's hard to believe that people, let alone just Hitler, could take these ideas seriously. As Hitler could see in his own regiment, Jewish Germans had volunteered enthusiastically for the army, had fought valiantly and had died in large numbers. Approximately 100,000 German Jews served in the army between 1914 and 1918, 18 per cent of the Jewish population—which was representative of Germany as a whole. Of these, 80 per cent served in the front lines and 12,000 of them died or went missing.[14] They were a great aid to the German war effort in terms of soldiers and economic production. Yet an extreme nationalist like Hitler could not blame the German people as a whole for their own doubts, so had to fall back upon and enormously magnify the supposed enemy he had first identified back in his Vienna days.

Hitler stewed in his anger in Munich, wanting to get back to his regiment and complaining that, unlike at the front, he could not find enough jam for his bread.[15] By the time he did return in March 1917, things were once again quiet for the List Regiment. Indeed, the summer and winter would once more see the regiment tangentially engaged in the great battles of that year—both of which to a more distant participant such as Adolf Hitler would have provided some proof that the war was turning in Germany's favour. The Allies launched two major efforts to break the trench stalemate on the Western Front in 1917: the Nivelle offensive in April and the Battle of Passchendaele in July. Both almost crushed the spirits of the attacking armies.

During the Nivelle offensive, overseen by the undeservedly

arrogant French general Robert Nivelle, the plan was to overwhelm German lines with mass artillery barrages, more than a million troops and even some of France's newest tanks.[16] He planned to use his guns to create a creeping barrage—a wall of fire surrounding his advancing troops, shielding them from German counterattacks while blasting a hole in the enemy's defences. The Germans, however, warned by Nivelle's public boasting, had more than ample time to prepare for the attack. They strengthened their defences in exactly the right places near the Aisne River, and the French offensive, inevitably, was a bloody fiasco. With the Germans waiting, brave French soldiers were scythed down as they moved forward, advancing about a mile before seeing their advance stopped dead. Nivelle's creeping barrage could not be coordinated on such a large scale, and many French soldiers were killed and wounded by their own shells. After a few weeks of slaughter, the French Army had had enough. Whole units started disobeying orders, refusing to attack. Eventually up to 40,000 soldiers took part in the mutiny. To try to quell the disaster, Nivelle was fired and some of the mutineers were shot. Things calmed down, but the French Army was in no shape to try another attack and would need the rest of the year to recover.

The British attack at Passchendaele was a little more successful, but at a steep cost. An attempt to drive the German forces off the high ground around Ypres and retake the Belgian coast, the offensive was still based on the idea of using overwhelming force to break German lines (which the British Army's General Staff hoped had been considerably weakened by the Nivelle offensive). When the British attack started in July there were some local advances, but inevitably things got bogged down. The summer weather was unusually atrocious, with sheets of rain turning the already soft soil of northern France and southern Belgium into acres of bog. These swampy fields were then pulverized by mass British artillery fire and transformed into a muddy goo, thick enough to swallow horses and the bodies of men, many of which were never found.[17] The result was a sea of immobility, with British troops struggling for hours in the open air to move short distances, exhausting themselves. When the Passchendaele attacks were finally called off, 300,000 British Empire troops were dead, wounded or missing. The government in London, including munitions minister Winston Churchill, was appalled. Churchill, who had been at the front only a little over a year before, had not wanted to launch any offensive in 1917. He responded to the slaughter of Passchendaele by composing his papers on the importance of movement over firepower and the necessity of delaying any more attacks until British troops could be better protected—waiting until 1919 at the earliest.

Such high-level planning was far beyond the remit of Corporal Adolf Hitler. He had only a passing experience of Passchendaele.[18] The List Regiment was originally stationed in part of the line that came under attack, though it was quickly transferred to a much quieter sector in Alsace.* In his own mind, however, the performance of the German Army had provided reasons enough for growing optimism. Based on his experiences in the three years since his baptism of fire, Hitler believed that Germany had developed the equipment, built the army and created the international situation to win the war. He still had some nagging doubts about the commitment of the German home front to the cause, but until almost the end of the war he was able to suppress these.

When it came to equipment, he remained focused on the value of the biggest and strongest, fascinated as always with heavy pieces of machinery that carried a big punch. Like Mussolini, Hitler believed that the political/national commitment of the soldier (the will) was a critical element in victory. However, unlike Mussolini, Hitler had a much greater focus on the importance of military equipment in determining the outcome of modern battles. During World War II, he criticized German decision makers in 1916 and 1917 for putting too much stress on getting soldiers to the front, and in doing so neglecting to prioritize crucial areas of war production back in Germany. "During the first war we had to wait until 1918 before the Army consented to release forty thousand workmen needed urgently for the construction of submarines," he said. "In 1917 the military authorities refused to make available the men required for the manufacture

---

* It was during the transfer to Alsace that Hitler lost his dog Foxl.

of tanks. In this the High Command committed a fatal error, sacrificing a potentially tremendous improvement in war technique in order to avoid a decrease in their available man-power." After this meditation, he added for emphasis that "the decisive factor in any war is the possession of the technically superior weapons."[19]

The need for superior weapons was something that oozed from Hitler's strategic pores, though he had a particular and skewed idea of what was superior. This can best be seen in his constant focus on heavy artillery, which would have massive ramifications in shaping German production in World War II. Hitler's fascination with the value of artillery, the source of his 1916 injury, only grew the more time he spent on the Western Front.

This focus was shared by many other German soldiers. Adolf Meyer served in the List Regiment and later became a committed Nazi. In the 1930s he wrote a hagiographic description of Hitler's service in the regiment which has no value as a work about Hitler. However, Meyer confirmed one thing that was probably true—that the appearance of new German heavy artillery was an important factor in the mental condition of the troops. He connected the upsurge in the general morale of the regiment in late 1917 and early 1918 to the appearance of more heavy artillery, such as the Paris Gun.[20] These guns, which sported barrels so long that they had to be suspended with cables, were the largest artillery weapons of the war. They were capable of hurling shells twenty-five miles up into the air—touching the stratosphere—and their enormous firing arc allowed their shot to reach out for a distance of more than eighty miles.[21] Meyer claims that when the soldiers were told of this new wonder weapon they were dumbfounded—elated that they could now bombard Paris from the Western Front.[22]

Hitler was even more convinced than Meyer of the value of heavy guns. One of his favourites was the archetypical heavy German gun of the war, the Big Bertha. As a convinced nationalist, Hitler was sure that the 42cm gun, which he had seen devastate French villages and British lines in 1914, was already the best in the world, far outclassing anything the French possessed. Yet even with this superiority, he believed that Germany needed to press on in making larger, heavier and more powerful guns like the Big Bertha. In *Mein Kampf*, he would lecture about how having better, similarly sized weapons to the enemy was never enough. Germany's armed forces should not be reaching the same level as its enemies, but always seeking to achieve "superior fighting power."[23]

Even though he had never once been at sea, Hitler was so convinced about his rightness on this question that he even condemned the German Navy for building vessels carrying what he considered under-sized guns. Germany had built the second-largest battlefleet in the world by 1914, based on a force of formidable dreadnoughts. In constructing those battleships, the Germans tried to balance protection and firepower, making them survivable with greater armoured plates and more watertight subdivisions than their British counterparts, but in exchange having slightly smaller guns. To Hitler, this balance was a terrible choice, and the German Navy should have opted first and foremost for the most powerful guns, as the only way to succeed in war was to attack. "The neglect of superior artillery power and superior speed lay entirely in the absolutely erroneous so-called 'idea of risk,'" he wrote in *Mein Kampf*. "The navy leadership by the very form in which it expanded the fleet renounced attack and thus from the outset inevitably assumed the defensive. But in this they also renounced the ultimate success which is and can only be forever in attack."[24]

Hitler's fascination with the largest, heaviest firepower reveals something common in dictators: a stress on strength, without a corresponding ability to understand rational trade-offs. The problem with the Big Bertha was that it was so heavy, weighing almost fifty tons, that moving and setting it up was enormously time-consuming, and ammunition was extremely difficult to produce in large quantities. Also, its use was limited. While it could be effective against large, pre-1914 fortifications, its value in an era of dispersed trench warfare was reduced. Its reputation rested as much on mythology as anything else, and by the end of the war, to those who understood artillery, the Big Bertha's importance had been downgraded and it was considered mostly outmoded.[25]

As for the Paris Gun, rarely has so much been written about something so pointless (and expensive). To propel a shell so far as to hit

Paris, the Germans could only include a small amount of explosive in the casing, making the rounds mostly annoyances that only solidified the reputation the Germans had constructed for themselves of point-less brutality. Someone with a much more rational understanding of cost-effectiveness in war was Captain William Leahy, Franklin Roosevelt's friend who would later serve as the president's chief of staff and chairman of the Joint Chiefs of Staff during World War II. Leahy visited Paris in the summer of 1918 as part of a fact-finding mission to the Allies, and experienced a Paris Gun in action. The day after he arrived the Germans starting bombarding Paris from a distance "said to be 65 or 70 miles," Leahy recalled. The attack started in the morning and lasted for a day, with a shell landing every twenty minutes or so. One hit very close to where Leahy was working, killing "two women, one child, and some horses."[26]

Though the casualties were tragic, Leahy thought the German strikes were useless and expensive. "The damage done by these long-range guns is negligible compared to the effort which must be expended to fire them. The projectile evidently carries a small explosive charge that is not capable of producing any destructive effect beyond a few yards from its point of impact . . . It is not likely that many people in Paris ever know anything about the effect of the bombardment or pay any attention to it."[27] Hitler, however, loved such weaponry, and would eventually pour money into brutally expensive, showy distractions during World War II.

Hitler's judgements on German naval artillery were even more lacking in evidence. The German Navy before World War I, in giving high priority to protection, had built some of the sturdiest, most difficult-to-sink battleships in the world. This was revealed during the Battle of Jutland, the greatest battleship clash in history. When the British Grand Fleet and German High Seas Fleet met in the North Sea in 1916, the British discovered that doing serious damage to a German battleship, with its solid, compartmentalized protec-tion, was no easy task.* Even though the Germans were severely

---

* To be fair, it was not easy for the Germans to damage fully protected British battleships either at Jutland. What was clear, and where Hitler was definitely

outgunned, their ships dealt more damage than they took. This was almost entirely down to the fact that the British had more ships designed to Hitler's tastes than the Germans—battlecruisers with super-heavy guns but relatively slight protection. At Jutland, all three of the British dreadnoughts sunk were battlecruisers, as it was shown that having a big gun without adequate protection was extraordinarily risky.

Hitler's obsession with weight and firepower transferred seamlessly to the tank. Tanks first made their appearance on the Western Front in 1916, when the British used them in the Battle of the Somme. In many ways the creation of Winston Churchill, tanks were thought to be a key to unlocking the trench stalemate on the Western Front. The truth was less glamorous. Though the first British tank attack caused panic in German lines, tanks were still a long way from being the famous blitzkrieg vehicles of World War II. They were slow, averaging less than four miles an hour, broke down easily, and had difficulty manoeuvring around large ditches and obstructions.

The Germans were quick to discover these problems, once they eventually decided to react. At first they did not rush to build their own tanks, thinking they could counter the problem with armour-piercing bullets and artillery. Only in 1918 did anything like a proper German tank appear—the Sturmpanzerwagen A7V. More like a mobile armoured fort than what we now know as a tank, the A7V weighed thirty tons, carried a crew of seventeen soldiers and one officer, and was bristling with armaments. Its sloping armour, which reached almost down to the ground, made it look like a large metal train carriage as it plodded along—which revealed one of its problems. It was prone to breakdowns and had great difficulty operating on anything other than decent roads. Hitler, however, had few doubts. He believed that Germany should have poured more effort into building tanks sooner, even reducing the number of available soldiers if it meant that tank production could have risen earlier and

---

mistaken, was that ships which prioritized firepower over protection were the most vulnerable and were destroyed and sunk in alarming numbers.

more rapidly.[28] In 1942, he expounded on his ideas on tank design, making direct reference to World War I and the need to prioritize firepower over mobility: "At the end of the first World War, experience had shown that only the heaviest and most thickly armoured tank had any value. This didn't prevent people, as soon as peace had returned, from setting about constructing ultra-light tanks. Within our own frontiers we have a network of perfect roads, and this encourages us to believe that speed is a decisive factor."[29]

Hitler was able to understand the value of speed when it came to aircraft, but beyond that he was mostly ignorant about the new technology that was starting to exert influence over the World War I battlefield. Hitler had seen planes in action from early in the war, though at first did not see them as particularly important. He witnessed them dropping propaganda leaflets and scouting, but rarely intruding into combat. This changed in 1916–17 when he started paying attention to aircraft in a combat role. It was during this time that his basic chauvinism about the relative value of German equipment and technology asserted itself. Like many Germans, he was captivated by the exploits of the Red Baron, Manfred von Richthofen. Flying in his distinctive three-wing Fokker, Richthofen led the most famous German fighter wing of the war, which included a young Hermann Göring, whom Hitler would make the head of the German Luftwaffe and name his successor. Hitler later claimed to have watched Richthofen in action during the Battle of Arras in 1917, when the Red Baron and his superior German fighters "totally cleared out the sky. British squadrons came through and were absolutely beaten back." He said he saw an entire flight of ten British aircraft shot "down to the last one." In a sign that he had been growing aware of the power of aircraft to control movement on the battlefield, he remembered that the Red Baron's mastery of the air gave German troops "total freedom."[30] This faith in German technical superiority was something Hitler would cling to from his time on the Western Front until the end of World War II. As he told his generals confidently in 1942, "In the technique of armament, we will always be superior to the others."[31]

If Hitler's faith in the excellence of German equipment only grew during the course of the war, he also believed that the geopolitical situation had moved very much in Germany's favour by late 1917—another reason for his optimism. Hitler had said almost nothing on international politics before this, with his international view best summarized as: Germany is best, Austria is a hopeless degenerate, and the Allies are enemies. Yet he now looked at Europe and calculated that Germany was in much stronger shape than at any time since 1914. On the Italian Front the great German-Austrian victory of Caporetto, which had caused Mussolini such panic, made it seem that Italy could be driven from the war in short order. Even more importantly, it confirmed to Hitler that the German Army had a significant qualitative advantage over its enemies and could break through Allied lines.[32] Overshadowing even this, however, was the Bolshevik revolution and the withdrawal of Russia from the alliance of Germany's enemies. With Stalin playing his role in creating the USSR by withdrawing from the war, Germany had secured what looked like a smashing victory. This allowed for what seemed to Hitler to be "endless transports of men and material" rolling towards the Western Front from Russia.[33]

Adding these factors together, it might not have been unreasonable for a German infantryman with a narrow field of vision to think his army was about to unleash the "final conclusion of the eternal struggle."[34] Yet as the first half of 1918 would demonstrate, Germany had strung together a number of advantages that were enough to win some battles, but nowhere enough to win the war. Germany did transfer a million troops from the Eastern Front to the west after the Bolsheviks sued for peace. The new German commanders in the west, Field Marshal Paul von Hindenburg and his chief of staff, General Erich Ludendorff, were determined to use these troops to break French resistance—and Hitler and the List Regiment would eventually be part of the action.

The most famous German tactic to be used in the attempt was actually a throwback to pre-industrial problem-solving. Instead of trying to batter the French into submission with modern weapons, Hindenburg and Ludendorff's 1918 offensives used less obvious methods. Highly trained German soldiers, referred to as storm troopers, would instead infiltrate Allied lines as quietly as possible.* They would bypass heavily defended areas, and locate gaps. Only then would the offensive begin, with a short, sharp bombardment including high explosives and poison gases to immobilize the defenders. This would provide a window for larger masses of German infantry to surge through the gaps, breaking the stranglehold of the trench lines.

At first this is exactly what happened. When the German attack opened on March 21, a major Western Front breakthrough was achieved for the first time since 1914. Moving over much of the same territory that had seen soldiers scrape and die for hundreds of yards during the Battle of the Somme, the Germans pushed first British then French troops out of their defences and into a general retreat. Cut off and confused, Allied soldiers became disoriented and large numbers became prisoners. On March 21, 21,000 British soldiers were captured, the highest number of any day in the war—and total British casualties after the first three days were 53,000, which almost matched the gory heights suffered during the first day of the Battle of the Somme.[35] Soon a section of the front almost forty miles wide had been split open and an ominous-looking bulge appeared, as German troops, their morale rising by the moment, restarted their march south and west.[36] Before the first phase of operations ended, the Germans had advanced almost thirty miles. Certain British strategy-makers started wondering if France would be driven out of the war like Russia.

Hitler followed all of this excitedly, but took part in none of the original attacks. Not considered particularly combat-effective, the List Regiment was kept in reserve and the first offensives were undertaken by some of the most experienced "elite" troops the German Army could find. And while these better troops achieved a remarkable feat of arms, what Hitler did not realize was that it was all pointless. The Germans were going to lose World War I regardless, because the balance of world power had swung so dramatically

---

* Hitler's Nazi Party would later name those who were part of the SA, its paramilitary wing, Storm Troopers as a tribute to this type of warfare.

against them that even these impressive advances were but minor blips in the inexorable process of the coming German defeat. This was apparent to some German soldiers in the field who, when they took the British trenches, were stunned to see how well equipped their enemy had become. Even Hitler himself remarked on the huge quantities of food that the British had stockpiled.

The fatal flaw in Hindenburg and Ludendorff's plan and why the Germans never could have won the war in 1918, regardless of Adolf Hitler's optimism, was that Germany was too weak. By this time the Allies were far more powerful, with more soldiers, far more equipment and a resource base that dwarfed what Germany could tap. Even with all the losses the Allies seemed to suffer in 1917, including the withdrawal of Russia from the war, the entry of the United States on the Allied side meant that the war could only have one outcome—and that would be a German defeat. If anything, the German offensives of 1918 only hastened German collapse because they led to extraordinarily high losses amongst the best troops in the German Army.

In only the first two weeks of the fighting, the spring offensives cost the Germans 250,000 casualties—and while Allied casualties were slightly higher, they could make up their losses while the Germans were already scraping the bottom of the barrel.[37] In fact, all Hindenburg and Ludendorff could do was commit more and more of their dwindling reserves to try to break through, and hope that this might somehow lead to victory. So they regrouped and German soldiers were sent forward once again to find gaps in the Allied lines.

The results showed how pointless the offensives had been in the first place. The Germans were able to break through French lines in a May offensive and create another bulge that reached down towards Paris, but they never came close to taking the French capital. As the Allies became more comfortable dealing with the new German methods, and more British and French troops were rushed to the battle area joined by large numbers of fresh American forces, the German offensives produced less and less and the lifeblood literally flowed out of their war effort. By the time Hindenburg and Ludendorff ended the attacks, almost 900,000 of their soldiers had been killed, wounded or captured. It was the highest toll that the Germans would suffer in any series of battles in the war, and a sign of the catastrophic defeat that the German Army leadership had inflicted on themselves.

Hitler understood none of this. His position behind the lines allowed him to obsess about the stories of German advances and tactical triumphs and not understand that these triumphs were only hastening defeat. Hitler and his comrades could see the elite troops train for the attack and heard the survivors' stories of triumph, but they remained safe. Their main combat experience occurred in the middle of July, during what was known as the Second Battle of the Marne, a final desperate German attempt to create one more breakthrough and take Paris. It was a failure, but even then the List Regiment avoided the worst of the fighting, suffering only 482 casualties, which was a lower number than the regiment had suffered in 1914.[38] Hitler, however, only saw that for four months the German Army had been going forward, taking more territory than at any time for years. To him this was all a sign of a magnificent success, and that by the summer of 1918 "victory was as nearly in our grasp as it was in that of our adversaries."[39]

With the failure to take Paris during the Second Battle of the Marne, all German offensives on the Western Front were halted. The List Regiment took up a defensive position near Le Cateau and Hitler assumed that German attacks would soon be restarted. He even received his second Iron Cross, for which he was recommended by a Jewish-German officer, Lieutenant Hugo Gutmann. Then, crucially, Hitler was rotated back to Germany, as if the war was set to continue for years. The German Army, deciding it needed radio communications for future operations, was taking dispatchers like Hitler and retraining them as radio operators. On 15 August he left the regiment and thus was away from the front when the situation in the west transformed.

As Hitler was leaving the front, the Allies had started their counterattacks to retake the lands lost to the German offensives. These attacks, sometimes called the Hundred Days Offensive, eventually culminated in the collapse of the German Army a few months later. For the first time in the war, a truly integrated and modern military force was sent into action. The British, French and Americans not only had many more soldiers; they now had thousands of tanks working with thousands of aircraft combined with infantry and masses of artillery. Though the first of the Allied attacks started on August 8, it was not until the end of the month, when Hitler was safely back in Germany, that the German lines started collapsing.

The Germany he returned to was if anything even more defeatist than the one he had encountered in 1916. He could not believe that the German newspapers were so pessimistic, when only a few weeks earlier the German Army had reached the Marne and seemed poised to take Paris. Moreover, factory workers making armaments, whom Hitler believed had had their minds poisoned by Marxists, chose this moment to go on strike.[40] In Hitler's world, the rot had once again set in on the home front, and not in the army that he loved so much. The proper solution would have been to execute more malcontents, and in his mind the German authorities were too tolerant. "The triumph of gangsterdom in 1918 can be explained," he wrote. "During four years of war great gaps were formed amongst the best of us. And whilst we were at the front, criminality flourished at home. Death sentences were very rare, and in short all that needed to be done was to open the gates of the prisons when it was necessary to find leaders for the revolutionary masses."[41]

Hitler's obsession with the dissent and dissatisfaction he encountered back in Germany decisively shaped his belief about how the war ended. He believed that he had left a mostly victorious army at a front where things seemed finely balanced, only to find Germans at home being led to betray the efforts of this army in the field. When he returned to the List Regiment at the end of September, once again stationed near the town of Ypres, and soon found the army in retreat, he established a causal connection between the loss of will in Germany itself and the eventual failure of its army. Things were made worse when Hitler was the recipient of a British mustard gas attack on October 15 and received his second significant injury of the war. Partially blinded, almost certainly traumatized, Hitler was sent back to Germany and treated in a military hospital at Pasewalk.

It was here that he heard about the German request for armistice (actually a surrender) a few weeks later. His mental state at the time was one of shock and disbelief. He might even have had a breakdown. At Pasewalk he was treated not just for the effects of the mustard gas attack but also for "war hysteria," and there was talk that he was hypnotized as part of his treatment.[42] Even allowing for the hyperbole of his rhetoric in *Mein Kampf*, he was clearly devastated by the news that Germany lost the war. To answer the question of why this disaster had occurred, Hitler fell back on the conspiracy theories he had been nursing for years and magnified them to enormous proportions. An internal, criminal enemy had poisoned the mind of the German people, leading them to betray the valiant troops at the front and transforming a possible war-winning situation into a humiliating defeat.

For the rest of his life Hitler would obsess about this fictional imagined betrayal, throughout World War II ranting about how the criminals of 1918 had stabbed the German Army in the back by poisoning the minds of the German people (who once again had revealed their Achilles heel). "A people, taken en masse, is neither wholly good nor wholly bad," he declared. "It possesses neither the courage to be wholly admirable nor the wickedness to be wholly evil. It is the extremes at each end of the scale that decide the level of the average. If the good are decimated while the evil are preserved, then it is quite possible, as happened in Germany in 1918, for a handful of a few hundred evil vagabonds to do violence to a whole nation."[43]

Once formed, this view of the internal enemy being the cause of German defeat, even when the Germans were militarily superior, never left him. In his unpublished second book, Hitler was even more explicit on this point, writing: "The collapse which the German Folk suffered in 1918 lies, as I want once more to establish here, not in the overthrow of its military organisation, or in the loss of its weapons, but rather in its inner decay."[44]

This is the crucial piece of the puzzle in understanding Hitler as a war leader in World War II. It combined his grasp of how to win wars (heavy equipment based on German technology which carried the biggest punch possible) with how Germany lost this one (home front weakened and then betrayed by evil influences—particularly

Jews). The combination of these ideas also seems to have been the motivation he needed to change professions. If Hitler went into the army in 1914 still thinking he would become a great artist or architect, by 1918 he had decided to immerse himself in politics. The army even helped this transformation. Unlike most German soldiers, Hitler manoeuvred to stay in the army for years after the war and was not actually discharged until March 1920.* What the army did in the intervening period was protect him, feed him, and train him to turn what earlier in his life would have seemed deranged rantings into a fanatical political movement.

In this career path Hitler was helped by the political chaos and instability that he entered when he returned to Munich at the end of November 1918.[45] In a madhouse like post-war Germany, a madman had a distinct advantage, and Hitler found himself in one of the few moments in history where his special skills as a ranting, manic mouthpiece for conspiracy theories was a great asset. The end of the war had left Bavaria without a government, and revolution(s) ensued as society seemed to lose all bearings. At first the socialist left seized power, led by Kurt Eisner, a Jew, who declared a Bavarian republic. Eisner not only admitted that Germany was guilty for starting World War I; he called for cooperation between the Bavarian government and the newly formed German soviets, which were aping the behaviour of the soviets formed at the start of the Russian Revolution.[46] As Hitler chose to stay in the army in a Bavarian regiment, he legally became a servant of Eisner's regime. It was during this phase that the army decided that Hitler would make a decent propagandist and sent him for training to learn how to communicate with the troops. It thus seems likely that his first speeches were given in favour of Eisner's "democratic-republican state."[47]

Eisner was assassinated in February 1919, and this was followed by six months of even more brutal convulsions. There existed a communist group which proclaimed Bavaria a new Soviet state and tried to ally the country with Soviet Russia. Strongly nationalist and

---

* It was also possible that Hitler worked for the army's military intelligence wing after the war.

right-wing elements in the army started organizing in opposition to the communists—and this provided a crucial entrée for Hitler into extreme national politics. He was taken in by one of these factions in the army, given even more training in speaking and propaganda, and sent out to make sure that those soldiers who allied with the nationalists thought the right thoughts.

It was in these speeches to the soldiers that he started publicly voicing the antisemitism that had lurked within him for years. He attacked the phantom Jewish menace with such force that an officer eventually asked him to tone down his rhetoric in case it offended some of the other soldiers.[48] This one rebuke did not stop him. In perhaps the first written political letter of Hitler's from after the war, he can be found arguing for the "elimination of the Jews altogether."[49]

Hitler's speeches, full of antisemitism as they were, were normally extremely popular, and he rose in the estimation of both officers and men. On September 12, 1919, as part of his political activities, he was sent to observe/spy on one of the many new political movements that were popping up across Munich, the German Workers' Party. A small, fringe group that met in one of the least salubrious of Munich's beer halls, the party represented a mishmash of patriotic nationalism combined with anti-capitalism. At first Hitler was unimpressed with the sparse turnout and weak speeches he heard. But when a visiting speaker piped up and starting arguing for Bavarian independence, Hitler became enraged. In a frenzy, he denounced the idea. The party chairman, impressed by the power of Hitler's rhetoric, supposedly exclaimed, "Goodness, he's got a gob. We could use him."[50] Hitler was invited to speak at the next party meeting. In a while the German Workers' Party would become the National Socialist German Workers' Party, and Hitler would be its leader—the Nazi Party had been created.

When Hitler left the army, he devoted himself fully to the party and, in particular, to using the party to make himself powerful. Like Mussolini, Hitler saw a party not so much as a receptacle of beliefs, but a vehicle to amplify his beliefs and magnify the authority of its leader. The war had given him the confidence, the training and the overall mindset to transform the Nazi Party from a small group of cranks yelling at each other in a beer hall into a powerful political force that would eventually take power by tapping into a huge well of popular resentment and fear. The first part of that process began in Munich between 1920 and 1923, when Hitler, using flamboyant speeches, grew the Nazi Party into a regional force, strong enough to launch a violent coup. The speeches on the page seem little more than a mishmash of conspiracy theories, bad history and childish economic theories. The stab-in-the-back myth pervaded them, and the usual target was the Jews who had brought Germany to its knees when victory was within its grasp.

As part of this theorizing, and obsessing about the Jews, Hitler started thinking about foreign policy as part of grand strategy. He was completely amoral, viewing foreign policy solely as a means to raise Germany to greatness. It was one of the reasons he decided to abandon Austria as soon as he could. "The more particularly I concerned myself with questions of foreign policy, the more my conviction rose and took root that this political formation could result in nothing but the misfortune of Germanism. More and more clearly I saw at last that the fate of the German nation would no longer be decided here, but in the Reich itself."[51] Hitler believed that the war had taught him that Germany needed a far better idea of how to integrate itself in an alliance structure. In the run-up to 1914, Germany had run the worst kind of alliance politics. It had anchored itself to a weak Austria, which could not supply the Reich with resources and could do precious little to help the Reich expand its borders. It had ended up in this predicament because it could not achieve an alliance with one of the two nations that Germany needed to be friends with: Britain and Russia. Of the two, an alliance with Britain was to Hitler the key goal of German policy, and would be so throughout his rise to power. He believed that Britain could now be won over to Germany's side due to fears that France would be too powerful and dominate the European continent. In his second book he described not only the benefits of a British alliance for Germany, but also the best way to bring that about: making sure there was no direct naval competition between the two countries.[52]

Russia was also a possible short-term ally, but any alliance with Russia would eventually collapse as Germany turned east. What

Hitler was dead set against (and would remain so until 1940) was Germany getting involved in a war with both Britain and Russia at the same time—the two-front disaster that had helped lose World War I. Of course, Hitler believed that before Germany could have an alliance with Britain, it needed to crush Jewish influence, which, even after having devastated Germany by the stab in the back in 1918, was dead set on stopping friendship between the two states. "Little interest as England, from a British state viewpoint, may have in a further annihilation of Germany," he wrote, "that of the international stock exchange Jews in such a development is great."[53]

One of Hitler's earliest speeches, given in September 1922, showed him giving free rein to his twisted, international, antisemitic world view. "We in Germany have come to this: that sixty million people see their destiny to lie at the will of a few dozen Jewish bankers," he declared. One can imagine him eyes blazing, his arms making sweeping, theatrical gestures as he whipped himself and his audience into a frenzy against this enemy that had supposedly lost them the war. The Jews had poisoned the German mind, he insisted, by tricking the German people using globalized buzzwords such as "democracy" and "world peace." This had led directly to German defeat by disintegrating German "race-consciousness" and breeding "cowardice."

Hitler's solution was direct and unspeakably grotesque: "We must call to account the November criminals of 1918. It cannot be that two million Germans should have fallen in vain and that afterwards one should sit down as friends at the same table with traitors. No, we do not pardon, we demand—Vengeance!"[54]

Hitler would eventually take his vengeance. This World War I soldier was convinced he had the right strategic blueprint to lead Germany to victory in the next war. He was convinced he knew the kinds of weapons Germany would need to win a new war and he knew how they should be used. He believed he had an understanding of geopolitics and who Germany should ally with (and who it should fight). Moreover, he knew who Germany's real enemies were and how they had to be confronted and eradicated. To a sane, rational outsider, it must have been difficult to imagine that a time would come when Hitler would actually put his plan into action.

11.   Interlude: The Interwar Years

Between the end of the Russo-Polish War in 1921 and the outbreak of World War II in 1939, four of the five grand strategists who would control the latter rose to the heights of political power in their countries. Adolf Hitler, Joseph Stalin, Benito Mussolini and Franklin Roosevelt ended up creating many of the decision-making structures and militaries that would be at their disposal when the war started. Only Winston Churchill was mostly an outsider in this process.

Benito Mussolini

Benito Mussolini in many ways pulled off the greatest trick of all, until he foolishly called his own bluff in 1940. Seizing power in 1922, he rapidly transformed Italy into a dictatorship by 1925. As Il Duce ("the Leader"—the moniker he chose for himself), Mussolini craved recognition for Italy as a great power. He talked grandly of creating a vast Italian empire in Africa, or turning the Mediterranean into an Italian sea and remaking Italians into a martial, hard race worthy of his leadership. As part of this effort Mussolini created a myth about himself as an efficient organizer—a vision that endures in some circles up until today. This Mussolini "made the trains run on time," as the cliché about him goes, and for the first time since unification made Italy a respected great power. It certainly led to some cringeworthy profiles in the interwar period, as some prominent journalists and writers from the United States penned horribly obsequious profiles of Mussolini that made him sound like everything he wanted to be.

In truth, what Mussolini did was borrow and spend massive amounts of money, nationalize much of the Italian economy and bombard the Italian people with endless slogans and programmes which showcased his efforts. It was all good theatre, but he did little if anything to transform Italy into a relatively greater economic or military power. While there was a boom in Italy in the late 1920s (as there was in many places in Europe and North America), Italy was one of the most affected countries when the Great Depression hit. Overall, Italy's per capita GDP declined relative to other European powers during Mussolini's rule.[1] Italian steel production, vital to the making of modern weapons, remained stagnant.

If Mussolini did nothing to improve the fundamentals of Italy's economic production, he likewise allowed the Italian military to trundle along with a few headline-catching stunts but little increase to its relative strength. The interwar period saw the transformation of advanced militaries into at least partially mechanized forces. Italy tried to keep pace with this, but had trouble making advanced equipment with a full complement of advanced machinery. For instance, while the Italians numerically had a large number of aircraft on hand when World War II started, half of their fighters were primitive biplanes that would have been more at home in the skies over World War I battlefields. Most demoralizing, while Italy had developed a number of excellent airframes for their modern planes, they could not power them with engines strong enough to take advantage of their superior characteristics—making them easy prey to more advanced enemy aircraft. Italian tanks, on the other hand, were generally terrible, under-engined and under-gunned, so much so that even their enemies would later feel twinges of sadness for the Italian crews forced to serve in them. Even the Italian Navy, which produced a number of excellent warships during the period of Mussolini's rule, was never able to create modern systems able to allow the fleet to operate efficiently at sea—like, say, a Japanese naval unit.

Mussolini, however, chose to ignore all of these deficiencies and tried to bluff his way into great power status. For a while he succeeded. With Britain and France preoccupied by the Great Depression, which made them both more cautious of international confrontation, Mussolini sent military forces into Ethiopia and then Spain. The invasion of Ethiopia in October 1935 showed how far Italy had to go to be a first-rank military power. Mussolini attacked with hundreds of thousands of troops, backed by Italy's best aircraft, and even then he struggled to advance against Ethiopian forces which were without modern weaponry and had to rely on foot couriers for communication. To help his attack, Mussolini approved the use of poison gas and sanctioned a campaign of atrocity against Ethiopians that comes close to the definition of genocide. Still, it took Italian forces a year and a half to conquer Ethiopia, though Mussolini had gambled correctly that Britain and France would do little more than scold him in return.

As the war was winding down, Mussolini turned his eyes to Spain, where a civil war was raging between a left-wing Republican government and Nationalist forces led by General Francisco Franco. Understanding that Franco was imposing something close to Spanish fascism, Mussolini became an enthusiastic supporter, at first providing a large amount of weaponry but then dispatching Italian forces to fight. Most famously, he allowed Italian Air Force units to bomb Spanish cities.

The intervention exposed the fundamental weaknesses in Italy's power status that Mussolini had been unable to correct. Hitler's Germany also backed Franco, and even though the Italians provided more overall aid, Franco pivoted more and more to his German paymaster. Having Mussolini's backing was not considered nearly so important.

Indeed, Mussolini himself was pivoting towards Hitler to try to realize his ambitions of making Italy a great power. When Hitler had first come to power and talked about bringing all German people into his Reich, Mussolini had been appalled and seemed willing to take a strong anti-German line. However, as time went on and Hitler showed himself to be an effective revisionist leader, Mussolini started sliding more and more into his orbit. Most crucially, when Hitler decided to seize Austria militarily in 1938, Mussolini acquiesced and refused to intervene—for which Hitler was eternally grateful. From that point on, Mussolini seems to have thrown in with his fellow fascist dictator, though in a way that highlighted Italian weakness, not strength. He would do Hitler's bidding, as he did later in 1938 during the Munich Crisis, when he pretended to be a broker between Hitler and the western Allies. He used his prestige to propose a compromise between the German dictator and the British prime minister Neville Chamberlain and French premier Édouard Daladier by which they would agree to give Hitler what he wanted in exchange for a meaningless pledge of peace. Mussolini enjoyed the plaudits for having arranged the deal, though he received little concrete in return other than the ability to pick up crumbs from the Germans' table when they were offered. And that was the dilemma he faced when World War II started in Europe. He had made Italy seem to be a great power, and himself a great leader, but he had done nothing to create the substance of power to back up his actions when he needed it most.

Joseph Stalin

Stalin's rise to absolute power started just after Mussolini's. When the dust settled at the end of the Russo-Polish War and the Bolsheviks got down to the nitty-gritty of governing, it became apparent that Stalin's paranoid organizing had made him far more powerful in the party than outwardly more well-known and celebrated figures like Leon Trotsky. Stalin, partly abetted by Trotsky's political incompetence and strongly supported by Lenin, became the general secretary of the Communist Party in 1922. This role, which allowed him to control party bureaucracy, gave him enormous powers of patronage. He used this power to promote his acolytes such as Viacheslav Molotov and ruthlessly cull supporters of others such as Trotsky. The only person who might have stopped Stalin's rise at this point was Lenin himself, but the long-time Bolshevik leader had been growing weaker since 1921, and in 1923 had a massive stroke which left him in a wheelchair and from which he would never recover. It's unclear whether or not Lenin had soured on Stalin by this time; Trotsky certainly liked to claim that he had. If so, there was little that even Lenin, weak and out of touch, could have done. Stalin controlled access to and from the dying leader and had established such a strong core of support in the party's Central Committee that he was untouchable. When Lenin died in January 1924, Stalin was free to do almost anything he wanted.

What he did was play the different sides of the Bolshevik Party against each other to remove any possible impediments. At first he sided with "rightists" such as his old friend Lev Kamenev and the head of the Petrograd (now Leningrad) party office Grigory Zinoviev. This allowed him to crush Trotsky.* Then, with his great rival out of the way, he sided with some of the remaining leftists against the rightists, and chopped Kamenev and Zinoviev down. By the late 1920s the Communist Party was his and his alone.

What followed showed that Stalin had reached the point not only where he wanted to have power and humiliate his rivals, but where he wanted to kill anyone or anything that he believed represented a challenge to his rule and his vision of Marxism. He attempted to radically remake the Soviet economy at this time. When it came to agriculture, he ended Lenin's more moderate policies of allowing peasants to own their own land and brought in forced collectivization. It was a disaster and millions starved to death. Stalin was forced to backtrack temporarily, and used the respite to prepare to destroy anyone and anything that he believed stood in his way. The result was the great purges of the 1930s.

Stalin had the party and country combed by his secret police to uncover (mostly fake) plots involving anti-Stalinist forces. He had hundreds of thousands, maybe millions, of these alleged traitors killed, often after using the most grotesque forms of torture to exact fictitious confessions of betrayal which were aired during pantomime show trials. In the end he ended up killing or driving to suicide many of his old friends such as Kamenev, his second wife Nadia Allilueva and practically anyone else who knew what he was really like or how he made disastrous mistakes throughout his career. The result was that he was left with a coterie of creatures to do his bidding—who could not advise him with any sort of detachment, but who would follow his direction slavishly. Though, in a way, that had been the point of the purges to begin with.

---

* At first Stalin did not always kill his enemies in the party. Trotsky was eventually forced into exile and others were arrested. It took Stalin a few more years before he would only be satisfied with blood sacrifices.

If Stalin was allowing his ideological, paranoid side to kill many more people than Mussolini would have considered, he also prepared the USSR far more formidably for a modern war, both industrially and diplomatically, than the Italian. Stalin forced through at a remarkable pace the industrialization of the country, building up a large steel industry, for instance, and putting into place manufacturing facilities to produce large quantities of solid, if not the highest-quality, war materiel. By the end of the decade, the Soviet Union was one of world's larger producers of industrial goods, had a big and functioning rail network and had on hand an enormous stock of tanks and artillery pieces.

Stalin even had under his control one of the most intellectually engaged armed forces in the world. During the 1920s and early 1930s the Red Army was one of the most creative armies in the world in terms of trying to integrate doctrinally the changes in warfare brought about by the creation of better tanks and aircraft. Successful Civil War officers, including most famously Marshal Tukhachevsky, developed cutting-edge theories—such as deep battle, which envisaged something akin to blitzkrieg tactics, using mass formations of industrial, combustion-engine equipment to cut through enemy lines swiftly. Much of this expertise was geared towards fighting a war against Germany; indeed, the USSR had plans to launch a forward, pre-emptive invasion of eastern Europe. By 1937, the USSR was more well prepared to fight Nazi Germany than any other country in the world.

But then Stalin threw this great advantage away in a fit of murderous paranoia. Starting in 1937 he instituted a widespread purge in the Red Army, killing most of the senior commanders (including Tukhachevsky). In particular, he targeted those classes of officers he had distrusted since his days in Tsaritsyn—those who had served in the Tsar's army and those with advanced skills. In the end three out of the Red Army's five marshals, eleven of its thirteen army commanders, and fifty-seven of its eighty-five corps commanders were liquidated. In their place, Stalin promoted those with little experience of senior command but who hailed from the kind of poor, uneducated classes that he favoured. Many of these were mediocrities—led by his own crony Klim Voroshilov, who was now the most important officer in the entire Red Army.

Stalin also watched the rise of Hitler with less dread than one would have thought. Though ostensibly an anti-Hitlerite, Stalin seemed to view the German dictator not as a particularly aggressive enemy, but as just one of many different faces of capitalism that he needed to manipulate for his own ends. He kept lines of communications open both with the British and French and with the Nazis, assuming that they were all potential enemies and it would be best to have them fight each other, leaving the Soviet Union to pick up the pieces.

Adolf Hitler

Unlike Mussolini and Stalin, it took Adolf Hitler a while to seize political power. After his failed coup attempt in Munich in 1923, the Nazi Party remained on the fringes of German politics until 1929, and Hitler seemed more a radical crank than a future leader. The advent of the Great Depression, however, supercharged Hitler's message of resentment towards Jews and the Versailles Treaty, and provided many Germans with a simple way to explain their misfortune. Riding this wave of resentment, the Nazis transformed quickly into the largest party in Germany, and in January 1933 Hitler was invited to lead a coalition of right-wing parties as the new chancellor.

Within weeks he transformed Germany into a dictatorship. When the German parliament building, the Reichstag, was set ablaze in February, most likely by a communist sympathizer, Hitler acted immediately. He had emergency legislation passed which gave him dictatorial powers and then asked the German people to acquiesce in their loss of freedom in a referendum—which they duly did. Now unchecked, Hitler purged the Nazi Party of any possible rivals and, much like Mussolini, embarked on a spree of deficit spending to win over the German people to their new reality. From that point on he started preparing Germany both for expansion and to fight a great war in the future, and the German state and armed forces that went to war in 1939 strongly bore his imprint.

The World War I corporal obsessed with the stab-in-the-back myth started his rule with a plan that would severely handicap Germany as a power in World War II. Convinced that Jewish Germans were a threat to his view of a unified state, Hitler brought into force a series of ever harsher antisemitic laws which at this point were mostly intended to force German Jews to leave the country. He was wildly and self-destructively successful. Between 1933 and 1939 more than half of Germany's population of just over half a million Jews emigrated, embittered and afraid, usually with only a few items that they could carry in a suitcase. This not only deprived the German state of a large number of people who had just shown their patriotism in the last world war; it hobbled German science and technology. Those leaving included many of the greatest minds of their generation—brilliant physicists, engineers, doctors and other scientists—not only depriving Germany of their skills but often adding them to states that would soon be Hitler's enemies. For instance, Albert Einstein, Leo Szilard and Edward Teller, who would help in different ways to build the atom bomb for the United States during the war, left Germany for America because of Hitler's policies. In the history of warfare, it is impossible to come up with a more catastrophically wrong-headed decision.

Hitler's military build-up, which saw a huge amount of resources transferred into the armaments sector, also strongly mirrored his earlier perceptions of war and power. On the one hand the build-up was undertaken with his eyes firmly on maintaining domestic support. The general rise in government spending meant that the average German experienced an improvement in living standards; and jobs, which the Great Depression had made difficult to find, were now plentiful. Of course, it was still early days, and the massive spend meant that Hitler for a while could have his cake of increasing armament spending and let the German people eat it too when it came to keeping them employed and better supported.

What Hitler had built showed just how important his wartime experiences were in shaping his outlook. He was more than pleased to see the army transform itself by building newer tanks and grouping itself into armoured panzer divisions. He was also an early and enthusiastic supporter of the creation of a new German air force, the Luftwaffe. He provided a great deal of money to Hermann Göring to get the new service up and running, and in many ways the growth of the Luftwaffe represented the most successful German military growth of the post-1933 years. That being said, the Luftwaffe as created was almost entirely a tactically driven force, with smaller aircraft (fighters or two-engine bombers) whose job it was to attack the armed forces of the other side. When it was asked to fight a strategic war, trying to cut shipping lanes or hit economic targets, it would be found woefully lacking.

The navy that Hitler started building also came almost directly from his earlier perceptions of war. On the one hand, Hitler did use the fleet to try to reach a deal with the UK in his quixotic quest to secure an Anglo-German alliance. In 1935 he agreed to a treaty with the British limiting the German Navy to 35 per cent of the strength of the Royal Navy. What he then supported—working with the head of the German Navy, Admiral Erich Raeder—was a surface fleet force with ever larger guns. He seemed more than happy to spend few resources building up submarines, and when he invaded Poland in 1939 the Germans had only a pitiful force of somewhere between twenty and thirty ocean-going U-boats available for operations.* What the Germans were building, however, were mammoth battleships such as the *Bismarck* and *Tirpitz*, the two largest built in Europe, which could fire the massive broadsides that Hitler had argued twenty years earlier should be the goal of any German fleet. As it turned out, both battleships would be unimportant in the course of the war.

Where Hitler was never able to reach his ultimate goal, however, was in creating the right international situation that would allow him to achieve his push eastward for Lebensraum (a German word meaning "living space")—an ethnically pure German empire. His assumption that the UK and France could be separated, which would allow him to have an agreement with the UK, never materialized because of his

---

* Admiral Dönitz, the head of the U-boat force, estimated that he would need 300 operational U-boats to win the war at sea.

aggressive foreign policy. Keen to bring all Germans together in one state, he regularly created crises such as the remilitarization of the Rhineland (1936) and the Anschluss with Austria (1938), which, while they were not met by a Franco-British military response, helped keep the two western powers together even as they found ways to try to work with Hitler—a policy known as appeasement.

Appeasement reached its high point in late 1938 during the crisis over the Sudetenland, the German-speaking part of Czechoslovakia. When Hitler sat down with Chamberlain, Daladier and Mussolini in Munich, to try to resolve the crisis, the British and French agreed to see the Sudetenland given to Germany, assuming that this would be the end of Germany's territorial ambitions. When, just a few months later, Hitler marched into the rest of what was left of Czechoslovakia, the British and French decided that they would react more forcefully if Hitler pushed against Poland. Hitler was not willing to wait. He started agitating in 1939 to have the city of Danzig, which had a German population but was surrounded by Polish-dominated countryside, and which had been named a free city by the Versailles Treaty, handed over to him. At this point the British and French decided not to back down, leaving Hitler with the dilemma about what to do when his expectations were not being met.

Franklin Roosevelt

Franklin Roosevelt was elected president of the United States of America only a few months before Hitler became chancellor of Germany, but the intervening years had been far more transformative for him as an individual than they had been for Hitler. Even though Roosevelt had been on the losing side of the 1920 presidential election, he acquitted himself so well that he was widely recognized as a rising star for the Democrats. His rise was brutally interrupted less than a year later when, during a summer vacation on Campobello, he developed polio. In a matter of days he lost the ability to walk—a devastating blow to someone who based a lot of his appeal on his energy and forcefulness.

After a few years of emotional adjustment, during which Roosevelt became more sensitive to the needs of the less well-off and those with handicaps, he re-entered the political world in 1928 when he ran for and won the governorship of New York state, one of the most prominent positions in the country. After the Great Depression started after the stock market crash of 1929, Roosevelt understood that the Democrats would be in pole position to win the White House in the 1932 election and decided to throw his hat into the ring for the ultimate prize. Running on a platform of optimism, little engagement with the outside world and low military spending, he was a transcendent campaigner. He won the Democratic nomination and then stormed to a landslide election victory over the sitting Republican president, Herbert Hoover.

In his first term, Roosevelt was overwhelmingly focused on domestic issues, and launched an unprecedented peacetime plan that included growing the regulatory power of the state, providing a social safety net, and reflating the US economy with a huge rise in government spending on a range of major infrastructure projects. Known as the New Deal, it was one of the few governmental programmes in US history that could truly be called radical. Even in this ambitious proposal to reshape American society, Roosevelt's old Mahanian instincts asserted themselves. Within a year he repudiated his non-militarist stance and embarked on a large naval spending plan, focused primarily on warship construction. During a time of financial hardship and growing military threats in both Europe and Asia, Roosevelt's agenda strengthened the US Navy while providing desperately needed industrial jobs in shipyards up and down the country.

It would be the start of Roosevelt's military preparations for World War II, and would reveal the enduring legacy of his earlier experiences. He overwhelmingly pressed for the development of American sea and air power while spending little on the army. During his second term, he once again pushed for the construction of the most powerful navy in the world, just as he had in 1916. He set in motion plans to build more warships than any president in history, adding not only battleships but aircraft carriers, smaller vessels and, crucially, logistical support vessels to the list of ships being built.

At the same time, spending on military aircraft rose significantly after 1936, eventually outstripping that on ships for the navy. Much of this funding provided the US with the foundations of the most effective strategic bombing force in the world. This included the design and building of the best pre-war bomber, the B-17, the construction of the best bombsight, the Norden, and the development of the best strategic air doctrine, which emerged from the Air Corps Tactical School in Maxwell, Alabama.

If Roosevelt did a credible job of preparing the US to fight his preferred air-sea war in these years, he remained cautious, maybe too cautious, when it came to the domestic politics of the conflict. The Great Depression had given a major boost to isolationist sentiments within the United States, all while Roosevelt was growing worried that the nation might have to intervene in two areas in the world of great strategic concern.

The first was to help China in its ongoing struggle for independence against Japan. In 1937 the Japanese Army decided to invade northern China of its own volition, unleashing one of the largest wars of brutal conquest in history. Japanese forces moved relentlessly through coastal China and started heading inland, pushing the Nationalist Chinese government deeper and deeper into the interior of the country. To Franklin Roosevelt, this was a strategic disaster. He had always believed that at some point China would modernize and become a great global power, and when that happened he wanted the United States to be China's closest partner. Japanese aggression threatened to upend all of this.

At the same time, Roosevelt was alarmed by the growth of Nazi Germany. He understood that Germany represented the one power that might overthrow Europe's strategic equilibrium by dominating the continent, and as Hitler expanded German strength, adding new people and territory to the Reich, Roosevelt was keen that someone stand up to the Nazi dictator.

The only problem for Roosevelt was that he was unwilling to take anything but the most timid steps to intervene. He condemned Japan and Germany, and urged others like Great Britain to be more forceful when it came to confronting the latter, but he refused to have the

United States do anything material at the same time. He calculated that politically there was no advantage to a more forceful policy, and did almost nothing to try to push isolationist elements to rethink their strategic priorities. Even when Congress passed the most isolationist legislation in US history, the Neutrality Acts, which Roosevelt considered to be dangerous and foolish, he eventually signed the bills rather than investing much of his enormous political capital to fight them off. It was the great Roosevelt conundrum. He was preparing the United States materially to confront Nazism and Japanese expansion, but at the same time he was being restrained in policy and political terms. Always fearful of the opinions of the American people, he would wait and hope events allowed him to be the kind of strategic leader that he wanted to be.

Winston Churchill

Winston Churchill was the only World War II leader not in power when Adolf Hitler ordered the German Army to cross the border of Poland on September 1, 1939. Indeed, the timing of the invasion saved Churchill from becoming a footnote in British history. At the end of World War I, Churchill still seemed a politician poised to rise to the top of the power pyramid. With Lloyd George as prime minister, Churchill was made the secretary of state for war (and air) in 1919 and then colonial secretary in 1921. Both positions showed that he remained as imperially centred as always. He was one of the great hawks on Ireland, disastrously supporting the use of paramilitaries to try to maintain British rule. When it came to the empire further afield, he spent much of his time thinking about how to use new technologies such as airpower to enforce British rule.

In 1922, the Lloyd George government fell from power and Churchill lost his seat in Dundee to an anti-alcohol campaigner. When he rejoined Parliament in 1924, he had miraculously come back to the Conservative Party, which he had abandoned in 1904. As a sign that the switch had not damaged his status, Churchill was named Chancellor of the Exchequer in Prime Minister Stanley

Baldwin's government. The second or third highest office of state (depending on how you ranked it with the foreign secretary), the Chancellor of the Exchequer controlled the budget, and for a few years Churchill transformed into a committed opponent of military spending, successfully reducing the number of warships that the Royal Navy was allowed to build and strongly endorsing the ten-year rule—which argued that the UK did not have to plan for a major war for at least a ten-year window. He was also stridently anti-American, believing that the United States was not to be trusted, and even argued that Britain would be better off improving relations with Japan than appeasing what he believed were unfair American demands for naval equality with Britain.

As Chancellor of the Exchequer, he was not a great success politically. Churchill showed little interest in or flair for financial policy, falling back on basic orthodoxy for most of his policy decisions. He seemed heartless to a growing number of poor workers in Britain's industrial heartlands and took a particularly hard line against strike action, especially the general strike of 1926.

By 1929, he was considered such a compromised and unpopular chancellor that Baldwin was looking for a way to demote him. He considered sending Churchill to the India Office, but before that could happen the Conservatives lost that year's election. For Churchill, this defeat had all the markings of the end of his political career. Though the Conservatives returned to power as part of different national coalitions from 1931 to 1939, the party showed no desire to have Churchill amongst its office-holders. Indeed, as time went on, he seemed ever more a man on the fringes, agitating for issues that he cared about but having only a small base of support willing to fight along with him.

The two issues he most cared about were the defence of the British Empire and opposition to the expansion of Nazi Germany. The first was always the closest to his heart, and Churchill might have been at his most disagreeably imperialist in the 1930s. Harking back to his earliest experience of war, when he fought to keep India British, in the 1930s he violently attacked the notion of Indian self-rule, which was becoming popular at the time. Any plan that involved giving the

Indians some say in their governance, while staying within the British Empire, was to him not only strategic madness; it was a dangerous concession to non-white groups of people. He continued to argue that Indians were incapable of honest self-government, and so it remained Britain's mission to maintain the empire. In this sense Churchill was articulating a more and more extreme vision of imperial power and dominance than most mainstream politicians of that time.

As he was doubling down on his imperial vision of British dominance, he was also arguing for a much greater British response to the growing militarism and aggression of Adolf Hitler—for many of the same reasons. From the mid-1930s Churchill became Britain's most famous opponent of appeasement. When the Munich Agreement was agreed by Neville Chamberlain, handing the Sudetenland over to Hitler and crippling Czechoslovakia, Churchill made perhaps his greatest speech of the entire period. He attacked what he called a shabby, self-defeating agreement with Hitler that not only betrayed the Czechs, but threatened to make Germany too strong and would only lead to more aggression. Far better to have a coordinated response to Hitler, even involving Stalin's Soviet Union, than allow Germany to get any stronger.

In that way, his stance against appeasement was not a stance in favour of democracy; it was a stance in favour of a balance of power in Europe. At the same time that he was so critical of Hitler, for instance, he could say extremely kind and supportive things about Benito Mussolini.

Until almost 1939, that was Churchill's fate. To many, he seemed maybe most like a Victorian imperial dinosaur, raging against modernizing the empire while raging for war with Germany. It might have been the epitaph of his career, had Adolf Hitler not stepped in and done exactly what Churchill needed him to do.

12. Hitler, Stalin and the Nazi–Soviet Pact

"I have them! I have them!" Adolf Hitler blurted, probably slapping his thigh.[1] Sitting amongst his favourite acolytes in his kitsch Bavarian mountain retreat, he had just received the news he had been waiting for all summer.[2] For weeks he had gently courted Joseph Stalin, hoping to arrange a strategic pact between National Socialist Germany and the Bolshevik Soviet Union. Now, in late August 1939, Stalin had agreed to talk. Hitler could see all the pieces of his grand strategy falling into place.

Almost 1,500 miles to the east, Stalin was just as excited. Once he had been convinced that Hitler really wanted to make a deal, he had greedily taken control of the negotiations. In response to a personal request from Hitler, he invited the Nazi foreign secretary, Joachim von Ribbentrop, to come to Moscow. In only a few hours, the two men hammered out one of the most cynical pacts in history. Stalin agreed to transform the USSR from, outwardly, the world's greatest opponent of Nazism into by far its most important supporter—and in return received more than half of Poland and the Baltic states as booty.[3]

Unlike the teetotal Hitler, Stalin decided to celebrate his triumph with strong drink. When the negotiations concluded, he had bottles of the best Russian champagne wheeled in and the Bolsheviks and Nazis had a party. After a few rounds of toasts, the Soviet dictator, with that glint in his eye that could either mean mirth or death, told one Nazi functionary, "Let's drink to the new anti-Cominternist—Stalin!"[4] Stalin also raised a toast to Hitler himself, saying, "I know how much the German people loves its Führer; I want therefore to drink to his health."[5]

Hitler and Stalin were so pleased with themselves because they were each convinced that they had pulled off a strategic coup, one that came directly from their early experiences of war. Hitler believed he had prevented the one thing he had most feared, the factor that had led to Germany's defeat in World War I: a two-front war for Germany. With the Soviets no longer a threat, he could point his military forces westward, consolidating his firepower on the British menace he anticipated. The threat would be too great for London, forcing them to accept his attack on Poland. Stalin, meanwhile, believed he had achieved what Lenin had in 1918: turned the capitalist powers against each other. Now Germany would come to blows with Britain and France, and the two capitalist forces would exhaust themselves in a bloody war. His Soviet Union would stand aside, husbanding its strength, ready to take advantage of the resulting carnage.

The signing of the Nazi–Soviet Pact started World War II in Europe, and determined much of its course. It did not bring about the war or the world that either Hitler or Stalin thought he was creating. Both had stumbled badly. Stalin almost paid with his life in 1941, and Hitler definitely did in 1945.

Adolf Hitler's grand-strategic vision for Germany had almost always been based on an eventual war in Europe, one that would secure for the German people a massive land empire, free of Jews and other "undesirables," on which to settle more Germans. This empire would also provide access to natural resources that could not be cut off by sea power—the lack of which was, in Hitler's mind, one of the fundamental weaknesses of Germany's geographic position.[6] This need for a vast, contiguous land empire, referred to by Hitler as Lebensraum (living space), would allow the Nazis to create a world power capable of matching and then exceeding that of the United States and the British Empire.[7] Though Hitler occasionally mused about constructing a large overseas empire somewhere like Africa, this vision never held his focus for that long. It was to the east in Europe that he believed Germany's destiny lay.

To achieve his vision of Lebensraum, Hitler harped on the need for Germany to have good relations with Great Britain. He was convinced that Britain and Germany had reinforcing national interests and that he should be able to secure an agreement between the two as part of his plan for German national greatness. In Hitler's second, never-published book, he devoted an entire chapter to discussing the importance of an alliance between Germany and Britain.[8] In his (spectacularly flawed) analysis of British policy, he claimed that the United Kingdom would not be threatened by a European continent dominated by a German army as long as the Royal Navy's hold on the seas was accepted, and that Britain would not "fundamentally oppose a European great power of preeminent military significance, as long as the foreign policy aims of this power are obviously of a strictly continental nature."[9]

In Hitler's world view, the great mistake that Germany had made before 1914 was in challenging British naval supremacy, transforming Britain from Germany's greatest potential ally into its greatest enemy. To Hitler, the greatest success of German foreign policy would be to reach an agreement with Britain, whereby Germany would support Britain's global position and help maintain its empire, and in exchange the British would allow the Germans a free hand on the continent of Europe and accept German expansion to the east. When Hitler took power, he went to great lengths to realize that vision.

One of the best, and most overlooked, ways of understanding grand strategy is not to be distracted by speeches or even written plans, which are often the smoke and mirrors of policy. Instead, one should start by looking at how armed forces are organized and what equipment is built for them. These structural and material choices involve the commitment of significant amounts of money, and they involve decisions that affect the way societies are impacted more than plans or speeches. Once made, it is much harder to change them.

By the start of 1939, Hitler had been in power for six years and in that time had spent vast sums creating a German military very much in his image—that of a World War I soldier with a belief in the innate superiority of firepower and German technology. It was a land-centric force built to fight battles with France and the USSR, complete with one of the most powerful air forces in the world, if not the most. The land-warfare-centric nature of Germany's air force stood out, because different air forces in the interwar period took different paths. The USA and UK, for instance, started developing aircraft and doctrines based around the idea of strategic bombing—the long-distance targeting of an enemy's industrial or population base a long way from the battlefield. The Luftwaffe, though it would have liked to have the option to plan for a strategic air war, was tied very much to the coat-tails of the German Army. As such, the Germans had no plans, at the start of the war, to fight an air campaign against Britain.[10]

But at least Germany spent significant resources on the Luftwaffe, which was mostly not the case for its pre-war naval forces. Spending on the fleet normally made up less than 10 per cent of the annual expense on German armaments. Indeed, since coming to power, Hitler had mostly tried to use naval policy as a way of reaching out to Great Britain, or at least trying to reassure the British that he had no intention of competing with them. In 1935 he signed the Anglo-German Naval Agreement, under which he promised to limit any future growth of the German navy to 35 per cent of the Royal Navy in each class of warship (a ratio far smaller than that achieved by the Germans before 1914). Even after this agreement, he hardly rushed to build his small fleet. Only in 1939 were the first two large German warships launched—relatively small, hybrid battleships/battlecruisers named *Scharnhorst* and *Gneisenau*. The famous battleship *Bismarck*, the first real capital ship the Germans would build after World War I, and one that could match the best British battleships, would not be commissioned until August 1940, and her sister ship *Tirpitz* would not be ready for action until 1941. Hitler's naval build-up was so slow that once he started taking naval issues seriously, in early 1939, he put in place a plan that meant it would be many years before the German Navy was ready for any kind of real war with the British. At that point he supported a building programme, sometimes referred to as Plan Z, under which Germany would construct a formidable naval force. By 1944 or 1945 they would have six more super-battleships and a number of aircraft carriers ready for action.

The end result of this attempt to reach a deal with Britain on the high seas meant that, when the war did start, Hitler possessed a navy that was nowhere close to being able to fight with the British on or under the ocean. Though the German Navy would later pose a significant challenge to the British with its U-boats, much as it had done during World War I, at the start of the war the Germans had only a small force, fewer than forty boats, only some of which were the ocean-going type needed to wage a proper trade war against Britain. Moreover, only a few others were in the process of being built. During all of 1939, Germany would complete only twenty-three U-boats of different classes, for a combined displacement of less than 12,000 tons.[11] Germany's submarine force was so small that Albert Speer, who would become Hitler's munitions minister in 1942, claimed it was a convincing indication that Hitler was not expecting a war with Britain in 1939.

If Hitler's military build-up was uniquely ill-suited to fighting Britain, it complemented many of his public and private pronouncements. Whereas Hitler would regularly refer to Bolshevism or communism as an "infection," he so often spoke of his respect, even affection, for Great Britain—which he always referred to as "England"—that he comes across as needy.[12] Before 1939, he regularly told journalists, diplomats and even random visitors that he would be happy to safeguard the future of the British Empire, and that he believed Britain and Germany were natural allies. In 1934 he gave an interview to British journalist George Ward Price, who wrote for the *Daily Mail*, one of the most widely read UK newspapers.* Hitler started by cooing to Price, "If England does not attack us, we will never have any differences with England." When Price expressed scepticism and wondered if Germany coveted some of Britain's overseas colonies, Hitler acted hurt, saying he "would not demand the life of a single German in order to gain any colony," and moreover that he welcomed an increase in British naval and air strength. "The English," he assured Price, "can double or quadruple their fleet, they can make it any size they choose; it is no affair of ours, because we do not intend to attack them." A few moments later he added, in a maudlin touch, that the "National Socialist Movement would view a war against England as a crime against the race."[13] At the same time, in

---

* Price seems to have been one of Hitler's favourite outlets for communicating his ideas to the British people. He sat down for five interviews with the British journalist between 1934 and 1938.

private Hitler spoke just as keenly about his desire for a deal with Britain. In 1936 he told the visiting Aga Khan that he was willing to make a "most generous" offer that if "England gives us a free hand on the continent, we will not meddle in its affairs overseas."[14]

All of Hitler's mooning over a deal with Britain did not mean that he thought war was an impossibility—far from it. The longer the British continued to rebuff what he considered his very reasonable offers of friendship, the more hurt he became. By 1937 he started to muse about a possible war between the two, though one that would be in the distant future. In a typically long-winded monologue to a gathered group of senior military officers, recorded in what is known as the Hossbach Memorandum, Hitler mentioned the possibility of a war with Britain sometime between 1943 and 1945. These years represented to him the optimum period for a large war, based on his rearmament plans. Even in this case it was not to be a preferred war, as the goal of his policy was to take over living space to the east for future German colonization and settlement. There was nothing that indicated that he wanted, or even expected, a war with Britain.

In 1939, one of the reasons Hitler believed that the Nazi–Soviet Pact made war with Britain unlikely was that he had become accustomed to the British prime minister, Neville Chamberlain, going to great lengths to avoid a conflict—something Hitler had definitely internalized. Starting with the early 1938 Anschluss (the illegal incorporation of Austria into the Third Reich) and culminating with the famous and grubby deal to dismember Czechoslovakia at the Munich Conference a few months later, he had seen the British agree to wholesale repudiations of the Versailles Treaty and the significant expansion of German power—as long as German aggression was kept on land and aimed east. At the same time, he had seen the British unwilling to make a deal with Stalin to try to surround Germany.

This helps explain one of the most testosterone-laden boasts Hitler would ever make. At Munich, Chamberlain and Édouard Daladier had basically ordered the Czechoslovak government to hand over the mostly German-speaking areas known as the Sudetenland, and at the same time allowed Slovakia to set up a separate state—leaving a rump Czecho-Slovak Republic. Once the deal was agreed, Hitler—one of history's great bullshit artists—started telling his acolytes it was actually a defeat, as he had been cruelly deprived of the war that he really wanted at the time.

This was not about Hitler's hope for a general war, but a limited war against just Czechoslovakia, with the British and French stepping aside. He seemed to completely misunderstand what Chamberlain expected from him after Munich. During the war Hitler would continue to argue that Chamberlain shared a basic understanding with him of what was in the British national interest. Hitler was convinced that a deal could have been reached between the two, if only Chamberlain had called a British general election immediately after Munich. In 1942, Hitler told his nightly gathering of fawning officers that if Chamberlain had held an election then and run on a peace-with-Germany platform, the British people would have rallied behind him: "If Chamberlain, on his return from Munich, had based elections on the choice between war and peace, he'd have obtained a crushing majority in favour of peace."[15] As Hitler saw it, Chamberlain's failure meant that the irrational anti-Germans such as Churchill—aided as always by the worldwide Jewish conspiracy—were able to recover, and push Chamberlain to be too aggressive over Poland.

Hitler's vision, as so often was the case, was wrong. He failed to understand that Chamberlain believed that Munich had settled the Czechoslovak issue, and when Hitler reneged on the deal a few months later by marching in and seizing the rest of the country, it was Chamberlain who called an end to any more deals. Perhaps the best sign of this was that after Hitler seized all of Czechslovakia, Chamberlain, with reluctance, started inching towards doing his own deal with Stalin. The question was, as always, would Chamberlain be willing to pay the steep price that Stalin would undoubtedly demand?

While Hitler had been expanding eastwards in 1937 and 1938, Stalin was weighing his options in his own special way. One reason he so brutally purged his officer corps just before the Nazi–Soviet Pact was because he became suspicious, on the flimsiest of evidence, that the Red Army had been penetrated by a network of foreign spies who would betray the country in any war.[16]

There has been a huge amount of scholarship about the personalities and actions of these two dictators, much of which stresses the similarities in their methods. They were certainly both genocidally inclined.[17] And they did share certain qualities. Most importantly, by 1939 both dictators had created echo chambers for their strategic decision-making, surrounding themselves with people who would automatically agree with them, and indeed praise their supposed genius, reinforcing their strategic confidence and their sense of historic greatness.

In the run-up to the invasion of Poland, Hitler relied more and more on his toady Ribbentrop, who also favoured war and would always reassure Hitler that Britain could be kept out of any conflict. Hitler, whose ego was already massive, started telling people that everything now depended on him and him alone, and that he needed to act in case he died early and Germany was deprived of his historic leadership.

Stalin, if anything, had an even lower tolerance for dissent, killing most of the people he disagreed with as well as many people who he thought disagreed with him but didn't. By 1939 he had created an echo chamber that was ever more supportive of his move to improve relations with the Nazis. In May that year he demoted one of the few pro-Allied voices left in the government, the foreign minister Maxim Litvinov, and replaced him with the much more pro-German Viacheslav Molotov. Other, younger members of his inner circle were mostly party functionaries who had risen up under his dictatorship and owed their positions entirely to his support.[18] Terrified that they might say something that would cause Stalin to doubt their loyalty, they reinforced all of his prejudices and allowed him to control all the levers of Soviet foreign and strategic policy. While Stalin was normally careful not to go around telling everyone how wonderful he was, he allowed everyone else to tell him that instead. Indeed, praising Stalin's foresight and genius while massaging his ego became one of the most important tasks of the Soviet state and media. In the late 1930s and early 1940s, for instance, many of the films portraying his (completely fictional) brilliance during the Russian Civil War were made, including *Oborona Tsaritsyna* (*The Defence of Tsaritsyn*).

Even with these similarities, there was an important difference in
the dictators' strategic outlook. Where Hitler believed that Britain
and Germany had common interests and should cooperate, Stalin
looked at every country he could not control as an enemy. He was
not a realist in a classical manner, as he filtered everything through
his ideological lens. If we might call Hitler's strategic outlook one of
grandiose racism, Stalin's would best be termed practical paranoia.

One of the best examples of this was his dealings with Japan and
China between 1937 and 1939. Stalin was keen to maintain good relations with Japan, and at the same time keep it emmeshed in the war it
had unleashed with China in 1937. What he did not want, therefore,
was to further weaken the already chaotic Chinese Nationalist regime
of Chiang Kai-shek, which was leading the fight against the Japanese.
He therefore ordered the Chinese Communists led by Mao Zedong,
who could have made an attempt to oust the weak Chiang, to instead
support the Chinese Nationalists in order to keep the Japanese
engaged. At one point Stalin even saved Chiang from potentially
being killed, when the Chinese leader was captured by forces with
strong links to the Chinese Communists.[19] Ultimately, communism
and communists were there to serve Stalin's interests, not the other
way around.

When it came to Europe, always a greater concern, Stalin had been
trying to play the Germans off against the British and French for
years. Even though the Nazis were outwardly anti-Bolshevik, Stalin
always considered making a deal with them as likely as making a
temporary deal with the British and French. Yet Stalin's first preoccupation in 1938 was vanquishing the internal enemy, and that
included in his armed forces. Stalin's military build-up and policies
reveal as much about his view of war and strategy as do Hitler's—and
in this case they showcase both extremes of Stalin's behaviour.

The practical Stalin, who had come to understand the importance
of modern equipment and logistics, had started building up a relatively impressive land force. By the mid-1930s the Red Army had
made significant advances in the production of its military equipment, with a growing number of modern tanks and some decent
modern aircraft designs.[20] While it was a force that could not fulfil

the doctrinal expectations of Marshal Tukhachevsky's deep battle concept, it was still a force to be reckoned with, and there was the prospect of even more impressive development in the coming years.

But then, Stalin, wanting to destroy any possible centre that could oppose his power, chopped off the head of his armed forces. Judging that the more senior the officer, the more dangerous he was, Stalin killed well over half of the Soviet Union's most senior commanders and a frightening number of its middle ranks. Though a few officers of talent were left, such as Georgii Zhukov, who would go on to distinguish himself as one of the finest commanders in the war, the depth of talent in the Red Army had been devastated. Both in its strengths and weaknesses, it was now clearly "Stalin's army."[21]

In Stalin's mind, the strengths of the Red Army after his purges put him in exactly the situation he wished to be: able to bargain between the Germans and the British/French. Not only did he believe that all capitalist powers were his enemy; he was convinced that they were each other's enemies as well. He saw the late 1930s, long before the German invasion of Poland, as a period of globalized, interconnected capitalist war between two different camps. In March 1939, in one of his more detailed expositions, he outlined this vision to the Communist Party's Central Committee. "A new imperialist war is already in its second year, a war waged over a huge territory stretching from Shanghai to Gibraltar," he wrote. Furthermore, Stalin believed the economically stronger but politically weaker, previously dominant powers of the UK, France and the US were being challenged by the "aggressive" Germany, Japan and Italy.[22] The aggressive powers had triumphed so far in the Spanish Civil War, the Italian invasion of Ethiopia, the Japanese invasion of China, and the German expansion into Austria and Czechoslovakia.[23]

However, now this crisis was reaching a delicate stage. Stalin understood that Germany was the most important in Europe of the aggressive powers, and argued that, as Nazi rearmament was so far along, the Germans would have to continue with their aggression or soon head down a relative "downward path." The question was therefore whether the UK, France and the US would toughen up and fight back more assertively. So far, Stalin reasoned, because of domestic politics as much as anything else, the group had adopted a policy of "non-intervention" which had played into Germany and Japan's hands in particular. That policy had been a mistake. "Far be it for me," he stated, "to moralize on the policy of non-intervention, to talk of treason, treachery and so on. It would be naive to preach morals to people who recognize no human morality. Politics is politics, as the old, case-hardened bourgeois diplomats say."[24]

Stalin was determined to make sure that he triumphed in the great political game by playing the two sides against each other. He had been dropping hints about his willingness to make a deal with Hitler for years. He had always believed an arrangement with the Nazis was possible—and in some ways preferable. The Germans and Soviets had built up a strong relationship in the 1920s, with the former allowed to illegally train a military force on Soviet territory to escape the prying eyes of the Versailles Treaty, and in exchange the latter receiving some high-quality military equipment which helped along Soviet technological development. Stalin also saw advantages in working with Hitler in that it would definitely preclude a British–German grouping against him, and as a fellow dictator he seemed to believe he could speak more directly with Hitler than with democratic politicians.

Outwardly, however, it was the British and French with whom he did the most talking. One of the reasons for his obvious frustration with the non-interventionists was that he would have been willing to take part in a more forceful reaction on their part. He certainly had made it known to Chamberlain in 1938 that he would have been willing to join forces to keep the Germans out of Czechoslovakia, though working with Stalin was so distasteful to Chamberlain that the Briton preferred cutting a deal with Hitler in this case. In 1939, however, the British and French now seemed to understand that they needed to reach out to Stalin in some way, to at least make it look like they were interested in setting up an anti-Hitler coalition. The problem was that they did so in the most incompetent way possible.

The story of the British–French negotiations with Stalin in the spring and summer of 1939 is painful. Stalin continued to express a willingness to join an anti-German coalition, and proposed terms regularly to the western Allies.[25] His minimum price was Britain and France supporting the absorption of the Baltic states (Latvia, Lithuania and Estonia) into the Soviet Union.[26] To the practical Stalin, western reluctance to sign away these small, weak states was astounding.[27]

Poland was also a real problem. The Polish government, whom the British and French were trying to protect, did not want Soviet troops on their soil and would have seen the abandonment of the Baltics as a sell-out of the highest order. Still, the talks trundled on, and in early August, as the Polish crisis was worsening, the British and French sent a delegation to Moscow. It made things worse. Instead of sending their envoys by plane, the British showed their lack of urgency by using a slow steamer instead. When the British team eventually arrived in Moscow, the Soviets found that they were not even empowered to make a deal.[28]

Stalin had had enough. With the British and French unwilling, in his mind, to offer any realistic concessions, he decided to play the German card—which is exactly what Hitler had been hoping. The Germans had been quietly approaching the Soviets since May. As the Polish crisis ratcheted up and German troops took up positions to invade, Hitler retreated to the Obersalzberg in Bavaria to indulge his passion for bourgeois living and monologues. At his isolated retreat he would sleep late, eat cake, go for walks in the countryside, watch trashy films, and endlessly harangue his chosen companions with his crackpot historical ideas. As the time for action started getting closer, and his overtures to the British in particular kept getting knocked back, the tension built (which usually led to the monologues getting even more obsessive). Hitler told Ribbentrop, with whom he was in regular contact, to start pressing the Soviets to talk. Ribbentrop sent a letter to Molotov making it clear that a far-reaching deal could be reached, as the "capitalist democracies" were as much the enemy of National Socialist Germany as they were of the Communist USSR.[29]

When Stalin reciprocated, letting Hitler know he was willing to talk, the results were swift. On August 21, Hitler asked Stalin to invite Ribbentrop to Moscow, saying that a protocol between the two countries dividing up Poland and the Baltics could be "settled substantially in the shortest possible time." Stalin wrote back almost immediately, and Ribbentrop was on a plane heading east a few hours later. There the deal was struck with extraordinary speed.

Hitler, believing that he had prevented war with Britain, was euphoric, but only a few days later he plunged into a depression because of a decision by Benito Mussolini. Hitler had assumed that the Nazi–Soviet Pact had so changed the balance in Germany's favour that Italy was bound to fight beside him when he attacked Poland. Earlier in 1939, Mussolini had signed a "Pact of Steel" with Hitler, which pledged both countries to fight for each other almost regardless of the provocation.[30] Hitler had been keeping in regular contact with Mussolini since hosting his son-in-law, the Italian foreign minister Count Galeazzo Ciano, at Obersalzberg on August 12 and 13.[31] Hitler made it clear to Ciano that he "had decided to strike, and strike he will."[32] At the same time, Hitler's self-absorption made the Italian believe that the Germans did not see them as partners, but simply tools to help them draw off enemy power once Hitler went to war. When Ciano returned to Rome he met a Mussolini who, for the only time in the war, made the right strategic choice.

The Italian dictator, torn between his admiration for German power and his feeling of being infantilized by the Germans, was also worried about the state of Italy's armed forces. Deficiencies in equipment and training had him believing that they were far from being ready for war.[33] Moreover, Mussolini still had no idea what he would be going to war to achieve, had no strategic goals, and was unsure if Germany could win. As such, he craftily dodged Hitler's call to arms.

Mussolini compiled an extraordinary list of munitions and raw materials—Ciano said it was "long enough to kill a bull"—and sent it to the Germans, saying he could only go to war if he received it all. The list was so extensive that it would have crippled the German war effort had its terms been met. Mussolini's manoeuvre left Hitler stunned and downcast.[34] He would now have to attack Poland without the support of the one power he had expected to stand by him.

Hitler had always believed that the Italian fleet and air force would be a useful tool to deter the British from joining the war against him. When he received Mussolini's unmeetable demands, he "believed his plans had been ruined." In "dismay" Hitler "postponed the assault on Poland" and for a brief moment lost his nerve. Mussolini had pulled off an important strategic coup—keeping Italy out of any war it didn't need to enter.[35]

Hitler, however, could not wait for Mussolini to change his mind. Having agreed the Nazi–Soviet Pact, his massive ego and his diplomatic manoeuvrings had painted him into a corner from which he could not escape. For weeks—actually years—before the invasion, he had been boasting to his generals about his personal genius and foresight.[36] He kept telling them that he would know the best time to strike, and that his personal intervention would make sure that all worked out. Having thus prepared them for the invasion, and told them that the Nazi–Soviet Pact was the final piece of the puzzle, backing out now would undermine his claim to strategic genius.

Furthermore, if he didn't attack Poland, his deal with Stalin would be unfulfilled. Plus, he reasoned, the British might not join the war against him. Admitting that the British were definitely going to fight him would be to admit that he had been wrong all along—something Hitler would never do. So, after hesitating for a day, Hitler once again authorized an attack against Poland, to start on September 1. He was willing to risk war with Britain, even if he still did not want it. Hitler met with the visiting Swedish emissary (and good friend of Göring's) Birger Dahlerus. As Hitler was about to launch the German Army against Poland he lamented, "Herr Dahlerus, you know England so well, can you give me any reason for my perpetual failure to come to an agreement with her?"[37]

Hitler's strategic failure here was one of the reasons he lost World War II. He had seen Britain the way he wanted that country to be, not the way it was. It was a tendency he would show time and time again. He had created a system around himself that reinforced his ego, and he found it impossible to reckon with being wrong. But he was wrong, and soon Germany would find itself launched into a war in possession of a brilliant land army but a seriously deficient air-sea force, which would fail spectacularly a year later when it was asked to fight an enemy Hitler had assumed and hoped he would not have to fight.

If Hitler had a crisis just a few days after the pact, in Moscow the

mood remained upbeat for longer. Mikhail Smirtiukov, a junior officer in the Sovnarkom (the Soviet council of ministers), had not taken
part in the talks but had seen Molotov walking through the Kremlin.
He later recalled the excitement the pact had created. Once the deal
was signed, the Soviet leadership was gripped by "euphoria," feeling
that "they had grabbed God by the beard." They had "grabbed a piece
of Poland" and "got the Baltic states," and had hardly had to lift a
finger.[38]

Stalin shared in this euphoria. He certainly accepted that Hitler
might attack the Soviet Union at some point, but he believed he had
turned Hitler away for now—and in a way that could be devastating
for the Germans. According to Nikita Khrushchev, one of Stalin's
new men who had risen up completely due to his patronage and was
now on the cusp of real power in Stalin's court, the Soviet dictator
exclaimed: "Well, who will deceive whom? We will deceive Hitler!"[39]

It was a comforting thought, but deceptively so. Stalin hadn't
deceived Hitler; he had strengthened him by relieving him of the
worry that the USSR might join a two-front war. Some have
defended Stalin's choice, arguing that he had to opt for a pact with
the Nazis, as the British and French never offered a concrete deal.[40]
That is true—but Stalin did not have to make a deal with either side,
particularly the one that openly coveted Soviet lands. By viewing all
capitalist powers as enemies, he had failed to understand that one—
Hitler's Germany—wanted to wipe him off the face of the earth, while
others, such as Britain and France, had no such ambitions. He had,
wittingly, made it more likely that Hitler would be able to do that.

13. Churchill, Hitler and the Battle of Britain

On the late afternoon of May 16, 1940, Winston Churchill flew into Paris, arriving for the first time as prime minister of the United Kingdom. He had risen to the position only six days earlier, finally attaining the office he had dreamed of since he first entered politics. He could not have chosen a worse time—though that was why he was there in the first place. Neville Chamberlain, prime minister when the war started, had shown himself to be a rather uninspiring war leader. In April 1940, the Germans had launched successful invasions of Norway and Denmark, and his support in the Conservative Party had started to collapse. Chamberlain's political position quickly became untenable and, with reluctance, he had turned the reins of power over to Churchill.[1]

When Churchill took office, the Western Front was starting to collapse. The German Army had just broken through French and Belgian lines in the Ardennes forest, and its panzer spearheads, backed by the most powerful tactical air force in the world, were beginning their race for the English Channel. With the situation so precarious, Churchill made his hurried trip to Paris to consult with the French leadership. When he landed at Le Bourget Airport, he encountered a people both stunned by the speed at which things were unravelling at the front and yet not fully grasping the depth of their peril. One of the first things Churchill was told was that the French were having difficulty getting troops to the endangered parts of the front, because of a strike of Belgian railway workers. He told his hosts to "shoot the workers."[2]

By 5.30 p.m. Churchill had been driven into the centre of Paris to meet with the French leadership at the legendary French foreign ministry building on the Quai d'Orsay. The Second Empire style of the mid-nineteenth-century rooms was a jarring accompaniment to a meeting of men on the edge. No one could relax enough to sit down, so they all milled around playing their parts in the tragedy. General Maurice Gamelin, the hopeless French Army commander-in-chief, started with a brief outline of the unfolding disaster. Speaking matter-of-factly, he said the only way to stop the rapidly advancing Germans was for the British to flood the battle area with their aircraft. Only a massive infusion of fresh planes, Gamelin pleaded, would provide cover to the French soldiers being relentlessly bombed by the Luftwaffe and allow the Allies to strike back by attacking the vulnerable German supply dumps.[3]

Churchill hedged. He promised to send a few more RAF squadrons to aid the French but no more. He would keep the bulk of British aircraft in Britain, where they would remain for home protection. Though he did not say this openly, Churchill was already thinking about a war in the event that France was overrun.* When Paul Reynaud, the feisty French premier, asked what would happen if the Germans turned their air force on Britain, Churchill was remarkably sanguine. As he told the French, "as long as the British could hold command of the air over England and could control the seas of the world, they were confident of the ultimate results, and it would always be possible to carry on."[4] As Churchill understood it, protecting Britain was the path to eventual victory, and if that meant France fell in 1940, as terrible as that was, it could not be avoided.

Adolf Hitler could not have viewed the events of May 1940 more differently. For Hitler, victory over France was a war-determining event that spelled Britain's doom, and he revelled in it. Just over a month after Churchill visited Paris, Hitler entered the city as a conqueror. He fulfilled a lifelong dream by spending the day as a tourist accompanied by his court architect Albert Speer and the Nazi sculptor Arno Breker. Hitler spent most of his time indulging his fetish for nineteenth-century grandeur.[5] He was most excited by the chance to

---

* It is important to realize that Churchill, and also Franklin Roosevelt, looked at France and French power from both a European and a global perspective. Even if France fell to the Germans, they both assumed that French resistance could continue in some form in the vast French empire stretching from North Africa through the Caribbean to South-East Asia.

visit Napoleon's tomb with its extraordinary, dark red marble sarcophagus and the hyper-ornate Palais Garnier, the home of the Paris Opera. He also visited the Eiffel Tower, pausing for some holiday pictures, and the enormous white, neo-Byzantine cathedral Sacré-Coeur in Montmartre. Indulging his casual psychopathy, Hitler admitted that he had considered wiping Paris off the map, but decided that he would spare the city—for now.[6] Instead, he would make sure that German cities were made even more gaudy.

One thing that did not seem to worry Hitler much was eventual victory over Britain. On July 21, he met with Field Marshal Walter von Brauchitsch, the commander-in-chief of the German Army. Hitler pontificated to the senior commander about how Britain's position was "hopeless. The war is won by us. A reversal in the prospects of success is impossible."[7] Why, then, was Winston Churchill refusing to accept this reality? Hitler guessed that Churchill had yet to ask for terms because of hopes for intervention by the US or Russia. Hitler was sure he would soon put an end to those dreams. He ordered that Britain be "reduced" through air and sea assault by the middle of September, and then invaded by a massive force.[8] He was probably already planning his day of sightseeing in London.

In a short space of time, Churchill and Hitler had articulated their diametrically opposed visions of how wars are won. Some of Churchill's confidence on May 16 was performative. He was trying to buck up his French allies, and personally he had yet to grasp just how dire the situation was. His generally upbeat assessment had emerged mostly from his lifetime experiences. He had developed a global, imperial, technological and economic understanding of war. In his world, the power(s) who controlled world trade and resources and had access to the greatest production base with the best technology would win in the end. Individual battles were important in as much as they affected this balance. Though the fall of France was a terrible experience for Churchill and made World War II a much longer and bloodier affair, it did surprisingly little to change the global calculus of production and supply. In one way Hitler was right; Churchill did think that, as long as the United States and the British Empire remained unconquered, the UK could and probably would end up on the winning side.

Hitler, meanwhile, with his experience firmly grounded in the army, possessed a battle-centric understanding of war and had a misguided faith in the importance of heavy firepower, German technology and racial superiority. He could not imagine any power in Europe, including Britain, resisting him once the German Army had defeated France. From the start of the war his confidence in the German soldier and German Army, along with his vision of his own genius, had grown exponentially. Only five days after the last of the Polish armed forces had been forced to surrender in October 1939, Hitler was urging his generals to prepare for an attack on the Western Front as soon as possible.* He read out a memorandum saying, "We must make the French and British give battle and beat them. Only in this way can our superiority in leadership, training and materiel be applied to full advantage."[9] Once he had given the French and British armies a "beating" in the west, Hitler argued, the British would "be ready to talk" and accept German superiority on the continent.[10]

Hitler was already thinking about the post-war world. He told Speer, who had designed and was overseeing the building of many of his most grandiose constructions, not to redirect any of the significant resources under his direction into supporting the German war effort. Hitler wanted work to continue on his ego projects even if it weakened his armed forces. This was also, perhaps, indicative of Hitler's nagging concern about the German people's willingness to wage war on his behalf. He had never forgotten that the German people, albeit tricked by "evil" Jews, had lost their will and betrayed the German Army in 1918. He was thus determined to make sure that they were not deprived of too much during the war—be it food or distraction.

Hitler combined his confidence in German superiority and his lingering suspicion about the German people's desire for war in the

---

* Polish forces remaining in Poland, that is. Many Polish soldiers and pilots were able to escape and carry on the fight, with great bravery, against Germany from France and Britain. During the Battle of Britain, the famous Polish No. 303 Squadron RAF could even claim the highest number of shot-downs of all sixty-six Allied fighter squadrons.

last speech he would give before attacking France. An address delivered at the Berlin Sportpalast to German officers on May 3 was on the one hand typical, militarist, racist populism. On the other, Hitler clearly felt the need to reassure his audience that the attack on France—indeed the entire war—was the right thing to do. The German "warrior" was the "best-equipped soldier in the world," with the best training and the best leadership.[11] Thus the German "Volk" could be reassured that victory was obtainable and would not "collapse" as it had done in 1918. Hold your nerve, Hitler was trying to convince the German people, and victory over France and Britain would follow.

Sharing with Hitler one particular response, Churchill believed that the opening months of the war vindicated his strategic outlook. And he rather surprisingly found himself able to act on his strategic concepts. Less than a year earlier, Churchill had still been existing on the fringes of Conservative party politics, arguing with anyone he could find against Chamberlain's policy of appeasement. But the more Hitler lived up to Churchill's picture of him as the expansionist thug who could not be bargained with, the more Churchill's prospects brightened. When war looked all but inevitable in August 1939, Chamberlain had invited Churchill back into the cabinet as First Lord of the Admiralty, the exact post Churchill had held when World War I started.

The sense of historical symmetry was something Churchill adored. He rushed into the Admiralty building off Whitehall to find the First Lord's office almost the same as he had left it. Many of the same ship models were on display and many of the same pictures hung on the walls. To complete the sense of returning home, Churchill ordered much of his favourite old furniture and fittings to be taken out of storage. He was particularly delighted when, in a long-ignored box, hidden behind an old sofa, he discovered the same charts that he had left there in 1915.[12]

While quickly returning the Admiralty to its World War I appearance, Churchill also showed that he remained, partly, the same erratic, impulsive strategist who had sabotaged his first tenure there. If Joseph Stalin had a strategic vision that was fundamentally paranoid but could be practical when his paranoia allowed it, Churchill was the opposite. Overall he had quite a prudent and considered strategic outlook, which he always threatened to derail with rash impulses and a constant need for action. Part of him remained the rambunctious child, always eager to be doing something—usually, the more dangerous and daring, the better.

Immediately he started revisiting some of the most dangerous plans he had contemplated a quarter-century earlier. One of the first was to force entry for British naval forces into the Baltic, to try to cut trade between Germany and Scandinavia (codenamed Operation Catherine in 1939–40). He started pressing for action on this just a few days after taking office, and returned to it regularly until the Germans attacked Denmark and Norway. If anything, any British attack on the German coast would have been a more difficult job in World War II than World War I, as German aircraft meant that British warships operating so close to Germany faced even greater dangers.

Churchill also started dabbling again with plans to inject British power into Turkey or the Balkans. He had visions of setting up a large alliance across Turkey and the Balkans to take the war to Germany (and perhaps the USSR). In October 1939 he ordered the First Sea Lord, Admiral Sir Dudley Pound, to explore plans for sending a large naval force through the Dardanelles into the Black Sea, to present a threat to Soviet naval forces stationed there. Thankfully, these plans went nowhere.

If the peripatetic Churchill fired up immediately after taking office, so did the more measured grand strategist. It's fascinating to see that one of the first people with whom Churchill started corresponding after becoming First Lord of the Admiralty for the second time was Franklin Delano Roosevelt. On September 11, rather unusually, FDR wrote to Churchill to congratulate him on his new appointment—and, even more unusually, asked Churchill to keep him personally informed of developments in the war at sea, which he said could be sent in reports included in sealed diplomatic pouches.[13] Churchill, needless to say, was elated and, with War Cabinet approval, struck up an unprecedented correspondence with the American president that soon even involved the still very rare transatlantic phone call.★

These early contacts helped establish a strategic understanding between the two that would last until Roosevelt's death. The correspondence, which was almost entirely about the naval war, showed just how fascinated both were with sea power, which was broadening out to air power, and displayed a fundamental understanding that keeping the North Atlantic open would be decisive in the outcome of the war. In one of Churchill's first letters he tried to impress on Roosevelt the importance of British successes with sonar (referred to as "Asdic"), and at the same time to belittle the effectiveness of German air attacks on shipping, saying that the Germans obviously did not have a high-quality bombsight.[14] He later sent Roosevelt stories of sea engagements, most famously the sinking of *Admiral Graf Spee*, as well as other technical reports. Roosevelt was obviously keenly interested in what he was being told, and in February 1940 introduced more of a personal note into their correspondence, telling Churchill how much he wished he could "talk things over with you in person."[15]

Another area in which Churchill quickly established himself after returning to the Admiralty was as an authentic voice of resistance to Germany. As opposed to the subdued and schoolmasterly Chamberlain, he spoke about British defiance in bright colours, with the added authority of his past experiences of war. He also used his new bully pulpit to re-emphasize his commitment to empire. Churchill tried to impress on the British people a similar outlook. One of the last articles he published before becoming prime minister, in March 1940, was an imperialist homage in the *Sunday Dispatch* entitled "The Mysteries of Empire."[16] The empire which had been "founded by war and conquest" was now serving its purpose of keeping Britain strong. Thousands of young, fit soldiers from Canada, Australia, New Zealand and South Africa were at that very moment volunteering to

---

★ Before this Roosevelt–Churchill correspondence it is impossible to find direct communications flowing back and forth between the US president and a cabinet member (non-prime minister) in the British government.

fight for Britain. The key to keeping this vital imperial edifice together—Churchill wanted to impress on the British public—was giving the white dominions political equality. Nothing was said about non-white-dominated parts of the empire such as India, as these were undoubtedly to remain under London's rule.

Churchill's way with words was one of the reasons he was considered the natural choice to replace Chamberlain when the latter's standing crumbled after the German invasions of Norway and Denmark.* When Churchill took office he was probably more experienced than any other war leader in history. He possessed decades of political service, having served as munitions minister, war secretary, air secretary, colonial secretary and Chancellor of the Exchequer, as well as First Lord of the Admiralty. He had also fought in four wars and observed many others. This vast experience helped him politically from the start. One thing Churchill did that paid real dividends in this war (even if it might have led to his political defeat in 1945) was to create a truly national government by bringing the opposition Labour Party fully into the cabinet and giving it a number of major offices.[17]

Churchill's experience and the strategic mindset it created, with one possible wobble, allowed him to retain faith in Britain achieving victory even with the fall of France. The one wobble for Churchill— and more so members of his War Cabinet—happened in the midst of the Dunkirk crisis in late May 1940, when British forces were being hastily evacuated from the continent and French capitulation seemed imminent. The idea of seeking a negotiated settlement with Hitler was seriously discussed in the War Cabinet and received at least some support from the foreign secretary, Lord Halifax,[18] who proposed approaching Mussolini to see if the Italian dictator might help broker a deal.[19] Churchill expressed doubts about such a move, but did admit

---

* Chamberlain, of course, did not see it that way, and would have far preferred that his successor be the wan foreign secretary, Lord Halifax. Churchill, however, would not agree to this, and so Chamberlain was given no choice but to move aside for him.

on May 26 that it was something that the War Cabinet should "consider."[20]

This one expression of doubt was followed up a few hours later with one of Churchill's strongest statements that Britain should carry on fighting, regardless of the fall of France. The minutes note that he told the War Cabinet that "we were in a different position from France. In the first place, we still had powers of resistance and attack, which they had not. In the second place, they would likely be offered decent terms by Germany, which we should not. If France could not defend herself, it was better that she should get out of the war rather than she should drag us into a settlement . . ."[21]★

Why Churchill remained confident was that he believed that Britain could and would retain control of the air and sea around the British Isles, and as long as that was the case, the Germans could be held at bay. Just a few days after the French request for an armistice, in late June 1940, Churchill laid out to Jan Smuts, an old opponent from the Boer War—and now good friend, prime minister of South Africa and supporter of the British Empire—his vision of what would happen in the coming months. There would be a Battle of Britain, the British would win it, and then Hitler would be forced to turn to the east and attack the Soviet Union. "Obviously we have first to repulse any attack on Great Britain by invasion, and should ourselves be able to maintain our development of Air Power. This can only be settled by trial. If Hitler fails to beat us here, he will probably recoil eastwards."[22]

Churchill's confident vision of the war in 1940, even after the fall of France, is doubly interesting because he was being fed information at the time that grossly overestimated both the Luftwaffe's strength and German aircraft production. Over the course of the war, British intelligence was usually pretty accurate in its estimates of German strength, but in the summer of 1940 they miscalculated. They assumed each German air unit had many more aircraft than it did,

---

★ It also shows how mistaken Churchill could be—Hitler would almost certainly have offered Britain better terms than France, and he remained interested in co-operating with Britain as part of his new Europe.

and estimated that German industry was being mobilized with the immediacy that the British themselves were showing.

The disparity between what Churchill assumed Britain was facing and the reality of the German threat was stark. At the beginning of the Battle of Britain it was estimated that the Germans had approximately 5,400 aircraft ready for operations against the United Kingdom. The real number was roughly half as large.[23] British estimates of German aircraft production were even more out of kilter. Just before the Battle of Britain the British were estimating that the Germans were producing 1,300 aircraft a month. In reality the German monthly average for 1940 was 401.

One of the reasons that the British were so mistaken about German air power was probably because Churchill was pushing British production to unprecedented heights. With his understanding that ultimate British victory would be built on the ability of the United Kingdom to control the airspace around the British Isles and western Europe, Churchill had made fighter-aircraft production the nation's highest priority almost as soon as he took office. He appointed Lord Beaverbrook, one of the most forceful members of the cabinet, as minister of air production, and told him to do what was necessary to produce as many fighters as possible. British output rocketed. Between July and December 1940, Britain built 2,779 fighters, almost as many as Germany was able to build during the entire year.[24] Indeed while British production of aircraft was increasing at a rapid pace, German construction flatlined throughout 1940 and well into 1941, averaging a little over 400 a month (all types) when the similar British figure by the end of 1940 was over 1,000.[25] The British advantage in aircraft production that Churchill set in place in 1940 would continue for almost the entire war and play an enormous role in achieving the Allied victory Churchill was able to imagine in the darkest hour.

While Winston Churchill was marshalling his ideas for a protracted, global conflict that he believed would end with a British victory, Adolf Hitler was trying to choose the quickest way to drive Britain out of the war. However, having neglected to prepare Germany to fight Britain, he was left making up strategy on the hoof—with disastrous results. Hitler started seriously to discuss plans to attack Britain in June 1940, and two options were contemplated: a direct invasion (codenamed Operation Sea Lion), or air/sea attacks alone. When it came to an actual seaborne assault, Hitler showed some caution. He seemed aware that the German Navy had no proper landing craft, his army had never practised maritime assault and the Royal Navy severely outclassed the German surface fleet. Indeed, the amateurishness with which the Germans went about trying to establish an invasion force is what makes their preparations stand out in the annals of World War II. They ultimately planned to put far more troops ashore in Britain in 1940, ten full divisions, than the US and UK did on D-Day in 1944. However, they had nothing like the necessary specialist equipment to do this effectively. Admiral Karl Dönitz, the commander of Germany's submarine force, and later head of the entire navy and then Hitler's named successor as chancellor, admitted that the Germans would have to land their troops with "boats and river vessels which we found in French rivers and canals." Not entirely without reason, he quickly came to the conclusion that any German invasion of Britain was "militarily impossible."[26] This view was also shared by senior army commanders. When he was asked whether it was a mistake not to have attempted an invasion of Britain, General Alfred Jodl, who would serve as one of Hitler's most important military officers until the last days in the bunker, gave a withering reply, saying, "I cannot consider that a mistake because at that time I gave him a situation appraisal in which I advised against it."[27]

While Hitler refused to say that an invasion was impossible, he was clearly concerned with all that it entailed. On July 11, when he discussed the details of invasion-planning with Admiral Erich Raeder, he said he considered any invasion a "last resort."[28] Hitler's longest exposition on the subject of invading Britain was given to Raeder ten days later: "The invasion of Britain is an exceptionally daring undertaking, because even if the way is short, this is not just a river crossing, but a crossing of the sea which is dominated by the enemy . . . operational surprise cannot be expected; a defensively prepared and utterly determined enemy faces us and dominates the sea area which we must use. For the Army operation 40 divisions will be required; the most difficult part will be the continued reinforcement of material and stores. We cannot count on supplies of any kind being available to us in England." Furthermore, Hitler added, as he regularly did throughout this time, the Luftwaffe had to establish "complete mastery of this air" over the battle area.[29]

What Hitler did not understand, but would soon be forced to realize, was that none of his conditions could ever be met no matter what he chose to do. The Germans simply lacked the equipment to pull an invasion off. For instance, the German U-boat force whose job it would have been to patrol the entire coast of southern England for weeks had only a handful of submarines that it could deploy at any time. Dönitz himself discounted the possibility of Germany invading Britain in 1940 because the number of U-boats operational at any one time in the main combat areas around the British Isles averaged between two and eight. Indeed, he believed that the German U-boat force would not be in fit shape to pose a real threat to Britain until 1942.[30]

If the naval forces were lacking, Hitler still assumed that his all-conquering Luftwaffe was up to the task. One area where Hitler did have a basic grasp of what an invasion would require was his belief that Germany would have to gain total air supremacy over at least southern England and the English Channel if Britain were to be driven from the war. That being said, his understanding of air power was still very much that of a front-line infantry soldier. The German air force he had created had shown itself to be a brilliant enactor of tactical warfare in 1940—excelling in the direct attack on enemy armies. Hitler seemed to assume that this ability would magically translate to strategic attacks against Britain. One of his constant refrains from the Polish campaign onwards was about the power of German dive bombers—most famously the gull-winged and be-whistled Junkers Ju 87 Stuka. He believed that dive bombers were the most effective form of air attack and wanted them to be given key roles in the battle against the UK.* Indeed, dive bombers, flying

---

* Hitler's fascination with dive bombers would prove a major impediment to the modernization of German air power during the war. Two of the most expensive

Stalin at the outbreak of the Russian Revolution in 1917. By this time, he was already
a leading Bolshevik and one of the few people trusted by Lenin.

Franklin Roosevelt visiting the Western Front in France in 1918. Roosevelt was disgusted by t' smells and dirt of the land war and much preferred the more modern war at sea.

Roosevelt in London in 1918. He met many of the UK's political elite including the King, though one of the few people he met whom he disliked was Churchill.

Roosevelt saw aircraft in action in France in 1918, and from then on was fascinated by their military potential.

Churchill as Minister of Munitions in 1918 visiting armaments workers in Glasgow. During one of the most important periods for understanding his military strategy, Churchill focused on building weapons to help Britain win the war.

Franklin Roosevelt running for vice president on the Democratic ticket in 1920. An effective and energetic campaigner, Roosevelt ended up losing to the Republicans, who ran against joining the League of Nations.

Hitler right after World War I, still in his uniform as a soldier, working as part of the propaganda wing of the Bavarian armed forces.

Mussolini in 1922 not long after seizing power. He was the first of the strategists to become sole leader.

A mythical depiction of Stalin in the trenches of Tsaritsyn, painted by the Soviet artist
Mitrofan Grekov in 1934, at a time when offending Stalin could be fatal.
This was how Stalin wanted his military experience to be portrayed.

A very happy Stalin (*second from right*) after agreeing to the Nazi–Soviet Pact. On Stalin's right is the Nazi Foreign Minister, Ribbentrop, and on Stalin's left is his old crony Molotov.

WONDER HOW LONG THE HONEYMOON WILL LAST?

The signing of the pact stunned much of the Western world, leaving people to wonder if it would last.

Hitler with Albert Speer on his right, visiting the Eiffel Tower
in a conquered France in June 1940.

Hitler and Mussolini meet in Munich in June 1940. Though ostensibly
equal dictators, Hitler was already starting to dominate.

unopposed in good conditions, could drop a small payload very accurately. Yet as the Battle of Britain would show, they were extremely vulnerable and had to be quickly withdrawn from a contested airspace. On August 18, 1940, for example, during a raid on England's south coast, a force of just over 100 Stukas suffered a catastrophic loss rate of 21 per cent, and the aircraft were assigned to secondary duties shortly afterwards.[31]

Even better German aircraft than the primitive Stuka dive bomber were not up to the specific tasks that would be expected in any campaign to drive Britain from the war. The best German fighter, the Messerschmitt Me 109 (also known as the Bf 109), was an excellent dogfighter but had a very short range—so short that it could not escort German bombers particularly far into the skies over Britain, and, if it had to enter air-to-air combat, could only fly for a few minutes before having to return to its bases in France. German bombers, the bulk of which were two-engine Heinkel He 111s and Dornier Do 17s, were small by Allied standards (with bombloads approximately one-quarter of the heavy four-engine bombers the British and Americans used to bomb Germany from 1942 onwards). Moreover, they were relatively lightly armed and protected, making them much easier to shoot down than Allied bombers.

Overall, it was a force that had no ability to win an air war over southern England, as was quickly shown. When it came to the air campaign for the Battle of Britain, one thing the Germans did do right was come up with probably the most sensible plan possible. They laid out two prime targets at the start. They would first try to cripple the RAF in southern England; and then, having gained mastery in the skies, attack Britain's port system. Luftwaffe General Karl Koller, who served as chief of staff to Luftflotte 3, the main German air-striking force during the Battle of Britain, laid out the plan for Allied interrogators after the war. The principal German "strategic

---

and advanced aircraft Germany would build, the four-engine heavy bomber Heinkel He 177 and the first operational jet fighter, the Messerschmitt Me 262, had their production severely hampered by Hitler's desire that both have a dive-bombing capability.

objective . . . was the destruction of British ports and shipping." After gaining command of the air, the London docks and other major harbours were to be devastated, and a combined offensive with German U-boats was to further destroy British shipping. Of course, as Koller also admitted, lack of planning for any air-sea war with Britain meant that Germany didn't have the long-range reconnaissance or attack aircraft that would have been needed to support the U-boat campaign at sea.[32]

The Germans quickly found that even though they had a sensible plan, they had no way of putting it into operation with the equipment at hand. Using the ends-ways-means strategic paradigm, they had developed a very good sense of what was needed to try to drive Britain from the war; they just completely lacked the means to realize the ends—and, no matter what they did, they would continue to do so for years.

The Battle of Britain ended up being a multi-stage affair where the Germans started with one objective, found they could not come anywhere close to achieving it, so switched to another objective, only to fail at that too. The opening attacks in July and early August aimed to cripple the RAF by damaging its airfields and radar sites and whittling down its number of fighters. But after a few weeks of that, the Germans found that they were losing aircraft faster than the British. They switched their targeting to aircraft production facilities, which often involved their bombers flying unescorted into the Midlands— where their losses stayed very high and the results of their raids were minimal. When these production attacks were deemed too dangerous, the Luftwaffe went back to attacking airfields while trying to damage ports. Finally, starting in September, the Germans resorted to attacks on London and made one final attempt to try to damage as many RAF planes as possible—only to come up short here as well. They were simply running short on front-line aircraft, and could no longer be competitive in the daylight skies over Britain.[33] As Koller would later lament: "In any event, the Luftwaffe was forced to dissipate its energies on attacks of many types of objectives. The target selection was clearly erroneous."[34]

All Hitler showed during the Battle of Britain was how far out of his depth he was in this kind of war—and deep down he might have known it. Being so ineffective in damaging the British gnawed away at Hitler and revealed the one thing he was terrified of more than anything else: it showed to the German people the limits of his abilities and the war machine he had created. This helps explain one of the most ridiculous, if typically histrionic, of his outbursts during the battle.

In late August 1940, the RAF launched its first bombing raids on Berlin.[35] Small by 1942 or 1943 standards, these raids did minimal damage. About eighty bombers took part in the first attack, only fifty of which reached Berlin. They hit nothing of military value and their most famous casualty was an elephant in the Berlin Zoo. Hitler, however, was apoplectic. His first major speech after the attack was given on September 4 on the opening of the 1940 German winter relief effort. It was full of Mussolini-like braggadocio: "And should the Royal Air Force drop two thousand, or three thousand, or four thousand kilograms of bombs, then we will now drop 150,000; 180,000; 230,000; 300,000; 400,000; yes, one million kilograms in a single night. And should they declare they will greatly increase their attacks on our cities, then we will erase their cities!"[36]

Hitler had no ability to do any such thing. He just could not admit the truth to himself or the German people. Instead, on September 14, as plans for any invasion were quietly being shelved, Hitler once again preferred to deceive himself and others that victory over Britain was just around the corner. The Luftwaffe had, he told his generals, accomplished things "beyond praise." If the Germans could count on only a few more days of good weather, then "a decisive result will be achieved." For good measure he added, "We have a good chance to force Britain to her knees."[37]

In fact, the Luftwaffe was just about to throw in the towel. A few days after Hitler's latest boast about imminent victory, the air force switched targets once again and focused on the high-altitude, night-time bombing of London and some other British cities. The fires they caused looked spectacular and the world's media, particularly in the US, made a great deal about how London was under siege from German assault. Yet news accounts missed the point entirely. In an effort to reduce crippling German losses, Hitler's bombers were flying too high to see their targets, and were thus dropping bombs indiscriminately, hoping to hit something useful. They rarely did. Indeed, by the end of 1940, it is remarkable how little damage the Germans had done to the fundamentals of the British war effort.

Night-time bombing was basically all the Luftwaffe would do for the rest of the 1940–41 winter, after which the remaining bombers were mostly switched to the Eastern Front to take part in the attack on the Soviet Union. The night-time attacks were the only way that they could keep losses down to a manageable level and keep functioning.[38] In the end, the Luftwaffe, according to its leading commanders, simply suffered too many losses against the British from July through September 1940.[39] General Werner Kreipe, later the head of all Luftwaffe pilot training, said the air force was "simply astonished" at their huge losses, particularly for bombers.[40] General Werner Junck, who was in charge of all fighters for Luftflotte 3 in the summer of 1940, described the Battle of Britain as an "air-Verdun" for the Luftwaffe—where the Germans were the losers.[41]

Hitler was so thoroughly defeated in the Battle of Britain that he was basically left with two options. He could retool his entire war industry and try to create the masses of air-sea weapons he would need to beat Britain. This would take many years at the earliest, and even then, as long as Britain had access to US resources, it was not a clear-cut path to victory. The other option was to fall back on his preferred land-army understanding of war. He took the easier choice and decided to attack Stalin and the USSR.

Hitler had been widely sharing his suspicions that one of the reasons Churchill continued to fight was that the British prime minister eventually hoped to work out a deal with Russia.[42] On July 21, 1940, Hitler gave Walther von Brauchitsch, the German Army's commander-in-chief, a long-winded description of why Britain had put "hope in Russia."[43] Moreover, Hitler was convinced that Stalin would eventually be receptive to any British overture, to keep Germany from getting too strong. Thus now was the time to start anticipating the "Russian problem." Hitler ordered the German Army to start planning its invasion of the Soviet Union.[44]

From that point on, the need to thwart Britain by removing the USSR as a strategic consideration became a constant refrain of Hitler's. As he said on July 31 when explaining his decision to start detailed planning to attack the USSR: "All that Russia needs to do is to hint that she does not care to have a strong Germany, and the British will take hope, like the one about to go under, that the situation will undergo a radical change within six or eight months. With Russia smashed, Britain's last hope would be shattered."[45]

Thus attacking the USSR in 1941 came directly out of Hitler's failure to defeat Britain in the Battle of Britain in 1940, and it showed how his inability to fight Britain had boxed him in. Hitler's strategic vision coming out of World War I, which was reinforced regularly during the interwar period, had been that Germany should avoid a two-front war, especially if Britain was one of its enemies. Now, Hitler was deliberately starting a two-front war, adding a front against the USSR when he was already at war with Britain. He simply could not stand to do what would be required to actually fight Britain, which he knew would be too costly and take too long.

If the Battle of Britain caused Hitler to change strategic tack out of frustration, it proved very heartening to Churchill and those around him. As the battle developed, those on the inside of the British government could see that Germany did not have the tools to defeat the United Kingdom. Lord Beaverbrook, one of Churchill's most important ministers at the time and the man in charge of fighter aircraft construction, wrote to a friend on August 30 (when supposedly the battle was entering its most dramatic phase): "The German air offensive is at present the thing that occupies the public's mind to the exclusion of almost everything. Yet, looked upon as a serious military operation its effect is small. Production in the aircraft factories is affected more by the sirens than by the bombs and not much by either."[46]

Indeed, what the battle did was reconfirm Churchill's strategic perceptions, in many ways going back to his experience as minister for war production in 1918. By October, when the results of the Battle of Britain seemed certain, Churchill started imagining how the UK would eventually achieve victory. On the one hand, he knew it would not be easy and would require a huge amount of aid and probably an alliance with the United States. At the same time, the role for Britain in that victory was almost identical to the one that he had imagined two decades earlier. The British should concentrate on technology and machines, avoid large infantry engagements and strain every sinew to control the air and sea space around Britain and Europe.

On October 15, Churchill wrote a note for the War Cabinet about the priorities for British war production. The top two were to maintain air-sea control. There was communications and radar, what Churchill called the "Radio sphere," and aircraft production. When it came to the army, Churchill wanted the focus to remain on a small number of highly mechanized armoured divisions. As he said, the British "cannot hope to compete with the enemy in numbers of men, and must therefore rely upon an exceptional proportion of armoured fighting vehicles."[47]

Two weeks later, Churchill went further and tried to put meat on the bones of his victory plan. In a detailed minute to the War Cabinet, he laid out a three-year plan to bring the fight to the Germans.[48] The rest of 1940 and most of 1941 would be spent building up Britain's material strength (very much hoping that the United States would be supportive). The most important thing was that Britain "must keep our sea communications open" and the United Kingdom (including Ireland) secure.[49]

From this foundation, a fightback could be created. British forces would work to bolster their position in the Mediterranean and begin the first serious air assault on Germany. By 1942, Britain would have a total of fifty-five divisions ready for operation, and could consider serious amphibious operations somewhere against Hitler's Europe.

When the time came to strike back, Churchill would be ready.

14. Mussolini, Churchill and Greece, 1940–41

Benito Mussolini could have died in an ornate bed, surrounded by weeping disciples, attended by the finest medical practitioners Italy could provide. His death could have been mourned by heaving masses of black-clad Fascists, his funeral attended by ranks of global dignitaries, and his body interred in some enormous modernist mausoleum placed on an Apennine mountaintop or maybe in the middle of the Roman Forum. Too much, you say? This is exactly what happened when Spanish dictator Francisco Franco died in 1975, and Mussolini in 1939 was considered a far greater personality than the Spaniard ever was. The reason that Franco died in his bed surrounded by the trappings of power and was then entombed in a hollowed-out mountain, and Mussolini was gunned down on a shabby street corner and his corpse abused by an angry mob, was that Franco ultimately refused to cast his lot fully with Adolf Hitler, while Mussolini could not resist the urge to do so.★

The irony for Mussolini was that at the start of World War II he made the smart choice. When Hitler came calling in August 1939, Mussolini, fearing that his military was not up to the rigours of a world war, wriggled out of joining the war. The Italian could not, however, stay the course, and this reveals almost everything one needs to know about him as a grand strategist. Though Hitler, Stalin, Roosevelt and Churchill could all speak and act in contradictory, impulsive ways, Mussolini stands out in this regard. As war approached, he both wanted to join and did not, believed that the Italians would and could fight while worrying that they really did not want to, and even thought almost simultaneously that Germany

---

★ Franco certainly flirted with formally joining the Axis as a belligerent, but his demands for such a move were considered so exorbitant that Hitler never considered it a deal worth making.

was bound to win and lose. His decision-making could be equally erratic, with fateful decisions made quickly, after little considered thought and based on hopes more than realities.

He shared these different impulses with both his mistress, Clara Petacci, and his son-in-law, foreign secretary and widely assumed successor, Galeazzo Ciano. With the twenty-seven-year-old Petacci, the fifty-six-year-old Mussolini ruminated about his fear of impending death and his need to accomplish great things before it was too late. This tension was perhaps the formative personal drive that Mussolini had at this time. By 1939 he been in power for seventeen years, longer than any of the other war leaders, and in many ways he had carved out a reputation as the most successful of the lot. To many he seemed to be a deft if brutal manoeuvrer who had made Italy into a respected great power. He was credited with expanding the Italian Empire in Africa, helping Franco make Spain fascist, and overall transforming Italy into a nation of weight in European power politics. In many circles he was considered the man who had prevented war in 1938 with his mediation of the Munich Crisis, and when war started in 1939 he was thought to be one of the only politicians capable of brokering a new peace deal in Europe. *The Times* editorialized on September 26, 1939, that Mussolini had "worked throughout the crisis, before and since the invasion of Poland, as a sincere advocate of peace."[1]

When Hitler conquered Poland without Italy, however, Mussolini started to fear that he was missing out not as a peacemaker (which was never really his forte) but as a conqueror (not his greatest skill either, it must be said). Moreover, the dictator who had cultivated such a hyper-masculine image worried that he had humiliated himself by not living up to the terms of the Pact of Steel.[2] He lamented to Petacci in November 1939, "I have no time: I am in a great hurry. I won't be able to carry out all I had planned. I won't be able. My work will be incomplete."[3] This fear of needing to act soon kept haunting him. In March 1940 he confided even more emotionally to Petacci: "I sense death in life. One day this sand will be trampled by other footprints, the stars will rise and fall . . . the dead eyes will not be capable of admiring the sublime spectacle of this wonderful nature, and I will be eaten by worms."[4]

Though part of Mussolini was afraid he had missed out on an opportunity by not declaring war in 1939, until it was clear that Germany was going to conquer France, his practical side kept these fears in check. In discussions with his foreign secretary, Mussolini admitted that he might pay a steep price by siding with Hitler. The day before he told Petacci that he feared dying too soon, Mussolini heard rumours that the Germans were about to attack Belgium and Holland. Mussolini considered such a move reckless. If Hitler did attack, Germany "would be totally discredited and . . . in Italy there would be such a wave of hatred for Germany as to make anybody think twice."[5] Just a few days after he wrote of his worm-food worries, Mussolini fretted that the Germans had bitten off far more than they could chew, but admitted to being terrified in case they did win. According to his son-in-law Ciano, Mussolini wanted to "dissuade Hitler from his land offensive, an idea he returns to over and over again." It would be "unbearable if the Germans forces really entered the struggle."[6] Mussolini was so conflicted that he even dabbled with trying to play the great peacemaker. In February 1940, when things seemed very much to be at a stalemate in the west, he ridiculed the British, French and Germans equally. He told Petacci that all three powers were "submerged by stupidity which rises, rises, increases and submerges. Yes, all this could have been avoided; all they had to do was follow me . . ."[7]

By the time the Germans were poised to attack in the west, Mussolini had built himself up into a state of high tension, with the contradictory sides of his nature in conflict. When news of German successes started coming in, however, all that nervous energy released and Mussolini immediately transitioned from caution to bombast, and then to war. On May 3, 1940, stories of German conquests in Norway "literally exalt[ed] the Duce" according to Ciano, who claimed Mussolini was now certain of German victory.[8]* When reports of the first successful German attacks in France appeared a

---

* What makes this so interesting is that, on the day when Mussolini first seemed certain of German victory, he received a message from Franco saying that Spain was going to remain neutral in all cases.

few days later, Mussolini spoke of "his certainty about rapid success of the Nazi armies and also his decision to intervene." Ciano, a notoriously slippery character whose claims even in his diary need to be treated with caution, claimed that when he tried to dampen down Mussolini's ardour for going to war by Hitler's side, this "served only to annoy him." The likelihood of Italy declaring war was "growing stronger and stronger."[9]

Three days later, in typical Mussolini fashion, the dictator declared that he had never had any doubts about German victory and that Italy must join the war immediately to make up for not supporting Hitler the previous September. "Some months ago I said that the Allies had lost the victory. Today I tell you that they have lost the war. We Italians are already sufficiently dishonoured. Any delay is inconceivable. We have no time to lose. Within a month I shall declare war."[10]

In this case, Mussolini was as good as his word. On June 10, in a moment that represented the realization of a lifetime's "dream," he appeared on the balcony of his headquarters on Piazza Venezia in Rome and, before a massed audience that had been assembled to reassure him that the decision was correct, declared war against Britain and France.[11] The Italian people were not so dreamy. There was still a strong anti-German sentiment detected in the countryside and certain large cities, and many people remained resolutely opposed to the war.[12] Mussolini no longer cared, however, as the lure of victory was too strong.

Mussolini had fallen for the great trap that lies in wait for political leaders, and dictators more than others—he had talked himself into believing what he wanted to be true, even if he understood it might not be. Though there has been some argument that Mussolini joined the war out of a sense of Fascist/National Socialist ideology, it does seem that it was more a calculated gamble to try to gain glory and booty by coasting in Hitler's slipstream.[13] What had stayed Mussolini's hand in 1939 were two rational calculations. The first was that the Italian military and Italian people, even after seventeen years of his rule, were not ready to take part in a full-scale modern war. The second was that defeating Britain would be a very tricky undertaking, and Italy needed to be very careful about getting into a war in the Mediterranean against a superior air-sea power. His worries about the state of the Italian military showed Mussolini had the capacity to override his impulsive side—if only temporarily.

One of the dilemmas posed by Mussolini's strategic successes in the 1930s was that they made it seem like Italy really was one of the great powers, now capable of throwing its weight around at the top table of Europe with Britain, France, Germany and the USSR. It was not. Italy remained what it had been, going into World War I, a medium-sized economic power with a mixed record in technological innovation and without the ability to equip and support a top-of-the-line, full-range military. Italian steel production, for instance, was equal to Belgium's, about one-third of France's and one-eighth of Germany's.[14] Meanwhile, its fuel production was even worse, with domestic coal production able to meet less than a third of its domestic requirements, and an almost non-existent petroleum output.[15] Though Mussolini and his Fascist acolytes liked to boast of their economic record, in truth they had left the country exposed. Italy would "pay dearly for its fascist experience."[16]

The industrial/economic weakness translated to the Italian armed forces. The army had only flimsy light tanks and a handful of trucks, and the air force showed just how far Italy was getting by on bluff. Though it had more than 3,000 aircraft listed on its records, fewer than 200 were modern fighters (the large majority of Italian fighters were still biplanes). The most modern of these, the Fiat G.50 Freccia, one of Italy's best, had an excellent and manoeuvrable airframe but an underpowered engine (a regular problem in Italian aircraft). It could not compete with the best British or German fighters of the day. The Italian bomber force fared little better. Though the Italians had some excellent modern bombers, they had developed no strategic plans for their use. When the war came, they were used in widely varied theatres, but they achieved little of note.[17] The only service to have front-line equipment comparable to the great powers was the navy, which had a number of excellent individual units—from Littorio-class fifteen-inch battleships to some of the best midget submarines in the world. Still, these naval units lacked radar or sonar, and were without the kinds of support systems, such as advanced naval aviation, that could be found in the best navies in the world at the time.

Mussolini was aware of many of these shortcomings. Even before the Germans attacked Poland he had started complaining that the army and air force had been deliberately sending him false estimates of their strengths.[18] In January 1940 he claimed that the air force had exaggerated the number of operational aircraft it possessed by a factor of three.[19] Mussolini's understanding about the limitations of his military was matched by a realization that a significant section of the Italian people were actively hostile towards the prospect of going to war. Even after almost two decades in power, he had not succeeded in turning the Italians into the southern European Prussians he wanted them to be. No matter how many military parades, bloodthirsty speeches and over-the-top, tacky imperial buildings he constructed, they remained sceptical of his closeness with Germany and had little desire to go to war with France and Britain—as Mussolini was regularly told by many different sources.[20]

By April 1940 Mussolini was so angry at the reluctance of the Italians to play the role he wanted that he started attacking his own people: "I hate this Italian rabble! While up there [in Europe] the armies crush on each other, here people live in fear and serenity . . . I checked the temperature of this people for eight months, I counted its pulse, and I have to say they disgust me. They are cowards and weak, they are afraid."[21] Mussolini even started talking about joining the war to teach the Italians a lesson—to purify and punish them by making them experience combat. In a harking back to his rhetoric of 1915–18, he once again saw war as a great test of Italian mettle, a process that would wipe out the weak and allow for a new, more militarized country to emerge. As Mussolini told a gathering of his closest political associates in 1940: "A nation that shirks the supreme test of its history is a nation of swine."[22]

Mussolini's faith in unquantifiable will and his commitment to justifying his decision for war, even in the face of his knowledge of Italy's military and political shortcomings, were replicated in the vagueness of his comprehension of strategic ways and ends. For years he had equated his Fascist rule with a re-creating of the greatness of imperial Rome. As war approached, his desire to be seen as a modern-day Julius Caesar or Augustus sharpened.[23] Yet the specifics of what a new Roman Empire would be were fungible, driven by a general desire for more territory, naked opportunism and Mussolini's erratic behaviour. He wanted Italy to be the dominant power in the Mediterranean with a large, maybe even the largest, empire in the Balkans and North and North-East Africa. He had only the vaguest notions of how to realize this dream, let alone which specific territories would be included within it.

One reality of which he was at least partly aware was that if he did declare war and set out to enlarge Italy's position, he would be Germany's less-strong partner—and this tormented him. Even though Mussolini liked to act as the senior dictator in Europe, he understood that his military resources were significantly smaller than Hitler's. As such, he realized his plans for expansion and defeating the British would inevitably be based to a large degree on following in Germany's wake. The trick would be doing this while still retaining some political autonomy.

In one of his few strategic musings that seemed coherent at the time, Mussolini outlined what he called a "parallel" war.[24] This would be an Italian war, with specific Italian aims, to be waged in alliance with but somehow separate from those of Nazi Germany. The two linked powers would pursue their own goals, cooperating for their greater benefit but crucially—Mussolini hoped—retaining some independence of action in deciding where and when to act. The idea of a parallel war was probably the best strategic notion that any war-like Italian leader could have come up with. The only problem was that Italy had nowhere near the means necessary to wage it. Within a few months the whole parallel war edifice collapsed, and Mussolini found himself waging what can only be called a supplicant's war.

The story of the transformation from parallel war to supplicant's war reveals how much Mussolini's stress on will and the purifying power of war had played a brutal but very just trick on him. Immediately after his June 10 declaration, Mussolini ordered his army to invade a collapsing France. He wanted to seize as much of south-eastern France as possible before the Germans finished the job of destroying the bulk of the French Army. Mussolini had massed approximately 300,000 soldiers on the French border with Italy, assuming that they could overwhelm the much smaller French forces arrayed against them. For the first—but certainly not the last—time in the war, his plans unravelled almost immediately.

When Italian forces crossed the border, nearly simultaneously with Mussolini's declaration of war, they were almost immediately crippled by the manifold shortcomings of their leader's military build-up.[25] Poor equipment, absent leadership and the lack of an understanding of modern combined-arms warfare, to say nothing of the determined resistance of the few French troops in the area, stymied their efforts.[26] The Italian soldiers were being ordered to fight on terrain that negated any numerical advantage they possessed, and which highlighted the shoddy state of much of their equipment. Forced to funnel their advance through a small number of steep-sided Alpine passes, the Italian attack broke down into different uncoordinated thrusts. Italian equipment was so poor that many soldiers lacked protection for the mountainous environment and, even in June, suffered from frostbite. After seizing a few kilometres of French territory, the attack ground to a halt, at a cost of many thousands of Italian dead.[27]

Mussolini tried to pretend it had been a great success, and decided to ask for more booty from a defeated France. The Italians even requested that the Germans fly Italian soldiers to positions deeper in France so they could make a claim for more land. The German response was withering. General Franz Halder, chief of the General Staff of the German Army, claimed the whole thing was "the cheapest kind of fraud" and made it plain that he would not have his name "connected with that sort of trickery."[28]* Hitler also had little sympathy for the blundering of Mussolini's first campaign. Though he

---

* As an indication of just how perverted the sense of honour was in the German Army during this period, a few months before Halder believed it was shoddy to help his Italian allies, he had listened without objection while Hitler outlined his plans to turn the Poles into a captive slave race.

had real warmth for Mussolini personally, he was damning about the Italian's delaying of his declaration of war until France was about to fall. Hitler told a group of army officers that the Italian move was "the worst declaration of war in this world . . . I would not have thought the Duce so primitive."[29]

When the French did ask for terms a few days after the Italian entry into the war, Hitler barely lifted a finger to help his "closest" ally. Italy was allocated a tiny little occupation zone of France, with fewer than 30,000 people, centred on the resort town of Nice. Indeed, Hitler was already trying to decide whether throwing crumbs to Mussolini was more important than trying to re-create France as a player in his new Europe. If the Italian was going to wage his parallel war with any kind of success, it would have to happen somewhere else, and his armed forces would have to show that they were up to the task.

As it turned out, that would be in the Eastern Mediterranean, and this time the most important opponent would not be a collapsing France but a still-powerful Britain being led by Winston Churchill. And to make things worse, Mussolini would choose to fight in the one area that Churchill had long considered strategically vital to the maintenance and, if possible, strengthening of the British Empire.

Even during the height of the Battle of Britain, Churchill had his eyes on the Eastern Mediterranean as the strategic throughway of the British Empire. He spent a great deal of time beefing up forces in the region, even transferring air and sea units from the UK itself while the Battle of Britain was raging. Later, when he believed that the Battle of Britain had been won, Churchill accelerated this build-up. In his important October 31, 1940 strategic review, Churchill made it clear that, other than the defence of the British Isles themselves, the Middle East and Eastern Mediterranean would be the highest priority. "We had already sent 72,000 men to the Middle East; and 53,000 more would arrive from this country and from other parts of the Empire by the end of the year. More than half our best tanks had been sent to the Middle East, and in spite of the great air battles over this country, we were in the process of firstly re-equipping and then increasing our air forces overseas."[30]

Churchill's commitment to the war in the Mediterranean meant that the Italians and British ended up having their first land fights in the border areas between the Italian colony of Libya and the British protectorate/colony of Egypt. These early engagements were insignificant, as no one had originally expected the region to be a major theatre of war. In September 1940, Italian forces, again poorly equipped and hesitatingly led, advanced a few miles into Egypt. They established some fortified positions around the coastal town of Sidi Barrani, raised the Italian flag and declared victory.[31] Yet they did almost no damage to British forces, and from that point on showed little desire to push deeper into Egypt. Mussolini, when he heard of these limited successes, was, according to Ciano, "radiant with joy."[32] Indeed, this tiny advance was part of a great period of Italian optimism, in the summer of 1940.[33] Mussolini's foreign ministry drew up fantastical plans for victory, with a post-war Fascist Italy having a huge sphere of influence—taking in not only Egypt and Sudan, but a huge arc of the Middle East stretching from Palestine through Iraq.

Certainly, Mussolini's appetite for greater conquest and glory had been whetted, and he decided next to strike into Greece, to solidify his control over the Eastern Mediterranean. This choice was one of the most disastrous of any grand-strategic leader in the war, and one that Mussolini had earlier rejected. Greece was run by the proto-fascist Ioannis Metaxas, who was trying to keep the country out of the war by keeping open lines of communication with both the British and the Axis powers. At first the balancing act seemed to be working. In 1939, even after Hitler had gone to war, Mussolini dismissed the idea of attacking Greece, calling the country "too poor for us to covet."[34]

By the late summer of 1940, Mussolini was no longer thinking this. As Italy had a land border with Greece through the Italian colony of Albania, Greece was one of the few countries that Mussolini could attack without having to worry about interference from the Royal Navy. Mussolini liked to argue that Greece represented maybe the last strategic opportunity for Britain on the European continent, and by seizing it Italy would lock the British out. Greece also held symbolic meaning for an Italian who loved the idea of re-creating the Roman Empire, as the seizure of Greece had been one of the important milestones in classical Rome's march to greatness. Above all, Mussolini convinced himself that the invasion of Greece would be a straightforward and simple affair, something that Italy could pull off without German aid. He could launch it as part of his parallel war without having to rely on Hitler. Indeed, partly he liked the idea of paying Hitler back a little for treating Italy as an after-thought in Germany's strategic planning. In maybe the most pathetic comment made by one of the grand strategists during the war, Mussolini admitted that he, for once, wanted to be the big man on the European continent. "Hitler always faces me with a *fait accompli*. This time I am going to pay him back with his own coin. He will find out from the papers that I have occupied Greece."[35]

Mussolini might have wanted to play the sole conqueror over Greece, but his strategic planning revealed how little he understood modern war. His brutal inadequacies can best be seen in one of the final planning meetings held between him and his senior military commanders, on October 15, eleven days before the attack on Greece was supposed to begin.[36]★ Even though the invasion was imminent, major details that should have been worked out much earlier were still up in the air, including how much of Greece should be seized. Mussolini admitted this by telling his commanders that they needed to "define the lines of the action."[37] Originally, Mussolini said, he had wanted to seize Epirus, the north-west part of Greece directly bor-dering Albania, as well as the Ionian Islands and maybe the city of Thessaloniki in the east. Now, however, that was not going to be enough, and he was thinking about taking the entire country.

Mussolini's ambitions were growing because he was becoming increasingly convinced that the Greeks would collapse not long after the invasion. The Italians would outnumber the Greeks by more than two to one, and the Greeks had no tanks and aircraft. Moreover, the Greeks were divided and lacked spirit, their society split between a fabulously wealthy "plutocratic ruling and political class" and a large

---

★ The attack was originally supposed to start on October 26, though in the end it started on October 28.

mass of "indifferent" poor.[38] Mussolini was assured the only hope the Greeks had to put up any worthwhile resistance would be if the British and their air force intervened.

If the Greeks were seen as a negligible concern, Mussolini was also assured that his soldiers were champing at the bit to attack. Sebastiano Visconti Prasca, the commanding general of Italian forces in Albania, exclaimed that the spirit of the troops was "extremely high. Enthusiasm is at its peak." Prasca boasted that the only discipline problems he had to deal with came from Italian soldiers who had an "excess of desire to fight."[39] Showing just how he had forgotten his own experiences of front-line duty in World War I and the doubts he had faced then, Mussolini accepted these absurd statements at face value. He asked a few questions and let the conversation peter out. Indeed, he was more interested in how his conquest should be staged almost as a theatrical procession than in the nitty-gritty of strategic planning. He ended the meeting laying out an operation that was supposed to reach the Greek capital in a matter of weeks. "To sum it up: offensive in Epirus, observation and pressure over Thessaloniki, and . . . march on Athens."[40]

This meeting revealed that Mussolini was fully in the grip of dictator's disease: making plans in an echo chamber, the role of which was to confirm and not challenge the opinions of the leader. Some in the room on October 15 had doubts about the attack but were unwilling to tell the truth to Mussolini's face. Marshal Pietro Badoglio, the long-standing chief of the Italian General Staff, attended the meeting and was bullish. Two days later, however, he went to Ciano saying that the heads of the armed services believed that Italian forces in Albania were not strong enough for the task, and pleaded for the invasion to be cancelled.[41] Ciano, a strong supporter of the attack, passed on Badoglio's misgivings to Mussolini the next day. Hearing the doubts, the Italian dictator exploded "in a violent outburst of rage." He would personally take the field, he said, "to witness the incredible shame of Italians who are afraid of Greeks."[42] If Badoglio wanted to resign, that was fine by Mussolini. Of course, when the marshal came face to face with Mussolini later that day, he lost his nerve and refused to repeat any of the doubts he had communicated to Ciano. Mussolini was going to have his moment as a conqueror.

He enjoyed it for a few hours. On October 28, Italian forces crossed the Greek border. At that moment, Mussolini was meeting with Hitler in Florence. The Nazi dictator was making one of his few forays outside of Germany, to see Franco, Pétain and now Mussolini about the construction of the new Europe. By the time he reached Florence, Hitler was irritable, having found Franco's exorbitant demands particularly stomach-turning. He was immediately set upon by Mussolini, who informed him, dictator to dictator, that Italian forces were now invading Greece. Hitler was furious, but kept outward composure and wished Mussolini well.[43] To his German staff, he was withering. He had already decided that if Mussolini attacked Greece, the Italians would be "on their own."[44] Hitler refused to declare war against the Greeks as he should have done according to the Pact of Steel.

Mussolini had his parallel war, but the results quickly turned into a hugely magnified version of his attack on France. After a few days of tentative advances into Greece, the Italian Army was stymied by the mountainous terrain and determined Greek resistance.[45] Italian soldiers, too few in number, were once again let down by their primitive supply systems and lack of combined-arms support, while Greek soldiers, who were well prepared for the attack, were in excellent morale. Two weeks after the invasion, things deteriorated alarmingly for the Italians. On 13 November the Greeks launched a major counterattack, and soon Mussolini's forces were in full retreat. By the end of 1940 the Italian Army had been ejected from Greece entirely and the Greeks had advanced more than twenty miles into Albania. By February 1941 the line had been pushed back even further and the Greeks were in control of southern Albania and starting a new offensive.[46]

Humiliated again by the disaster he had unleashed, Mussolini desperately tried to stem the tide. He made the war against Greece Italy's number-one priority, rushing troops to the theatre and starving other fronts—such as the one in North Africa against the British.[47] By February there were almost 380,000 Italian soldiers in Albania, and at the same time there were fewer than 125,000 in North Africa. These mass reinforcements did help stop the Greek advance, but the hastily built-up Italian forces suffered huge losses. In the six months following the invasion, Italy suffered three times as many casualties as the British and Germans combined—and the overwhelming majority of these came from the fighting in Greece and Albania.[48]

One of the people most conflicted by Mussolini's invasion of Greece was Winston Churchill. When Mussolini attacked, the Greeks asked the British for support, presenting Churchill with arguably his first major strategic dilemma as prime minister. He was tempted by the thought of turning Greece into a new battle area to take on the Axis. Since World War I he had thought of the Balkans as a fruitful area for Britain in order to bleed Germany and its allies. In 1940 and early 1941, Churchill had visions of a united front in the Balkans, involving not just Greece but also Turkey and Yugoslavia. With that in mind, almost immediately after hearing about Mussolini's invasion, Churchill started drawing up plans to get military aid to the Greeks.[49] At the same time, Churchill's dashing side was now being regularly held in check by a prudent cost-benefit analysis of whether any British intervention was worth the risk. The problem Churchill quickly identified in this case was that Adolf Hitler might choose to help his faltering ally Italy and send in a large force of his own.[50] The prospect of a large land war against the Wehrmacht in and around Greece made Churchill's stomach turn.

Churchill's caution played a significant role in limiting the amount of aid he initially sent to the Greeks, which amounted to a few aircraft and some ammunition.[51] He was reluctant to dispatch a large British land force, and prevaricated on the question for months. As the Greek Army pushed the Italians back into Albania, the pressure on Churchill to send troops increased. In January 1941, even with the recognition that Mussolini's failure might bring an intervention by the German Army, Churchill argued that the war in North Africa be downgraded to make sure that substantial support was given to the Greeks.[52] By February, Churchill was deep into discussions with the Greek government to dispatch a large force, even offering 100,000 soldiers.[53] On March 2, 1941, he took the plunge, and British troop transports starting arriving in the Greek port of Piraeus. By April, almost 60,000 British Empire forces were in the country, many coming directly from the battlefields of Libya.

Still, Churchill was torn. Occasionally he would talk about Britain leading a large pan-Balkans coalition to take on the Germans. At one time he calculated that the UK, with its Greek allies, and possibly aided by Turkey and Yugoslavia, could muster seventy divisions in the region, while the Germans, he believed, could send only thirty.[54] Moreover, German troops would have to pass over tricky terrain where they had no pre-existing communications routes. Yet these flashes of optimism were balanced with sober reflection. If the Germans really did significantly intervene, Churchill worried, numerical superiority for the Anglo-Greeks would not matter and Greece was doomed.[55] Even after British troops arrived in Greece, Churchill proposed telling the Greeks that "they were free to make terms with Germany" if it meant that Britain would be relieved from the obligation to send in its army.[56]

He was right to be cautious. The story of Churchill's intervention in Greece is often seen as a debacle—though, if so, it was not one that led to the significant degradation of British strength. The story of the British withdrawal from Greece was directly tied to his great fear coming true: Hitler sending a large force into the region to save his Italian ally.

The situation deteriorated badly for the British almost as soon as their troops started arriving in Greece. The event that caused the collapse happened to the north, in Yugoslavia. In late March 1941, Yugoslav officers staged a coup against their government, which had just agreed to join the Axis. For Hitler, this was a sign that he needed to act. He had earlier watched the Italian collapse in Greece with derision as much as anything else. While still occasionally defending Mussolini, Hitler believed that the disastrous results of the invasion revealed the complete void at the top of Italy's leadership.[57] Just in case they were needed, Hitler started sending military forces to Bulgaria, a new member of the Axis, to warn the Greeks not to press their luck. Now, with the coup in Yugoslavia and the Italians still rocked back on their heels in Albania, he chose to deal with the entire region at once.

In what can only be called an impressive logistical operation, a large German force (many of which had been deployed to invade the Soviet Union) was switched to points up and down the northern and eastern border of Yugoslavia and along the north-eastern border of Greece. By April 6 they were in place and, supported by their Balkan allies and the Italians, the Germans attacked. The German Army moved with extraordinary speed, plunging deep into Yugoslavia and Greece in a matter of days.

Churchill determined that the prudent course of action was to get his troops out as quickly as possible.[58] By April 17, he was pushing the War Cabinet on this, calling for the 59,000 British soldiers to be evacuated quickly, even if it meant that they would have to leave behind most of their artillery and tanks.[59] The withdrawal itself, while chaotic—as are all rushed withdrawals—worked tolerably well considering the German Army was approaching. By the end of April more than 50,000 British soldiers had been removed, with the rest having been killed or captured in Greece.* Far from seeing this as a great setback, however, Churchill seemed mostly relieved. He reported the news positively to the House of Commons, even downplaying the fact that the British had been forced to leave behind their tanks, explaining that the Germans were already "not short of heavy equipment."[60]

He was right. The British intervention in Greece could have been much worse if Churchill had decided to stay and fight, pouring in more resources. The Germans would have had strong air superiority over the Greek mainland, making the manoeuvre of British forces difficult. In many ways the greatest disaster that the British faced at that time was not in mainland Greece, but across the sea on the island of Crete. And Churchill was not to blame for that. Relatively well defended by the British Army, Crete was attacked by a German airborne assault on May 20.[61] Indecisive British commanders did not strike back quickly against the light German troops, and instead abandoned Crete's main airfield to the attackers. The Germans were

* At first Churchill reported that only 45,000 had been evacuated, but the figure now seems to be closer to 50,000.

thus able to create a lifeline to their paratroopers and provide them with air protection. British troops either surrendered or were evacuated by the beginning of June.

Mussolini was not so lucky as the Germans. Though he would end up the "conqueror" of Greece and get his victory parade in Athens, his catastrophic invasion and need to be bailed out by Adolf Hitler spelled the end of any parallel war—and the infantilization of Italy within the Axis, which was made brutally clear to him just days after the British pulled out of Crete. On June 1, the two dictators held a summit to assess the state of the war, meeting at the Brenner Pass. Once again, they acted as friends, with Mussolini given the greatest respect and treated like an equal. It was all a show. Hitler even put on quite the acting job, claiming that he was unsure what he would do next. Ciano wrote in his summary that "Hitler has no precise plan of action. Russia, Turkey, Spain, are all subsidiary elements: complements or dispersion of forces, but it is not there that one can find the solution of a problem." Mussolini showed his complete ignorance of Hitler's immediate plans by confidently stating that the Germans wanted to have a "compromise peace" and were now "sick of victories."[62] Hitler was many things, but sick of victory and viewing Russia as subsidiary were not amongst them. He had spent most of the last nine months preparing to launch the invasion of the Soviet Union, his largest invasion to date. At this point, Mussolini simply did not matter.

The Greece fiasco ended as a disastrous triumph for Mussolini and a successful failure for Churchill. The former had relied on bluster and the power of will to conquer a country he could not, while the latter understood what was important for his nation and what was subsidiary, and was willing to cut and run and accept the criticism that came down upon him. Churchill was dealing with the substance of power, while Mussolini was still obsessed with the style.

15.   Stalin, Hitler and Barbarossa

Was his time up? For two days Joseph Stalin had sat hidden away in his heavily guarded dacha outside Moscow, fearing a retribution that he very much deserved. Just over a week earlier, Adolf Hitler had done the one thing Stalin had stated over and over again the Nazi dictator would never do: attack the Soviet Union while still at war with Great Britain. Stalin had spent the last few months scoffing at the stream of reports flooding his desk warning that the Germans were poised to attack. In increasingly coarse and colourful language, he had dismissed the intelligence as either a mistake or a deliberate British plot to sow distrust between the USSR and Nazi Germany.[1]

On June 22, 1941, Stalin was shown to be the fool. In one of the most famous military operations in history, the Germans rolled into Soviet territory and launched an invasion codenamed Barbarossa. Using a combined-arms understanding honed in earlier campaigns, the German Army, relying on four large armoured spearheads backed by the tactical air power of the Luftwaffe, immediately started carving up the numerous but often inert Red Army forces Stalin had placed on the border. After only a few days the Germans had advanced over 100 miles into the Soviet Union and trapped a large number of Soviet armies around the Belarusian capital of Minsk. The road to Moscow seemed open. Stalin, paralysed both by the awareness of his own failures and his long-standing fear of the power of the German Army, panicked. On June 28 he retreated into a shell and stopped communicating with the rest of the Soviet state.

Stalin expected that those below him in the Soviet government would do what he would undoubtedly have done to someone who had erred so catastrophically: arrest him, blame him, and then execute him after a public show trial. Stalin had built his power on such brutal methods practised on an epic scale, and it was his choices, and his alone, that had brought the Soviet Union to this perilous state.

On June 30, when other senior members of his government, led by Viacheslav Molotov, showed up at Stalin's dacha, the Soviet dictator feared the worst. They found him sitting warily but passively in an armchair, staring ahead with a strange look on his face. "Why did you come . . . who is in charge?" Stalin reportedly asked. The response was a shock. They had come to beg Stalin to come back to the Kremlin and exercise supreme command, paralysed as they were without his direction. His subordinates had been so conditioned in the psychologically emasculating crucible of his regime that they could not function without his rule, even after his grand strategy had failed so disastrously. In one way, it was the sign of one of the greatest "successes" of Stalin's rule—the way in which he had made himself indispensable. He had so thoroughly destroyed any potential rival, many physically but some mentally, that even when he was vulnerable the Soviet system could not produce a person or group strong enough to try to oust him from power.

The strategic decision-making that led up to Barbarossa for both Stalin and Hitler revealed the one great difference between them that explains how one ended the war as part of a victorious coalition and the other had his corpse cremated in a shallow pit in the middle of a destroyed capital. Stalin's paranoia in situations allowed him to grasp American and British hands to save himself when Hitler was shown to be the greater threat, while Hitler's megalomania pushed the German to double down on his self-perceived strategic genius and continue to wage a war he could not win. This difference also helps explain how Barbarossa worked out as it did. Hitler, in charge of the greater war machine in 1941, was not honest about how he had been forced to make the strategic choices that he had, and fought a campaign based on what he hoped would happen. Stalin, faced with a catastrophe of his own making, adjusted to save himself and his rule by being practical and doing what needed to be done.

To be fair, Stalin needed a lot of saving. From the moment he agreed to the Nazi–Soviet pact, Stalin had acted in a way that aped Hitler but also made an attack by Nazi Germany on the Soviet Union more likely—and more likely to happen sooner. He immediately put into place an ambitious interpretation of the Nazi–Soviet Pact and moved to take over any area he considered in the Soviet interest, using methods similar to Hitler's. Indeed, Stalin publicly associated himself with the German dictator. He portrayed the world as a competition between status quo powers such as Britain and France and revanchist powers, which Stalin said included both the USSR and Nazi Germany.[2] He even told the Soviet people that they needed to accept that "Hitlerism" as an ideology was a permanent part of the world. When the French press published a speech that was not real but nevertheless correctly described Stalin's expansionist aims, Stalin responded in November 1939 by publishing a statement in *Pravda* saying he stood with Hitler. In it, he declared:

a) [It was] not Germany [who] attacked France and England, but France and England [who] attacked Germany, taking responsibility for the current war.

b) After the start of hostilities, Germany turned to France and England with peace proposals, and the Soviet Union openly supported Germany's peace proposals . . .

c) The ruling circles of France and England rudely rejected both the peace proposals of Germany and the attempts of the Soviet Union to achieve an early end to the war.[3]

In associating himself so openly with Hitler, Stalin was only speaking the truth. If anything, his methods for securing national expansion were even more brazen than the Nazi leader's. After seizing his slice of Poland, which was larger than the German zone, Stalin bullied the Baltic states of Estonia, Latvia and Lithuania into accepting Soviet domination.[4] He did not invade them outright (at first), but instead forced them to sign mutual defence treaties which turned over military bases in all three to the USSR, and then proceeded to flood the Baltic states with tens of thousands of occupying Red Army soldiers. Stalin was so heavy-handed that even Hitler was a little surprised.

In making such moves, Stalin was not just associating himself with Hitler's methods; he was threatening Germany strategically more than any other power left on the European continent—in a way that Stalin himself seemed unable to comprehend. Starting with the

Baltics but then spreading out to Finland and Romania, Stalin moved to establish Soviet dominance in areas the control of which threatened Germany's ability to wage war economically and strategically. The first of these other adventures—Stalin's invasion of Finland—threatened to extend Soviet power into an area which could impact the vital supply of Swedish iron ore to the German economy. At the same time as making Stalin look grasping, it would expose him to military ridicule—never a good combination.

According to the secret protocol of the Nazi–Soviet Pact, Finland and the Baltic states were in the Soviet sphere of interest.[5] Stalin interpreted such statements to mean he could do what he wanted to such countries, and moved to compel the Finns to accept his supremacy. He treated Finland with the contempt he felt for all small nations. He had been pressuring the Finns for a while to cede part of their southern coast to the Soviet Union, arguing that this was vital in order to provide security to the port of Leningrad. However, as Poland was falling he decided to just take what he wanted.[6] In October 1939 Stalin demanded not only a large slice of Finnish territory, but the right to base Soviet troops in Finland itself.[7]* The Finns refused, which was fine by Stalin as he could now invade. He ordered the Red Army to start massing on the Finnish border for what he assumed would be a straightforward, quick and gloriously victorious campaign.

He had, just as Mussolini would a year later in Greece, fooled himself into believing what he wanted to be true. The build-up for the Russian invasion of Finland was a rushed and slipshod process, and Stalin threw together an inadequately led and equipped invasion force. He pushed the pace so relentlessly that a large number of the Red Army forces were still not in place when the attack started on November 30.[8] To Stalin it should have made no difference. He believed that the Finns, in what would be called the Winter War, would be conquered by Soviet forces "in a week or two."[9]

---

* In exchange for relatively heavily populated (for Finland) areas near Leningrad, Stalin did offer to hand over an even larger part of Soviet territory, which was to the north and almost unpopulated.

The results were not quite as disastrous as Mussolini's invasion of Greece—but almost. The Finns had only a handful of tanks, little modern artillery and hardly any aircraft, but they were competently led, had prepared excellent defensive positions, and were perfectly at home fighting in some of the most inhospitable battle areas on earth. The winter of 1939–40 was brutally cold even by Finnish standards, with temperatures reaching as low as −50 Celsius. Soviet forces, on the other hand, were incompetently directed—starting with their overall commander, Stalin's old crony from his Tsaritsyn days and now Marshal of the Soviet Union, Klim Voroshilov. Much of the most modern Soviet equipment, including aircraft, could not be used in the very few hours of light available at that high latitude in December and January, and the intense cold often led to Red Army vehicles breaking down.

For weeks Soviet attacks were knocked back along the lines by the Finns. The Red Army advanced a few kilometres here and there, even fewer than the Italians would into Greece and at an even higher cost in casualties than the Italians would suffer. The Finns, fighting within what was called the Mannerheim Line (named after their leading commander), befuddled the confused and ill-prepared Soviet attackers, massacring them from unseen positions and leaving thousands of wounded Red Army soldiers to freeze to death in the dense Finnish forests. Internationally the effectiveness of Finnish resistance, and Stalin's open thuggishness, made the Finns a sensation. They won the admiration of a broad coalition that included Franklin Roosevelt, Winston Churchill, Adolf Hitler and Benito Mussolini.

Humiliated, Stalin had to stop the attacks in early 1940. Having been punched in the face, he finally understood the formidable task he had taken on and assembled a force strong enough to obliterate Finnish lines. Relying in particular on massed artillery, the Soviets threw overwhelming firepower into the fight.[10] By early March 1940 the Mannerheim Line had been pulverized and Finnish forces were in retreat. The Finnish government called for negotiations and Stalin agreed. In relatively short order the two sides concluded the Moscow Peace Treaty, in which Finland was forced to hand over more territory than Stalin had originally demanded. In a sign of how difficult the war had been, Stalin left the rest of Finland as an independent state.

Soviet casualties were extreme by the standards of World War II to that time, with well over 100,000 dead and missing and an additional 200,000 wounded.[11] This meant that in attacking small Finland, Stalin had lost more than twice as many soldiers as Hitler had lost in taking Poland, Denmark, Norway, Holland, Belgium and France—a fact that was not lost on the Germans.[12] Hitler watched the poor performance of the Red Army in the Winter War with a keen—one might even say overexcited—eye. He had long considered Russia, fighting alone, to be too weak to stand up to Germany. After the Russian performance in Finland, coming fast on the heels of Stalin's extraordinary purge of his own officer corps, Hitler decided that the Red Army was even less of a threat—for now. It helps explain his great strategic pivot just a few months later, in the summer of 1940, when he decided to invade the USSR the next year even without being able to drive the British out of the war.

When Hitler started seriously contemplating Barbarossa, he spoke as if destroying the Red Army and seizing European Russia would be quick and easy. On July 22, 1940, Hitler first ordered his generals to start detailed planning. He stated that a significantly smaller army would be needed to crush the Soviets than had been needed to conquer France a month before. Thinking that the Red Army could only rely on 50–75 good divisions, Hitler believed that 80–100 German divisions would be sufficient to "crush" the Soviets and penetrate far enough into the USSR to "smash" the key areas of strategic resistance. As Germany would need such a relatively small force, Hitler also believed that it would take only "4–6 weeks" to assemble his armies.[13]

It is also worth noting how the Soviets' weak performance in Finland transformed the value of the Finns in Hitler's mind. In the summer of 1940 he started asking for studies of Finland's military strength, and imagining using Finland as a significant ally in his plans to attack Stalin.* By August 1940 Hitler was willing to break the Nazi–Soviet Pact clause that put Finland in the Soviet sphere, by

---

* In his more grandiose moments before launching Barbarossa, Hitler contemplated giving a large amount of Russian territory to Finland after the war—basically all the territory to the port of Murmansk.

providing Finland with significant military aid in the forms of arms, ammunitions and even two of Germany's mountain divisions.[14] If Stalin ever thought about attacking Finland again, Hitler had made it clear that Germany might be willing to help the Finns.

The growth of Hitler's dismissiveness of Soviet military capabilities was mirrored by a growing irritation at what he saw as Stalin's overreaching, expansionist goals. As France was about to collapse in late June 1940, Stalin used the opportunity to invade the eastern Romanian province of Bessarabia. As with Finland, the Nazi–Soviet Pact proclaimed that Bessarabia was an area of Soviet and not German interest.[15] Still, the fact that Stalin used this as a justification to simply march in and seize a part of Romania seemed unnecessarily threatening. General Halder, for one, was dumbfounded when Stalin made his move, having thought the Soviets had no intention of physically occupying the territory.[16]

It is not clear whether Stalin understood just how dangerous this move looked to Hitler. In encroaching into Romania, Stalin was menacing one of the most important strategic resource areas for Germany anywhere in the world. Romania possessed the largest working oil fields on the European continent (outside of Russia), and as Germany had precious little oil itself, guaranteeing access to Romanian oil was crucial to Germany retaining strategic autonomy in the war. After Stalin pounced on Bessarabia, Hitler spent considerably more time integrating the rest of Romania into his strategic calculus. During the July 22, 1940 meeting when Hitler first laid out a strategic rationale and force allocation for the invasion of the USSR, he made it clear that one of the highest priorities for the operation was the "protection of Romanian oil fields."[17]

If Stalin's strategic blunders and grasping expansion served only to make a German attack more likely, his mistakes, at least in the case of the Winter War, did provide one significant benefit in terms of the Soviet ability to resist a German invasion. They exposed the enormous weaknesses that had been built up in the Red Army over the past few years—particularly after Stalin's purges had destroyed so many talented professionals. Stalin, now no longer fearful that the

Red Army represented a threat to his rule, and faced with clear evidence of the massive shortcomings in his armed forces, was able to activate his practical side after the war with Finland and push for important reforms in both command and equipment that would pay significant benefits from 1941 onwards. He now admitted that his experiences in Tsaritsyn had provided a flawed view of "modern warfare" and that the Red Army needed a new mindset and new equipment.[18] As he claimed in a detailed study of the deficiencies of the Red Army in light of the Finland fiasco: "It is precisely the cult of the tradition and experience of the civil war, which must be put to an end and prevented our command staff from reorganizing in a new way, on the rails of modern war."[19]

When it came to the manning of the Red Army, Stalin argued that the "cult" of the Civil War had led to planning being impromptu and based on political hopes over reality—both with disastrous effect. Attacks could be made prematurely (Stalin was openly admitting the failures of the Winter War in starting too soon—though avoiding personal blame, of course), because commanders did not understand that material supremacy was more important in carrying the day than revolutionary zeal. What material supremacy was needed? Here Stalin was very clear. The Red Army needed to upgrade its heavy firepower across the board—from planes, to tanks, to the small arms carried by each soldier. The "first thing" he focused on was the weapons system that had proved decisive in the war against Finland and would be one of the Red Army's most successful components in the war against Germany—heavy artillery. "In modern warfare, artillery is God," Stalin wrote. "Artillery decides the fate of war, mass artillery."[20]

After artillery, Stalin believed that the Red Army needed to drastically upgrade its tactical air support, not by "hundreds" of aircraft but by "thousands." Stalin, like most of the grand strategists, was relatively unschooled in types of aircraft and their uses, but he had come to believe that having air control over the battle area was a key part of victory. Then there was the need for ever more "massive" tanks, again in their many thousands. These needed to be "thick-skinned" and powerful, to work with the artillery to overwhelm the enemy.* It was an important meditation, and Stalin would put his money where his mouth was. From the end of the war with Finland until Barbarossa was launched, the Red Army would push forward with this plan for modernization, which would make it more combat-effective when the Germans crossed the border—and considerably more combat-effective as the war continued.

To improve the Red Army's human assets, training was made more combat-realistic, military discipline was imposed, and commanders' prerogatives to take action were strengthened.[21] When it came to firepower, new, heavier weapons systems were developed with greater urgency, to give the Red Army the advantage that Stalin craved. The first generation of Soviet ground-attack aircraft, the Ilyushin Il-2—the most produced aircraft variant of any type during the war—was brought from the prototype to the operational state at this time. More functional than top-line when compared to British or German aircraft, the Il-2 would provide the Red Army with useful air support during such famous battles as Stalingrad and Kursk.

Stalin's personal interventions paid particular dividends with the improvement and increased equipping of heavy artillery and mortars. Now no longer relying on reconditioned Tsarist-era equipment, the Red Army started receiving a regular supply of more robust modern artillery—from the excellent 76mm gun that would serve with great effectiveness during the war to the large 80mm trench mortar.[22] Of all the equipment upgrades at this time, probably the most well known to military historians is the new generation of medium and heavy tanks that in some ways surpassed those of the Germans. The legendary T-34 medium tank (which was not much lighter than a heavy tank by the standards of the time) came into operation in 1940, and by 1941 Soviet industry was gearing up to produce this reliable, well-protected AFV (armoured fighting vehicle) in numbers that would dwarf what the Germans were able to produce

---

* Stalin's focus on the largest and most powerful also covered infantry weapons. He believed that the Red Army needed new "massive" mortars and new automatic/semi-automatic rifles. The stress was on firepower.

of similarly sized vehicles. Overall, the Red Army upgraded its equipment considerably between 1939 and 1941, and provided the capacity and understanding to upgrade even more between 1941 and 1945.[23] In this way, Stalin transformed the disaster of the Winter War into an opportunity.

Stalin's focus on heavy firepower was an area that showed some similarities to Hitler, with the crucial difference being that the Soviet leader possessed an ability to adapt. At this point in the war, Hitler believed Germany had already shown its superiority in heavy equipment and firepower, and he seemed content to press on with the weapons they already had. Looking at his plans for Barbarossa as they developed between the summer of 1940 and June 1941, what stands out is his complacency—the extraordinary confidence he displayed in the German Army's abilities and Germany's place in the world. In an overarching sense, Hitler believed that his successes to this point showed that German industrial production was not just the best in Europe, but the best in the world. He went overboard both in private and in public with his vision of German strength. On November 8, 1940, in an address to Nazi Party members, he played up German power to a ridiculous degree: "German productive capacities are the highest in the world. And we will not leave matters at that, since we are in a position today to mobilize nearly all of Europe, and that I am doing this in the industrial sphere you can take for granted . . . We are better prepared for the future than ever before."[24]

He was just as effusive when speaking to his leading generals. He made the same boast to them in January 1941, claiming that the British, for one, were fooling themselves when they talked about British industrial prowess, because in Hitler's estimation Germany was "the biggest industrial nation in the world."[25] Actually, Germany was nowhere close to being the largest industrial power in the world, and it would never be. Britain was still significantly outproducing the Germans in aircraft, the largest element of industrial production for the warring powers, while the USSR was outproducing it for AFV and artillery and the US was showing the ability to outproduce it in everything. The real problem Germany was starting to face was that it was nowhere near mobilizing its resources effectively to properly

equip the German Army for an invasion of the USSR—unless it
ended quickly.[26]

When it came to equipment, Hitler was just as sure that he possessed the tools to crush the Soviets. In particular he and his generals
were convinced that Germany had pronounced advantages in tanks
and aircraft. German tanks were supposedly superior to their Russian
counterparts in armour protection and speed, with much better
optical sights and radio equipment.[27] German aircraft, meanwhile,
were considered at least a generation ahead of their Soviet counterparts. Even though the Luftwaffe had been decisively defeated in the
Battle of Britain, Hitler assumed German air power, even if outnumbered significantly by the Soviets, would easily best their opponents.
When the sums were done in February 1941, Hitler was told that
Russian aircraft were expected to outnumber German aircraft during
Barbarossa by almost two to one (more than 4,000 Soviet airplanes to
approximately 2,300 German) but that the Russian aircraft were
so "inferior" or "obsolete" that they posed little threat.[28] While some
of these estimations were right, particularly in terms of aircraft quality, the Germans would get a rude awakening when they encountered
the newest generation of Soviet tanks.

It is important to remember the overconfidence that Hitler displayed in German equipment at this time, because it helps put the
idea that Hitler had decided to attack the USSR to pre-empt a Soviet
attack on Germany in its proper context. Hitler did mention a few
times his fear of letting Russia get too strong, though there was a lack
of immediacy to his expressions. In February 1941 he told some officers that he was "stunned" by reports on Soviet plans to increase their
air power in the future and this was a reason to strike soon. However
he later added that the real reason he needed to strike now was that,
after defeating Britain, the German people might lose interest in any
extension of the war to include the USSR.[29]

Hitler remained, as he had been since the summer of 1940, boxed
in by his inability to come up with a plan to defeat Britain. His frustration, even while the master of most of the European continent,
was always a higher consideration than pre-empting an attack by
Stalin. The anger and irritation he felt towards Britain was so strong

that it gnawed away at him. He would try to process his frustration by oscillating between boasts that Britain was doomed to defeat and the occasional wistful longing that Britain might still become the valued ally he had always wanted it to be. In November 1940 Hitler stated he was reluctant to allow Vichy France to become a German ally because he hoped to "negotiate an understanding with England at the expense of France."[30] To those around Hitler, this desire was "always" in his mind—and indeed a month later Hitler once again repeated to a military gathering the idea of making Britain Germany's great ally to control France in the future (and all of Europe for that matter).[31]

Hitler's continuing desire to have Britain by his side was probably heightened the more he saw his powerlessness to force the country to make peace. The story of the war against Britain in late 1940 and the first six months of 1941 was a continuation of that established during the fall of France and the Battle of Britain. In places where Hitler could engage on land using the German Army, he could win—such as in the Balkans and Greece. As soon as the war shifted to the sea and the air, however, the Germans found themselves frustrated. Though it is not always portrayed that way, during 1941 Britain was growing in strength and winning the air-sea war. The U-boat campaign in the North Atlantic, which had seemed to hold promise for the Germans in the summer of 1940, levelled off in terms of sinkings in the first six months of 1941, before going into a decline as the Royal Navy's ability to protect convoys grew numerically and qualitatively. The number of radar-equipped escort vessels available for convoy duty grew significantly, long-range aircraft started playing an important role and German U-boats started to be sunk in such high numbers that surface attacks were stopped in March 1941. In the air, the British turned the tables on the Germans, and while Luftwaffe attacks on British cities became less of a problem, British attacks on German cities grew to the point that they became increasingly embarrassing for Hitler, who liked to talk endlessly about how he was winning the war. That year also highlighted how in many ways Britain was the superior air power, as it launched a significant number of heavy, four-engine bombers—most famously the Halifaxes and later the

Lancasters.* Germany, meanwhile, was unable to efficiently produce a four-engine bomber at any time in the war.

Britain's growing strength in the air had even punctuated the last great diplomatic set piece between Nazi Germany and the Soviet Union before the German invasion: Molotov's visit to Berlin in November 1940. In a lavish display for the time, the Soviet foreign secretary was welcomed at Berlin's grand Anhalter Bahnhof with all the proper trappings, including an orchestra performing "The Internationale," the worldwide anthem of communism. [32]† Yet for all their pomp, the talks were some of the more bizarre in diplomatic history.

The outward purpose of Molotov's visit was to see if there were grounds to formalize the Nazi–Soviet alliance, even to the point of including the Soviet Union in the Axis pact. This was something which intrigued Stalin, and so the strongly anti-British Molotov was at least approaching the talks with a smattering of good faith. Hitler, however, was negotiating while massing more and more troops on the Russian border. The only question he seemed to have was whether Stalin might offer him something that would negate the need for an invasion. It was a meeting of predator and prey.

For two full days, November 12 and 13, the Soviets and Nazis talked past each other, each focusing on their individual concerns, testing the sincerity of the other side. Hitler and Joachim von Ribbentrop spent their time trying to entice Molotov with dreams of a divvied-up post-war British Empire, with the Soviets given India as part of their booty. Molotov, no dreamer, focused on the more immediate issues of German support for Finland, a recognition of Soviet interest in Romania and the Balkans and, maybe most annoyingly for the Germans, an effort to get the Nazis to agree to hand over the Bosporus to the USSR. [33] Things reached a head during the final evening. Warnings of a British bombing attack forced the negotiators into a cramped air-raid shelter below the German foreign ministry, a fitting reminder that Hitler and Ribbentrop had no real

---

* Lancasters would not become available for operations until 1942.

† The Anhalter Bahnhof was destroyed by the end of the war, except for one small section of wall which can still be seen in Berlin today.

power to offer anything of substance. When Ribbentrop again bloviated about what Germany would give to the Soviets once Britain had been beaten, Molotov pointed out that the Germans "were assuming that the war against England had actually already been won."[34] No agreement was reached.

For Hitler, the end of the talks with Molotov helped erase any lingering doubts he had about launching Barbarossa. The Soviet Union was not only weak—it was obstructive; it refused to accept his vision of the world while at the same time trying to expand into areas that threatened Germany. He brought these different strands of his strategic mindset together with his frustration with Britain during one of his longest and most self-obsessed monologues, given to his officers on March 30, 1941. For two and a half hours in his enormous office in the Reich Chancellery, Hitler outlined his geo-strategic rationale for Barbarossa. It was a bewildering combination of overconfidence, delusion and the deepest self-regard. He started his overview with the itch he could never scratch—the need to pay the British back for not agreeing to be his friend and for having the temerity not to lose the Battle of Britain. This, Hitler claimed, was their great "mistake," and having not grasped the hand of friendship offered to them, the British were left putting their hopes in the US and Russia. The US, Hitler confidently told his generals, would not reach maximum production for four years, so could be put aside for now. Russia, on the other hand, was close by, still weak, and its conquest would solve all of Germany's "land problems." Having conquered Russia, Germany could devote itself entirely to the war against Britain, giving the Nazis two years to completely focus on "tasks in the air and on the oceans."[35]★

When it came to conquering the USSR, the main problem would

★ It is worth noting that while Hitler was beginning to understand how poorly he had constructed his armed forces to fight Britain in an air-sea war, he still continued to underestimate the United States' ability to produce air-sea weapons. He told his officers that it would take the US four years to increase war production to maximum levels, and even then he doubted the Americans would be able to ship everything across the Atlantic.

be the "vastness" of the country, not the Red Army or Stalinist state. Soviet armed forces had a great deal of equipment but most of it was old and lagged behind the Germans in technological sophistication. The great majority of Soviet tanks were "obsolete" and the Soviet air force was mostly "outmoded."[36] Beyond the material weaknesses, Hitler also believed that Bolshevism was so unpopular in much of the Soviet Union that many of the different nationalities, such as the Ukrainians, would look at the Germans as liberators. Perhaps the most quoted line of Hitler's overall vision of the USSR is "We have only to kick in the door . . . and the whole rotten structure will come crashing down."[37] Moreover, he told his officers that, when faced with heavy German firepower and superior technology, the Russians would "crumple under the massive impact of our tanks and planes."[38] Indeed, what he said most often in 1941 was that, when faced by a modern German onslaught, the Russians would "collapse."

It was easily Hitler's greatest failure in the planning of Barbarossa. He was preparing to invade the largest country in the world with an army in some ways less effective than the one he had sent against France a year earlier. While the German Army had more soldiers and tanks, the stresses of the air-sea war against Britain meant that the Luftwaffe force available to attack the USSR was smaller by almost half than the one used in May 1940 against France and the Low Countries. Then, the Luftwaffe had deployed almost 4,000 aircraft. Now, for the looming attack against Stalin, the air force had approximately 2,300 planes available.[39]

Hitler's overconfidence persisted regardless of what he faced. Even after he had to delay the invasion of Russia by a month because Mussolini dragged him into attacking Yugoslavia and Greece, he seemed unconcerned about Stalin's military. When asked about whether the USSR might take advantage of Germany having to attack in the Balkans because of Mussolini's disastrous war with Greece, he replied that he had "no reason for anxiety."[40] Just one week before Barbarossa itself was launched, Hitler delivered a detailed monologue on the political reasons behind the invasion, which boiled down to the fact that he calculated that "Russia's collapse would induce England to give in."[41]

While Hitler was hardening in his strategic belief that he needed to attack Stalin, the Soviet dictator believed the opposite was the case. During the first half of 1941, he engaged in an increasingly sur-real contest to convince himself that all the different reports he was receiving about German preparations for an invasion, which would reach primal scream levels in the weeks before June 22, were wrong. Stalin really seemed to believe that he could convince Hitler that he remained a worthwhile proto-ally of the Axis. As part of this, he went out of his way to insult Churchill and the British. In May 1941 Stalin removed official Soviet recognition of the pre-war govern-ments of Belgium, Norway and Yugoslavia, all of which were recognized by Britain. Moreover, he had the Soviet press lambast the British ambassador to Moscow, Sir Stafford Cripps, for trying to undermine the great unity binding Germany and the USSR.[42] Yet no matter what he did, more and more reports were delivered to Stalin saying that Hitler was preparing to attack.

The sheer volume of such reports was staggering.[43] Stalin received warnings from Soviet agents around the world, perhaps most fam-ously Richard Sorge, the legendary Soviet spy in the German embassy in Japan. Foreign embassies in Moscow had also been penetrated by Stalin's counterintelligence services, producing, particularly from the Germans, a great deal of confirmatory information. Two days before the invasion commenced, the German ambassador to the USSR, Friedrich von der Schulenburg, was recorded by Soviet eavesdropping equipment claiming that Hitler was about to attack.[44]

The rumblings were hard to ignore. Even the British directly passed on to Stalin information they had about German intentions, which he dismissed as a plot to poison the well between himself and Hitler. It was as if Stalin had to believe that Hitler was not going to attack, as the truth would reveal to himself, and the rest of the world, that he had bungled his strategy badly. Stalin became so enraged by the warnings of a German betrayal that he became abusive, exclaiming at one point when given a report lifted from a German source: "You can send your 'source' . . . back to his f-ing mother. This is not a source but a disinformation . . ."[45]

With his own eyes and ears sealed, Stalin took steps to put his self-deception into action in such a way that he actively aided the Germans in their invasion. He forbade the air force from trying to intercept German reconnaissance flights illegally entering Soviet airspace.[46] Thus the Luftwaffe was able to fly unmolested over western Russia, amassing a detailed picture of the disposition of Russian forces and the terrain the German Army would first encounter. He also kept trainloads of supplies running regularly into Germany, feeding the German war effort and allowing the Germans to create stockpiles of vital raw materials they could tap once Barbarossa began and they lost access to Soviet sources. He even refused to let the large Red Army formations that were stationed on the border directly across from the German Army take up readiness positions.[47] As such, they were woefully unprepared when the Germans did attack.

The reason Stalin was so dogmatic about his seemingly wilful blindness to German intentions is still challenging. Some historians have argued that Stalin trusted Hitler too much, a charge that Molotov for one rejected decades after the dictator's death, saying, "Stalin trusted Hitler? He didn't trust his own people!"[48] Indeed, Stalin probably didn't trust Hitler—but he did trust Joseph Stalin. Since August 1939, when he signed the Nazi–Soviet Pact, he had claimed that there was no way that Germany would attack the USSR while still at war with Great Britain, and he had based his entire policy of helping Germany on that assumption. He needed to be right, because the implications of his being wrong seemed too much for him to accept.

Of course, even dictators find that not everything they want comes to pass. On June 22, 1941, almost to the moment that many of the sources had foretold, the Germans invaded the Soviet Union. Stalin was devastated, though once the shock wore off and he remained in power, he did everything practical to protect himself. He instantly accepted offers of friendship and aid from his two great enemies, Britain and the United States. He reintroduced older Russian customs to rally the Soviet people, even allowing churches to reopen. Having been shown to be in error, he would do what he needed to do in the moment to protect himself. If he lost the battle with Hitler in the short term, he would win in the long run.

16.   Roosevelt, Hitler and the Road to War

On August 30, 1939, Franklin Delano Roosevelt made his first strides towards war with Adolf Hitler. With the Nazi dictator poised to invade Poland, the American president was thinking about the strategic structure he needed to guide the United States to victory. He had pondered this question for years, long suspecting that Hitler's voracious hunger for expansion would end in tears. Roosevelt was also sure about how he wanted the United States to fight in a war—a sea-air war to control global lines of communication. Yet the president worried that the American system of government might complicate his efforts to get his plans enacted. As would later be shown, he had very different views of war and warfare from many in his own government. The War Department, which oversaw the US Army, favoured the creation of a large land army and an early invasion of France. What Roosevelt wanted, therefore, was a governmental structure, headed by someone he trusted, to do the dirty work of coordinating the American armed services—both enforcing his plans and simplifying his life. He also knew exactly who he wanted in that post. And so, on August 30, Roosevelt invited into the Oval Office for a private chat his old friend from Woodrow Wilson's Navy Department, William Leahy.*

Now an admiral, the sixty-four-year-old Leahy was set to retire the following day as Roosevelt's chief of naval operations and leave for Puerto Rico to serve as the president's handpicked governor. Over the previous years, the two had had many private chats in the White House, as Leahy had become Roosevelt's most important naval adviser. The meeting on August 30 felt different, more intense. The two spent an hour analysing the likelihood of war in Europe and

* Roosevelt rarely called Leahy by his formal title, preferring the informal "Bill," while Leahy always referred to Roosevelt as "Mr. President."

the role the United States should play in it. Roosevelt understood that he and Leahy shared a very similar strategic mindset—and, maybe even more importantly, that he could trust the admiral. Eventually, Roosevelt leaned in and let Leahy in on a secret. If the United States should become "seriously involved in the European difficulty," Roosevelt wanted Leahy to take charge of a "four-man War Board, with the duty of coordinating the work of the State, War and Navy Departments."[1] Roosevelt, in a rather remarkable formulation, was creating a position that would eventually morph into both the present-day national security adviser and chairman of the Joint Chiefs of Staff.*

The president would be as good as his word. When the United States joined World War II after the Japanese attacked Pearl Harbor, Leahy was serving as the US ambassador to Vichy France. Roosevelt called him back to Washington as soon as was politically possible, and named him chief of staff to the commander-in-chief and the "senior member" of the Joint Chiefs of Staff.†

This kind of manoeuvring reveals much about Roosevelt as a war leader. More than two years before the US joined the fight, hemmed in by public opposition to war, he was already trying to imagine a wartime policy structure. He was in many ways one of the most far-sighted and prepared of all the grand strategists. His selection of Leahy as his closest adviser shows how greatly the president valued strategic coherence at the top. The two shared identical visions of how the United States should fight a world war, a strategic mind-meld that went back to their friendship in the Navy Department. Both believed that the US must establish control over the world's lines of communication, at sea and in the air, as the first step towards victory. Alfred Thayer Mahan's vision, which had driven both men's actions before and during World War I, had been broadened to take

---

* Roosevelt had already discussed Leahy taking on a role as his senior adviser and aide in case of war, back in April 1939, but was much less specific than he was on August 30.

† The formal position of Chairman of the Joint Chiefs of Staff was created by an act of Congress and did not go into effect until 1948.

in air power, but the basic idea of controlling communications remained. Neither was enamoured of large armies or land battles. They wanted to use air and sea machines to weaken enemy resistance before using land power as selectively as possible to bring any war to a close.

As president, Roosevelt had been much more intimately involved with the details of the navy build-up of the late 1930s than with anything to do with the army. With the Japanese invading China and Hitler rattling his sabre in Europe, Roosevelt pushed for a greatly expanded fleet. In 1938, this pressure resulted in a Naval Expansion Act which called for a 20 per cent rise in naval shipbuilding across the board.[2] It seemed a massive increase for the time, but would be dwarfed by what Roosevelt would do for the navy two years later.

If in 1939 Roosevelt was convinced he knew how the United States would win any war, he was less sure about how to exercise control over the American grand strategy. In particular, he wanted to coordinate the armed services with the State Department to put his ideas into action. He could see trouble arising here. A man of great suspicion, Roosevelt normally hid his true feelings behind a mask—usually one of charm. He would establish an air of faux intimacy with people, making them think he valued their ideas and friendship, when in fact he often looked at them as a means to an end. He therefore disliked openly disagreeing with members of his own government, even when there were serious policy differences. As war approached, this was particularly the case with his cabinet members with power over strategic affairs—the secretaries of state, navy and war. He valued these secretaries for political reasons more than anything else: Cordell Hull, the long-time secretary of state and a power in the Democratic Party; and Henry Stimson and Frank Knox, both pro-British Republicans who had recently been named secretaries of war and the navy in a show of bipartisanship. But Roosevelt had little trust in their strategic views and wanted to reduce their influence. It was one of the reasons he started preparing Leahy for the post of chief of staff years before Pearl Harbor—he wanted to make sure that if the United States went to war, it was Franklin Roosevelt's war that it fought.

Two days after Roosevelt and Leahy's White House meeting, Hitler invaded Poland and Roosevelt at once began to stake out a clear pro-Allied position. In a public address on September 3, he repudiated Woodrow Wilson's famous plea in August 1914 that Americans be neutral "in thought." As Roosevelt told his fellow Americans, "Even a neutral has a right to take account of facts. Even a neutral cannot be asked to close his mind or his conscience."[3] If Roosevelt was openly rooting for a British–French victory, he also believed at this point that US entry into the war was not necessary for such an outcome. He certainly did not want to risk too much of his political capital by aggressively pushing intervention on behalf of the British and French. Roosevelt was pleased when in November 1939 Congress amended the Neutrality Acts, which had made trade with warring nations impossible, to allow the Allies to purchase US-made munitions on a cash-and-carry basis, but otherwise he waited to see what would happen.

The fall of France changed everything. Roosevelt had seemed relatively sanguine about the prospects of hemming in Hitler, with the French and British armies seemingly solidly deployed in a better position than they had been during the last world war. Yet when the German Army shattered French lines, seized Paris and dictated terms that pushed France out of the war, Roosevelt saw his strategic calculations upended almost overnight. It changed his vision of how wars were fought and what the United States would need to do to make sure Hitler did not win this one.

The fall of France was the event that made it clear to Roosevelt that the airplane was now at least the equal of the ship in determining the outcome of modern war. As the German invasion streaked forward, he heard horrific accounts of the impact of German tactical air power, with many stories coming directly from the US ambassador to France, William Bullitt. The ambassador relayed reports of French army units breaking under the power of Hitler's Luftwaffe, as well as columns of fleeing French civilians mercilessly attacked from the air. The coming months would only cement this transition in favour of air power in Roosevelt's mind, as he was told stories of the bombing of British cities by the Luftwaffe.

In response, Roosevelt raised the production of aircraft to the highest priority possible. Pushing for a massive increase in US defence spending, he told the American people in July 1940, just as Winston Churchill was gearing up to fight the Battle of Britain, that France's defeat had altered everything. The "changes in the world situation are so great and so profound," he said, that the United States needed to prepare to defend not only itself but the entire western hemisphere against Nazi aggression. The US Navy, he insisted, needed to be made strong enough "to meet any possible combination of hostile naval forces."[4]

Roosevelt's other priority was by far the most expensive. He called the United States to more than triple the size of its existing air capabilities by adding 15,000 planes to the US Army Air Forces and 4,000 to the US Navy. Moreover, as he stressed, he did not want to add just numbers; he wanted to strengthen America's ability to build aircraft to such a degree that the country would dwarf other nations, with the ability to churn out 50,000 aircraft annually.

The fall of France also made clear to Roosevelt that the United States would eventually have to join the war to defeat Nazi Germany. He never said so openly, careful to wear the mask of non-combatant before the American people and never committing himself to a warpath (much to Winston Churchill's dismay). But Roosevelt's caginess was not a sign that he was undecided. Politically, he needed Hitler to give him the pretext to take that next step, and until the Nazi dictator did so, Roosevelt was left showing the US public one face and trying very hard to show Hitler another.

At first, Hitler seemed uncertain about Roosevelt's commitment to the Allied cause. Between the invasion of Poland and Roosevelt's re-election in November 1940, Hitler spoke in his habitual contradictory way about a possible war with the United States. At times he assumed Roosevelt could never gain the public support for war, while at others he would talk about the US joining Britain as a real possibility. When Hitler did envisage war with the US, he did not instantly shy away. He was more concerned that it happen on his terms, when he was ready and when he believed that American power could not be deployed to Europe quickly or materially enough to stop him. In that sense, he revealed a fundamentally flawed vision of the United States. He respected America's ability to exert power, but he also became increasingly convinced that his own strategic genius and a German-dominated Europe would be able to fend off anything that Roosevelt could throw at him.

Privately, Hitler never seemed to be able to make up his mind as to whether the United States was a racially impure nation of "mongrel" softies who were too far away from Europe to interfere in the war, or an economic powerhouse he needed to fear and maybe even emulate.[5] He liked to boast that German cars were far better than their American counterparts, which he labelled as junk. On the other hand, he was a voracious consumer of Hollywood movies, particularly westerns. His obsession had a major impact on his understanding of the US, as he was known to refer to the Depression-era classic *The Grapes of Wrath* to make the case that America was too divided and weak to ever want to get into a war against him.

Outwardly, however, Hitler seemed anything but conflicted. Though he and Roosevelt never met, they communicated with each other through public declarations and speeches. In April 1939, Roosevelt issued a public statement in which he asked Hitler to refrain from militarily threatening Germany's neighbours. A few days later, in a lengthy and mocking address to the Reichstag, Hitler ridiculed the American president.[6] Referring back to the previous world war, he accused Roosevelt of overlooking the fact that it was the United States who had made war on Germany, not for self-defence but "for the realization of capitalist interests." The US, he declared, was more warlike and interventionist than Nazi Germany, and Roosevelt was the one who represented more of a threat to the peace of Europe than Adolf Hitler did to the United States. Near the end, Hitler caused hooting amongst the Nazi deputies when he exclaimed with mock sincerity that he would "not like to let this opportunity pass without extending assurances" to Roosevelt "that any and all allegations of a planned German attack on American territories or an intervention [are] pure swindle and crude fabrication."[7]

When war broke out, Hitler at first seemed unconcerned about the possibility of the US joining the Allies—so much so that he continued to snub Roosevelt's very public attempts to intervene. Immediately after Hitler launched the invasion of Poland, Roosevelt publicly called on all the combatants to refrain from bombing civilian targets. Hitler's Luftwaffe bombed the residence of the US ambassador in Poland a few days later.[8] Even Roosevelt's corresponding increase in military spending after the fall of France did not seem to worry Hitler. He spoke of Roosevelt, the United States or American power rarely. When he did mention them, he tried to seem blasé, believing that if the United States did start throwing its weight around, it would only be in a limited fashion. On October 15, 1940, Hitler, during one of his regular monologues based around the assumption that the war had already been won and Britain was defeated, confidently claimed that the US would "furnish only war materials" for Britain and any discussion of America entering the war was just a "big bluff."[9]

That being said, Hitler was aware that Roosevelt was up for re-election in 1940 and that this might matter. On the eve of the election, Hitler prophesied that the United States might enter the war at some point, though it would not happen until 1942 at the earliest.[10] He followed this up a week after Roosevelt's re-election by going further and providing some of his first concrete—if unorthodox—ideas about what a German–American war would look like. Hitler told Admiral Erich Raeder, the head of the German Navy, to plan to seize the Azores islands off the coast of North Africa, explaining that the chain would afford him "the only facility for attacking America, if she should enter the war, with a modern plane of the Messerschmitt type, which has a range of 12,600 km."[11]★ This idea of attacking America from the Azores took deep root. In late May 1941, while making final preparations for Barbarossa, Hitler once again instructed the navy to come up with plans to take the Azores—even though the navy believed it would be impossible to hold the islands against

---

★ Hitler was referring to the prototype development of the Me 264, sometimes referred to as the *Amerikabomber*. A typically wasteful Nazi glamour project, the plane was expensive and impractical, and was eventually shelved in favour of more immediate concerns.

British and American attacks. Hitler didn't care about the navy's objections, still believing that the islands were the only way to attack the US with long-range bombers, and that Germany might find itself needing to do so by the autumn.[12]

In this way, Hitler showed that he had some grasp of Roosevelt's real outlook, and how much Roosevelt detested him and his regime. For the post-election Franklin Roosevelt would indeed be very different from the pre-election version in terms of how far he was willing to go to help Britain and do everything possible to get his own nation ready for war—and the even greater lengths he would go to with Hitler to convince him of his intentions. Before the vote, Roosevelt had remained politically cautious, wary that, for the first time since he became president, the next election might be close. His Republican challenger, Wendell Willkie, was a strong campaigner, and many Republicans (if not Willkie himself) accused the president of being too willing to intervene in the European war. These isolationist attacks worried the president, and it was why he went out of his way until the night of the vote to assure Americans that their boys would not die in any "foreign war."

Once safely re-elected, and by a comfortable majority of 449 electoral votes to 82, Roosevelt was free to put on a more aggressive mask. After taking some time in November to "refuel" his ideas on the war in Europe, by December a far more bellicose Roosevelt started to reveal himself.[13] Speaking over the radio during one of his regular "fireside chats," Roosevelt spoke to Hitler, even if he refused to use the German dictator's name. Where Hitler used mockery towards Roosevelt, the president spoke of the Nazi dictator with loathing. Roosevelt described the Germans as aiming to conquer the world, led by a man who lied and deceived with "pious frauds," and who could only be stopped by the barrel of a gun.[14] He still tried to assure the American people that if he went after Hitler directly, they would not be needed to fire the weapons to bring Hitler down, but that they would have to produce them, pay for them and in many cases ship them to Britain. The British people were the "spearhead of resistance" against Hitler's plan for world conquest, according to Roosevelt, and it was up to the United States to make sure that they received such support. Roosevelt's address became known as the "Arsenal of Democracy" speech.

Roosevelt's firm conviction that Britain could not under any circumstances be allowed to fall was transmitted to Europe through two of the three people he trusted most at the time: William Leahy and Harry Hopkins.* Indeed, these two, both destined to play major roles in the Roosevelt White House, were dispatched on separate diplomatic missions just after Roosevelt's re-election, to make it clear around Europe that America was going to make its power felt.

Leahy, in December 1940, was plucked from his sinecure as the US-appointed governor of Puerto Rico (where he had been overseeing the drawing-up of plans to create a massive new naval base on the island) to become Roosevelt's new US ambassador to Vichy France. Roosevelt chose Leahy because he felt the admiral could be trusted to follow his wishes exactly. Just to be sure, before Leahy left for France, Roosevelt invited his friend for another long, private meeting in the White House to discuss policy. For a few hours the two chatted alone in the president's study, Leahy mostly listening as Roosevelt laid out his vision of the war and what he wanted Leahy to accomplish in France.

The depth of Roosevelt's conviction made such an impression that Leahy asked for, and received, a detailed letter outlining the president's wishes. It is one of the best, clearest and most honest examples of how Roosevelt viewed the war at the time.[15] Much of the letter is a testimony to the president's continuing obsession with naval power. Even though France seemed very much defeated and demoralized, Roosevelt was worried that the Vichy government, led by the octogenarian World War I hero Marshal Philippe Pétain, could be a real asset for Nazi Germany. The president believed that if Hitler could get his hands on the French fleet, it would be a blow to the British (and the United States), complicating the war at sea. Since the collapse of French resistance, Roosevelt had tried to get promises from

---

* The third was Under Secretary of State Sumner Welles, who was a lifetime friend of the president and was so close to Roosevelt that it caused resentment in the rest of the State Department, particularly from Cordell Hull.

Pétain that the large and functional French fleet might not be handed over to Germany. But no matter what Pétain promised him, Roosevelt was worried. He therefore told Leahy that keeping the French Navy out of Hitler's hands was of "prime importance" to the United States and the defence of the western hemisphere.

Overall, what Roosevelt wanted Leahy to do in France was to make absolutely clear to Pétain (and the rest of Europe if possible) that the US was going to make sure that Hitler and Mussolini were defeated no matter what. The new ambassador was to tell everyone that the position of the United States government (i.e. Roosevelt) was a "firm conviction that only by the defeat of the powers control-ling the destiny of Germany and Italy can the world live in liberty, peace and prosperity; that civilization cannot progress with a return to totalitarianism." How was this to happen? The US, for now, would start flooding Britain with whatever arms it needed; Roosevelt would be guaranteeing the United Kingdom "all possible assistance short of war." To make sure this specific message was heard loud and clear, Leahy was told to periodically "bring to the attention of Mar-shal Petain and members of the Government concrete information regarding the American program to this end."[16]

Leahy took this message to heart, and from the moment he arrived in France he kept up a steady drumbeat, saying that the US would make sure that Hitler did not win the war. Meanwhile, the president sent Hopkins, his closest adviser at the time, to go and see Winston Churchill and find out exactly what Britain needed to make sure the Nazis were defeated. Hopkins had first met Roosevelt in 1931, when Roosevelt was governor of New York and Hopkins an ambitious and determined social reformer who had come to the state from Iowa to ply his trade. The two connected, with Hopkins developing an acute sense of how to appeal to Roosevelt and the two sharing a willing-ness to try anything to help combat the extreme poverty that plagued New York during the Great Depression.

When Roosevelt became president in 1933, he summoned Hop-kins to Washington, and for the next seven years Hopkins established himself as one of the very few people Roosevelt trusted. At first Hopkins held a number of major positions in the New Deal bureaucracy, but eventually the formal roles ended and Hopkins moved into the White House to serve the president as a constant adviser, social companion and general political factotum. Using Hopkins in this way was typical Roosevelt management. Hopkins was his man and his alone, and because of that was actually far more influential than those with formal cabinet posts, who could be independent actors and politicians in their own right. In this case, by using Hopkins to go directly to Churchill, Roosevelt was basically cutting Secretary of State Cordell Hull, who was ostensibly in charge of US foreign relations, entirely out of the loop.

When Hopkins arrived, Churchill was confused why the president had sent him this emaciated, chain-smoking, enigmatic, anti-imperialist social reformer. But he quickly understood the immense influence Hopkins wielded as a direct conduit to Roosevelt.[17] Once he did, Churchill barely let Hopkins out of his sight, bringing the American with him on weekends to Chequers, the official country house of the prime minister (and a place that Hopkins considered the coldest house he had ever stayed in), and shepherding him around London.* Hopkins originally was to stay in Britain for two weeks, but the work was so intense and considered so important that he stayed for six. When Hopkins left, Churchill was abnormally effusive, and cabled Roosevelt telling the president he could now understand "why he is so close to you."[18]

Churchill had understood through Hopkins just how committed Roosevelt was to an Allied victory. This was brought home to him just a few weeks after Hopkins's departure, when the US Congress passed the most important peacetime strategic bill in US history: the Lend-Lease Act of March 1941. First proposed by Roosevelt around the time he was meeting with Leahy and before his Arsenal of Democracy address, Lend-Lease was a plan to allow Roosevelt to hand over any military equipment to any country he believed was vital to US security. Between 1941 and 1945, the US would send $49 billion

---

* One of Hopkins's weekends with Churchill was actually spent at Ditchley Park, as Churchill's security staff would not let him stay at Chequers if there was a full moon—because of the fear that the Luftwaffe might try to attack the famous house.

of aid—mostly to Britain, but also with large amounts sent to the Soviet Union and Nationalist China.

Lend-Lease began the process of tying the UK into the US economy (in some ways making it a subsidiary of it), and went a long way to setting up the preconditions for US entry into the war. Still, that would take another eight months, and that alone tells an interesting story of Roosevelt and Hitler as war leaders.

Both knew a clash between their nations was all but inevitable, but each was trying to pave the road to war based largely on his World War I experiences. Roosevelt, forever wary of the fickle nature of US public opinion, spent the coming months escalating his rhetorical and economic conflict with Hitler's Germany into a quasi-military one, but always holding back from taking the ultimate step in the hope that it would be Hitler who fired the first shot. And this manoeuvring exposed the one problem he was never willing to face—how to get the United States in the war if Hitler did not solve this political problem for him.

Hitler, on the other hand, wanted to wait to fire that shot until he felt he had established the kind of Europe he wanted—one with him as lord and master, with access to the continent's entire resource base. By 1941 he seemed more than willing to accept a war with the United States, though he hoped to delay it until he could be sure it would see Germany having conquered the USSR so that it would not be faced with a two-front war.

Unlike in 1940, Hitler regularly spoke of war with America in 1941. He seemed to accept Roosevelt's statements from the Arsenal of Democracy speech through the passage of Lend-Lease as a strong signal that war was coming. On January 8, 1941, fewer than two weeks after the speech in which Roosevelt had called him a liar and threat to the world, Hitler called a conference of the heads of his armed forces, the army (Heer), navy (Kriegsmarine) and air force (Luftwaffe), at his Berghof residence in Obersalzberg.[19] Ostensibly held to discuss his plans for the Balkans and North Africa, the meeting gave Hitler yet another opportunity to proclaim his own geopolitical brilliance. Part of this brilliance was assuring his generals and admirals that if war with the United States did happen, he could master the situation.

Don't worry about the US joining Great Britain, Hitler said. The productive possibilities of a German-dominated Europe were significantly superior. He was "firmly convinced that Europe's armament and economic resources offer[ed] far greater possibilities" than the combined force of the UK and US.[20] Of course, that meant that he had to defeat Stalin first. If Germany found itself at war with Britain, America and the USSR, the situation would be "very complicated."[21] Therefore, his next move, unless he could finally convince Britain to make peace, would be to conquer the USSR. Having done that, Germany would be safe in its continent-wide sinecure.

This meditation on the need to conquer Soviet resources before the US joined the war became a regular part of Hitler's talks. In discussions with the head of the German Navy, Admiral Raeder, Hitler wondered if he might tempt the Japanese to take military action to divert the Americans and the British. In March 1941, Raeder spoke about how Japan "must" be encouraged to attack the British naval base at Singapore "at once" because the US was not yet "prepared to wage war."[22] In April, Hitler echoed this call and asked how Japan could be "induced to attack Singapore."[23]

More fatefully, around the same time, Hitler—through his foreign secretary, Ribbentrop—started urging the Japanese to move into southern Vietnam.[24] Then part of the French Empire, Vietnam was supposedly the imperial territory of the Vichy regime, but the French had no way to defend it against Japanese power. In the second half of 1940 the Japanese had moved forces into northern Vietnam but had left the south unoccupied. By 1941, they had started gazing southwards as the weak Vichy forces looked to be incapable of stopping them; taking the south would be a necessary step if Japan intended to strike down towards Singapore, then part of the Dutch East Indies. Hitler could see such a move as exactly what he wanted to distract the United States, and he assured the Japanese that he would support them if any southward movement resulted in war with America.

Hitler's policy set the clock ticking. When Germany attacked the Soviet Union, it set in motion Japanese action and American counteraction that led directly to Pearl Harbor. In the first place, the invasion of the Soviet Union convinced Roosevelt that he needed to up the stakes in confronting Hitler. On July 11, during one of his late-night chats with Harry Hopkins, he ripped a map of the North Atlantic from a copy of *National Geographic* and drew a line dividing the ocean into two unequal parts.[25] The smaller segment extended from Europe, around the United Kingdom, and out into the ocean. The larger part covered the remaining two-thirds of the vital waterway, including everything from the US and Canadian coasts to the east of Greenland and Iceland.

Roosevelt was dividing the Atlantic into American and British zones. He was proposing that the United States, completely against all laws of war for neutral powers, take over the protection of commerce in its area, greatly reducing the responsibility of the Royal Navy and allowing the British to provide far greater protection for merchant ships in British and European waters. Sure, Hitler might order attacks in Roosevelt's soon-to-be-declared American zone, but that would give the president his *casus belli*. If for some reason Hitler didn't attack, Roosevelt at least would have simplified British lives.

Having drawn his map, Roosevelt ordered Hopkins to head immediately to Britain to see Churchill to communicate his plan, and then to head to the Soviet Union to see Joseph Stalin to let the Soviet dictator know that the United States was willing to provide him with a massive amount of support in his fight against Hitler. Roosevelt was stitching together the grand coalition.

If Barbarossa upped Roosevelt's aggression, it likewise made the Japanese more risk-prone. They finally decided to take south Vietnam, on the assumption that a German victory in Europe was all but assured. On 28 July, Japanese forces started occupying the south of the country, having forced the Vichy regime to acquiesce.

Roosevelt, in retaliation, dropped an economic bomb on Japan. He not only froze all Japanese assets in the United States; he embargoed the sale of oil from the US (a move quickly copied by Winston Churchill). With the stroke of a pen, Roosevelt cut off 75 per cent of Japan's overseas trade and shut off the source of 88 per cent of Japan's overseas oil. He forced the Japanese to face the most fateful of choices: either give in humiliatingly to his demands for a withdrawal, or go to war to get oil to keep their economy and military functioning. They would soon choose the latter.

Roosevelt might never have foreseen that Japan would take the extraordinarily risky step of going to war with America, whose economy was maybe twenty times larger than their own. But he was willing to take the risk, open to anything to get into the war—and still feeling he could not do it directly until someone else fired first.

The continuation of his dilemma was made clear just over a week after sanctioning the Japanese. Aboard a warship moored off the coast of Newfoundland, Roosevelt greeted Winston Churchill at one of the most famous summits of World War II, known at the Argentia Conference. Churchill had hoped to secure a commitment from Roosevelt to get the United States into the war. Instead, he was subjected to the classic Roosevelt charm. The president spoke warm words about US support for Britain but refused to say anything that smacked of a definite commitment to fight. Their only real achievement was a joint statement of principles, which came to be known as the Atlantic Charter. Using high-sounding phrases, the two leaders expressed their support for democracy and freedom, though in truth the charter was as anti-imperialist as it was anti-Nazi. Churchill, however, signed, wary of doing anything to offend the charming American president. When the conference was over, the British prime minister felt let down as much as anything else.[26]

In a way, Churchill was right to feel let down. Roosevelt was still playing a game of making common cause with Britain, threatening Hitler verbally, trying to goad the Germans into action, but baulking at declaring war first. And Hitler, for a while, seemed determined not to give the president that satisfaction. After Argentia, Roosevelt sent US warships to patrol the Atlantic, soon clashing with German submarines. On September 4, a rather confused engagement occurred when a German U-boat and a US destroyer, the *Greer*, got into action. Exactly what happened is not entirely clear, but Roosevelt portrayed it as a dastardly German attack on a US ship that was keeping the peace. On September 11, the president initiated a shoot-on-sight policy in the American zone, allowing US ships to attack anything they thought was a target.

Hitler's response showed just how Roosevelt's actions had convinced him that the Americans would soon join the war. The early successes of Barbarossa, which saw German forces encircle and destroy a large number of Russian armies, had seemed to convince Hitler that victory over the Soviets was imminent. On September 17, less than a week after Roosevelt issued his shoot-on-sight policy, Hitler and Admiral Raeder sat down with Ribbentrop and senior German Army officers to analyse Roosevelt's actions.[27] Raeder gave a detailed report on the situation in the North Atlantic in light of Roosevelt's new policy, claiming that the president had basically turned the entire Atlantic into an American lake. He advised that Germany hurry a war with the US into existence by challenging Roosevelt's policy and calling for a US neutrality zone to be respected only to twenty miles from the US coast. Beyond that, the German fleet, including its submarines, would be at liberty to attack any ship it wanted.

Hitler's response was hardly negative. Wanting only to buy a little more time, he told Raeder that the Russian invasion should be settled by the end of the month, and therefore he wanted no engagements that could lead to a major clash with America before the "middle of October."[28]

In the end, the catalyst Roosevelt had been looking for came not in the Atlantic but in the Pacific. When the Japanese attacked Pearl Harbor on December 7, 1941, the president was shocked and angry, but ready to act.[29] He responded by immediately declaring war on Japan—but not on Germany. Roosevelt could not imagine that Hitler would not do him the favour of declaring war first.[30] Four days later, on December 11, fully conditioned by Roosevelt's decisions and relying on his own optimistic vision of German power, Hitler declared war on the United States. Roosevelt had worn his mask perfectly, and the US was now in a war with Germany—exactly as he had wanted it to be.

17. Roosevelt, Churchill, Hitler and the Air-Sea Super-Battlefield

After December 7, 1941, neither Franklin Roosevelt nor Winston Churchill had any doubts about the outcome of World War II. They were both convinced that Germany, Italy and Japan would all be crushed. What they disagreed about, sometimes bitterly, was the best way to do the crushing. They had a number of very different strategic priorities, which led to some exhausting arguments about the best way to bring the war to the heart of Nazi/Fascist Europe. Yet for all of these disagreements, they were bound by one thing, and this always held them together during the most difficult times. In the end, it led them to create the closest and most well-coordinated alliance in modern military history.

The thing that held Roosevelt and Churchill together was their belief that what happened on the battlefields of Europe was secondary. As long as the Allies controlled world communications, both were convinced they were on the road to victory. As such, they judged that by the time large British and American land armies became locked in combat with Germany somewhere on the continent (and they disagreed strongly on where that should be), this would represent the death throes of the Nazi and Italian empires. It was therefore the air and sea strangulation of Germany and Italy, preceding this land war, that would be crucial in determining the length and severity of the conflict.

This communications struggle, which happened over a vast area, can be termed the air-sea super-battlefield. It was an extreme contest in terms of length, breadth, depth and effort.[1] It stretched from ports in South and North America across the entire Atlantic Ocean. It reached up around Norway to Murmansk, and through the Strait of Gibraltar to the Suez Canal. It covered skies over Europe, from the south of Italy to the Baltic coast—and, crucially, over the main cities and industrial centres of Germany. This air-sea super-battlefield consumed far more industrial production than the famous land war, sometimes by a significant amount. Germany devoted a minimum of two-thirds of its annual war production to air-sea weapons and ammunition, and by 1944 this figure would be over 70 per cent. For the United States and United Kingdom, the figure was even higher.[2]

Their earlier experiences with war had taught both Roosevelt and Churchill the vital importance of controlling the air-sea super-battlefield—and in that way they had a massive advantage over Adolf Hitler, with his more parochial war and life experiences. Hitler's view of air-sea power was, particularly for the first few years of the war—before the reality of Allied air-sea power bashed him one too many times over the head—mostly as a simple extension of the land war. He never seemed to see air-sea power as Churchill and Roosevelt did: a way to control the flow of civilian goods and military supplies and equipment. For all his exposure to modern weapons and technology, he remained an infantry soldier, his understanding of war still stuck in the trenches of the last war. "The arms of the future?" he asked his audience rhetorically one evening in August 1941, before, naturally, answering himself: "In the first place, the land army, then aviation and, in the third place only, the navy."[3]

The reasons Hitler gave for his rankings betray his limited comprehension of military power. Even though his own war economy was devoting more resources to the production of aircraft than anything else, he saw air power almost exclusively as a form of mobile artillery—useful for supporting troops on the battlefield, or occasionally as a means to terrorize enemy populations. As for the navy, he had seen most of his warships sunk or driven to seek refuge in port, including the famous battleship *Bismarck*, which had been destroyed by British air and sea power less than three months earlier. With doubts about the value of a surface fleet, Hitler launched an attack on the "big warship" concept entirely. "The navy . . . has not changed, so to speak, since the first World War. There is something tragic in the fact that the battleship, that monument of human ingenuity, has lost its entire *raison d'etre* . . ."[4]

Six days after Pearl Harbor, on December 13, 1941, Winston

Churchill boarded the massive British battleship *Duke of York* and, amid deep swells and the gale force winds of the North Atlantic winter, journeyed to his first meeting with Franklin Roosevelt as wartime allies. On December 22, the battleship docked at the Norfolk Navy Yard and Churchill hurried north to Washington, where he was quickly installed in the White House. For the next three weeks, during what was codenamed the Arcadia Conference, he lived cheek by jowl with Roosevelt—dining, talking, smoking and at times even walking in on one another while in a state of undress.

The two made an odd pair. Roosevelt, the accommodating American, kept on hand a large supply of champagne, brandy and whisky. Churchill made himself at home in the White House, setting up his own map room (which Roosevelt later emulated by establishing his own, right next to the Oval Office) and continuing his preferred habit of lengthy, alcohol-fuelled chats that lingered late into the evening.[5] These went on longer than the sleep-loving Roosevelt would have preferred, but he—often accompanied by Harry Hopkins, who also lived in the White House—did his best to keep up.* These evening chats were in many ways the most important discussions of the conference, and allowed the war leaders to try to work out their differences away from everyone but the trusted Hopkins.[6]

During these chats, and the more formal meetings with their officials, the two strategists grappled with problems present and future—and tried to imagine what they would need in order to fight the war going forward. Much of the conference covered functional issues as the leaders tried to establish a more formal structure for Anglo-American war leadership, including joint boards for shipping and natural resources, and a combined chiefs of staff, so that all military operations would be planned as cooperatively as possible.

---

* During this conference Roosevelt began the process of limiting the truly important conversations to meetings of just himself and select advisers such as Hopkins. He invited cabinet ministers such as Henry Stimson to attend larger meetings, but quickly decided they were unhelpful and made sure not to involve them in future conferences, such as the Casablanca and Tehran/Cairo Conferences, whenever possible.

Beyond structure, the leaders had to think of how to win the war in as few years as possible. As Roosevelt said early on in the discussions, they needed to look forward at least two years, because anything they decided on, be it for "planes, tanks [or] ammunition," would not be produced in the quantities needed to complete a war-winning strategy until then.[7] Indeed, over the three weeks of the conference, Churchill and Roosevelt spent hours alone or with their advisers trying to get a handle on this vast question.

Shipping and the control of the sea figured in almost every discussion in different ways, with both leaders displaying their detailed knowledge—at times even showing off a little to each other. On January 4, 1942, Roosevelt and Churchill sat down with their military leaders for one of the more wide-ranging discussions. They touched on a variety of issues, focusing on "Army-Navy" operations, which Roosevelt highlighted as having important "political considerations" (a Rooseveltian way of saying that they were damn important).[8] One of the most important operations they were considering was codenamed Gymnast (a British amphibious operation to seize French North Africa) or Super-Gymnast (if the Americans joined too). Both Roosevelt and Churchill showed off their naval thinking as if they were once again assistant secretary of the navy and First Lord of the Admiralty respectively. Roosevelt wanted to be informed about the "sea conditions" in the possible invasion area, and was told that at this time of year there would be "large surf with a heavy roll."[9] Churchill, on the other hand, went into detail about whether aircraft carriers were going to be used, saying it was an important consideration because carrier vulnerability to German U-boat attacks meant that "the time factor for unloading would have to be reduced."[10] The evening was devoted to air power.

After the formal conference ended, the leaders decamped back to the private rooms of the White House, and the commanding general of the US Army Air Forces, Henry A. "Hap" Arnold, was brought by for private meetings. He started with Hopkins, almost as a warm-up session to prepare for his encounters with the two warlords. The two went through the details of the US air production programme and deployment plans, and then the general met alone with Churchill to discuss the building and allocation of aircraft in the United States to be sent to Britain. Churchill seemed satisfied and then, somewhat to Arnold's surprise, asked the American to comment on the British air command structure, telling him that some important personnel changes were coming up in the RAF, which Arnold was to keep in confidence.[11]

Then Arnold was moved on to the president's study for the highlight of the evening, a forty-five-minute tête-à-tête with Roosevelt. They covered all the important questions of the day when it came to air power. Roosevelt quizzed his senior air commander about aircraft deployment, wondering how many were heading to Ireland, England and North Africa. Roosevelt was, as always, particularly interested in the specifics of the USAAF's aircraft building programme, wanting to get as many aircraft constructed and deployed as soon as possible. Eventually Roosevelt turned to Arnold and asked "whether or not . . . we could reach" the planned-for US aircraft building target "and what obstacles there might be in our path." Arnold tried to reassure the president that things were under control, and later recalled that at the end of the meeting Roosevelt was in agreement with the building plan in "every respect."[12] Though this was not the end of the story. Arnold's building programme would eventually fall far short of its goals, and Roosevelt's angry, energetic reaction to this failure would show just how deeply invested he was in the air war at that time—more so even than Churchill, and a world away from Adolf Hitler with his limited strategic horizons.

The clear differences between Hitler on the one hand and Roosevelt and Churchill on the other would determine the next two years of World War II. These differences extended beyond visions of the air-sea war to important methods and tendencies in the exercise of strategic power. Arnold's experiences of Roosevelt and Churchill on January 4 were typical of how both operated. They were generally on the lookout for information to help them make decisions—and they normally (Roosevelt more than Churchill) were careful to limit their decisions to the higher levels of grand strategy. They both threw their weight around on overall decisions on the creation and application of military power, leaving the details to those below them. They would thus decide priorities for building programmes, shaping the militaries to their strategic outlooks, but would allow their militaries to decide on the specifics of each piece of equipment. Roosevelt, for instance, was determined that the United States control the air and made sure that America invested billions in the construction of aircraft. He left it up to the Army Air Forces and US Navy (which ended up fielding one of the largest air forces in the world) to determine the types and specifications of the aircraft needed to achieve dominance.

When it came to the application of military power, they acted similarly. They each had clear ideas of where the war should be fought. Churchill hoped to focus mostly on North Africa and then the Mediterranean from 1942 into 1944. When it came time to plan for the famous operations, such as the Battle of El-Alamein or the invasion of Sicily, he allowed the theatre commanders to get on with the job in the way that they saw fit. Roosevelt, if anything, was even less intrusive. He would occasionally make decisions on theatre actions—most famously perhaps in the Pacific war in 1944, when he decided to support an invasion of the Philippines over an attack into Taiwan—but he almost always left the specific decision of how to launch operations to his commanders.

In this way both Roosevelt and Churchill had an understanding of their strengths and weaknesses in a way that was alien to Adolf Hitler. Hitler was convinced of his own genius, and suspicious about giving too much power to others. Where Roosevelt and Churchill often liked to ask questions and welcomed debate, Hitler favoured his own tedious monologues and surrounded himself with advisers who enthusiastically agreed with everything he said. He therefore felt free to meddle incessantly with decisions on all levels, and even to set up competing power structures leading to strategic incoherence that he would use to his own advantage. As such, he would not only decide what to build, but would also interject his ideas into the smallest details of equipment and planning. One of the best examples was his decision to take what would be the first operational jet-fighter aircraft in the world, the Messerschmitt Me 262, and delay its eventual appearance in the skies over Germany in a vain and foolish attempt to change the aircraft into a dive bomber, so that he could have a weapon to use to pay Britain back for bombing German cities.

When it came to military operations, Hitler could take control of units anywhere up and down the line, ordering them around even when he had no knowledge of the terrain or the combat conditions they were experiencing. He would regularly demand units undertake operations they had no chance of fulfilling—ordering them to hold fast under all circumstances. It was like watching a high-school boy playing war games on a map.

When it came to air-sea power, Hitler's interference and need for control played a major role in hastening Germany's defeat. Roosevelt and Churchill, on the other hand, made a material difference, helping to ensure that the Allies won the air-sea war as comprehensively as possible. The first step in their road to victory in the air-sea war was to guarantee Allied control over the movement of goods and supplies across the Atlantic Ocean. To do this, they had to come up with a way to contain the threat posed by the Germans in the Battle of the Atlantic.

This battle, mostly conducted by submarines on the German side, but occasionally by surface vessels and long-range aircraft, was the most efficient and modern campaign that Germany could ever have waged. The sinking of Allied merchant ships as they transited from the Americas to Britain achieved a number of things that simple battlefield destruction never could. It destroyed a large amount of raw materials before they reached Britain or America, therefore reducing the production of war equipment in factories there in the first place. The targets also included merchant ships laden with finished munitions destined for the battlefields of North Africa or Europe, thus depriving Allied soldiers of being able to use them against German or Italian soldiers. Finally, the German campaign forced the British and Americans to divert massive amounts of military equipment into building up their own anti-submarine capabilities and merchant shipping capacity—so much so that this was one of the most expensive campaigns the Allies would fight in 1942 and the first half of 1943. No mere land battle could ever have had that kind of holistic impact.

Hitler, however, didn't understand this until far too late. His interest in the sea war was spasmodic and prejudicial. Going into World War II, his focus had been almost entirely on the construction of surface vessels, not submarines. Even when shown how vulnerable German surface vessels were to British air-sea power during the first two years of the war, the amount invested in German submarine production still lagged. Had Hitler bothered to prioritize building U-boats earlier, they could have been an extremely potent weapon against Britain's ability to wage war.

The invasion of Norway and the fall of France in April–June 1940 had given Germany access to naval bases that allowed them to outflank the Royal Navy on both sides of the British Isles. But, possessing fewer than forty operational submarines, the Germans failed to make the most of the advantage. The new German bases did temporarily lead to a rise in sinkings, as the British had too few escort vessels, but thanks to Churchill's prioritizing the war at sea, the Royal Navy soon gained access to more and better escort vessels, and German sinkings in the second half of 1941 fell to their lowest since the fall of France.

Once the United States joined the war, Hitler was left with the reality of being faced with the world's largest industrial power. This reality was almost too much for him to comprehend. Coming out of the Arcadia Conference, Roosevelt and Churchill had agreed that merchant shipping would be given high priority in construction, and they announced ambitious plans to ensure that enough material and manpower could be shipped to Europe for an invasion by 1944 at the latest.[13] Indeed, in 1942, US shipbuilders alone produced approximately 5.5 million tons of merchant ships, and they would more than double this figure in 1943.

Hitler, however, remained in denial, and refused to accept that the Allies could produce merchant ships at anything like that pace. He and his naval advisers searched for the flimsiest excuses to try to justify their scepticism. In May 1942, Admiral Karl Dönitz, the commander of Germany's U-boat force, claimed that the US and UK together could only build five million tons of merchant ships in 1942 as a whole.[14]

Hitler agreed. In September, during a conference held specifically to discuss what was a worsening situation in the war against Anglo-American shipping in the Atlantic, Hitler stated with conviction—and no evidence—that "the monthly rate of [merchant] sinkings will continue to be so high that the enemy will not be able to replace his losses by new construction." Furthermore, Hitler claimed that it was impossible for the Allies to build merchant ships anywhere as quickly as their "propaganda" was claiming. "Even if the enemy should succeed in launching ships relatively fast, he would still not have the necessary engines, auxiliary engines, other equipment and, most of all, crews for those ships."[15] Quite why the Allies would lack the engines was never specified. It was all wishful thinking, pretending to be wisdom.

When Hitler was not living in this state of denial, he often distracted himself with amateurish dabbling in issues of naval building and technology. For the first six months of 1942, he spent much of his time with his naval advisers imagining the construction of a German fleet of aircraft carriers. Even though Germany had not yet completed a single carrier, and had no experience whatsoever operating and maintaining one, let alone building effective carrier aircraft and operating a carrier as part of a naval task force, Hitler imagined creating a range of different flat-tops. In March, he told his armed forces high command, including Admiral Raeder, that work on building carriers was "urgently needed" and that he would direct the Luftwaffe to make the development of carrier aircraft a priority.[16] In April he discussed with Raeder the completion of the one German aircraft carrier, *Graf Zeppelin*, under construction. Even when the admiral said the carrier would not be "completed before the winter of 1943" because of problems making all the new equipment such as launch catapults, Hitler brushed his concerns aside.[17] He claimed that "in general the Armed Forces set their requirements too high," and went on to talk about the importance of Germany starting to develop carrier torpedo planes.[18] By May, Hitler took his dreams to even more extreme lengths, saying that the best way for Germany to get into naval aviation was to build four escort carriers (none were under construction at the time) and start the mass production of carrier aircraft (even though none had even reached the prototype stage).[19] In June, to satisfy this fantasy, the navy briefed Hitler about plans to start immediately collecting the materials to build his four aircraft carriers, which were named, in homage to Hitler's vision of German military greatness and European subjugation, *Europa*, *Potsdam*, *Seydlitz* and *Gneisenau*.[20]

While he was imagining this new fleet of aircraft carriers, Hitler was also convincing himself that he understood the mechanics of ship propulsion much better than naval engineers. In maybe the most extraordinary example of his musings about naval vessels, at a June 1942 dinner attended by Admiral Theodor Krancke, commander of the pocket battleship *Admiral Scheer*, Hitler questioned whether the naval profession really understood its business at all. With no knowledge of the impact of drag, aerodynamic shape or laws of diminishing returns, Hitler lectured the admiral about ship propulsion:

> You cannot deny that the design and method of propulsion of the present-day ship are out of date. With warships we have already come to the point where an addition of driving power does not lead to a corresponding increase of efficiency. You find that a battleship of over 45,000 tons with 136,000 horsepower engines steams at 30 knots, while an aircraft carrier of half the size with 200,000 horsepower engines raises only 35 knots! Something, obviously, is wrong with the mathematics . . . I can only hope that our naval experts will at last allow themselves to be persuaded that their current methods of ship design and construction are out of date.[21]

In the end, of course, Hitler would complete no aircraft carriers, and would not rewrite the laws of surface-ship propulsion. But the first six months of 1942 afforded him the ability to dream that everything was under control. At the end of the previous year, the entry of the United States into the war had provided the Germans with one great opportunity. To try to recover from the humiliation of the Japanese attack on Pearl Harbor and halt Japanese expansion, the US Navy had deliberately prioritized the war in the Pacific. The Atlantic theatre was therefore starved of American escort vessels, making convoy protection impossible anywhere near the United States. Left to their own devices, merchant ships were massacred as they cruised in a vast area from the Gulf of Mexico and up the eastern seaboard of the US. The resulting losses were historic, as a very small number of German submarines were able to patrol at will in such a target-rich environment that they had to ration torpedoes. In the end, the Germans sank 526 vessels weighing a combined 2,832,000 tons between January and June 1942, the highest half-yearly toll they would ever achieve during the war.[22]

This massacre was Franklin Roosevelt's worst moment as a grand strategist during the war. As his preferred choice to coordinate the armed forces, Admiral Leahy, was stuck in France as ambassador and would not make it back to the United States until June, Roosevelt was left on his own trying to act as referee between the US Army, led by George Marshall, and the US Navy, led by Ernest King. King, in charge of US naval vessels, was determined to send everything possible to the Pacific, and refused to institute a convoy system to protect merchant vessels anywhere on the east coast—even though the United States had ostensibly promised to fight a Germany First war. Marshall, determined to build up forces in Britain for an early assault on the continent of Europe, raged against this lack of protection and beseeched Roosevelt to order King to start convoys. Torn between his two most senior commanders, Roosevelt prevaricated. Unable to use his charm to square the army–navy circle, he left the services to run themselves, with the result that King refused to send enough vessels to the Atlantic to institute a convoy system.

American paralysis on the convoy question caused Churchill real despair. Throughout the spring of 1942 he badgered and cajoled Roosevelt and Hopkins to do something, anything, to make the US Navy transfer escorts from the Pacific to the Atlantic. He even offered to send British vessels to patrol off the US coast, but that offer went nowhere. In the end it took until the summer for Roosevelt to order King to start convoys—by which point King was happy to comply. The production of new American vessels meant that he didn't have to transfer anything meaningful from the Pacific to make it happen. Almost immediately after the convoys were instituted, sinkings by German submarines off the American coast plummeted.

Roosevelt found the whole experience frustrating and exhausting—exactly the kind of decision-making problem he loathed, and why he had started discussing appointing Leahy his coordinator of strategic policy in 1939. Thankfully for Roosevelt, it was not something that would be repeated. By June 1942 he was able to get Leahy back from Vichy France, and in July named him to be his chief of staff and senior member of the Joint Chiefs of Staff (later renamed chairman of the joint chiefs).* From that point on, Roosevelt was able to use Leahy as the enforcer of his strategic wishes, and this cut down hugely on the amount of time he spent interacting with King and Marshall.[23] There would be no repeats of the shipping massacre of early 1942.

Having scuttled the German threat off the US coast, Roosevelt and Churchill were determined to do everything in their power to make sure that this never happened again. On paper it looked like things could get much worse in 1943.[24] They started receiving reports that German submarine numbers were poised to leap ahead—and the reports were right. In the summer of 1942, Hitler finally grasped the importance of the war at sea, and made U-boats one of the highest-priority production items. Soon, newly constructed German submarines would be hunting in the North Atlantic.[25]

It had finally dawned on Hitler that a weak U-boat force would make it much harder to stop war materiel and resources from North and South America from crossing the Atlantic, a threat that could cause all his plans to collapse. In June, he recognized for the first time that "the submarine war will in the end decide the outcome of the war."[26] In July, he called for the release of soldiers who had expertise in submarine construction back into the factories to help with production.[27] By September, he was holding conferences devoted almost entirely to the submarine war.

---

* Leahy's full title was Chief of Staff to the Commander-in-Chief of the United States. In many ways its closest equivalent today would be National Security Adviser, as Leahy would meet the president every morning and brief him on the state of the world.

In this, however, he was more than matched by the extraordinary efforts of Roosevelt and Churchill. They were well aware that Germany was going to see a great increase in submarine construction in 1943. Churchill provided Roosevelt in October 1942 with an excellent summary of his views on how the Battle of the Atlantic and the war at sea in general would evolve the following year. The war against the U-boats was "our worst danger" anywhere in the war, he stated. "There will be many more U-boats [in 1943] and they will range more widely . . . No ocean passage will be safe."[28]

Churchill's solution to the problem was clear, simple and expensive: build as many escort vessels as possible and put the increasing number of merchant ships into well-defended convoys. In this effort Churchill needed Roosevelt, as US production facilities had the capacity for significant expansion. In response, Roosevelt, if anything, exceeded expectations (by too much in the end). Even though the US was in the midst of a major war production crisis and all major priorities were being evaluated, the president, working with Leahy, made sure that escort vessels were near the top (just below aircraft and aircraft carriers). Indeed, in the second half of 1942 the amount spent on escort vessels was greater than the spending on all larger warships such as cruisers, battleships and aircraft carriers combined.[29]

The irony of this situation was that Churchill and Roosevelt were actually overpreparing, as Hitler's earlier policies made the German submarine build-up far less powerful than it appeared on paper. While the number of German submarines did jump enormously in 1943, basically doubling in the year between April 1942 and April 1943, Hitler's earlier lack of interest meant that Germany-built boats were unable to compete with the far more advanced British and American technology and tactics.[30] Hitler's new submarines were easy for Allied subs to find and destroy.

The Battle of the Atlantic between 1940 and 1943 was dominated by the Type VII U-boat, upgraded with technological advances such as Metox radar detectors but overall a pre-war design with significant drawbacks. Painfully slow when submerged, it was incapable of catching up with newer Allied merchant ships, as well as the much swifter new escort vessels being churned out of American and British shipyards. Though the Germans increased production, they were mass-producing antiquated, deficient equipment.[31]

This deficiency was to be cruelly exposed, as the British and Americans were about to upgrade their anti-submarine capabilities significantly in 1943. The previous two years of anti-submarine warfare had given the Royal Navy in particular a remarkable understanding of the importance of convoy size and speed in neutralizing the U-boat threat (the faster the convoy, the safer it was; and the larger it was, the easier it was to defend). Moreover, Allied improvements in radar and sonar made it easier to spot German U-boats. Anti-submarine weapons were also growing increasingly effective, with better depth charges and even ship-launched mortar systems. Finally, and maybe most importantly, the Allies were about to throw more and more air power into the anti-submarine war.

The role of aircraft in detecting and destroying submarines had grown throughout 1941 and into 1942. Aircraft, particularly specially modified long-range B-24 Liberator bombers, could find submarines with radar, alerting convoys to lurking threats, and were also able to swoop down on their unsuspecting prey before the U-boats knew they were being targeted. The effectiveness of these planes meant that by the second half of 1942 German U-boats could only operate in a relatively small area in the middle of the North Atlantic, sometimes called the North Atlantic gap, without fear of air attack. Even this area was erased by 1943 with the introduction of Allied auxiliary aircraft carriers.

The stage was set, therefore, for the culmination of the Battle of the Atlantic in 1943, though it would be a far different and less dramatic end (if far more clear-cut and simple) than Hitler, Churchill or Roosevelt had ever imagined. That was because of Allied strategic leadership having provided the right equipment and letting the naval specialists get on with the job. When the German U-boats started appearing in large numbers in the spring of 1943, they were massacred by advanced, layered convoy protection. After that, the Battle of the Atlantic ended quickly and decisively in a matter of weeks. By May the Germans had thrown in the towel, and the U-boats were withdrawn from the crucial North Atlantic waterways.

The overall arms build-up for the crushing of Germany and Italy could therefore proceed without much hindrance at all for the rest of the war.

At that point, there was a great switch in the air-sea super-battlefield—transitioning from the more defensive use of air-sea power to control the communications in the Atlantic, to the offensive use of air power over Germany. This, known as the Combined Bomber Offensive, was one of the most controversial military campaigns of World War II. It involved the employment of large fleets of four-engine British and American bombers (such as the British Lancaster and the US B-17) to devastate the German homeland through direct attack from the air. These bombers had two major roles in 1943. The British, coming at night, made area attacks on larger German cities. The aim was to ravage large parts of German urban areas, killing, wounding and otherwise confounding German workers, and at the same time destroying as many buildings as possible to damage overall German resistance. The US bombers, coming by day, were aimed more specifically at German areas of production, such as factories. The expectation was that by selectively devastating the ability of the Germans to produce items of war, such as aircraft or ball bearings, the whole structure of German warfighting would be brought to collapse.

The role that both Churchill and Roosevelt played in this was similar to the one they played in the war at sea, if even less intrusive. Roosevelt in particular was a fascinating contrast when it came to air power—on one hand its greatest champion, but, on the other, hands off when it came to the details. After deciding in 1940 that the dominance of air power was at least as important as dominating the seas, he had made the building of aircraft perhaps the most important American production goal. But he played almost no role in determining how those aircraft would be used. Instead, he allowed Hap Arnold to devise US air strategy towards Germany, usually content only to be informed and venturing just the occasional opinion.

Churchill was a bit more involved with the details, though even he usually deferred to the air staff over all technical and strategic issues. One of the best examples of this is that the RAF, under Bomber

Command led by Air Marshal Arthur Harris, conducted a three-year campaign of bombing German cities. Churchill was unconvinced that this was the best use of air power and questioned it with his senior commanders—such as the chief of the Air Staff, Air Marshal Charles Portal—a number of times. However, he never pressed his objections very far, and the RAF was generally left to run the bombing of Germany however it saw best.

Hitler's approach to air strategy could not have been more different. As with sea power, he was meddling and destructive. As the Allied bomber threat loomed, he seemed incapable of thinking seriously about the implications of a combined British and American air assault. Instead of preparing for the large bomber fleets his enemy was sure to produce by countering them with German fighter planes, he fantasized about building a great, expensive force of German bombers and attacking Britain. "If I had a bomber capable of flying at more than seven hundred and fifty [kilometres] an hour," he said in February 1942, "I'd have supremacy everywhere. This aircraft wouldn't have to be armed, for it would be faster than the fastest fighters. In our manufacturing schedules, therefore, we should first attack the problem of bombers, instead of giving priority to fighters."[32]

Hitler's fantasy was translated into policy: until 1943, the Germans prioritized bomber production over all other aircraft.[33] This included trying to build the most expensive flop of the war, the four-engine He 177. Hitler spoke glowingly about the bomber's theoretical ability to obliterate London.[34] Terribly designed and massively expensive, the project never yielded an aircraft that could be sent into combat. By 1944, even Hitler would be forced to admit that all his desire and resources had only created an airplane that he called "garbage" and "the biggest piece of junk."[35] By then, of course, the damage had been done.

It was only once the Combined Bomber Offensive really took off in the summer of 1943 that Hitler understood the reality of his situation. The firebombing of Hamburg in July resulted in almost 40,000 Germans killed and many times that wounded. Yet Hitler's first instinct was to lash out and show that he could strike back. He took his ire out on his military staff, attacking what could have been a successful operation—the use of sea mines to block British ports—and instead insisting that Germany needed to punish British civilians. "Terror must be broken by terror!" he ranted. "We have to make counterattacks—everything else is nonsense. All the mining is worthless, in my view; it doesn't affect the masses, and even over there it doesn't affect the people. It doesn't affect us, either."[36]

Hitler poured resources into a weapon to strike back at Britain: the famous V-2 rocket. This weapons programme, the most expensive that Germany would ever attempt, was a technological marvel. Yet the rockets could never be built in anything like the numbers needed to have a major effect on the war, and though they caused a sensation when they were launched, they were responsible for killing fewer than 3,000 people in the UK. In building them, the Germans spent resources equivalent to making 20,000 front-line fighter planes—a massive amount that could have made a difference in the air war over Germany.[37]

In 1943 Hitler did embark on building and maintaining defensive systems to try to regain control over Germany's skies. In fact, he made it the top military priority. Facing a three-front war (one in Russia, one in Italy and the Mediterranean and one over Germany), he decided that the battlefields where his armies were engaged, including the Eastern Front, were to be stripped of fighter cover, and as many aircraft as possible were to be rushed back home. Between June and September 1943, the percentage of German fighters defending Germany and western Europe jumped from about 50 per cent to 70 per cent. German armies, meanwhile, were basically left to fend for themselves against Allied air power. Hitler also started, finally, prioritizing the production of German fighters, though the numbers would not start rising steeply until 1944.

Hitler's other interjection into the air war at this time showed that for all his claims of being technologically conversant, he remained at heart a World War I, artillery-obsessed soldier. During his years in the trenches, he had developed a fascination with anti-air artillery—or flak, as it was often called.[38] A quarter-century later, still enamoured with the idea, Hitler funnelled resources into building anti-air weaponry. By 1944, about 10 per cent of all of Germany's military production was devoted to making anti-air weapons and ammunition.[39] Even though there is often an idea that much of Germany's anti-air weaponry was sent to the front lines, in truth the vast majority was used in-country to protect Germany against British and American bombers. Considering the massive investment Hitler made, flak had only a marginal effect in hindering the strategic bombing campaign.

The investment in flak was typical of Hitler's failures in war production. He would choose a technology he was convinced was effective, usually based on a World War I understanding of warfare which valued firepower over mobility. He would then pour resources into that choice. Because he had such misplaced confidence in the superiority of German technology, he assumed that the new weapon would help turn the course of the war. From heavy tanks and massive anti-aircraft weaponry, to jet fighters and warships, he was sure of his choices. But, typically, he made the wrong choices, right through to the very end of the war. Even as his world came crashing down around him in late 1944, he assured those he spoke with that German technology was the best and German weapons were about to change the course of the war.[40] It was nonsense.

In the end, Roosevelt and Churchill were right, both conceptually and organizationally, when it came to the air-sea war. They recognized the enormous importance of this campaign and made sure that appropriate resources were devoted to it early enough to make a major difference. What's more, they recognized the limits of their leadership, and rarely interfered where their expertise ended. They allowed their military advisers to determine the technological specifications of what was built and decide how this equipment should best be used. Hitler never understood this, and constantly sabotaged Germany's own conduct of the air-sea war by forcing his ideas into the strategic mix. Thankfully.

18. Mussolini, Churchill, Roosevelt and Empire in the Mediterranean

If Winston Churchill was the happiest man in the world when news of the Japanese attack on Pearl Harbor reached Europe, Benito Mussolini was not the unhappiest. Though one might think that the idea of Italy fighting a war against the greatest economic and industrial power in the world—a rival to the entire European continent—should have caused Mussolini worry if not outright panic, he reacted to the news with outward satisfaction. He had been expecting the announcement for days, he said, and had already made up his mind that a greater war would help him realize his strategic goals.

On December 3, 1941, just days before the attack, the Japanese ambassador in Rome had asked for a formal audience with the Italian dictator. In a meeting infused with tension, the diplomat read out a long declaration, the purpose of which was to announce to Mussolini, and the Italian foreign secretary Count Galeazzo Ciano, that Japanese negotiations with Franklin Roosevelt had reached an impasse. As such, he made clear, Japan had little option other than to go to war with the United States, and the ambassador asked Mussolini formally whether Italy would "declare war on the United States as soon as the conflict begins."[1]

Most people in the room were struck by the gravity of the moment. The Italian interpreter was so nervous he ended up "trembling like a leaf." Ciano tried to calculate just how such a great world war would culminate; he hoped the Axis would emerge victorious, but he had an idea of the cost they would pay if they didn't. Mussolini, however, was more content than nervous. "Thus we arrive at the war between continents which I had foreseen since September 1939," he boasted.[2]*

---

* There is no evidence that Mussolini had actually believed a great world war was inevitable in 1939. Indeed, his decision to keep Italy out of the war at that

Five days later, early in the morning of December 8, news of the attack reached Rome. Now the Italian dictator was "happy," claiming that he had long desired clarification of America's wartime position.[3] When Italy declared war on the United States on December 11, Mussolini continued to radiate confidence. He told the Italians it was a great "privilege" for them to fight side by side with the Japanese. Moreover, he declared that the Axis countries had the "moral and material resources" necessary for victory, and exhorted: "Italians! Once more arise and be worthy of the historical hour! We shall win."[4]

The reason for Mussolini's pleasure at the prospect of another world war, even one involving the United States, was that he viewed such a war as the best way to protect and enlarge the great Italian empire after which he had always lusted. What the war had taught him so far, however, was that Italy was too weak on its own to create an empire fit for his ego. Lacking the interest, let alone the intellectual capability, to prepare Italy properly to wage a modern war, Mussolini decided it was best to slipstream behind his more powerful allies, picking up the scraps of territory around the Mediterranean and North Africa that the Germans did not themselves covet. Remaining the same man he had been during World War I, he decided that acting the world leader was the best way to become one—and while he would try to convince the Italian people to be military-minded, he would ultimately get by with what he could pilfer from his ally. And he had great hopes for his thievery. In late 1941 Mussolini seemed convinced that a German victory over the USSR was inevitable, freeing up the Nazis to send a massive amount of force into the Mediterranean and North Africa. Moreover, he believed the Japanese would be a major asset. For years Mussolini had maintained a healthy respect for Japanese power. In 1937, he had spoken of the Japanese as "invulnerable" from American attack.[5] Just before Pearl Harbor, he had given an interview to a Fascist journalist in which he discussed how Japanese capabilities, along with

---

point—the most sensible grand-strategic position he ever took—would indicate he was not at all convinced that a great war would happen or that it would be in Italy's interest.

Germany's, had put Italy in an excellent strategic situation. Basically, Italy would vampirically triumph off their allies' "will" and military successes. "Russia has lost and is losing ground, England has lost ground, we are engaged in a bitter fight, but the accounts must be settled at the end," he said. "In the end, the active will exceed the passive, for Italy and Germany are allied with Japan, which is a very powerful country, which will, at the right time, make its own huge weight count."[6]

Winston Churchill could not have looked upon America's entry into the war any more differently. He had complete confidence that, with the United States in the war, Germany, Japan and Italy would be ground to a pulp. Having honed in World War I his understanding of industrial war and the potential of full US mobilization, for Churchill victory was now assured. Not long after Pearl Harbor, he started talking about a possible German collapse in 1944 or even 1943. Japan, meanwhile, would be dispensed with quickly once Germany's doom had been achieved.

Furthermore, Churchill felt that having America as a full combatant was the best way to ensure the existence of a strong, cohesive British Empire. At the age of sixty-seven, when it came to empire, he had changed little from the twenty-three-year-old who first went to war in India's Malakand valley. For all of Churchill's rhetoric of fighting for freedom, the continuation of the British Empire remained the single most powerful driving force in his strategic and emotional mindset. Many of his most famous speeches given during the war were warnings to his fellow Britons about the importance of the continuation of empire. In his "Finest Hour" speech in May 1940, he maintained that without victory over Nazi Germany there was no possibility that the British Empire would endure.[7] In November 1942, just as news of the great victory at El-Alamein came in, Churchill exclaimed that he had "not become the King's First Minister in order to preside over the liquidation of the British Empire."[8]

He also understood that victory in World War II did not guarantee that the empire would long survive. The United Kingdom had the smallest population of all the main powers except Italy, and its land mass, without the empire, was by far the smallest. Without its empire, even a victorious Britain would, Churchill feared, be dwarfed by the mega-powers of the US and the USSR.

Churchill knew that parts of the empire—in particular, determined parts of Indian society—were threatening to break up what he loved most. The Indian Congress Party, with such leaders as Mahatma Gandhi and Jawaharlal Nehru, had been growing progressively more influential and assertive in its campaign for independence.[9] They offered to support Britain in its war effort in exchange for Indian independence after the war. Churchill, in response, was determined that India, and the rest of the empire, not be given up without a struggle. Thus, if Britain lost too many soldiers on the battlefields, or was simply too exhausted at the end of the war, it would be almost as damaging for Britain's ability to hold its empire as would losing the war. Like Mussolini, therefore, Churchill was hoping to manipulate his allies to serve his imperial ambitions.

Overall, this was one of the great factors driving him to demand that the Mediterranean/North Africa theatre be the greatest area of Allied offensive operations. Making this the prime area in the land war would achieve a host of objectives, including keeping British casualties down. His own experiences of facing the German Army in the fields of France in 1916 had made him queasy at the idea of sending massed ranks of British soldiers back there in the 1940s. As such, Churchill was more than happy to let the USSR carry the can in the European land war. Far better for the Americans and the British to concentrate on doing what they did best—fighting the air-sea war with machines over mass manpower.

Churchill's desire to turn the Mediterranean and North Africa into a major area of British effort manifested itself almost immediately after the fall of France. While Churchill always understood that the Battle of Britain had to be won and that the Battle of the Atlantic was the foundational struggle that had to be successfully conducted above all else, when it came to striking back at the Axis he turned to the Mediterranean. Even as the Battle of Britain was being waged, he started planning to transfer British forces to the region to be able to undertake offensive operations.[10]

Churchill's prioritizing of the Mediterranean meant that from the summer of 1940 until December 1941, a great imperial struggle went on between the British and the Italians. For the next three years of the war, the British Army fought many more Italian soldiers than German—mostly in Africa, but also in Greece and eventually Sicily and Italy itself. The outcome of these campaigns was mixed, such as in Greece. However, one of the most clear-cut British triumphs was the seizing of all of Italian East Africa.

Mussolini's African empire centred on Ethiopia, and had mostly been assembled in the 1930s using horrific tactics and weapons, including the Mussolini-ordered use of poison gas.[11] In early 1941, the British, working with Ethiopian and Sudanese forces, attacked Italian East Africa from the north. This humiliating campaign cost the Italians approximately 300,000 troops, the vast majority of whom were captured and not killed. Mussolini watched the loss of one of the crown jewels of his empire in horror. In July 1941, with most of Ethiopia already under British control, he swore "hatred against the British for all time" and claimed that the region would be reconquered regardless of the cost.[12] If this was going to happen, however, it would have to start with a campaign already underway in North Africa.

The Desert War, as the fighting there came to be known, rolled back and forth across much of Libya and Egypt from 1940 to 1942. In January 1941, a well-prepared British Army—supported by many dominion troops, most famously from Australia and New Zealand—launched an attack on the Italian forces that had crept over the border into Egypt from Libya. Almost immediately the British had the Italians in headlong retreat. Soon, half of Libya was in British hands and an Italian collapse looked imminent. Mussolini, desperate, begged Hitler for help, and the Germans sent a few divisions led by General Erwin Rommel. Though the Italians would still supply the bulk of the manpower, the German forces led by Rommel, who would soon gain the nickname the Desert Fox for his exploits, turned the tide. Soon the British invasion of Libya had not just stopped, but gone into reverse. For the rest of 1941 the forces see-sawed through western Libya, with Rommel eventually advancing all the way to the Egyptian border before his forward movement was stopped.

Thankfully for Churchill, Hitler was far more preoccupied with the invasion of the USSR than with Mussolini's needs, so Rommel was given little additional support to press on.[13]

And then Pearl Harbor happened, and Churchill was determined to get the United States involved as much as possible in the Desert War. The first meetings of the Allied leaders after the Japanese attack, at the Arcadia Conference, represented a golden opportunity for Churchill to convince Roosevelt to make a major commitment to this war in North Africa and the Mediterranean. Churchill believed that he had a very strong hand to play. A few weeks before Pearl Harbor, the British had launched Operation Crusader, a large-scale offensive against Rommel's forces. Though the British suffered heavy tank losses, they eventually wore down Rommel's troops. By the time Churchill was sailing on the *Duke of York* to Washington, the Germans and Italians had been forced back a long way into Libya. Churchill could thus argue that Roosevelt should support this great success.

While on board the battleship, Churchill took advantage of the relative peace and isolation to write a strategy summary and propose a joint Anglo-American plan for 1942.[14] In many ways the document outlined a grand strategy that he would argue for—first successfully and then increasingly desperately—for the next two years. When Churchill looked at the great land war in Europe, he stated openly that Stalin and the USSR should carry the main burden. The British and Americans, he argued, could provide aid but should not yet consider sending ground forces onto the European continent.* "Neither Great Britain nor the United States have any part to play in this event except to make sure that we send, without fail and punctually, the supplies we have promised," he wrote.[15]

Having argued against a land war in Europe, Churchill outlined an

---

* There was one exception to this rule—if the USSR seemed on the point of collapse. If that seemed to be the case in 1942, both Churchill and Roosevelt discussed making almost a desperate invasion of France to try to draw off as many German forces as possible and provide Stalin with hope. Of course, things never came close to reaching such a point.

expansive vision of a war in North Africa. Over many paragraphs he discussed an American invasion of French North Africa, a continuing British offensive from Libya, and even, if possible, the defection of a significant number of Vichy French forces in the region to the Allied cause. If such a strategy were prioritized, he argued, by the end of 1942 the entire coastline of North Africa from Morocco on the Atlantic to the Suez Canal in Egypt—a distance of more than 2,000 miles—would be safely under the control of the British and the Americans.

Churchill's justifications for this were imperial as much as anything else. Such a strategy would secure British communications across the Mediterranean through the Suez Canal, into the Indian Ocean, and onwards to Britain's Pacific empire.[16] Any discussion of deploying significant forces to Europe, beyond bombers, would have to wait until 1943 at the earliest and, Churchill hoped, might prove unnecessary. Maybe, he argued, Hitler's regime could be brought to the point of collapse through the application of Allied air and sea power from the south and west, and the power of Stalin's Red Army pressing back from the east—making any Anglo-American invasion of the continent superfluous, or more of a mopping-up operation.

When Churchill arrived in Washington for the Arcadia Conference, he immediately started pressing a Mediterranean/North African-centric strategic vision on Franklin Roosevelt. On December 23, the two grand strategists and their military teams met in the White House for one of the first times. The British prime minister presented his overall vision of the war, admitting that Britain was "short in manpower" and that this would shape their plans. One of his hopes was that the Americans would take over a number of responsibilities from the UK, including the defence of Iceland. He also welcomed the idea of sending some American troops to the UK and Ireland as soon as possible.

He then turned to his great passion, North Africa. Trying to create an air of excitement, Churchill claimed that matters in the region were "coming to a head quickly."[17] No longer seeming so worried about manpower, Churchill claimed he had an additional 55,000 British soldiers, with transports, ready for action at a moment's notice. Hopeful of enticing Roosevelt to act with him, he proposed an American landing in French Morocco. Roosevelt stonewalled this idea. He made positive noises as he usually did, but threw some chaff in the air about a possible landing at Agadir, and mentioned some complications that needed to be considered. Churchill, however, would not back down. Not understanding Roosevelt's hesitation, he pressed for action in North Africa, saying the British "expedition was ready."

Roosevelt was unmoved, and refused to commit. It was not, however, because he was opposed in principle to the idea of a major North African campaign. As he told Hap Arnold a few hours later when the two chatted privately, the real issue was timing. FDR didn't want to invade the French colonies in North Africa at present if it would trigger a direct war with Vichy France and lead to greater French support for the Nazis.[18] This was not Roosevelt being supportive of or interested in protecting the French (or indeed British) Empire at this time—far from it. It was purely tactical, as he was trying to balance a number of different political and strategic calculations.

Roosevelt was if anything hardening what was already a passionate anti-imperial stance. When it came to empires and colonialism, Roosevelt, as he aged, was becoming a bit of a radical. More and more empires seemed to him to be exploitative, demeaning, and ultimately destructive to the future security of the world (and thus the United States). In his first term as president, he had signed a bill to make the Philippines independent by 1946—and he had meant it. In his mind, World War II represented the great struggle between the world of those who wanted to create empires (Nazi Germany, Fascist Italy and Imperial Japan) and the Allies whose job it would be to usher in the post-imperial era—even if in the case of the British they did not realize it. It was not by accident that Roosevelt forced Churchill in the 1941 Atlantic Charter to sign up to a document that was implicitly anti-empire. It spoke of the right of "all peoples to choose the form of government under which they will live."[19]

Getting into the war only intensified Roosevelt's loathing of empire and his belief that the war needed to bring an end to colonialism, whether practised by America's enemies or allies.[20] One of his most shocking experiences in the war was in early 1943, when he was on his way to the Casablanca Conference. To make the journey, Roosevelt had to fly in hops from the US to the Caribbean, then across the Atlantic to British Gambia, before heading north to Morocco. Passing through Gambia, he witnessed local labourers heading to work in the fields—a scene of poverty and exploitation that left him shaken. He said nothing about it to Churchill, but one night early during Casablanca he had a private chat with his son El-liott. Chain-smoking during the cool of an African evening, he got progressively more angry describing what he had witnessed. "The natives were just getting to work. In rags . . . glum-looking . . . I was told that the prevailing wages for these men was one and nine. One shilling, ninepence. Less than fifty cents." Roosevelt then added: "They're given a half-cup of rice . . . Dirt. Disease. Very high mortal-ity rate. I asked. Life expectancy—you'd never guess what it is. Twenty-six years. Those people are treated worse than the livestock. Their cattle live longer!"[21]

Not content to describe the squalor of the British Empire in Gambia, Roosevelt moved on to the British Empire globally. "The thing is . . . the colonial system means war. Exploit the resources of an India, a Burma, a Java; take all the wealth out of those countries, but never put anything back into them, things like education, decent standards of living, minimum health requirements—all you're doing is storing up the kinds of trouble that leads to war."[22]

Roosevelt provided the British prime minister with strong glimpses of his thinking about the British Empire in general, includ-ing the need to consider Indian independence after the war. In early 1942, not long after the Washington summit ended, the president brought up the subject in a number of different ways to a clearly irri-tated Churchill.[23] In February, Roosevelt offered to try to mediate between the British government and Indian nationalists.[24] A few weeks later, he rather cheekily sent Churchill a pamphlet that argued that India at that point was very similar to the United States when it declared independence.[25]

But no matter how much Roosevelt had grown to despise empire, he first and foremost wanted to win the war. This is what eventually drove him to pivot in the summer of 1942 and support Churchill's favoured plan for the invasion of North Africa. This move is one of the most important, if not always best understood, strategic choices that Roosevelt made in the war. On the outside it happened almost out of the blue, when the president—who had seemingly been sitting on the fence between supporting what Churchill wanted and what his own army wanted—opted in July for an invasion of French North Africa, later codenamed Operation Torch. Indeed, Churchill believed that he made all the difference in swinging Roosevelt into backing the operation, because of the power of his arguments.[26]

Roosevelt's decision in favour of Torch was actually something that he had been considering for more than a year. He had made the strategic importance of North Africa clear to William Leahy when he had appointed the admiral ambassador to Vichy France, and the president had sent a special envoy, Robert Murphy, to French North Africa to keep him informed of what was happening in the region. Leahy, who was always closely attuned to Roosevelt's thinking, was the first person to urge the president, in May 1941, to consider an invasion of French North Africa. According to Leahy, 250,000 soldiers backed up by American air and sea power could seize Morocco and Algeria before the Germans could react, shortening the time needed to defeat Germany "by half." Using much the same language that Churchill would use seven months later, Leahy argued that "some day, to win the war superior pressure must be applied at a weak point in the German military campaign . . . Today the vulnerable spot is North Africa."[27]

The reason Roosevelt did not act then, and still refused to act in early 1942, was not that he was opposed to the operation; it was just the preconditions were not yet right. Before Pearl Harbor there had been no chance he was going to do something so daring as getting the US into the war in the face of so much domestic opposition. And once the US was in, he had to deal with the reality that the heads of his army and navy were dead set against any invasion of North Africa. In fact, the US Army was practically apoplectic at the idea. Secretary of War Henry Stimson, writing with the full support of generals George Marshall and Hap Arnold, sent Roosevelt a paper during the

Arcadia Conference outlining US strategic priorities. For the army, securing the North Atlantic to allow a build-up of US air and land forces in the UK was easily the dominant concern.[28] North Africa was hardly mentioned, and the Desert War in Egypt was shunted aside as a British imperial concern that the US should stay away from. "While this area [Egypt] is of immense importance psychologically to the British Empire and perhaps strategically as a possible though unfavorable front for an attack on Hitler in Europe, it seems to me of the least important to us as a combat area. We should of course continue our supplies to the British. In my opinion we should not divert armed forces to that area . . ."[29]

Marshall and the US Army had a very direct strategy in mind to win the war. They advocated securing the North Atlantic, having a massive build-up in the United Kingdom and then invading France/north-west Europe at the earliest possible moment. He was entirely confident in the strategic rightness of Germany First, and believed that expending forces either in the Pacific or North Africa was wasteful. For Admiral King, Operation Torch was a drain on resources that he wanted to be sent to the Pacific. He saw the war against Japan as the US Navy's highest priority, and was loath to send significant naval forces to the Atlantic—especially while the Japanese seemed to be doing so well in pressing the US Navy back.

Roosevelt, therefore, stood practically alone at the top of the US strategic structure in seeing the advantages of a North African invasion. Yet his reasons for supporting the invasion are easy to see when you approach it from his point of view. Not only did he have a long-term strategic understanding of the importance of the region, but an invasion fit his priorities politically and militarily. Being the extraordinarily successful domestic politician that he was, Roosevelt was determined to keep US casualties as low as possible. Attempting an early, risky invasion of France had no appeal to him (unless it looked like the USSR was going to collapse, in which case desperate measures were to be attempted). Like Churchill, he had his own memories of the battlefields of the Western Front, and he had a healthy respect for what the German Army could accomplish. Roosevelt would therefore only support an invasion of Europe when the time was right, but that would be 1943 at the earliest—or, even more likely, 1944.

In the interval, an invasion of North Africa would allow the US Army to learn its craft while also showing the American public that the US was willing to take on the enemy. With the US having one of the world's smallest armies on a per capita basis before 1939, very few US soldiers (including generals George Marshall and Dwight Eisenhower) had any real combat experience. Invading North Africa would let them learn in an environment more difficult for the Germans to reinforce, preparing them for fighting in Europe in the future. Moreover, as Roosevelt admitted at Arcadia, an invasion of North Africa would show the American people that the US was willing to get in the fight—albeit in a prudent, Rooseveltian manner.

Finally, invading North Africa, as opposed to having a massive build-up in the UK in preparation for the invasion of Europe, would allow Roosevelt to maintain and indeed reinforce American forces in the Pacific. Though he was a believer in the policy of Germany First, by which the United States should concentrate first on defeating the Nazis and then turn to defeat Japan, he also felt that he could not let the Japanese run wild in the Pacific. The early Japanese victories that had come in the wake of Pearl Harbor, including the defeat of US forces in the Philippines, Guam and Wake Island, made Roosevelt desperate to be seen to be hitting back at Japan. All in all, North Africa was a powerful strategic cocktail for the president.

The problem Roosevelt had with Torch was bringing the rest of his military team along with him. His pre-war fears of having a disparate structure that he could not control had been realized. The War and Navy Departments often had their own agendas, and the Joint Chiefs of Staff, the new body he had put together to bring order to the process, was dysfunctional. Its two leading figures, Marshall and King, had almost entirely divergent views on how the war should be fought, and as they could not resolve their differences, it was left to Roosevelt to referee between them—a job the president loathed.

The appointment of Leahy as Chairman of the Joint Chiefs in July 1942, and maybe even more importantly the first and only Chief of Staff to the Commander-in-Chief in US history, allowed Roosevelt to exercise the control over strategic policy that he had always craved. He immediately used that power to imprint his vision of grand strategy on the government, by forcing Marshall, King and the rest to bend to his wishes. And his wishes were for an invasion of North Africa. Leahy and Roosevelt at once set about planning the operation, meeting continually from late June through to mid-July.[30]★

Marshall and King did not understand Roosevelt. When rumours that the president was now seriously considering the operation in North Africa reached their ears, they were determined to stop it in its tracks. Along with Arnold, they drew up a memorandum asking Roosevelt to drop his plans for the region and instead focus on the build-up in the UK in preparation for an invasion of the European continent.[31] Much to their astonishment, the president fired back and put them in their place, letting them know that Torch was his choice to make, he had made it, and they had to accept that or they could leave. Or, to be more accurate, he had Leahy tell them this on his behalf.

Roosevelt cut back significantly on the amount of time he spent interacting with Marshall and King, even refusing to write to them directly.[32] Instead, he channelled his communications through Leahy, turning his friend/admiral into both an enforcer to get his wishes fulfilled and his shield to absorb all the complaints that the other senior officers wanted to make to the president. Roosevelt was therefore spared the constant squabbles and relatively minor-detail discussions that Hitler, Stalin, Mussolini and to a certain degree Churchill were involved in. He could concentrate on the larger questions, and not get tied down in the minutiae, which was not his forte.

If Roosevelt in the summer of 1942 was getting his strategic house in order, and aligning himself with Winston Churchill in making the war in North Africa a major priority for the Anglo-American alliance, Benito Mussolini was stuck hoping for his allies to win him his

★ Roosevelt formally offered Leahy the post of chief of staff to the commander in chief on July 6 1942, and from then on Leahy would provide the president with his daily morning briefing and accompany him on most of his official and even private trips.

empire. The strategic differences between the three could not have been more stark. Churchill and Roosevelt had coherent, if very different, reasons for fighting in the region, and had the forces on hand to effect their plans. Mussolini was increasingly detached from strategic reality, living on hopes and dreams and having almost no power to influence events.

Part of Mussolini was well aware of his powerlessness and had enough of a grasp on reality to know that, with the British and Americans throwing force into the Mediterranean, his regime—indeed his very life—was very much on borrowed time. Nervous and stressed, he suffered from extreme stomach upsets, at times able to eat only sparingly, leading to weight loss. He was so worried about his condition that shortly after the Americans landed in North Africa and the British had Rommel on the run in Libya, Mussolini said he would meet with Hitler only if he could have his meals in private. He didn't want the Germans to see his pitiful diet of just "rice and milk."[33]

Mussolini's inability to control his own fate and that of his empire began to sour not just his health but his strategic partnership as well. According to Ciano, for much of 1942 Mussolini affected a pronounced "anti-German" outlook.[34] He would criticize German slights, was jealous of German successes and felt increasingly emasculated in the presence of senior German leaders, including Hitler himself. Yet Mussolini was also completely dependent on the Germans, and had to hope for their success in spite of himself. For the previous year he had used Italian troops as pawns to try to convince Hitler that he was still a useful ally. When Hitler invaded the Soviet Union in June 1941, Mussolini had been determined to send a large Italian army to help the Germans. He made this choice even after Hitler had humiliated him by refusing to let him in on the plans for attack, even though they had met just before Barbarossa commenced. Further, he was being humiliated because Mussolini understood that the Germans did not want the Italian troops—but that did not matter, as Mussolini had to be seen to be important even if he really wasn't. As Ciano rather pathetically admitted, "The Duce realizes that Hitler did not welcome the participation of our troops on the Russian front, but he insists on sending them just the same." Mussolini's reasoning was all about prestige—either the war would end soon through a compromise that would save the balance of power and thus his position, or it would "last a long time, permitting us by force of arms to regain our lost prestige."[35]

To help restore Mussolini's prestige, hundreds of thousands of Italian troops were sent east in the next year and a half, and placed under German command. As usual, the Italians were often poorly equipped and completely unprepared for the environment in which they were supposed to fight. That seemed to matter little to Mussolini. He needed German support for his own plans for greatness, and if he had to sacrifice masses of his own citizens, so be it. He admitted his almost total dependence on the Germans to Ciano in May 1942, even after the first year of Barbarossa had failed to see Hitler knock Stalin out of the war. "The German machine is still formidably powerful, but has suffered great wear. Now it will make a new and imposing effort. It must attain its goal."[36] For Mussolini, the key was to gain German help to stem the British, who after the success of Operation Crusader had, by mid-January, advanced halfway through Libya—to Mussolini, the "bastion" of his empire.[37]

For a while it looked like Mussolini's hopes were based on some reality. The British advance from Crusader eventually stalled because of overstretched supply lines. On January 21, 1942, Rommel, with a reinforced German–Italian army, counterattacked. He soon had the British Eighth Army, famously known as the Desert Rats, rocked backwards. Over the coming six months Rommel would win a series of engagements and drive the British further back into Egypt than they had been at any time in the war. By the time his offensive ran out of steam in July 1942, also suffering from overstretched supply lines, Rommel's army had driven to just outside the small town of El-Alamein in Egypt, only 150 miles from the capital Cairo. There, things seemed to freeze.

Mussolini was pleased with Rommel's victories, but chafed at the fact the success was being ascribed to the German general (now field marshal) instead of Mussolini's own brilliance. On 26 June, Ciano noted that the situation was "appearing more and more as a German rather than an Italian victory."[38] It would be the last time Mussolini could talk about victory.

Though the lines in the desert seemed static over the next few months, the reality was that the Axis was about to be crushed. With Roosevelt and Churchill having made their choices, overwhelming force was being sent to the region, bookending Rommel's army. The British Eighth Army, now under the command of Bernard Montgomery, was reinforced with hundreds of new tanks—both British and American—and masses of artillery. The Royal Air Force in the theatre was raised to unprecedented strength, providing a crucial advantage. Thousands of miles to the west, the US started accumulating the largest ground force it had assembled since World War I, along with the shipping and air power needed to get these troops ashore. It was the kind of force that had never before been seen in the region—and meant that the coming campaign could have only one outcome.

The first indication of the catastrophe that was to befall Mussolini was Montgomery's attack at El-Alamein starting in late October. Methodically using his forces and much greater firepower, Montgomery had the Eighth Army grind down Rommel's forces without mercy. By the end of the first week of November, Rommel had few vehicles left and his army was breaking. Soon, the Italians and Germans were driven back to the border of Libya, with no hope this time of ever returning. On the other side of North Africa, starting on November 6, the other hammer fell—US forces started landing up and down the coast of French Morocco and Algeria. Though French soldiers resisted in places, in others they seemed willing to collaborate with the Americans. By the middle of November, US troops had secured all their landing ports and could begin preparing to march on the rear of Rommel's forces.

In just a few weeks, Axis fortunes in the desert had transformed. Though the Germans would send large reinforcements to Rommel, there was no way that they could possibly match the Anglo-American forces ranged against them. The reality of the war that Hitler and Mussolini had got themselves into was now clear—there were too many places that needed force and not nearly enough to go around.

On the Eastern Front, the Germans were in another debilitating fight. German forces, which had launched an offensive into southern

Russia and the Caucasus in the summer of 1942, had been stymied at the Russian city of Stalingrad. Fewer than two weeks after the Torch landings in North Africa, the Russians counterattacked on both sides of the city. With a savage assault that took a heavy toll on the Italian troops that Mussolini had sent to Russia in order to win favour with Hitler, the Russians trapped the entire German 6th Army in Stalingrad. And if that were not enough, the Allies were strengthening their grip over the North Atlantic and beginning to exert more pressure over the skies of western Europe. And all the while, more and more force would soon come streaming across from the United States.

Mussolini could not admit this reality; if anything, he clung even more tightly to the strategic dream world he had inhabited all year. He spoke at times as if greatness and an Italian empire still beckoned. In early December 1942, after reading one of Churchill's speeches, Mussolini claimed that "Churchill's address honours me because it proves that I am the real antagonist of Great Britain."[39] Several days later, he spoke about a "quick victory" being just around the corner in North Africa.[40]

In late January 1943, when the news from Stalingrad was getting bleak for the Germans, Mussolini had to keep up the idea that Hitler would soon be able to send him forces to help salvage the situation in the desert. Five days before the pitiful remnants of the 6th Army surrendered to Stalin's armies, Mussolini confidently declared that the Germans had the "men, resources and energy to dominate the situation."[41] Even after the Germans had surrendered at Stalingrad, Mussolini kept talking like things were fine. To show how little he valued his own soldiers, in March 1943 he urged Hitler to make better use of the Italian forces in Russia and deploy them more often for dangerous combat missions.[42]

There was certainly part of Mussolini that was aware that he was living a lie. For all his attempts to portray confidence, his health declined further. He underwent electrotherapy, suffered severe stomach pains and looked progressively haggard. Ciano, who tried to portray Mussolini somewhat positively, guessed that the dictator's poor condition was down to the anxiety of the situation and "nervousness."[43] Mussolini grew morbid at times, and his attempts to project positivity vanished. In those cases, he often blamed the Italian people for not fighting with the valour that he wanted from them. When news first started coming in of the terrible street-by-street fighting in Stalingrad, Mussolini, "depressed," claimed that he would like his forces to fight like that in Tripoli in Libya, but that "this will not happen."[44]

Blaming others was all that Mussolini had left. With his dreams vanishing, he would moan to his mistress Clara Petacci about the inadequacy of the Italian Army, the cowardice of his officers and the overall weakness of the Italian race.[45] In public speeches he railed against the soft middle classes, and in very Nazi-like language ascribed Italy's problems to the physically and mentally weak elements in its society.[46] Over the coming months there would be no respite—just military catastrophe upon military catastrophe. In May 1943 the remaining 260,000 Italian and German troops left in North Africa— to say nothing of a large force of armoured vehicles—were forced to surrender. All in all, from October 1942 until May 1943, the British and Americans destroyed a force in the desert not dissimilar to the one destroyed by the Russians at Stalingrad. Then the British, Americans and Canadians invaded Sicily, and Mussolini's rule collapsed almost overnight.

Over the weekend of July 24–25, 1943, the Fascist Grand Council stripped Mussolini of his position as party leader, with even his son-in-law Ciano voting against him. The king removed his governmental authority, and Mussolini was arrested.[47] He was either too tired or too deluded to understand his predicament. Still telling those around him that Germany had a real chance of winning the war, he docilely accepted his captivity. Though Hitler would "free" his fellow fascist a month and a half later and put Mussolini in charge of a supposedly new Italian state—the Italian Social Republic—Mussolini's influence was over. All he could do was live a little while longer, executing some of his supposed enemies, such as Ciano, but having no authority whatsoever to decide the grand strategy of the war. Hitler would do that for him.

It was a swift end for the grand strategist who had been shaped in the Italian Army of World War I. There he had learned that acting with swagger and bravado could help him rise to power. He then took this experience and translated it to international politics, pretending to be the head of a major international power—and for a while he had carried off the bluff. Now, however, the limits of his World War I experience had been ruthlessly exposed. Having based so much of his leadership on acting as a great world leader, and trying to pretend that "will" would make Italy great, he could not acknowledge his own terrible failings. He was left blaming the Italian people for the disaster he had created. As his world was collapsing around him in June 1943, he admitted only one mistake. "My fault is that I gave an Empire to the Italians 40 years too early."[48] It was never Mussolini's fault.

19. Hitler, Stalin and the Eastern Front

When Adolf Hitler launched Operation Barbarossa in 1941, Joseph Stalin learned a hard lesson in humility. Before June 22 he had thought he was the clever one—that he had played off the two greatest European capitalist powers, Germany and Britain, against each other. Hitler had now shown him in the clearest possible manner that this was nonsense, that it was Stalin who had been tricked. Hitler had turned on Stalin when the latter was friendless, and the German Army was streaking into the USSR, destroying Red Army units and capturing major Soviet cities. With the very survival of his regime at stake, Stalin's paranoia was overcome by his practical side. One of the strange benefits of his emotional crisis at the start of the invasion, when Stalin wondered if his colleagues were going to depose him, was that when they did not he seemed to be able to work with them for the rest of the war without being crippled by suspicion. The same thing happened, on a lesser scale, internationally. If in his darkest hour, when they could have abandoned him, Roosevelt and Churchill were instead offering support, he was going to take it—indeed beg for it. He had learned from his experiences in the Russian Civil War that you could make major blunders, but as long as you ended up winning, those errors could be erased from history. He was determined to do the same thing again.

When it came to help, the real prize on offer was from the beating heart of worldwide capitalism, the United States of America. Winston Churchill had stepped up immediately after June 22, pledging to help Stalin with British aid and creating a military alliance between the two countries. However, Britain was also fighting for its own survival in the summer of 1941 and did not have a great deal of spare resources to offer. The United States was different. Franklin Roosevelt was in control of the greatest economy in the world, with huge untapped reserves, and seemed interested in helping. Moreover, his closest adviser and personal emissary, Harry Hopkins, had been already planning on going to London when Hitler attacked. Hopkins quickly made plans to add Moscow to his itinerary, to meet with Stalin and get a better picture of where things stood. Stalin was going to do anything possible to make the meeting a success.

Stalin and Hopkins first met on July 28, and the Soviet dictator could not have been more gracious. Even though the war on the Eastern Front remained in a state of crisis for the Red Army, he promised the American that he would be available to meet from 6 p.m. to 7 p.m. every day that Hopkins was in Moscow.[1] This was not enough, and their meetings ended up stretching on for hours. Stalin also made his own air-raid shelter available to Hopkins, and had it liberally stocked with champagne, caviar, chocolates and cigarettes.[2] They would need that shelter sooner than they might have liked, though Stalin was able to use the experience to make a statement about the value of his friendship.

Moscow was subjected to a Luftwaffe bombing raid almost immediately after Hopkins arrived (Soviet sources believed news of Hopkins's visit had leaked). Stalin and Hopkins were quickly driven from the Kremlin to the nearby metro station where the air-raid shelter was located. Once there, Stalin refused to allow his head of state security, Lavrentii Beria, a notorious murderer, to lead them down to safety. With a wave of his hand, Stalin told Beria, "Go away, coward."[3] He then proceeded to stand out in the open, watching the German planes defiantly. Hopkins stood with him. Soon, Russian anti-air fire hit two German bombers in rapid succession, and the Nazi aircraft fell out of the sky in clear sight. Stalin turned to Hopkins and said, "So it will be with anyone who comes to us with a sword. And whoever is kind, we accept him as a dear guest."[4]

This bit of theatre worked, and Stalin was able to convince Hopkins of his desire to fight Hitler to the bitter end and his willingness to work with Roosevelt and the United States. That only a few weeks ago he had been savaging capitalism was now unimportant. The Soviet dictator went to great lengths to praise Roosevelt and talk up the prospects for future cooperation between the USSR and the US. He even told Hopkins that he believed Roosevelt "had more influence with the common people of the world today than any other force."[5]

Not only was Hopkins convinced of Stalin's sincerity, but he became the greatest supporter of aid to assist the USSR in its struggle. This aid, which Roosevelt would also personally support, would be passed as part of the famous Lend-Lease programme.[6] It provided Stalin with many types of war equipment that the Red Army would have had trouble producing on its own, including 400,000 jeeps and trucks, 14,000 airplanes, 13,000 tanks, and massive amounts of raw materials including so much aluminium that the Soviets could make many tens of thousands of aircraft on their own. The final value of the Lend-Lease aid given to Stalin's forces has been calculated at $11.3 billion—an enormous sum by the standards of the time.[7]

At the exact moment Stalin and Hopkins were working out the practical details of an eventual shared victory, Adolf Hitler was living in a fantasy. On the evening of July 28, he regaled his evening audience about how he had already won the war, and how he would soon remake the world. The campaign on the Eastern Front had just finished its fifth week, and German armies were about to start a major operational pause, yet Hitler assured his listeners that he had everything under control. "The reason I'm not worrying about the struggle on the Eastern Front," he said, "is that everything that happens there is developing in the way that I've always thought desirable." Indeed, everything they were witnessing on the battlefields of Russia seemed to confirm his genius: "At the outbreak of the first World War, many people thought we ought to look towards the mineral riches of the West, the raw materials of colonies, and the gold. For my part, I always thought that having the sun in the East was the essential thing for us."[8] Hitler then revealed something that basically summarized his grand-strategy-making from then until the end of the war: "I have no reason to modify my point of view."[9]

By this point in the war, imposing his views was Hitler's strategic modus operandi. Where Stalin was in the process of learning where he needed to defer and rely on others, Hitler was concentrating ever more power in his own hands, looking at others as impediments who were thwarting his genius. It was the formative difference between the two as war leaders.

Germany's military successes at the start of Barbarossa had inflated Hitler's already monstrous ego. He saw an all-conquering German Army vindicating his ideas on war, race, religion, economics—pretty much any issue that came into his mind. What's more, the fight in the east further convinced him that his World War I prejudices, that firepower and protection trumped mobility and speed, were correct. Interestingly, one of his main assumptions about German superiority proved to be a myth. Hitler always claimed that one of the reasons the USSR would collapse was the weakness and shoddiness of Red Army equipment when compared to the excellence of that of the German Army. Barbarossa showed that when it came to tanks, at least, the Soviet Union was far ahead. The T-34 at this time had greater firepower, and was generally heavier, faster, and simpler to produce and maintain than its German equivalents.[10] Hitler was determined that a new generation of German tanks be built to be better than the T-34 or anything else they expected the Soviets to have. He didn't care about having a faster or more manoeuvrable tank, of course. He wanted a heavier one with stronger armour and a more powerful gun.[11]

Soon, to placate Hitler, the German arms industry produced two new powerful designs, the Panzer VI (Tiger) and Panzer V (Panther). Expensive, highly technical and, especially in the case of the Tiger, super heavy, the tanks could only be manufactured in small numbers, and by the time they started appearing on battlefields in 1943, their firepower advantage could be negated in different ways.

Hitler's World War I experience had also taught him vital lessons in command, or so he thought. Looking back, he liked to think he was cleverer than the German high command had been in that war, and that he understood how to keep German losses low, as opposed to the slaughter of the trenches. He liked to attack previous German decisions, such as the launching of the Battle of Verdun, calling it "lunacy" and saying that he would never sacrifice his soldiers uselessly.[12] But while Hitler spoke as if the war in Russia was a confirmation of his strategic vision, it became clear that the basic assumption on which he had based his campaign planning was wrong. Far from being a rotten house that the German Army would easily kick down, Soviet resistance, if at times more valiant than skilful, was fierce. The idea that the Germans could wrap the campaign up in sixteen weeks as planned was nonsense, and soon Hitler would be sacrificing German soldiers' lives at a pace that exceeded World War I. The German Army was forced continually to stop, regroup and resupply, as the wastage of its military equipment was far higher than they had ever imagined, and it risked outrunning the ability of Hitler's weak logistical corps to keep up with the army's advances. During these operational pauses, Hitler started flexing his command muscles and destroying what was left of the German Army's independence.

His most controversial decision came during the first operational pause in August. At that point much of the German Army's high command wanted to attack Moscow, to seize the Soviet capital and split the front line into two. Hitler, however, considered Moscow a "secondary" objective and proposed attacking southwards into Ukraine. He argued that it was more important to seize Ukraine's economic resources. When confronted with an objection to this idea by many of his generals, he reacted angrily. He was going to direct the war his way, and the army would have to get in line. He started accusing the army of failing him and made it clear that he was going to take charge.[13]

In the end he got his way, with mixed results. On the one hand the immediate result was a major German victory in Ukraine which included the capture of 600,000 Red Army troops. On the other hand the decision did mean that by the time the German Army geared up for its attempt to seize Moscow, it was very late in the year and the Russian winter was looming. The offensive towards Moscow began in October and would become the main focus of fighting on the Eastern Front for the next five months—in ways that Hitler never anticipated. At first the German Army seemed once again to be triumphant. They cut through Red Army lines and captured masses of Soviet troops—approximately another 600,000. By the end of November the Germans were approaching Moscow, but then three things combined and led to Germany's first major setback in the land war since they had crossed the border into Poland.

First, they once again started struggling with supplies. German troops were trying to advance far in front of established rail lines, and without trains the German ability to get needed supplies to the front began to fail. This was actually a major fault of Hitler's. His focus on heavy weaponry and firepower over mobility had made truck production a very low priority in Germany. The German Army that invaded Russia only had enough trucks to properly equip about one-tenth of its units, with the rest having to make do with horse and cart.

At the same time that German supply lines were creaking, the harsh Russian winter started earlier than expected. And then the Russians started counterattacking in force in a planned and organized manner, something the Germans had never experienced before. Having learned something from their early failed battles, Soviet commanders, led by the famous general Georgii Zhukov, had accumulated a large army around Moscow, and waited for the Germans to extend themselves before launching a series of counteroffensives.[14] While elements of the German Army were close enough to Moscow by early December that they reached the tramlines that stretched into the Soviet capital, they would never be able to take the city.

On December 6 the Red Army counterattacked in massive force. Outnumbering the overextended and exhausted German troops by 2.5 to 1, Zhukov's armies—many of them fresh from Siberia, where they had avoided combat—stopped the Germans in their tracks and shocked the German high command.[15] At the same time, the temperature plummeted. One German soldier recalled that it reached −46 degrees Celsius that day.[16] German troops caught up in the attack were exhausted and frozen. Now finding themselves poorly supplied, lacking winter protection and facing a reinforced and aggressive enemy, they started to fall back in places, though they held in others. Senior German officers suffered nervous breakdowns while understrength units on both sides of Moscow switched instantly from attack to defence, desperate just to survive in the face of the Soviet assault.[17]

This reverse caused the opposite of humility in Hitler—and when faced with the first real setback in his land war on the European continent, he failed the basic test of war leadership. When stories started coming in of the faltering German advance and the first signs of a possible Russian counterattack, Hitler became angry and unbalanced and started issuing the first of his famous no-retreat orders—ones he would repeat up until the moment he committed suicide in Berlin three and a half years later. One of the first examples of this was on November 30. Hitler lost control when he heard news that Soviet counterattacks had caused the 1st Panzer Army, which was driving towards Moscow from the south, to pull back to keep from getting encircled. According to Franz Halder, the army's chief of staff, Hitler was "in a state of extreme agitation." Refusing to let his generals speak, Hitler did all the "talking, pouring out reproaches as abuse, and shouting orders as fast as they come into his head." The orders were all variations on the same theme: Hitler forbidding "withdrawals" or allowing his armies to "fall back."[18]

As things became more difficult in December and the true strength of the Russian counterattack was revealed, Hitler tried to escape blame for having underestimated the Red Army. On December 8, he issued a Führer directive ordering his armies to stop attacking and instead take up defensive positions up and down the line. The reason given was not the Soviet counterattack but the "severe winter weather which has come surprisingly early in the East, and the consequent difficulties in bringing up supplies."[19] Blaming the weather didn't keep the Soviets from pressing, however, and more and more German units had to retreat. In response, Hitler repeated the same order over and over—no retreat, stand your ground, and die in place if needed.[20]

Unable to shoulder any of the blame himself, he now started blaming his generals, claiming that they were either weak or deceiving him. On December 19, he decided to neuter army interference as much as possible by abolishing the post of Commander-in-Chief of the German Army and assumed direct control himself. This meant that General Halder now reported directly to him.[21] Hitler even boasted that operational command was so easy that anyone could do it.[22] He had by now completely infantilized the armed forces, and for the rest of the war would increasingly surround himself only with officers who told him what he wanted to hear.

With one fewer check in place, Hitler continued to order the troops outside of Moscow not to retreat, regardless of the freezing weather. On December 20, he held forth at "great length" on the need to hold the line. "Every man must fight back where he stands."[23] He also referred to his own World War I experiences. When General Heinz Guderian, who was commanding one of the Panzergruppen aimed at Moscow, said that his troops could not entrench because the ground was frozen for at least five feet below the surface, Hitler suggested that the soldiers use howitzers to blast craters to use as trenches. After all, Hitler said, this is what German troops had done on the Western Front in World War I.[24] He seemed incapable of understanding that the conditions in Russia could be that different to those he had experienced himself as a soldier.

This "hold fast and die in place" order quickly became part of Hitler's self-reinforcing myth of greatness—almost like he was trying to expunge the disaster that had befallen the German Army in 1918. He believed that it was his will and determination that saved the German Army from catastrophe outside of Moscow, that rallied the troops and prevented a great defeat. It was a view without substance, but has lived on partly because it was repeated so much. Yet it makes no sense. In the first place, many German soldiers did retreat. The German Army, under pressure from the Russians, disregarded Hitler's stand-and-die order a number of times. By late January, even he was forced to admit the reality, and authorized a significant withdrawal of German forces from outside of Moscow.[25] The upshot of all this was that the German Army found itself much further from Moscow in the spring of 1942 than it had been in December 1941. In some cases it was now more than 100 miles further west, and Moscow was so secure that Hitler would never be able to threaten it again.[26]

A reflective war leader might have tried to understand what had happened in the winter of 1941–42 and learn from it. The German Army had been overextended because of overconfidence in its own abilities and a drastic underestimation of its enemy's. Yet the lesson that Hitler took from all this was that he had been right all along—that it was his greatness that saved the day. In fact, once things settled down on the Eastern Front in 1942, he returned to his earlier, already disproved perception that the Russians were about to collapse and could not take the pounding much longer. He told his secretary that it would soon be shown that the Russian lines were "a quite thin veil" and that it would be discovered that "Russian resistance will not endure."[27] What was needed, of course, was more direct control from him, to make sure his weak-kneed generals fought with the will and conviction needed to crush the weakening Red Army.

Someone heading in an opposite direction from Adolf Hitler was Joseph Stalin. Stalin's meeting with Harry Hopkins was just one example of how he reacted to adversity not by doubling down on his own brilliance, but by trying to cultivate and benefit from the support of others. This was not because of any change of personality; it was because he had calculated, accurately, that the chances of his personal survival and that of the USSR (and then later of their further successes) would be better assured by taking help where he could get it, even if this showed him doing things that ideologically or personally he had not done before.

Having been played so spectacularly by Hitler up until 22 June, afterwards Stalin became arguably the most successful manoeuvrer on the international stage. His meeting with Hopkins was only the start of his ingratiating himself with US and British policymakers in such a way that these two great capitalist powers provided massive support for the Bolshevik Soviet Union. When it came to cultivating Roosevelt, until November 1943 Stalin had to act through intermediaries (primarily Hopkins) and telegrams. He did so very successfully.

When it came to the British, Stalin was able to arrange a meeting with Churchill more than a year earlier than his eventual meeting with Roosevelt, and in a way that allowed him control while making him seem to be agreeable. Stalin understood how eager Churchill and Roosevelt were to meet with him, and leveraged their eagerness in psychological as well as material ways. One of the reasons for this leverage was that Stalin was pathologically afraid of flying. With

Roosevelt, in late 1943, he made the president travel halfway around the world, from Washington to Tehran, the furthest a US president had ever travelled in office. Stalin could take a train to the Soviet city of Baku, from where it was a very short flight over the border into Iran. Even then, Stalin was wary. When he arrived at Baku there were two large C-47 transports (American-made) waiting to fly him to Tehran. The one that he was supposed to fly on was to be piloted by a general of the Soviet Air Force, but Stalin noticed that the other was to be piloted by a younger man, a colonel. On the spot he switched planes, saying that "generals rarely fly planes."[28] He would take his chances with the colonel.

When it came to meeting Churchill in August 1942, Stalin had also called the logistical shots. The prime minister offered to come to the USSR for the meeting, but because of the state of the war he had to take a long, circuitous route, starting in London and heading south to Gibraltar and then east to Cairo before heading north into the USSR. To give himself a little break, Churchill proposed that they meet in Astrakhan in the Caucasus, which was 800 miles closer to Cairo than Moscow.[29] Stalin said no. He was far too busy with his "intense struggle" with Hitler, so Churchill would have to travel all the way to the Soviet capital if he wanted to meet.[30] Churchill agreed.

The meeting between the two showed that Stalin understood what he could get and what was impossible. As with Hopkins a year before, he was a generous host, providing Churchill with accommodations stuffed with delicacies and drink, including copious amounts of "caviar and vodka."[31] When they sat down for their first face-to-face encounter, Stalin played the supplicant. The situation on the Eastern Front was difficult, he claimed; the Germans were moving swiftly across the southern Russian steppe on their way towards the city of Stalingrad, and into the Caucasus to try to seize the centre of Soviet oil production. Stalin desperately wanted the western Allies to launch a cross-Channel invasion to relieve the pressure.

Churchill, however, was dead set against the operation and talked about how the British and Americans lacked the forces to try something as ambitious as a cross-Channel attack. Stalin, looking "very glum," wondered if the Allies might try something smaller—seizing the Channel Islands, or threatening to land a force on the French coast.[32] Anything to draw even a handful of German troops away from the Eastern Front would do.

Churchill continued to throw up objections. The Anglo-American forces were simply not ready to invade France and, Churchill added, they were going to concentrate on his favoured area of the Mediterranean. Though Stalin was not convinced fighting in the Mediterranean would make a difference, he understood he was not going to get his way and gave up. "Mr. Stalin (who looked glummer still) said that if we could not make a landing in France this year, he was not entitled to demand it or insist upon it," Churchill recorded.[33]

In the short term, Stalin would settle for as much Lend-Lease support as possible and let Churchill keep his focus on the Mediterranean. Churchill, however, did not seem to understand Stalin's manoeuvring. When he returned to his room that night and spoke to his advisers, he adopted the vision of the nineteenth-century aristocrat and saw Stalin as some unsophisticated simpleton—"a peasant whom he knew how to handle."[34] It was wishful thinking on Churchill's part. Stalin simply understood the power balance between them. When the two leaders got together again fifteen months later in Tehran, Stalin would ruthlessly turn the tables. In a much more powerful position, he would brutally apply pressure on Churchill to get his way.*

Stalin's willingness to defer to Churchill in 1942 matched his other very careful international balancing act during this time: his handling of Japan. Even though he was now an ally of the United States and United Kingdom, both of which were locked into a bitter war with the Japanese, Stalin was keen that, for the moment, the USSR avoid war with Japan. He ordered his army to do nothing to provoke Japanese troops over the border in China, and confirmed his commitment to a non-aggression treaty he had agreed with Japan in April 1941.[35] He understood that an Allied victory would give him the ability to expand his influence in East Asia, and while he was assuring the Japanese of his good intentions, he was planning to attack them when the moment was right—as he told the British and Americans. In the

---

* See Chapter 20.

meantime, he was more than happy to let the US and UK do the heavy lifting in the Pacific, and would only swoop in to grab spoils at the end when the Japanese could no longer fight back.[36]

It was another example of how Stalin, more than any other war leader, successfully manipulated other powers to serve his needs. His grand-strategic successes were recognized within the Soviet military leadership, and helped cement his personal power. When looking back on Stalin's leadership twenty years after the war, Zhukov remarked how comfortable Stalin was with international relations (in his language, "strategy" and "politics") from the very start. "Stalin understood strategic issues from the very beginning of the war. The strategy was close to his usual sphere—politics—and the more directly the questions of strategy overlapped political questions, the more confident he felt to resolve them." However, Zhukov offered one pointed criticism. "In the beginning of the war, Stalin poorly understood matters of operational art."[37]

This criticism, certainly merited, also revealed one of the great differences between Hitler and Stalin as war leaders. Stalin had the capacity to learn. In 1941 and early 1942, Hitler and Stalin were quite similar as military commanders. Like Hitler, Stalin started with a desire to micromanage his armies. He was continually in touch by telegraph and telephone with officers in the field, and made it clear that he was watching their movements closely.[38] He gave orders that were to be followed down through the ranks, robbing his commanders of independence and making himself responsible for many of the disasters that befell the Red Army in the first year after Barbarossa. For the rest of 1941, he had the Soviet media present a far more optimistic picture of the war than actually existed, leading to panic at times when the population discovered the Germans were much closer than they had been led to believe.[39]

Even before Hitler developed his hold-at-all-costs command vision in December 1941, Stalin had tried, with disastrous results, to implement an identical forward policy. When the Germans invaded, the Red Army forces opposed to them were pushed very far towards the border, as Stalin liked to have his forces in a "forward" position.[40] One of the reasons the opening weeks of Barbarossa were so spectacularly successful for the Germans was that Stalin had not only pushed his troops right to the border; he had forbidden them to get combat-ready, worried that such a move would be seen as too provocative by Hitler. Thus, once the German armoured spearheads broke through the forward Red Army lines, there was little the Soviets could do to keep from being encircled.

This initial disaster was followed by an even greater Stalin-exacerbated catastrophe. When Hitler rejected his generals' advice to head to Moscow and in August decided to attack into Ukraine instead, he encountered another group of Soviet armies there that Stalin had primed for defeat. Not only were these Red Army troops once again being micromanaged by Stalin, but he also continued to forbid all retreat. Moreover, his choice for theatre command was disastrous: one of his old cronies from the Civil War, Marshal Semion Budennyi. A one-time cavalry officer with a fabulous moustache, Budennyi had been an asset to Stalin in the great purges and his loyalty had been rewarded with houses, money, medals and power. Dashing he might have been, but Budennyi was also incompetent, and when faced with the best strike force of the German Army in 1941, he froze. Holding tight to Stalin's orders not to retreat, Budennyi presented the Wehrmacht with an inert mass of troops centred on Kyiv. The Germans quickly surrounded these stationary armies and mass surrenders started not long after. As well as the more than 600,000 prisoners seized by the Germans, Budennyi's forces suffered hundreds of thousands of killed and wounded, leaving overall losses at well over a million. Perhaps the only positive thing for Stalin was that Hitler took this victory as a confirmation of his own strategic genius.

From that point onwards, Stalin would never be quite so inflexible, but for many months he remained rash, still prone to micromanagement and too aggressive when prudence was in order. After the Red Army's initial successes around Moscow in December and early January, Stalin started thinking about a military campaign for 1942. He was convinced that the Red Army's limited successes meant that the German Army was in dire straits; and much like Hitler a year before, he thought if he gave it one great shove, the whole enemy line would collapse. On 10 January 1942, Stalin produced an overall strategic vision which he circulated to the senior Red Army commanders. They were to prepare to go on the offensive, to give the Germans no respite and hopefully defeat the German Army before the end of the year. He wrote:

> After the Red Army had succeeded in exhausting the Nazi troops enough, it launched a counteroffensive and drove the German invaders west.
>
> In order to delay our advance, the Germans went on the defensive and began to build defensive lines with trenches, barriers, and field fortifications. The Germans are counting on delaying our offensive until spring, so that in the spring, having gathered strength, they will again go on the offensive against the Red Army. The Germans therefore want to buy some time and get a respite.
>
> Our task is not to give the Germans that respite, to drive them west without stopping, to force them to use up their reserves before spring, when we will have new large reserves, and the Germans will have no more reserves, and to achieve in such way the complete defeat of the Nazi troops in 1942.[41]

Stalin was dreaming. Though the Red Army had fought well around Moscow and the German Army needed rest, the Soviets still had a long way to go to be able to launch successful combined-operations warfare, while the Germans remained operationally strong. However, driven forward by Stalin's optimism, the Red Army prepared a series of offensives up and down the line for the first months of 1942. When presented with plans for more limited operations, Stalin at first preferred a larger, riskier offensive.[42] The result of his preferences was another series of Red Army disasters, in particular what is known as the Second Battle of Kharkiv.

On May 12, a Soviet force of more than 750,000 solders, outnumbering German forces by more than 2 to 1, and approximately 1,000 tanks, which outnumbered the Germans 1.5 to 1, attacked.[43] Unfortunately for them, the attacks towards Kharkiv had unwittingly been launched near where the Germans were preparing some of their forces for their summer offensive. This included the 6th Army led by

General Friedrich Paulus. In a few days the Germans not only blunted the Soviet attack; they counterattacked with such force that the Red Army found its surviving forces pushed well back from where they started. By the middle of June, Red Army losses in the battle were "catastrophic," with almost 280,000 soldiers lost from all causes and practically the entire force of tanks they had started with wiped out.[44] It was one of the greatest defeats that any army in the war would suffer in 1942.

It would also be one of the last defeats the Red Army would ever suffer. The next fourteen months would see two of the most famous campaigns of World War II, resulting in the battles of Stalingrad and Kursk—engagements that spelled the end of any forward movement for the German Army on the Eastern Front. One of the most important reasons why both of these battles turned out the way that they did was that Stalin evolved as a commander, while Hitler remained the same.

The Battle of Stalingrad might be the best example of this. This famous campaign came about because of the results of the overly ambitious German summer offensive of 1942. Once again there had been a big debate between Hitler and some of his generals about what the German Army should do. When it came to going on the offensive, some generals were wary and others proposed a relatively modest offensive towards the city of Stalingrad, which at the time of the Russian Civil War had been Tsaritsyn, the site of Stalin's first and most famous military command. Hitler, however, considered such an operation too cautious, and devised a far more ambitious plan, which was codenamed Case Blue. This operation would aim for Stalingrad with one force, but more to secure the northern flank of the German Army. Another large German force would advance almost 1,000 miles from its start point. This force would strike deep into the Caucasus, taking Stalin's most productive oilfields and aiming for the city of Baku on the Caspian Sea. The plan was certainly bold.

At first things seemed to go well. When Case Blue began, the Red Army had been so weakened by the Second Battle of Kharkiv that it was in no shape to put up much resistance. The Germans moved forward with relative ease, advancing over hundreds of miles of Russian steppe—flat lands with few distinguishing characteristics. Some days the German advance was only limited by the amount of fuel they could put in their tanks. This early success made Hitler even more cocksure, and he abused those who argued for caution. On July 23, Halder, who had an increasingly fractious relationship with the dictator, let loose in his diary. After Hitler had exploded "in a fit of insane rage" and hurled "the gravest reproaches" against the German General Staff for questioning some of his plans, Halder remarked, "The chronic tendency to underrate enemy capabilities is gradually assuming grotesque proportions and develops into a positive danger."[45]

For a while it didn't seem to matter. The 6th Army reached the outskirts of Stalingrad by the end of August, and then started the job of trying to clear Soviet forces out of the city itself. It was a far more difficult task than expected. The Red Army, which had mostly retreated quietly before this, made the Germans pay for every inch of the difficult urban terrain, defending from houses and factories. By the end of September, Halder (who was just about to be fired by Hitler) admitted that the 6th Army's assault troops in Stalingrad were "approaching exhaustion."[46] Still, Hitler ordered that the city be seized, so the Germans continued to attack.

Hitler seemed fascinated with capturing the city named after his fellow dictator, and wanted it taken regardless of cost. Paulus complied, sending most of the best troops into the city, and leaving the flanks of his army outside the city to be defended by weaker troops from Germany's allies, including Romanians and hundreds of thousands of Italian troops that Mussolini had sent to show Hitler how important he was.

By November victory was seemingly in Hitler's grasp, and there was boasting on German radio about the Wehrmacht having captured the city named after Stalin. Then the Soviets struck. In an operation codenamed Uranus, powerful Soviet forces, which had been methodically accumulated, struck on both sides of Stalingrad. They avoided the powerful German units, and shattered the Romanians and Italians. They blasted such holes in the Axis lines and moved so quickly that by the end of month the Red Army had surrounded the 6th Army in the city. It was a textbook example of modern break-out, exploitation and encirclement armoured warfare.

For Stalin it was a sign that the more straightforwardly aggressive school of military command—holding your ground at all costs or advancing straight towards the enemy—was at an end. He had allowed Red Army commanders to retreat, draw the Germans in and, when ready, counterattack weak areas of the Axis line and surround an entire army. Marshal Zhukov, for one, was impressed: "From the time of Stalingrad, Stalin adhered to his own approach to the problems of encirclement and destruction of German troops. The course of the Stalingrad operation sunk into his memory, and he repeatedly returned to this experience."[47]

Now the struggle was on between Hitler and Stalin for the fate of the 6th Army—entombed as it was in Stalingrad. Stalin was generally happy to let the commanders on the spot control the campaign, as long as they kept the 6th Army pinned down and surrounded and blunted the expected German counterattack. Hitler, however, wanted total control. As he considered retreat to be humiliating, he forbade any possibility of the 6th Army fighting its way out of the pocket, which came to be called the Kessel. Instead, he spent his time desperately coming up with ways to try to hold on to all his gains.*

When Hitler first heard stories of a large Russian counterattack, he downplayed the threat, saying the Red Army would never be strong enough to keep the German Army from mastering the situation. "Our generals are making their old mistakes again," he told Albert Speer. "They always overestimate the strength of the Russians."[48] Basically, as long as he could scrape together some relief troops, the Russians would prove too weak and he would save the day again. "In the short or long run the Russians will simply come to a halt. They'll run down. Meanwhile we shall throw in a few fresh divisions; that will put things right."[49]

When his first overconfident prediction proved nonsense, Hitler rooted around for anything that would allow him to hold the city

* *Der Kessel* in German is a kettle or boiler—i.e. a pot where liquid can be heated to boiling.

and relieve the 6th Army. What he decided revealed how little he understood modern war, but also how he had corrupted the German strategy-making system to tell him what he wanted to hear—even if it was a lie. Looking for ideas, Hitler turned to his deputy and Luftwaffe commander-in-chief Hermann Göring and asked if Stalingrad could be supplied by air. Göring had been hardwired by this point to tell Hitler only what the dictator wanted to hear, and simply lied outright to make Hitler feel better for a moment. "My Leader! I personally guarantee the supplying of Stalingrad by air. You can rely on that."[50]

Göring was speaking nonsense, as he probably knew and many of Hitler's generals suspected. The 6th Army needed 300 tons of supplies a day to function, and the idea that the Luftwaffe could manage that in the middle of a Russian winter, flying from forward bases with a limited number of aircraft, was fantasy. A quick calculation of planes available and cargo loads would have made that apparent. The Germans actually averaged deliveries of just over 100 tons a day, which left the 6th Army to waste away.[51] Its soldiers were not just surrounded; they were starving to death, chronically short of ammunition and basic supplies. Hitler, however, preferred to accept Göring's assurances without inquiring too much and without asking for a calculation.[52] He did not want to know the truth.

Having been given the lie he needed to keep the 6th Army from breaking out and retreating, Hitler put his hopes in attacking with a German relief force. It was almost as fanciful an idea as supplying by air. The German Army was exhausted after months of constant moving and fighting, and its other most powerful units were by then deep in the Caucasus, hundreds of miles away. Hitler did raise a force and sent it forward on December 12. It made some decent gains at first, but was soon stopped by the strength of the large Soviet forces around Stalingrad, and by the end of the month it was being pushed back, having never been as close as fifty kilometres to the trapped German forces. At that point the only realistic option was for the 6th Army to abandon Stalingrad and fight its way to safety.

Hitler would have none of it, however. Retreat would be failure and dishonour; far better for the 6th Army to fight and die in place.

And so that's what it did—until it could take it no more and did the one thing Hitler forbade. On February 2, 1943, what was left of Paulus's troops, as well as Paulus himself, surrendered. It was Hitler's catastrophic leadership that had caused the disaster—a direct result of him taking supreme command of the army a year before.[53] It was also the first time an entire German army had capitulated in World War II. It would not be the last.

Overall, Hitler had taken a difficult situation and made it infinitely worse. His standfast order and fantasy plan to supply the 6th Army by air had failed catastrophically. Yet, once again, he blamed everyone around him for the failure, and used it to further dismiss any dissenting voices. He was now an agent rushing Germany to epochal defeat. Stalin, on the other hand, was becoming increasingly comfortable with the big picture and developing into an asset as a commander where before he had caused real problems. During the Stalingrad campaign he had shown flexibility in not calling for holding at all costs, and for allowing retreats and waiting for well-planned counterattacks. Unlike Hitler he stepped back from micromanaging, allowing his commanders with better knowledge the freedom they needed to manage the situation.

Stalin's performance as commander in late 1942 and 1943 during the Stalingrad campaign stood out to many of his senior commanders. Marshal Aleksander Vassilevskii, who became Stalin's military chief of staff during the war, and worked very closely with him, was actually specific in dating the most important change in Stalin's behaviour to "September 1942," which he called a "turning point." From that point on, Stalin seemed confident enough to listen more and allow for greater collective decision-making. Vassilevskii said it was most noticeable because the gruff Stalin was now given more realistic pictures of what was happening at the front, and would regularly exclaim, "Damn it, why didn't you tell me this [earlier]!"[54] Later, Vassilevskii added: "The war must have taught him a lot. He seems to have realized that he could be wrong, and his decisions may not always be the best and that the knowledge and experience of others can also be useful."[55] Zhukov also noted a marked change in Stalin as a commander at this time and, like Vassilevskii, considered the Stalingrad campaign to be a "milestone" for Stalin as a war leader. "I felt that he had a better grasp of operational issues in the last period of the Battle of Stalingrad, and by the time of the Kursk Salient it was already possible to say without exaggeration that he felt quite confident in these matters too."[56]

Zhukov's reference to Kursk, the great tank battle that would be Hitler's last attempt at a large offensive in the east, was apt. After the disaster of Stalingrad, the Germans gave up all the territory they had seized in 1942, and in the summer of 1943 found themselves basically at the same place they had been a year earlier. Hitler, however, wanted to launch another attack. In this case it was clear that the growing strength of the Red Army meant that German ambitions would have to be scaled back. Hitler decided on an offensive to cut off a large bulge of Red Army territory that erupted right in the middle of the German line, a protrusion known as the Kursk salient.

It was also to be a test of Hitler's quest for the heaviest, most powerful tanks. His preferences had led the Tiger, originally planned to weigh fifty tons, to reach a massive seventy-five tons.[57] The Panther, meanwhile, which was supposed to be more manoeuvrable, grew from thirty tons originally to almost forty-five. Hitler was more than satisfied with the upweighting and believed that they were just the weapons to help reinvigorate the German effort on the Eastern Front. Indeed, he kept putting off the Kursk offensive, codenamed Operation Citadel, to make sure that his new heavy tanks would appear in enough numbers to make a difference.[58]

Sadly for Hitler, the delay to get his new beasts in action might have only made things more difficult for the German Army. The extra time allowed Stalin and the Red Army to cram the Kursk salient so full of soldiers and equipment that the Germans had no chance to break their lines. The German Tigers were mechanically unreliable, yet over the protests of General Guderian, the inspector general of all German panzers, Hitler ordered that they still be thrown into the fight.[59] What developed was a relatively short and bloody slugfest. The Germans, even with their new Panthers and Tigers, advanced only small amounts on either side of the salient. They did destroy a great deal of Soviet equipment, but the Russian defences held. In the end, after fewer than two weeks, Hitler called the offensive off. With little prospect of a breakthrough, and with news coming in of the Anglo-American landing in Sicily, he had lost the appetite to continue.

Stalin's overall strategic command before and during Citadel showed him to be a very different beast. He had started talking with Zhukov and other Soviet generals about the possibility of a German Kursk offensive in April. Though Stalin personally believed Moscow was a more likely German target, he had allowed the Red Army to prioritize building up the Kursk defences, as the generals thought that was the more likely area for Hitler to attack.[60] This meant that the Soviets poured forces in exactly the right place at the right time to be ready for the Germans.

As the time for the German offensive drew near, Stalin had some doubts. Wondering if the Red Army could withstand a new mass German offensive, he seemed to favour a pre-emptive Red Army assault before the Germans were ready. His generals opposed this, believing that the Red Army was now strong and professional enough to withstand the German attack—so once again Stalin gave way. Looking back on it after Stalin's death, and after the Soviet Communist Party had been officially de-Stalinized, Vassilevskii was still impressed by how Stalin had been willing to go against his instinct on the advice of the military professionals. "Stalin was worried, and he did not hide it, whether our troops could withstand the blow of large masses of fascist tanks," he recalled. "However, it was no longer 1941. The Red Army was tempered in battles, had acquired vast combat experience, had excellent weapons and excellent military equipment. Now the Nazis were afraid of us. And the hesitation was cast aside. A thorough analysis of the situation and foresight of the development of events made it possible to draw the correct conclusion: the main forces should be concentrated north and south of Kursk, to bleed out the enemy here in a defensive battle, and then go on the counter-offensive and defeat him."[61]

The difference between Stalin and Hitler could not have been more stark. The results of Kursk also spelled the end of Hitler as an offensive grand strategist in World War II. Though Nazi Germany would fight on for twenty-two more months, it was led by a desperate and increasingly self-sabotaging dictator who would make increasingly erratic and stupid decisions, exclude other voices, and sacrifice his people for his own vision of national greatness. If Mussolini was the most pathetic of the grand strategists, Hitler was the most delusional.

20. Churchill, Roosevelt, Stalin and the Cross-Channel Invasion

In the late afternoon of January 23, 1943, in the Anfa hotel in Casablanca, Morocco, the president of the United States, prime minister of the United Kingdom and their most important military advisers sat down together for a session of back-slapping and self-congratulation. A rounded modernist structure with touches of art deco, the hotel would have looked at home in Miami Beach, and for the previous nine days it had housed a group of the most important strategists in the world. After a gruelling negotiation process, the British and American teams had thrashed out a consensus on how to take the war forward in 1943, and it was time to dot the i's and cross the t's. Of everyone in the room, Winston Churchill was the most effusive. He claimed it was the "first instance he knew of" when a group such as this had worked together so closely, free from political "considerations," to come together to back one strategic vision.[1] The military head of the British armed forces, General Sir Alan Brooke, later Lord Alanbrooke, recorded the congratulations in his diary, saying that Churchill and Roosevelt had commended the combined chiefs of staff for producing "the most complete plan for a world-wide war that has even been conceived."[2]

It was no surprise that Churchill was so happy, as the European strategy endorsed at the Casablanca Conference (codenamed Symbol) was practically a word-for-word endorsement of what he wanted. It has even been called his "Royal Flush."[3] The discussion that took place over the next two hours on that January afternoon was basically a recitation of his priority list. Overall, the war in Europe dominated the agreements, with the Pacific relegated to a few words at the end. When it came to Europe, the two issues which took up the lion's share of strategic vision were how to get aid to Russia so that Stalin could keep fighting the land war, and a plan to fight in the Mediterranean in 1943.

Churchill's plan to continue making the Mediterranean the focus for Anglo-American efforts, thus providing the best protection for the British Empire and keeping British casualties low, had been confirmed by Roosevelt and the Americans as well. The only 1943 offensive operation that received definite authorization at Casablanca was codenamed Husky, an amphibious assault on the island of Sicily. It was exactly what he had pushed for, and Churchill even talked about speeding up preparations for Husky and moving the date forward. Whereas the tentative target date for Husky was July, he suggested June was possible and added that he was "sure that the force could be sent earlier."[4]

Casablanca was the exact moment that Churchill reached the apex of his authority as a grand strategist in World War II. Ever since Roosevelt had opted for Torch, the war seemed to be going Churchill's way. With an invasion of Sicily set, who knew whether there would ever need to be an invasion of France? Maybe, Churchill hoped, Mussolini's rule would collapse when Husky was launched, and this would allow the war to be quickly broadened to the Italian mainland.* Anglo-American land forces could make their main effort for the rest of the war in the area which Churchill called, rather inaptly, the "soft underbelly" of Europe. In truth, it was a rugged landscape cut by a series of mountains and regular patches of dangerous terrain, which provided great cover for defensive forces. But it was where Churchill was determined to fight, keen to do anything not to repeat the slaughter in France of World War I.

In the end Churchill's hopes for making the Mediterranean the most important theatre for the defeat of Germany were not to be. Though Roosevelt said all the right words at Casablanca, Churchill had not grasped the president's underlying motivations. Roosevelt remained convinced that, in all but exceptional circumstances, D-Day (a cross-Channel invasion of France/north-west Europe) was going to happen. Unless Italy collapsed so spectacularly that the Allies

---

* It is important to realize that at Casablanca there was no agreement that an invasion of Sicily would be followed by an invasion of Italy as a whole. That decision was to be left for a later date.

could get almost up to the Alps, the president felt an invasion of France would be necessary to destroy Hitler's Nazi empire.[5] As such, the Casablanca decision to focus on the Mediterranean was to FDR a step in preparing for a cross-Channel attack, not a move to pre-empt one. Soon his feelings would be better understood by the British. Alanbrooke ended up stunned by how quickly the Mediterranean consensus unravelled after Casablanca. As he wrote about the Anglo-American grand strategists in a postscript to his diary, "as soon as we parted, we began to drift away from each other, and misunderstandings grew up between us."[6]

The truth is that there was never the kind of consensus that Alanbrooke or Churchill believed there to be. What had to happen was that a difference of opinion within the US decision-making structure needed first to be reconciled, and once that happened Roosevelt basically battered Churchill into submission, eventually even utilizing Joseph Stalin to crush any remaining hope out of the British prime minister.

The story of how Roosevelt forced Churchill to agree to D-Day, and in the process became the dominant grand strategist of the war, played out in 1943 over the various grand-strategy conferences held after Casablanca. The two leaders would meet again in Washington, DC (codenamed Trident) in May, Quebec City (codenamed Quadrant) in August and Cairo/Tehran (codenamed Sextant/Eureka) in November–December. Together these conferences determined the final shape of World War II. They were also a gruelling series of meetings that tested Roosevelt and Churchill in extreme ways. Everything from the long trips to reach the locations, the meetings themselves, the constant need to humour local dignitaries, the heavy meals with lots of alcohol, and the even heavier smoking, took a great toll. The president would leave Cairo in December 1943 in a state of utter exhaustion, and in many ways was never the same confident, forceful commander-in-chief he had been before Casablanca. Churchill would be so worn out by the process that he emotionally broke down at the same time.

The issue that Roosevelt was still trying to finesse at Casablanca was that, once again, he disagreed with the strong feelings of his own army. George Marshall remained what he had been in 1942—determined to invade France as soon as possible—and at the time of Casablanca he believed this meant in 1943. Even if the United States did not have the force to invade and liberate all of France, Marshall argued an attempt could be made to seize the Brittany peninsula. This would allow the Allies to build up enough force to break out into the rest of France in 1944.

Roosevelt was wary. While he eventually expected to invade France, he only wanted to try when he was sure the effort would succeed and not end in heavy casualties. By the time of Casablanca, he seemed more and more convinced that 1944 would be the right year. However, having humiliated Marshall once by overruling him when it came to Torch, Roosevelt wanted to operate with a defter touch than he had in the summer of 1942, when he had basically bludgeoned the army into line. When Roosevelt sat down with his joint chiefs on January 7, 1943, to prepare for Casablanca, the president fell back on his well-worn mask of agreeability. In the meeting, Marshall, predictably, made a direct argument for an invasion of Brittany. He wanted to go ahead even if the operation resulted in heavy American casualties. The US "could replace troops" that were lost, Marshall argued, and it would be worth it for such a high-priority objective.[7] Inside, Roosevelt probably blanched when he heard this, but instead of disagreeing he talked around Marshall's plan. Yes, the US should support a build-up of force in England, Roosevelt said, but could not commit at present to what to do with those troops. How about, Roosevelt suggested, any decision on exactly what to do be delayed "for a month or two."[8]

Having expressed his doubts and called for the final decision to be deferred until after Casablanca, Roosevelt could now rely on the ever-loyal William Leahy to back him up. The admiral immediately jumped in to support FDR's position, saying it had "considerable merit." If anything, in private Leahy was even more sceptical than the president about the prospect of invading France in 1943. He considered any such operation to be premature, as the Allies could not guarantee overwhelming air and sea power (from the point of view of January 1943), and thus there was a possibility of it being a bloody disaster. He saw no reason for the US to take part in an event that could result in "failure or great loss of life."[9]

The president's doubts, reinforced by his chief of staff, helped explain Churchill's great success at Casablanca. There was no unity in the American delegation at Symbol, and as such in the negotiations Marshall was basically hung out to dry.* It suited Roosevelt, as well as Leahy—and to a certain degree Admiral King—to allow the British to do the heavy lifting to keep the main focus of operations in 1943 in the Mediterranean, and to avoid a major build-up for a cross-Channel invasion happening too soon.† However, once the British did Roosevelt's dirty work for him by blocking an invasion of France in 1943, the president decided to act and guarantee one in 1944.

One of Roosevelt's first moves when he returned from Casablanca was to push a more united American negotiating stance for Trident. The president understood that in opting for Husky as the main effort in the summer of 1943 he might have prevented a cross-Channel invasion that year, but he in no way guaranteed it for the next. In the words of Leahy, who analysed the results of the conference with Roosevelt once back in Washington, it was believed that the Casablanca decisions had achieved "little of value to ending the war."[10] Determined now to make sure Trident accomplished exactly what he wanted, Roosevelt charged the joint chiefs with coming up with a series of clear strategy papers that would guide their actions during the next conference.

What the chiefs offered, under Leahy's constant prodding, might best be termed overkill. A series of strategy documents were produced over the coming months, outlining in great detail what the US position now was, how it differed from the British and what the US

---

* Leahy fell sick on the way to Casablanca, and had to stay in the Caribbean to recover, missing the entire conference. For Roosevelt this was a major blow, and he complained to his cousin that "I shall miss him as he is such an old friend and a wise counsellor."

† King offered Marshall some lukewarm support for an invasion of France in 1943, but it was a clear secondary concern for him. He was mostly concerned with getting the strategic freedom necessary to fight the war against Japan the way he wanted, and with the equipment he wanted.

expected to achieve at Trident. The chiefs reviewed every possible invasion route through the Mediterranean and rejected them all for multiple reasons. Indeed, they went on to attack the idea of spending any force to the east of Sicily in the Mediterranean, and said that a build-up in the UK to be able to launch an attack on France/north-west Europe in 1944 constituted the US's "basic strategy against Germany, and must not be delayed or otherwise prejudiced by other undertakings in Europe."[11]

For maybe the first time, the joint chiefs clearly spelled out that the Mediterranean strategy Churchill was proposing was geared more towards protecting the British Empire than defeating the Axis. When Roosevelt was briefed by Leahy and the other chiefs about preparations for Trident on 1 May, Leahy admitted that they were fearful that "Great Britain is desirous of confining allied military effort in Europe to the Mediterranean area in order that England may exercise control thereof, regardless of what the terms of peace may be."[12]

Fully believing that Churchill's focus on the Mediterranean was imperial, the chiefs, with Roosevelt's evident approval, argued that if Churchill continued to "insist on undertaking commitments in the Mediterranean, which the United States considers prejudicial to the over-all concept of the earliest defeat of Germany and the ultimate defeat of Japan," then the two countries should go their own ways strategically.[13] In such a scenario, "the British will be informed that the United States may be forced to revise its basic strategy and extend its operations and commitments in the Pacific."[14] Basically, the chiefs were saying that if Churchill continued to press broadening the war in the Mediterranean and not prioritize a build-up for D-Day in 1944, the US would go its own way in the war and leave them to it.* The reports were all forwarded to the president, and at Trident the US delegation would follow their prescription to the letter.

---

* It is worth noting that the joint chiefs' suspicion of Churchill's imperial strategy extended to the Pacific. They believed that the British were not interested in helping China resist Japanese aggression (a huge interest of Roosevelt's) because the British Empire was not directly concerned.

Churchill had no way of knowing that his entire strategic vision was about to be savagely attacked. He left Casablanca in high spirits, determined to build on the agreements by making the Mediterranean even more central. One of Churchill's great hopes was to secure the Eastern Mediterranean by convincing Turkey to join the fight, and he decided to speak directly with representatives of the Turkish government. Instead of heading back to London, he embarked for Cairo, en route to Turkey.[15] After a terribly bumpy overnight flight, Churchill arrived in the Egyptian capital and demanded breakfast right away. When offered a cup of tea, he rejected it with a scowl and asked for a tumbler of white wine, which he downed at once. He then exclaimed, "Ah, that is good, but you know, I have already had two whiskies and soda and two cigars this morning."[16] When he arrived in Turkey, he pressed his case with his normal vigour, though the Turks remained cautious.

For the next few months Churchill would continue to operate as if the Casablanca Conference represented a strategic consensus that the Mediterranean would continue to be the main theatre for Allied operations. His big priority with Roosevelt was to convince the president to expand the aims of Operation Husky. As approved at Casablanca, the plan was to seize only Sicily, but Churchill started arguing for a full-scale invasion of the Italian mainland (the exact thing that Leahy and the joint chiefs were worried that he was aiming to do). In April, Churchill wrote to Roosevelt saying that while Husky had been seen as an "end to itself," it would be a huge lost opportunity if the British and Americans stopped in Sicily. If it seemed possible, the Allies should make an immediate effort to seize as much of Italy as they could—even, Churchill offered rather optimistically, as far north as "the Brenner [Pass] or along the French Riviera."[17]

Overall, Churchill's preparations for Trident could not have been more different to Roosevelt's. While Roosevelt was methodically planning, Churchill seemed to coast. On May 5 he travelled north from London to just outside Glasgow, where he boarded the famous liner *Queen Mary* for the transatlantic crossing. Rather bizarrely, the large ship carried not only the grand-strategic leadership of the

United Kingdom, but also five thousand German prisoners of war on their way to North America for internment. Though the *Queen Mary* was no warship, her high speed made her invulnerable to German U-boat attacks, and Churchill could cross the ocean both safely and in some comfort. Much of his time on board was spent in strategy discussions, with the prime minister wondering how he could fend off expected American requests to spend greater effort in the Pacific— in particular getting support to China, which he considered a waste. Churchill and his chiefs were united in the view that the invasion of Sicily approved at Casablanca should be followed up with an invasion of the Italian mainland.[18] They had no interest in a cross-Channel invasion of France. Roosevelt had other ideas.

The Trident conference opened in an unseasonably hot and humid Washington on May 12, with the president, prime minister and their military teams cloistered together in the White House.[19] Roosevelt began the meeting with a note of triumph, pointing out that the war in North Africa was about to end in a "satisfactory conclusion." He then turned to Churchill and asked the prime minister to provide an overview of his thoughts. Indulging a little in the recent victories, Churchill said the alliance should now agree on one goal, or "first objective," and that was the Mediterranean. The "great prize there," Churchill claimed to Roosevelt, was "to get Italy out of the war by whatever means might be best."[20] Crushing Mussolini would damage German morale, letting the Germans know that they were facing "the beginning of their doom."

Looking eastwards in the Mediterranean, Churchill argued that the fall of Italy would secure the Balkans for the Allies, might bring Turkey into the war, would draw German troops away from Russia and would even help the Americans in their war against the Japanese Navy, as it would free up many British warships to go to the Pacific. An invasion of France, even in 1944, held no appeal. The minutes from the meeting note that "Churchill said that he could not pretend that the problem of landing on the Channel coast had been solved as the German defences would be formid-able. The difficult beaches, with the great rise and fall of the tide, the strength of the enemy's defences, the number of his reserves and the ease of his communications, all made the task one that must not be underrated."[21]

It was in some ways a tour de force. Even Leahy, who had an entirely different strategic vision from Churchill's, called the presentation "convincing."[22] But in this case eloquence would not matter. When Churchill finished, Roosevelt thanked him, and proceeded, with a typical light touch, to disagree point by point.* Attacking Italy might be all well and good, Roosevelt said, but the Allies should not make it their first priority as it would be a "drain" on resources. Instead, the British and Americans should "definitely" focus on the build-up of force to invade France in the "spring of 1944."[23]

The strategic break between the two leaders had been made, and the rest of the conference revolved around it. This fundamental strategic difference gave Trident a completely different feel from Symbol. Now the Americans were united, dogged and entirely inflexible. For the British, it was shocking and a little disheartening. Churchill and Alanbrooke both kept pressing the case for a major Mediterranean operation in 1943 and arguing against widescale preparations for an invasion of France in 1944, but became increasingly frustrated when their arguments were met by a solid wall of American opposition. For Churchill, this was particularly upsetting, as being forced to commit to an invasion of France was the one thing of which he was most terrified.

Churchill expressed his fears most succinctly not to the Americans, but to the delegates of the British Empire who were also in Washington. On May 20, he hosted a meeting with representatives from Canada, Australia, South Africa, New Zealand and India.[24] Ranging widely, Churchill started with upbeat assessments of the war at sea and in the air. When it turned to the land war and plans for the invasion of France, however, his tone darkened. Reimagining the carnage of World War I, he was worried that a great war in France would repeat the slaughter of almost thirty years ago. Churchill told the dominion leaders that any invasion would find "the French shore

---

* Roosevelt also disagreed with Churchill about the importance of China, which he made clear in this and other discussions at Trident.

bristling with cannon, secured by currents, and having the protection of a 30-foot tide and unduly flat beaches [and it] must be regarded as a deadly coast. If the Germans could oppose an attack with an active mobile reserve we might meet with disaster."[25]

Churchill's fears were never going to sway Roosevelt, however; the president was willing to do anything that needed to be done to break British resistance. With such a deep split between the two delegations, Leahy suggested that the military chiefs submit separate reports to Churchill and Roosevelt, basically decoupling British and American strategy.[26] This caused a crisis, and the chiefs had to go into a session during which no minutes were kept. In the end, the British were forced kicking and screaming to accept the American demand that the number-one priority in the European theatre be the build-up for an invasion of France in a year's time. The final report, submitted to Roosevelt and Churchill on May 25, after discussing the importance of defeating the German submarine menace and supporting the Combined Bomber Offensive, turned to preparations for the land war against Germany.[27] The first priority was the assembly of a minimum of twenty-nine divisions in the UK, ready to launch a cross-Channel invasion by May 1, 1944. To make this possible, troops were to be pulled out of the Mediterranean after Husky. Four American and three British divisions were to be prepared for shipment to the UK by the autumn, and operations in the Mediterranean would have to get by with what was left.

Churchill had to give way, despite his most ardent wishes, because of the raw power of the United States. American industrial production and mobilization were beginning to make an impact, and soon the UK would become a junior partner in almost all theatres. Still, for the rest of 1943 Churchill argued, sometimes majestically, sometimes self-destructively, to hold back approval for a D-Day in France. For someone whose career had been built on always coming back from failure, Trident alone was never going to be the end of the story.

For a few glorious weeks in the summer of 1943, it seemed that Benito Mussolini's strategic incompetence might offer Churchill a lifeline. The results of Trident meant that the only opportunity Churchill would have to broaden the war into the Italian mainland in

1943 would be an Italian collapse. Lo and behold, when Husky was launched on the evening of July 9–10, it did lead to an implosion of the Italian state. With Italy's war having had its foundations entirely eroded by Mussolini's fantasy strategy, and with no one believing that he had any way to prevent imminent defeat, the Italian dictator was left politically defenceless. Two weeks later, in concert with the Italian king, leading members of the Fascist Party deposed Mussolini and opened negotiations with the Allies.

The collapse of the Fascist Party itself followed almost immediately. In many ways built entirely on Mussolini's personality, once he had been deposed the party had no purpose, and the Italian government devolved to the army and the king, a brotherhood of incompetents. For a moment it seemed to Churchill, and to many Americans as well, that Italy as a unitary state might switch sides. Roosevelt in late July did think that such a development was worthy of consideration and could lead to a revision in Allied strategy.[28] Plans were drawn up to quickly get troops into southern Italy as part of a plan to seize as much of the country as possible.

These events in Italy supercharged the atmosphere at the next grand-strategic conference, Quadrant, which started in Quebec City in Canada on August 17. The Americans still clung to their belief that preparing for the cross-Channel invasion in 1944 was the top priority for Europe, but did admit that "in view of very recent developments in Italy, the ultimate consequences of which are as yet unpredictable," this strategy was now to be regarded as "tentative."[29] With the wind back in his sails, Winston Churchill was revitalized. At Quebec, he did not ask for the cancellation of the cross-Channel invasion; he just pressed for an agreement to make any such operation provisional—its ultimate fate to be subject to change if the situation in Italy called for it. He even partially succeeded. Though the Quebec agreements on the surface did restate, as the Americans wanted, that plans for a cross-Channel invasion remained the number-one strategic priority for the attack on Hitler, they also approved an attempt to invade Italy in September 1943. Churchill took his cue from this, and when he and Roosevelt sat down with their military chiefs on August 23 to go through the final conclusions, the prime minister was bullish.[30]

Having secured support for an invasion of Italy, he had a vision of reaching the far north of the country. Churchill claimed that the Germans, who were desperately trying to shore up resistance, were planning on only holding a line stretching from Ravenna to Genoa, hundreds of miles north of Rome. He called for immediate action to invade the mainland, claiming that "the further north in Italy the United Nations [the Allies] were able to progress," the more support they would get from Italian partisans and the easier any campaign would be.[31]

Churchill at Quebec was also consistent in arguing that a cross-Channel attack was now provisional. His first comment on planning for Overlord (the codename given to the invasion of France) was that he "wished it definitely understood that British acceptance" of the plan "included the proviso that the operation could only be carried out in the event that certain conditions regarding German strength were met."[32] These conditions were that the number of German divisions and the strength of the Luftwaffe had to be considered small enough that success was guaranteed. Otherwise, Churchill threatened, he would pull the plug on the whole operation.

Roosevelt listened, strangely silent. His performance at Quebec was possibly the first sign that his strength was ebbing. He attended few of the larger strategy meetings, preferring to have small meetings with key figures, including Churchill and Leahy. In the larger meetings he did attend, he spoke infrequently; and when he did speak, he said little. Roosevelt seemed to be conserving his strength and letting the chiefs do all the arguing.

For Churchill, what Mussolini giveth, Adolf Hitler taketh away. The German dictator watched the fall of his fellow fascist and decided to act. He did not want to control only northern Italy, as Churchill had assumed, but as much of the Italian landmass as he could, at the same time bringing back Mussolini as well. From almost the moment Hitler heard about the planned invasion of Sicily, he started making preparations to get more German troops into Italy; indeed, one of the reasons he called off the Kursk offensive on the Eastern Front was that he needed troops for just this purpose.[33]

Hitler sent these troops into Italy over the objections of the country's new leadership, led by Marshal Pietro Badoglio, one of Mussolini's most senior and least skilled officers. When Badoglio and the king then went ahead and signed an armistice with the Allies on September 3, Hitler was ready. German troops disarmed all Italian troops they considered disloyal, and soon the Germans had units deployed almost all the way down through southern Italy to below Naples. On September 12, Hitler ordered a daring raid, made up of German paratroopers and Waffen-SS commandos, to pluck Mussolini from the mountaintop hideaway where the Italian government had stashed him. He soon had his old ally reinstated, in charge of a new Italian state. Mussolini had no real power to speak of, other than to kill those whom he considered traitors. One of those who would be executed was Ciano, his son-in-law and presumed successor for many years. However, outside of a very narrow area of rule, Mussolini was an irrelevance in the making of World War II grand strategy and his state was seen as an appendage of Hitler's.

This extraordinary transformation meant that when US and British troops started landing on the Italian mainland, instead of being welcomed by friendly Italians, they were met by angry Germans. In particular, the US landing at Salerno, which started on September 9, ran into well-positioned German troops who caused a great number of US casualties. At one point it looked like the landing might even fail. Instead of moving quickly into northern Italy, the Allies found themselves stuck deep in the south, fighting northwards through some of the worst terrain possible. By December, when fighting started winding down for the winter, the lines had stabilized with the Germans in an excellent defensive position about 100 miles south of Rome.

Hitler's quick response meant the end of Churchill's hopes to forestall a cross-Channel invasion in 1944. When things bogged down in Italy, Roosevelt lost any hope that fighting there offered the opportunity to break Hitler's power, and he redoubled his commitment to D-Day. This hardening of the American position set the stage for the final grand-strategic conferences of the war: the two meetings in Cairo and one in Tehran which started in late November.

These meetings were actually three quite different conferences,

Winston Churchill, now Prime Minister, visits bomb damage in Ramsgate, Kent, in August 1940.

Roosevelt delivering a radio address in 1941 (the arm band was a sign of mourning for his mother, who had just died). He spent much of the year trying to maneuver the United States into the war on his terms.

Mussolini meets the Spanish dictator Francisco Franco in 1941. Franco was clever enough not to join up with Hitler completely, while Mussolini at this time was fully committed to his German ally.

Stalin and Churchill meet in Moscow in 1942. When these two met without Roosevelt, they could be more direct in their dealings.

oosevelt and Churchill fishing and smoking together during a break in the Trident Conference of May 1943. Though their relationship was often portrayed to the outside world as close and cooperative, they disagreed profoundly at times on issues of grand strategy and empire.

Hitler with his mistress and later wife, Eva Braun, in 1942. As the war turned more against him, he railed more and more against his generals and sought the company of Braun, who worshipped him.

Mussolini inspecting German troops in Sicily in 1942. By this point Mussolini's rule was entirely dependent on German military power.

Roosevelt and Churchill meet at Casablanca in January 1943. Churchill was delighted with the agreements reached there, while Roosevelt was not.

Churchill and Roosevelt, now joined by Stalin, meet at Tehran in December 1943. At this conference Roosevelt, joined by Stalin, forced Churchill to accept their strategy for an invasion of France in 1944.

After the Allied invasion of Sicily in July 1943, Mussolini lost power and was imprisoned by Italian authorities. In September, German forces released him and a delighted Hitler welcomed the shrunken Mussolini.

One of the last pictures of Hitler and Mussolini together. The two inspect the bomb damage to Hitler's headquarters after the July 1944 attempt to kill the German dictator. Each would live for only a few more months.

In July 1944, Roosevelt went to meet his leading Pacific commanders, General Douglas MacArthur and Admiral Chester Nimitz. Roosevelt had weakened considerably since 1943 and had lost a great deal of weight.

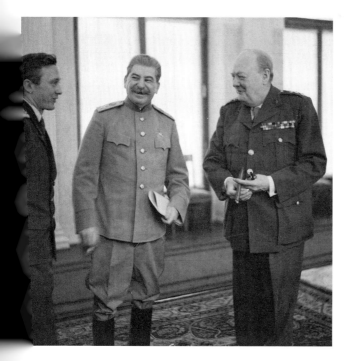

Stalin and Churchill meet at the Yalta Conference in February 1945. Though they smiled for the cameras, the two strategists were growing estranged because of their clashing views of the postwar world.

One of the last pictures of Roosevelt, Stalin and Churchill, together at Yalta. Sitting on Roosevelt's right was Admiral William Leahy, who spent much of the conference by Roosevelt's side.

each of which had a different cast of characters and a very different tone. The First Cairo Conference, which went on from November 23 to 26, focused more on the war in the Pacific than anything else. Churchill and Roosevelt were joined by the Chinese leader, Chiang Kai-shek, and much of the discussions revolved around what should be done to help China. When Churchill tried to discuss the war in Europe, Roosevelt put him off. The US delegation dropped ominous hints to the British that they were waiting for Stalin and Tehran to bring up the question, though it is unclear whether Churchill understood what was waiting for him.[34]

On November 27, Roosevelt and Churchill boarded planes and flew to the Iranian capital of Tehran. Waiting for them there was Joseph Stalin. Roosevelt now put into action a plan he had been thinking about for years. He was convinced that Stalin distrusted the British in general and Churchill in particular, and that he, Franklin Roosevelt, would be seen as a fair intermediary among the Allies. In March 1942, Roosevelt had made that clear to Churchill himself. "I know you will not mind me being brutally frank," he told the prime minister. "I think I can personally handle Stalin better than either your Foreign Office or my State Department. Stalin hates the guts of all your top people." Then Roosevelt added a hope based on his own self-confidence and centrality to events more than any evidence: "He thinks he likes me better, and I hope he will continue to do so."[35]

In disparaging the British and his own diplomatic service, Roosevelt was only being honest. He really did think it was his personal ability to persuade and connect that would keep Stalin on board, and so he went into Tehran determined to put some clear blue water between himself and Churchill. The two greatest areas of difference that he would use to appeal to Stalin were visions of empire and plans for a cross-Channel invasion. Roosevelt's determination to show he was not a Churchill clone became clear from the moment that the American and Soviet leaders first met.

Upon his arrival in Tehran, Roosevelt was taken to the US embassy, where he was to stay for the conference's duration. Almost as soon as he got there, he was given a message by Soviet sources saying that there was an assassination plot brewing against him, followed up with a kind offer to house the president in the large and heavily fortified Soviet diplomatic compound. Even though Roosevelt was placing himself completely before the eyes and ears of Joseph Stalin—an extraordinary position to be in for an American president—the offer was accepted. Soon Roosevelt and his two most trusted advisers, Harry Hopkins and William Leahy, were driven surreptitiously to the Soviet compound, where they would live for the rest of the conference.

The benefit of the move for Roosevelt was to show Stalin that he trusted him while allowing the two of them to meet in private, which they immediately did. At 3:30 in the afternoon of November 28, the two men came face to face for the first time. Roosevelt, eager to please and more than a little excited, welcomed Stalin, exclaiming, "I am glad to see you. I have tried for a long time to bring this about."[36] It was only the truth.

For the next hour Roosevelt worked to establish a connection with Stalin by finding common areas of support, and one common area of hate. The first thing he did was to state that he was committed to helping Stalin by supporting a cross-Channel invasion. He told the Soviet leader that he wanted "to bring about the removal of 30 or 40 German divisions from the Eastern front," and that was an issue he would press in Tehran.[37] This was all music to Stalin's ears. The Soviet leader had long wanted the Allies to invade France, and looked at the war in the Mediterranean as a sideshow to the great contest for control of Europe.

Then, after a quick chat about the war in the Pacific, Roosevelt's desire for intimacy took an anti-imperialist turn. The president started lashing out at the colonial policies of the French in Vietnam, stating that after a century of French rule, "the inhabitants were worse off than they had been before."[38] To this Stalin heartily agreed. Roosevelt then brought up the British Empire, in a more oblique way, but also one that clearly aligned him with Stalin. The president was said to have told Stalin that in the future he would like to talk about the status of India, and that he (FDR) "felt the best solution would be reform from the bottom, somewhat on the Soviet line."[39] So much for respecting Churchill's empire.

Roosevelt was constructing an American–Soviet strategic bloc to grind Churchill down over the coming days. The first time the president spoke at a meeting of the Big Three leaders together (which started just after his private meeting with Stalin), he delved right into European strategy, stating that his goal was to relieve pressure on Stalin's army on the Eastern Front—and to do that, he had pledged to support a cross-Channel invasion to be launched on May 1, 1944.[40] Stalin, primed, piped up right away to support Roosevelt, and in the process insulted Churchill's hope for a larger Mediterranean effort. Stalin said he "did not consider that Italy was a suitable place from which to attempt to attack Germany proper." He then added that he believed that "Hitler was endeavoring to retain as many allied Divisions as possible in Italy where no decision could be reached, and that the best method in Soviet opinion was getting at the heart of Germany with an attack through northern or northwestern France," supported if possible by a drive through southern France.[41]

With Roosevelt and Stalin aligned, Churchill had no room to manoeuvre. Of course, that did not stop him from trying. He attempted to interest Stalin a few times in the idea that fighting in Italy or even the Eastern Mediterranean offered the best chance for strategic success, but it was pointless. Stalin was if anything even more supportive of Overlord than Roosevelt. Things got so bad that, by the end of the conference, Stalin was openly, if gently, mocking Churchill's attempts to wriggle out of Overlord. The final banquet ended up being a rather raucous affair, with many toasts and alcohol flowing freely. The American diplomat Charles Bohlen, who also acted as Roosevelt's interpreter at times, was so struck by Stalin's rough treatment of the British prime minister that he made a special note about it. Observing the leaders in action, he said the "most notable feature of the dinner" was that "Marshal Stalin lost no opportunity to get in a dig at Mr. Churchill."[42] Stalin teased Churchill for being pro-German, for underestimating the intelligence of Russians and, Bohlen added, expressed "his displeasure at the British attitude on the question of Overlord."[43]

If Stalin was willing to needle Churchill about his perceived lack of commitment to Overlord, he also put Roosevelt on the spot at one point, pressuring the president to do everything possible to get the operation underway. Though Roosevelt was a supporter of Overlord, he had not yet formally chosen a commander for the operation. The unspoken assumption was that General George Marshall would be given the assignment, which would allow him to crown his career with perhaps the most important battle command in US history. In return, the present commander-in-chief in the Mediterranean, General Dwight Eisenhower, would come back to Washington to take Marshall's post as chief of staff of the army.

Roosevelt equivocated, even though it was reported that Marshall had already started packing up his furniture in anticipation of the appointment. By this point in the war the president hated change, and was quite comfortable with how his strategic decision-making structure operated. The idea of working with new personalities had no appeal. Stalin, however, was impatient. If you really want Overlord to happen, he said to Roosevelt on November 29, it needs a commander quickly or "nothing will come" of it. Roosevelt understood that he would have to act soon.

Overlord may have been confirmed, but Churchill still had one final opportunity to lobby for his Mediterranean plan. With the Tehran Conference done, the British and American delegations flew back to Cairo for one more series of talks. This Second Cairo Conference was probably the most hated meeting of the war. The Americans wanted to get home, while Churchill, forced to accept the reality of Overlord, tried one more time to get the Americans interested in the Eastern Mediterranean.[44] As an exhausted and irritated Roosevelt listened, Churchill tried to wrangle a commitment to devote more resources to the region if Turkey could be convinced to enter the war on the Allies' behalf. The president, not even bothering to hide his feelings at having to go round and round in circles about the region, summarized the situation as follows:

a. Nothing should be done to hinder Overlord.
b. Nothing should be done to hinder Anvil.*

---

* Anvil was the codename for the Anglo-American landing in southern France that was to happen after Overlord had established itself. It occurred, but by the time the

c. By hook or by crook we should scrape up sufficient landing craft to operate in the Eastern Mediterranean if Turkey came into the war.[45]

Roosevelt just wanted to get home and end the incessant talking. In the end, the final report of the combined chiefs, issued on December 5, could basically have been dictated by the president. "Overlord and Anvil are the supreme operations for 1944. They must be carried out during May 1944. Nothing must be undertaken in any other part of the world which hazards the success of these two operations."[46]

When the Second Cairo Conference adjourned on December 6, 1943, it was the end of a process that, when it came to the war in Europe, had seen Franklin Roosevelt dominate Allied grand strategy. If this gave him satisfaction, however, he seemed unable to enjoy it. He had one more major decision he had to make. Unwilling to accept any change to his Washington circle of wartime leadership, Roosevelt decided to keep George Marshall as his army chief of staff. Dwight Eisenhower would thus get the great honour of commanding Allied forces in the liberation of western Europe. With that difficult choice made, Roosevelt was incapable of more work. He was flown across the length of North Africa, before boarding USS *Iowa*, one of America's largest battleships, for the voyage home. He chose to rest for the entire crossing, spending his time either in bed or on deck, taking in the sea air. It was a worrying sign of what was to come.

Winston Churchill also headed out across North Africa, en route to review troops on the Italian Front. Yet after stopping in at General Eisenhower's villa near the historic city of Carthage in Tunisia, he collapsed. For days he lingered in bed, suffering from excruciating headaches and light-headedness. His staff worried he had contracted pneumonia as well.[47] Medical specialists were brought in, but his condition seemed to worsen. The physical and emotional strain of 1943 had been too much for him. His most serious symptoms make it sound like he was suffering from what we would today call panic attacks. He

---

troops moved inland from southern France the German Army was already in retreat towards Germany, so it proved relatively unimportant.

would become breathless and his heart raced dangerously. At one point he even thought he might be dying. Yet he never stopped thinking about the war and strategy. Having been forced to accept the overall loss of his strategic vision, Churchill understood where the war was heading. "If I die," he said to his daughter Sarah during one of the most worrying moments, "don't worry—the war is won."[48]

It would just be won in a way that he had not wanted to happen.

21. Stalin, Roosevelt, Churchill and the Post-War World

By 1944, Franklin Roosevelt was firmly established as the senior leader of the Allied alliance against Germany and Japan—as much as a dying man could be firmly entrenched in anything. Though both Winston Churchill and Joseph Stalin were older and had more experience of military matters, both understood that it was Roosevelt whom they needed to cultivate. Both, in their own ways, also deferred to him. Churchill had spent as much of the war as possible with Roosevelt, thinking his own personal presence and charisma would win the president over to supporting his positions. Stalin, who had far less time with Roosevelt, was always more respectful of the president than he was of the prime minister. Whereas Stalin could tease or even insult Churchill, he treated Roosevelt more seriously. When the Soviet security services assigned codenames to the two men, Churchill was named "Boar" and Roosevelt "Captain."[1] Considering the Soviet intelligence services were hyper-sensitive about keeping Stalin happy, it's unlikely these choices were accidental.

Before the two first met, Stalin had clearly been a little nervous. His translator recalled that while preparing for the Tehran Conference, Stalin had seemed uncharacteristically tense:

> Stalin went up to the table, casually threw a box of cigarettes on it. He lit a match and lit an extinguished cigarette. Then, with a slow gesture, he put out the match, pointed it to the sofa and said:
>
> "Here, I will sit on the edge. Roosevelt will be brought in a wheelchair, let him sit to the left of the chair where you will sit."
>
> "Sure," I replied.
>
> I have translated Stalin more than once, but I have never heard him attach such importance to such details. Perhaps he was nervous about meeting Roosevelt.[2]

When the two did finally meet face to face, Stalin went out of his way to convince Roosevelt of his sincerity and friendship. Stalin's long-time head of security, the thuggish Nikolai Vlasik, remembered Stalin being extremely solicitous of Roosevelt at Tehran. One of the highlights of the conference was when Churchill presented Stalin with a specially forged, bejewelled longsword commissioned on behalf of the British people and state to commemorate the people of Stalingrad for their historic victory. "Solemn was the ceremony of presenting the sword on behalf of the English King George VI to the people of the heroic Stalingrad. Having accepted the sword from Churchill, Stalin took it out of its scabbard and kissed it. Thanking Churchill for the gift, Stalin went up to Roosevelt and showed him the sword. In general, Stalin treated Roosevelt very attentively and warmly, apparently appreciating in him the sincerity and goodwill that he showed during all the negotiations."[3] Later in the conference, Stalin heard Roosevelt praise the Soviet champagne that was being served. Stalin immediately told Vlasik to have a case prepared to present to the president.

Stalin's desire to cultivate Roosevelt was not a sign that he particularly trusted or even liked the president. What he understood, which Churchill did as well, was that Roosevelt held more influence over not only how the war would be won but also the shape of the post-war world. American power through Lend-Lease and the direct application of US force was vital to both the Soviet and British war efforts, and in the post-war world American power might be even greater as the US would possess a greater global economic dominance than practically any other country or empire in history. In that sense, Stalin saw Roosevelt as the most important, but in a way most threatening, person with whom he had to deal.

One of the greatest comparisons that Stalin ever made between Roosevelt and Churchill was the 1944 description he gave Milovan Djilas, the Yugoslavian emissary in Moscow and committed communist who at this time practically worshipped Stalin. "Perhaps you think that just because we are the allies of the English we have forgotten who they are and who Churchill is," he said. "There's nothing they like better than to trick their allies. During the First World War they constantly tricked the Russians and the French. And Churchill? Churchill is the kind of man who will pick your pocket of a kopeck if you don't watch him. Yes, pick your pocket of a kopeck! By God, pick your pocket of a kopeck! And Roosevelt? Roosevelt is not like that. He dips in his hand only for bigger coins."[4]*

Franklin Roosevelt understood his powerful position, and in many ways revelled in it. He was convinced, as he had been since World War I, that the United States needed to play a major peacekeeping role in the world, and he wanted to be the person to determine the shape of that role for as long as possible. The one problem, which he did not want to fully face, was that his health made that distinctly unlikely.

When Roosevelt returned to Washington at the end of 1943, he could barely work. The strain of two years of continual war leadership had been too much for a man who, because of his infirmity, took little exercise, and who liked both a drink and a cigarette (in particular the latter). His blood pressure could soar to dangerous levels, and he was showing signs of advanced coronary disease. A walking time bomb, he could have dropped dead at almost any moment.

For the first four months of 1944, Roosevelt decided to take a break to restore his health. He spent long periods away from the White House, either in Warm Springs, Georgia, or the long-time Roosevelt family home in Hyde Park, New York. When there was no improvement he spent an entire month, sleeping twelve hours a day, at financier Bernard Baruch's secluded estate in rural South Carolina. When he returned to Washington in early May, he had still hardly improved. He even confided to William Leahy, Roosevelt's most important adviser and constant companion, that he was not sure he had the strength to carry on. "Bill, I just hate to run again for election . . . Perhaps the war will by that time have progressed to a point that will make it unnecessary for me to be a candidate."[5]

Yet not long after this, he decided he had no choice. The prospect of giving up power, of becoming a respected but secondary figure in the creation of a new post-war world order, was simply too terrifying

* A kopeck was the smallest unit of Soviet currency; 100 kopecks made up a rouble.

for him. Though one does not want to analyse Roosevelt's psyche too much, part of him seemed to believe that, as long as he was president, he could not really die. After all, the world needed him, Churchill and Stalin needed him—who else but Franklin Roosevelt, with his charm, subtle mind and political understanding, could really hold together all the different forces needed to establish a new era of global peace?

So, in 1944, Roosevelt would make one of the most selfish choices in international relations history, something so profoundly self-centred that historians still shy away from addressing it. He not only decided to run for office while dying; he decided to change vice president to someone he did not like, would not confide in and would not prepare in any way to be president. Worried that the incumbent vice president, Henry Wallace, was seen as too left-wing, Roosevelt chose the more moderate Harry Truman to be his running mate. Politically it was an astute choice. Truman hailed from Missouri, and had the political common touch that nicely complemented Roosevelt's aristocratic presence. Truman could help Roosevelt in the Midwest and upper South, areas not particularly enamoured with the more radical Wallace.

Truman, by his own estimation, had almost no experience in international relations, and Roosevelt would make sure he got none. The election of 1944 happened on November 7. Between that day and Roosevelt's death on April 12, 1945, the president is recorded in his appointments diary meeting with Truman only six times—and only once, on December 21, would the two meet alone.[6] Roosevelt seemed to actively avoid including his vice president in his plans, such as the famous Yalta Conference which occurred in February 1945. He was basically saying that he, and only he, could lead the United States and the world in this crisis, and therefore he must live. If he did die—well, *après moi, le déluge*.

One of the reasons this lack of consultation ended up being so extraordinary is that Roosevelt never wrote down, and rarely discussed, a concrete vision for the post-war world. He usually dazzled people with broad, amorphous concepts of keeping order through the "four policemen" (USA, USSR, UK and China), and talked hopefully about the creation of the United Nations, but he avoided trying to answer the difficult questions. Would US forces be permanently deployed in Europe at the end of the war? Should Germany be permanently divided? Would a military alliance with the USSR continue, and if so would the United States accept Soviet domination of eastern Europe? What would the post-war world settlement look like in Asia/Pacific? Would European empires such as the Dutch or French be allowed to reconstruct themselves? Would US forces go into areas formerly occupied by Japan? How would China be one of the world's policemen if it had such a chaotic political situation? If he had clear answers to these questions, Roosevelt kept them to himself. As Leahy admitted in his memoirs, "There were times when I felt that if I could find anybody except Roosevelt who knew what America wanted, it would be an astonishing discovery."[7]

In refusing to provide the US government with an idea of concrete war aims and purposes, Roosevelt was making a mockery of the Clausewitzian notion of strategy being a connection between ends, ways and means. Roosevelt, more than any war leader, had a clear idea of ways and means—fighting the war with air-sea power and many machines over soldiers, etc.—but they seemed disconnected from the ends. The ends were what he wanted at any given moment.

If Roosevelt was becoming in many ways more secretive about what he wanted from the war for the United States, Joseph Stalin was willing to be more direct. He wanted security and strength, and preferred direct control over amorphous international guarantees and understandings. Away from Roosevelt and what seemed to Stalin the president's more airy-fairy ideas, the Soviet dictator made this very clear. Stalin's greatest moment of clarity was probably in October 1944 when he met alone with Churchill in Moscow. Roosevelt was preoccupied with his re-election and the idea of making a long trip to Moscow at that point had no appeal, so he was happy to skip it. What Stalin and Churchill did without him, however, was revealing.

Only a few weeks before, Churchill had taken part in some of the most frustrating meetings he would ever have with Roosevelt. Between September 12 and 16 they had attended another formal summit in Quebec City (codenamed Octagon), which saw the two leaders, for the first time, clash bitterly about the future shape of

Germany—and by extension Europe. Before the conference began, Roosevelt had been persuaded by his secretary of the treasury and long-time friend, Henry Morgenthau, to support Morgenthau's plan to radically transform Germany after the war. Morgenthau's idea to permanently bring peace to Europe involved depriving Germany of all its industry. He proposed the destruction of basically every factory in the country—the largest industrial power in Europe (and second-largest industrial power in the world)—and the transformation of Germany into what was essentially a giant farm.[8]

At Quebec, Roosevelt suggested that Churchill endorse the Morgenthau Plan, arguing that even leaving Germany owning something as humble as a furniture factory would provide the industrial basis for the rebirth of German military power. Churchill was aghast, and when the two clashed about the idea in a small private meeting he spoke forcefully against the plan. Creating a weak and useless Germany in the heart of Europe created some obvious dangers for Britain. Not only would that mean that the enormous Red Army, now on the borders of Germany itself, would be able to dominate the continent once the United States pulled out after the war, but deindustrializing Germany would also rob Britain of its largest pre-war trading partner on the continent. Yet Roosevelt was by this point simply too powerful for Churchill to outwardly oppose, and in the end the British prime minister initialled a document that seemed to commit him to supporting Morgenthau. Churchill probably had no intention of ever following through.★

At Hyde Park a few days later, Roosevelt and Churchill's differences were also laid bare on one of the greatest, most secret questions of the day: the future of nuclear power and weaponry. For maybe the first time, the two men had a frank, detailed and private discussion about the state of the nuclear weapons project that was producing the world's first atomic bombs. They also discussed the future of atomic power, and to what degree Britain, which had provided much

---

★ Roosevelt lost interest in the Morgenthau Plan not long after Octagon, when it became clear just how controversial it would be. With the 1944 election approaching, he quietly dropped it.

of the early research on atomic energy, would be allowed access to any finished bomb or technology. Once again, Roosevelt's position caused alarm bells to start ringing for Churchill.

And then Churchill arrived in Moscow on October 9 to meet with Stalin for what was nicknamed the Tolstoy Conference. On the surface it was just another of the grand-strategic confraternities of the war. Churchill went to the Bolshoi Ballet and the Russian food gave him diarrhoea. There were official meetings which were often attended by the US ambassador to the Soviet Union, Averell Harriman. These were mostly safe affairs during which Churchill and Stalin behaved themselves and tried to pretend that they were looking for a peace based on Rooseveltian concepts. When Stalin and Churchill were alone, however, they behaved differently. Stalin, who had treated Churchill rather roughly at Tehran, was now far more accommodating. The two were both night owls by this stage in their lives, and Stalin used that, as well as their common love of tobacco and alcohol, to show Churchill special favour. He even did something he had hardly ever done before and invited Churchill to come to his private flat in the Kremlin for evening chats. One night, while Churchill smoked a huge Burmese cigar, the prime minister brought up the fact that, at the end of World War I, he had been the greatest advocate for and organizer of British intervention in Russia to try to thwart the Russian Revolution. When he asked if Stalin held a grudge against him for this, Stalin replied with the old Russian proverb "who mentions the past loses an eye." This equivalent of "let bygones be bygones" did not seem to assure Churchill, who asked Stalin for forgiveness. "But can you forgive me personally for organizing the campaigns of the Entente?" The committed atheist Stalin answered enigmatically: "It's not for me to forgive you . . . May God forgive you."[9]

One night during their private chats, both men looked to the future and talked about a Europe without the possible influence of Roosevelt and the United States. Their conversations to this point had shown that there were a number of major areas of tension between Churchill and Stalin, often surrounding the future of Germany and the fate of Poland. Understanding that Britain was "powerless in the face of Russia" when it came to Poland, Churchill accepted that the lands

Stalin had seized through the Nazi–Soviet Pact were never going to be returned.[10] However, remaining as Mediterranean-focused as always, he was not going to give way so easily on Greece and the Balkans. The result was the famous "Percentages Agreement," which saw Churchill and Stalin dividing up the region into spheres of interest.

There are two recollections of how this came about, and they agree almost exactly on the substance with a few differences in detail. The Soviet recollection, which was written down by Stalin's interpreter, started with Stalin and Churchill both expressing irritation at Roosevelt's dominant position:

> Stalin recalled Roosevelt's wish that any decisions of the current meeting be considered "preliminary."
>
> "Between you and I," picked up the prime minister, "there are no secrets from the president. I even welcome the presence of Harriman at a number of our talks. However, this should not prevent us from having intimate conversations."
>
> "It seems to me," Stalin noted understandingly, "that the United States claims too many rights for itself, leaving the Soviet Union and Great Britain limited opportunities."[11]

Having bonded, Churchill steered the conversation to the fate of south-eastern Europe. "Let us settle our affairs in the Balkans," he said to Stalin. "Your armies are in Romania and Bulgaria. We have interests, missions and agents there. Don't let us get at cross-purposes in small ways. So far as Britain and Russia are concerned, how would it do for you to have ninety per cent predominance in Romania, for us to have ninety per cent of the say in Greece, and go fifty-fifty about Yugoslavia?"[12]

Having made his opening offer, Churchill took out a sheet of paper and wrote down the percentages of influence that each country would have throughout the region, adding for good measure that Hungary would be divided 50/50 between the two while Stalin would be given a 75/25 predominance in Bulgaria.[13] Stalin looked over Churchill's sheet quickly and made a large tick of agreement upon it in blue pencil. Churchill then got nervous. Understanding that Roosevelt would find any such agreement anathema, he suggested that the sheet be destroyed. Stalin seemed nonplussed. "No," he said to Churchill, "you keep it." And that was that.

This Percentages Agreement represents perhaps the truest picture of how Stalin and Churchill would have liked to conduct negotiations between themselves. When compared to Roosevelt, they certainly had more concrete aims in mind for the war. For Churchill it was the maintenance of Britain and the British Empire as a great power. For Stalin it was the expansion of the Soviet Union as much as possible in eastern, central and southern Europe. Neither had much time for a Rooseveltian notion of international goodwill and cooperation. In fact, in a telegram that was dispatched by them both not long after the meeting, no mention of the Percentages Agreement was made.[14]

If the Percentages Agreement better represented how Stalin and Churchill would have liked to order the post-war world, it was also a political and personal pipe dream. Roosevelt would never have agreed to such an arrangement for political reasons as much as anything else, and so the three would have to gather together to see if the American president could be brought on board in devising a more workable framework for post-war Europe and the world. They would need to reconcile Churchill and Stalin's quite concrete strategic aims with Roosevelt's more amorphous ones.

The result of this difference would be the Yalta Conference, codenamed Argonaut, easily the most controversial of all the grand-strategic meetings of the war, held from February 4 to 11, 1945, in Crimea. To this day, Yalta generates heated discussion about just what was agreed— or to put it more accurately, what the three practitioners thought they were agreeing to.[15] In some ways the problem was not the conference itself, the conclusions of which were not seen by any of the Big Three as "definitive" at the time.[16] The real problem was that Roosevelt died not long after, and as he kept the real meaning of the deals he made so close to the vest, his successor, Harry Truman, ended up having to intuit Roosevelt's intentions.

Certainly, the three men who gathered for this meeting were very different than the three who had first led their countries into war in 1940 and 1941. Roosevelt had aged noticeably, but the intense pressures of running their own countries' war efforts had also taken a toll on Stalin and Churchill. Stalin's ageing had become perceptible to those around him by 1943. When Hopkins saw Stalin at Tehran he had remarked how greyer the Soviet dictator looked.[17] As the war went on, Stalin fell ill more regularly, and when he became ill it took him considerably longer to recover. More and more he would retreat to his dacha outside of Moscow and work from there.[18] This was one of the reasons he started to rely on his staff to do more of the work (which was not in and of itself a bad thing). By 1945, Stalin's heart had also started giving him trouble.*

Churchill had increasing bouts of ill health during the war, which was not surprising as he was the leader who had to do the most travelling. While Roosevelt made three trips out of North America to see Churchill and Stalin (Casablanca, Cairo/Tehran and Yalta), Churchill visited North America many times and made two gruelling trips to the Soviet Union as well. All this activity seemed to weaken his immune system, and he caught pneumonia a number of times between Tehran and Yalta, regularly ran high fevers, and, though he continued to work, there were signs that his mind was wandering.[19]

Of course, compared to Roosevelt, both Stalin and Churchill would have been considered to be in stable health. By the time of Yalta the American president was nearing the end. His run for re-election in 1944 had taken what little energy he had. Though he only made a relatively small number of campaign appearances, when the election was over he was incapable of sustained work. On the few days that he was in the office between early November and the start of 1945, he would normally not come down from his White House bedroom to the Oval Office until noon or just before. He would meet Leahy for his daily briefing on the war, have lunch, rush through a few meetings and be done by four or five in the afternoon. And those were his workdays, which were rare enough as it was. Between November 27 and New Year's Eve, Roosevelt spent only four days in the White House.[20]

* Stalin would actually suffer a heart attack at the start of the Potsdam Conference (July 1945) with Churchill and Truman.

The president's true condition was kept from the American people. When he had to be seen in public, such as for his inauguration on January 20, 1945, he spoke only for a few minutes before being whisked into the White House. There was no parade and little celebration.[21] By the time Roosevelt reached Yalta, he seemed even worse. He had lost more weight, had large, puffy black bags under his eyes, and needed constant rest. Some members of the British delegation, who had last seen the president at Quebec, were shocked by his deterioration in such a short time. One of Churchill's secretaries, upon seeing Roosevelt, remarked that he "was hardly in this world at all."[22]

With the Allies in firm control of the seas, this time Roosevelt could now sail directly into the Mediterranean and head to the island of Malta, where he met with his chiefs of staff and eventually Winston Churchill in preparation for the trip to the Soviet Union. Everything possible was done to make Roosevelt comfortable. Though women were forbidden from travelling on US warships, Roosevelt's daughter, Anna, was given special permission to accompany her father. Once Roosevelt reached Malta, he rested for a few days and met with Churchill, and then flew on to Yalta. The flight was made in the newly completed presidential airplane, christened the *Sacred Cow*, with a specially installed elevator so that Roosevelt could be comfortably whisked on board without having to be carried up a flight of stairs. Even then, the president's health was so precarious, with his blood pressure threatening to shoot up to dangerous levels at any moment, that the aircraft was given strict instructions only to fly at low altitude.

If Roosevelt was unwell and exhausted, Churchill was full of "foreboding."[23] The approaching conference filled him with dread. When he wrote to his wife from Malta, Churchill could only see a world of problems—some that would be made worse by the end of the war in Europe. Indian nationalism had partly been repressed by the war, but now threatened to burst back into life, and Churchill felt "despair about the British connection" with the jewel in the imperial crown.[24] Throughout Europe he could also only see problems, from a potential communist insurgency in Greece—still in his mind a key area of British interest—to the intractable conundrum of how to control post-war Germany with the enormous Red Army poised to seize much of the country.

Stalin was in a better mood. Not only could he take a train to the summit, but events on the battlefield in January 1945 had given him a strong hand to play in the upcoming negotiations. On January 12, Red Army forces, led partly by Marshal Zhukov, had launched another overwhelming offensive. Starting from just outside the Polish capital, Warsaw, Russian forces used their tanks, aircraft and artillery in expert combination to shatter German lines in Poland.[25] Hitler, in his growing paranoia and distrust of the military, decided to entrust overall command of many of the forces in this region to the head of the SS—and his executioner-in-chief—Heinrich Himmler. Though Himmler might have been able to arrange the murders of millions of Jews, Romani and homosexuals, when faced with an enemy that could fire back he was a disaster. Frozen in incompetence as Soviet forces shattered German lines, Himmler did nothing. In a matter of weeks, Soviet forces had conquered almost all of pre-war Poland. By the time the Big Three sat down at Yalta, Russian forces had reached the Oder River, the present-day border between Poland and Germany. They were now lurking fewer than 100 miles from Berlin. Once they had reorganized and rested for their next offensive, the German capital was bound to fall. Hitler had once again accelerated Germany's demise.

The conquest of most of Poland before the Yalta Conference was an enormous advantage for Stalin in the upcoming talks. He knew "what sort of Poland he wished to build," and was in no mood to compromise.[26] That being said, he did his best to be a gracious host. Yalta, located at the southern tip of Crimea, was one of the most temperate cities in the Soviet Union. Thankfully for Roosevelt and Churchill, both of whom came to spend more and more time in warmer climates as they aged, the weather was fine for February. It averaged around 5 degrees Celsius in the day—far from cold for the USSR—and the Soviets, to flatter the president, referred to it as "Roosevelt weather."[27]

During Tsarist times, Yalta had been a favoured summer destination of the Russian aristocracy, to say nothing of the tsar himself.

Churchill and Roosevelt were housed in some of the most lavish nineteenth-century palaces built during the city's opulent heyday. Though the area had only been liberated from the Germans a few months before, in true Stalinist fashion huge numbers of workers (many of them POWs) and resources were poured into fixing everything up like the war had never happened. Of course, also in true Stalinist fashion, while they did a remarkable job on the major venues, there were signs of desolation all around, and the level of cleanliness left a lot to be desired. Leahy, for one, complained of the insects plaguing the buildings, including mattresses infested with bedbugs. His had to be heavily dosed with the now-banned insecticide DDT.

Roosevelt and Churchill flew into Yalta separately from Malta on February 3, and both were rather surprised to find that the venues for the talks lay a few hours' drive from the airfield, along rather winding country roads through snowy hills. Already tired, they had to endure this journey, made all the more surreal by the fact that the road for the entire way was lined with smart-looking Red Army soldiers who would snap to attention whenever one of the cars drove by. As a nod to Roosevelt's infirmity and his seniority, the daily talks were held in his residence, the Livadia Palace—an enormous white wedding cake of a building that had been built on the orders of the last tsar, Nicholas II.

The key actors at Yalta would be Roosevelt and Stalin. Churchill's positions were well known, but by this time Britain lacked the military or financial power to compel either the United States or the USSR to do what it wanted. On the other hand, Stalin still needed US support from Lend-Lease and was eager to join the war in the Pacific almost immediately after Germany was defeated. He thus could not disregard Roosevelt's opinion. Roosevelt was still planning on the continuation of the US–USSR wartime alliance in some form after the war, as a guarantee of world peace.

As at Tehran, Roosevelt used his first private meeting with Stalin to assure the Soviet dictator that they had many things in common. They talked just before the formal opening of the conference, and practically the first thing he said to Stalin was that seeing the destruction the

Germans had caused to Crimea made him "bloodthirsty." To prove his anger, he asked Stalin to make a toast at one of the events to "the execution of 50,000 German officers."[28]★ Then, to once again try to differentiate himself from imperialist Britain, as well as the French, Roosevelt proceeded to throw Churchill under the bus. He claimed that the British were trying to re-establish France as a great power with a large army facing eastwards (towards the Red Army) to help provide Britain with security. As the official US minutes state: "The President said he would now tell the Marshal something indiscreet, since he would not wish to say it in front of Prime Minister Churchill, namely that the British for two years have had the idea of artificially building up France into a strong power ... He said the British were a peculiar people and wished to have their cake and eat it too."[29]

It was all a little sad on the part of the dying president—but it was also indicative of his desire to reach a deal with Stalin. To begin with, things seemed to go well enough in that regard. The first plenary meeting of the leaders with their closest advisers celebrated the fact that they were about to win the war. It was a military overview of the war in Europe, and thus a story of the inevitable crushing of Hitler's Germany. The different leaders praised the performance of each other's militaries and talked about close coordination in the final stages of the war in Europe.

With the military overview out of the way, the leaders turned to the post-war world. Stalin voiced a view of great power politics—that it was these three men who should decide on the future, and not spend time listening to the views of smaller states. On the evening of February 4, Roosevelt, Churchill and Stalin met for a relaxed and cheerful dinner in the Livadia Palace. As the food was served and the drinks passed around, "Marshal Stalin made it quite plain on a number of occasions that he felt that the three Great Powers which had borne

---

★ At Tehran, Stalin had made a toast calling for the summary execution of 50,000 German officers, a move that caused Churchill to be outraged, which Roosevelt undoubtedly knew. The fact that the president would then encourage Stalin to do something that had so angered Churchill before was one of Roosevelt's more grotesque attempts at triangulation during the conferences.

the brunt of the war and had liberated from German domination the small powers should have the unanimous right to preserve the peace of the world." Roosevelt spoke relatively little, but he did provide Stalin with support, agreeing that "the Great Powers bore the greater responsibility and that the peace should be written by the Three Powers represented at the table."[30] Churchill was uncomfortable. Not wanting to contradict Stalin outright, he argued instead that it was incumbent on the great powers to listen to the small, to show some humility (though it was never clear how his vision of empire fit into this vision). Stalin, seemingly amused, started teasing Churchill about possibly losing the next election.

For the rest of the conference the Big Three decided the fate of the rest of the world—and a great deal of that was done amicably. Though Roosevelt, Stalin and Churchill had different priorities when it came to the fate of Germany, the creation of the new United Nations and even the end of the war in the Pacific, they found ways to either settle or cover over those differences for the time being. Starting on February 5, much of their conversation focused on the post-war fate of Germany. There were some differences of opinion— primarily about whether Germany should be dismembered or not. Stalin, who was opposed to it, wanted to put off any such decision until the future. He asked if Roosevelt, who had spoken in favour of German dismemberment at Tehran, still held to that position. Roosevelt said he did, but did not want to make a big deal of it now. In fact, postponing any such decision was easy, as the key first step— the division of Germany (and of Berlin as well) into clearly defined occupation zones—had already been made. The Big Three had maps presented which showed where the British, US and Soviet zones would be, and they were more than happy with those. Maybe the most interesting statement made in the discussion was Roosevelt's claim that American troops would not stay in Europe for more than the next two years. Hearing that, Churchill responded that maybe France should now be built up with a strong army. Stalin said that was fine, but France was not to be given a major say in the control of Germany.[31]

Another major issue that was settled was the plan for Stalin to have the USSR enter the war against Japan. With victory over Germany now looking set for the spring, he was keen to get into the Pacific and take as many spoils as possible from the collapsing Japan. However, he framed Soviet participation in the war as fulfilling a pledge of assistance that he had made to the Americans years earlier. By this time, as Roosevelt and Leahy well knew, the US had no need for any Russian help to defeat the Japanese, and they had even talked about the war in the Pacific as being in its final phases. As Leahy said to the president when the issue was discussed, the Japanese "are already licked. We don't have to land in Japan, we don't have to do anything more to them."[32] Roosevelt used identical, if more diplomatic, language at Yalta, trying to downplay the need for any Soviet aid to end the war with Japan. He told Stalin that "he hoped it would not be necessary actually to invade the Japanese Islands" to end the war.[33] Stalin, however, had no desire to take the hint, and continued to press his offer of unneeded assistance. Hoisted on his own petard, Roosevelt could do nothing but gratefully accept Stalin's help through gritted teeth. Of course, Stalin had a definite price in mind. In the final agreements, it was stated that the USSR, in exchange for entering the war, would get the rest of Sakhalin, the Kuril Islands and control over the Chinese port of Dairen, as well as the railroad that stretched from the USSR to the port.[34]

If the issues of Germany and Japan were handled relatively amicably, it quickly became apparent that Poland would be a very different matter. The second plenary, on February 6, started with a discussion about the new United Nations. Both Stalin and Churchill seemed to understand how important it was to Roosevelt, even if they were less concerned with it themselves. Stalin even admitted to having been so busy that he had not had time to read the detailed outline of the UN structure produced at the conference at Dumbarton Oaks.[35] Then the fate of Poland was brought up, and the tension in the room increased.

The Polish problem for Stalin, Roosevelt and Churchill was in one way straightforward and in another basically intractable. There was agreement that Poland as a state would be re-created after the war, but that it would be re-created much further to the west. Roosevelt and Churchill had accepted that Stalin would keep the lands he had secured in his dirty deal with Hitler, and in exchange the new Poland would be given a large bit of what had been eastern Germany.* The political structure of this new Poland was an entirely different matter. Throughout the war, the US and the UK had recognized the pre-war Polish government in exile, sometimes referred to as the London government. Stalin, remembering his own military defeat at the hands of the pre-war Polish state, had moved immediately to install a new communist government called the Lublin Committee.[36]

The question of which Polish government would rule became the great, if at times softly spoken, confrontation of Yalta. When the issue first came up, Roosevelt gave what looks to be his longest address of the whole conference. Gathering what strength he had, and trying to appear his normal reasonable and charming self, he proposed the creation of a multi-party interim presidential council, with representatives of five different parties including the strongly pro-Soviet ones.[37] This body would rule Poland until new elections could be held. Churchill then piled in with his normal eloquence. He spoke even more forcefully for a free and independent Poland. "It is," Churchill said, "the earnest desire of the British Government that Poland be mistress in her own house and captain of her own soul."[38]

Stalin could not have cared less about Roosevelt's charm or Churchill's eloquence. By this point in the war, after his experiences at Tehran and during the percentages discussion with Churchill, Stalin had calculated that his supremacy in eastern Europe had been accepted by the Americans and British.[39] When he spoke he made it clear that the fate of Poland was one of "strategic security not only because Poland was a bordering country but because throughout history Poland had been the corridor for attack on Russia." Then Stalin stuck the knife in deep. He too wanted a democratic Poland—indeed he wanted it more than Churchill or Roosevelt. As far as he could see from Poland, the Lublin Poles were governing freely and efficiently, and moreover they were helping the Red Army keep its rear areas

---

* When Roosevelt first mentioned Poland, he did make an attempt to convince Stalin to leave Lviv in the re-created Polish state. The effort went nowhere and Roosevelt let it drop.

safe and patrolled. The London Poles, however, were threatening to end this harmony and create an insurgency behind Soviet lines. They were, in essence, doing Hitler's work. "When I compare what the agents of the Lublin government have done and what the agents of the London government have done I see the first are good and the second bad. We want tranquillity in our rear. We will support the government which gives us peace in our rear, and as a military man I could not do otherwise."[40]

Stalin had thrown down the gauntlet, and the discussion, even though it would go on for days longer, never changed. The Red Army was in Poland, Stalin commanded the Red Army, he wanted the Lublin government in power and would not countenance any influence from the pre-war Polish state. He had also put Roosevelt and Churchill in an almost impossible bind. They could either accept his terms, or in essence break the alliance. As he and they knew, there was nothing that could be done to force Stalin to change the composition of a Polish government.

Roosevelt, however, was determined to try. The next day when they returned to the question, he started by discarding the entire London government to appease Stalin. He was "not so concerned on the question of the continuity of the government. There really hasn't been any Polish government since 1939." Instead, let us create a new Polish government, he argued, "like a breath of fresh air."[41] Roosevelt had understood that the Lublin government was going to be powerful no matter what, and was proposing only to balance it by setting up a new commission, half made up of the Lublin government and half made up of other parties, to come and meet with the leaders and discuss establishing a new provisional government. Stalin, knowing that it would benefit him to act reasonably, did not dismiss Roosevelt out of hand, but pointed out that collecting that group would take time. He then stalled. On and on it went. Roosevelt even sent Stalin a private letter trying to arrange a deal. It would be a great help to him domestically, he pleaded, if he could tell the American people that Poland would have a multi-party, democratic government.[42]

Roosevelt was only speaking the truth. He very much did want some concession in order to make it easier for him to sell any Polish agreement to the American people. Even if he understood that Stalin was going to install a government basically of his own choosing and on his own terms, Stalin's inability to understand that Roosevelt had such political needs shows that his evolution as a strategist had only gone so far. He just could not believe that Roosevelt really needed to answer to any other authority—after all, Stalin had never needed to. As Stalin once said to Molotov, "Roosevelt refers to Congress. He thinks that I will believe that he is really afraid of it and therefore cannot agree to [our demands]. It's just that he doesn't want to and hides behind Congress. Nonsense! He is the military leader, the supreme commander-in-chief. Who dares to object to him? It is convenient for him to hide behind parliament. But he won't fool me."[43]

It was a sign of how close Stalin was to screwing everything up. If he had operated cannily since Hitler invaded, because his practical side had suppressed his paranoid side in a need to survive, as the war was ending and victory assured, the old Stalin was coming out. He couldn't understand that Roosevelt really did want some sign that Stalin could be flexible—to show the American people, but also to validate Roosevelt's view of his own importance. However, all Stalin could see was Roosevelt asking him to make a concession that Stalin did not want or have to make, and as such he basically stonewalled the president. Though Roosevelt would press him for the rest of the conference, in the end Stalin made only the most minor of concessions. He agreed to include language in the final communiqué that the Lublin government would be "broadened" to include democratic elements. This meant almost nothing, as Stalin had already stated that the Lublin government represented true democracy, with the unspoken point that capitalist states were not really democratic. After the conference, Stalin told Lavrentii Beria, his head of secret police, that he had not "moved one inch" in making this deal with Roosevelt.[44] This agreement on Poland was historic, as it also established the basic framework for Soviet rule of eastern Europe. Where the Red Army was ascendant and where Stalin said the USSR had a security interest, he could do what he wanted to make a government that suited his interests.

Roosevelt took this slight personally, but he just did not know what else to do.* He was too sick and too exhausted to keep up the fight. The person who understood that best was Leahy. At the start of the conference, worried that he could fully trust no one else, Roosevelt had named Leahy a member of both the plenary council and the military council, which meant that the admiral attended all the meetings of Yalta—including the small ones involving the Big Three and a handful of aides. When he asked Leahy to do this, Roosevelt had said, "Bill, I wish you would attend all these political meetings in order that we may have someone in whom I have full confidence who will remember everything that we have done."[45] Leahy thus witnessed the fight over Poland in its gory detail, spending almost every minute of the conference with the president. When Roosevelt could stand the fighting no longer and threw in the towel with Stalin, it was to Leahy that he admitted the truth. When Leahy commented that the language agreed on Poland basically allowed Stalin to do whatever he wanted, all Roosevelt could do was concede. He didn't have the strength for anything else—"I know it, Bill, but I'm too tired to fight any more."[46]†

* Churchill was actually slightly more hopeful at first than Roosevelt. When he returned to London he spoke as if there was a real possibility that Stalin would allow more pluralism into the Polish government. However, he soon realized that was not to be the case.

† In Leahy's published memoir he relayed a sanitized version of this statement, recording Roosevelt saying that it was "the best I can do for Poland." However he seems to have told the real version to a confidant at the time—the reporter Constantine Brown, who published it in his memoirs later.

Epilogue

The Strategists' War

By the end of the Yalta Conference, Joseph Stalin had to feel pleased. In fewer than four years his international position had transformed, and his own actions were responsible for much of the change. He had moved on from the self-created disaster of aiding Hitler in attacking his country, to now forcing the US president and the British prime minister to accept his domination of eastern Europe. Stalin was now lord and master of more territory than imperial Russia had ever controlled. In the process, he had used US and British aid to grow in strength, and to create the largest army in the world. It was the greatest example of why he went from the worst of the grand strategists up until 1941 to arguably the best by the time of Yalta.

Then, Stalin threatened to destroy everything he had accomplished. After Yalta, he began to drift away from even making a pretence of cooperation with the US and UK. His earlier strategic successes had come from an ability to practically react to a dynamic situation by tailoring his actions to suit the needs of his allies, particularly Roosevelt. He started to openly subjugate eastern Europe and not even pay lip service to the needs of Franklin Roosevelt or Winston Churchill.[1] Stalin even stopped treating Roosevelt with the consideration and tact he had almost always displayed. He deeply insulted the president by refusing to allow US officers into Poland to look after American POWs who had been liberated from the German camps.[2] Soon, Stalin would go even further. He accused Roosevelt, bizarrely, of planning to betray him by cutting a deal with Hitler.

This was about as insulting a charge as Stalin could have made towards the American president. In Roosevelt's mind, he had bent over backwards to reach out to Stalin, and so Stalin accusing him of the most heinous betrayal stung deeply. Finally, it seemed Roosevelt had had enough and his tone towards Stalin changed markedly in

March 1945.[3] His final telegrams to Stalin were the sternest and most forthright he would send during the entire war.★ He spoke of his "astonishment" that Stalin would think Roosevelt would betray him through making a separate peace.[4] In a long telegram about Poland, he basically accused Stalin of lying to him at Yalta and refusing to actually allow other elements into the Lublin committee: "I cannot reconcile this either with our agreement or our discussions."[5]

Winston Churchill was delighted with Roosevelt's firmer tone. He had quickly soured on Yalta, and pushed the president to make a "firm and blunt stand" alongside him against Stalin.[6] Things were shaping up for a confrontation. And then, on April 12, as Roosevelt was once again on vacation—this time at his compound in Warm Springs—the president complained of a headache, slumped back in his chair, and died. US policy was thus put in the hands of Harry Truman, who had no idea what Roosevelt had really wanted to achieve or how he had planned to achieve it. Over the coming three years, Truman would take this ignorance, combined with Stalin's return to strategic overreach and blundering, and in the process create the Cold War that Roosevelt had always been keen to avoid.

In some ways this instability in policy- and decision-making should come as no surprise to anyone who saw the grand strategists in action. By 1945 they had stamped the world with their personal visions, for good or for ill. They had determined, mostly, what their countries had to fight with, where they would fight, and, though it wasn't always clear, for what they were supposedly fighting.

In evaluating their behaviour as leaders it's best to start with consistently the two worst, Adolf Hitler and Benito Mussolini. Not only were they the worst as they selected grand strategies that led to catastrophic defeat and the planned and unplanned deaths of millions, but they actively made things worse for their nations' war efforts. Even though they might seem different, in many ways the strategic disasters

---

★ By this point in the war, Leahy, as Roosevelt's chief of staff, was writing or at least approving all the telegrams that were going out under Roosevelt's name. This often made the telegrams more direct and less soothing, as Leahy was much blunter in his assessment of Stalin's aims.

they unleashed came from very similar impulses. Both dictators had come out of World War I determined to transform their respective nations into great empires, and believed that their personal genius would be a key element in that transformation. Both created deeply flawed war machines. Hitler the World War I infantry soldier, with a love of heavy weaponry, and Mussolini the soldier-propagandist, who stressed will and commitment over materiel, created their armies without enough mobility. Both also preferred to see their enemies as they wanted to see them and not as they were, and believed that their personal intervention and "will" would help achieve victory. This trait left them both struggling to adapt to the dynamic part of strategy-making, as they clung to their earlier preconceptions rather than adjusting to what their enemies were doing. From Hitler's starting a war he did not expect, to Mussolini's joining a war he had misjudged, the two transformed what might have been a continent-dominating alliance into a worldwide catastrophe. In 1940, Hitler's farcical handling of the Battle of Britain was outdone by Mussolini's farcical invasion of Greece. Then in 1941 they both, with their eyes very wide open, not only started (or in Mussolini's case joined) a war against the USSR based on the hope of swift Soviet collapse; they also prepared for a war with the US with no idea of what they were unleashing. From that point onwards, all they could do was try to slow down their inevitable defeat. Yet they almost certainly hastened it. From directly intervening on the battlefield, to wasting money building inappropriate weaponry, to living in dream worlds where everything was going to be all right, Hitler and Mussolini are a textbook case of how leaders should not, but sadly do too often, behave.

The victors in the war—Roosevelt, Stalin and Churchill—were much better as grand strategists, even with their evident flaws. In many ways Churchill was the most tragic. If anyone could be said to have had a definite end in mind for the war, it was Churchill. The continuing existence of the British Empire, which had been the focus of his military experiences in India, Sudan and South Africa, remained the strategic goal of all of Churchill's policies. As such it was vital to him that Great Britain remain amongst the leading powers of the world, and during World War II he did everything possible to ensure this. He helped craft a large and powerful air-sea force and worked closely with an even stronger US ally. However, he completely lost the fight after 1943 when Roosevelt and Stalin stomped on his strategic vision and forced him to support a cross-Channel invasion. The irony for all of this is that, while Churchill's great fears about what a large land war in Europe would mean ended up overblown, his intended ends were overtaken by the tides of history. British casualties in European fighting in 1944 and 1945 were not crippling, and British equipment losses were manageable, but the empire broke apart regardless. A few months after Yalta, in a stinging rebuke to Churchill, the British people opted for a socialist Labour government over his Conservatives. And the empire itself was never going to be held. India, which Churchill had always seen as the crux of empire and where he had first seen war as a young man in 1897, would become independent by 1947. Churchill could fulminate and mourn the changes, but there was nothing he could do to stop them.

Roosevelt and Stalin were different. Roosevelt was probably the greatest success of all the grand strategists in the ways and means of modern war. With his World War I experience of mass industrial war, combined with his fine political nose for the concerns of the American electorate, he constructed an awesome war-fighting force, based overwhelmingly on machines and a relatively small number of combat forces. His forces crushed the economic life out of the Axis with air-sea power, while at the same time allowing him to provide massive aid to both the UK and the USSR. This method of war-fighting was also remarkably humane for his fellow citizens. The United States lost just over 400,000 military personnel in the war, a remarkably low number in comparison to the size of the population and the casualties suffered by most other countries.[7]*

If Roosevelt succeeded in these parts of the war, the ends he had in

---

* The Soviet Union lost approximately 10 million military personnel in the war, the Germans 5.5 million, and the United Kingdom 384,000 (and the British population was about one-third of the US). The relatively small number of US and UK military deaths speaks to the more modern, machine-oriented way that they waged war, which was discussed in Chapter 17.

mind still remain difficult to ascertain. He certainly wanted to establish a cooperative relationship with his fellow Allied leaders, including Stalin, that he expected would endure after the war ended. Yet the fundamentals of that cooperative relationship were in many ways based on his personal charm and existence. There was no plan to put them in place without Franklin Roosevelt, and when he died his aims died along with him.

Stalin's success and failures are so stark that they do make him stand out. He displayed both sides of his nature as a strategist—sides that had come to the fore from the Russian Revolution through the end of the war with Poland. In the first two years of World War II he came close to destroying his own regime and rule. He helped unleash Hitler on the continent, and continued to feed and water the Nazi war machine up until the moment Hitler turned around and attacked him. Yet when faced with possible destruction he adapted, unlike Hitler. He cultivated new allies, exploited them for their massive resources, and learned when his interference in the Soviet war effort could be counterproductive as well as productive. The result of his evolution can be seen in the extreme recovery in the Soviet position between 1942 and 1945.

Ultimately, Stalin remained the same hyper-suspicious strategist he revealed himself to be at Tsaritsyn in 1918, however. Once the crisis passed and he felt more secure, he dropped his cooperative restraint and took policy stances that drove an increasing wedge between himself and Roosevelt, and then Truman. Stalin squandered what could have been one of the great victories of World War II—the permanent anchoring of the USSR as part of the dominant grouping of states. His paranoia would help break up the wartime alliance, eventually launch a Cold War that the USSR could never sustain, and see the break-up of his empire decades later. In that way, it might be fair to term him the worst-best-worst grand strategist of the war.

In the end, what does the overall experience of the grand strategists of World War II tell us in general about the making of strategy? First, it reveals that being a grand strategist in war is a dangerous job—certainly more dangerous than being a front-line soldier in many branches of the armed services. By the end of the war, three of the five were dead: Hitler by suicide, Mussolini gunned down on a street corner and Roosevelt whose body failed after all his exertions. Even the two survivors, Churchill and Stalin, had aged greatly because of the stress of war leadership. Neither was the same forceful figure after the war that he had been when it started.

This high death toll also reveals another lesson: grand strategy in World War II was far more personal than we might believe. Though these five men were supposedly parts within large, well-staffed states with layers of bureaucracy, they individually made the crucial choices over strategy and most of the time were able to see those choices enacted. As such, the idea of there being a clear and logical national strategy remains a positivist dream but an actual myth.

That is important. If we are going to be honest about national behaviour—then, now and in the future—we have to try to understand the minds of the individual leaders who make the crucial choices. Though we use phrases like "national interest" or "greater good," these are abstract concepts in grand-strategy-making. Hitler, Stalin, Mussolini, Churchill and Roosevelt had very personal notions of what national interest was; in some cases, notions that led to the lives of their fellow citizens being made far worse. All of them also believed that they were personally indispensable in terms of making their countries greater, and all imposed their own visions on their states during the course of the war. As such, they regularly acted like their personal views of the world were in the national interest of their countries, when they were decidedly not.

If we want to understand strategy, we must also understand the strategist.

Select Bibliography

I would like to start with a brief apology to all the authors whose books are not on this list. This bibliography includes only books or articles which ended up in the notes. In the process of keeping the book manageable, much ended up being cut, and many books which I've enjoyed and found fascinating will not be listed here. The same goes for published primary and archival sources.

Archival and Governmental Papers (non-published sources)

UK

Admiralty Papers (ADM), UK National Archives, London
Cabinet Papers (CAB), UK National Archives, London
Winston Churchill Mss, Chartwell papers, Churchill Archives Online (Char)
Ministry of Munitions Records (MUN), UK National Archives, London
Prime Minister's Papers (PREM), UK National Archives, London
Templewood Mss (Samuel Hoare), Cambridge University Library
War Office Papers (WAR), UK National Archives, London

USA

Harry Hopkins Papers, Franklin Roosevelt Presidential Library, Hyde Park, NY
Joint Chiefs of Staff, Minutes and Papers (USA), NARA, US National Archives, College Park, MD
Ernest King Papers, Library of Congress, Washington, DC
William Leahy Diary, Library of Congress, Washington, DC
William Leahy Papers, Naval History and Heritage Command, Washington, DC

Franklin Roosevelt Mss, FDR Presidential Library, Hyde Park, NY; and online through FDR Presidential Files, accessed through https://www.fdrlibrary.org/

United States Strategic Bombing Survey Mss (USSBS), Washington, DC

War Department Papers (WO) (USA), NARA, US National Archives, College Park, MD

Published Memoirs, Diaries, Documents; Books and Articles

Addison, Paul, "The Political Beliefs of Winston Churchill," *Transactions of the Royal Historical Society*, Vol. 30 (1980)

Allard, Dean, "Anglo-American Naval Differences During World War I," *Military Affairs*, Vol. 44, No. 2 (April 1980)

Allen, Keith, "Sharing Scarcity: Bread Rationing and the First World War in Berlin 1914–23," *Journal of Social History*, Vol. 32, No. 2 (Winter 1998)

Alliluyeva, Svetlana, *Only One Year* (London: Hutchinson, 1969)

American Battle Monuments Commission, "The Allied North Sea Mine Barrage of World War I," June 11, 2018.

Arielli, Nir, *Fascist Italy and the Middle East, 1933–40* (Basingstoke: Palgrave, 2010)

Baer, George, *One Hundred Years of Sea Power: The U.S. Navy, 1890–1990* (Stanford: Stanford University Press, 1994)

Beiriger, Eugene E., "Building a Navy 'Second to None': The U.S. Naval Act of 1916, American Attitudes toward Great Britain, and the First World War," *British Journal for Military History*, Vol. 3, No. 3 (2017)

Bekker, Cajus, *Hitler's Naval War* (London: Macdonald, 1974)

Bell, Christopher M., *Churchill and the Dardanelles* (Oxford: Oxford University Press, 2017)

——, *Churchill and Sea Power* (Oxford: Oxford University Press, 2013)

Below, Nicolaus von, *At Hitler's Side: The Memoirs of Hitler's Luftwaffe Adjutant* (London: Frontline Books, 2010)

Berezhkov, V. M., *Kak ia stal perevodchikom Stalina* (Moscow: DEM, 1993)

Best, Geoffrey, *Churchill: A Study in Greatness* (London: Hambledon and London, 2001)

Bol'shevistskoe rukovodstvo. Perepiska. 1912–1927. Sbornik dokumentov (Moscow: ROSSPEN, 1996)

Bosworth, R. J. B., *Claretta: Mussolini's Last Lover* (New Haven: Yale University Press, 2017)

——, *Mussolini* (London: Arnold, 2002)

——, *Mussolini and the Eclipse of Italian Fascism: From Dictatorship to Populism* (New Haven: Yale University Press, 2021)

Bottai, Giuseppe, *Diary 1935–1944* (Rome: BUR, 2006)

Brinkley, Alan, *Franklin Delano Roosevelt* (Oxford: Oxford University Press, 2010)

Broadberry, Stephen, and Mark Harrison (eds), *The Economics of World War I* (Cambridge: Cambridge University Press, 2005)

Brown, Constantine, *The Coming of the Whirlwind* (Chicago: Henry Regnery Company, 1964)

Buckley, Christopher, *Greece and Crete 1941* (London: HMSO, 1952)

Burgwyn, H. James, *Mussolini Warlord: Failed Dreams of Empire 1940–1943* (New York: Enigma Books, 2012)

Carley, Michael J., "End of the 'Low, Dishonest Decade': Failure of the Anglo-Franco-Soviet Alliance in 1939," *Europe-Asia Studies*, Vol. 45, No. 2 (1993)

Carr, John C., *The Defence and Fall of Greece: 1940–1941* (Barnsley: Pen and Sword, 2013)

Carruthers, Bob (ed.), *Hitler's Wartime Orders: The Complete Führer Directives: 1939–1945* (Barnsley: Pen and Sword, 2018)

Carter, Nick, *Modern Italy in Historical Perspective* (London: Bloomsbury, 2010)

Churchill, Randolph, *Winston S. Churchill*, Vol. 1 (London: Heinemann, 1966), and companion volumes.

Churchill, Winston, *My Early Life* (London: Eland, 1930)

——, *The River War: An Account of the Reconquest of the Sudan* (1902), https://www.gutenberg.org/files/4943/4943-h/4943-h.htm.

——, *The Second World War*, Vol. IV, (London: Cassell, 1951)

——, *The Story of the Malakand Field Force: An Episode of the Frontier War* (1898), https://www.gutenberg.org/files/9404/9404-h/9404-h.htm.

——, *The World Crisis*, 5 vols (London: Thornton Butterworth, 1923–31)

Ciano, Galeazzo, *The Ciano Diaries*, ed. Hugh Gibson, introduction by Sumner Welles (London: Simon and Schuster, 2001) (Ciano Diaries)

Citino, Robert M., *The Wehrmacht's Last Stand: The German Campaigns of 1944–1945* (Lawrence: University Press of Kansas, 2018)

Coker, Jeffrey, *Franklin Roosevelt: A Biography* (Westport: Greenwood Press, 2005)

Conquest, Robert, *Stalin: Breaker of Nations* (London: Weidenfeld and Nicolson, 1991)

Corner, Paul, *The Fascist Party and Popular Opinion in Mussolini's Italy* (Oxford: Oxford University Press, 2012)

Dallek, Robert, *Franklin D. Roosevelt: A Political Life* (London: Allen Lane, 2017)

——, *Franklin D. Roosevelt and American Foreign Policy* (Oxford: Oxford University Press, 1979)

Danchev, Alex, and Daniel Todman (eds), *War Diaries 1939–1945, Field Marshal Lord Alanbrooke* (London: Weidenfeld and Nicolson, 2001) (Alanbrooke Diaries)

Daniels, Josephus, *The Wilson Era: Years of Peace 1910–1917* (Chapel Hill: UNC Press, 1944)

——, *The Wilson Era: Years of War and After 1917–1923* (Chapel Hill: UNC Press, 1946)

Davies, Norman, *White Eagle, Red Star: The Polish–Soviet War of 1919–20* (London: Macdonald, 1972)

Djilas, Milovan, *Conversations with Stalin* (New York: Penguin, 1967)

Dockter, Warren, *Churchill and the Islamic World: Orientalism, Empire and Diplomacy in the Middle East* (London: IB Tauris, 2015)

Dokumenty o geroicheskoi oborone Tsaritsyna v 1918 godu (Moscow: Gospolitizdat, 1942)

Dolezalek, Alexander (ed.), *Moskau–Berlin–Streng geheim: Wie Stalin und Hitler Osteuropa unter sich aufteilten, 1939 bis 1941*, Vol. 6 (Lindhorst: Askania, 1989)

Domarus, Max (ed.), *Hitler: Speeches and Proclamations 1932–1945: The Chronicle of a Dictatorship*, 4 vols (Wauconda: Bolchazy-Carducci Publishers, 1990–2004)

Dulles, Foster Rhea, and Gerald Ridinger, "The Anti-Colonial Policies of Franklin D. Roosevelt," *Political Science Quarterly*, Vol. 70, No. 1 (1955)

Dunn, Walter S., *Hitler's Nemesis: The Red Army, 1930–1945* (Westport: Praeger, 1994)

Ebner, Michael, *Ordinary Violence in Mussolini's Italy* (Cambridge: Cambridge University Press, 2011)

Elizarov, M. A., "Vosstanie na forte 'Krasnaia gorka' v iune 1919. Pravda I legendy," *Morskoi sbornik*, Vol. 4 (2009)

Este, Carlo d', *Warlord: A Life of Churchill at War, 1874–1945* (London: Allen Lane, 2009)

Farrell, Nicholas, *Mussolini* (London: Weidenfeld and Nicolson, 2003)

Felice, Renzo De, *Mussolini il rivoluzionario* (Turin: Einaudi, 1965)

Fenby, Jonathan, *Alliance: The Inside Story of How Roosevelt, Stalin, and Churchill Won One War and Began Another* (London: Simon and Schuster, 2007)

Figes, Orlando, *A People's Tragedy: A History of the Russian Revolution* (New York: Penguin, 1998)

Flood, Charles B., "Lance Corporal Adolf Hitler on the Western Front 1914–1918," *The Kentucky Review*, Vol. 5, No. 3 (1985)

Foreign Relations of the United States (FRUS), various volumes; online copies at https://search.library.wisc.edu/digital/AFRUS.

Freidel, Frank, *Franklin Roosevelt: A Rendezvous with Destiny* (New York: Little, Brown, 1990)

Fritz, Stephen G., *The First Soldier: Hitler as Military Leader* (New Haven: Yale University Press, 2018)

Fuehrer Conferences on Naval Affairs, volumes for 1940–42 (UK Admiralty, 1947)

Ganin, A. V., "Arest I osvobozhdeniesotrudnikov shtaba Severokavkazkogo voennogo okruga v avguste 1918 g," *Zhurnal rossiiskikh I vostochnoevropeiskikh istorichskikh issledovanii*, Vol. 3, No. 10 (2010)

Gellately, Robert, *Stalin's Curse: Battling for Communism in War and Cold War* (Oxford: Oxford University Press, 2015)

Germany and the Second World War (Oxford: Oxford University Press), various volumes.

Gilbert, Martin, *Churchill and America* (New York: Simon and Schuster, 2005)

——, *Winston S. Churchill*, vols 3–8 (London: Heinemann, 1971–88)

——(ed.), *The Churchill War Papers*, 3 vols (London: Heinemann, 1993–2000)

Glantz, David M., *Kharkov 1942: Anatomy of a Military Disaster through Soviet Eyes* (Shepperton: Ian Allan, 1998)

Glei, Dana, Silvia Bruzzone and Graziella Caselli, "Effects of War Losses on Mortality Estimates for Italy: A First Attempt," *Demographic Research*, Vol. 13, No. 15 (November 2005)

Goeschel, Christian, *Mussolini and Hitler: The Forging of the Fascist Alliance* (New Haven: Yale University Press, 2018)

Gooch, John, *The Italian Army and the First World War* (Cambridge: Cambridge University Press, 2014)

——, *Mussolini's War: Fascist Italy from Triumph to Collapse 1935–1943* (London: Allen Lane, 2020)

Gorodetsky, Gabriel, *Grand Delusion: Stalin and the German Invasion of Russia* (New Haven: Yale University Press, 2001)

Greenberg, Joshua, " 'Comrades and Brothers': Churchill, Stalin and the Moscow Conference of 1942," International Churchill Society, September 24, 2019.

Gundle, Stephen et al. (eds), *The Cult of the Duce: Mussolini and the Italians* (Manchester: Manchester University Press, 2013)

Halder, Franz, *The Private War Journal of General Franz Halder 1939–1942*, 9 vols (Nuremberg: Office of the Chief Counsel for War Crimes, 1947) (Halder Diaries)

Harvey, A. D., "The Bomber Offensive that Never Took Off," *Air Power History*, Vol. 63, No. 3 (Fall 2016)

Hasegawa, Tsuyoshi, "Soviet Policy Towards Japan During World War II," *Cahiers du monde russe*, Vol. 52, No. 2/3 (2011)

Hastings, Max, *Finest Years: Churchill as Warlord 1940–45* (London: Harper Press, 2009)

Heiber, Helmut, David Glantz and Gerhard Weinberg (eds), *Hitler and His Generals: Military Conferences 1942–1945* (London: Enigma Books, 2004)

Hill, Alexander, *The Red Army and the Second World War* (Cambridge: Cambridge University Press, 2017)

Hitler, Adolf, *Mein Kampf* (Boston and New York: Mariner Books, 1999)

Holland, James, *The Battle of Britain: Five Months that Changed History, May–October 1940* (London: Bantam Press, 2010)

Isakov, I. S., *Krasnaia gorka. Stalinskaia operatsiia, 13–16 Iunia 1919* (Moscow: Voenizdat, 1946)

Iz istorii Grazhdanskoi voiny v SSSR. 1918–1922: Sbornik documentov i materialov. T.2. Mart 1919–Fevral' 1920 (Moscow: Sovetskaia Rossiia, 1961)

Jablonsky, David, *Churchill, the Great Game and Total War* (London: Frank Cass, 1991)

Jäckel, Eberhard, *Hitler's World View: A Blueprint for Power* (Cambridge: Harvard University Press, 1981)

—— and Axel Kuhn (eds), *Hitler Sämtliche Aufzeichnungen 1905–24* (Stuttgart: Deutsche Verlags-Anstalt, 1980)

Jackson, Ashley, *Churchill* (London: Quercus, 2011)

James, Robert Rhodes (ed.), *Winston S. Churchill: His Complete Speeches 1897–1963*, Vol. 1 (London: Chelsea House, 1974)

Jankowski, Paul, *Verdun: The Longest Battle of the Great War* (Oxford: Oxford University Press, 2014)

Kaiser, David, *No End Save Victory: How FDR Led the Nation into War* (New York: Basic Books, 2018)

Keegan, John, *The First World War: An Illustrated History* (London: Pimlico, 2002)

Kershaw, Ian, *Hitler 1889–1936: Hubris* (New York: W. W. Norton, 1999)

——, *Hitler 1936–1945: Nemesis* (New York: W. W. Norton, 2000)

Khlevniuk, Oleg V., *Stalin: New Biography of a Dictator* (New Haven: Yale University Press, 2015)

——, "Stalin at War: Sources and Their Interpretation," *Cahiers du monde russe*, Vol. 52, No. 2/3 (2011)

Khrushchev, N. S., *The Crimes of the Stalin Era: Special Report to the 20th Congress of the Communist Party of the Soviet Union* (New York: New Leader, 1956)

——, *Vremia, Liudi, Vlast' (Vospominania)*, Vol. 1 (Moscow: Moskovskie Novosti, 1999)

Kimball, Warren (ed.), *Churchill and Roosevelt: The Complete Correspondence*, 3 vols (Princeton: Princeton University Press, 1984)

Kitchen, Martin, *The German Offensives of 1918* (Stroud: Tempus, 2005)

——, *Speer: Hitler's Architect* (New Haven: Yale University Press, 2015)

Knight, Jonathan, "Churchill and the Approach to Mussolini and Hitler in May 1940: A Note," *British Journal of International Studies*, Vol. 3 (1997)

Knox, Dudley W., *A History of the United States Navy* (New York: G. P. Putnam's, 1948)

Kotkin, Stephen, *Stalin, Vol. 1: Paradoxes of Power 1878–1928* (New York: Penguin, 2015)

——, *Stalin, Vol. 2: Waiting for Hitler 1928–1941* (London: Penguin, 2017)

Kozlov, A., "Tsaritsynskii 'opyt,'" *Istoriki otvechaiut na voprosy*, Vol. 2 (Moscow: Moskovskii rabochii, 1990)

Kubizek, August, *The Young Hitler I Knew* (New York: Frontline Books, 2011)

Kumanev, G. A., *Govoriat stalinskie narkomy* (Smolensk: Rusich, 2005)

Kuzmin, N., "Ob odnoi nevypolnennoi directive Glavkoma (iz istorii Sovetsko-polskoi voiny 1920 goda)," *Voenno-istoricheskii zhurnal*, Vol. 9 (1962)

Lamb, Richard, *Mussolini and the British* (London: John Murray, 1997)

Laqueur, Walter, *Stalin: The Glasnost Revelations* (London: Unwin and Hyman, 1990)

Lautemann, W., and M. Schlenke (eds), *Geschichte in Quellen: Weltkriege und Revolutionen 1914–1945*, Vol. 5 (Munich: Bayerischer Schulbuch-Verlag, 1961)

Leahy, William, *I Was There: The Personal Story of the Chief of Staff to Presidents Roosevelt and Truman Based on His Notes and Diaries at the Time* (New York: McGraw-Hill, 1950)

Legran, B. V., *Stalin v Tsaritsyne*, Seriia "Revoliutsionnye memuary" (2019), https://www.litres.ru/book/boris-legran/stalin-v-caricyne-42348004/

Leutze, James, *Bargaining for Supremacy: Anglo-American Naval Cooperation 1937–1941* (Chapel Hill: UNC Press, 1978)

Levy, Herbert, *Henry Morgenthau Jr.: The Remarkable Life of FDR's Secretary of the Treasury* (New York: Skyhorse Publishing, 2010)

Lloyd, Nick, *Passchendaele: A New History* (London: Penguin, 2017)

Lloyd George, David, *War Memoirs of Lloyd George*, Vol. 1 (London: Odhams Press, 1938), https://archive.org/details/warmemoirsvolume035284mbp/page/n3/mode/2up.

Longerich, Peter, *Hitler: A Life* (Oxford: Oxford University Press, 2019)

Lumsden, Malvern, "New Military Technology and the Erosion of International Law: The Case of the Dum-Dum Bullets Today," *Instant Research on Peace and Violence*, Vol. 4, No. 1 (1974)

Lussu, Emilio, *A Soldier on the Southern Front: The Classic Italian Memoir of World War I* (New York: Rizzoli, 2014)

McBride, William, *Technological Change and the United States Navy 1865–1945* (Baltimore: Johns Hopkins University Press, 2000)

McDermott, Kevin, and Matthew Stibbe (eds), *Stalinist Terror in Eastern Europe: Elite Purges and Mass Repression* (Manchester: Manchester University Press, 2010)

Macdonald, John, and Zeljko Cimpric, *Caporetto and the Isonzo Campaign: The Italian Front 1915–1918* (Barnsley: Pen and Sword, 2011)

MacIsaac, David (ed.), *The Strategic Bombing Survey* (New York: Garland, 1976)

Maiskii, I. M., *Vospominania sovetskogo diplomata, 1925–1945 gg* (Uzbekistan: Tashkent, 1980)

Master, Werner (ed.), *Hitler: Letters and Notes* (New York: Harper and Row, 1974)

Mawdsley, Evan, *The Russian Civil War* (London: Birlinn, 2008)

——, *Thunder in the East: The Nazi–Soviet War 1941–1945* (London: Bloomsbury, 2015)

—— and John Ferris (eds), *The Cambridge History of the Second World War* (Cambridge: Cambridge University Press, 2015)

Megargee, Geoffrey, *Barbarossa 1941: Hitler's War of Annihilation* (Stroud: Tempus, 2007)

Meyer, Adolf, *Mit Adolf Hitler im Bayerischen Reserve-Infanterie-Regiment 16 List* (Neustadt-Aisch: Georg Aupperle, 1934)

Mikoyan, A. I., *Tak bylo* (Moscow: Vagrius, 1999)

Millard, Candice, *Hero of Empire: The Making of Winston Churchill* (London: Allen Lane, 2017)

Monelli, Paolo, *Mussolini piccolo Borghese* (Milan: Garzanti, 1950)

Montefiore, Simon Sebag, *Young Stalin* (New York: Alfred Knopf, 2007)

Morgan, Ted, *Churchill: Young Man in a Hurry, 1874–1915* (London: Triad, 1984)

——, *FDR: A Biography* (New York: Simon and Schuster, 1985)

Murphy, David E., *Breaking Point of the French Army: The Nivelle Offensive of 1917* (Barnsley: Pen and Sword, 2015)

——, *What Stalin Knew: The Enigma of Barbarossa* (New Haven: Yale University Press, 2005)

Murray, Williamson, *Strategy for Defeat: The Luftwaffe 1933–1945* (Alabama: Air University Press, 1983)

Mussolini, Benito, *Diary* (Milan: Imperia, 1923)

——, *My Autobiography* (Milan: Borodino Books, 2017)

Naimark, Norman, *Stalin's Genocides* (Princeton: Princeton University Press, 2010)

Nelis, Jan, "Fascist Identity: Benito Mussolini and the Myth of 'Romanita,'" *The Classical World*, Vol. 100, No. 4 (Summer 2007)

Neville, Peter, *Mussolini* (London: Routledge, 2015)

Nossovitch, A. L., *Krasnyi Tsaritsyn. Vzgliad iznutri* (Moscow: AIRO-XXI, 2010)

Oborona Tsaritsyna. Sbornik statei I dokumentov (Stalingrad: Kraevoe knigo-izdatel'stvo, 1937)

O'Brien, Paul, *Mussolini in the First World War: The Journalist, the Soldier, the Fascist* (Oxford: Berg, 2005)

O'Brien, Phillips, *British and American Naval Power: Politics and Policy 1900–1936* (Westport: Praeger, 1998)

——, *How the War Was Won: Air–Sea Power and Allied Victory* (Cambridge: Cambridge University Press, 2015)

——, *The Second Most Powerful Man in the World* (New York: Dutton, 2019)

Offer, Avner, *The First World War: An Agrarian Interpretation* (Oxford: Clarendon Press, 1989)

Pakenham, Thomas, *The Boer War* (London: Weidenfeld and Nicolson, 1979)

Pechatnov, V. O., "Stalin, Roosevelt, Churchill: 'Bol'shaia Troika' cherez prizmu perepiski voennykj let,'" *Vestnik MGIMO Universiteta*, Vol. 5 (2009)

Petacci, Claretta, *Verso il disastro: Mussolini in guerra: diari 1939–1940*, ed. Mimmo Franzinelli (Milan: Rizzoli, 2011)

Pipes, Richard, *The Russian Revolution* (New York: Alfred Knopf, 1990)

Pitt, Barrie, *The Crucible of War: Western Desert 1941* (London: Jonathan Cape, 1980)

Plokhy, S. M., *Yalta: The Price of Peace* (New York: Penguin, 2010)

Pollock, John, *Kitchener: The Road to Omdurman* (London: Constable, 1998)

Radzinsky, Edward, *Stalin* (London: Hodder and Stoughton, 1996)

Raghavan, Srinath, *India's War: The Making of Modern South Asia 1939–1945* (London: Allen Lane, 2016)

Resis, Albert, "The Churchill-Stalin Secret 'Percentages' Agreement on the Balkans, Moscow, October 1944," *American Historical Review*, Vol. 83, No. 2 (April 1978)

—— (ed.), *Molotov Remembers: Inside Kremlin Politics, Conversations with Felix Chuev* (Chicago: Ivan R. Dee Publishers, 1993)

Reynolds, David, and Vladimir Pechatnov (eds), *The Kremlin Letters: Stalin's Wartime Correspondence with Churchill and Roosevelt* (New Haven: Yale University Press, 2018)

Ridley, Jasper, *Mussolini* (London: Constable, 1997)

Rieber, Alfred, *Stalin and the Struggle for Supremacy in Eurasia* (Cambridge: Cambridge University Press, 2015)

Romanych, Marc, and Martin Rupp, *42cm "Big Bertha" and German Siege Artillery of World War I* (London: Bloomsbury, 2014)

Roosevelt, Elliott, *As He Saw It* (New York: Duell, Sloan and Pierce, 1946)

—— (ed.), *FDR: His Personal Letters* (New York: Duell, Sloan and Pierce, 1947)

Rose, Kenneth D., *The Great War and Americans in Europe, 1914–1917* (New York: Routledge, 2017)

Roskill, Stephen, *The War at Sea*, 4 vols (London: HMSO, 1954–61)

Russell, Douglas S., *Winston Churchill, Soldier: The Military Life of a Gentleman at War* (London: Conway, 2006)

Sadkovich, James, "The Italo-Greek War in Context: Italian Priorities and Axis Diplomacy," *Journal of Contemporary History*, Vol. 28, No. 3 (July 1993)

——, "Understanding Defeat: Reappraising Italy's Role in World War II," *Journal of Contemporary History*, Vol. 24, No. 1 (January 1989)

Scala, Spencer Di, and Emilio Gentile (eds), *Mussolini 1883–1915* (New York: Palgrave Macmillan, 2016)

Schindler, John R., *Isonzo: The Forgotten Sacrifice of the Great War* (Westport: Praeger, 2001)

Schmider, Klaus H., *Hitler's Fatal Miscalculation: Why Germany Declared War on the United States* (Cambridge: Cambridge University Press, 2021)

Schneider, James S., *The Structure of Strategic Revolution: Total War and the Roots of the Soviet Warfare State* (Novato: Presidio Press, 1994)

Schroeder, Christa, *He Was My Chief: The Memoirs of Adolf Hitler's Secretary* (Barnsley: Frontline Books, 2012)

Sherwood, Robert E., *Roosevelt and Hopkins: An Intimate History* (New York: The Universal Library, 1948)

——, *The White House Papers of Harry L. Hopkins* (London: Eyre and Spottiswoode, 1948)

Shtemenko, S. M., *General'nyi Shtab v gody voiny* (Moscow: Voenizdat, 1968)

Sica, Emanuele, "June 1940: The Italian Army and the Battle of the Alps," *Canadian Journal of History*, Vol. 47, No. 2 (2012)

Simms, Brendan, *Hitler: Only the World Was Enough* (London: Allen Lane, 2019)

Simonov, K., *GlaSami cheloveka moego pokoleniia: Razmyshleniia o I. V. Staline.* (Moscow: Kniga, 1990)

Smith, Denis Mack, *Modern Italy: A Political History* (New Haven: Yale University Press, 1997)

——, *Mussolini: A Biography* (New York: Alfred Knopf, 1982)

Andrei Evgen'evich Snesarev. Zhizn' i nauchnaia deiatel'nost' (Moscow: Nauka, 1973)

Snyder, Timothy, *Bloodlands: Europe Between Hitler and Stalin* (London: The Bodley Head, 2011)

—— and Ray Brandon (eds), *Stalin and Europe: Imitation and Domination 1928–1953* (Oxford: Oxford University Press, 2014)

Speer, Albert, *Inside the Third Reich* (London: Weidenfeld and Nicolson, 2009)

Spiers, Edward M., *Engines for Empire: The Victorian Military and Its Use of Railways* (Manchester: Manchester University Press, 2015)

——, *Sudan: The Reconquest Reappraised* (London: Frank Cass, 1998)

Spring, D. W., "The Soviet Decision for War against Finland, 20 November 1939," *Soviet Studies*, Vol. 38, No. 2 (April 1986)

Stahel, David, *The Battle for Moscow* (Cambridge: Cambridge University Press, 2015)

——, *Operation Barbarossa and Hitler's Defeat in the East* (Cambridge: Cambridge University Press, 2013)

——, *Retreat from Moscow: A New History of Germany's Winter Campaign, 1941–1942* (New York: Picador, 2019)

Stalin, Joseph, *Anarchism or Socialism?* (1906–7), https://www.marxists.org/reference/archive/stalin/works/1906/12/x01.htm.

——, *Sochineniia*, Vol. 14 (Moscow: Izdatel'stvo "Pisatel," 1997)

——, *Sochineniia*, Vol. 17 (Tver: Nauchno-izdatel'skaia kompaniia "Severnaia korona," 2004)

Stefan, Charles G., "Yalta Revisited: An Update on the Diplomacy of FDR and His Wartime Summit Partners," *Presidential Studies Quarterly*, Vol. 23, No. 4 (Fall 1993)

Stone, David, *Twilight of the Gods: The Decline and Fall of the German General Staff in World War II* (London: Conway, 2011)

Strachan, Hew, *The First World War*, Vol. 1 (Oxford: Oxford University Press, 2001)

Stratigakos, Despina, *Hitler at Home* (New Haven: Yale University Press, 2015)

Sumida, Jon Tetsuro, *Inventing Grand Strategy and Teaching Command: The Classic Works of Alfred Thayer Mahan Reconsidered* (Baltimore: Johns Hopkins University Press, 1997)

Susmel, Edoardo and Duilio (eds), *Opera omnia di Benito Mussolini*, 44 vols (Florence, Rome: La Fenice, 1951–80)

Terraine, John, *The U-Boat Wars, 1916–1945* (New York: Henry Holt, 1989)

Thompson, Mark, *The White War: Life and Death on the Italian Front, 1915–1919* (London: Faber and Faber, 2009)

Tolstoy, Nikolai, *Stalin's Secret War* (London: Jonathan Cape, 1981)

Toniolo, Giovanni (ed.), *The Oxford Handbook of the Italian Economy Since Unification* (Oxford: Oxford University Press, 2013)

Toye, Richard, *Churchill's Empire: The World That Made Him and the World He Made* (London: Pan Books, 2010)

——, "'The Riddle of the Frontier': Winston Churchill, the Malakand Field Force and the Rhetoric of Imperial Expansion," *Historical Research*, Vol. 84, No. 225 (2011)

Trevor-Roper, Hugh, *Hitler's Table Talk, 1941–1944* (New York: Enigma Books, 2000)

Trotsky, Leon, *My Life* (1930), https://www.marxists.org/archive/trotsky/1930/mylife/

Tucker, Robert, *Stalin in Power* (New York: W. W. Norton, 1992)

——, *Stalin as Revolutionary* (New York: W. W. Norton, 1992)

Ulam, Adam, *Stalin, the Man and his Era* (London: IB Tauris, 1989)

Ullrich, Volker, *Hitler: Ascent 1889–1939* (London: The Bodley Head, 2016)

——, *Hitler: Downfall 1939–1945* (London: Vintage, 2020)

Vale, J. A., and J. W. Scadding, "In Carthage Ruins: The Illness of Sir Winston Churchill at Carthage, December 1943," *Journal of the Royal College of Physicians, Edinburgh*, Vol. 47 (2017)

Vassilevskii, A. M., *Delo Vsei Zhizni* (Moscow: Politizdat, 1978)

Vlasik, N. A., "Vospominaniia o I. V. Staline," *Istoricheskii vestnik*, Vol. 5, No. 152 (2013)

Watt, Donald C., "Britain and the Historiography of the Yalta Conference and the Cold War," *Diplomatic History*, Vol. 13, No. 1 (Winter 1989)

Weber, Thomas, *Becoming Hitler: The Making of a Nazi* (Oxford: Oxford University Press, 2017)

——, *Hitler's First War: Adolf Hitler, the List Regiment and the First World War* (Oxford: Oxford University Press, 2010)

Weinberg, Gerhard, "Hitler's Image of the United States," *American Historical Review*, Vol. 69, No. 4 (July 1964)

——, "The Nazi–Soviet Pacts: A Half-Century Later," *Foreign Affairs*, Vol. 68, No. 4 (Fall 1989)

—— (ed.), *Hitler's Second Book: The Unpublished Sequel to Mein Kampf* (New York: Enigma Books, 2006)

Wheatcroft, Geoffrey, *Churchill's Shadow: An Astonishing Life and a Dangerous Legacy* (London: The Bodley Head, 2021)

Whitewood, Peter, *The Red Army and the Great Terror: Stalin's Purge of the Soviet Military* (Lawrence: University Press of Kansas, 2015)

Wilcox, Vanda, *Morale and the Italian Army during the First World War* (Cambridge: Cambridge University Press, 2016)

Wilson, A. N., *Hitler: A Short Biography* (London: Harper Press, 2012)

Woolner, David B., *The Last 100 Days: FDR at War and Peace* (New York: Basic Books, 2019)

Zhilin, V. A. et al (eds), *Bitva pod Moskvoi: Khronika, fakty, liudi,* 2 vols (Moscow: Ol'ma Press, 2002)

Zhukov, G. K., *Vospominania i razmyshleniia*, Vol. 3 (Moscow: Izdatel'stvo Agenstva Pechati Novosti, 1986)

Notes

Introduction: Strategy, War and Personality

1 Hugh Trevor-Roper, *Hitler's Table Talk, 1941–1944* (New York: Enigma Books, 2000), p. 94.
2 Ibid.
3 Ibid., p. 634.
4 Phillips O'Brien, *How the War Was Won: Air-Sea Power and Allied Victory* (Cambridge: Cambridge University Press, 2015), pp. 197–215.

1. Winston Churchill: The Making of an Imperial Strategist

1 Winston Churchill, *The Story of the Malakand Field Force: An Episode of the Frontier War*, Chapter 1. This book was first published in 1898. There is a copy online through Gutenberg which is accessible at: https://www.gutenberg.org/files/9404/9404-h/9404-h.htm.
2 Ibid., Chapter 3.
3 Churchill to Barnes, September 14, 1897, in Randolph Churchill, *Winston S. Churchill*, Vol. 1 (London: Heinemann, 1966), Companion Vol. 2, pp. 786–7. From here on, these source volumes will be labelled *WSC*.
4 Carlo d'Este, *Warlord: A Life of Churchill at War, 1874–1945* (London: Allen Lane, 2009), p. 77.
5 Churchill to Duchess of Marlborough, October 25, 1897, *WSC*, Vol. 1, Companion 2, pp. 809–10.
6 Churchill to Mother, October 2, 1897, *WSC*, Vol. 1, Companion 2, pp. 796–7.
7 Churchill, *The Story of the Malakand Field Force*, Chapter 17.
8 Malvern Lumsden, "New Military Technology and the Erosion of International Law: The Case of the Dum-Dum Bullets Today," *Instant Research on Peace and Violence*, Vol. 4, No. 1 (1974), p. 17.

9 Winston Churchill, *My Early Life* (London: Eland, 1930). This is from the Apple Books copy I have, Chapter XI.

10 Churchill, *The Story of the Malakand Field Force*, Chapter 12.

11 Churchill, *My Early Life*, Chapter XI.

12 Churchill to Mother, January 19, 1898, *WSC*, Vol. 1, Companion 2, pp. 859–60.

13 Richard Toye has produced a number of superb works on Churchill over his career, and one article in particular shows how he was not as sceptical about the Forward Policy as some have claimed. Richard Toye, "'The Riddle of the Frontier': Winston Churchill, the Malakand Field Force and the Rhetoric of Imperial Expansion," *Historical Research* Vol. 84, No. 225, Nov. 2011, pp. 494, 499, 508. See also Toye, *Churchill's Empire: The World That Made Him and the World He Made* (London: Pan Books, 2010), pp. 42–5. For the best challenge to some of Toye's ideas see Warren Dockter, *Churchill and the Islamic World: Orientalism, Empire and Diplomacy in the Middle East* (London: I. B. Tauris, 2015), p. 29.

14 *WSC*, Vol. 1, Companion 1, p. 43.

15 *WSC*, Vol. 1, p. 189.

16 Ibid., p. 196.

17 Ibid., p. 242.

18 Churchill, *My Early Life*, Chapter VI.

19 Churchill to Duchess of Marlborough, October 25, 1897, *WSC*, Vol. 1, Companion 2, pp. 809–10.

20 Candice Millard, *Hero of Empire: The Making of Winston Churchill* (London: Allen Lane, 2017), p. 9.

21 *WSC*, Vol. 1, pp. 266–7.

22 Churchill, *My Early Life*, Chapter VI.

23 Ibid.

24 *WSC*, Vol. 1, Companion 1, p. 603.

25 Ibid., p. 617.

26 Churchill, *My Early Life*, Chapter VI.

27 Ibid.

28 *WSC*, Vol. 1, p. 279.

29 *WSC*, Vol. 1, Companion 1, p. 617.

30 *WSC*, Vol. 1, p. 278.

31 Churchill, *My Early Life*, Chapter VIII.

32 *WSC*, Vol. 1, Companion 2, p. 774.

33 Robert Rhodes James (ed.), *Winston S. Churchill: His Complete Speeches 1897–1963*, Vol. 1 (London: Chelsea House, 1974), p. 25; Churchill to Mother, December 22, 1897, in *WSC*, Vol. 1, Companion 2, p. 839.

34 James, *Winston S. Churchill: His Complete Speeches*, p. 30.

35 Churchill, *My Early Life*, Chapter IX.

36 Churchill to Brother, December 2, 1897, *WSC*, Vol. 1, Companion 2, pp. 835–6.

37 James, *Winston S. Churchill: His Complete Speeches*, p. 25; Churchill to Mother, December 22, 1897, in *WSC*, Vol. 1, Companion 2, p. 839.

38 Martin Gilbert, *Churchill and America* (New York: Simon and Schuster, 2005), p. xxiv.

39 Churchill to Mother, May 22, 1898, *WSC*, Vol. 1, Companion 2, p. 937. Churchill was most upset at the United States at this time because he felt the US was being too aggressive against Spain over Cuba.

40 Churchill to Mother, March 2, 1899, *WSC*, Vol. 1, Companion 2, p. 1013.

41 Geoffrey Best, *Churchill: A Study in Greatness* (London: Hambledon and London, 2001), p. 12.

42 Churchill to Mother, October 25, 1897, *WSC*, Vol. 1, Companion 2, p. 937.

43 Churchill, *My Early Life*, Chapter XIII.

44 Edward M. Spiers, *Engines for Empire: The Victorian Military and Its Use of Railways* (Manchester: Manchester University Press, 2015). Chapter 6 tells the whole story of the construction of this vital strategic route through some of the most inhospitable terrain on earth.

45 Churchill wrote a very dramatic history of his experiences and the Battle of Omdurman itself, and published it very quickly after the war was over. See Winston Churchill, *The River War: An Account of the Reconquest of the Sudan*. There is a copy of the 1902 version available online at https://www.gutenberg.org/files/4943/4943-h/4943-h.htm.

46 Churchill, *My Early Life*, Chapter XV.

47 John Pollock, *Kitchener: The Road to Omdurman* (London: Constable, 1998), p. 131.

48 Toye, *Churchill's Empire*, p. 57.

49 Churchill, *The River War*, Chapter XV.

50 Churchill to Mother, September 4, 1898, *WSC*, Vol. 1, Companion 2, p. 973.

51 David Jablonsky, *Churchill, the Great Game and Total War* (London: Frank Cass, 1991), p. 37.

52 Edward M. Spiers, *Sudan: The Reconquest Reappraised* (London: Frank Cass, 1998), p. 71.

53 Churchill to Mother, September 17, 1898, *WSC*, Vol. 1, Companion 2, p. 980.

54 Ted Morgan, *Churchill: Young Man in a Hurry, 1874–1915* (London: Triad, 1984), p. 95.

55 Toye, *Churchill's Empire*, pp. 63–4.

56 Address to the electors of Oldham, June 24, 1899, *WSC*, Vol. 1, Companion 2, p. 1032.

57 Chartwell papers, Churchill Archives Online, Char 1/19, November 1897, Churchill article draft, "Our Account with the Boers."

58 Toye, *Churchill's Empire*, p. 65.

59 Letter to Mother, October 25, 1899, *WSC*, Vol. 1, Companion 2, p. 1056.

60 Thomas Pakenham, *The Boer War* (London: Weidenfeld and Nicolson, 1979), pp. 246–9.

61 Churchill, published letter to *Natal Witness*, March 29, 1900, *WSC*, Vol. 1, Companion 2, p. 1163.

62 Churchill to unknown, March 22, 1900, *WSC*, Vol. 1, Companion 2, p. 1160.

63 Churchill to Mother, May 16, 1898, *WSC*, Vol. 1, Companion 2, pp. 931–2.

64 National Churchill Museum, "Winston Churchill, The Glow Worm," https://www.nationalchurchillmuseum.org/winston-churchill-leadership-the-glow-worm.html.

65 Churchill, *My Early Life*, Chapter X.

2. Joseph Stalin: The Making of an Ideological Strategist

1 Robert Tucker, *Stalin as Revolutionary* (New York: W. W. Norton, 1992), p. 159.

2 Adam Ulam, *Stalin, the Man and his Era* (London: IB Tauris, 1989), pp. 19–20.

3 Svetlana Alliluyeva, *Only One Year* (London: Hutchinson, 1969), p. 340.

4 Stephen Kotkin, *Stalin, Vol. 1: Paradoxes of power 1878–1928* (New York: Penguin, 2015) pp. 36–7.

5 For a copy of Joseph Stalin, *Anarchism or Socialism?* (1906–7) see https://www.marxists.org/reference/archive/stalin/works/1906/12/x01.htm.

6 Alfred Rieber, *Stalin and the Struggle for Supremacy in Eurasia* (Cambridge: Cambridge University Press, 2015), p. 11.

7 Kotkin, *Stalin, Vol. 1*, p. 123.

8 Simon Sebag Montefiore, *Young Stalin* (New York: Alfred Knopf, 2007), p. 180.

9 Ibid., p. 131.

10 Leon Trotsky, *My Life* (1930), Chapter 28. Online copy accessible at: https://www.marxists.org/archive/trotsky/1930/mylife/ch28.htm; https://www.nybooks.com/articles/2007/11/08/rise-of-a-gangster/

11 Trotsky, *My Life*, Chapter 24 https://www.marxists.org/archive/trotsky/1930/mylife/ch24.htm.

12 Richard Pipes, *The Russian Revolution* (New York: Alfred Knopf, 1990), p. 388.

13 Stalin, "The War," *Pravda*, March 16, 1917. Online copy accessible at: https://www.marxists.org/reference/archive/stalin/works/1917/03/16.htm.

14 Tucker, *Stalin as Revolutionary*, p. 168.

15 Oleg V. Khlevniuk, *Stalin: New Biography of a Dictator* (New Haven: Yale University Press, 2015), p. 46.

16 Tucker, *Stalin as Revolutionary*, p. 170.

17 Ibid., pp. 173–4.

18 Stalin, "The Counterrevolution is Mobilizing," October 10, 1917. Online copy accessible at: https://www.marxists.org/reference/archive/stalin/works/1917/10/10.htm.

19 Kotkin, *Stalin, Vol. 1*, pp. 224–5.

20 Stalin, "What Do We Need?," October 24, 1917. Online copy accessible at: https://www.marxists.org/reference/archive/stalin/works/1917/10/24.htm.

21 Kotkin, *Stalin, Vol. 1*, p. 226.

22 Tucker, *Stalin as Revolutionary*, p. 178.

23 Orlando Figes, *A People's Tragedy: The Russian Revolution* (New York: Penguin, 1998), p. 548.

24 Stalin, "Either—Or," August 25, 1917. Online copy accessible at: https://www.marxists.org/reference/archive/stalin/works/1917/08/25-2.htm.

25 Stalin to Lenin, June 7, 1918. Online copy accessible at: https://www.marxists.org/reference/archive/stalin/works/1918/06/07.htm.

26 Legran, *Stalin v Tsaritsyne*, Seriia "Revoliutsionnye memuary," 2019, https://www.litres.ru/book/boris-legran/stalin-v-caricyne-42348004/, p. 87.

27 Ibid.

28 Kotkin, *Stalin, Vol. 1*, p. 302.

29 Legran, *Stalin v Tsaritsyne*, p. 87.

30 A. L. Nossovitch, *Krasnyi Tsaritsyn. Vzgliad iznutri* (Moscow: AIRO-XXI, 2010), p. 27.

31 Kotkin, *Stalin, Vol. 1*, p. 304.

32 Khlevniuk, *Stalin: New Biography*, p. 57.

33 It now seems more than likely that Alekseev was guilty of spying for the Whites, though the evidence for that would have been unknown to Stalin. For more on that, see A. V. Ganin, "Arest I osvobozhdenie-sotrudnikov shtaba Severo-kavkazkogo voennogo okruga v avguste 1918 g," *Zhurnal rossiiskikh I vostochnoevropeiskikh istorichskikh issledovanii* Vol. 3, No. 10 (2010), pp. 32–51.

34 Nossovitch, *Krasnyi Tsaritsyn. Vzgliad iznutri*, p. 28.

35 Kotkin, *Stalin, Vol. 1*, p. 306.

36 Khlevniuk, *Stalin: New Biography*, p. 58.

37 Lenin's Speech at the Closed Session of the VIII Congress of the R.C.P.(b), March 21, 1919, *Izvestiia TsK KPSS*, Vol. 11 (1989), p. 168.

38 S. M. Budennyi, "Slovo o starshem druge," in *Andrei Evgen'evich Snesarev. Zhizn' i nauchnaia deiatel'nost'* (Moscow: Nauka, 1973), pp. 5–9.

39 Stalin to Lenin, July 10, 1918. Online copy accessible at: https://www.marxists.org/reference/archive/stalin/works/1918/07/10.htm.

40 Robert Conquest, *Stalin: Breaker of Nations* (London: Weidenfeld and Nicolson, 1991), p. 78.

41 Stalin to Sverdlov, August 31, 1918. Online copy accessible at: https://www.marxists.org/reference/archive/stalin/works/1918/08/31b.htm.

42 Conquest, *Stalin: Breaker of Nations*, p. 81.

3. Franklin Roosevelt: The Young Maritime Strategist

1 FDR to Sara Roosevelt, 1887, http://www.fdrlibrary.marist.edu/_resources/images/sign/fdr_2.pdf.

2 Ted Morgan, *FDR: A Biography* (New York: Simon and Schuster, 1985), p. 175.

3 FDR Assistant Secretary of the Navy (ASN) Files, Personal File, Diary, handwritten entry, July 11, 1918.

4 Jon Tetsuro Sumida, *Inventing Grand Strategy and Teaching Command: The Classic Works of Alfred Thayer Mahan Reconsidered* (Baltimore: Johns Hopkins University Press, 1997), pp. 1–2.

5 Elliot Roosevelt (ed.), *FDR: His Personal Letters* (New York: Duell, Sloan and Pearce, 1947), Vol. 1, p. 161.

6 Ibid., p. 192.

7 Ibid., p. 200.

8 Ibid., p. 358.

9 Ibid., p. 378.

10 Frank Freidel, *Franklin Roosevelt: A Rendezvous with Destiny* (New York: Little, Brown, 1990), p. 10.

11 Ibid., p. 11.

12 Josephus Daniels, *The Wilson Era: Years of Peace 1910–1917* (Chapel Hill: UNC Press, 1944), p. 126.

13 Jeffrey Coker, *Franklin Roosevelt: A Biography* (Westport: Greenwood Press, 2005), p. 30.

14 Phillips O'Brien, *The Second Most Powerful Man in the World* (New York: Dutton, 2019), p. 42.

15 Coker, *Franklin Roosevelt: A Biography*, pp. 35–6.

16 Freidel, *Franklin Roosevelt: A Rendezvous with Destiny*, p. 28; Morgan, *FDR: A Biography*, p. 154.

17 FDR ASN Files, FDR to TR, May 10, 1913.

18 FDR ASN Files, article draft (probably 1917).

19 TR quote, October 16, 1916, https://www.theodorerooseveltcenter.org/Learn-About-TR/TR-Quotes.

20 FDR ASN, FDR to Mahan, May 28, 1914.

21 FDR ASN, FDR to Mahan, July 17, 1914; Mahan to FDR, August 2 and 4, 1914.

22 FDR ASN 3, 1915 article draft on purpose of US Navy.

23 FDR ASN 3, article draft about Montcalm victory at Oswego, undated.

24 FDR ASN, Family File, undated lecture notes on the American Navy in the Revolution (looks to be around 1911).

25 FDR ASN 3, article draft on purpose of US Navy, undated.

26 Elliot Roosevelt, *FDR: His Personal Letters*, Vol. 2, p. 238.

27 Ibid., p. 243.

28 Morgan, *FDR*, p. 166.

29 FDR ASN 3, "Notes for Battleships vs Submarines."

30 Ibid.

31 FDR ASN, FDR to Daniels, August 3, 1915.

32 Eugene E. Beiriger, "Building a Navy 'Second to None': The U.S. Naval Act of 1916, American Attitudes toward Great Britain, and the First World War," *British Journal for Military History,* Vol. 3, No. 3 (2017), p. 8.

33 FDR ASN, Family, assorted articles, draft of 1915/16 article, undated but has to be in that period.

34 *New York Times*, March 28, 1916.

35 FDR ASN 1, handwritten list of battleships in light of 1916 programme (undated).

36 *New York Times*, October 8, 1916, p. 6, in FDR speech file online: http://www.fdrlibrary.marist.edu/_resources/images/msf/msf00059.

37 FDR ASN, FDR to Leahy, October 26, 1916.

38 FDR ASN 4, Diary notes, March 11, 1917.

4. Benito Mussolini: The Birth of a Nationalist Strategist

1 Benito Mussolini, *Diary* (Milan: Imperia, 1923), September 16, 1916.

2 During Mussolini's rule, Predappio would be turned into a major site of fascist pilgrimage, with thousands visiting annually. See Sofia Serenelli, "A Town for the Cult of the Duce: Predappio as a Site of Pilgrimage," in Stephen Gundle et al. (eds), *The Cult of the Duce: Mussolini and the Italians* (Manchester: Manchester University Press, 2013), pp. 93–109.

3 Philip Cannistraro, "Father and Son," in Spencer Di Scala and Emilio Gentile (eds), *Mussolini 1883–1915* (New York: Palgrave Macmillan, 2016) pp. 44–7.

4 Ibid., p. 47.

5 Ibid., p. 49.

6 Peter Neville, *Mussolini* (London: Routledge, 2015), pp. 18–19.

7 Paolo Monelli, *Mussolini piccolo Borghese* (Milan: Garzanti, 1950), p. 16.

8 Ibid.

9 Benito Mussolini, *My Autobiography* (Milan: Borodino Books, 2017) Chapter 3.

10 Monelli, *Mussolini*, p. 23.

11 Cannistraro, "Father and Son," p. 59.

12 Simone Visconti, "A Romangol in Switzerland," in Di Scala and Gentile, pp. 65–96.

13 Monelli, *Mussolini*, p. 39.

14 Mussolini, *My Autobiography*, Chapter 2.

15 Ibid.

16 Monelli, *Mussolini*, p. 61.

17 R. J. B. Bosworth, *Mussolini* (London: Arnold, 2002), p. 116.

18 Rupert Colley, "Ida Dalser—Mussolini's First Wife," https://rupertcolley.com/2014/12/03/ida-dalser-a-brief-biography/.

19 Monelli, *Mussolini*, p. 74.

20 "La gara degli armamenti," *Avanti!*, February 21, 1913, in Edoardo and Duilio Susmelt (eds), *Opera Omniadi Benito Mussolini*, Vol. XXX (Florence: La Fenice, 1960), p. 108.

21 "In tema di neutralità: al nostro posto!," *Avanti!*, August 16, 1914, *Opera Omnia*, VI, p. 331.

22 "Un accordo anglo-franco-russo per la discussione delle condizioni di pace," *Avanti!*, September 7, 1914, *Opera Omnia*, XI, pp. 359–60.

23 Nicholas Farrell, *Mussolini* (London: Weidenfeld & Nicolson, 2003), pp. 56–8.

24 Monelli, *Mussolini*, p. 93.

25 Richard Lamb, *Mussolini and the British* (London: John Murray, 1997), p. 20.

26 Bosworth, *Mussolini*, p. 106.

27 "L'altra sponda," *Il Popolo d'Italia*, May 26, 1915, *Opera Omnia*, XI, p. 3.

28 Paul O'Brien, *Mussolini in the First World War: The Journalist, the Soldier, the Fascist* (Oxford: Berg, 2005), p. 63.

29 Denis Mack Smith, *Mussolini: A Biography* (New York: Alfred Knopf, 1982), p. 27.

30 "L'altra sponda."

31 John Gooch, *The Italian Army and the First World War* (Cambridge: Cambridge University Press, 2014), p. 90.

32 Ibid., pp. 103–6.

33 Mark Thompson, *The White War: Life and Death on the Italian Front, 1915–1919* (London: Faber and Faber, 2009), pp. 66–8.

34 Gooch, *The Italian Army*, p. 100.

35 Bosworth, *Mussolini*, p. 114.

36 Mussolini, *Diary*, September 19, 1915, pp. 27–32.

37 Ibid., October 18, 1915, pp. 24–6.

38 Ibid., September 17, 1915, pp. 21–4.

39 Ibid., September 19, 1915, pp. 27–32.

40 John Macdonald and Zeljko Cimpric, *Caporetto and the Isonzo Campaign: The Italian Front 1915–1918* (Barnsley: Pen and Sword, 2011), Chapter 11.

41 Thompson, *The White War*, pp. 128–130.

42 Mussolini, *Diary*, October 24, 1915, pp. 72–3.

43 John R. Schindler, *Isonzo: The Forgotten Sacrifice of the Great War* (Westport: Praeger, 2001), p. 103.

44 Mussolini, *Diary*, October 24, 1915, pp. 72–3.

45 Schindler, *Isonzo*, p. 124.

46 Mussolini, *Diary*, October 23, 1915, pp. 70–72.

47 Ibid., April 4, 1916, pp. 129–30.

48 Ibid.

5. Adolf Hitler: Art and War

1 August Kubizek, *The Young Hitler I Knew* (New York: Frontline Books, 2011), p. 232.

2 Ian Kershaw, *Hitler 1889–1936: Hubris* (New York: W. W. Norton, 1999), p. 11.

3 Trevor-Roper, *Hitler's Table Talk*, p. 164.

4 Ibid., p. 608.

5 Ibid., p. 359.

6 Kubizek, *The Young Hitler I Knew*, p. 29.

7 Kershaw, *Hubris*, p. 24.

8 Peter Longerich, *Hitler: A Life* (Oxford: Oxford University Press, 2019), p. 21.

9 Volker Ullrich, *Hitler: Ascent 1889–1939* (London: The Bodley Head, 2016), pp. 30–1.

10 Trevor-Roper, *Hitler's Table Talk*, p. 333.

11 Kubizek, *The Young Hitler I Knew*, p. 160.

12 Ibid., p. 194.

13 Ibid., p. 227.

14 Trevor-Roper, *Hitler's Table Talk*, p. 480.

15 Adolf Hitler, *Mein Kampf* (Boston and New York: Mariner Books, 1999), p. 56.

16 Trevor-Roper, *Hitler's Table Talk*, p. 712.

17 Hitler, *Mein Kampf*, p. 270.

18 Ibid., p. 291.

19 Ibid., p. 41.

20 Trevor-Roper, *Hitler's Table Talk*, p. 112.

21 Ibid., p. 361.

22 Ibid.

23 Kershaw, *Hubris*, p. 37.

24 Kubizek, *The Young Hitler I Knew*, p. 207.

25 Trevor-Roper, *Hitler's Table Talk*, p. 97.

26 Kershaw, *Hubris*, p. 84.

27 For a discussion of Hoffmann doctoring the picture, see https://www.warhistoryonline.com/war-articles/famous-adolf-hitler-photo-odeons platz-fake.html.

28 Trevor-Roper, *Hitler's Table Talk*, p. 44.

29 By far the best work which goes into the history of the List Regiment as a whole, and Hitler's experiences in it, is Thomas Weber, *Hitler's First War: Adolf Hitler, the List Regiment and the First World War* (Oxford: Oxford University Press, 2010).

30 Weber, *Hitler's First War*, pp. 17–19.

31 Trevor-Roper, *Hitler's Table Talk*, p. 7.

32 Werner Master (ed.), *Hitler: Letters and Notes* (New York: Harper and Row, 1974), Hitler to Frau Popp, October 20, 1914, p. 43.

33 Hew Strachan, *The First World* War, Vol. 1 (Oxford: Oxford University Press, 2001), pp. 242–62.

34 Master, *Letters and Notes*, Hitler to Popp, January 26, 1915, pp. 60–63.

35 Weber, *Hitler's First War*, pp. 44–5.

36 Master, *Letters and Notes*, Hitler to Popp, January 26, 1915, p. 60. Hitler described the artillery needed to win the battle in more specific detail to Popp than he did in the overall more detailed letter to Hepp.

37 Weber, *Hitler's First War*, pp. 48–9.

38 Hitler, *Mein Kampf*, p. 165.

39 Master, *Letters and Notes*, Hitler to Hepp, February 5, 1915, p. 90.

40 Weber, *Hitler's First War*, p. 53.

41 Charles B. Flood, "Lance Corporal Adolf Hitler on the Western Front 1914–1918," *The Kentucky Review*, Vol. 5, No. 3 (1985).

42 Brendan Simms, "Against a 'World of Enemies': The Impact of the First World War on the Development of Hitler's Ideology," *International Affairs*, Vol. 90, No. 2 (March 2014), p. 322.

43 Longerich, *Hitler: A Life*, p. 40.

44 Flood, "Lance Corporal Adolf Hitler," pp. 10–11.

45 Weber, *Hitler's First War*, pp. 87–9.

46 Master, *Letters and Notes*, Hitler to Hepp, February 5, 1915, p. 88.

47 Kenneth D. Rose, *The Great War and Americans in Europe, 1914–1917* (New York: Routledge, 2017), p. 161.

48 Trevor-Roper, *Hitler's Table Talk*, pp. 232–3.

49 Master, *Letters and Notes*, Hitler to Hepp, February 5, 1915, p. 88.

50 Trevor-Roper, *Hitler's Table Talk*, p. 56.

51 Ibid., pp. 183–4.

52 See https://www.theworldwar.org/learn/wwi/artillery.

53 See https://weaponsandwarfare.com/2019/07/02/wwi-spotting-for-the-armys-big-guns-i/.

6. Winston Churchill: Learning Strategic Restraint

1 Avner Offer, *The First World War: An Agrarian Interpretation* (Oxford: Clarendon Press, 1989), p. 36.

2 Phillips O'Brien, *British and American Naval Power: Politics and Policy 1900–1936* (Westport: Praeger, 1998), p. 35.

3 Char 2/64/9, Churchill to Asquith, August 3, 1914.

4 *WSC*, Vol. 3, Companion 1, Asquith to Venetia Stanley, October 3, 1914, pp. 158–9.

5 Douglas S. Russell, *Winston Churchill, Soldier: The Military Life of a Gentleman at War* (London: Conway, 2006), p. 351.

6 *WSC*, Vol. 3, Companion 1, Churchill to Grey and Kitchener, October 3, 1914, pp. 160–161.

7 Ibid., Asquith to Stanley, October 7, 1914, p. 177.

8 Ibid., October 5, 1914, pp. 165–6.

9 Ibid., October 7, 1914, pp. 177–8.

10 Ibid.

11 Ibid., Margot Asquith recollection, p. 283.

12 Char 2/75/159, Dardanelles Enquiry, p. 6.

13 Char 8/75, Churchill to Asquith, December 29, 1914.

14 *WSC*, Vol. 3, Companion 1, Richmond recollection, p. 216.

15 Char 8/75, Churchill to Asquith, December 29, 1914.

16 Char 2/75/159, Dardanelles Enquiry, p. 6.

17 *WSC*, Vol. 3, Companion 1, War Council Minutes, November 25, 1914, p. 278.

18 Christopher M. Bell, *Churchill and the Dardenelles* (Oxford: Oxford University Press, 2017), p. 362.

19 *WSC*, Vol. 3, Companion 1, Churchill to War Cabinet, March 3, 1915, p. 614.

20 Ibid., Margot Asquith recollection, p. 524.

21 Char 2/75/159, Dardanelles Enquiry, p. 6.

22 *WSC*, Vol. 3, Companion 2, John Churchill to WSC, May 4, 1915, p. 844.

23 Russell, *Winston Churchill, Soldier*, p. 360.

24 *WSC*, Vol. 3, Companion 2, letter to Clementine Churchill, December 15, 1915, p. 1329.

25 Ibid., "Variants of the Offensive," December 3, 1915, pp. 1303–7.

26 MUN 5/210, Churchill to Asquith, January 5, 1915.

27 *WSC*, Vol. 3, Companion 2, Churchill to Clementine, January 6, 1916, p. 1358.

28 Martin Gilbert, *Winston S. Churchill*, Vol. 3 (London: Heinemann, 1971), p. 623.

29 Companion, 1914–16, Vol. 2, Churchill to Clementine, January 13, 1916, p. 1354.

30 Ibid., February 14, 1916, p. 1423.

31 Ibid., December 8, 1915, p. 1318.

32 Ibid., February 8, 1916, p. 1416.

33 Ibid., April 14, 1916, p. 1488.

34 Ibid., November 23, 1915, p. 1286.

35 Ibid., January 28, 1916, p. 1402.

36 Ibid., January 20, 1916, p. 1386.

37 Ibid., Churchill to Fergusson, May 6, 1916, p. 1499.

38 Ibid., Churchill to Smith, August 1, 1916, pp. 1534–9.

39 David Lloyd George, *War Memoirs of Lloyd George*, Vol. 1 (London: Odhams Press, 1938), pp. 635–6.

40 Paul Addison, "The Political Beliefs of Winston Churchill," *Transactions of the Royal Historical Society*, Vol. 30 (1980), p. 26.

41 *WSC*, Vol. 4, Companion 1, Churchill to Archibald Sinclair, December 29, 1917, p. 222.

42 Char 8/105, "Munitions Possibilities of 1918."

43 Winston Churchill, *The World Crisis, Vol. 3: 1916–1918* (London: Thornton Butterworth, 1927), Chapter XII.

44 Char 8/105, "Munitions Possibilities of 1918."

45 MUN 5/131, Churchill Memo, December 8, 1917.

7. Joseph Stalin and the Strategy of Practicality

1 Stalin to Lenin, August 4, 1918. Online copy accessible at: https://www.marxists.org/reference/archive/stalin/works/1918/08/04.htm.

2 Ibid.

3 Ibid.

4 James S. Schneider, *The Structure of Strategic Revolution: Total War and the Roots of the Soviet Warfare State* (Novato: Presidio Press, 1994), pp. 234–5.

5 Tucker, *Stalin as Revolutionary*, p. 195.

6 Nossovitch, *Krasnyi Tsaritsyn*, p. 27.

7 Khlevniuk, *Stalin: New Biography*, p. 56.

8 Stalin to Lenin, August 31, 1918. Online copy accessible at: https://www.marxists.org/reference/archive/stalin/works/1918/08/31.htm.

9 *Dokumenty o geroicheskoi oborone Tsaritsyna v 1918 godu* (Moscow: Gospolitizdat, 1942), p. 159.

10 A. Kozlov, "Tsaritsynskii 'opyt,'" *Istoriki otvechaiut na voprosy*, Vol. 2 (Moscow: Moskovskii rabochii, 1990), pp. 244–53, https://scepsis.net/library/id_492.html.

11 *Oborona Tsaritsyna: Sbornik statei I dokumentov* (Stalingrad: Kraevoe knigoizdatel'stvo, 1937), pp. 330–31.

12 Kozlov, "Tsaritsynskii 'opyt.'"

13 Kotkin, *Stalin, Vol. 1*, p. 309.

14 Khlevniuk, *Stalin: New Biography*, p. 58.

15 Stalin, "The South of Russia," *Pravda*, October 30, 1918. Online copy accessible at: https://www.marxists.org/reference/archive/stalin/works/1918/10/30.htm.

16 Ibid.

17 Inscription on the draft of K. E. Voroshilov's article "Stalin and the Red Army," December 1929, in Stalin, *Sochineniia*, Vol. 17 (Tver: Nauchno-izdatel'skaia Kompaniia "Severnaia Korona," 2004), p. 326.

18 Figes, *A People's Tragedy*, p. 571.

19 Stalin, "The South of Russia."

20 Kotkin, *Stalin, Vol 1*, p. 314

21 Figes, *A People's Tragedy*, p. 586.

22 Kotkin, *Stalin, Vol. 1*, p. 314.

23 Report to Comrade Lenin by the Commission of the Party Central Committee and the Council of Defence on the Reasons for the Fall of Perm in December 1918. Online copy accessible at: https://www.marxists.org/reference/archive/stalin/works/1919/01/31b.htm.

24 Ibid.

25 Ibid.

26 Kotkin, *Stalin, Vol. 1*, pp. 320–1.

27 Evan Mawdsley, *The Russian Civil War* (London: Birlinn, 2008), pp. 196–7.

28 *Iz istorii Grazhdanskoi voiny v SSSR. 1918–1922: Sbornik documentov i materialov. T. 2. Mart 1919–Fevral' 1920* (Moscow: Sovetskaia Rossiia, 1961), p. 324.

29 M. A. Elizarov, "Vosstanie na forte 'Krasnaia gorka' v iune 1919, Pravda i legendy," *Morskoi sbornik*, Vol. 4 (2009), pp. 69–70.

30 I. S. Isakov, *Krasnaia gorka. Stalinskaia operatsiia 13–16 Iiunia 1919* (Moscow: Voenizdat, 1946), p. 40.

31 Stalin to Lenin, June 16, 1919. Online copy accessible at: https://www. marxists.org/reference/archive/stalin/works/1919/06/16.htm. See also *Iz istorii Grazhdanskoi voiny v SSSR*, p. 338.

32 N. S. Khrushchev, *The Crimes of the Stalin Era: Special Report to the 20th Congress of the Communist Party of the Soviet Union* (New York: New Leader, 1956), p. 57.

33 Kotkin, *Stalin, Vol. 1*, p. 331.

34 Mawdsley, *The Russian Civil War*, pp. 250–1.

35 Kotkin, *Stalin, Vol. 1*, p. 354.

36 Stalin, "The Entente's New Campaign Against Russia," *Pravda*, May 25–26, 1920. Online copy accessible at: https://www.marxists.org/ reference/archive/stalin/works/1920/05/25.htm.

37 Stalin, "The Situation on the Polish Front," *Pravda*, July 11, 1920. Online copy accessible at: https://www.marxists.org/reference/archive/stalin/ works/1920/07/11.htm.

38 *Bol'shevistskoe rukovodstvo. Perepiska. 1912–1927. Sbornik dokumentov* (Moscow: ROSSPEN, 1996), pp. 142–3.

39 *Iz istorii Grazhdanskoi voiny v SSSR*, pp. 338–9.

40 N. Kuzmin, "Ob odnoi nevypolnennoi directive Glavkoma (iz istorii Sovetsko-polskoi voiny 1920 goda)," *Voenno-istoricheskii zhurnal*, Vol. 9 (1962), pp. 62–3.

41 Ibid., pp. 55, 62.

42 Stalin to Lenin, August 13, 1920, in ibid., p. 62.

43 Norman Davies, *White Eagle, Red Star: The Polish–Soviet War of 1919–20* (London: McDonald, 1972), see Chapter 5, "The Battle of Warsaw," pp. 188–225.

44 Trotsky maintained that Stalin was almost singlehandedly responsible for losing the Battle of Warsaw through his focus on Lviv and neglect to aid Tukhachevsky. See Trotsky, *My Life*, Chapter 37, https://www .marxists.org/archive/trotsky/1930/mylife/ch37.htm.

45 Lenin's Speech at the IX Congress of the R.K.P. (b), September 22, 1920. See https://www.marxists.org/archive/lenin/works/1920/sep/22.htm.

46 *Bol'shevistskoe rukovodstvo. Perepiska. 1912–1927. Sbornik dokumentov* (Moscow: ROSSPEN, 1996), p. 160.

47 Ibid., pp. 160–1.

8. *Franklin Roosevelt and the Domestic Politics of Strategy*

1 FDR ASN, McCauley Narrative, p. 2.

2 This trip is one of the best documented of Roosevelt's pre-presidential life. Not only is there a large collection of letters that he wrote to his mother and wife, but there are detailed narratives written by two aides who accompanied him, Captain Edward, McCauley and Livingston Davis. All of these papers are in the Franklin Roosevelt presidential library.

3 FDR ASN, Roosevelt Diary, July 13, 1918.

4 FDR ASN, McCauley Narrative, p. 2.

5 FDR ASN, FDR Diary Notes, July 11, 1918.

6 FDR ASN, Roosevelt to Daniels, June 26, 1917.

7 FDR ASN, Roosevelt to Daniels, September 7, 1917.

8 *New York Times*, January 18, 1914, p. 3.

9 FDR ASN, Roosevelt article draft, June 1917. The original version of this article must have been written in later March or early April as Roosevelt speaks of the US about to enter the war against Germany.

10 Ibid.

11 Dean Allard, "Anglo-American Naval Differences During World War I," *Military Affairs*, Vol. 44, No. 2 (April 1980), p. 76.

12 John Terraine, *The U-Boat Wars, 1916–1945* (New York: Henry Holt, 1989), p. 113; "The Allied North Sea Mine Barrage of World War I," American Battle Monuments Commission, June 11, 2018, https://www.abmc.gov/news-events/news/allied-north-sea-mine-barrage-world-war-i. See also NHHC, https://www.history.navy.mil/browse-by-topic/wars-conflicts-and-operations/world-war-i/tech/north-sea-barrage.html.

13 FDR ASN, Roosevelt to Daniels, October 21, 1918, p. 6; many naval histories don't actually describe the process by which the decision was made, writing that the navy decided to support the mine barrage. George Baer, *One Hundred Years of Sea Power: The U.S. Navy, 1890–1990* (Stanford: Stanford University Press, 1994), p. 74.

14 Josephus Daniels, *The Wilson Era: Years of War and After 1917–1923* (Chapel Hill: UNC Press, 1946), p. 83.

15 FDR ASN, Roosevelt to Daniels, October 29, 1917.

16 Allard, "Anglo-American Naval Differences During World War I," p. 78.

17 Baer, *One Hundred Years of Sea Power*, p. 72.

18 FDR ASN, FDR to Wilson, October 29, 1917.

19 Daniels, *The Wilson Era*, pp. 116–117.

20 https://www.militaryfactory.com/armor/detail.asp?armor_id=770.

21 FDR ASN, McCauley Narrative, p. 22.

22 Elliot Roosevelt, *FDR: His Personal Letters*, Vol. 1, p. 373.

23 Ibid., p. 372.

24 Roosevelt's summer 1918 trip to Europe is probably the best docu-
    mented era of his time as ASN. Not only did he keep a detailed series
    of notes, much in diary form, but he also kept copies of the letters he
    wrote to Eleanor which provided more detail. There are also two sur-
    viving narratives from aides who accompanied him for parts of the
    journey, McCauley and Davis.

25 FDR ASN, Diary Notes, July 9, 1918.

26 FDR ASN, McCauley Narrative, p. 3.

27 FDR ASN, FDR to Eleanor Roosevelt, July 19, 1918.

28 FDR ASN, FDR to Daniels, July 27, 1918.

29 FDR ASN, FDR to Eleanor, July 30, 1918.

30 https://winstonchurchill.org/publications/finest-hour/finest-hour-172/
    churchill-and-roosevelt/.

31 Gilbert, *Churchill and America*, p. 77.

32 FDR ASN, Diary Notes, August 11, 1918.

33 FDR ASN, Diary Notes, July 24, 1918.

34 Baer, *One Hundred Years of Sea Power*, p. 75.

35 Dudley W. Knox, *A History of the United States Navy* (New York: G. P.
    Putnam's, 1948), p. 417.

36 FDR ASN, Diary Notes, August 4, 1918.

37 Ibid., August 6, 1918.

38 FDR ASN, Livingston Davis Report, p. 6.

39 FDR ASN, Diary Notes, August 6, 1918.

40 Ibid., August 7, 1918.

41 Ibid., August 4, 1918.

42 William McBride, *Technological Change and the United States Navy 1865–
    1945* (Baltimore: Johns Hopkins University Press, 2000), p. 130.

43 FDR ASN, Diary Notes, August 3, 1918.

44 Ibid., August 1, 1918 (strangely this notation is in a separate paragraph
    labelled August 1, but it clearly happens after the failed raid which is in
    the entry for August 3).

45 FDR ASN, McCauley Narrative, p. 20.

46 Ibid., p. 22.

47 FDR ASN, FDR to Daniels, November 14, 1918.

48 Baer, *One Hundred Years of Sea Power*, p. 75.

49 Knox, *A History of the United States Navy*, p. 418. Overall Knox has a far more positive analysis of the effectiveness of the North Sea mine barrage than most who have written about it.

50 *New York Times*, August 23, 1919.

51 Ibid., April 14, 1919.

52 Ibid., March 9, 1919.

53 Ibid., June 29, 1919.

54 In Roosevelt's acceptance speech, he started with a call for a stronger merchant marine. See Roosevelt Speech File, Acceptance Speech, August 9, 1920, http://www.fdrlibrary.marist.edu/_resources/images/msf/msf00134

55 FDR Speech File, Final Pre-Election Statement, October 31, 1920, http://www.fdrlibrary.marist.edu/_resources/images/msf/msf00236.

56 FDR ASN, FDR to Coleman, March 30, 1921.

57 FDR ASN, FDR to Peoples, January 16, 1926. See also FDR to Koon, March 9, 1928.

9. Benito Mussolini and Bluffing as Strategy

1 Mussolini, *Diary*, April 4, 1916, pp. 129–30.

2 Ibid., March 31, 1916, pp. 124–5.

3 Gooch, *The Italian Army*, pp. 99–100.

4 Emilio Lussu, *A Soldier on the Southern Front: The Classic Italian Memoir of World War I* (New York: Rizzoli, 2014), Chapter 2.

5 Mussolini, *Diary*, May 2, 1916 p. 149.

6 Ibid., April 30, 1916, p. 147.

7 Ibid., April 6, 1916, pp. 131–2.

8 Both Bosworth and Mack Smith, for instance, say very little about his time at the front and the reason for the absences.

9 Schindler, *Isonzo*, pp. 151–71.

10 Ibid., p. 191.

11 Mussolini, *Diary*, note to Part III.

12 Ibid., December 2, 1916.

13 Ibid., December 6, 1916.

14 Vanda Wilcox, *Morale and the Italian Army during the First World War* (Cambridge: Cambridge University Press, 2016), p. 131.

15 Dana Glei, Silvia Bruzzone and Graziella Caselli, "Effects of War Losses on Mortality Estimates for Italy: A First Attempt," *Demographic Research*, Vol. 13, No. 15 (November 2005), p. 373.

16 John Keegan, *The First World War: An Illustrated History* (London: Pimlico, 2002), p. 319.

17 Ibid.

18 Wilcox, *Morale and the Italian Army*, pp. 173–5.

19 Ibid., p. 178.

20 Ibid., pp. 99–100.

21 Renzo De Felice, *Mussolini il rivoluzionario* (Turin: Einaudi, 1965), p. 323.

22 Mussolini, *Diary*, December 31, 1916.

23 Ibid.

24 Ibid., December 30, 1916.

25 Ibid., January 21, 27–28, 1917.

26 Ibid., February 22, 1917.

27 Jasper Ridley, *Mussolini* (London: Constable, 1997), p. 79.

28 Bosworth, *Mussolini*, p. 118.

29 "Il morale," *Il Popolo d'Italia*, July 29, 1917.

30 *Il Popolo d'Italia*, December 27, 1916, *Opera Omnia*, VIII, pp. 271–2.

31 Smith, *Mussolini: A Biography*, p. 29.

32 "Spirito di decisione," *Il Popolo d'Italia*, June 17, 1917.

33 Mussolini, *Diary*, March 18, 1917, p. 112.

34 Thompson, *The White War*, p. 298.

35 Gooch, *The Italian Army*, p. 239.

36 Macdonald and Cimpric, *Caporetto and the Isonzo Campaign*, Chapter 20.

37 Gooch, *The Italian Army*, pp. 242–3.

38 Thompson, *The White War*, p. 318.

39 "Fronte al nemico!," *Il Popolo d'Italia*, October 28, 1917.

40 "Nella più dura delle ipotesi," *Il Popolo d'Italia*, October 30, 1917, *Opera Omnia*, X, pp. 5–7.

41 Wilcox, *Morale and the Italian Army*, pp. 143, 151.

42 Gooch, *The Italian Army*, pp. 248–56.

43 Francesco Galassi and Mark Harrison, "Italy at War, 1915–1918," in Stephen Broadberry and Mark Harrison (eds), *The Economics of World War I* (Cambridge: Cambridge University Press, 2005), p. 289.

44 Gooch, *The Italian Army*, p. 251.

45 Bosworth, *Mussolini*, p. 119.

46 "L'Italia è immortale," part of Mussolini's speech in Rome on February 24, 1918, reported in *Il Popolo d'Italia*, February 27, 1918, *Opera Omnia*, X, pp. 344–5.

47 "Wilson, dittatore," *Il Popolo d'Italia*, March 23, 1918, *Opera Omnia*, XII, p. 88.

48 "Mezzi e fini dell'intesa italo-jugoslava," speech in Milan, May 23, 1918, reported in *Il Popolo d'Italia*, March 24, 1918, *Opera Omnia*, XI, p. 88.

49 Smith, *Mussolini: A Biography*, p. 31.

50 Mussolini, *My Autobiography*, Chapter 5.

10. Adolf Hitler: Victory and Defeat

1 Master, *Letters and Notes*, p. 96.

2 Hitler, *Mein Kampf*, p. 194.

3 Ibid., p. 196.

4 Paul Jankowski, *Verdun: The Longest Battle of the Great War* (Oxford: Oxford University Press, 2014), p. 62. The author makes a persuasive case that the specific plan to simply bleed the French is more likely a post-war justification and that Falkenhayn spent a great deal of effort to seize Verdun itself and not just bleed the French.

5 https://www.iwm.org.uk/history/key-facts-about-the-battle-of-the-somme.

6 Weber, *Hitler's First War*, pp. 145–6.

7 Ibid., p. 153.

8 Trevor-Roper, *Hitler's Table Talk*, p. 169.

9 Hitler, *Mein Kampf*, p. 192.

10 Keith Allen, "Sharing Scarcity: Bread Rationing and the First World War in Berlin 1914–23," *Journal of Social History*, Vol. 32, No. 2 (Winter 1998), pp. 374–5.

11 "The German Food Situation," *Monthly Labor Review*, Vol. 53, No. 2 (August 1941), pp. 283–4.

12 Hitler, *Mein Kampf*, p. 192.

13 Ibid., pp. 193–4.

14 https://blog.nli.org.il/en/jewish_germany_army/.

15 Weber, *Hitler's First War*, p. 169.

16 David Murphy, *Breaking Point of the French Army: The Nivelle Offensive of 1917* (Barnsley: Pen and Sword, 2015), Chapter 3.

17 Nick Lloyd, *Passchendaele: A New History* (London: Penguin, 2017), pp. 4–5.

18 Weber, *Hitler's First War*, pp. 197–9.

19 Trevor-Roper, *Hitler's Table Talk*, pp. 600–1.

20 Adolf Meyer, *Mit Adolf Hitler in Bayerischen Reserve-Infanterie-Regiment 16 List* (Neustadt-Aisch: Geora Aupperle, 1934), pp. 83, 89.

21 https://www.warhistoryonline.com/featured/the-paris-gun.html.

22 Meyer, *Mit Hitler*, p. 70.

23 Hitler, *Mein Kampf*, pp. 273–4.

24 Ibid., p. 274.

25 Marc Romanych and Martin Rupp, *42cm "Big Bertha" and German Siege Artillery of World War I* (London: Bloomsbury, 2014), Introduction.

26 Leahy Diary (William Leahy Papers, Library of Congress), Vol. 1, pp. 232–3.

27 Ibid., p. 233.

28 Hitler, speech at an NSDAP assembly, January 4, 1921, Munich, in Eberhard Jäckel and Axel Kuhn (eds), *Hitler. Sämtliche Aufzeichnungen 1905–1924* (Stuttgart: Deutsche Verlags-Anstalt, 1980), p. 294.

29 Trevor-Roper, *Hitler's Table Talk*, p. 55.

30 Helmut Heiber, David Glantz and Gerhard Weinberg (eds), *Hitler and His Generals: Military Conferences 1942–1945* (London: Enigma Books, 2004), pp. 441–2.

31 Trevor-Roper, *Hitler's Table Talk*, p. 184.

32 Hitler, *Mein Kampf*, p. 196.

33 Ibid., p. 194.

34 Ibid.

35 Martin Kitchen, *The German Offensives of 1918* (Stroud: Tempus, 2005), p. 87.

36 Ibid., p. 92.

37 Ibid., p. 280.

38 Weber, *Hitler's First War*, p. 212.

39 Trevor-Roper, *Hitler's Table Talk*, p. 660.

40 Hitler, *Mein Kampf*, p. 195.

41 Trevor-Roper, *Hitler's Table Talk*, p. 29.

42 Weber, *Hitler's First War*, p. 221.

43 Trevor-Roper, *Hitler's Table Talk*, p. 639.

44 Gerhard L. Weinberg (ed.), *Hitler's Second Book: The Unpublished Sequel to Mein Kampf* (New York: Enigma Books, 2006), Chapter 8, p. 55.

45 Thomas Weber, *Becoming Hitler: The Making of a Nazi* (Oxford: Oxford University Press, 2017), pp. 5–9.

46 Ullrich, pp. 74–5.

47 Kershaw, *Hubris*, p. 118.

48 Ibid., p. 125.

49 Eberhard Jäckel, *Hitler's World View: A Blueprint for Power* (Cambridge: Harvard University Press, 1981), p. 48.

50 Kershaw, *Hubris*, p. 126.

51 Hitler, *Mein Kampf*, p. 123.

52 Weinberg, *Hitler's Second Book*, p. 166.

53 Hitler, *Mein Kampf*, p. 622.

54 Hitler speeches, September 18, 1922, quoted in W. Lautemann and M. Schlenke (eds), *Geschichte in Quellen: Weltkriege und Revolutionen 1914–1945*, Vol. 5 (Munich: Bayerischer Schulbuch-Verlag, 1961), p. 195.

11. *Interlude: The Interwar Years*

1 Paolo Malanima and Vera Zamagni, "150 Years of the Italian Economy 1861–2010," *Journal of Modern Italian Studies*, Vol. 15, No. 1 (2010); Harold James and Kevin H. O'Rourke, "Italy and the First Age of Globalization, 1861–1940," in Gianni Toniolo (ed.), *The Oxford Handbook of the Italian Economy Since Unification* (Oxford: Oxford University Press, 2013).

12. *Hitler, Stalin and the Nazi–Soviet Pact*

1 Albert Speer, *Inside the Third Reich* (London: Weidenfeld and Nicolson, 2009), p. 80.

2 Volker Ullrich, *Hitler: Downfall 1939–1945* (London: Vintage, 2020), p. 29.

3 Gerhard Weinberg, "The Nazi–Soviet Pacts: A Half-Century Later," *Foreign Affairs*, Vol. 68, No. 4 (Fall 1989), p. 176.

4 Albert Resis (ed.), *Molotov Remembers: Inside Kremlin Politics, Conversations with Felix Chuev* (Chicago: Ivan R. Dee Publishers, 1993), p. 12.

5 Letter by Andor Hencke, August 24, 1939, in Alexander Dolezalek (ed.), *Moskau–Berlin–Streng geheim: Wie Stalin und Hitler Osteuropa unter sich aufteilten. 1939 bis 1941*, Vol. 6 (Lindhorst: Askania, 1989), p. 77.

6 One of the best places to see Hitler's interest in creating a Lebensraum for the German people is in his unpublished second book. Chapter 6, which is devoted to Germany's future needs, starts with a detailed discussion of the need for living space.

7 Brendan Simms, *Hitler: Only the World Was Enough* (London: Allen Lane, 2019), pp. 383–4.

8 Weinberg, *Hitler's Second Book*, p. 174.

9 Ibid., p. 160.

10 Williamson Murray, *Strategy for Defeat: The Luftwaffe 1933–1945* (Alabama: Air University Press, 1983), pp. 18–19.

11 "Summary Report (European Report #1)," in David MacIsaac (ed.), *The Strategic Bombing Survey* (New York: Garland, 1976), Vol. 1, p. 68.

12 UPI Archives, July 19, 1940, https://www.upi.com/Archives/1940/07/19/Hitler-offers-Britain-peace-or-destruction/6824181303557/.

13 Hitler interview with Ward Price, August 5, 1934, quoted in Max Domarus (ed.), *Hitler: Speeches and Proclamations 1932–1945: The Chronicle of a Dictatorship*, 4 vols (Wauconda: Bolchazy-Carducci Publishers, 1990–2004), Vol. 1, pp. 511, 513.

14 Adolf Hitler, address on the anniversary of "Day of Coburg," October 15, 1937, quoted in Domarus, *Hitler*, Vol. 2, p. 956.

15 Trevor-Roper, *Hitler's Table Talk*, p. 254.

16 Peter Whitewood, *The Red Army and the Great Terror: Stalin's Purge of the Soviet Military* (Lawrence: University Press of Kansas, 2015), p. 277.

17 Norman Naimark, *Stalin's Genocides* (Princeton: Princeton University Press, 2010), pp. 121–30.

18 Kotkin, *Stalin, Vol. 2*, p. 579.

19 Ibid., pp. 361–2.

20 Alexander Hill, *The Red Army and the Second World War* (Cambridge: Cambridge University Press, 2017), p. 50.

21 Ibid., p. 76.

22 Stalin, report on work of Central Committee, March 10, 1939. Online copy accessible at: https://www.marxists.org/reference/archive/stalin/works/1939/03/10.htm.

23 Ibid.

24 Ibid.

25 I. M. Maiskii, *Vospominania sovetskogo diplomata, 1925–1945 gg* (Tashkent, "Uzbekistan," 1980), pp. 337–8.

26 Michael J. Carley, "End of the 'Low, Dishonest Decade': Failure of the Anglo-Franco-Soviet Alliance in 1939," *Europe-Asia Studies*, Vol. 45, No. 2 (1993), p. 323.

27 Kotkin, *Stalin, Vol. 2*, p. 648.

28 Carley, "End of the 'Low, Dishonest Decade,'" p. 328.

29 Ribbentrop to Schulenberg (German ambassador to the USSR), August 14, 1939, in Dolezalek, *Moskau–Berlin*, pp. 37–40, 39.

30 Christian Goeschel, *Mussolini and Hitler: The Forging of the Fascist Alliance* (New Haven: Yale University Press, 2018), pp. 157–8.

31 Galeazzo Ciano, *The Ciano Diaries*, ed. Hugh Gibson, introduction by Sumner Welles (London: Simon and Schuster, 2001), August 12, 1939.

32 Ibid.

33 Giuseppe Bottai, *Diary 1935–1944* (Rome: BUR, 2006), April 29, 1939, p. 147.

34 Ullrich, *Downfall*, p. 38.

35 Speer, *Inside the Third Reich*, p. 596.

36 Longerich, *Hitler: A Life*, p. 635.

37 Domarus, *Hitler*, p. 55.

38 "Do 90 let on ezdil v polikliniku na elektrichke," *Kommersant-Vlast'*, Vol. 11 (March 21, 2000), https://www.kommersant.ru/doc/16644.

39 Khrushchev, *Vremia, Liudi, Vlast (Vospominania)*, Vol. 1 (Moscow: Moskovskie Novosti, 1999), p. 271.

40 Kotkin, *Stalin, Vol. 2*, p. 674.

13. Churchill, Hitler and the Battle of Britain

1 Max Hastings, *Finest Years: Churchill as Warlord 1940–45* (London: Harper Press, 2009), pp. 1–3.

2 Gilbert, *Winston S. Churchill*, Vol. 6, p. 349.

3 Martin Gilbert (ed.), *The Churchill War Papers*, Vol. 2 (London: Heinemann, 1994), pp. 54–9.

4 Ibid., p. 57.

5 A. N. Wilson, *Hitler: A Short Biography* (London: Harper Press, 2012), p. 135.

6 Speer, *Inside the Third Reich*, p. 627.

7 Frauz Halder, *The Private War Journal of General Franz Halder 1939–1942* (Nuremberg: Office of the Chief Counsel for War Crimes, 1947), Vol. 4, Halder notes of Brauchitsch meeting with Hitler, p. 126, http://militera.lib.ru/db/o/pdf/halder_eng4.pdf.

8 Ibid., p. 127.

9 Halder Diaries, Vol. 2, Fuehrer conference, October 10, 1939, p. 25, http://militera.lib.ru/db/o/pdf/halder_eng2.pdf.

10 Ibid., October 17, 1939, p. 31.

11 Hitler, speech in the Berlin Sportpalast, May 3, 1940, in Domarus, *Hitler*, Vol. 3, p. 1985.

12 Gilbert, *Winston S. Churchill*, Vol. 6, p. 4.

13 Ibid., Vol. 1, p. 76.

14 Ibid., p. 247.

15 Ibid., p. 714.

16 Char 8/666, "The Mysteries of Empire," March 17, 1940.

17 Ashley Jackson, *Churchill* (London: Quercus, 2011), p. 255.

18 Jonathan Knight, "Churchill and the Approach to Mussolini and Hitler in May 1940: A Note," *British Journal of International Studies*, Vol. 3 (1997), pp. 92–6.

19 Gilbert, *Churchill War Papers*, Vol. 2, p. 156.

20 Ibid.

21 Ibid., p. 157.

22 Ibid., p. 429.

23 Phillips O'Brien, *How the War Was Won: Air–Sea Power and Allied Victory in World War II* (Cambridge: Cambridge University Press, 2015), pp. 120–1.

24 Ibid., pp. 123–4. The Germans produced 3,106 fighters during all of 1940.

25 USSBS, Koller Interview, May 23, 1945, p. 1.

26 USSBS, Dönitz Interview, June 28, 1945, p. 16.

27 USSBS, Jodl Interview, June 29, 1945, p. 7.

28 *Fuehrer Conferences on Naval Affairs: 1940*, (UK Admiralty, 1947) p. 65.

29 Ibid., p. 72.

30 USSBS, Dönitz Interview, June 28, 1945, p. 2.

31 "Stuka Attack!," *Air University Press*, November 5, 2020, https://www. airuniversity.af.edu/AUPress/Book-Reviews/Display/Article/2406538/ stuka-attack-the-dive-bombing-assault-on-england-during-the-battle-of-britain/.

32 USSBS, Koller Interview, May 23, 1945, p. 2.

33 Murray, *Strategy for Defeat*, p. 52.

34 USSBS, Koller Interview, May 23, 1945, p. 3.

35 James Holland, *The Battle of Britain: Five Months that Changed History, May–October 1940* (London: Bantam Press, 2010), pp. 489–98.

36 Hitler, appeal for the benefit of the Winterhilfswerk, September 4, 1940, in Domarus, *Hitler*, Vol. 3, p. 2086.

37 Halder Diaries, Vol. 4, summary of *Fuehrer* conference, September 14, 1940, p. 194.

38 USSBS, Junck Interview, May 19, 1945, p. 3.

39 WO 208-4340, Milch Interview notes, July 7, 1945, p. 6.

40 USSBS, Kreipe Interview, June 4, 1945, p. 3.

41 USSBS, Junck Interview, May 19, 1945, pp. 3–4.

42 Halder Diaries, Vol. 4, July 13, 1940, p. 117.

43 Ibid., July 22, 1940, p. 126.

44 Ibid., p. 128.

45 Ibid., July 31, 1940, p. 144.

46 Templewood Mss (Hoare) in Cambridge University Library. Beaverbrook to Hoare, August 30, 1940.

47 Gilbert, *Churchill War Papers*, Vol. 2, pp. 947-8.

48 Ibid., pp. 1010–12.

49 Ibid., p. 1012.

14. *Mussolini, Churchill and Greece, 1940–41*

1 *The Times*, September 26, 1939, p. 9.

2 Goeschel, *Mussolini and Hitler*, pp. 168–70.

3 Claretta Petacci, *Verso il disastro: Mussolini in guerra: diari 1939–1940* (Milan: Rizzoli, 2011), November 12, 1939, p. 239.

4 Ibid., March 4, 1940, p. 309.

5 Ciano Diaries, November 11, 1939, p. 169.

6 Ibid., March 12, 1940, p. 220.

7 Ibid., February 7, 1940, p. 205.

8 Ibid., May 3, 1940, p. 243.

9 Ibid., May 10, 1940, pp. 246–7.

10 Ibid., May 13, 1940, p. 249.

11 Ibid., May 29 and June 10, 1940, pp. 256, 263.

12 Paul Corner, *The Fascist Party and Popular Opinion in Mussolini's Italy* (Oxford: Oxford University Press, 2012), pp. 264–5.

13 R. J. B. Bosworth, *Mussolini and the Eclipse of Italian Fascism: From Dictatorship to Populism* (New Haven: Yale University Press, 2021), p. 246.

14 In 1938, the last full year of peace in Europe, Italy and Belgium produced approximately 2.3 million tons of steel each, France produced 6.2 million tons and Germany produced 17.9 million tons. See https://www.cvce.eu/content/publication/2000/11/17/b7bfeb8b-ec5a-45e3-9356-3309c9eaeb04/publishable_en.pdf.

15 James Sadkovich, "Understanding Defeat: Reappraising Italy's Role in World War II," *Journal of Contemporary History*, Vol. 24, No. 1 (January 1989), p. 32.

16 Nick Carter, *Modern Italy in Historical Perspective* (London: Bloomsbury, 2010), p. 133.

17 A. D. Harvey, "The Bomber Offensive that Never Took Off," *Air Power History*, Vol. 63, No. 3 (Fall 2016), p. 31.

18 Bottai, *Diary*, April 29, 1939, p. 147.

19 Ibid., January 23, 1940, p. 174.

20 Ciano Diaries, March 15, 1939, p. 44.

21 Petacci, *Verso il disastro*, p. 313.

22 Bottai, *Diary*, April 2, 1940, p. 184.

23 Jan Nelis, "Fascist Identity: Benito Mussolini and the Myth of 'Romanita,'" *The Classical World*, Vol. 100, No. 4 (Summer 2007), pp. 406–7.

24 Bottai, *Diary*, January 23, 1940, p. 174.

25 John Gooch, *Mussolini's War: Fascist Italy from Triumph to Collapse 1935–1943* (London: Allen Lane, 2020), pp. 98–104.

26 Emanuele Sica, "June 1940: The Italian Army and the Battle of the Alps," *Canadian Journal of History*, Vol. 47, No. 2 (2012), pp. 355–6.

27 Gooch, *Mussolini's War*, p. 100.

28 Halder Diaries, Vol. 4, June 24, 1940, p. 92.

29 Goeschel, *Mussolini and Hitler*, p. 184.

30 Gilbert, *Churchill War Papers*, Vol. 2, p. 1011.

31 Barrie Pitt, *The Crucible of War: Western Desert 1941* (London: Jonathan Cape, 1980), pp. 54, 72.

32 Ciano Diaries, September 17, 1940, p. 273.

33 Nir Arielli, *Fascist Italy and the Middle East, 1933–40* (Basingstoke: Palgrave, 2010), p. 1701.

34 Ciano Diaries, September 12, 1939, p. 143.

35 Ibid., October 12, 1940, p. 300.

36 *Riunione presso il Capo del Governo*, October 15, 1940, *D.D.I.*, IX Serie, Volume V, n. 728, pp. 699–705.

37 Ibid.

38 Ibid.

39 Ibid.

40 Ibid.

41 Ciano Diaries, October 17, 1940, pp. 301–2.

42 Ibid., October 18, 1940, p. 302.

43 Goeschel, *Mussolini and Hitler*, pp. 194–8.

44 Halder Diaries, Vol. 5, November 1, 1940, p. 4.

45 Christopher Buckley, *Greece and Crete 1941* (London: HMSO, 1952), pp. 8–10.

46 John C. Carr, *The Defence and Fall of Greece: 1940–1941* (Barnsley: Pen and Sword, 2013), p. 142.

47 James J. Sadkovich, "The Italo-Greek War in Context: Italian Priorities and Axis Diplomacy," *Journal of Contemporary History*, Vol. 28, No. 3 (July 1993), pp. 440–1.

48 Ibid., pp. 447–8.

49 Gilbert, *Churchill War Papers*, Vol. 2, p. 1006.

50 Ibid., p. 1139.

51 Ibid., p. 1105.

52 Ibid., Vol. 3, pp. 50, 65.

53 Buckley, *Greece and Crete*, p. 24.

54 Gilbert, *Churchill War Papers*, Vol. 3, p. 418.

55 Ibid., p. 305.

56 Gilbert, *Churchill War Papers*, Vol. 2, p. 310.

57 *Fuehrer Conferences on Naval Affairs: 1940*, December 27, 1940, p. 136.

58 Gilbert, *Churchill War Papers*, Vol. 3, p. 507.

59 Ibid., p. 509.

60 Ibid., p. 581.

61 https://www.iwm.org.uk/history/what-was-the-battle-of-crete.

62 Ciano Diaries, June 2, 1941, p. 361.

15. *Stalin, Hitler and Barbarossa*

1 David E. Murphy, *What Stalin Knew: The Enigma of Barbarossa* (New Haven: Yale University Press, 2005), p. 81.

2 Kotkin, *Stalin, Vol.2*, p. 698.

3 Reply to the Editor of *Pravda*, November 30, 1939, in Stalin, *Sochineniia*, Vol. 2 (Moscow: Izdatel'stvo "Pisatel," 1997), p. 343.

4 Khlevniuk, *Stalin: New Biography*, p. 171.

5 https://avalon.law.yale.edu/20th_century/addsepro.asp.

6 D. W. Spring, "The Soviet Decision for War against Finland, 30 November 1939," *Soviet Studies*, Vol. 38, No. 2 (April 1986), pp. 214–15.

7 Khlevniuk, *Stalin: New Biography*, p. 173.

8 Hill, *The Red Army and the Second World War*, p. 143.

9 A. I. Mikoyan, *Tak bylo* (Moscow: Vagrius, 1999), p. 385.

10 Hill, *The Red Army and the Second World War*, pp. 154–5.

11 The exact number of Soviet casualties is difficult to judge, but there seem to have been more than 126,000 "irrecoverable" losses (dead and missing) and a further 200,000 wounded. Hill, *The Red Army*, p. 167.

12 Ian Kershaw, *Hitler 1936–1945: Nemesis* (New York: W. W. Norton, 2000), p. 308.

13　Halder Diaries, Vol. 4, July 22, 1940, p. 128.

14　Ibid., August 22, 1940, p. 168.

15　Nazi-Soviet Non Aggression Pact, August 1939. Full text with secret protocol at: https://avalon.law.yale.edu/20th_century/addsepro.asp.

16　Halder Diaries, Vol. 4, June 27, 1940, p. 96.

17　Ibid., July 22, 1940, p. 128.

18　Speech at the Meeting of the Commanders of the Red Army, April 17, 1940 in Stalin, *Sochineniia*, Vol. 14, pp. 347–60.

19　Ibid.

20　Ibid.

21　Hill, *The Red Army*, pp. 172–4.

22　Ibid., pp. 181–2.

23　Murphy, *What Stalin Knew*, p. 245. Murphy argues that Stalin's reforms after the Finnish debacle made little difference before Barbarossa, but paid some dividends after the German invasion.

24　Hitler, speech in Löwenbräukeller, November 8, 1940, in Domarus, *Hitler*, p. 2117.

25　Halder Diaries, Vol. 5, January 16, 1941, p. 83.

26　*Germany and the Second World War* (Oxford: Oxford University Press, 2000), Vol. V, pp. 621, 639–40.

27　Halder Diaries, Vol. 5, December 23, 1940, p. 80.

28　Halder Diaries, Vol. 6, February 22, 1941, pp. 2–3.

29　Halder Diaries, Vol. 5, February 17, 1941, p. 117.

30　Ibid., November 17, 1940, p. 28.

31　Ibid., December 18, 1940, p. 75.

32　Gabriel Gorodestsky, *Grand Delusion: Stalin and the German Invasion of Russia* (New Haven: Yale University Press, 2001), p. 73.

33　Hitler–Molotov meetings in Berlin, November 12–13, 1940. Text accessible at: https://www.worldfuturefund.org/wffmaster/Reading/Germany/Hitler-Molotov%20Meetings.htm.

34　Ibid.

35　Halder Diaries, Vol. 6, March 30, 1941, pp. 41–2.

36　Ibid.

37　"Hitler's Russian Blunder," *New York Times*, July 21, 1981.

38　Halder Diaries, Vol. 6, March 30, 1941, p. 42.

39　O'Brien, *How the War Was Won*, p. 193.

40　Halder Diaries, Vol. 6, April 10, 1941, p. 63.

41 Ibid., June 14, 1941, p. 154.

42 Nikolai Tolstoy, *Stalin's Secret War* (London: Jonathan Cape, 1981), p. 214.

43 Murphy, *What Stalin Knew*. This book has whole chapters on the information that was collected for Stalin about German intentions. See, in particular, Chapters 9, 10, 11.

44 Ibid., pp. 111–12.

45 Khlevniuk, *Stalin: New Biography*, p. 188.

46 Murphy, *What Stalin Knew*, p. 162.

47 Geoffrey Megargee, *Barbarossa 1941: Hitler's War of Annihilation* (Stroud: Tempus, 2007), p. 70.

48 Resis, *Molotov Remembers*, p. 23.

16. Roosevelt, Hitler and the Road to War

1 Leahy Diary, August 30, 1939.

2 James Leutze, *Bargaining for Supremacy: Anglo-American Naval Cooperation 1937–1941* (Chapel Hill: UNC Press, 1978), p. 6.

3 FDR Mss, Speech Library, FDR Speech to the Nation, September 3, 1939, p. 7, http://www.fdrlibrary.marist.edu/_resources/images/msf/msf01279.

4 Ibid., July 10, 1940, http://www.fdrlibrary.marist.edu/_resources/images/msf/msf01334.

5 Gerhard Weinberg, "Hitler's Image of the United States," *American Historical Review*, Vol. 69, No. 4 (July 1964), p. 1009.

6 Hitler, speech to Reichstag, "A Reply to US President Roosevelt," April 28, 1939, in Domarus, *Hitler*, Vol. 3, p. 1586.

7 Ibid., p. 1591.

8 Weinberg, "Hitler's Image of the United States," p. 1014.

9 Halder Diaries, Vol. 4, October 15, 1940.

10 Klaus H. Schmider, *Hitler's Fatal Miscalculation: Why Germany Declared War on the United States* (Cambridge: Cambridge University Press, 2021), p. 94.

11 Alan Brinkley, *Franklin Delano Roosevelt* (Oxford: Oxford University Press, 2010), p. 72; *Fuehrer Conferences on Naval Affairs: 1940*, p. 123.

12 *Fuehrer Conferences on Naval Affairs: 1941*, p. 57.

13 Robert E. Sherwood, *The White House Papers of Harry L. Hopkins* (London: Eyre and Spottiswoode), Vol. 1, pp. 222–3.

14 Roosevelt, Arsenal of Democracy Speech, December 29, 1940, https://millercenter.org/the-presidency/presidential-speeches/december-29-1940-fireside-chat-16-arsenal-democracy#dp-expandable-text.

15 Leahy Diary, January 1, 1941, p. 4. There is a copy of the letter prepared for Leahy at the start of his diary for the year.

16 Ibid., p. 2.

16 Ibid., Roosevelt letter prepared for Leahy.

17 Sherwood, *The White House Papers of Harry L. Hopkins*, Vol. 1, p. 235.

18 Ibid., p. 261.

19 *Fuehrer Conferences on Naval Affairs: 1941*, p. 8.

20 Ibid., p. 11.

21 Ibid., p. 13.

22 Ibid., p. 37.

23 Ibid., p. 48.

24 *Germany and the Second World War*, Vol. VI, pp. 229–30.

25 Sherwood, *The White House Papers of Harry L. Hopkins*, Vol. 1, pp. 309–10.

26 Ernest King Papers, Box 20, Sumner Welles memoranda of talks, August 10 and 11, 1941.

27 *Fuehrer Conferences on Naval Affairs: 1941*, pp. 108–9.

28 Ibid., pp. 109–10.

29 Robert Dallek, *Franklin D. Roosevelt: A Political Life* (London: Allen Lane, 2017), p. 441.

30 David Kaiser, *No End Save Victory: How FDR Led the Nation into War* (New York: Basic Books, 2018), p. 332.

17. Roosevelt, Churchill, Hitler, Mussolini and the Air–Sea Super-Battlefield

1 O'Brien, *How the War Was Won*, p. 5.

2 Ibid., Chapter 1.

3 Trevor-Roper, *Hitler's Table Talk*, p. 27.

4 Ibid.

5 https://www.whitehousehistory.org/mr-churchill-in-the-white-house-1.

6 FRUS, The Conferences at Washington 1941–1942 and Casablanca 1943, Dinner meeting of Roosevelt, Churchill and Hopkins, December 23, 1941, p. 81, https://search.library.wisc.edu/digital/AUCDN2IRO KTVV68T/.

7 Ibid., White House Conference, December 23, 1941, p. 77, Arnold Notes.

8 Ibid., Meeting of Roosevelt, Churchill and advisers, January 4, 1942, p. 162.

9 Ibid., p. 165.

10 Ibid., p. 164.

11 Ibid., Arnold meetings with Hopkins, FDR and Churchill, January 4, 1942, p. 161.

12 Ibid., p. 160.

13 https://history.army.mil/books/wwii/csppp/ch11.htm.

14 *Fuehrer Conferences on Naval Affairs: 1942*, p. 43.

15 Ibid., p. 62.

16 Ibid., p. 18.

17 Ibid., p. 31.

18 Ibid.

19 Ibid., p. 45.

20 Ibid., p. 48.

21 Trevor-Roper, *Hitler's Table Talk*, pp. 509–10.

22 Stephen Roskill, *The War at Sea* (London: HMSO, 1956), Vol. 2, p. 486.

23 O'Brien, *The Second Most Powerful Man in the World*, p. 193.

24 Christopher M. Bell, *Churchill and Sea Power* (Oxford: Oxford University Press, 2013), p. 281. Bell says that late 1942 and early 1943 was only the second period in the war when Churchill was truly worried about how the Battle of the Atlantic was developing.

25 USSBS, Saur Interview, May 23, 1945, p. 3.

26 *Fuehrer Conferences on Naval Affairs: 1942*, p. 48.

27 Trevor-Roper, *Hitler's Table Talk*, pp. 274–5.

28 Warren Kimball (ed.), *Churchill and Roosevelt: The Complete Correspondence* (Princeton: Princeton University Press, 1984), Vol. 1, p. 649.

29 FDR Mss, PSF 172-2, War Progress Report, December 4, 1942, p. 16.

30 *Germany and the Second World War*, Vol. VI, pp. 348, 399–400.

31 Cajus Bekker, *Hitler's Naval War* (London: Macdonald, 1974), pp. 337–8.

32 Trevor-Roper, *Hitler's Table Talk*, p. 307.

33 Heiber et al., *Hitler and His Generals*.

34 Ibid., p. 189.

35 Ibid., p. 415.

36 Ibid., p. 186.

37 O'Brien, *How the War Was Won*, p. 349.

38 Nicolaus von Below, *At Hitler's Side: The Memoirs of Hitler's Luftwaffe Adjutant* (London: Frontline Books, 2010), pp. 148, 169–70, 182.

39 O'Brien, *How the War Was Won*, pp. 23–4.

40 Despina Stratigakos, *Hitler at Home* (New Haven: Yale University Press, 2015), p. 137.

18. Mussolini, Churchill, Roosevelt and Empire in the Mediterranean

1 Ciano Diaries, December 3, 1941, p. 414.

2 Ibid.

3 Ibid., December 8, 1941, p. 416.

4 Mussolini War Statement, December 11, 1941, https://www.jewish-virtuallibrary.org/mussolini-s-war-statement-december-1941.

5 "Brusselle," *Il Popolo d'Italia*, December 1, 1937, p. 25.

6 Meeting with Sandro Giuliani, November 4, 1941, in Edoardo and Duilio Susmel (eds), *Opera omnia di Benito Mussolini*, Vol. XXX (Florence: La Fenice, 1960), pp. 132–34.

7 Geoffrey Wheatcroft, *Churchill's Shadow: An Astonishing Life and a Dangerous Legacy* (London: The Bodley Head, 2021), p. 247.

8 Churchill, Mansion House speech, November 10, 1942, http://www.ibiblio.org/pha/policy/1942/421110b.html.

9 Srinath Raghavan, *India's War: The Making of Modern South Asia 1939–1945* (London: Allen Lane, 2016), pp. 7–11.

10 Gilbert, *Churchill War Papers*, Vol. 2, pp. 1010–12.

11 Denis Mack Smith, *Modern Italy: A Political History* (New Haven: Yale University Press, 1997), p. 387.

12 Ciano Diaries, July 5, 1941, p. 373.

13 John Gooch, "Mussolini's Strategy 1939–43," in Evan Mawdsley and John Ferris (eds), *The Cambridge History of the Second World War* (Cambridge: Cambridge University Press, 2015), p. 153.

14 FRUS, The Conferences at Washington 1941–1942 and Casablanca 1943, Churchill Memoranda, December 16–20, 1941.

15 Ibid., p. 22.

16 Ibid., p. 26.

17 Ibid., Meeting of Roosevelt and Churchill with Staff, December 23, 1941, p. 71.

18 Ibid., Meeting of Arnold and Roosevelt, December 23, 1941, p. 76.

19 *The Atlantic Charter*, August 1941, https://avalon.law.yale.edu/wwii/atlantic.asp.

20 Foster Rhea Dulles and Gerald Ridinger, "The Anti-Colonial Policies of Franklin D. Roosevelt," *Political Science Quarterly*, Vol. 70, No. 1 (1955), p. 1.

21 Elliott Roosevelt, *As He Saw It* (New York: Duell, Sloan and Pierce, 1946), p. 75.

22 Ibid., p. 74.

23 Robert Dallek, *Franklin D. Roosevelt and American Foreign Policy* (Oxford: Oxford University Press, 1979), pp. 323–5.

24 FDR Mss, PSF, FDR to Winant, February 1942, Hopkins to FDR, April 1942.

25 Hopkins Mss, 24, FDR to Churchill, March 10, 1942.

26 Winston Churchill, *The Second World War*, Vol. IV (London: Cassell, 1951), pp. 390–1.

27 Leahy Diary, May 22, 1941.

28 Stimson to Roosevelt, December 20, 1941 FRUS, The Conferences at Washington 1941–1942 and Casablanca 1943, https://search.library.wisc.edu/digital/AUCDN2IROKTVV68T/pages/AA3T3ZGRT7KQW29A.

29 Ibid.

30 O'Brien, *The Second Most Powerful Man in the World*, pp. 190–1.

31 War Department, Special Staff, NARA, Marshall, King, Arnold to FDR, July 10, 1942.

32 O'Brien, *The Second Most Powerful Man in the World*, p. 193.

33 Ciano Diaries, December 8, 1942, p. 553.

34 Ibid., April 11, 1942, p. 471.

35 Ibid., June 30, 1941, p. 372.

36 Ibid., May 2, 1942, p. 480.

37 Bottai, *Diary*, July 5, 1941, p. 276.

38 Ciano Diaries, June 26, 1942, p. 502.

39 Ibid., December 1, 1942, p. 550.

40 Ibid., December 9, 1942, p. 554.

41 Ibid., January 28, 1943, pp. 575–6.

42 H. James Burgwyn, *Mussolini Warlord: Failed Dreams of Empire 1940–1943* (New York: Enigma Books, 2012), pp. 210–11.

43 Ciano Diaries, January 8 and 9, 1943, pp. 567–8.

44 Ibid., January 5, 1943, p. 566.

45 R. J. B. Bosworth, *Claretta: Mussolini's Last Lover* (New Haven: Yale University Press, 2017), p. 168.

46 Michael Ebner, *Ordinary Violence in Mussolini's Italy* (Cambridge: Cambridge University Press, 2011), p. 213.

47 Gooch, *Mussolini's War*, p. 388.

48 Bottai, *Diary*, June 5, 1943, p. 381.

19. Hitler, Stalin and the Eastern Front

1 Sherwood, *The White House Papers of Harry L. Hopkins,* Vol. 1, p. 330.

2 Ibid., p. 332.

3 Kumanev, *Govoriat stalinskie narkomy* (Smolensk: Rusich, 2005), p. 329.

4 Ibid.

5 Sherwood, *The White House Papers of Harry L. Hopkins,* Vol. 1, p. 344.

6 Dallek, *Franklin D. Roosevelt: A Political Life*, p. 428.

7 "World War II Allies: US Lend-Lease to the Soviet Union 1941–45," US State Department (accessed July 15, 2022). https://ru.usembassy.gov/world-war-ii-allies-u-s-lend-lease-to-the-soviet-union-1941-1945.

8 Trevor-Roper, *Hitler's Table Talk*, p. 17.

9 Ibid.

10 Walter S. Dunn, *Hitler's Nemesis: The Red Army, 1930–1945* (Westport: Praeger, 1994), p. 7.

11 Speer, *Inside the Third Reich*, p. 233; Martin Kitchen, *Speer: Hitler's Architect* (New Haven: Yale University Press, 2015), pp. 145–8.

12 Trevor-Roper, *Hitler's Table Talk*, p. 55.

13 David Stahel, *Operation Barbarossa and Hitler's Defeat in the East* (Cambridge: Cambridge University Press, 2013), pp. 425–7. This is an excellent and thorough book for anyone interested in the early stages of Barbarossa.

14 David Stahel, *The Battle for Moscow* (Cambridge: Cambridge University Press, 2015), pp. 251–2.

15 David Stahel, *Retreat from Moscow: A New History of Germany's Winter Campaign, 1941–1942* (New York: Picador, 2019), pp. 17–18.

16 Ibid., p. 28.

17 Halder Diaries, Vol. 7, December 1, 1941, p. 196.

18 Ibid., November 30, 1941, p. 193.

19 Bob Carruthers (ed.), *Hitler's Wartime Orders: The Complete Führer Directives: 1939–1945* (Barnsley: Pen and Sword, 2018), p. 120.

20 Ullrich, *Downfall*, pp. 225–7.

21 Halder Diaries, Vol. 7, December 19, 1945, p. 233.

22 David Stone, *Twilight of the Gods: The Decline and Fall of the German General Staff in World War II* (London: Conway, 2011), p. 225.

23 Halder Diaries, Vol. 7, December 20, 1945, p. 235.

24 Kershaw, *Nemesis*, p. 454.

25 Halder Diaries, Vol. 7, January 13, 1942, p. 253.

26 Ullrich, *Downfall*, p. 230.

27 Christa Schroeder, *He Was My Chief: The Memoirs of Adolf Hitler's Secretary* (Barnsley: Frontline Books, 2012), p. 100.

28 S. M. Shtemenko, *General'nyi Shtab v gody voiny* (Moscow: Voenizdat, 1968), p. 148.

29 Gilbert, *Winston S. Churchill*, Vol. 7, p. 157.

30 Ibid., p. 158.

31 Joshua Greenberg, "Comrades and Brothers": Churchill, Stalin and the Moscow Conference of 1942, International Churchill Society, September 24, 2019, copy accessible at: https://winstonchurchill.org/publica tions/finest-hour-extras/comrades-and-brothers-churchill-stalin-and-the-moscow-conference-of-1942.

32 Gilbert, *Winston S. Churchill*, Vol. 7, pp. 176–7.

33 Ibid., p. 178.

34 Greenberg "Comrades and Brothers."

35 Tsuyoshi Hasegawa, "Soviet Policy Towards Japan During World War II," *Cahiers du monde russe*, Vol. 52, No. 2/3 (2011), p. 246.

36 Ibid., pp. 247–8.

37 K. Simonov, *Glazami cheloveka moego pokoleniia: Razmyshleniia o I. V. Staline* (Moscow: Kniga, 1990), p. 328.

38 Oleg Khlevniuk, "Stalin at War. Sources and Their Interpretation," *Cahiers du monde russe*, Vol. 52, No. 2/3 (2011).

39 Walter Laqueur, *Stalin: The Glasnost Revelations* (London: Unwin and Hyman, 1990), p. 221.

40 Evan Mawdsley, *Thunder in the East: The Nazi–Soviet War 1941–1945* (London: Bloomsbury, 2015), p. 39.

41 Zhilin, V. A. et al (eds), *Bitva pod Moskvoi: Khronika, fakty, liudi,* 2 vols (Moscow: Ol'ma Press, 2002), p. 313.

42 Shtemenko, *General'nyi Shtab v gody voiny,* pp. 37–8; A. M. Vassilevskii, *Delo Vsei Zhizni* (Moscow: Politizdat, 1978), p. 189.

43 David M. Glantz, *Kharkov 1942: Anatomy of a Military Disaster Through Soviet Eyes* (Shepperton: Ian Allan, 1998), pp. 111, 218.

44 Ibid., p. 218.

45 Halder Diaries, Vol. 7, July 23, 1942, p. 356.

46 Ibid., September 20, 1942, p. 396.

47 Simonov, *Glazami cheloveka moego pokoleniia,* p. 330.

48 Speer, *Inside the Third Reich,* p. 247.

49 Ibid.

50 Ibid.

51 Phillips O'Brien, "Logistics by Land and Air," in Mawdsley and Ferris, *Cambridge History of the Second World War,* Vol. 1, pp. 631–2.

52 Speer, *Inside the Third Reich,* p. 249.

53 Stephen G. Fritz, *The First Soldier: Hitler as Military Leader* (New Haven: Yale University Press, 2018), p. 277.

54 Vassilevskii, *Delo Vsei Zhizni,* p. 497.

55 Ibid., p. 502.

56 Simonov, *Glasami cheloveka moego pokoleniia,* p. 328.

57 Speer, *Inside the Third Reich,* p. 234.

58 Fritz, *The First Soldier,* pp. 289–90.

59 *Germany and the Second World War*, Vol. VIII, p. 158.

60 G. K. Zhukov, *Vospominania i razmyshleniia*, Vol. 3 (Moscow: Izdatel'stvo Agenstva Pechati Novosti, 1986) pp. 30–31.

61 Vassilevskii, *Delo Vsei Zhizni*, p. 305.

20. Churchill, Roosevelt, Stalin and the Cross-Channel Invasion

1 FRUS, The Conferences at Washington 1941–42 and Casablanca 1943, Minutes of Meeting of FDR, Churchill and Staff, January 23, 1943, p. 708.

2 Alanbrooke Diaries, January 23, 1943, p. 367.

3 Carlo d'Este, *Warlord: The Fighting Life of Winston Churchill, from Soldier to Statesman* (London: Penguin, 2010), p. 569.

4 FRUS, The Conferences at Washington 1941–42 and Casablanca 1943, Minutes of Meeting of FDR, Churchill and Staff, January 23, 1943, pp. 713–14.

5 Ibid. It's worth noting that in this meeting Roosevelt did speak about the need for a quick reaction in case Italy collapsed. He was not against an invasion of Italy, as events in July/August 1943 would confirm; he was just never convinced that even invading Italy would be able to drive Germany out of the war.

6 Alanbrooke Diaries, January 23, 1943, p. 368.

7 Joint Chiefs of Staff Minutes, meeting with FDR, January 7, 1943, p. 4.

8 Ibid., p. 6.

9 O'Brien, *The Second Most Powerful Man in the World*, p. 214.

10 Ibid., p. 219.

11 FDR Mss, PSF 2, "Recommended Line of Action at the Coming Conference," May 8, 1943.

12 Leahy Diary, May 2, 1943.

13 FDR Mss, PSF 2, "Recommended Line of Action at the Coming Conference."

14 Ibid.

15 Alanbrooke Diaries, January 30, 1943, p. 373.

16 Ibid., January 26, 1943, p. 370.

17 FRUS, Conferences at Washington and Quebec: 1943, Churchill to Roosevelt, April 5, 1943, p. 12, https://search.library.wisc.edu/digital/AEXCU76BOSUW6487/.

18 Churchill, *The Second World War*, Vol. IV, p. 701.

19 FRUS, Conferences at Washington and Quebec: 1943, Minutes of Meeting in White House, May 12, 1943, pp. 26–7.

20 Ibid., pp. 25–6.

21 Ibid., p. 27.

22 Leahy Diary, May 12, 1943.

23 FRUS, Minutes of Meeting in White House, May 12, 1943, p. 30.

24 PREM 3443/2 (UKNA), Minutes of Meeting with Dominions, May 20, 1943.

25 Ibid., p. 7.

26 O'Brien, *The Second Most Powerful Man in the World*, pp. 226–30.

27 FRUS, Conferences at Washington and Quebec: 1943, Report of Combined Chiefs to Roosevelt and Churchill, May 25, 1943.

28 Ibid., JCS (Joint Chiefs of Staff) Meeting, July 26, 1943.

29 Ibid., JCS Memo, Estimate of the Enemy Situation, August 7, 1943.

30 Ibid., Meeting of Churchill and FDR with CCS (Combined Chiefs of Staff), August 23, 1943.

31 Ibid., p. 945.

32 Ibid., p. 942.

33 *Germany and the Second World War*, Vol. VIII, p. 145.

34 Hastings, *Finest Years: Churchill as Warlord 1940–45*, p. 431.

35 David Reynolds and Vladimir Pechatnov (eds), *The Kremlin Letters: Stalin's Wartime Correspondence with Churchill and Roosevelt* (New Haven: Yale University Press, 2019), p. 95.

36 FRUS, The Conferences at Cairo and Tehran: 1943, Roosevelt–Stalin Meeting, November 28, 1943, p. 483.

37 Ibid.

38 Ibid., p. 485.

39 Ibid., p. 486.

40 Ibid., First Plenary Meeting, November 28, 1943, p. 489.

41 Ibid., p. 490.

42 Jonathan Fenby, *Alliance: The Inside Story of How Roosevelt, Stalin, and Churchill Won One War and Began Another* (London: Simon and Schuster, 2007), pp. 1–2.

43 FRUS, The Conferences at Cairo and Tehran: 1943, Bohlen Minutes, p. 553.

44 Ibid., Meeting of FDR and WSC and the CCS, December 4, 1943.

45 Ibid., p. 680.

46 Ibid., Report of Combined Chiefs of Staff, December 5, 1943, p. 796.

47 J. A. Vale and J. W. Scadding, "In Carthage Ruins: The Illness of Sir Winston Churchill at Carthage, December 1943," *Journal of the Royal College of Physicians, Edinburgh*, Vol. 47 (2017), pp. 288–95.

48 Gilbert, *Winston S. Churchill*, Vol. 7, p. 606.

21. *Stalin, Roosevelt, Churchill and the Post-War World*

1 V. O. Pechatnov, "Stalin, Roosevelt, Churchill: 'Bol'shaia Troika' cherez prizmu perepiski voennykh let," *Vestnik MGIMO Universiteta*, Vol. 5 (2009), p. 3.

2 V. M. Berezhkov, *Kak ia stal perevodchikom Stalina* (Moscow: DEM, 1993), p. 250.

3 N. A. Vlasik, "Vospominaniia o I. V. Staline," *Istoricheskii vestnik*, Vol. 5, No. 152 (2013), p. 60.

4 Milovan Djilas, *Conversations with Stalin* (New York: Penguin, 1967), p. 61.

5 Leahy Diary, August 16, 1944.

6 Roosevelt Day by Day, online version of appointments diary between November 7, 1944 and his death. It should be noted that one of these entries occurred on the day that Roosevelt and Truman were inaugurated, so even including it as a meeting where an issue might have been discussed is being kind. See http://www.fdrlibrary.marist.edu/daybyday/.

7 William Leahy, *I Was There: The Personal Story of the Chief of Staff to Presidents Roosevelt and Truman Based on his Notes and Diaries at the Time* (New York: McGraw-Hill, 1950), p. 187.

8 Herbert Levy, *Henry Morgenthau Jr.: The Remarkable Life of FDR's Secretary of the Treasury* (New York: Skyhorse Publishing, 2010), pp. 443–8.

9 Berezhkov, *Kak ia stal perevodchikom Stalina*, pp. 331–2.

10 Gilbert, *Winston S. Churchill*, Vol. 7, p. 1015.

11 Berezhkov, *Kak ia stal perevodchikom Stalina*, p. 322.

12 Churchill, *The Second World War*, Vol. VI, p. 198.

13 Albert Resis, "The Churchill-Stalin Secret 'Percentages' Agreement on the Balkans, Moscow, October 1944," *American Historical Review*, Vol. 83, No. 2 (April 1978), p. 368.

14 Churchill, *The Second World War*, Vol. VI, p. 199.

15 There are a range of different views on Yalta, basically stretching from those who believe that Roosevelt sold out Eastern Europe to Stalin to those who believe it was a sensible bargain. For just some of the views out there, see Donald C. Watt, "Britain and the Historiography of the Yalta Conference and the Cold War," *Diplomatic History*, Vol. 13, No. 1 (Winter 1989), pp. 67–98; Charles G. Stefan, "Yalta Revisited: An Update on the Diplomacy of FDR and His Wartime Summit Partners," *Presidential Studies Quarterly*, Vol. 23, No. 4 (Fall 1993), pp. 750–55.

16 Reynolds and Pechatnov, *The Kremlin Letters*, p. 547.

17 R. E. Sherwood, *Roosevelt and Hopkins: An Intimate History* (New York: The Universal Library, 1948), p. 377.

18 Khlevniuk, *Stalin: New Biography*, pp. 194–5.

19 Surviving War, Declining Health: Lincoln & Churchill, a project of the Lehrman Institute, accessible at: https://lincolnandchurchill.org/surviving-war-declining-health/.

20 Roosevelt was in Warm Springs, Georgia, from November 28 and did not get back to Washington until December 19. He then left for Hyde Park on December 23 and did not head back to Washington until December 30. See http://www.fdrlibrary.marist.edu/daybyday/.

21 David B. Woolner, *The Last 100 Days: FDR at War and Peace* (New York: Basic Books, 2019), p. 24.

22 Dallek, *Franklin D. Roosevelt: A Political Life*, p. 603.

23 Gilbert, *Winston S. Churchill*, Vol. 7, p. 1166.

24 Ibid.

25 Robert M. Citino, *The Wehrmacht's Last Stand: The German Campaigns of 1944–1945* (Lawrence: University Press of Kansas, 2018), pp. 423–5.

26 Timothy Snyder, *Bloodlands: Europe Between Hitler and Stalin* (London: The Bodley Head, 2011), p. 313.

27 FRUS, Conferences at Malta and Crimea: 1945, The President's Log at Yalta, pp. 558–9.

28 Ibid., Roosevelt–Stalin Meeting, February 4, 1943, p. 571.

29 Ibid., p. 572.

30 Ibid., Dinner Meeting, February 4, 1943, p. 589.

31 Ibid., Second Plenary, February 5, 1945, pp. 611–24.

32 Columbia University Oral History Archive, Thomas Hart Interview, 1:44.

33 Leahy Diary, February 8, 1945.

34 FRUS, Conferences at Malta and Crimea: 1945, Agreement Regarding Entry of Soviet Union into the War against Japan, February 11, 1945, p. 984.

35 Ibid., Third Plenary, February 6, 1945, p. 666.

36 Lukasz Kaminski, "Stalinism in Poland, 1944–1956," in Kevin McDermott and Matthew Stibbe (eds), *Stalinist Terror in Eastern Europe: Elite Purges and Mass Repression* (Manchester: Manchester University Press, 2010), pp. 79–83.

37 Roosevelt seems to have gone into the conference believing that a multi-party Poland was a possibility. See FRUS, Conferences at Malta and Crimea: 1945, Undated Memo from Secretary of State for FDR, p. 568.

38 Ibid., Third Plenary, February 6, 1945, p. 669.

39 Mark Kramer, "Stalin, Soviet Policy, and the Establishment of a Communist Bloc in Eastern Europe, 1941–1948," in Timothy Snyder and Ray Brandon (eds), *Stalin and Europe: Imitation and Domination 1928–1953* (Oxford: Oxford University Press, 2014), pp. 272–3.

40 FRUS, Conferences at Malta and Crimea: 1945, Third Plenary, February 6, 1945, p. 670.

41 Ibid., Matthews Minutes, February 7, 1945, p. 718.

42 Ibid., Letter from Roosevelt to Stalin, February 6, 1945, pp. 727–8.

43 Berezhkov, *Kak ia stal perevodchikom Stalina*, p. 253.

44 Robert Gellately, *Stalin's Curse: Battling for Communism in War and Cold War* (Oxford: Oxford University Press, 2015), p. 101.

45 Leahy, *I Was There*, p. 297.

46 Constantine Brown, *The Coming of the Whirlwind* (Chicago: Henry Regnery Company, 1964), p. 316.

Epilogue: The Strategists' War

1 S. M. Plokhy, *Yalta: The Price of Peace* (New York: Penguin, 2010), p. 375.

2 Conquest, *Stalin: Breaker of Nations*, p. 264.

3 Ibid., p. 265.

4 Reynolds and Pechatnov, *The Kremlin Letters*, p. 572.

5 Ibid., p. 567.

6 Dallek, *Franklin D. Roosevelt and American Foreign Policy*, p. 527.

7 For a list of national casualties in World War II, see: https://www. nationalww2museum.org/students-teachers/student-resources/research-starters/research-starters-worldwide-deaths-world-war.

Index